Your fully reengineered Microsoft Study Guide.

The all-new learning format of your Microsoft study guide delivers in-depth preparation for the exam—including full objective-by-objective review—along with great new study tools to help prepare you for the job. Features include:

- **Relevant exam objectives highlighted at the start of each chapter**

- **"Why This Chapter Matters" and "Real World" sidebars on how you can apply learning concepts to the job**

- **Case scenario exercises where you work through a multi-step, real-world solution**

- **Troubleshooting labs on a simulated operating system for practical field experience**

- **"Off the Record" sidebars bridge the gap between how things *should* work and how they *do* work**

- **Security Alerts and Planning Tips you can apply in the real world**

- **Complete objective-by-objective review section**

- **Exam highlights—key points and terms you should know**

- **Exam tips written by industry insiders**

Exam 70-284: Implementing and Managing Microsoft Exchange Server 2003

Objective	Pages
Installing, Configuring, and Troubleshooting Exchange Server 2003	
Prepare the environment for deployment of Exchange Server 2003	1-2 to 1-14, 2-3 to 2-27
Install, configure, and troubleshoot Exchange Server 2003	2-28 to 2-34
Install, configure, and troubleshoot Exchange Server 2003 in a clustered environment	6-29 to 6-34
Upgrade from Exchange Server 5.5 to Exchange Server 2003	5-3 to 5-25
Migrate from other messaging systems to Exchange Server 2003	5-3 to 5-42
■ Use the Migration Wizard to migrate from other messaging systems	
■ Migrate from other Exchange Server organizations	5-39 to 5-42, 5-39 to 5-42
Configure and troubleshoot Exchange Server 2003 for coexistence with other Exchange Server organizations	4-3 to 4-42
Configure and troubleshoot Exchange Server 2003 for coexistence with other messaging systems	5-26 to 5-38
Configure and troubleshoot for interoperability with other Simple Mail Transfer Protocol (SMTP) messaging systems	10-3 to 10-20
Managing, Monitoring, and Troubleshooting Exchange Servers	
Manage, monitor, and troubleshoot server health	13-3 to 13-42
Manage, monitor, and troubleshoot data storage	7-46 to 7-57, 13-35 to 13-42
Manage, monitor, and troubleshoot Exchange Server clusters	6-29 to 6-34, 4-16 to 4-25
Perform and troubleshoot backups and recovery	12-3 to 12-45
Remove a computer running Exchange Server from the organization	2-35 to 2-40
Managing, Monitoring, and Troubleshooting the Exchange Organization	
Manage and troubleshoot public folders	8-2 to 8-346
Manage and troubleshoot Internet protocol virtual servers	10-3 to 10-52
Manage and troubleshoot front-end and back-end servers	3-28 to 3-32, 6-29 to 6-34
Manage and troubleshoot connectivity	13-3 to 13-42, 14-4 to 14-35
Monitor, manage, and troubleshoot infrastructure performance	13-35 to 13-42, 3-21 to 3-27

Objective	Pages
Managing Security in the Exchange Environment	
Manage and troubleshoot connectivity across firewalls	3-28 to 3-32, 14-26 to 14-35
Manage audit settings and audit logs	11-12 to 11-21
Manage and troubleshoot permissions	11-3 to 11-11, 11-22 to 11-29, 2-3 to 2-18, 7-46 to 7-72
Manage and troubleshoot encryption and digital signatures	11-22 to 11-29
Detect and respond to security threats	13-35 to 13-42, 11-22 to 11-29
Managing Recipient Objects and Address Lists	
Manage recipient policies	7-58 to 7-72
Manage user objects	7-3 to 7-45, 7-58 to 7-72
Manage distribution and security groups	7-3 to 7-57
Manage contacts	7-3 to 7-45
Manage address lists	7-58 to 7-72
Managing and Monitoring Technologies that Support Microsoft Exchange Server 2003	
Diagnose problems arising from host resolution protocols	14-4 to 14-15
Diagnose problems arising from Active Directory issues	14-16 to 14-25
Diagnose network connectivity problems	14-36 to 14-44

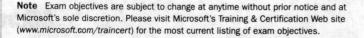

Note Exam objectives are subject to change at anytime without prior notice and at Microsoft's sole discretion. Please visit Microsoft's Training & Certification Web site (*www.microsoft.com/traincert*) for the most current listing of exam objectives.

Microsoft

MCSA/MCSE Self-Paced Training Kit (Exam 70-284): Implementing and Managing Microsoft® Exchange Server 2003

This Indian Reprint—Rs. 695.00
(Original U.S. Edition—Rs. 2030.00)

MCSA/MCSE SELF-PACED TRAINING KIT: EXAM 70-284—IMPLEMENTING AND MANAGING MICROSOFT® EXCHANGE SERVER 2003 (with CD-ROM)
by Will Willis and Ian McLean

Will Willis and Ian McLean

Prentice-Hall of India Private Limited
New Delhi - 110 001
2004

Published by Asoke K. Ghosh, Prentice-Hall of India Private Limited, M-97, Connaught Circus, New Delhi-110001 and Printed by Mohan Makhijani at Rekha Printers Private Limited, New Delhi-110020.

This Indian Reprint—Rs. 695.00
(Original U.S. Edition—Rs. 3024.00)

MCSA/MCSE SELF-PACED TRAINING KIT: Exam 70-284—IMPLEMENTING AND
MANAGING MICROSOFT® EXCHANGE SERVER 2003 (with CD-ROM)
by Will Willis and Ian McLean

This Eastern Economy Edition is the authorized, unabridged reprint published by Prentice-Hall of
India Private Limited, © 2004 by arrangement with original publisher, Microsoft Press, a division
of Microsoft Corporation, Redmond, Washington, U.S.A.

This edition is authorised for sale in Bangladesh, Bhutan, India, Maldives, Nepal and Sri Lanka only.

ISBN-81-203-2534-6

The export rights of this book are vested solely with the publisher.

Published by Asoke K. Ghosh, Prentice-Hall of India Private Limited, M-97, Connaught Circus,
New Delhi-110001 and Printed by Mohan Makhijani at Rekha Printers Private Limited,
New Delhi-110020.

Dedicated in memory of my dad (2/24/1949-9/14/2003), who not only was a father, but a close friend. He taught me to try my best at everything I do, and to not take anything for granted. There never is enough time in life, but I thank God for the time that we did have together.

—Will Willis

To Anne. My love and my life.

—Ian McLean

Will Willis

Will Willis, MCSE, A+ Certified Technician, Network+, B.A., is a Senior Network Administrator for an international software development company in the Dallas, Texas, area. He is responsible for the network and server infrastructure, for documentation, maintaining disaster recovery preparedness, antivirus strategies, firewalls and network security, infrastructure (servers, routers, switches, hubs, etc.) maintenance and upgrades, and ensuring the reliability and availability of network resources.

Will started out as a help desk tech, providing technical support over the phone for PC hardware and software, and later moved up to a desktop/LAN support specialist position working on an eight-person team to support a 3000+-user, multiple-site network. From that position, Will became a network manager, where he also administered multiple Active Directory domains and servers running BackOffice applications such as Exchange Server, IIS, Site Server, SQL Server, and SMS. He can be reached at *WWillis@Inside-Corner.com* and enjoys spending time with his family and writing and recording original music when not busy being a techie. Will has co-authored eight books and scores of technical articles. He has also written practice exams and tech-edited many titles. His first album of guitar-based instrumental music, *Darkness into Light*, was released in late 2002. Will is also a seminary student, pursuing a Master of Arts in theology. More information on Will can be found at *http://www.willwillis.us*.

Ian McLean

Ian McLean, MCSE, MCDBA, MCT, has more than 35 years experience in industry, commerce, and education. He started his career as an electronics engineer before going into distance learning and then education as a university professor. Currently he runs his own consultancy company. Ian has written 14 books, as well as many papers and technical articles. He has been working with networks since the early 1980s and with Microsoft network operating systems since 1997.

Contents at a Glance

1   Microsoft Exchange Server 2003 and Active Directory 1-1
2   Planning a Microsoft Exchange Server 2003 Infrastructure 2-1
3   Configuring a Microsoft Exchange Server 2003 Infrastructure 3-1
4   Coexistence with Microsoft Exchange Server 5.5 4-1
5   Migrating from Microsoft Exchange Server and Other Mail Systems . . . 5-1
6   Installing Microsoft Exchange Server 2003 Clusters and Front-End
    and Back-End Servers 6-1
7   Managing Recipient Objects and Address Lists 7-1
8   Public Folders 8-1
9   Virtual Servers 9-1
10 SMTP Protocol Configuration and Management 10-1
11 Microsoft Exchange Server 2003 Security 11-1
12 Backup and Restore 12-1
13 Monitoring Microsoft Exchange Server 2003 13-1
14 Troubleshooting Microsoft Exchange Server 2003 14-1

Glossary G-1

Index I-1

Practices

Preparing for Installation 2-8

Preparing Forests and Domains 2-15

Installing Exchange Server 2003 into a New Organization. 2-21

Performing an Unattended Installation of Exchange Server 2003. 2-31

Removing Exchange Server 2003 from an Organization 2-37

Post-Installation Considerations 3-8

Administrative and Routing Groups 3-17

Connecting Exchange Server 5.5 to Active Directory 4-8

Installing Exchange Server 2003 into an Existing Exchange Server 5.5
Organization 4-29

Troubleshooting Connectivity between Active Directory and Exchange Server 5.5 . . . 4-38

Upgrading from Exchange Server 5.5 and Exchange Server 2000 5-14

Configuring Exchange Server 2003 to Coexist with Other Messaging Systems. 5-33

Installing Exchange Server 2003 in a Clustered Environment 6-12

Managing an Exchange Server 2003 Cluster 6-23

Installing Exchange Server 2003 in a Front-End and Back-End Configuration. 6-32

Configuring Recipient Objects. 7-41

Configuring Information Stores. 7-54

Creating and Managing Address Lists and Recipient Policies 7-69

Creating Public Folders 8-8

Administering Public Folders 8-23

Public Folder Security 8-32

Enabling and Starting the POP3, IMAP4, and NNTP Services 9-15

Creating and Configuring Virtual Servers 9-25

Obtaining, Installing, and Associating a Certificate for an IMAP4 Virtual Server
on a Front-End Exchange Server 9-44

Configuring Authentication 9-45

Viewing and Managing Connected Users on an IMAP4 Virtual Server 9-53

Creating MX Records and Configuring an SMTP Connector 10-15

Configuring an SMTP Connector to Use a Relay Host for Outbound SMTP 10-18

Configuring SMTP Security and Demand-Dial Communications. 10-27

Message and Client Configuration 10-44

Configuring Exchange Server 2003 to Use RPC Over HTTP 11-5

Downloading Antivirus Software 11-20

Configuring the Junk E-Mail Feature in Outlook 2003 and Enabling Connection
Filtering 11-25

Deploying Digital Signature and Encryption Certificates 11-32

Creating and Using an Administrative Group 11-39

Enabling and Configuring Protocol Logging 11-53

Managing Storage 12-12

Performing Backups. 12-22

Recovering from a Disaster Using Restore. 12-37

Configuring Diagnostic Levels and the Monitoring And Status Utility 13-14

Using Performance and Protocol Logs and Managing Mailbox Limits. 13-28

Defragmenting Exchange Stores and Checking Their Integrity 13-39

Using the Netdiag and Dcdiag Command-Line Utilities 14-10

Configuring an Alert 14-21

Limiting Write and Delete Permissions to Public Folders 14-31

Checking That E-Mail is Encrypted 14-41

Managing the ARP Cache and Analyzing an ARP Packet 14-56

Troubleshooting Labs

Chapter 2 2-44

Chapter 4 4-44

Chapter 5 5-43

Chapter 7 7-75

Chapter 8 8-36

Chapter 9 9-56

Chapter 10 10-54

Chapter 11 11-58

Chapter 12 12-47

Chapter 13 13-44

Chapter 14 14-63

Contents

Acknowledgments xxvii

About This Book xxix

    Intended Audience xxix

    Prerequisites xxix

    About the CD-ROM. xxx

    Features of This Book xxxi

        Informational Notes. xxxi

        Notational Conventions xxxii

        Keyboard Conventions xxxiii

    Getting Started xxxiii

        Hardware Requirements. xxxiii

        Software Requirements xxxiv

        Setup Instructions. xxxiv

        The Readiness Review Suite xxxiv

        The eBook xxxv

    The Microsoft Certified Professional Program xxxv

        Certifications xxxv

        Requirements for Becoming a Microsoft Certified Professional xxxvi

    Technical Support xxxvii

    Evaluation Edition Software Support xxxviii

1   Microsoft Exchange Server 2003 and Active Directory   **1-1**

    Why This Chapter Matters 1-1

    Before You Begin. 1-1

    Lesson 1: Overview of Active Directory 1-2

        Active Directory Forests and Domains. 1-2

        Active Directory Sites 1-3

        Active Directory Schema 1-3

        Organizational Units 1-3

        Global Catalogs. 1-4

        Operations Masters. 1-5

        Lesson Review 1-6

        Lesson Summary 1-7

    Lesson 2: Exchange Server 2003 Integration with Active Directory 1-8

        Naming Contexts. 1-8

        Global Catalog Integration 1-9

Active Directory Group Integration. 1-10

Lesson Review 1-10

Lesson Summary 1-11

Lesson 3: Exchange Server 2003 and Windows Server 2003 Protocols and
Services Integration 1-12

Exchange Server 2003 and IIS 6 1-12

Lesson Review 1-14

Lesson Summary 1-14

Case Scenario Exercise 1-15

Requirement 1 1-15

Requirement 2 1-16

Chapter Summary 1-16

Exam Highlights 1-17

Key Points 1-17

Key Terms. 1-17

Questions and Answers 1-18

2   Planning a Microsoft Exchange Server 2003 Infrastructure   2-1

Why This Chapter Matters 2-1

Before You Begin. 2-2

Lesson 1: Installation Considerations 2-3

Supported Combinations of Exchange and Windows Server 2-3

Hardware Requirements. 2-5

Creating a Service Account 2-6

Installing Windows Services Required by Exchange Server 2003. 2-7

Practice: Preparing for Installation 2-8

Lesson Review 2-10

Lesson Summary 2-11

Lesson 2: Preparing Forests and Domains 2-12

ForestPrep 2-12

DomainPrep 2-15

Practice: Preparing Forests and Domains 2-15

Lesson Review 2-17

Lesson Summary 2-18

Lesson 3: Performing an Exchange Server 2003 Installation 2-19

Installation Types 2-19

Performing an Installation of Exchange Server 2003 into a New
Organization 2-21

Practice: Installing Exchange Server 2003 into a New Organization 2-21

Lesson Review 2-26

Lesson Summary 2-27

Lesson 4: Unattended Setup 2-28

Creating an .ini File for Unattended Setup 2-28

Performing an Unattended Installation of Exchange Server 2003 2-31

Practice: Performing an Unattended Installation of Exchange
Server 2003 2-31

Lesson Review 2-33

Lesson Summary 2-34

Lesson 5: Removing an Exchange Server 2003 Server from an Organization . . 2-35

Removing an Exchange Server 2003 Server Using the Microsoft
Exchange Installation Wizard 2-35

Forcibly Removing Exchange Server 2003 from an Organization 2-36

Practice: Removing Exchange Server 2003 from an Organization 2-37

Lesson Review 2-39

Lesson Summary 2-40

Case Scenario Exercise 2-40

Requirement 1 2-41

Requirement 2 2-42

Requirement 3 2-43

Troubleshooting Lab 2-44

Exercise 1: Unsuccessful Removal of Exchange Server 2003 2-44

Exercise 2: Correct the Problem and Remove Exchange Server 2003
Successfully 2-45

Chapter Summary 2-45

Exam Highlights 2-46

Key Points 2-46

Key Terms 2-46

Questions and Answers 2-47

3   Configuring a Microsoft Exchange Server 2003 Infrastructure   3-1

Why This Chapter Matters 3-1

Before You Begin 3-1

Lesson 1: Post-Installation Considerations 3-2

Exchange Server 2003 Services 3-2

Delegation of Authority 3-5

Administration from Client Workstations 3-7

Adding and Removing Exchange Server 2003 Components 3-8

Practice: Post-Installation Considerations 3-8

Lesson Review 3-10

Lesson Summary 3-12

Lesson 2: Administrative and Routing Groups 3-13
   Administrative Groups 3-13
   Routing Groups 3-15
   Practice: Administrative and Routing Groups 3-17
   Lesson Review 3-18
   Lesson Summary 3-19
Lesson 3: Mixed Mode and Native Mode 3-21
   Mixed Mode and Native Mode Concepts 3-21
   Mixed Mode Benefits and Limitations 3-22
   Native Mode Advantages 3-24
   Lesson Review 3-26
   Lesson Summary 3-27
Lesson 4: Front-End and Back-End Servers 3-28
   Front-End and Back-End Architecture 3-28
   Front-End and Back-End Scenarios 3-29
   Lesson Review 3-31
   Lesson Summary 3-32
Case Scenario Exercise 3-32
   Requirement 1 3-33
   Requirement 2 3-34
   Requirement 3 3-34
Chapter Summary 3-35
Exam Highlights 3-36
   Key Points 3-36
   Key Terms 3-36
Questions and Answers 3-37

4   Coexistence with Microsoft Exchange Server 5.5   4-1

Why This Chapter Matters 4-1
Before You Begin 4-2
Lesson 1: Connecting Exchange Server 5.5 to Active Directory 4-3
   Installing the Active Directory Connector 4-3
   Using the ADC Tools 4-5
   Setting Up a Connection Agreement Manually 4-6
   Practice: Connecting Exchange Server 5.5 to Active Directory 4-8
   Lesson Review 4-21
   Lesson Summary 4-22
Lesson 2: Installing Exchange Server 2003 into an Existing Exchange
Server 5.5 Organization 4-23
   Installing Exchange Server 2003 into an Exchange Server 5.5 Organization 4-23

Practice: Installing Exchange Server 2003 into an Existing Exchange
Server 5.5 Organization   4-29

Lesson Review   4-32

Lesson Summary   4-33

Lesson 3: Troubleshooting Connectivity Between Active Directory and Exchange
Server 5.5   4-34

Merging Duplicate Accounts   4-34

Troubleshooting the ADC   4-35

Troubleshooting the Site Replication Service   4-38

Practice: Troubleshooting Connectivity between Active Directory and
Exchange Server 5.5   4-38

Lesson Review   4-41

Lesson Summary   4-42

Case Scenario Exercise   4-42

Requirement 1   4-43

Requirement 2   4-43

Troubleshooting Lab   4-44

Exercise 1: Configure a Connection Agreement.   4-44

Exercise 2: Change the LDAP Port   4-44

Chapter Summary   4-45

Exam Highlights   4-45

Key Points   4-45

Key Terms.   4-46

Questions and Answers   4-47

5   Migrating from Microsoft Exchange Server and Other Mail Systems   5-1

Why This Chapter Matters   5-1

Before You Begin.   5-2

Lesson 1: Upgrading from Exchange Server 5.5 and Exchange Server 2000 . . .   5-3

Upgrading and Migrating an Exchange Server 5.5 Organization to
Exchange Server 2003   5-3

Upgrading and Migrating an Exchange 2000 Server Organization to
Exchange Server 2003   5-11

Practice: Upgrading from Exchange Server 5.5 and Exchange Server
2000   5-14

Lesson Review   5-24

Lesson Summary   5-25

Lesson 2: Configuring Exchange Server 2003 to Coexist with Other
Messaging Systems   5-26

Configuring Exchange Server 2003 to Coexist with Lotus Notes   5-26

Configuring Exchange Server 2003 to Coexist with X.400-Compliant

Messaging Systems 5-32

Practice: Configuring Exchange Server 2003 to Coexist with Other
Messaging Systems 5-33

Lesson Review 5-37

Lesson Summary 5-38

Lesson 3: Migrating from Other Messaging Systems 5-39

Using the Migration Wizard to Migrate from Other Messaging Systems . . . 5-39

Lesson Review 5-41

Lesson Summary 5-41

Case Scenario Exercise 5-42

Requirement 1 5-42

Requirement 2 5-43

Troubleshooting Lab 5-43

Exercise 1: Attempt to Migrate Mailboxes with the Migration Wizard 5-44

Exercise 2: Migrate Mailboxes with Active Directory Users And
Computers 5-44

Chapter Summary 5-44

Exam Highlights 5-45

Key Points 5-45

Key Terms 5-45

Questions and Answers 5-47

**6   Installing Microsoft Exchange Server 2003 Clusters and Front-End and
Back-End Servers   6-1**

Why This Chapter Matters 6-1

Before You Begin 6-2

Lesson 1: Installing Exchange Server 2003 in a Clustered Environment 6-3

Network Load Balancing and Microsoft Cluster Service 6-3

Exchange Server 2003 and Clustering 6-8

Installing Exchange Server 2003 on a Windows Server 2003 Cluster 6-11

Practice: Installing Exchange Server 2003 in a Clustered Environment . . . 6-12

Lesson Review 6-16

Lesson Summary 6-18

Lesson 2: Managing an Exchange Server 2003 Cluster 6-19

Creating an Exchange Server 2003 Virtual Server 6-19

Managing Exchange Server 2003 Clustered Services 6-20

Practice: Managing an Exchange Server 2003 Cluster 6-23

Lesson Review 6-27

Lesson Summary 6-28

Lesson 3: Installing Exchange Server 2003 in a Front-End and Back-End
Configuration 6-29
   Configuring Exchange Server 2003 as a Front-End Server. 6-29
   Front-End and Back-End Servers and Clustering. 6-30
   Practice: Installing Exchange Server 2003 in a Front-End and Back-End
   Configuration 6-32
   Lesson Review 6-33
   Lesson Summary 6-34
Case Scenario Exercise 6-34
   Requirement 1 6-35
   Requirement 2 6-35
Chapter Summary 6-36
Exam Highlights 6-36
   Key Points 6-37
   Key Terms. 6-37
Questions and Answers 6-38

7 Managing Recipient Objects and Address Lists   7-1

Why This Chapter Matters 7-1
Before You Begin. 7-2
Lesson 1: Configuring Recipient Objects 7-3
   Recipient Types. 7-3
   Managing Mailboxes 7-10
   Managing Mail-Enabled Groups 7-37
   Practice: Configuring Recipient Objects 7-41
   Lesson Review 7-43
   Lesson Summary 7-45
Lesson 2: Configuring Information Stores 7-46
   Understanding Storage Group Architecture 7-46
   Understanding the Use of Multiple Databases and Storage Groups. 7-47
   Adding Storage Groups and Databases. 7-48
   Moving Exchange Server 2003 Storage Groups and Databases 7-52
   Practice: Configuring Information Stores 7-54
   Lesson Review 7-55
   Lesson Summary 7-57
Lesson 3: Creating and Managing Address Lists and Recipient Policies. 7-58
   Creating and Modifying Address Lists 7-58
   Administering Address Lists. 7-62
   Managing a Recipient Update Service. 7-64
   Working with Offline Address Lists 7-66

Creating and Applying Recipient Policies 7-67

Practice: Creating and Managing Address Lists and Recipient Policies . . . 7-69

Lesson Review 7-70

Lesson Summary 7-72

Case Scenario Exercise 7-72

Requirement 1 7-74

Requirement 2 7-74

Requirement 3 7-75

Troubleshooting Lab 7-75

Exercise 1: Create a Recipient Policy 7-75

Exercise 2: Apply the Recipient Policy 7-76

Chapter Summary 7-76

Exam Highlights 7-77

Key Points 7-77

Key Terms 7-77

Questions and Answers 7-78

8   **Public Folders**   **8-1**

Why This Chapter Matters 8-1

Before You Begin 8-1

Lesson 1: Creating Public Folders 8-2

Using Public Folders 8-2

Creating Public Folders 8-3

Creating a Public Folder Tree 8-7

Practice: Creating Public Folders 8-8

Lesson Review 8-11

Lesson Summary 8-12

Lesson 2: Administering Public Folders 8-13

Managing E-Mail Properties for Public Folders 8-13

Setting Storage Limits on Public Folders 8-18

Moving Public Folders 8-19

Public Folder Replication 8-19

Practice: Administering Public Folders 8-23

Lesson Review 8-24

Lesson Summary 8-25

Lesson 3: Public Folder Security 8-26

Inherited and Assigned Permissions 8-26

Configuring Permissions 8-28

Practice: Public Folder Security 8-32

Lesson Review 8-33

Lesson Summary 8-34

Case Scenario Exercise 8-34

Requirement 1 8-35

Requirement 2 8-36

Requirement 3 8-36

Troubleshooting Lab 8-36

Exercise 1: Create a Public Folder and Test E-Mail 8-37

Exercise 2: Mail-Enable and Create an Additional E-Mail Address for a
Public Folder 8-37

Chapter Summary 8-37

Exam Highlights 8-38

Key Points 8-38

Key Terms. 8-38

Questions and Answers 8-40

9   Virtual Servers   9-1

Why This Chapter Matters 9-1

Before You Begin. 9-2

Lesson 1: Overview of Exchange Server 2003 Virtual Servers 9-3

Virtual Servers in a Windows Clustering Environment. 9-3

Virtual Servers in a Network Load Balancing Environment 9-4

Exchange Virtual Server Requirements 9-4

Overview of POP3 Virtual Servers 9-5

Overview of IMAP4 Virtual Servers 9-7

Overview of NNTP Virtual Servers 9-8

Overview of HTTP Virtual Servers 9-11

Overview of SMTP Virtual Servers. 9-14

Practice: Enabling and Starting the POP3, IMAP4, and NNTP Services. . . . 9-15

Lesson Review 9-19

Lesson Summary 9-19

Lesson 2: Configuring Virtual Server Settings 9-20

Creating Additional Virtual Servers 9-20

Configuring Virtual Server Settings 9-21

Front-End and Back-End Configuration 9-24

Practice: Creating and Configuring Virtual Servers 9-25

Lesson Review 9-39

Lesson Summary 9-39

Lesson 3: Configuring Authentication 9-41

Configuring Virtual Server Authentication Methods. 9-41

Configuring Client Access to Virtual Server Protocols 9-43

Practice: Obtaining, Installing, and Associating a Certificate for an
IMAP4 Virtual Server on a Front-End Exchange Server 9-44
Practice: Configuring Authentication 9-45
Lesson Review 9-50
Lesson Summary 9-51
Lesson 4: Maintaining Virtual Servers 9-52
Virtual Server Status 9-52
Viewing Connected Users and Terminating Connections 9-52
Diagnostic Logging 9-53
Practice: Viewing and Managing Connected Users on an IMAP4 Virtual
Server 9-53
Lesson Review 9-53
Lesson Summary 9-54
Case Scenario Exercise 9-54
Requirement 1 9-55
Requirement 2 9-56
Requirement 3 9-56
Troubleshooting Lab 9-56
Chapter Summary 9-58
Exam Highlights 9-59
Key Points 9-59
Key Terms 9-59
Questions and Answers 9-60

10   **SMTP Protocol Configuration and Management**   **10-1**
Why This Chapter Matters 10-1
Before You Begin 10-2
Lesson 1: Managing SMTP Message Transfer Support 10-3
How SMTP Implements a Connection 10-3
How ESMTP Implements a Connection 10-5
Configuring DNS to Support SMTP 10-9
Configuring Internet Connectivity 10-11
Configuring SMTP Relays 10-12
Practice: Creating MX Records and Configuring an SMTP Connector 10-15
Practice: Configuring an SMTP Connector to Use a Relay Host for
Outbound SMTP 10-18
Lesson Review 10-19
Lesson Summary 10-20
Lesson 2: Configuring SMTP Security and Advanced Options 10-21
Configuring Connections 10-21

Securing SMTP Traffic 10-23
Practice: Configuring SMTP Security and Demand-Dial
Communications 10-27
Lesson Review 10-34
Lesson Summary 10-35
Lesson 3: Configuring Interoperability with Other SMTP Messaging
Systems 10-36
Configuring Global Settings 10-37
Supporting HTTP Clients 10-39
Supporting IMAP4 Clients 10-41
Supporting POP3 Clients 10-42
Supporting NNTP Clients 10-43
Practice: Message and Client Configuration. 10-44
Lesson Review 10-51
Lesson Summary 10-51
Case Scenario Exercise 10-52
Requirement 1 10-53
Requirement 2 10-53
Requirement 3 10-54
Troubleshooting Lab 10-54
Chapter Summary 10-56
Exam Highlights 10-56
Key Points 10-56
Key Terms. 10-57
Questions and Answers 10-58

11 Microsoft Exchange Server 2003 Security   **11-1**

Why This Chapter Matters 11-1
Before You Begin. 11-2
Lesson 1: Managing Connectivity Across Firewalls 11-3
How a Firewall Works. 11-3
MAPI Client Connection Through a Firewall 11-5
Practice: Configuring Exchange Server 2003 to Use RPC Over HTTP 11-5
Lesson Review 11-11
Lesson Summary 11-11
Lesson 2: Protecting Against Computer Viruses. 11-12
Viruses, Worms, and Trojan Horses 11-12
Preparing an Antivirus Strategy. 11-13
Choosing Antivirus Software. 11-16
Virus-Clean Policies and Procedures 11-16

Security Updates. 11-18

Practice: Downloading Antivirus Software 11-20

Lesson Review 11-20

Lesson Summary 11-21

Lesson 3: Securing Mailboxes 11-22

Message Filtering 11-22

Guidelines for Securing Mailboxes 11-24

Practice: Configuring the Junk E-Mail Feature in Outlook 2003 and
Enabling Connection Filtering 11-25

Lesson Review 11-29

Lesson Summary 11-29

Lesson 4: Implementing Digital Signature and Encryption Capabilities. 11-30

Digital Signature and Encryption. 11-30

Practice: Deploying Digital Signature and Encryption Certificates. 11-32

Lesson Review 11-35

Lesson Summary 11-35

Lesson 5: Configuring Administrative Permissions 11-36

Administrative Groups 11-36

The Exchange Administration Delegation Wizard 11-37

Advanced Security Permissions 11-38

Practice: Creating and Using an Administrative Group 11-39

Lesson Review 11-44

Lesson Summary 11-45

Lesson 6: Disabling Services and Protocol Logging 11-46

Services Used by Exchange Server 2003 11-46

Protocol Logging 11-51

Practice: Enabling and Configuring Protocol Logging. 11-53

Lesson Review 11-55

Lesson Summary 11-56

Case Scenario Exercise. 11-56

Requirement 1 11-57

Requirement 2 11-57

Requirement 3 11-58

Troubleshooting Lab 11-58

Chapter Summary. 11-61

Exam Highlights 11-61

Key Points 11-61

Key Terms. 11-62

Questions and Answers. 11-63

12   Backup and Restore   12-1

Why This Chapter Matters 12-1

Before You Begin. 12-1

Lesson 1: Managing Data Storage 12-3

How Exchange Server 2003 Manages Data. 12-3

How Transaction Logs Protect Your Data 12-8

Storage Technologies 12-10

Practice: Managing Storage 12-12

Lesson Review 12-14

Lesson Summary 12-15

Lesson 2: Backing Up Exchange Server 2003 12-16

Types of Data to Back Up. 12-16

Backup Strategies. 12-17

Performing Backups 12-19

Practice: Performing Backups. 12-22

Lesson Review 12-26

Lesson Summary 12-27

Lesson 3: Restoring Exchange Server 2003 12-28

Recovering Databases. 12-28

Backing Up and Restoring System State Data 12-36

Restoring Entire Servers 12-36

Performing a Trial Restore 12-37

Practice: Recovering from a Disaster Using Restore. 12-37

Lesson Review 12-44

Lesson Summary 12-45

Case Scenario Exercise. 12-45

Requirement 1 12-46

Requirement 2 12-46

Requirement 3 12-47

Troubleshooting Lab 12-47

Chapter Summary 12-49

Exam Highlights 12-50

Key Points 12-50

Key Terms. 12-50

Questions and Answers 12-51

13   Monitoring Microsoft Exchange Server 2003   13-1

Why This Chapter Matters 13-1

Before You Begin. 13-2

Lesson 1: Performing Daily Exchange Server 2003 Monitoring and
Maintenance. 13-3
    Daily Monitoring Tasks. 13-3
    Event Viewer. 13-8
    The Monitoring And Status Utility 13-11
    Queue Viewer 13-11
    Practice: Configuring Diagnostic Levels and the Monitoring And Status
    Utility 13-14
    Lesson Review 13-18
    Lesson Summary 13-19
Lesson 2: Performing Scheduled Exchange Server 2003 Monitoring and
Maintenance. 13-20
    Scheduled Maintenance Tasks 13-20
    The Performance Console 13-22
    Protocol Logs 13-23
    HTTP Monitor 13-25
    Mailbox Limits 13-26
    The Badmail Folder 13-27
    The Postmaster Mailbox 13-27
    Practice: Using Performance and Protocol Logs and Managing Mailbox
    Limits. 13-28
    Lesson Review 13-33
    Lesson Summary 13-33
Lesson 3: Performing On-Demand Exchange Server 2003 Monitoring and
Maintenance. 13-35
    On-Demand Maintenance Tasks 13-35
    Offline Defragmentation. 13-36
    Verifying Exchange Store Integrity 13-37
    Checking Queues 13-38
    Exchange Server 2003 Management Tools 13-38
    Practice: Defragmenting Exchange Stores and Checking Their Integrity . . 13-39
    Lesson Review 13-41
    Lesson Summary 13-42
Case Scenario Exercise 13-42
    Requirement 1 13-43
    Requirement 2 13-43
    Requirement 3 13-44
Troubleshooting Lab 13-44
    Exercise 1: Install and Use Network Monitor 13-45
Chapter Summary 13-50

Exam Highlights 13-51
    Key Points 13-51
    Key Terms. 13-51
Questions and Answers 13-53

14   Troubleshooting Microsoft Exchange Server 2003   14-1

Why This Chapter Matters 14-2
Before You Begin. 14-2
Lesson 1: Troubleshooting Exchange Server 2003 Server Migration and
Interoperability 14-4
    Troubleshooting Installation 14-4
    Removing an Exchange Server 2003 Server 14-7
    Troubleshooting Connectivity 14-8
    Troubleshooting Migration 14-8
    Troubleshooting Interoperability 14-9
    Practice: Using the Netdiag and Dcdiag Command-Line Utilities 14-10
    Lesson Review 14-14
    Lesson Summary 14-15
Lesson 2: Troubleshooting Exchange Server 2003 Servers 14-16
    Troubleshooting Server Health 14-16
    Troubleshooting Data Storage 14-18
    Troubleshooting Clusters 14-19
    Troubleshooting Backup and Restore 14-20
    Practice: Configuring an Alert. 14-21
    Lesson Review 14-24
    Lesson Summary 14-25
Lesson 3: Troubleshooting the Exchange Server 2003 Organization 14-26
    Troubleshooting Public Folders 14-26
    Troubleshooting Virtual Servers 14-28
    Troubleshooting Front-End and Back-End Servers 14-29
    Troubleshooting Connectivity 14-30
    Practice: Limiting Write and Delete Permissions to Public Folders 14-31
    Lesson Review 14-34
    Lesson Summary 14-35
Lesson 4: Troubleshooting Security 14-36
    Troubleshooting Connectivity Across Firewalls 14-36
    Troubleshooting Permissions 14-39
    Troubleshooting Encryption and Digital Signatures 14-40
    Practice: Checking That E-Mail is Encrypted. 14-41
    Lesson Review 14-44

      Lesson Summary 14-44

Lesson 5: Troubleshooting Technologies That Support Exchange Server
2003 14-45

      Troubleshooting Host Resolution 14-45

      Troubleshooting DNS 14-48

      Troubleshooting Active Directory Issues 14-51

      Troubleshooting Network Connectivity 14-52

      Practice: Managing the ARP Cache and Analyzing an ARP Packet 14-56

      Lesson Review 14-59

      Lesson Summary 14-60

Case Scenario Exercise 14-60

      Requirement 1 14-61

      Requirement 2 14-62

      Requirement 3 14-62

Troubleshooting Lab 14-63

Chapter Summary 14-66

Exam Highlights 14-67

      Key Points 14-67

      Key Terms 14-67

Questions and Answers 14-68

Glossary G-1

Index I-1

Acknowledgments

Writing a book is often a strenuous task, particularly when it is in addition to being a full-time IT professional, ¾-time seminary student, and full-time husband and father. The full gamut of emotions come into play: joy, depression, frustration, exhilaration, humility, and pride. I cannot thank my wife Melissa enough for her support when it seemed like from one day to the next she'd never know what my mood would be. I can be a big pain in the rear, but she rarely complains. I'd also like to thank my kids Duncan and Rebekah, who even at 5 years old and 18 months teach me that life is usually a lot simpler than we make it out to be. Seeing the world through their eyes helps me not to worry so much about the things I can't control.

I'd like to also thank my dad, Bill Willis. His fun-loving attitude towards life had a way of draining away life's stress when he was around. He passed away all too young, while I was working on this book, and it has been a great loss in my life. To my mom, Ann, and my sister Alexandra, thanks for everything you guys have done for me over the years.

Thanks to Bill and Melba Duncan for being there for us. Your generosity never goes unnoticed or unappreciated. Donna, you're like a sister to me; thanks for being someone I can talk to about practically anything. It means a lot to me.

Thanks to the gang at CertTutor.net. The tutors and members of the site form a community that doesn't come easily in the online world. There are too many good people to list everyone individually, but those I am close to know who they are. Special thanks to Lisa Arase, who has been a good friend who is always willing to listen while I ramble on about anything and everything.

Thanks to my lifelong friends: Kim Larsen, Ken Lord, Charles Thompson, Matt Rutherford, Nick Smith, Ian Worcester, Phil Martinelle, Brian Howard, Jimmy Crider, Chad Rolph, Shane Cook, and Matt Bird.

Thanks to everyone at Trinity Southern Baptist Church who has had a positive influence on my life.

Thanks to Annie Miller, Gary Cloninger, Patrick Nesbitt, Ray Street, Bill Thurlow, George Shepherd, and Rick Heffel. You guys make coming to work in the morning something I look forward to.

I feel like I could fill an entire chapter thanking the people who have meant something to me and who influenced me along the way. To everyone I didn't have room to mention specifically, know that you are in my thoughts and prayers.

Will Willis

Writing a book is a team effort, and my part of this one owes much to the outstanding people with whom I worked at Microsoft Press. Kathy Harding, my acquisitions editor, trusted me with the project initially, and gave me a whole heap of encouragement and support, especially in the difficult first stages.

Melissa von Tschudi-Sutton, my copy editor, spotted all sorts of inconsistencies that I'd missed, corrected my English, explained the corrections (which was of enormous assistance) and maintained a consistent Microsoft style that contributed greatly to the quality of the book. Melissa went well beyond the call of duty when I was unsure of elements to be added, and contributed far more to the book than any author can expect of an editor.

The whole operation was managed most efficiently by my project manager at nSight Publishing Services, Susan McClung. Susan made sure that everything was done on time and to specification. She also contributed greatly to the style and consistency of the work and was firm in her handling of an author with an unfortunate tendency to fly off at a tangent.

The mainstay of this entire project was Julie Pickering, my project manager at Microsoft Learning, a true professional who guided and encouraged me through the days when I knew I was never going to get the thing finished. Julie had the impossible job of interfacing between an author who was fortunate to get three hours sleep in a night (and can get bad-tempered at the best of times) and a production team struggling to meet tight deadlines. She handled this task with unfailing tact, courtesy, and kindness.

I also owe a great deal to Chris Russo, my technical editor. Chris's comments were always pertinent and perceptive, and his suggestions added much value to the book. When working to a tight deadline, errors can creep in, and it was an enormous comfort to have someone with Chris's exceptional ability and deep technical knowledge minding my back.

I have known Will Willis for some considerable time—even before we became fellow tutors on the CertTutor forum. I have always admired Will's work, but this is our first joint book. It is an honor to have my name on the same cover as an author of Will's stature.

There are few creatures more antisocial than an author in mid-book. I would have gotten nowhere without the support of my lovely wife, Anne. She has been through this process many times before, and will go through it all again—and still she loves me. I'm a lucky guy.

Ian McLean

About This Book

Welcome to *MCSA/MCSE Self-Paced Training Kit (Exam 70-284): Implementing and Managing Microsoft Exchange Server 2003*. This training kit is designed to provide the knowledge you need in order to pass the 70-284 certification exam and to train you to implement, manage, and administer Exchange Server 2003 effectively in a real-world environment. After all, passing an exam is of little value if you cannot translate that knowledge into real-world Exchange Server administration skills. To assist you in this pursuit, this training kit combines a mixture of theory, practical insight, real-world examples, hands-on exercises, and questions designed to reinforce what you've learned.

Note For more information about becoming a Microsoft Certified Professional, see the section entitled "The Microsoft Certified Professional Program" later in this introduction.

Intended Audience

This book was developed for information technology (IT) professionals who plan to take the related Microsoft Certified Professional Exam 70-284: Implementing and Managing Microsoft Exchange Server 2003, as well as IT professionals who design, implement, manage, and maintain Exchange Server solutions in Microsoft Windows–based environments.

Note Exam skills tested are subject to change without prior notice and at the sole discretion of Microsoft.

Prerequisites

This training kit requires that students meet the following prerequisites:

A candidate for this exam should have at least one year of experience implementing and managing an Exchange Server messaging system in environments that have the following characteristics:

- 250 to 5,000 or more users

- Three or more physical locations

- Network services and resources such as multiple versions of Exchange Server, Active Directory directory service, a proxy server, a firewall, other messaging systems, Domain Name System (DNS), Internet access, an intranet, and mobile client computers

■ Network services and resources such as multiple versions of Exchange Server, Active Directory directory service, a proxy server, a firewall, other messaging systems, Domain Name System (DNS), Internet access, an intranet, and mobile client computers

■ Two or more computers running Exchange Server

■ Connectivity requirements such as connecting branch offices and individual users in remote locations to the corporate network and connecting corporate networks to the Internet

About the CD-ROM

For your use, this book includes a Supplemental CD-ROM, which contains a variety of informational aids to complement the book content:

■ The Microsoft Press Readiness Review Suite Powered by MeasureUp. This suite of practice tests and objective reviews contains questions of varying degrees of complexity and offers multiple testing modes. You can assess your understanding of the concepts presented in this book and use the results to develop a learning plan that meets your needs.

■ An electronic version of this book (eBook). For information about using the eBook, see the section titled "The eBook" later in this introduction.

■ An eBook of the *Microsoft Encyclopedia of Security* provides complete and up-to-date reference material for security.

Features of This Book

Each chapter identifies the exam objectives that are covered within the chapter, provides an overview of why the topics matter by identifying how the information is applied in the real world, and lists any prerequisites that must be met to complete the lessons presented in the chapter.

The chapters are divided into lessons. Lessons contain practices that include one or more hands-on exercises. These exercises give you an opportunity to use the skills being presented or explore the part of the application being described.

After the lessons, you are given an opportunity to apply what you've learned in a case scenario exercise. In this exercise, you work through a multi-step solution for a realistic case scenario. You are also given an opportunity to work through a troubleshooting lab that explores difficulties you might encounter when applying what you've learned on the job.

Each chapter ends with a summary of key concepts and a section listing key topics and terms you need to know before taking the exam. This section summarizes the key topics you've learned, with a focus on demonstrating that knowledge on the exam.

Real World   Helpful Information

You will find sidebars like this one that contain related information you might find helpful. "Real World" sidebars contain specific information gained through the experience of IT professionals just like you.

Informational Notes

Several types of reader aids appear throughout the training kit.

Tip   Contains methods of performing a task more quickly or in a not-so-obvious way.

Important   Contains information that is essential to completing a task.

Note   Contains supplemental information.

Caution   Contains valuable information about possible loss of data; be sure to read this information carefully.

Warning   Contains critical information about possible physical injury; be sure to read this information carefully.

See Also   Contains references to other sources of information.

Planning   Contains hints and useful information that should help you to plan the implementation.

Security Alert   Highlights information you need to know to maximize security in your work environment.

Exam Tip   Flags information you should know before taking the certification exam.

Off the Record   Contains practical advice about the real-world implications of information presented in the lesson.

Notational Conventions

The following conventions are used throughout this book.

- Characters or commands that you type appear in **bold** type.

- *Italic* in syntax statements indicates placeholders for variable information. Italic is also used for book titles.

- Names of files and folders appear in Title caps, except when you are to type them directly. Unless otherwise indicated, you can use all lowercase letters when you type a file name in a dialog box or at a command prompt.

- Most file name extensions appear in all lowercase.

- Acronyms appear in all uppercase.

- Monospace type represents code samples, examples of screen text, or entries that you might type at a command prompt or in initialization files.

- Square brackets [ ] are used in syntax statements to enclose optional items. For example, [*filename*] in command syntax indicates that you can choose to type a file name with the command. Type only the information within the brackets, not the brackets themselves.

- Braces { } are used in syntax statements to enclose required items. Type only the information within the braces, not the braces themselves.

Keyboard Conventions

- A plus sign (+) between two key names means that you must press those keys at the same time. For example, "Press ALT+TAB" means that you hold down ALT while you press TAB.

- A comma (,) between two or more key names means that you must press each of the keys consecutively, not together. For example, "Press ALT, F, X" means that you press and release each key in sequence. "Press ALT+W, L" means that you first press ALT and W at the same time, and then release them and press L.

Getting Started

This training kit contains hands-on exercises to help you go from simply understanding the theory behind the concepts being discussed to developing the hands-on skills necessary to implement and manage Exchange Server 2003 in different real-world environments. Use this section to prepare your self-paced training environment.

To complete some of these procedures, you must have two networked computers or be connected to a larger network. Both computers must be capable of running Microsoft Windows Server 2003 and Exchange Server 2003.

> **Caution** Several exercises might require you to make changes to your servers. This might have undesirable results if you are connected to a larger network. Check with your network administrator before attempting these exercises.

Hardware Requirements

Each computer must have the following minimum configuration. All hardware should be on the Microsoft Windows Server 2003 Hardware Compatibility List:

- Pentium 133 or better
- 256 megabytes (MB) of random access memory (RAM)
- 200 MB free hard disk space on the system drive
- 500 MB free hard disk space on the partition Exchange Server 2003 is installed on
- CD-ROM drive or DVD drive
- Microsoft Mouse or compatible pointing device

Setup Instructions

Set up your computer according to the manufacturer's instructions.

For the exercises that require networked computers, you need to make sure the computers can communicate with each other. The configuration of the computers will change depending on the requirements for the chapter; therefore, the required configurations will be given at the beginning of each chapter. Most chapters require two computers that can be configured as servers, though in some instances a third computer will be required.

Caution If your computers are part of a larger network, you must verify with your network administrator that the computer names, domain name, and other information used in setting up Windows Server 2003 and Exchange Server 2003 do not conflict with network operations. If they do conflict, ask your network administrator to provide alternative values and use those values throughout all the exercises in this training kit.

The Readiness Review Suite

The CD-ROM includes a practice test made up of 300 sample exam questions and an objective-by-objective review with an additional 125 questions. Use these tools to reinforce your learning and to identify any areas in which you need to gain more experience before taking the exam.

▶ **To install the practice test and objective review**

1. Insert the Supplemental CD-ROM into your CD-ROM drive.

Note If AutoRun is disabled on your machine, refer to the Readme.txt file on the CD-ROM.

2. Click Readiness Review Suite on the user interface menu.

The eBook

The CD-ROM includes an electronic version of the training kit. The eBook is in portable document format (PDF) and can be viewed using Adobe Acrobat Reader.

▶ **To use the eBook**

1. Insert the Supplemental CD-ROM into your CD-ROM drive.

Note If AutoRun is disabled on your machine, refer to the Readme.txt file on the CD-ROM.

2. Click Training Kit eBook on the user interface menu. You can also review any of the other eBooks that are provided for your use.

The Microsoft Certified Professional Program

The Microsoft Certified Professional (MCP) program provides the best method to prove your command of current Microsoft products and technologies. The exams and corresponding certifications are developed to validate your mastery of critical competencies as you design and develop, or implement and support, solutions with Microsoft products and technologies. Computer professionals who become Microsoft certified are recognized as experts and are sought after industrywide. Certification brings a variety of benefits to the individual and to employers and organizations.

> **See Also** For a full list of MCP benefits, go to *http://www.microsoft.com/traincert/start/itpro.asp.*

Certifications

The Microsoft Certified Professional program offers multiple certifications, based on specific areas of technical expertise:

- **Microsoft Certified Professional (MCP)** Demonstrated in-depth knowledge of at least one Microsoft Windows operating system or architecturally significant platform. An MCP is qualified to implement a Microsoft product or technology as part of a business solution for an organization.

- **Microsoft Certified Solution Developer (MCSD)** Microsoft Certified Solution Developer (MCSD). Professional developers qualified to analyze, design, and develop enterprise business solutions with Microsoft development tools and technologies including the Microsoft .NET Framework.

- **Microsoft Certified Application Developer (MCAD)** Professional developers qualified to develop, test, deploy, and maintain powerful applications using Microsoft tools and technologies including Microsoft Visual Studio .NET and XML Web services.

- **Microsoft Certified Systems Engineer (MCSE)** Qualified to effectively analyze the business requirements, and design and implement the infrastructure for business solutions based on the Microsoft Windows and Microsoft Server 2003 operating system.

- **Microsoft Certified Systems Administrator (MCSA)** Individuals with the skills to manage and troubleshoot existing network and system environments based on the Microsoft Windows and Microsoft Server 2003 operating systems.

- **Microsoft Certified Database Administrator (MCDBA)**   Individuals who design, implement, and administer Microsoft SQL Server databases.

- **Microsoft Certified Trainer (MCT)**   Instructionally and technically qualified to deliver Microsoft Official Curriculum through a Microsoft Certified Technical Education Center (CTEC).

Requirements for Becoming a Microsoft Certified Professional

The certification requirements differ for each certification and are specific to the products and job functions addressed by the certification.

To become a Microsoft Certified Professional, you must pass rigorous certification exams that provide a valid and reliable measure of technical proficiency and expertise. These exams are designed to test your expertise and ability to perform a role or task with a product, and are developed with the input of professionals in the industry. Questions in the exams reflect how Microsoft products are used in actual organizations, giving them "real-world" relevance.

- Microsoft Certified Product (MCPs) candidates are required to pass one current Microsoft certification exam. Candidates can pass additional Microsoft certification exams to further qualify their skills with other Microsoft products, development tools, or desktop applications.

- Microsoft Certified Solution Developers (MCSDs) are required to pass three core exams and one elective exam. (MCSD for Microsoft .NET candidates are required to pass four core exams and one elective.)

- Microsoft Certified Application Developers (MCADs) are required to pass two core exams and one elective exam in an area of specialization.

- Microsoft Certified Systems Engineers (MCSEs) are required to pass five core exams and two elective exams.

- Microsoft Certified Systems Administrators (MCSAs) are required to pass three core exams and one elective exam that provide a valid and reliable measure of technical proficiency and expertise.

- Microsoft Certified Database Administrators (MCDBAs) are required to pass three core exams and one elective exam that provide a valid and reliable measure of technical proficiency and expertise.

- Microsoft Certified Trainers (MCTs) are required to meet instructional and technical requirements specific to each Microsoft Official Curriculum course they are certified to deliver. The MCT program requires ongoing training to meet the requirements for the annual renewal of certification. For more information about becoming a Microsoft Certified Trainer, visit *http://www.microsoft.com/traincert/mcp/mct/* or contact a regional service center near you.

Technical Support

Every effort has been made to ensure the accuracy of this book and the contents of the companion disc. If you have comments, questions, or ideas regarding this book or the companion disc, please send them to Microsoft Press using either of the following methods:

E-mail: tkinput@microsoft.com

Postal Mail: Microsoft Press
                   Attn: *MCSA/MCSE Self-Paced Training Kit (Exam 70-284):*
                   Implementing and Managing Microsoft Exchange Server 2003, Editor
                   One Microsoft Way
                   Redmond, WA 98052-6399

For additional support information regarding this book and the CD-ROM (including answers to commonly asked questions about installation and use), visit the Microsoft Press Technical Support Web site at *http://www.microsoft.com/mspress/support/*. To connect directly to the Microsoft Press Knowledge Base and enter a query, visit *http://www.microsoft.com/mspress/support/search.asp*. For support information regarding Microsoft software, please connect to *http://support.microsoft.com/*.

1 Microsoft Exchange Server 2003 and Active Directory

Exam Objectives in this Chapter:

- Prepare the environment for the Exchange Server deployment

Why This Chapter Matters

With Microsoft Exchange Server 5.5 and earlier, the administration of Exchange Server was independent of the Microsoft Windows NT Server structure. Exchange Server had its own directory, and it was tied to Windows NT only for mailbox authentication purposes. A mailbox was not directly related to a user object in Windows NT and could be associated with any user or security group. In fact, it was common for an NT domain user account to be associated with multiple mailboxes.

Beginning with Microsoft Exchange Server 2000, there is a much tighter integration between Exchange Server and the Windows domain infrastructure, which is based on Active Directory directory service. This is also true in Exchange Server 2003. As a result, the importance of understanding Active Directory as an Exchange administrator cannot be overstated. This chapter introduces you to the concepts behind Active Directory and describes how Exchange Server 2003 integrates with it.

Lessons in this Chapter:

- Lesson 1: Overview of Active Directory 1-2
- Lesson 2: Exchange Server 2003 Integration with Active Directory 1-8
- Lesson 3: Exchange Server 2003 and Windows Server 2003 Protocols and Services Integration 1-12

Before You Begin

This chapter is primarily concerned with concepts that you will need to understand and consider prior to deploying Exchange Server 2003. The focus is conceptual rather than instructional, but it is important to understand how Exchange Server 2003 relates to Active Directory in order to be an effective administrator. While there are no hands-on exercises in this chapter, the fundamental concepts in this chapter will prepare you for what comes later in the training kit.

Lesson 1: Overview of Active Directory

Active Directory, first introduced with Microsoft Windows 2000 Server, allows administrators to create a more flexible network structure than what was previously available with Windows operating systems for servers. Active Directory is a directory service, and the benefits of a directory service–based approach to network design is that it allows for large distributed network environments that have a common centralized authority for network security. Active Directory provides a single point of management for Windows-based user accounts, clients, servers, and applications.

After this lesson, you will be able to

■ Understand Active Directory forests and domains

■ Understand sites

■ Understand the Active Directory schema

■ Understand organizational units (OUs)

■ Understand global catalogs

■ Understand operations masters

Estimated lesson time: 20 minutes

Active Directory Forests and Domains

The primary security boundary for Active Directory is the forest, which contains domain trees. There can be one or more domain trees in a forest, though the first domain is designated as the forest root domain. Domains in Active Directory are identified through their Domain Name System (DNS) names rather than the NetBIOS naming scheme that was prevalent in Windows NT Server 4 and earlier. An example of a DNS domain name is *contoso.com*. A domain tree can contain multiple domains that share a common namespace. For example, *contoso.com*, *marketing.contoso.com*, *sales.contoso.com*, and *europe.sales.contoso.com* are all a part of the same domain tree. The *marketing.contoso.com* domain is a child domain of *contoso.com*, the parent domain. Since a forest can contain multiple domain trees, you could also have a domain tree for *fabrikam.com* in the same forest as the *contoso.com* domain tree.

Regardless of the number of domain trees in a forest, there is centralized administration at the forest level with permissions to all domain trees. Each forest has an Enterprise Admins group as well as a Schema Admins group. Members of these groups have authority over all the domain trees in the forest. Each domain has a Domain Admins group, and administrators in a parent domain automatically have administrative permissions to all child domains through automatic transitive trust relationships.

This type of structure is known as a hierarchical structure, since there can be multiple levels. This differs from the flat structure of Windows NT domains, which did not support parent-child relationships between domains.

Active Directory Sites

With the amount of replication that takes place between domain controllers and the amount of querying of data that is done in Active Directory, it is important for computers and services to have a way of identifying Active Directory resources that are located on the same local area network (LAN) versus resources that are on a different LAN separated by a wide area network (WAN) connection. Active Directory uses the concept of sites to make this distinction. Sites contain Active Directory resources that are all connected by reliable high-speed bandwidth—a minimum of 10 megabytes (MB). Site membership is used in the logon process as a computer attempts to locate a domain controller in its own site first; in replication (intrasite replication occurs immediately, and intersite replication is scheduled); in accessing global catalogs (discussed in the section entitled "Global Catalogs," later in this lesson); and in the Exchange Server 2003 messaging infrastructure.

Active Directory Schema

One of the defining elements of a forest is a common schema. The schema is a definition of the types of objects that are allowed within a directory and the attributes that are associated with those objects. These definitions must be consistent across domains in order for the security policies and access rights to function correctly.

There are two types of definitions within the schema: attributes and classes, also known as schema objects and metadata. Attributes are defined only once, and then can be applied to multiple classes as needed. The object classes, or metadata, are used to define objects. For example, the Users class requires certain attributes such as user name, password, groups, and so on. A particular user account is simply an Active Directory object that has those attributes defined.

A class is simply a generic framework for objects. It is a collection of attributes, such as Logon Name and Home Directory for user accounts or Description and Network Address for computer accounts. Active Directory comes standard with a predefined set of attributes and classes that fit the needs for many network environments. In addition, network administrators can extend the schema by defining additional attributes and extending the classes within the directory.

Organizational Units

One of the enhancements within Active Directory is the ability to organize the network in a logical manner and hide the physical structure of the network from the end users.

Active Directory uses a special container known as an organizational unit (OU) to organize objects within a domain for the purpose of administration. OUs can be used to split a domain into administrative divisions that mirror the functional or physical separations within the company.

An OU can contain user accounts, computers, printers, shared folders, applications, and any other object within the domain. OUs can be used to separate administrative functions within a domain without granting administrative rights to the whole domain. This was something that couldn't be done prior to Active Directory.

An OU is the smallest element to which you can assign administrative rights. This means that OUs can be used to delegate authority and control within a domain; in essence, OUs function as subdomains without the creation of additional domains.

Global Catalogs

Domain controllers keep a complete copy of the Active Directory database for a domain, so that information about each object in the domain is readily available to users and services. This works well within a domain but poses problems when crossing domain trees. Active Directory solves this issue with a special limited database known as the *global catalog*. The global catalog stores partial replicas of the directories of other domains. The catalog is stored on domain controllers that have been designated as global catalog servers. These servers also maintain the normal database for their domain.

Function of the Global Catalog

The global catalog has two primary functions within Active Directory. These functions relate to the logon capability and queries within Active Directory.

Within a multidomain environment that is running in Windows 2000 Native mode or the Windows Server 2003 functional level, a global catalog is required for logging on to the network. The global catalog provides universal group membership information for the user account that is attempting to log on to the network. If the global catalog is not available during the logon attempt and the user account is external to the local domain, the user will only be allowed to log on to the local machine.

If the account is part of the local domain, the domain controllers for the local domain will handle the authentication request. The global catalog is required only when a user account or object needs to be authenticated by another domain.

Querying generates the majority of Active Directory traffic, and queries for objects (printers, services, and so on) occur much more often than database updates. Within a simple single-domain environment, the directory is readily available for these queries. However, in a highly complex, multidomain environment, having every query search through each domain would generate an unreasonable amount of network traffic.

The global catalog maintains a subset of the directory information available within every domain in the forest. This allows queries to be handled by the nearest global catalog, saving time and bandwidth. If more than one domain controller is a global catalog server, the response time for the queries improves. The tradeoff is that each additional global catalog server increases the amount of replication overhead within the network.

> **Note**   The global catalog is a read-only database, unlike the normal Active Directory database.

Global Catalog Servers

Active Directory automatically creates a global catalog on the first domain controller within a forest. Each forest requires at least one global catalog. In an environment with multiple sites, it is good practice to designate a domain controller in each site to function as a global catalog server. While any domain controller can be configured as a global catalog server, a sense of balance is necessary when designating these servers. As the number of global catalog servers increases, the response time to user inquiries decreases. However, the replication requirements within the environment increase as the number of global catalog servers increases.

Operations Masters

Much of the replication within an Active Directory environment is multimaster replication, which means that the domain controllers are all peers. This is in contrast to earlier versions of Windows NT, in which a primary domain controller (PDC) was responsible for recording all changes to the security policy and replicating those changes to the backup domain controllers (BDCs).

Some operations are impractical in a multimaster environment. Active Directory handles these operations by allowing only a single domain controller to make these types of changes. This domain controller is known as an *operations master*. There are five different operations master roles in Active Directory: Schema Master, Domain Naming Master, Relative ID Master, PDC Emulator, and Infrastructure Master. The Schema Master and Domain Naming Master roles function at the forest level and exist only once in a forest. The Relative ID Master, PDC Emulator, and Infrastructure Master roles function at the domain level and exist in each domain in the forest. The functions of the operations master roles are as follows:

- The Schema Master role controls all the updates and modifications to the schema itself. The schema controls the definition of each object in the directory and the object's associated attributes.

- The Domain Naming Master role controls the addition or removal of domains from the forest.

- The Relative ID (RID) Master role controls the sequence number for the domain controllers within the domain. The master assigns a unique sequence of RIDs to each of the domain controllers. When a new object is created by a domain controller, the object is assigned a security ID (SID). The SID must be unique within the domain and is generated by combining a domain SID and a RID. The domain SID is a constant ID within the domain, while the RID is assigned to the object by the domain controller. When the domain controller uses all the RIDs that the RID Master has assigned, the domain controller receives another sequence of RIDs from the RID Master. If the RID Master is unavailable and a domain controller exhausts its pool, it will be unable to create additional objects.

- The PDC Emulator role is used whenever a domain contains non–Active Directory computers. It acts as a Windows NT PDC for legacy client operating systems, as well as for Windows NT BDCs. The PDC Emulator processes password changes and receives preferential treatment within the domain for password updates. If another domain controller is unable to authenticate a user due to a bad password, the request is forwarded to the PDC Emulator.

- The Infrastructure Master role is responsible for maintaining all inter-domain object references. In other words, the Infrastructure Master informs certain objects (such as groups) that other objects (such as users in another domain) have been moved, changed, or otherwise modified. This update is needed only in a multiple domain environment. If there is only a single domain, then all domain controllers already know of the update, and this role is unnecessary. Likewise, if all domain controllers are also global catalog servers, the domain controllers are aware of the updates and do not need the assistance of the Infrastructure Master.

By default, Active Directory assigns all five of these operations master roles to the first domain controller installed in a forest. In a simple network environment, these roles may remain with that first domain controller. As the network environment expands, some of the roles will need to be reassigned to other domain controllers.

Lesson Review

The following questions are intended to reinforce key information presented in this lesson. If you are unable to answer a question, review the lesson materials and then try the question again. You can find answers to the questions in the "Questions and Answers" section at the end of this chapter.

1. You are developing a deployment plan for Exchange Server 2003. You have been asked to ensure that the *contoso.com* and *fabrikam.com* domain trees that are part of the same forest can be included in the same Exchange Server 2003 organization. Is this possible with the existing Active Directory structure, or will you need to change the Active Directory structure first?

2. You are an Exchange Server 2003 administrator. You regularly create new user accounts for contractors, but periodically you receive an error that the object cannot be created. Usually you are able to cancel the process and try again later or to create the new account from another server. Since the process works most of the time, you know it isn't a configuration problem or permissions problem. What else might be causing the problem?

    a. The PDC Emulator is unavailable

    b. The RID Master is unavailable

    c. The Schema Master is unavailable

    d. The Infrastructure Master is unavailable

3. The CIO for your company returns from a Windows Server 2003 seminar and is anxious to share his new knowledge. He says you should make all of the servers in your Active Directory forest global catalog servers because it will improve the response time to user queries, especially with Exchange Server 2003. He feels that this will help significantly since your organization has four domain trees with multiple child domains in each. Do you agree with him? Why or why not?

    _____

    _____

Lesson Summary

- Active Directory is a hierarchical structured database that replaced the flat structure of Windows NT domains.

- Global catalog servers are used to allow Active Directory queries to cross domains.

- There are five operations masters roles. The Schema Master and Domain Naming Master roles are forest-wide, while the PDC Emulator, Infrastructure Master, and RID Master roles are domain-wide.

- Sites are used to control the replication topology by defining whether resources in Active Directory are connected by high-speed or low-speed links.

- The schema defines the types of objects that are allowed in Active Directory, as well as the attributes the objects can have.

Lesson 2: Exchange Server 2003 Integration with Active Directory

Exchange Server 2003 is tightly integrated with Active Directory, in that Exchange Server 2003 uses Active Directory as the storage mechanism for its data (although Exchange Server 2003 still uses its own databases for storing the content of messages and transaction logs). This is different from Exchange Server 5.5 (and earlier versions), which maintained its own directory and databases independent of the operating system and even maintained its own replication infrastructure. In order to deploy Exchange Server 2003 effectively in an Active Directory environment, you must first understand how Exchange Server 2003 stores data in Active Directory.

After this lesson, you will be able to

- Understand how Active Directory is partitioned into naming contexts
- Understand how Exchange Server 2003 uses global catalog servers
- Understand how Exchange Server 2003 leverages Active Directory groups

Estimated lesson time: 15 minutes

Naming Contexts

Active Directory is partitioned into naming contexts. The three naming contexts are

- Domain
- Configuration
- Schema

These naming contexts provide boundaries for and structure to the Active Directory database and can have their own replication and permissions configuration.

Domain Naming Context

The domain naming context is where all the domain objects for Exchange Server 2003 are stored. These objects include recipient objects like users, groups, and contacts. Exchange Server 2003 extends the attributes Active Directory includes for these types of objects, meaning that, in contrast to Exchange Server 5.5, Exchange Server 2003 mailboxes and Active Directory user accounts are not separate objects. For example, with Exchange Server 2003, you mailbox-enable a user account rather than create a mailbox object in Exchange Server and associate a user account with the mailbox.

Configuration Naming Context

The configuration naming context stores information about the physical structure of the Exchange organization, such as routing groups and connectors. Active Directory replicates this data to all domain controllers in the forest, which marks the security boundary of an Exchange organization.

Schema Naming Context

The schema naming context contains information about all of the object classes and their attributes that can be stored in Active Directory. This data is replicated to all domain controllers in a forest. During the deployment of Exchange Server 2003, the Active Directory schema is extended to include the classes and attributes specific to Exchange Server 2003. A visible example of the schema extensions is in the Exchange-specific options that are available in a user account in the Active Directory Users And Computers console after the installation of Exchange Server 2003.

Global Catalog Integration

Exchange Server 2003 uses two services—DSProxy and DSAccess—to access the global catalog.

DSProxy

While Microsoft Outlook 2000 and 2003 clients can access a global catalog directly, other clients cannot. So Exchange Server 2003 provides a proxy service called DSProxy to function as an intermediary between the client and the global catalog. DSProxy works as a facilitator to allow Outlook clients to access information within Active Directory through the Name Service Provider Interface (NSPI). In addition, the DSProxy service supports older Messaging Application Programming Interface (MAPI) clients by forwarding requests directly from the client to the global catalog server. DSProxy does not examine the request; instead, it blindly forwards the request and then returns the results. The process is transparent to the user.

DSAccess

Exchange Server 2003 shares global catalog functionality with other Active Directory services, so it is important to reduce the impact of Exchange Server 2003 queries. DSAccess implements a directory access cache that stores recently accessed information for a configurable length of time. This reduces the number of queries made to global catalog servers. Increasing the cache and timeout period too much can cause problems with out-of-date data, while a cache that is too small and a short timeout period can cause performance problems, as well.

Active Directory Group Integration

The use of security groups and distribution groups is another feature in which Exchange Server 2003 integrates with Active Directory. Versions of Exchange Server prior to Exchange Server 2000 maintained their own distribution lists, which contained recipients that were members of the Exchange organization (mailboxes, custom recipients, and other distribution lists). These distribution lists existed only within Exchange and were unrelated to the Windows user accounts database. Exchange Server 2003 does not maintain its own distribution lists. Instead, Active Directory security groups and distribution groups are extended to support e-mail addresses. In this way, the group can be used as a mail recipient, with the message being distributed to each member of the group.

Lesson Review

The following questions are intended to reinforce key information presented in this lesson. If you are unable to answer a question, review the lesson materials and then try the question again. You can find answers to the questions in the "Questions and Answers" section at the end of this chapter.

1. You are an Exchange Server 2003 consultant that has been contacted by Contoso, Ltd., to help analyze their network environment and make recommendations as they prepare to migrate from Windows NT Server 4 and Exchange Server 5.5 to Windows Server 2003 Active Directory and Exchange Server 2003. They are concerned about total cost of ownership (TCO), especially as it concerns having to duplicate user information between Windows and Exchange. What advice can you give them about this concern?

   _____

   _____

2. Which Active Directory naming context is responsible for the storage of Exchange Server 2003 recipient objects?

   a. The domain naming context

   b. The schema naming context

   c. The configuration naming context

3. What is the primary function of the DSAccess service?

    a. To provide access to Active Directory information for Microsoft Outlook and MAPI clients.

    b. To store information about all Active Directory objects and their attributes.

    c. To store information about routing groups and connectors used to access other sites in the Exchange organization.

    d. To implement a directory cache to reduce the number of global catalog queries.

Lesson Summary

- The domain naming context stores information about Exchange Server 2003 recipient objects.

- The configuration naming context stores information about Exchange Server 2003 routing groups and connectors.

- The schema naming context stores information about all Active Directory objects and their attributes.

- Exchange Server 2003 uses Active Directory security groups and distribution groups rather than maintaining its own distribution lists.

Lesson 3: Exchange Server 2003 and Windows Server 2003 Protocols and Services Integration

In addition to being designed to integrate with Active Directory, Exchange Server 2003 is designed to integrate with services provided by the Windows server operating systems. Exchange Server 2003 can be installed on computers running Windows 2000 Server, but to take advantage of all of the new functionality, you must use Windows Server 2003. Because Windows 2000 Server and Windows Server 2003 include messaging transport capabilities such as Simple Mail Transport Protocol (SMTP), Network News Transfer Protocol (NNTP), and Hypertext Transfer Protocol (HTTP), Exchange Server 2003 uses these Windows services rather than duplicating the services with its own. This is in contrast to Exchange Server 5.5 (and earlier versions), which used Internet Information Services (IIS) for Outlook Web Access (OWA) and newsgroup access, but not for much else.

After this lesson, you will be able to

■ Understand how Exchange Server 2003 uses the features of IIS 6

Estimated lesson time: 15 minutes

Exchange Server 2003 and IIS 6

IIS is included with Windows operating systems for servers and provides some core services for Exchange Server 2003. Windows Server 2003 includes Internet Information Services (IIS) 6. This new version of IIS introduces Worker Process Isolation Mode, which offers greater reliability and security to Web servers. Worker Process Isolation Mode ensures that all of the authentication, authorization, Web application processes, and Internet Server Application Programming Interface (ISAPI) extensions that are associated with a particular application are isolated from all other applications. When you install Exchange Server 2003 on a computer running Windows Server 2003, the Exchange Server 2003 Setup program automatically sets IIS 6 to Worker Process Isolation Mode. Setup also enables certain ISAPI extensions. By default, during Windows Server 2003 installation, ISAPI extensions are not allowed to load. This is different from previous versions of Windows and IIS, which were less secure in their default configurations. Exchange Server 2003 requires certain ISAPI extensions, however, for features such as OWA, WebDAV, and Exchange Web Forms. Exchange Server 2003 Setup enables and configures the required ISAPI extensions, with no intervention required.

The integration of Exchange Server 2003 with IIS services includes the following:

■ SMTP

■ NNTP

■ World Wide Web Service

The SMTP Service

Unlike Exchange Server 5.5 and earlier versions, Exchange Server 2003 does not provide its own SMTP services. Windows 2000 Server and Windows Server 2003 include a core SMTP service with IIS 5 and 6, respectively, and Exchange Server 2003 relies on this service to provide e-mail services. Exchange simply extends the built-in SMTP service to provide the necessary additional functionality.

Windows Server 2003 also includes a Post Office Protocol 3 (POP3) service, which is listed in the Windows Components Wizard as Email Services. This service is not used by Exchange Server 2003 and should not be installed if you are deploying Exchange Server 2003, which includes more robust POP3 support as well as Internet Message Access Protocol 4 (IMAP4) support.

There are a number of new enhancements in the Exchange Server 2003 SMTP service, with the most exciting for network administrators being native support for Real-Time Blacklists (RBLs) and improved antivirus support. Fighting spam and viruses is a time-consuming process for administrators, and the enhanced functionality eases the administrative burden.

The NNTP Service

Exchange Server 2003 also relies on the IIS built-in NNTP service. The NNTP service provides user access to newsgroups either internally or on the Internet. Access to newsgroups is made available through Exchange Server 2003 public folders, with security configured through the Exchange Server 2003 organization. The NNTP service is also useful for sharing public folders between organizations. Exchange Server 2003 does not modify or extend the IIS NNTP service, as it does the SMTP service.

The World Wide Web Service

OWA integrates into IIS and doesn't even have to be installed on the same server as Exchange Server 2003. Because of the integration, services can be installed almost anywhere within Active Directory, providing flexibility and a very scalable messaging solution. OWA provides client access to an Exchange mailbox through a Web browser. The HTTP protocol, which is part of the World Wide Web Service, is the transport used for OWA functionality.

Users running Microsoft Internet Explorer 5 or later can take advantage of a number of new enhancements to OWA. A common complaint with previous versions of OWA was regarding the lack of basic Outlook features, such as spell checker, support for mail rules, support for digital signatures, marking messages as read/unread, and public folder support. These features have been included with the Exchange Server 2003 version of OWA. Some features, such as digital signatures, specifically require Internet

Explorer 6 SP1 or greater, but most features work with Internet Explorer 5, as well. There is still a basic version of OWA that can be used by other Web browsers.

A new feature exclusive to Exchange Server 2003 running on Windows Server 2003 is the ability to use Outlook 2003 to connect to Exchange Server 2003 servers using the HTTP protocol. This is known as "RPC over HTTP." In previous versions of Exchange Server and IIS, if a remote user needed to connect to a corporate Exchange server using the Outlook client rather than OWA, they would have to establish a virtual private network (VPN) connection first. This was because the communication between the client and server took place only over remote procedure call (RPC). Another requirement for client computers to use RPC over HTTP is that they must be running Windows XP Professional SP1 or later.

Lesson Review

The following questions are intended to reinforce key information presented in this lesson. If you are unable to answer a question, review the lesson materials and then try the question again. You can find answers to the questions in the "Questions and Answers" section at the end of this chapter.

1. You are the Exchange administrator for Contoso, Ltd. You are planning the deployment of Exchange Server 2003 into your Windows Server 2003 Active Directory domain. The IT director questions you about the effect that Exchange Server 2003 will have on IIS security, concerned that installing Exchange Server 2003 will cause IIS to be less secure. How do you address his concerns?

   _____

   _____

2. Which of the following Windows Server 2003 services is not used by Exchange Server 2003 to support the messaging infrastructure?

   a. SMTP

   b. POP3

   c. World Wide Web Service

   d. NNTP

Lesson Summary

- Exchange Server 2003 leverages several Windows Server 2003 protocols and services rather than duplicating them.

- The new Worker Process Isolation Mode feature of IIS 6 provides better security and reliability by isolating an application's authentication, processes, and extensions.

- Outlook Web Access (OWA) has been greatly enhanced when used with Internet Explorer 6 SP1 or later, providing much of the functionality previously found only in the Outlook client.

Case Scenario Exercise

Wide World Importers is a company that operates under different names in different countries. In addition to the *wideworldimporters.com* domain name, they also operate under *contoso.com*, *fabrikam.com*, *adatum.com*, and *litwareinc.com*.

The consortium of companies has been operating in a Windows NT 4 domain environment running Exchange Server 5.5 SP4. Each company has its own domain, with all domains trusting the *wideworldimporters.com* domain for the parent company. The present arrangement has led to a lot of duplication of administrative effort, and the support costs of maintaining five distinct Windows NT domains and Exchange organizations have increased to unacceptable levels. As a result, the decision has been made to migrate to Windows Server 2003 and Active Directory, and to migrate from Exchange Server 5.5 to Exchange Server 2003. You have been hired as a consultant in order to facilitate the entire project.

- **Requirement 1** Management has determined that by reducing the duplication of resources and administrative effort, it will reduce the support costs for the organization. One of your key responsibilities is to ensure that the network administrators for *wideworldimporters.com* can administer all of the domains effectively without a network of complex trust relationships in place. Furthermore, they want all the companies to share a common global address list rather than having five separate lists.

- **Requirement 2** Some of the companies that comprise Wide World Importers are located in countries where there are toll charges for accessing the Internet. So, even though there are VPN connections between company locations, it is important to minimize the usage of the WAN connections for non-user-generated network traffic during business hours, when toll charges are the highest.

Requirement 1

The first requirement involves planning the Active Directory infrastructure to support the company's needs.

1. Describe the forest and domain infrastructure you would recommend that would result in the most efficient level of administration.

2. Explain how the number of Active Directory forests would affect the deployment of Exchange Server 2003.

_____

_____

Requirement 2

The second requirement involves minimizing the usage of toll-based WAN connections during business hours.

1. Describe a feature of Active Directory that you can use to organize resources in a way that will allow you to minimize usage of WAN bandwidth for non-user-generated network traffic during business hours.

_____

_____

2. How would the use of sites in this situation affect the placement of global catalog servers?

_____

_____

Chapter Summary

- Active Directory is a hierarchical database that provides directory services to users and client computers within the directory.

- The Active Directory schema defines the types of objects allowed in Active Directory, as well as their attributes.

- Active Directory logically groups resources into a forest, which can contain multiple domain trees.

- Sites are used to define resources that are connected by high-speed LAN bandwidth versus resources connected by lower-speed WAN bandwidth.

- Global catalog servers provide an efficient means of querying for resources across domains within a forest.

- Active Directory is partitioned into three naming contexts: schema, domain, and configuration.

- DSProxy and DSAccess function as intermediaries between a global catalog server and an Exchange Server 2003 client.

- Exchange Server 2003 integrates with the SMTP, NNTP, and World Wide Web services of Windows Server 2003 and IIS.

Exam Highlights

Before taking the exam, review the key points and terms that are presented in this chapter. You need to know this information.

Key Points

- RPC over HTTP works only when the client computer is running Windows XP Professional SP1 or later and Outlook 2003, and the Exchange Server 2003 server is running on Windows Server 2003.

- You can have only a single Exchange Server 2003 organization in an Active Directory forest, and an organization cannot span forests.

Key Terms

naming context   Active Directory is partitioned into three naming contexts: the schema naming context, the domain naming context, and the configuration naming context. Each naming context is responsible for storing different types of Active Directory data.

operations master   Active Directory functions mostly in a multimaster manner, where each domain controller is a peer. However, some functions cannot be reliably performed in a multimaster manner, so Active Directory implements them as single-master roles. The Schema Master role and the Domain Naming Master role exist only once in a forest. The Infrastructure Master role, the RID Master role, and the PDC Emulator role exist on a domain controller in each domain in the forest.

Questions and Answers

Page
1-6   **Lesson 1 Review**

1. You are developing a deployment plan for Exchange Server 2003. You have been asked to ensure that the *contoso.com* and *fabrikam.com* domain trees that are part of the same forest can be included in the same Exchange Server 2003 organization. Is this possible with the existing Active Directory structure, or will you need to change the Active Directory structure first?

   The security boundary for an Exchange Server 2003 organization is the forest rather than the domain, so you will be able to include the two domain trees in the same Exchange Server 2003 organization. If the domain trees were in separate forests, you would have to first migrate one domain into the other forest in order to be able to place them both in the same organization.

2. You are an Exchange Server 2003 administrator. You regularly create new user accounts for contractors, but periodically you receive an error that the object cannot be created. Usually you are able to cancel the process and try again later or to create the new account from another server. Since the process works most of the time, you know it isn't a configuration problem or permissions problem. What else might be causing the problem?

   a. The PDC Emulator is unavailable

   b. The RID Master is unavailable

   c. The Schema Master is unavailable

   d. The Infrastructure Master is unavailable

   The correct answer is b.

3. The CIO for your company returns from a Windows Server 2003 seminar and is anxious to share his new knowledge. He says you should make all of the servers in your Active Directory forest global catalog servers because it will improve the response time to user queries, especially with Exchange Server 2003. He feels that this will help significantly since your organization has four domain trees with multiple child domains in each. Do you agree with him? Why or why not?

   While more global catalog servers would theoretically improve the response time to user queries, replication traffic on the network would increase. Depending on the network, this additional traffic could have a detrimental effect that outweighs the benefits of using additional global catalog servers. There is a balance between too few and too many global catalog servers.

Page
1-10

Lesson 2 Review

1. You are an Exchange Server 2003 consultant that has been contacted by Contoso, Ltd., to help analyze their network environment and make recommendations as they prepare to migrate from Windows NT Server 4 and Exchange Server 5.5 to Windows Server 2003 Active Directory and Exchange Server 2003. They are concerned about total cost of ownership (TCO), especially as it concerns having to duplicate user information between Windows and Exchange. What advice can you give them about this concern?

   In contrast to Exchange Server 5.5, which maintained its own directory, Exchange Server 2003 integrates with Active Directory. As a result, there is no need to maintain separate user databases. Exchange Server 2003 extends the Active Directory schema so that user objects can be configured with Exchange-specific information, such as e-mail addresses, mailboxes, and so on. The end result is a single point of user management with no duplication of effort between the Windows environment and the Exchange environment.

2. Which Active Directory naming context is responsible for the storage of Exchange Server 2003 recipient objects?

   a. The domain naming context

   b. The schema naming context

   c. The configuration naming context

   The correct answer is a.

3. What is the primary function of the DSAccess service?

   a. To provide access to Active Directory information for Microsoft Outlook and MAPI clients.

   b. To store information about all Active Directory objects and their attributes.

   c. To store information about routing groups and connectors used to access other sites in the Exchange organization.

   d. To implement a directory cache to reduce the number of global catalog queries.

   The correct answer is d.

Lesson 3 Review

1. You are the Exchange administrator for Contoso, Ltd. You are planning the deployment of Exchange Server 2003 into your Windows Server 2003 Active Directory domain. The IT director questions you about the effect that Exchange Server 2003 will have on IIS security, concerned that installing Exchange Server 2003 will cause IIS to be less secure. How do you address his concerns?

   IIS security has been a problem in the past, but IIS 6 includes the Worker Process Isolation Mode, which provides greater security by isolating all the processes and extensions associated with an application. When Exchange Server 2003 is installed, it automatically configures IIS to operate in this more secure mode.

2. Which of the following Windows Server 2003 services is not used by Exchange Server 2003 to support the messaging infrastructure?

   a. SMTP

   b. POP3

   c. World Wide Web Service

   d. NNTP

   The correct answer is b.

Case Scenario Exercise: Requirement 1

1. Describe the forest and domain infrastructure you would recommend that would result in the most efficient level of administration.

   Because management wants to reduce the duplication of administrative effort and also have a centralized IT department that is able to administer all domains, it would be best to implement Active Directory as a single forest. A forest can have multiple domain trees, which would be ideal for this situation, since each domain tree in the forest would share a common Schema Admins and Enterprise Admins security group. Local domain administration can still be performed by members of each individual Domain Admins group, allowing a level of decentralized administration, as well.

2. Explain how the number of Active Directory forests would affect the deployment of Exchange Server 2003.

   The security boundary for an Exchange Server 2003 organization is the forest, so if there are multiple forests, then there need to be multiple Exchange organizations. This would fail to meet the needs of the company, which requires that each domain be a part of the same Exchange organization in order to share a common global address list. A single forest structure with multiple domain trees would allow each domain to be in the same Exchange organization, and Exchange Server 2003 can support multiple domains in the same organization.

Case Scenario Exercise: Requirement 2

1. Describe a feature of Active Directory that you can use to organize resources in a way that will allow you to minimize usage of WAN bandwidth for non-user-generated network traffic during business hours.

   Active Directory uses sites to group resources that are connected by high-speed LAN bandwidth. Within a site, non-user-generated network traffic such as replication between domain controllers takes place immediately when a change is made. However, replication traffic between sites can be scheduled. By using scheduling, you can schedule non-user-generated network traffic to take place outside of business hours, thereby reducing costs.

2. How would the use of sites in this situation affect the placement of global catalog servers?

   In order to minimize the use of WAN bandwidth further, you would want to make at least one domain controller in each site a global catalog server. This would prevent Active Directory from being sent across the WAN connection.

2 Planning a Microsoft Exchange Server 2003 Infrastructure

Exam Objectives in this Chapter:

- Prepare the environment for the Microsoft Exchange Server 2003 deployment
- Install, configure, and troubleshoot Exchange Server 2003
- Remove a computer running Exchange Server 2003 from an organization
- Manage and troubleshoot permissions

Why This Chapter Matters

One of the most fundamental aspects of deploying a new network application—especially one as complicated as Exchange Server 2003—is planning. Lack of planning and flaws in the planning stage are the leading causes of implementation failure and other significant problems.

Exchange Server 2003 integrates extensively with Active Directory directory service, which makes proper planning even more important. In this chapter, you'll learn what you should consider when planning an Exchange Server 2003 deployment, including preparing the Active Directory forest and domain for an Exchange Server 2003 installation. You will also install Exchange Server 2003.

In the next several chapters, you will install Exchange Server 2003 into a number of environments: a clean installation (this chapter); to coexist with Microsoft Exchange Server 5.5 in an existing organization (Chapter 4); upgrading or migrating to Exchange Server 2003 from Exchange Server 5.5, Microsoft Exchange 2000 Server, and foreign messaging systems (Chapter 5); and finally you will install Exchange Server 2003 in a clustered environment (Chapter 6).

Lessons in this Chapter:

- Lesson 1: Installation Considerations 2-3
- Lesson 2: Preparing Forests and Domains 2-12
- Lesson 3: Performing an Exchange Server 2003 Installation. 2-19
- Lesson 4: Unattended Setup 2-28
- Lesson 5: Removing an Exchange Server 2003 Server from an Organization . . . 2-35

Before You Begin

To perform the exercises in this chapter, you will need the following:

- Two servers running Microsoft Windows Server 2003, Enterprise Edition, that meet the hardware requirements, installed and configured as Server01 and Server02 in the *contoso.com* domain

- Administrative rights to the server, including membership in the Schema Admins group

- Exchange Server 2003 software

Lesson 1: Installation Considerations

With Exchange Server 5.5 and earlier, deploying Exchange Server in your organization was much like deploying any other application. Planning was important, but the actual installation was typical. With Exchange 2000 Server, there was a dramatic change with tighter integration between the messaging platform (Exchange 2000 Server) and the server operating system (Microsoft Windows 2000 Server). Deployment of Exchange was dependent on your Windows 2000 Server infrastructure, and you couldn't effectively manage Exchange 2000 Server without dealing with Windows 2000 Server and Active Directory. Exchange Server 2003 builds on this concept. As a result, you must be acutely aware of how Active Directory and Domain Name System (DNS) work, and how Exchange Server 2003 utilizes the services of the server operating system. Also, since you can install Exchange Server 2003 on a computer running Windows 2000 Server (with SP3 or later) or Windows Server 2003, you must be aware of how the version of Windows you are running will affect what functionality is available.

After this lesson, you will be able to

- Understand what versions of Exchange Server run on what versions of Windows 2000 Server and Windows Server 2003
- Identify the hardware requirements necessary for successful deployment of Exchange Server 2003
- Configure a service account for use with Exchange Server 2003
- Install the necessary Windows Server components required by Exchange Server 2003

Estimated lesson time: 30 minutes

Supported Combinations of Exchange and Windows Server

Depending on your organization, you might have a number of server configurations that affect how you will deploy Exchange Server 2003. The following list shows the different combinations of Exchange versions and Microsoft Windows versions that are supported:

- Exchange Server 5.5

    ❑ Windows NT 4 Server, Windows 2000 Server (any service pack)

    ❑ Not Active Directory-aware but can replicate data to and from Active Directory with the Active Directory Connector (ADC).

- Exchange 2000 Server

    ❑ Windows 2000 Server (SP1 or later)

❏ Can be installed on a member server or domain controller but requires Active Directory.

■ Exchange Server 2003

❏ Windows 2000 Server (SP3 or later)

❏ Windows Server 2003

❏ Can be installed on a member server or domain controller but requires Active Directory.

Tip Because the only version of Exchange Server that will run on Windows Server 2003 is Exchange Server 2003, you will need to upgrade your Exchange environment to Exchange Server 2003 prior to upgrading the Windows Server operating system to Windows Server 2003.

It is worth noting that when deploying Exchange Server 2003, Windows 2000 Server with SP3 or later and Windows Server 2003 are not equal. To take full advantage of the functionality of Exchange Server 2003, you must run it on a Windows Server 2003 server. In fact, complete functionality requires Windows Server 2003, Enterprise Edition. The following list identifies features of Exchange Server 2003 that are supported when installed on a server running Windows Server 2003 but that are not supported on Windows 2000 Server:

■ Mount points overcome the 24-drive letter limitation of previous versions of Windows.

■ Volume Shadow Copy service for database backup (requires Windows Volume Shadow Copy service backup application vendor).

■ Internet Protocol Security (IPSec) support for front-end and back-end clusters.

■ Cross-forest Kerberos authentication with Microsoft Outlook 2003 (requires Microsoft Metadirectory Services 2003 and Outlook 2003).

■ Internet Information Server (IIS) 6 enhanced security and dedicated application mode.

■ Hypertext Transfer Protocol (HTTP) access from Outlook 2003.

■ Real-time collaboration (requires Real-Time Collaboration service).

■ Microsoft SharePoint Portal Server Web Parts (requires SharePoint Portal Server, Microsoft Windows SharePoint Services, or both).

The following list identifies functions that are available only when running Exchange Server 2003 on Windows Server 2003, Enterprise Edition:

- Supports 8-way PIII Xeon Processors
- Supports 8-way P4 XeonMP Processors (hyper-threaded)
- Up to 8-node clustering
- Mount point support

Hardware Requirements

There are several factors that affect the hardware requirements for Exchange Server 2003: the number of users that will be accessing the server; the size and number of messages transferred on a daily basis (not to mention during peak usage periods); availability requirements; and so on. These factors will have a significant influence on the type of hardware you use for your deployment. However, Table 2-1 contains some minimum hardware requirements.

Table 2-1   Minimum Hardware Requirements for Exchange Server 2003

Component	Minimum requirements
Processor	Pentium 133
Operating system	Windows 2000 Server + SP3
Memory	256 megabyte (MB)
Disk space	200 MB on system drive, 500 MB on partition where Exchange Server 2003 is installed
Drive	CD-ROM drive
Display	VGA or better
File system	All partitions involving Exchange Server 2003 must be NTFS file system (NTFS), including ■ System partition ■ Partition storing Exchange binaries ■ Partition containing Exchange database files ■ Partition containing Exchange transaction logs ■ Partitions containing other Exchange files

While Table 2-1 contains the minimum requirements to install Exchange Server 2003, that configuration is sufficient for only the smallest of Exchange environments supporting only a handful of users, or for testing in a lab. In most cases, the Microsoft-recommended requirements for Exchange Server 2003 in Table 2-2 are a more reasonable starting point. However, remember that this is only a starting point; your organization's specific needs will dictate your system requirements.

Table 2-2   Recommended Hardware Requirements for Exchange Server 2003

Component	Recommended requirements
Processor	Pentium III 500 (Exchange Server 2003, Standard Edition) Pentium III 733 (Exchange Server 2003, Enterprise Edition)
Operating system	Windows Server 2003
Memory	512 MB
Disk space	200 MB on system drive, 500 MB on partition where Exchange Server 2003 is installed. Separate physical disks for the Exchange binaries, database files, and transaction logs.
Drive	CD-ROM drive
Display	SVGA or better
File system	All partitions involving Exchange must be NTFS, including ■ System partition ■ Partition storing Exchange binaries ■ Partition containing Exchange database files ■ Partition containing Exchange transaction logs ■ Partitions containing other Exchange files

Tip   Installing Exchange Server 2003 on an existing server will increase the burden on that server. You should use System Monitor to establish a performance baseline for your server prior to installing Exchange Server 2003 to determine if the server hardware is adequate to support Exchange and also so you can later determine the effect that the Exchange Server 2003 installation has had on your server's overall performance.

Creating a Service Account

Another consideration when installing Exchange Server 2003 is the creation of a dedicated service account. One reason for using a dedicated service account is related to security auditing. When you run services under the Administrator or System account, it is more difficult to tell by viewing the Security log in the Event Viewer whether an entry is being generated by a user actively performing a task as the administrator or a service performing a task unattended. With a service account, you can see specifically what is being done by the Exchange services. Also, you can quickly identify situations where someone might be trying to log on interactively with the service account to gain administrative permissions to the domain.

Table 2-3 shows the permissions that are required of a user account in order to perform the installation-related tasks. With all the permissions required to deploy Exchange Server 2003 successfully, it is clear that the security account Exchange services run under is quite powerful.

Table 2-3   Permissions and Roles Required to Perform Exchange Installation Tasks

Task	Required permissions or roles
Run ForestPrep for the first time in a forest (this updates the schema)	Member of the Schema Admins and Enterprise Admins groups
Run ForestPrep (other than the first time)	Exchange Full Administrator permissions at the Exchange organization level
Run DomainPrep	Member of the Domain Admins group in the target domain
Install the first server in a domain	Exchange Full Administrator permissions at the Exchange organization level
Install additional servers in a domain	Exchange Full Administrator permissions at the administrative group level Machine account added to the Exchange Domain Servers group
Install a server with the Site Replication Service (SRS) enabled	Exchange Full Administrator permissions at the Exchange organization level

When creating a service account, you will want to select the User Cannot Change Password option. This is a security precaution that prevents a malicious user from logging on interactively with the service and attempting to seize the account by changing the password. It also has the effect of requiring password changes to be made by an administrator through the Active Directory Users And Computers console. Another option to choose is Password Never Expires. You don't want the service account to be subject to the domain password policy, which usually requires passwords to be changed on a periodic basis. Any password change to the service account must be carefully planned. Since the account is not being used to log on to a server interactively, you won't receive a warning telling you the password will expire in so many days.

Installing Windows Services Required by Exchange Server 2003

Prior to installing Exchange Server 2003, there are certain Windows Server 2003 components that must be enabled on the server because of the level of integration Exchange has with Active Directory and the Windows operating systems. For Setup to complete successfully, you must have the following services installed and enabled on your server:

- Microsoft .NET Framework
- Microsoft ASP.NET
- World Wide Web service
- Simple Mail Transfer Protocol (SMTP) service
- Network News Transfer Protocol (NNTP) service

The configuration will vary depending on whether your server platform is Windows 2000 Server or Windows Server 2003. If you are installing Exchange Server 2003 onto a server running Windows 2000 Server, Setup automatically installs and enables the .NET Framework and ASP.NET services. This is because these services were not available when Windows 2000 Server was released. Since Windows Server 2003 has the .NET Framework built into the operating system and has ASP.NET available through the Add/Remove Windows Components Wizard, the Microsoft Exchange Installation Wizard will not install these components on that platform. Instead, you must manually enable these components on Windows Server 2003.

With Windows 2000 Server, the World Wide Web service and SMTP service were automatically installed and enabled as part of a default installation of the operating system. By default in Windows Server 2003, these services are not installed. So, if you are installing Exchange Server 2003 onto a system running Windows 2000 Server, it is likely that the only service you will need to add is the NNTP service. With Windows Server 2003, none of the above-mentioned services are installed and enabled, so you must add all of them.

Practice: Preparing for Installation

In this practice, you will first create a service account that you will use later to install Exchange Server 2003, and then you will configure the required Windows Server 2003 server components to support the Exchange Server 2003 installation.

Exercise 1: Create a Service Account

1. Log on to your Windows Server 2003 system as an administrator.

2. From the Start menu, point to Administrative Tools, and then select the Active Directory Users And Computers console.

3. Expand the appropriate domain on the left side and right-click the Users container. Point to New on the shortcut menu, and then click User.

4. Provide the required information, entering **svc_xch** as the name of the service account. Click Next to continue.

5. Create a strong password, with a minimum of seven characters and meeting the complexity requirements required by Windows Server 2003. Configure the account password so that it will never expire, and so that it can't be changed by the user. Click Next to continue, and then click Finish.

Security Alert   Strong passwords are required by default in Windows Server 2003, which is a change from previous versions of Windows. Best practices are to have a password of at least seven characters and which contains a combination of uppercase and lowercase letters, numbers, and special characters.

6. Double-click the new user account that you just created and go to the Member Of tab. Click Add, and add this account to the following groups:

□ Schema Admins

□ Enterprise Admins

□ Domain Admins

7. Click OK, and then click OK again to finish.

Exercise 2: Install Windows Components Required by Exchange Server 2003

1. From the Start menu, point to Settings, and then click Control Panel. Next, click Add Or Remove Programs.

2. Click Add Or Remove Windows Components to start the Windows Components Wizard.

3. Click the Application Server component, and then click Details.

4. Select the check box for ASP.NET and click OK.

5. Scroll down to Internet Information Services (IIS) and click Details.

6. Select the check boxes to select the following components:

□ NNTP service

□ SMTP service

□ World Wide Web service

7. Click OK to return to the Application Server components, and then click OK again to return to the main Windows Components Wizard page.

8. Complete the wizard to install the components.

ASP is a component of IIS, and is installed by default when you install the World Wide Web Service. However, you must enable ASP in the Internet Information Services console even though it is installed. To do this, perform the following steps:

1. Start and select All Programs, and then go into Administrative Tools and start the Internet Information Services (IIS) Manager console.

2. When the console opens, expand the local computer (if it isn't already), and then select Web Service Extensions.

3. Select ASP (which will have the version of the extensions in parenthesis), and then click Allow, as shown in Figure 2-1.

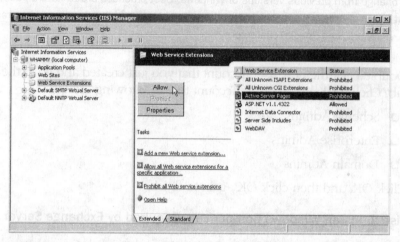

Figure 2-1   Enabling ASP in the IIS Manager console

Lesson Review

The following questions are intended to reinforce key information presented in this lesson. If you are unable to answer a question, review the lesson materials and then try the question again. You can find answers to the questions in the "Questions and Answers" section at the end of this chapter.

1. You are heading up a team of systems and network administrators that is planning to deploy Exchange Server 2003 in an environment where e-mail has to date been hosted by the organization's Internet service provider (ISP). One of the administrators asks you why you should bother creating a service account for Exchange instead of simply using the domain's Administrator account. What are two reasons you can give him to justify using a separate account?

_____

_____

2. You are planning to set up a couple of lab computers using old computers that aren't in use anymore in order to test and practice with Exchange Server 2003. What is the minimum amount of random access memory (RAM) your systems will need to have in order to install Exchange Server 2003?

   a. 64 MB

   b. 128 MB

   c. 256 MB

   d. 512 MB

3. Which of the following platforms are able to support an installation of Exchange Server 2003? (Choose all that apply.)

    a. Windows NT 4

    b. Windows NT 4 SP6a

    c. Windows 2000 Server SP1

    d. Windows 2000 Server SP3

    e. Windows 2000 Server SP4

    f. Windows Server 2003, Standard Edition

    g. Windows Server 2003, Enterprise Edition

    h. Windows Server 2003 SP1

4. You install Exchange Server 2003 onto a Windows Server 2003 file server that has a Pentium III–450 MHz processor, 512 MB of RAM, and a RAID 5 disk array. After a couple of weeks, users begin complaining that working with documents on the server is very sluggish during the middle of the day. What can you do to improve performance?

_____

_____

Lesson Summary

- Exchange Server 2003 can be installed on systems running Windows 2000 Server SP3 or later or Windows Server 2003. Some functionality is lost when using Windows 2000 Server.

- Exchange Server 2003 is the only version of Exchange Server that can run on Windows Server 2003.

- A dedicated service account should be used for the Exchange Server 2003 installation.

- Because of the integration of Active Directory and Windows 2000 Server and Windows Server 2003, several Windows components must be installed and enabled to support the Exchange Server 2003 installation.

Lesson 2: Preparing Forests and Domains

After having prepared a service account and installed the Windows components required by Exchange Server 2003, the next step is to prepare Active Directory for the Exchange installation. Preparing Active Directory involves running ForestPrep and DomainPrep, two utilities that prepare the forest and domains, respectively.

After this lesson, you will be able to

- Understand the changes made by ForestPrep
- Run ForestPrep in an Active Directory forest
- Understand the changes made by DomainPrep
- Run DomainPrep in each Active Directory domain in which Exchange Server 2003 will be installed

Estimated lesson time: 60 minutes

ForestPrep

Active Directory consists of three partitions that store data: the schema partition, the configuration partition, and the domain partition. Prior to installing Exchange Server 2003, you need to use ForestPrep and DomainPrep to prepare these Active Directory partitions.

> **Off the Record**   You can install Exchange Server 2003 and have it go through ForestPrep and DomainPrep at the time of installation, but it is important to note that these two functions can take a significant amount of time to complete (an hour or more depending on your hardware and network). In addition, you may not even run ForestPrep and DomainPrep on the same servers on which you will actually be installing Exchange Server 2003. You may also be in a multidomain situation where different levels of administrative permissions are held by different people, so one administrator might run ForestPrep while a second administrator runs DomainPrep in one domain and a third administrator runs DomainPrep in another domain. Therefore, you will want to complete the preparation of Active Directory prior to installing the Exchange Server 2003 application to ensure the smoothest possible installation process.

ForestPrep updates the schema and configuration partitions in Active Directory. Therefore, the account used to run ForestPrep must be a member of the Schema Admins and Enterprise Admins security groups. Specifically, ForestPrep is a setup switch for Exchange that, when run, extends the Active Directory schema to include Exchange

Server 2003–specific classes and attributes. With Exchange 2000 Server, ForestPrep also created the Exchange organization container, but this has changed with Exchange Server 2003. As a result, you no longer have to specify an organization name until you actually install Exchange Server 2003.

> **Exam Tip**   It is required that you run ForestPrep in the forest root domain because Forest-Prep must be able to contact the server with the Schema Master operations master role, which is the first domain controller installed in a forest (unless you've transferred the role to another domain controller). When you run ForestPrep, it checks whether it is being run in the Correct domain. If it isn't, it tells you which domain contains the Schema Master, and Forest-Prep ends.

To run ForestPrep, insert the Exchange Server 2003 installation CD, and from the Run command line, type the command shown in Figure 2-2, substituting the drive letter for your CD-ROM drive if it isn't D. You'll be doing this in the practice at the end of the lesson.

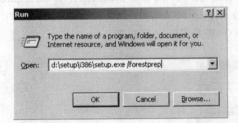

Figure 2-2   Starting the ForestPrep Setup command

Once you start Setup with the /forestprep switch, Setup will copy temporary files to your hard drive and then open the Microsoft Exchange Installation Wizard. After reading the Welcome page, click Next.

Next, you are presented with the End User License Agreement (EULA). Take the time to read it; there is important information regarding the product's licensing. Once you've read the agreement, click the I Agree option, and then click Next.

At this point, the wizard brings you to the component selection portion of Setup. Since you ran Setup with the /forestprep switch, the component selection will be filled in automatically and you will not be able to make any other selections. However, you can choose to change the installation directory if the default doesn't suit your needs. This is shown in Figure 2-3.

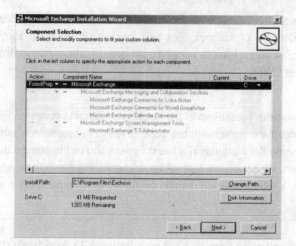

Figure 2-3 The Component Selection portion of Setup

After confirming the component selection and installation directory, enter the account that you will use to install Exchange Server 2003. The account will be granted the Exchange Full Administrator role and will be given the authority to delegate other Exchange administrator roles. As shown in Figure 2-4, by default, Setup will try to use the account that you are currently logged on with.

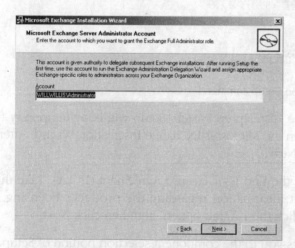

Figure 2-4 Identifying the service account that will be given Exchange Full Administrator permissions

Click Next, and ForestPrep begins. Because it is modifying the Active Directory schema, there is no way to cancel the ForestPrep process once it begins. You'll see the progress being made, but remember that it is not unusual for ForestPrep to take an hour or more to complete. When it does finish, you will see the completion dialog box. Simply click Finish, and the ForestPrep portion of Setup is done.

DomainPrep

Running DomainPrep is much the same as running ForestPrep, except that you use the /domainprep switch instead (you'll do this in the practice at the end of the lesson). The only difference you will see in the wizard is in the component selection screen, which now has DomainPrep selected for the action. Again, you cannot select any other components. If you changed your installation directory during ForestPrep and the change isn't updated here, simply change the installation directory to match what you chose earlier.

While the DomainPrep Setup switch may seem to do the same thing as ForestPrep on the surface, its purpose is different. Whereas ForestPrep prepared the schema and configuration partitions of Active Directory, DomainPrep prepares the domain partition. Another key difference is that while ForestPrep is run once (in the forest root domain) for the entire forest, DomainPrep must be run in each of the following domains:

- The forest root domain
- All domains that will contain Exchange Server 2003
- All domains that will contain Exchange mailbox-enabled objects (users and groups), even if the domain does not have its own Exchange Server 2003 server

The DomainPrep switch creates the groups and permissions required by Exchange Server 2003. Two security groups are created by DomainPrep:

- **Exchange Enterprise Servers**   A domain local group that contains all Exchange servers running in the forest
- **Exchange Domain Servers**   A global group that contains all Exchange servers running in the domain you have selected

To run DomainPrep, you must use a user account that is a member of the Domain Admins group in the local domain.

Practice: Preparing Forests and Domains

In this practice, you will prepare Active Directory for the Exchange Server 2003 installation by running ForestPrep and DomainPrep.

Exercise 1: Run ForestPrep

1. Log on to your Windows Server 2003 server with an Administrator account that belongs to the Schema Admins and Enterprise Admins security groups.
2. Insert the Exchange Server 2003 installation CD into the CD-ROM drive.

3. From the Run command line, execute the command **D:\setup\i386\setup.exe/ forestprep**. (Substitute your CD-ROM drive letter for D if it is different.)

4. When the Welcome page of the Microsoft Exchange Installation Wizard appears, click Next to continue.

5. Read the EULA and click I Agree, and then click Next.

6. On the Component Selection page, verify that ForestPrep is selected for the action. Change the installation path if necessary and click Next.

7. When prompted for the account to be used to install Exchange Server 2003, enter the account you want to use if it isn't the default, and click Next to continue.

8. Once the ForestPrep process finishes and you see the completion dialog box, click Finish to end the wizard. If a screen still appears prompting you to click Next when the installation is done, do so, and then click Finish.

Exercise 2: Run DomainPrep

1. Log on to your Windows Server 2003 server with an Administrator account that belongs to the Domain Admins group (if you logged off after the ForestPrep exercise).

2. With the Exchange Server 2003 installation CD in the CD-ROM drive, from the Start menu, click Run, and then type **D:\setup\i386\setup.exe/domainprep** (substitute D with the drive letter for your CD-ROM drive, if different).

3. When the Welcome page of the Microsoft Exchange Installation Wizard appears, click Next to continue.

4. Read the EULA and click I Agree, and then click Next.

5. On the Component Selection page, verify that DomainPrep is selected for the action. Change the installation path if necessary and click Next.

6. When prompted for the user account to be used for installing Exchange Server 2003, enter the account you want to use if it isn't the default, and click Next to continue.

7. Once the DomainPrep process finishes and you see the completion dialog box, click Finish to end the wizard. If a screen still appears prompting you to click Next when the installation is done, do so, and then click Finish.

Lesson Review

The following questions are intended to reinforce key information presented in this lesson. If you are unable to answer a question, review the lesson materials and then try the question again. You can find answers to the questions in the "Questions and Answers" section at the end of this chapter.

1. You are part of a team that is deploying Exchange Server 2003 in your organization. Your role is to delegate the Exchange Full Administrator role to the team after another administrator prepares Active Directory with ForestPrep and DomainPrep. The administrator informs you that the process has completed successfully, so you log in with the designated service account and attempt to delegate the Exchange administrator roles. However, you find that you are unable to delegate and need to determine why. What would you check?

   _____

   _____

2. Which of the following are domains in an enterprise where you would need to run DomainPrep?

   a. The Schema Master domain controller

   b. Each domain in the forest where you install Exchange Server 2003

   c. Each 'omain in the forest

   d. Each domain that will contain mailbox-enabled objects

   e. The forest root domain

3. What are the two Active Directory partitions that are updated when running ForestPrep?

   _____

   _____

4. You have been asked to prepare your Windows Server 2003 Active Directory forest for a pending Exchange Server 2003 deployment. Your forest consists of the domains *contoso.com*, *dallas.contoso.com*, *boston.contoso.com*, and *seattle.contoso.com*. You are located in Dallas and log on to the *dallas.contoso.com* domain with the domain's Administrator account, which also belongs to the Schema Admins and Enterprise Admins groups. You run ForestPrep, but Setup generates an error and aborts. Why might this have happened?

   _____

   _____

Lesson Summary

- The user account you use to run ForestPrep must be a member of the Schema Admins and Enterprise Admins security groups.

- The user account you use to run DomainPrep must be a member of the Domain Admins group in the domain you are running Setup in.

- ForestPrep is run once to update the entire forest, and DomainPrep is run in each domain that will have Exchange Server 2003 servers or mailbox-enabled objects.

- DomainPrep creates two security groups when run: Exchange Enterprise Servers and Exchange Domain Servers.

Lesson 3: Performing an Exchange Server 2003 Installation

The installation of Exchange Server 2003 is critical, yet many administrators take the installation process far too casually. One of the most important choices you make during the installation of Exchange is the creation of the organization name because once your organization is up and running, it is very difficult to change the configuration without causing severe disruption to your users. Therefore, it is important to carefully step through each part of the installation process.

After this lesson, you will be able to

- Understand the types of installations you can perform
- Successfully install Exchange Server 2003 into a new organization

Estimated lesson time: 45 minutes

Installation Types

There are two primary types of installations available when the Microsoft Exchange Installation Wizard starts. They are:

- **Create a New Exchange Organization**   This installation type is the topic of this chapter.

- **Join Or Upgrade An Existing Exchange Server 5.5 Organization**   This installation type, which also includes coexisting with and upgrading Exchange 2000 Server, is the topic of Chapters 4 and 5.

The following list identifies the available switches that can be used with the Microsoft Exchange Installation Wizard (Setup.exe), and their function:

- **/ChooseDC** *dcname*   Specifies a domain controller to be used during Setup for the reading and writing of Active Directory information. This switch is especially useful when you are installing multiple Exchange Server 2003 servers simultaneously in the same domain, such as in a lab or classroom environment. You can force each Setup instance to use the same domain controller, which results in the computer accounts for each Exchange Server 2003 server being created in the Exchange Domain Servers group on one server and then replicated out from there to other domain controllers. Without using this switch, you would have multiple domain controllers being used and replication clashes as a result, which could prevent some Exchange servers from being able to start their services properly after Setup completes.

- **/DisasterRecovery**   Recovers an Exchange installation after the server's configuration has been restored from backup. Using this switch causes Setup to skip re-registering the server with Active Directory and writing any data to Active Directory. Instead, Setup reinstalls the Exchange binaries, so you can then restore the information stores from backup and re-mount them.

> **See Also**   Chapter 12, "Backup and Restore," discusses recovering Exchange Server 2003 from disaster in much more detail.

- **/ForestPrep**   Prepares the Active Directory forest for the Exchange Server 2003 installation. You only need to run this once in a forest.

- **/DomainPrep**   Prepares each Active Directory domain that will have an Exchange Server 2003 installation, or mailbox-enabled objects such as user accounts. DomainPrep is run in each domain that fits the criteria.

- **/?**   Displays a list of all of the command-line switches with a brief explanation of their function.

- **/CreateUnattend** *filename.ini* –   Creates an .ini file where *filename.ini* is the name of the file that will contain all the information necessary to perform an unattended installation of Exchange Server 2003. In Lesson 4, you will create an unattended installation .ini file and use it to install Exchange Server 2003.

- **/EncryptedMode** –   Encrypts the .ini file to protect it from being read by unauthorized personnel.

- **/UnattendFile** *filename.ini* –   Performs an unattended installation using the .ini file specified. This switch can be further modified by other Setup switches related to unattended installation.

- **/Password** *password* –   Specifies the password of the currently logged on user as a Setup switch, which will auto-logon rather than prompting you during Setup.

- **/ShowUI** –   Displays the wizard user interface even though Setup is running in unattended mode; this switch is used in conjunction with the /UnattendFile switch.

> **Tip**   This is useful if you want to monitor the installation visually without having to intervene, or if your unattended installation is failing and you need to see where in the process the failure is occurring.

- **/NoEventLog**   Prevents Setup from writing any event information to the Windows event logs (System, Application, or Security). Routine messages generated by the Setup program won't create additional clutter in the event logs.

- **/NoErrorLogging** – Disables any error logging during Setup.
- **/All** – Enables all Exchange components for an install, upgrade, or reinstall.

> **Tip** Use this switch if you need to force the installation or reinstallation of a component that the Setup utility wasn't making available.

Performing an Installation of Exchange Server 2003 into a New Organization

After running ForestPrep and DomainPrep, you are ready to begin installing Exchange Server 2003. The previous Setup switches provide a lot of flexibility in managing the behavior of the Setup program. However, the first type of installation you will perform is installing Exchange Server 2003 without any Setup switches into a new organization. When you do this, a new Exchange Server 2003 organization will be created in the forest. Because Active Directory supports only one Exchange Server organization per forest, you can create a new organization in a forest only if one does not already exist.

Practice: Installing Exchange Server 2003 into a New Organization

In this practice, you will complete the exercise of installing Exchange Server 2003 on the Windows Server 2003 server on which you previously ran ForestPrep and Domain-Prep. While it is tempting to install every available component when performing an installation, at this time, you will perform a typical installation. Later you will add additional components, as necessary. Installing Exchange Server 2003 into a new organization is the simplest installation since there are no coexistence issues to manage.

Exercise 1: Run the Microsoft Exchange Installation Wizard to Install Exchange Server 2003

Before you begin, make sure you either have the Exchange Server 2003 installation CD in the CD-ROM drive or have reliable access to the source files for the installation. In the real world, you would likely be installing directly from a local CD-ROM.

To begin installing Exchange Server 2003, you need to have completed the pre-installation tasks that were discussed in Lessons 1 and 2 of this chapter. If you have not yet completed the tasks, do so before proceeding.

1. With the Exchange Server 2003 installation CD in the CD-ROM drive, go to the run line and execute **<drive>:\setup\i386\setup.exe** (where *<drive>* is your CD-ROM drive). Do not use any of the installation switches here.

   The first page you will see is the Welcome page for the Microsoft Exchange Installation Wizard. This page describes the basic functions of the wizard and prompts you to click Next to continue with Setup.

2. You are prompted to read and agree to the End User License Agreement (EULA). This is a step that many administrators skip, but as the person installing the software, you should understand what you are agreeing to when you click I Agree. After you read through the EULA, click I Agree, and then click Next.

> **Important**   Licensing is one of the most misunderstood aspects of systems administration, and failing to read and understand the EULA is the primary cause. IT professionals who install and support the software must be able to accurately convey licensing details to both management and end users. IT professionals are often caught in the middle between users who believe they need every program the company owns installed on their computers and management that doesn't understand why it needs to buy copies for both the users' office computers and home computers when they can't physically use both systems at the same time. Failure to properly understand and abide by EULAs has resulted in many problems for companies, and when companies have problems, often their administrators are blamed.
>
> So while it may seem tedious and a waste of time to read the EULA on a product you're going to install, by doing so, you are fulfilling your responsibility as an administrator.

3. On the Component Selection page, shown in Figure 2-5, you can choose the Exchange Server 2003 components that you want to install. You can also change the installation directory.

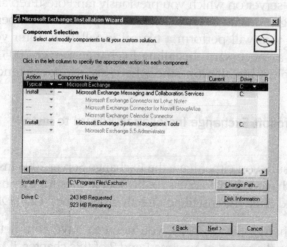

Figure 2-5   The Component Selection page

4. Click the Action column to the left of the Microsoft Exchange component. A drop-down menu presents the installation options, such as Typical, Custom, or Minimum.

When you select one of the options, the subcomponents are automatically updated to match your basic choice. For example, a Typical installation would install the Microsoft Exchange Messaging and Collaboration Services and the Microsoft Exchange System Tools subcomponents. If you choose a Custom installation, you manually choose the components you want to install. If you choose a Typical installation and then want to add a component, such as the Microsoft Exchange 5.5 Administrator, you'll have to change Typical to Custom in the Action column. Otherwise, any component you attempt to select that isn't part of a Typical installation will only give you the option for "none."

5. In the Action column, click Typical, and then click Next. You are prompted to choose the installation type, as shown in Figure 2-6. Here you indicate whether you are performing a new or an upgrade installation. Click Create A New Exchange Organization, and then click Next.

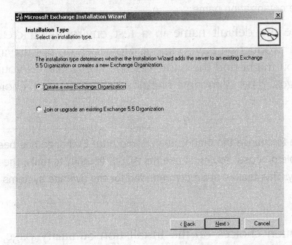

Figure 2-6   Creating a new organization or installing into an existing organization

6. In the Organization Name box, type a name for your organization, and then click Next. As shown in Figure 2-7, First Organization is the default name.

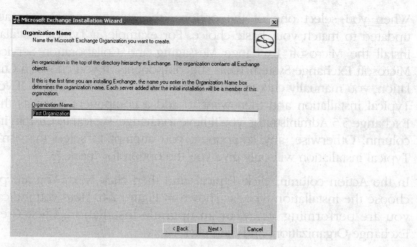

Figure 2-7   Defining the organization name

While you might use the default name in a test environment, create a more descriptive name in a production environment. However, do not use a name that is too restrictive or you might find the name doesn't apply later as your organization grows or changes. The company name is often a good choice for the organization name.

Note   It is not impossible to change the organization name after Exchange has been installed, but it isn't a simple process. You must use the ADSIEdit utility to make the changes in Active Directory manually. This task is not recommended for the average systems administrator.

7. Confirm your installation choices on the Installation Summary page, shown in Figure 2-8. This is your chance to review the component choices you've made and to decide whether to move forward with the installation or to go back and make changes. After you confirm your installation choices, click Next.

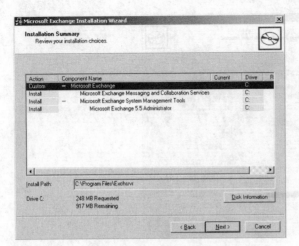

Figure 2-8   Confirming your installation choices

8. Review the Exchange Server licensing agreement shown in Figure 2-9. This agreement is different from the EULA and is specific to Exchange Server 2003 client access licensing requirements. Exchange Server 2003 supports Per Seat Licensing only. Click the option I Agree That I Have Read And Will Be Bound By The License Agreements For This Product, then click Next, and then click Next at the Installation Summary page to begin installing Exchange Server 2003.

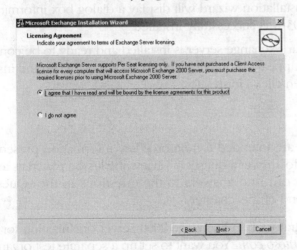

Figure 2-9   Exchange Server Per Seat licensing agreement

Setup begins installing the components you selected. As shown in Figure 2-10, you can monitor the progress of the installation and see what task Setup is currently performing.

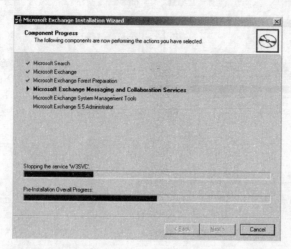

Figure 2-10   Tracking the progress of the installation

Because you performed the pre-installation tasks of running ForestPrep and DomainPrep, Setup will progress quickly to the Microsoft Exchange Messaging and Collaboration Services task after verifying the initial information in Active Directory. If you had not run ForestPrep in advance, Setup would do it for you in the Microsoft Exchange Forest Preparation stage, and it would take just as long as it did when you ran it separately—potentially an hour or more. After Setup finishes its tasks, the installation wizard will display a dialog box informing you that Exchange Server 2003 was successfully installed.

9. Click Finish, and your Exchange server is installed and ready to be configured for use. If a screen still appears prompting you to click Next when the installation is done, do so, and then click Finish.

Lesson Review

The following questions are intended to reinforce key information presented in this lesson. If you are unable to answer a question, review the lesson materials and then try the question again. You can find answers to the questions in the "Questions and Answers" section at the end of this chapter.

1. You are the administrator of an Exchange 2000 Server organization for the Active Directory domain *contoso.com*. You want to set up a separate test organization for Exchange Server 2003. You install a Windows Server 2003 server and join it to the domain and then attempt to install Exchange Server 2003 (since it is a test environment, you run ForestPrep and DomainPrep at the same time that you install the program). However, Setup only gives you the option to join an existing Exchange Server organization. Why?

2. In which of the following circumstances would you install Exchange Server 2003 into a new organization? (Choose two.)

    a. Exchange Server 2003 must coexist with Exchange Server 5.5 or Exchange Server 2000.

    b. You are preparing to migrate from Lotus Notes.

    c. You are setting up e-mail for a new company that is just opening.

    d. You already have an existing Exchange Server 2003 organization and need to install a second server to reduce the load on the first server.

3. Which of the following is not a valid Setup switch for Exchange Server 2003?

    a. /disasterrecovery

    b. /choosedc

    c. /?

    d. /forceremoval

    e. /noerrorlog

    f. /noeventlog

    g. /all

Lesson Summary

- The Microsoft Exchange Installation Wizard allows you to create a new organization or to join an existing Exchange Server 5.5 organization.

- Exchange Server 2003 is licensed in Per Seat mode only.

- Choose an organization name that is reflective of the organization but not so restrictive that a reorganization or other corporate change is likely to make it out of date.

- Changing the organization name after installation can be accomplished manually with ADSIEdit, but it is not recommended.

- Setup.exe can be modified with a number of switches to change the way it runs.

Lesson 4: Unattended Setup

You've now used the Microsoft Exchange Installation Wizard to manually install Exchange Server 2003. In this lesson, you will install a second server into your organization using the unattended method of installation. In the real world, unattended installations are very useful when you need to perform an installation remotely. By supplying someone on site with the installation media and the .ini file for the unattended installation, that person can run Setup without any intervention, ensuring that settings are not inadvertently selected or modified.

Unattended installations are also useful when you were deploying a number of new Exchange servers in an existing organization. With the ability to also perform unattended installations of Windows Server 2003, you can save time deploying multiple servers by automating the entire installation process.

After this lesson, you will be able to

■ Create an .ini file for use with an unattended installation

■ Successfully install Exchange Server 2003 using the /unattendfile switch

Estimated lesson time: 60 minutes

Creating an .ini File for Unattended Setup

Creating an unattended installation file can be very useful for deploying Exchange Server 2003. The process of creating the file is essentially the same as the process for a manual setup: selecting the components you want to install and the installation path; choosing whether to create a new organization or to join an existing one; agreeing to the licensing; and so on. However, rather than beginning installation of the components after you confirm your installation choices on the Installation Summary dialog box, the Microsoft Exchange Installation Wizard writes the configuration to an .ini file, which is a text file formatted specifically for use with the /unattendfile Setup switch.

 Planning An unattended installation will not eliminate the need for the pre-installation work that is required for installing Exchange Server 2003. You still have to ensure that the Windows server installation has the required components installed and configured to support the Exchange installation. You must meet any requirements, such as permissions, to perform the installation.

In this lesson, you will add a second Exchange Server 2003 server to the existing forest and domain. You can also use the unattended installation to create a new organization, which is similar to what you did in Lesson 3 with the manual installation. The only

limitation when creating a new organization with an unattended installation file is that the file is not reusable because Setup would not be able to create the organization on subsequent installations. Therefore, creating an unattended installation file is more useful for additional installations after the creation of the organization.

> **Note**   If you have only a single lab computer to work with, you can alternatively uninstall Exchange Server 2003 and then perform the following steps to create an unattended installation file to use in setting up a new organization. The process would be similar to the manual installation, including choosing the same options. However, this will not allow you to add the server to an existing organization, which is covered in a section and practice later in this chapter.

You can choose any name for the .ini file; however, the extension should be .ini. While technically you can use any extension, such as .txt, the format is that of an .ini file and it is recommended to leave the extension as such for consistency. Creating an .ini file for an unattended installation will be covered in the practice at the end of this lesson.

Unless there is a specific need for all your unattended installations to have custom components installed, choose a Typical installation. If you change the installation path for Exchange Server 2003, it will apply to all servers on which you run the unattended installation. Plan carefully to ensure that the Windows servers are configured consistently with their drives and partitions.

When you are deploying a test environment of Exchange Server 2003, it isn't sufficient to set up a separate lab server in an existing production forest or domain; you must set up a separate Active Directory forest for testing. Otherwise, you may be faced with unwanted forest level settings that are difficult to get rid of when you go to a live deployment of Exchange Server 2003.

> **Exam Tip**   Watch for exam scenarios where an option is to install a second Exchange Server 2003 organization into an existing forest. Because of the nature of the Exchange Server 2003 integration with Active Directory, a forest can support only a single Exchange organization.

When you run Setup and create an Unattend.ini file, you are creating a text file that contains the configuration settings you selected. Since it is a text file, you can view Unattend.ini in Microsoft Notepad. When you do, you'll see something similar to the following: "This Unattend.ini file was created using a Typical installation onto a new server in an Active Directory domain, which already has another domain controller running an Exchange 2003 organization." Because you selected a Typical installation, fields for components that aren't being installed are blank. The [InstallOrder] subsection tells you which components are being installed.

> **Note** The following example has been edited for length. The real file is much longer, as you can see by viewing it on your system.

```
[Version]
Signature="$Windows NT$"
Provider="Microsoft Exchange"
[CompleteComponentList]
exsetdata.dll
srchcomp.dll

 [PreInstallOrder]
gfn_mid microsoft search
gfn_mid microsoft exchange
gfn_mid microsoft exchange server component
gfn_mid microsoft exchange system management tools

[InstallOrder]
gfn_mid microsoft search
gfn_mid microsoft exchange
gfn_mid microsoft exchange server component
gfn_mid microsoft exchange system management tools

[PostInstallOrder]
gfn_mid microsoft search
gfn_mid microsoft exchange
gfn_mid microsoft exchange server component
gfn_mid microsoft exchange system management tools

[Component Error List]
[gfn_mid microsoft search]
gfn_pid stockprop hidden=1

[Additional Global Property Names]
{DF8FF64A-1967-4871-9E32-CA2F819BAB81},HWNDForLoadingDialog,0,0

[Global Properties]
gfn_pid core password=
gfn_pid core autologon=0
gfn_pid core autologon previously enabled=0
gfn_pid core user name=Will Willis
gfn_pid core organization=
gfn_pid core pid 20=111-1111111
gfn_pid core pid 30=J6T48-XCF7K-QCGKD-QV887-4BJYB
gfn_pid core license file=eula.txt
gfn_pid core suite directory=C:\Program Files\Microsoft Integration
gfn_pid core post reboot=0
gfn_pid core suite name=Microsoft Exchange
gfn_pid core disk requirement=31457280
gfn_pid core progress show subs=1
gfn_pid core progress show tasks=0
gfn_pid core ask for pre install=0
gfn_pid core ask for post install=0
gfn_pid core suite mode=0
```

```
gfn_pid core suite baseline=0
gfn_pid core install scenario baseline=0
gfn_pid core force disk space ok=0
gfn_pid core ignore final disk space check=0
gfn_pid core registry=Software\Microsoft\Microsoft Integration\3D5A0E1C-B6DA-42a7-A871-
03CD2E30FEA3\SetupData
gfn_pid core no error log=0
gfn_pid core no event log=0
gfn_pid core system drive=C:
gfn_pid core program files=C:\Program Files\
gfn_pid encrypted mode=0
{E0C022B6-2029-11D3-8DFC-00C04F797FB8}=10
{CDD00162-2E69-11D3-A829-00C04FB1799F}=3D5A0E1C-B6DA-42a7-A871-03CD2E30FEA3
{CDD00163-2E69-11D3-A829-00C04FB1799F}=
{AA62DF98-3F2C-11D3-887B-00C04F8ECDD6}=0
{F24FCE05-8B5C-472F-9F53-9C9BB3DE50AF}=7
gfn_pid core dont install suite files=0
{9843461C-2F7A-4000-B91C-2DDD224C9E91}=c:\Unattend.ini
{DF8FF64A-1967-4871-9E32-CA2F819BAB81}=0
[Scenario Factory]
ActiveScenario={8BED5C7A-CDC9-11D2-92F4-00C04F79F1A8}
```

You can edit this file manually to make changes to the installation behavior, such as if you want Setup to install the server into a specific administrative or routing group. Other options you might configure are those under the [Global Properties] subsection, such as changing the installation path. If you do edit the file, ensure that Notepad doesn't add a .txt extension when you save the file.

Performing an Unattended Installation of Exchange Server 2003

Using an unattended installation .ini file is a matter of using the /UnattendFile Setup switch with the correct Unattend.ini file. The following command line is an example of starting an unattended installation with the Unattend.ini file on a floppy disk in drive A and the Exchange Server 2003 CD in the D drive:

```
D:\setup\i386\setup.exe /unattendfile a:\unattend.ini
```

After executing the command, Setup will run without any input required. It is not a "silent" installation without user interface displayed; the progress window opens, and you can see the installation tasks being performed. Unlike a manual installation, Setup will not prompt you when it is finished installing Exchange Server 2003. Setup quits automatically when complete.

Practice: Performing an Unattended Installation of Exchange Server 2003

In this practice, you will create a file named Unattend.ini and then install Exchange Server 2003 using the file. The procedure will result in a second Exchange 2003 server being installed in your organization.

Exercise 1: Create an Unattend.ini Configuration File

1. From the Start menu, click Run and type the following command (substitute the drive letter for your CD-ROM drive if it is not D, and substitute C:\ with the path to your unattend.ini file if it is different):

   D:\setup\i386\setup.exe /createunattend c:\Unattend.ini

   The Microsoft Exchange Installation Wizard starts as if you ran Setup.exe without any switches.

2. At the Welcome page, click Next, accept the license agreement, and then click Next to open the Component Selection page.

3. In the Action column for the Microsoft Exchange component, click Typical, and then click Next.

4. If the Installation Type page is displayed, select Join Or Upgrade An Existing Exchange 5.5 Organization, and then click Next.

   Whether you have the option of choosing to create a new Exchange organization or upgrade to or join an existing Exchange organization depends on whether Setup detects an existing Exchange organization in the forest. If Setup detects an existing Exchange organization, it will automatically default to joining an existing organization and will not prompt you to choose. This is because an Active Directory forest can support only a single Exchange organization.

5. Review the Installation Summary, and then click Next.

6. Accept the licensing agreement and click Next to finish.

   Setup writes your choices into a configuration file with the path you specified and displays a message stating that Setup completed successfully.

Exercise 2: Perform an Unattended Installation of Exchange Server 2003

1. From the Start menu, click Run and type the following command (change drive D to match your CD-ROM drive letter, and change drive C to match the location where you have stored the unattended installation file, if necessary):

   D:\setup.i386\setup.exe /UnattendFile c:\Unattend.ini

2. Monitor the installation, seeing that Setup utilizes the custom settings from the Unattend.ini file, including installing the Microsoft Exchange 5.5 Administrator program.

   After Setup completes, from the Start menu, point to All Programs, then point to Microsoft Exchange, and start Exchange System Manager. View the organization in Exchange System Manager, verifying that the new server is installed into the organization by expanding the Servers container. Quit the program.

Lesson Review

The following questions are intended to reinforce key information presented in this lesson. If you are unable to answer a question, review the lesson materials and try the question again. You can find answers to the questions in the "Questions and Answers" section at the end of this chapter.

1. You are attempting to create a file called Unattend.ini in order to automate the deployment of Exchange Server 2003 servers in your organization. You currently do not have an Exchange Server 2003 organization. You run Setup with the /createunattend switch and create the Unattend.ini file, which works perfectly when you install your first Exchange Server 2003 server. However, subsequent installations to servers in the same domain fail using the Unattend.ini file. Why might this be happening?

   _____

   _____

2. You are the Exchange administrator for a single-forest/single-domain organization that spans three locations. You create an Unattend.ini file for use in deploying additional Exchange Server 2003 servers in your Exchange organization, which already consists of two Exchange Server 2003 servers at the main location. The other two locations have junior administrators who have been delegated the ability to administer accounts and computer objects in the domain, which they normally do by logging on to their local domain controllers. You verify that the necessary Windows components are installed on the remote servers to support Exchange Server 2003, copy the Unattend.ini file to the local hard drive on each server, and create a batch file for the local junior administrators to run on their server once they insert the Exchange Server 2003 installation CD that executes Setup with the required /unattendfile Setup switch. One junior administrator runs the batch file, and Exchange Server 2003 Setup completes successfully. The other junior administrator calls you and tells you that Setup failed. Why might that have happened?

   _____

   _____

3. Identify the two things that are incorrect about the following command line:

   `d:\setup\i386\setup.exe /createunattendfile unattend.txt`

   _____

   _____

4. You have been asked to coordinate the installation of Exchange Server 2003 on servers at six remote offices. The personnel performing the installation are with a consulting firm, and you won't be physically present during the installations. You want to limit their access to the organization's sensitive security information, yet allow the consultants to successfully install the product. Describe how you will meet these requirements.

_____

_____

Lesson Summary

- Unattended installations are useful for rapidly deploying subsequent Exchange Server 2003 installations into an existing organization.

- Unattended installations are great for delegating the task of installing the Exchange Server 2003 binaries to a lower-level IT professional or for deploying Exchange Server 2003 at a remote location.

- Performing an unattended installation is subject to the same prerequisites (permissions, Windows components, and so on) as performing a manual installation.

- An Active Directory forest can support only a single Exchange Server 2003 organization, so an Unattend.ini file that is used to create an organization cannot be used for subsequent installations.

- An Unattend.ini file is a specially-formatted text file that can be read and manually edited in Notepad after its creation, if changes are necessary.

Lesson 5: Removing an Exchange Server 2003 Server from an Organization

Certain situations may require you to remove a server from an Exchange organization, such as retiring an aging server in favor of a newer and faster server or phasing out a previous version of Exchange that has been migrated to Exchange Server 2003. In this lesson, you will learn how to remove an Exchange Server 2003 server from an Exchange organization.

After this lesson, you will be able to

- Remove an Exchange Server 2003 server from an organization using the Microsoft Exchange Installation Wizard
- Forcibly remove an Exchange Server 2003 server from an organization

Estimated lesson time: 30 minutes

Removing an Exchange Server 2003 Server Using the Microsoft Exchange Installation Wizard

The usual way to remove an Exchange Server 2003 server from an organization is with the Microsoft Exchange Installation Wizard. This is the preferred removal method because Setup is able to read and write information to Active Directory and to remove all references to the server. However, to use the Microsoft Exchange Installation Wizard, there are some prerequisites that must be met.

- You must move all mailboxes to another Exchange server in the organization or remove them from each user account.

- The server must not be a bridgehead server or routing group master. If it is, the role must first be transferred to another Exchange server in the routing group.

- The server must not be a part of any connection agreements.

- The server must not have any connectors installed and in use.

If you attempt to set the Microsoft Exchange component to Remove in the Microsoft Exchange Installation Wizard, and your server does not meet the prerequisites, Setup displays an error message advising you of the problem. Figure 2-11 shows an example of an error when there are user mailboxes on the server that you are trying to remove.

Figure 2-11   A Microsoft Exchange Installation Wizard error message

To complete the removal, you need to correct the situation, such as by moving user mailboxes to another Exchange server in the organization. A common pitfall is that the administrator account has a mailbox created for it automatically when Exchange Server 2003 is installed. So, even if you install and then immediately attempt to uninstall the mailbox, you will need to first delete it. Once you have done this, you can start the wizard again. It will run and complete in much the same way as when installing Exchange Server 2003.

Forcibly Removing Exchange Server 2003 from an Organization

Unfortunately, in the real world, things don't always go as planned. It is possible that, for one reason or another, Active Directory will determine that you don't meet the prerequisites, even when you are sure that you do. You might have a situation, for example, where you have many mailboxes on your Exchange Server 2003 server but you know you don't need any of them and you don't want to take the time to manually delete them.

In such situations, you have the option to forcibly remove an Exchange Server 2003 server from an organization by using the Exchange System Manager console. Before proceeding, stop all of the Exchange Server services. Right-click on the server you want to remove in the console, point to All Tasks, and then click Remove Server. The installation wizard will warn you that proceeding will result in a loss of mailbox, public folder, and configuration data, and that you should uninstall using Add Or Remove Programs instead.

If you click Yes, Exchange Server 2003 will ignore its built-in checks for protecting data and will remove itself from the server and from Active Directory, with the accompanying loss of data that entails. This is a last-resort tool—one you would use if you were unable to perform a removal with the Microsoft Exchange Installation Wizard.

> **Important**   Using the Remove Server task only removes the references to the server in Active Directory. There are additional steps that must be taken to completely remove Exchange Server 2003 from the server itself. As always, care must be taken when editing the registry, since incorrect changes to the registry can result in problems up to and including having to reinstall the operating system. Furthermore, because forcibly removing Exchange Server is not the recommended way of uninstalling, you will want to reinstall the system if at all possible to ensure there are no lingering effects from this procedure.

To finish removing the Exchange Server 2003 server, there are a number of steps to be completed. First, you will have to disable all of the Microsoft Exchange Server services on the server (rather than just stopping them). Then there are several registry keys that need to be deleted. If you are not using the IIS components required by Exchange Server 2003 for anything else, remove those as well.

Once you have completed these tasks, reboot the server and delete the folder structure and contents for the Exchange Server installation. Finish cleaning up by reapplying service packs and patches, and if the Exchange Server 2003 server was installed in an Exchange Server 5.5 site, delete the object in Exchange 5.5 Administrator. You will walk through these steps in the practice at the end of this lesson. At this point, you can either reinstall Exchange Server 2003, if necessary, or reassign the server for some other purpose.

Practice: Removing Exchange Server 2003 from an Organization

Because you have not yet added mailboxes to your server or connected to other platforms, you should be able to remove your server using the Microsoft Exchange Installation Wizard. The only caveat is that during installation, Exchange Server 2003 creates an e-mail address for the account used to install the program (often the Administrator account). You will have to remove this address prior to running Setup. In the practice, you will use the installation wizard to remove an Exchange Server 2003 installation, and then you will forcibly remove the other Exchange Server 2003 installation.

Exercise 1: Remove Exchange Server 2003

1. Log on to the server with an account that has Exchange Full Administrator permissions as well as Schema Admin, Enterprise Admin, and Domain Admin permissions.

2. Start Active Directory Users And Computers. Right-click on the user account you used to install Exchange Server 2003, and click Properties. On the General tab, remove the e-mail address listed.

3. Start the Microsoft Exchange Installation Wizard from the Exchange Server 2003 installation CD.

4. Work through the installation wizard, and when you reach the Component Selection page, click the Action column next to the Microsoft Exchange component and select Remove.

5. Allow the installation wizard to remove the Exchange Server 2003 installation, and monitor its progress as it runs through the steps. Quit the installation wizard when it completes.

Exercise 2: Forcibly Remove Exchange Server 2003 from an Organization

1. Disable all Microsoft Exchange services on the server, and then delete the following registry keys (HKEY_LOCAL_MACHINE has been shortened to HKLM for formatting purposes):

   ❑ HKLM \SOFTWARE\Microsoft\ESE98

   ❑ HKLM \SOFTWARE\Microsoft\Exchange

   ❑ HKLM \SYSTEM\CurrentControlSet\Services\DAVEX

   ❑ HKLM \SYSTEM\CurrentControlSet\Services\EXIFS

   ❑ HKLM \SYSTEM\CurrentControlSet\Services\ExIPC

   ❑ HKLM \SYSTEM\CurrentControlSet\Services\EXOLEDB

   ❑ HKLM \SYSTEM\CurrentControlSet\Services\MSExchangeMU

   ❑ HKLM \SYSTEM\CurrentControlSet\Services\MSExchangeES

   ❑ HKLM \SYSTEM\CurrentControlSet\Services\IMAP4Svc

   ❑ HKLM \SYSTEM\CurrentControlSet\Services\MSExchangeAL

   ❑ HKLM \SYSTEM\CurrentControlSet\Services\MSExchangeDSAccess

   ❑ HKLM \SYSTEM\CurrentControlSet\Services\MSExchangeIS

   ❑ HKLM \SYSTEM\CurrentControlSet\Services\MSExchangeMGMT

   ❑ HKLM \SYSTEM\CurrentControlSet\Services\MSExchangeMTA

   ❑ HKLM \SYSTEM\CurrentControlSet\Services\POP3Svc

   ❑ HKLM \SYSTEM\CurrentControlSet\Services\MSExchangeFBPublish

   ❑ HKLM \SYSTEM\CurrentControlSet\Services\RESvc

   ❑ HKLM \SYSTEM\CurrentControlSet\Services\MSExchangeSRS

   ❑ HKLM \SYSTEM\CurrentControlSet\Services\MSExchangeS

   ❑ HKLM \SYSTEM\CurrentControlSet\Services\MSExchangeTransport

   ❑ HKLM \SYSTEM\CurrentControlSet\Services\MSExchangeWEB

2. Remove the IIS components SMTP, NNTP, and World Wide Web service (if not needed by other components on the server), and remove the Metabase.bin file from the *Systemroot*\System32\Inetsrv folder. *Systemroot* refers to the folder that Windows is installed into, such as C:\WINNT.

3. Restart the server.

4. Rename the \Exchsrvr folder structures on all drives. For example, rename C:\Exchsrvr to C:\Exchsrvrold. This is necessary if you have anything you want to save, such as log files. Alternatively, you could delete the directory structure.

5. Reapply any service packs and security patches previously installed on the server.

> **Note**   If you installed the Exchange Server 2003 server into an existing Exchange 5.5 site, you will need to delete the Exchange Server 2003 server object from the Exchange 5.5 Administrator program by selecting it, then clicking File, and then clicking Delete.

6. Open the Exchange System Manager (the console is not in the Exchsrvr folder structure, so you didn't delete it in step 4) and navigate to your server.

7. Right-click the server, point to All Tasks, and click Remove Server.

8. Confirm the removal of the Exchange Server 2003 data from Active Directory.

9. Close Exchange System Manager.

Lesson Review

The following questions are intended to reinforce key information presented in this lesson. If you are unable to answer a question, review the lesson materials and try the question again. You can find answers to the questions in the "Questions and Answers" section at the end of this chapter.

1. You are an Exchange administrator who is trying to remove an Exchange Server 2003 server from your organization, but the Microsoft Exchange Installation Wizard is giving an error that it can't remove the server. The error states that user mailboxes exist on the server. What should you do?

_____

_____

2. Which of the following tasks are not *required* in a manual removal of Exchange Server 2003? (Choose two.)

   a. Delete the \Exchsrvr folder

   b. Use the Microsoft Exchange Installation Wizard

   c. Delete Registry keys

   d. Remove Windows Server components

   e. Use Exchange System Manager

   f. Reinstall Windows

   g. Disable services

3. You are an Exchange administrator who is trying to remove Exchange Server 2003 from a server that is performing poorly and running very low on disk space. The server belongs to an existing organization. You run the Microsoft Exchange

Installation Wizard and attempt to set the Microsoft Exchange component to Remove, but it fails. You realize that the server contains approximately 500 mailboxes belonging to former employees of the company, and you don't need the data. You decide to forcibly remove Exchange Server 2003 rather than address the mailbox problem, and you go into Exchange System Manager and use the Remove Server task to remove the server. Now, every time you reboot, it takes a long time logging in and then the Messenger Service displays a screen informing you that at least one service failed to start. You also notice that disk space usage on the server has not changed since you removed the server. What can you do to correct the server problems?

_____

_____

Lesson Summary

- Removing an Exchange Server 2003 server from an organization is usually accomplished by using the Microsoft Exchange Installation Wizard, or it can be removed forcibly using a manual process.

- There are prerequisites that must be met before the Microsoft Exchange Installation Wizard will allow Exchange Server 2003 to be removed.

- Forcibly removing a server is considered a last resort and should be done only if you can't get the Microsoft Exchange Installation Wizard to work even after ensuring the prerequisites are met.

Case Scenario Exercise

Contoso, Inc., is a company that has a sales office in Dallas, Texas, which is also the company's national headquarters. The company also has six manufacturing plants at various locations in the United States. Contoso is an old, traditional company that has been run by an executive team firmly entrenched in the 1960s way of doing business. As a result, technology has been viewed as little more than a necessary evil, and only the corporate office in Dallas has e-mail services—an archaic DOS-based peer-to-peer program that runs on NetBIOS Extended User Interface (NetBEUI) and is non-Internet aware.

Recently, the CEO retired and was replaced by an energetic visionary who wants to bring Contoso into the 21st century. He has the full support of board members and shareholders, who recognize that if Contoso is to survive in the new economy, it needs to update its technology infrastructure and be able to utilize the Internet to work with partners.

You have been contracted to perform the deployment of Exchange Server 2003 at the corporate office, which will be the first part of the deployment. Given the challenges of trying to migrate Contoso's proprietary e-mail system, as well as the company's desire to start fresh, executive management has given you the directive to simply deploy Exchange Server 2003 and Outlook 2003 with a clean install. Users will be able to access the proprietary system for history and reference purposes, but message transfer functionality will be disabled once Exchange Server is deployed and functional.

- **Requirement 1**   Initially, the manufacturing plants will connect to Exchange remotely using Internet Message Access Protocol 4 (IMAP4) and Outlook Web Access (OWA) over a virtual private network (VPN) connection between the plants and the corporate office. At a later date, the plants will have their own local Exchange Server 2003 servers installed into the Contoso organization. Contoso consists of a single forest with each branch location having its own child domain to the main *contoso.com* domain. To support the Contoso organization, which consists of roughly 15,000 employees, you have been asked to install 10 Exchange Server 2003 servers at the corporate office. Corporate users who have been using e-mail have been informed by management that their existing e-mail will be set to read-only for reference but not migrated over to Exchange Server 2003. Management wants a clean start on the new e-mail organization.

- **Requirement 2**   The server group has already purchased the servers for deployment of Exchange Server 2003 and placed them at each location. The servers have state-of-the-art hardware and are installed with Windows Server 2003, Enterprise Edition and configured as member servers in the appropriate domains. Windows Server 2003 has been installed on the servers with its default configuration. You need to add any Windows Server 2003 services or components that will be necessary to support the Exchange Server 2003 installations.

- **Requirement 3**   Since the Enterprise Admins group in Dallas manages the Active Directory infrastructure and controls access to the schema, you will need to coordinate with the group to run ForestPrep and DomainPrep. To accomplish this, you will have a service account created that has the necessary permissions, and you will use this service account to run ForestPrep and DomainPrep and to perform the Exchange Server 2003 installations.

Requirement 1

The first requirement involves installing Exchange Server 2003 on 10 servers at the corporate office.

1. Describe how you would deploy the 10 servers in a way that is consistent and efficient.

_____

_____

2. Which of the following tasks must you perform on *each* server prior to installing Exchange Server 2003 on Windows Server 2003 servers in the *contoso.com* domain? (Choose all that apply.)

    a. Run the /ForestPrep Setup switch.

    b. Run the /DomainPrep Setup switch.

    c. Install the Microsoft ASP.NET Windows component.

    d. Install the SMTP component.

    e. Log on with an account that has at least Exchange Administrator rights.

    f. Log on with an account that has at least Exchange Full Administrator rights.

    g. Install the WWW service.

3. If you want to create an Unattend.ini file to be used later, but you want to ensure that no one is able to view sensitive Exchange organization information by opening the file in Notepad, what should you do?

    a. Put the Unattend.ini file on a floppy and lock it up.

    b. Run Setup with the /encryptedmode switch.

    c. Store the file in an Encrypting File System (EFS) protected folder.

    d. Wait to create the Unattend.ini file until you are ready to use it.

Requirement 2

The second requirement involves configuring the servers running Windows Server 2003 with the necessary components to support Exchange Server 2003.

1. Which of the following components must you install manually after a default Windows Server 2003 installation in order to be able to install Exchange Server 2003? (Choose all that apply.)

    a. Simple Network Time Protocol (SNTP)

    b. Simple Mail Transport Protocol (SMTP)

    c. Network News Transfer Protocol (NNTP)

    d. TCP/IP

    e. ASP.NET

    f. Domain Name Service (DNS)

    g. World Wide Web service

    h. E-mail services

2. Describe the process that you would use to install the required Windows Server 2003 components that you identified as necessary in the previous question.

_____

_____

Requirement 3

The third requirement involves coordinating the running of ForestPrep and DomainPrep.

1. The Enterprise Admins group in Dallas has approved your request for an Exchange service account and asks you what specific groups you want this svc_xch account placed in. What group membership is necessary to run Forest-Prep? (Choose all that apply.)

   a. Domain Admins

   b. Enterprise Admins

   c. Schema Admins

   d. Domain Users

   e. Exchange Full Administrator

   f. Exchange Enterprise Servers

2. What group membership is required to run DomainPrep?

   a. Domain Admins

   b. Enterprise Admins

   c. Schema Admins

   d. Domain Users

   e. Exchange Full Administrator

   f. Exchange Enterprise Servers

3. Where in the Active Directory forest should you run ForestPrep and DomainPrep?

_____

_____

Troubleshooting Lab

In this lab, you will attempt to remove an Exchange Server 2003 server from an organization that has a user mailbox, which will cause Setup to fail. You will then correct the problem and successfully remove the server.

> **See Also**   Recipient management is covered in more detail later in Chapter 7, "Managing Recipient Objects and Address Lists," but what you need to know to complete the lab is supplied here.

Before proceeding with this lab, you must have two Exchange Server 2003 servers installed into the same organization, and on the second server, create one or more user mailboxes, as follows (*after* installing Exchange Server 2003):

1. Start the Active Directory Users And Computers console on the second server and navigate to the Users container.

2. Create a user account as usual, except with Exchange Server 2003 installed, you will have an additional prompt to create a mailbox. Confirm that you want to create a mailbox, and ensure that the mailbox store given by default is located on the server you will be removing.

3. Start Microsoft Internet Explorer on the server and go to *http:\\servername\exchange* (where *servername* is the name of your server), and then log on with the user account you just set up.

4. Send yourself an e-mail message to initialize the mailbox.

Exercise 1: Unsuccessful Removal of Exchange Server 2003

1. Log on to the Exchange Server 2003 server that you configured the mailbox on, and run Setup from the Exchange Server 2003 installation CD.

2. Proceed through the Microsoft Exchange Installation Wizard, and on the Component Selection page, attempt to assign the Remove action to the Microsoft Exchange component.

3. Note the error message that Setup will not continue because the server hosts one or more user mailboxes.

4. Exit the wizard.

Exercise 2: Correct the Problem and Remove Exchange Server 2003 Successfully

1. Start the Active Directory Users And Computers console.

2. Go to your user account, right-click it, and click Exchange Tasks.

3. From the task list that appears, click Move Mailbox.

4. The Server and Mailbox drop-down lists should default to your other server. If not, select them from the lists. Click Next to complete the process.

5. Once the mailbox is moved, run the Microsoft Exchange Installation Wizard again. Note that this time you can successfully assign the Remove action to the Microsoft Exchange component.

Chapter Summary

- Exchange Server 2003 can be installed manually or it can be scripted to install in unattended mode. To create an unattended configuration file, Setup is run with the /createunattend switch and goes through the Microsoft Exchange Installation Wizard. The configuration is written to an .ini file.

- Exchange Server 2003 has minimum hardware requirements of a Pentium 133 with 256 MB of RAM, NTFS partitions, and 200 MB of free disk space on the system drive and 500 MB of free disk space on the drive that will hold the Exchange binaries. However, this configuration is inadequate for anything other than basic testing and practicing with the software.

- Exchange Server 2003 can be installed on Windows 2000 Server SP3 or later or on Windows Server 2003. Not all functionality is available when Exchange Server 2003 is installed on Windows 2000 Server.

- Exchange Server 2003 is the only version that can run on Windows Server 2003.

- Prior to deploying the Exchange Server 2003 application, you must first prepare Active Directory by running ForestPrep and DomainPrep.

- An Exchange Server 2003 server can be removed from an organization by running the Microsoft Exchange Installation Wizard, but this requires that the server has no user mailboxes or connectors in use prior to removal.

- An Exchange Server 2003 server can be forcibly removed, if necessary, through a manual process that involves editing the registry, deleting the \Exchsrvr folders, uninstalling Windows Server components that support Exchange, stopping and disabling services, and removing the server data from Active Directory.

Exam Highlights

Before taking the exam, review the key points and terms that are presented in this chapter. Return to the lessons for additional practice.

Key Points

- An Active Directory forest can support only a single Exchange organization.
- Schema Admins permissions are required to run ForestPrep, and Domain Admins permissions are required to run DomainPrep.
- ForestPrep is run once, in the forest root domain, while DomainPrep is run in each domain that will have Exchange Server 2003 servers installed.
- A mailbox is created for the administrator account during the installation of Exchange Server 2003. This mailbox must be removed prior to attempting to uninstall the program using the installation wizard.
- A server performance baseline should be created prior to installing Exchange Server 2003, to ensure that the post-installation performance is adequate compared to the previous performance, and for troubleshooting purposes.

Key Terms

service account   A special account created for use by an application's services. Service accounts are used when specific security contexts are needed that you don't want to grant to an existing user account (such as the Administrator account), and you want to be able to specify account settings that will not be subject to domain policies.

Exchange organization   An Exchange organization defines the common security context for an Exchange Server 2003 infrastructure, much like an Active Directory forest. The organization is defined during the installation of the first Exchange Server 2003 server, and subsequent server installations can join the organization. Only one organization can exist per Active Directory forest.

ForestPrep   ForestPrep is a Setup switch that makes changes to the forest schema in order to support an Exchange Server 2003 server. ForestPrep creates the attributes and classes that define Exchange Server 2003 objects, such as mailboxes, and extends Active Directory so that existing objects gain Exchange Server 2003 functionality.

DomainPrep   DomainPrep is a Setup switch that makes changes to a domain to support an Exchange Server 2003 installation. DomainPrep creates two security groups when run, Exchange Enterprise Servers and Exchange Domain Servers, and the first installed server will be placed in both of these groups. The user account that runs DomainPrep must be a member of the Domain Admins group for the domain.

Questions and Answers

Page
2-10
Lesson 1 Review

1. You are heading up a team of systems and network administrators that is planning to deploy Exchange Server 2003 in an environment where e-mail has to date been hosted by the organization's Internet service provider (ISP). One of the administrators asks you why you should bother creating a service account for Exchange instead of simply using the domain's Administrator account. What are two reasons you can give him to justify using a separate account?

Service accounts differ from regular user accounts in that they are almost never used to log on to a server interactively. By using a dedicated service account, you can easily separate activities in the Security log that are generated by the service account from the events logged from someone actively using the Administrator account. In addition, the administrator password should be changed on a periodic basis as part of sound systems administration practices, whereas changing the password of a service account is rarely, if ever, done.

2. You are planning to set up a couple of lab computers using old computers that aren't in use anymore in order to test and practice with Exchange Server 2003. What is the minimum amount of random access memory (RAM) your systems will need to have in order to install Exchange Server 2003?

   a. 64 MB

   b. 128 MB

   c. 256 MB

   d. 512 MB

   The correct answer is c.

3. Which of the following platforms are able to support an installation of Exchange Server 2003? (Choose all that apply.)

   a. Windows NT 4

   b. Windows NT 4 SP6a

   c. Windows 2000 Server SP1

   d. Windows 2000 Server SP3

   e. Windows 2000 Server SP4

   f. Windows Server 2003, Standard Edition

   g. Windows Server 2003, Enterprise Edition

   h. Windows Server 2003 SP1

   The correct answers are d, e, f, g, and h.

4. You install Exchange Server 2003 onto a Windows Server 2003 file server that has a Pentium III–450 MHz processor, 512 MB of RAM, and a RAID 5 disk array. After a couple of weeks, users begin complaining that working with documents on the server is very sluggish during the middle of the day. What can you do to improve performance?

Exchange Server 2003 can add a significant performance burden to an existing server, especially one that is also performing other roles. In this situation, the server is performing poorly during peak usage periods, which suggests that it is underpowered. Adding a second processor, if possible, or upgrading to a faster processor would help alleviate the performance problems.

Page
2-17
Lesson 2 Review

1. You are part of a team that is deploying Exchange Server 2003 in your organization. Your role is to delegate the Exchange Full Administrator role to the team after another administrator prepares Active Directory with ForestPrep and DomainPrep. The administrator informs you that the process has completed successfully, so you log in with the designated service account and attempt to delegate the Exchange administrator roles. However, you find that you are unable to delegate and need to determine why. What would you check?

First you would want to check to make sure the account you were using had the appropriate level of permissions. If the administrator who ran ForestPrep forgot to replace the default name with the Exchange service account, ForestPrep would attempt to assign the Exchange Full Administrator role to the account in use (which would likely be the Administrator account). If this happened, when you logged on with the service account, it would not have been granted the Exchange Full Administrator role and therefore could not be used to delegate further administrator roles. You would need to use the same account specified during ForestPrep initially to delegate roles, and you could then delegate Exchange Full Administrator to the service account as well as delegate the roles to the other team members.

2. Which of the following are domains in an enterprise where you would need to run DomainPrep?

   a. The Schema Master domain controller

   b. Each domain in the forest where you install Exchange Server 2003

   c. Each domain in the forest

   d. Each domain that will contain mailbox-enabled objects

   e. The forest root domain

   The correct answers are b, d, and e.

3. What are the two Active Directory partitions that are updated when running ForestPrep?

   Schema and configuration.

4. You have been asked to prepare your Windows Server 2003 Active Directory forest for a pending Exchange Server 2003 deployment. Your forest consists of the domains *contoso.com*, *dallas.contoso.com*, *boston.contoso.com*, and *seattle.contoso.com*. You are located in Dallas and log on to the *dallas.contoso.com* domain with the domain's Administrator account, which also belongs to the Schema Admins and Enterprise Admins groups. You run ForestPrep, but Setup generates an error and aborts. Why might this have happened?

Since the user account being used is a member of the correct groups, this isn't a problem with permissions. ForestPrep is required to be run in the forest root domain (in this case *contoso.com*) because ForestPrep must be run in the same domain as the Schema Master. Since you attempted to run ForestPrep from the *dallas.contoso.com* domain, you are not running it in the right place and will get an error message to that effect during Setup.

Page 2-26 ## Lesson 3 Review

1. You are the administrator of an Exchange 2000 Server organization for the Active Directory domain *contoso.com*. You want to set up a separate test organization for Exchange Server 2003. You install a Windows Server 2003 server and join it to the domain and then attempt to install Exchange Server 2003 (since it is a test environment, you run ForestPrep and DomainPrep at the same time that you install the program). However, Setup only gives you the option to join an existing Exchange Server organization. Why?

Active Directory supports only a single Exchange Server organization per forest. Since a production organization already exists, Setup detects this and will only allow you to join an existing organization. In order to create a new organization, you need to make the server a domain controller in its own forest or install it into a forest that does not presently have an Exchange Server organization.

2. In which of the following circumstances would you install Exchange Server 2003 into a new organization? (Choose two.)

    a. Exchange Server 2003 must coexist with Exchange Server 5.5 or Exchange Server 2000.

    b. You are preparing to migrate from Lotus Notes.

    c. You are setting up e-mail for a new company that is just opening.

    d. You already have an existing Exchange Server 2003 organization and need to install a second server to reduce the load on the first server.

    The correct answers are b and c.

3. Which of the following is not a valid Setup switch for Exchange Server 2003?

   a. /disasterrecovery

   b. /choosedc

   c. /?

   d. /forceremoval

   e. /noerrorlog

   f. /noeventlog

   g. /all

   The correct answer is d.

Page
2-33

Lesson 4 Review

1. You are attempting to create a file called Unattend.ini in order to automate the deployment of Exchange Server 2003 servers in your organization. You currently do not have an Exchange Server 2003 organization. You run Setup with the /createunattend switch and create the Unattend.ini file, which works perfectly when you install your first Exchange Server 2003 server. However, subsequent installations to servers in the same domain fail using the Unattend.ini file. Why might this be happening?

   Active Directory can support only a single Exchange organization in a forest. When you created the Unattend.ini file, Setup detected that there was no existing organization so it prompted you to create a new Exchange organization or to join an existing one. Naturally, you would have chosen to create a new organization; otherwise, Setup would have failed when it could not contact an existing organization as part of the join process. However, subsequent server installations that attempt to use the Unattend.ini file fail because an Exchange organization now exists, and another cannot be created in the forest. You would need to create a new Unattend.ini file to support joining an existing Exchange organization.

2. You are the Exchange administrator for a single-forest/single-domain organization that spans three locations. You create an Unattend.ini file for use in deploying additional Exchange Server 2003 servers in your Exchange organization, which already consists of two Exchange Server 2003 servers at the main location. The other two locations have junior administrators who have been delegated the ability to administer accounts and computer objects in the domain, which they normally do by logging on to their local domain controllers. You verify that the necessary Windows components are installed on the remote servers to support Exchange Server 2003, copy the Unattend.ini file to the local hard drive on each server, and create a batch file for the local junior administrators to run on their server once they insert the Exchange Server 2003 installation CD that executes Setup with the required /unattendfile Setup switch. One junior administrator runs the batch file, and Exchange Server 2003 Setup completes successfully. The other junior administrator calls you and tells you that Setup failed. Why might that have happened?

The Unattend.ini file does not override the pre-installation requirements to install Exchange Server 2003. In this situation, you can eliminate the variables related to entering an incorrect command line or not having the Unattend.ini file in the right location because you performed those tasks yourself. You also verified that the necessary Windows components were installed. That leaves a permissions-related problem as the most likely cause, especially since the batch file worked in one location but not the other, yet all servers belong to the same domain. Probably the first junior administrator remembered to log on to the server using the service account you had set up, while the second junior administrator attempted to run the Setup batch file under their own logon account, which does not have the necessary Domain Admins level permissions to complete Setup.

3. Identify the two things that are incorrect about the following command line:

```
d:\setup\i386\setup.exe /createunattendfile unattend.txt
```

Knowing the correct syntax of a command is important to avoid unintended results. The two things wrong with the above command line are:

- The Setup switch should be /unattendfile to use a configuration file for performing an unattended installation and /createunattend for creating a configuration file. This command line combines the two switches.

- You must specify a path to the configuration file; no default path is assumed. So, you would need to specify c:\Unattend.ini or the appropriate path for your situation.

4. You have been asked to coordinate the installation of Exchange Server 2003 on servers at six remote offices. The personnel performing the installation are with a consulting firm, and you won't be physically present during the installations. You want to limit their access to the organization's sensitive security information, yet allow the consultants to successfully install the product. Describe how you will meet these requirements.

Because you will not be present, you will want to configure an unattended installation file for use by the consultants. In addition, to protect the file, you should use the /encryptedmode Setup switch. This will encrypt the file and prevent it from being opened in a text editor.

Page 2-39

Lesson 5 Review

1. You are an Exchange administrator who is trying to remove an Exchange Server 2003 server from your organization, but the Microsoft Exchange Installation Wizard is giving an error that it can't remove the server. The error states that user mailboxes exist on the server. What should you do?

Your best course of action would be to exit Setup, then start Exchange System Manager and move the mailboxes to another Exchange server in the organization. Then you should be able to run Setup again and successfully remove the server from the organization.

While you could forcibly remove the Exchange Server 2003 server even though the installation wizard is preventing you from uninstalling, it is not the recommended means of accomplishing the task. Forcible removal is considered a last resort when you are unable to get the installation wizard to work.

2. Which of the following tasks are not *required* in a manual removal of Exchange Server 2003? (Choose two.)

   a. Delete the \Exchsrvr folder

   b. Use the Microsoft Exchange Installation Wizard

   c. Delete Registry keys

   d. Remove Windows Server components

   e. Use Exchange System Manager

   f. Reinstall Windows

   g. Disable services

   The correct answers are b and f.

3. You are an Exchange administrator who is trying to remove Exchange Server 2003 from a server that is performing poorly and running very low on disk space. The server belongs to an existing organization. You run the Microsoft Exchange Installation Wizard and attempt to set the Microsoft Exchange component to Remove, but it fails. You realize that the server contains approximately 500 mailboxes belonging to former employees of the company, and you don't need the data. You decide to forcibly remove Exchange Server 2003 rather than address the mailbox problem, and you go into Exchange System Manager and use the Remove Server task to remove the server. Now, every time you reboot, it takes a long time logging in and then the Messenger Service displays a screen informing you that at least one service failed to start. You also notice that disk space usage on the server has not changed since you removed the server. What can you do to correct the server problems?

   Using the Remove Server option only removes the server from Active Directory. As a result, there are tasks that still need to be completed on the server. You will need to delete the \Exchsrvr folder structure to reclaim the disk space used by Exchange Server 2003 and to disable the Microsoft Exchange services on the server. This will stop the error messages about services being unable to start. In addition, you must delete a series of Registry keys to finish cleaning up Exchange Server 2003 from the server.

Page
2-41

Case Scenario Exercise: Requirement 1

1. Describe how you would deploy the 10 servers in a way that is consistent and efficient.

   You could install the first Exchange Server 2003 server into the organization manually and then create an Unattend.ini file to perform subsequent automated installations. Furthermore, you could use the /choosedc switch when you create the Unattend.ini file to specify a particular domain controller to be contacted, which would have all subsequent installations use the same domain controller to read and write Active Directory data. As an added benefit of this approach, servers 2 through 10 could all be installed simultaneously, dramatically reducing the time it takes to deploy the Exchange Server 2003 servers.

2. Which of the following tasks must you perform on *each* server prior to installing Exchange Server 2003 on Windows Server 2003 servers in the *contoso.com* domain? (Choose all that apply.)

   a. Run the /ForestPrep Setup switch.

   b. Run the /DomainPrep Setup switch.

   c. Install the Microsoft ASP.NET Windows component.

   d. Install the SMTP component.

   e. Log on with an account that has at least Exchange Administrator rights.

   f. Log on with an account that has at least Exchange Full Administrator rights.

   g. Install the WWW service.

The correct answers are c, d, g, and h.

3. If you want to create an Unattend.ini file to be used later, but you want to ensure that no one is able to view sensitive Exchange organization information by opening the file in Notepad, what should you do?

   a. Put the Unattend.ini file on a floppy and lock it up.

   b. Run Setup with the /encryptedmode switch.

   c. Store the file in an Encrypting File System (EFS) protected folder.

   d. Wait to create the Unattend.ini file until you are ready to use it.

The correct answer is b.

Page 2-42

Case Scenario Exercise: Requirement 2

1. Which of the following components must you install manually after a default Windows Server 2003 installation in order to be able to successfully install Exchange Server 2003? (Choose all that apply.)

   a. Simple Network Time Protocol (SNTP)

   b. Simple Mail Transport Protocol (SMTP)

   c. Network News Transfer Protocol (NNTP)

   d. TCP/IP

   e. ASP.NET

   f. Domain Name Service (DNS)

   g. World Wide Web service

   h. E-mail services

The correct answers are b, c, e, and g.

2. Describe the process that you would use to install the required Windows Server 2003 components that you identified as necessary in the previous question.

From the Start menu, select Control Panel, and then open Add Or Remove Programs. Then, click Add/Remove Windows Components to start the Windows Components Wizard. When the components selection opens, click Application Server, and then click Details. Add ASP.NET and click OK. Scroll down the list and select Internet Information Services and click Details. Add SMTP, NNTP, and World Wide Web service. Click OK, and then click OK again to install the components.

Page 2-43

Case Scenario Exercise: Requirement 3

1. The Enterprise Admins group in Dallas has approved your request for an Exchange service account and asks you what specific groups you want this svc_xch account placed in. What group membership is necessary to run ForestPrep? (Choose all that apply.)

a. Domain Admins

b. Enterprise Admins

c. Schema Admins

d. Domain Users

e. Exchange Full Administrator

f. Exchange Enterprise Servers

The correct answers are b and c.

2. What group membership is required to run DomainPrep?

a. Domain Admins

b. Enterprise Admins

c. Schema Admins

d. Domain Users

e. Exchange Full Administrator

f. Exchange Enterprise Servers

The correct answer is a.

3. Where in the Active Directory forest should you run ForestPrep and DomainPrep?

ForestPrep should be run once in the root domain of the forest, in this case *contoso.com*. DomainPrep must be run in each domain that will support servers running Exchange Server 2003 or mailbox-enabled objects. Therefore, you would run DomainPrep in the main corporate domain initially, and then in each of the domains supporting the branch offices prior to installing the first Exchange Server 2003 server in each domain.

3 Configuring a Microsoft Exchange Server 2003 Infrastructure

Exam Objectives in this Chapter:

- Prepare the environment for the Microsoft Exchange Server 2003 deployment
- Manage and troubleshoot front-end and back-end servers
- Install, configure, and troubleshoot Exchange Server 2003

Why This Chapter Matters

> Once Exchange Server 2003 is installed and a new organization is created, there are other deployment-related considerations such as delegating administrative authority, installing the administrative tools on a workstation, determining whether to keep Exchange Server 2003 in mixed mode or convert to native mode, setting up the administrative group and routing group structures, and so on. Most of this planning should be completed prior to installing the first Exchange Server 2003 server. In this chapter, you'll learn the post-installation tasks necessary to make the most efficient use of Exchange Server 2003 in an organization.

Lessons in this Chapter:

- Lesson 1: Post-Installation Considerations 3-2
- Lesson 2: Administrative and Routing Groups 3-13
- Lesson 3: Mixed Mode and Native Mode 3-21
- Lesson 4: Front-End and Back-End Servers 3-28

Before You Begin

The primary focus of this chapter is on the concepts that you will need to understand and consider prior to deploying Exchange Server 2003. However, there are some hands-on tasks and exercises in this chapter. To perform the exercises in this chapter, you will need to have completed the exercises in Chapter 2, "Planning a Microsoft Exchange Server 2003 Infrastructure."

Lesson 1: Post-Installation Considerations

After Exchange Server 2003 is installed, there are additional configuration steps to complete prior to setting up users, connecting routing groups, and performing other server administration tasks. For example, you may need to delegate administrative authority of Exchange Server 2003 to other IT personnel, or you may need to install Microsoft Exchange System Management Tools on a workstation. In this lesson, you will perform a number of post-installation tasks.

After this lesson, you will be able to

- Verify the Exchange Server 2003 services are installed and started and configure them to use the service account
- Delegate Exchange Full Administrator permissions
- Install Microsoft Exchange System Management Tools on a Microsoft Windows XP Professional workstation
- Install additional components that were not selected during the initial Exchange Server 2003 installation

Estimated lesson time: 45 minutes

Exchange Server 2003 Services

Several new services are installed as part of the Exchange Server 2003 installation process. Figure 3-1 shows these services and their default configuration for Startup Type, the account the services Log On As, and the current state of the service (started or stopped).

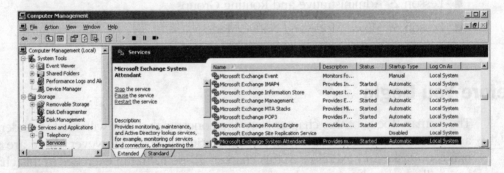

Figure 3-1   Exchange Server 2003 services

Table 3-1 lists and describes the services that are installed in a typical installation.

Table 3-1   Exchange Server 2003 Services and Their Function

Service	Description
Microsoft Exchange Event	Monitors folders and fires events for Microsoft Exchange Server 5.5–compatible server applications.
Microsoft Exchange IMAP4	Provides Internet Message Access Protocol 4 (IMAP4) services to clients. If this service is stopped, clients are unable to connect to the computer using the IMAP4 protocol.
Microsoft Exchange Information Store	Manages the Microsoft Exchange Information Store, including mailbox stores and public folder stores. If this service is stopped, mailbox stores and public folder stores on the computer are unavailable.
Microsoft Exchange Management	Provides Exchange management information using Windows Management Instrumentation (WMI). If this service is stopped, Exchange management information is unavailable using WMI.
Microsoft Exchange MTA Stacks	Provides Microsoft Exchange X.400 services. Exchange X.400 services are used for connecting to Exchange 5.5 servers and are used by other connectors (custom gateways). If this service is stopped, Exchange X.400 services are unavailable.
Microsoft Exchange POP3	Provides Post Office Protocol version 3 (POP3) services to clients. If this service is stopped, clients are unable to connect to the computer using the POP3 protocol.
Microsoft Exchange Routing Engine	Provides topology and routing information to Exchange Server 2003 servers. If this service is stopped, optimal routing of messages will not be available.
Microsoft Exchange Site Replication Service	Allows Exchange Server 2003 to coexist in an Exchange Server 5.5 site by presenting the Exchange Server 2003 server as an Exchange Server 5.5 directory service to other Exchange Server 5.5 servers. The Site Replication Service (SRS) is disabled by default and is useful only in mixed-mode organizations.
Microsoft Exchange System Attendant	Provides monitoring, maintenance, and Active Directory lookup services, for example, monitoring of services and connectors, defragmenting the Exchange store, and forwarding Active Directory lookups to a global catalog server. If this service is stopped, monitoring, maintenance, and lookup services are unavailable. If this service is disabled, any services that explicitly depend on it will fail to start.

Service Dependencies

Troubleshooting problems with Exchange Server 2003 often involves services that have stopped. A problem you are trying to solve might seem as though it is the result of one service failing, when the service in question stopped only because a service it was dependent upon stopped first. For example, if users could not log on to their Exchange Server 2003 server, you check the services and notice that the Information Store service has stopped. While the problem could be related to the Information Store service itself, you might also find that the Information Store service stopped only because the System Attendant service stopped. The System Attendant may have stopped because a service it depends upon stopped, and so on. Table 3-2 lists the dependencies for the Exchange Server 2003 services.

> **Exam Tip** You can view service dependencies through the Services management console, but for the exam, you should be able to identify the dependencies of each of the Exchange Server 2003 services. You may see scenarios where knowing the service dependencies is essential to determining the real problem and finding the correct answer.

Table 3-2 Exchange Server 2003 Service Dependencies

Service	Dependencies
Microsoft Exchange System Attendant	Event Log NTLM Security Support Provider Remote Procedure Call (RPC) RPC Locator Server Workstation
Microsoft Exchange Information Store	Microsoft Exchange System Attendant Exchange Installable File System (EXIFS)
Microsoft Exchange IMAP4	Internet Information Service (IIS) Admin Service
Microsoft Exchange POP3	IIS Admin Service
Microsoft Exchange MTA Stacks	Microsoft Exchange System Attendant
Microsoft Exchange Management	RPC WMI
Microsoft Exchange Routing Engine	IIS Admin Service
Microsoft Exchange Event	Microsoft Exchange Information Store

> **Tip**   There can be multiple levels of dependencies, where one service depends on another, which depends on another, and so forth. There are additional dependencies, as well, outside of the Exchange-specific services, such as the services that the IIS Admin Service depends on, and the services RPC depends on, and so on. When troubleshooting a service, first ensure that there are no other service dependencies in a stopped state.

Service Logon Accounts

In Figure 3-1, in the Log On As column, notice that by default Exchange Server 2003 uses the Local System account to start each of the services. The Local System account is a built-in account that has full administrative rights; most services are associated with this account by default. Applications such as Exchange Server 2003 use it automatically because it is a known account with the correct permissions. However, when you have multiple services sharing the same logon account, troubleshooting security can be more difficult. Therefore, it is recommended that you use a dedicated service account for your Exchange Server 2003 services. You will configure the services to use your dedicated service account later in this lesson.

Real World   Microsoft Exchange Server 2003 Services and Server Reboots

Anyone who has administered a version of Microsoft Exchange Server in the real world knows that rebooting a server running Exchange Server, whether on Microsoft Windows NT 4, Windows 2000 Server, or Windows Server 2003, can take much longer than normal. Exchange Server 2003 is no different, and if it is installed on a Windows Server 2003 server that functions as a global catalog server, the server can take as long as 10 minutes to reboot. If Exchange Server 2003 is installed on a member server, the process is not as lengthy, but it can still take significantly longer than rebooting a non-Exchange server.

A common workaround for this problem is to stop the Exchange services prior to initiating the server restart. To automate the process, many administrators use a batch file to stop the Exchange Server 2003 services and use the Shutdown.exe program (found in the Windows NT 4, Windows 2000 Server, or Windows Server 2003 Resource Kits) to completely script the reboot process. By doing so, the reboot process is dramatically sped up.

Delegation of Authority

Another post-installation consideration with Exchange Server 2003 is identifying the user accounts to which you will delegate administrative authority for the Exchange organization. When you installed Exchange Server 2003, the user account used was automatically given Exchange Full Administrator rights, which includes the ability to administer all configuration details of the Exchange organization and the ability to modify permissions. No other accounts are given rights to administer the Exchange organization. This means that any future administration has to be performed under the security context of the account that installed Exchange Server 2003. This is impractical and largely undesirable for a few reasons. First, if you have multiple Exchange administrators, you want to be able to track the activity of each administrator through the Security log. If all administrators use the same user account, it will be much more difficult to accomplish this. Another reason is that it will be necessary to distribute the service account password to every administrator, which will compromise security. In addition, each administrator will have the same level of permissions to the Exchange organization, which isn't desirable either.

The best practice is to delegate authority to the groups or individual users that need to administer the Exchange organization. The standard practice in system administration is to use security groups wherever possible for assigning permissions and to assign permissions to individual users only when absolutely necessary. By following these practices, an administrator is better able to manage and maintain security in an enterprise environment.

Exchange Server 2003 supports three administrative roles that can be delegated using Exchange System Manager: Exchange Full Administrator, which can manage anything in the organization including permissions; Exchange Administrator, which can manage everything in the organization except permissions; and Exchange View Only Administrator, which has read-only administrative access to the Exchange organization.

> **Security Alert**   Authority to administer Exchange Server 2003 can be delegated in one of two places: at the organization level (which grants the permissions to the entire organization) or at the administrative group level (which grants the permissions only to that administrative group). In a decentralized administrative model, you can delegate administrative rights to a division to manage their own administrative group without allowing them to have rights to any other administrative groups. And in a centralized administrative model, you can delegate administrative rights to the entire organization so that you don't have to repeat the delegation process for every administrative group that is added.

Administration from Client Workstations

Exchange administration tasks, including delegating authority, should not be performed directly from the server consoles. Secure environments strictly limit the ability to log on locally to a server, perhaps to only the Administrator account. Allowing regular user accounts to log on locally to servers, especially domain controllers, is not a recommended security practice.

If you have a workstation that meets the criteria, you can install Microsoft Exchange System Management Tools and administer the Exchange organization from there. Table 3-3 lists the system requirements necessary to install Microsoft Exchange System Management Tools. The requirements for non-Exchange servers are given, as well, in case you need to install the tools on a server that isn't running Exchange Server 2003. If a service pack level is given, the service pack is part of the requirements, and the tools cannot be installed on a system that isn't at that service pack level or later. A basic requirement for any management workstation is that it is a member of the same domain and forest as the Exchange organization.

Table 3-3 System Requirements for Running Microsoft Exchange System Management Tools

Operating system	Requirements
Windows XP Professional SP1	■ IIS snap-in component
	■ Simple Mail Transfer Protocol (SMTP) service component (disable SMTP service after installation; it is needed only for the snap-in and poses a security threat if left running)
	■ World Wide Web (WWW) service (required by SMTP; should be disabled after installation)
	■ Windows Server 2003 AdminPack (for Network News Transfer Protocol (NNTP) and Active Directory Users And Computers snap-ins)
Windows XP Professional SP2	■ IIS snap-in component
	■ IIS Manager component (provides SMTP now)
	■ Windows Server 2003 AdminPack
Windows 2000 Professional SP3	■ IIS snap-in component
	■ Windows 2000 Server AdminPack (provides SMTP, NNTP, and Active Directory Users And Computers snap-ins)
Windows 2000 Server SP3	■ IIS snap-in component
	■ SMTP service component (disable after installation)
	■ NNTP service component (disable after installation)
Windows Server 2003	■ IIS Manager component

The Microsoft Exchange System Management Tools installation is very similar to the Exchange Server 2003 installation. When your management workstation meets all the requirements, run Setup from the Exchange Server 2003 installation CD. The Microsoft Exchange Installation Wizard will start, and you will go to the Component Selection page and perform a Custom installation. The only component you need to select is Microsoft Exchange System Management Tools; however, if you will be managing any Exchange Server 5.5 servers, as well, you can also install the Microsoft Exchange 5.5 Administrator. Once Setup completes, you will be able to start Active Directory Users And Computers and Exchange System Manager and complete tasks using the rights that you have been delegated.

Adding and Removing Exchange Server 2003 Components

There might be times when you need to add or remove an Exchange Server 2003 component. Perhaps you installed the Microsoft Exchange Connector for Novell GroupWise as part of the process of migrating GroupWise to Exchange Server 2003, and with that process now complete, you want to remove the connector component. Or perhaps your company has recently acquired a company that has an Exchange 5.5 organization, and you need to install the Microsoft Exchange 5.5 Administrator in order to administer that site. Whatever the circumstance, the process of adding or removing an Exchange Server 2003 component involves re-running Exchange Server 2003 Setup and changing the selections on the Component Selection page of the Microsoft Exchange Installation Wizard.

> **Important** When planning to remove a component, it is necessary that you ensure the component is no longer in use in the organization. With connectors, that means making sure there are no existing connection agreements that utilize the connector (connection agreements are discussed in Chapter 4). If you attempt to remove a component that is currently in use, Setup will block the removal, and Setup will fail.

Usually adding or removing a component is as simple as running the Microsoft Exchange Installation Wizard. However, if the installation wizard won't allow you to add or remove a component and you know there shouldn't be a problem with it, there are ways to accomplish the task manually.

Practice: Post-Installation Considerations

In this practice, you will configure the Exchange Server 2003 services to use the service account you created in Chapter 2, create security groups for the administrative roles of Exchange Server 2003, and delegate authority to those groups. You will run Exchange Server 2003 Setup again and add the Microsoft Exchange 5.5 Administrator program to your first Exchange Server 2003 installation.

Exercise 1: Modify the Exchange Server 2003 Services

1. From the Start menu, point to All Programs, then point to Administrative Tools and start Services. Scroll down to the services that begin with Microsoft Exchange.

2. Double-click the Microsoft Exchange System Attendant service to bring up the properties, and then click the Log On tab.

3. Select the This Account option and browse to your service account.

4. Type the password for your service account and then confirm it. Click OK to return to Services.

5. Repeat the process for each of the Exchange Server 2003 services.

6. Restart the Microsoft Exchange System Attendant service, choosing Yes to restart all the other services in the process. Confirm that the services restart correctly using the service account rather than the Local System account.

Exercise 2: Delegate Administrative Authority

1. Start the Active Directory Users And Computers console and create the following Windows security groups:
   - ExchangeFullAdmins
   - ExchangeAdmins
   - ExchangeViewAdmins

2. From the Start menu, point to All Programs, and then point to Microsoft Exchange. Start Exchange System Manager.

3. Right-click on the organization name and click Properties. Select the check box to Display Administrative Groups, if it is not already selected. Click OK. Quit and reopen Exchange System Manager, if prompted.

4. Right-click the organization name and notice that Delegate Control is an option on the shortcut menu. Right-click an administrative group and notice the same option.

5. Right-click the organization name, and click Delegate Control. This will start the Exchange Administration Delegation Wizard. Click Next, and notice that only the account you used to install Exchange Server 2003 (and the account specified to be the Exchange Full Administrator during the installation, if they are not the same) has any permissions (Exchange Full Administrator).

6. Complete the wizard to add the ExchangeFullAdmins security group and assign it the role of Exchange Full Administrator.

7. Repeat the process and assign the ExchangeAdmins security group the role of Exchange Administrator and assign the ExchangeViewAdmins security group the role of Exchange View Only Administrator.

8. When finished, start Active Directory Users And Computers and create a personal user account for yourself. Make it a member of the ExchangeFullAdmins security group.

Exercise 3: Add Additional Exchange Server 2003 Components

1. On your first Exchange Server 2003 server, insert the Exchange Server 2003 installation CD and start Setup.

2. On the Component Selection page, check marks appear next to the installed components. Click the check mark next to the Microsoft Exchange component, and select Change from the drop-down list.

> **Tip**   You have to select Change at each component level or you will receive an error. You cannot set a child component to Change or Install without selecting its parent first.

3. In the Action column for Microsoft Exchange System Management Tools, click the check mark (which shows that the component is installed) and select Change from the drop-down list.

4. Click the Action column next to Microsoft Exchange 5.5 Administrator, and click Install.

5. Finish the wizard, and then verify that the Microsoft Exchange 5.5 Administrator is installed. You can find the program in the Microsoft Exchange menu, which is on the All Programs menu of the Start menu.

Lesson Review

The following questions are intended to reinforce key information presented in this lesson. If you are unable to answer a question, review the lesson materials and then try the question again. You can find answers to the questions in the "Questions and Answers" section at the end of this chapter.

1. You are the Exchange administrator for your organization. On Monday morning, users call to report that they are unable to open Microsoft Outlook; they receive an error message indicating that Exchange Server is unavailable. You check to see if the services are running and find that the Information Store service is stopped. You attempt to start it from Services and it fails, generating an error. Where do you begin troubleshooting?

_____

_____

2. Which of the following Microsoft operating systems meet the minimum requirements to install Microsoft Exchange System Management Tools?

   a. Windows XP Home SP2

   b. Windows XP Professional

   c. Windows XP Professional SP1

   d. Windows 98 SE

   e. Windows NT Workstation 4.0 SP6a

   f. Windows 2000 Professional SP2

   g. Windows 2000 Professional SP3

   h. Windows Millennium Edition (Windows Me)

3. You have been assigned the task of designing a more streamlined administrative structure for your Exchange Server 2003 organization. Your organization currently consists of 15 administrators who have various levels of administrative control of Exchange, assigned individually at the administrative group level as well as the organizational level, in some cases. What would be your best approach to this task?

   _____

   _____

4. You are an Exchange administrator for an organization that has five Exchange administrators who perform various tasks. There are no additional Exchange administration roles delegated outside of the service account that Exchange Server 2003 was installed with. You are trying to convince the senior Exchange administrator, who is more management-oriented than IT-oriented, to delegate administrative control to the individual administrators or, at a minimum, to create security groups and delegate control to the groups, but he is reluctant. His reasoning is that it is more secure if only a single user account has the Exchange Full Administrator role for the organization. How would you counter his argument?

   _____

   _____

Lesson Summary

- Services are often dependent on other services to run, so to effectively troubleshoot Exchange Server 2003, it is important to know which services rely on each other.

- Ideally, administrative control should be delegated to security groups rather than to individuals. Delegation of control is one of the first tasks that needs to be performed after installation in an organization that has multiple Exchange administrators.

- Microsoft Exchange System Management Tools can be installed on a client workstation that meets the operating system and component requirements.

- Administrative control can be delegated at either the organization level or the administrative group level.

- Exchange Server 2003 components can be added or removed by re-running Setup and changing the installed components.

Lesson 2: Administrative and Routing Groups

Another consideration when planning an Exchange Server 2003 deployment is the use of administrative and routing groups. For a single domain with a single Exchange server, not much planning is required, but administrative and routing groups are very important to plan for when you have larger, multi-location Exchange environments. The plan you devise for creating administrative and routing groups will affect how and where you install Exchange Server 2003.

After this lesson, you will be able to
- Understand administrative groups and their usage
- Create administrative groups
- Understand routing groups and their usage
- Create routing groups

Estimated lesson time: 20 minutes

Administrative Groups

Versions of Exchange Server prior to Exchange 2000 Server used the concept of *sites*, which defined the administrative and routing topology for an Exchange organization. Sites are familiar to administrators who have worked with Active Directory directory service, and the concept is very similar in defining the physical infrastructure of the organization. With Exchange Server 5.5, the administration model was tied directly to the routing and communication model, which was defined by the site. Beginning with Exchange 2000 Server and carried into Exchange Server 2003, the site concept is divided into administrative groups and routing groups. One limitation of the use of sites in previous versions of Exchange Server was that the administrative requirements of a large organization might not fit neatly within the site structure. As a result, the management of the administrative roles was more complicated, for example, in a situation where sites were defined geographically but administration was centralized. However, the centralized administration was delegated in a way that individual administrators were responsible for different sites. Exchange Server 5.5 sites are inflexible, so it is cumbersome in situations such as this to divide the administration in a way that goes against the site layout. With Exchange Server 2003, administrative groups are used to define the administrative topology of the Exchange organization. This is not tied to the physical topology, since in many organizations the administrative topology is different from the physical topology. It is possible for the administrative and routing group topology to correspond, but Exchange Server 2003 gives you the flexibility to separate them, if necessary.

> **Planning** The use of administrative groups requires Exchange Server 2003, Enterprise Edition. Exchange Server 2003, Standard Edition, is limited to a single administrative group containing a single storage group consisting of one mailbox store and one public folder store.

Administrative groups can contain any of the following types of objects:

- Servers
- Policies
- Routing groups
- Public folder trees

> **Note** Since small to mid-sized companies don't have a need for administrative groups, by default they are disabled. You have to enable the displaying of administrative groups in the Exchange System Manager utility. Right-click on the Organization name, click Properties, and then select the check box to Enable Administrative Groups.

You can think of an administrative group as a collection of the previous types of objects that have been organized into a container for simplified administration. You assign permissions to the administrative group rather than to the individual objects. This simplifies administration, for example, if you had 25 servers throughout Texas that all needed to have the same permissions, you could add them to a single administrative group rather than configuring the permissions individually on each server. This simplification is especially important when you consider ongoing administration of the organization after the initial configuration. If your company hires a new administrator and you need to add her to the list of administrators, it would be much simpler to do it once on an administrative group than having to configure each server.

Administrative Models

Administrative groups should be planned for prior to installing Exchange Server 2003, though they can be implemented before and after installation. The main reason it is important to plan your administrative groups prior to installing Exchange is because over the long term, it will be easier to support your organization and will require less administrative effort if you get it right the first time. In addition, there is less chance of users experiencing service disruptions because you need to reconfigure something.

Depending on your organization's needs, there are different administrative models you can use: a *centralized* model, a *decentralized* model, or a *mixed* model that utilizes features of both. The centralized administrative model is most commonly used in small to mid-sized companies that have a limited number of IT personnel, but it can also be used in larger organizations that want to have their Exchange environment managed centrally by a few individuals. In a centralized model, there may be only one or two administrative groups used. Administrative groups do not have to follow the physical topology of an organization, so adding every server in a global organization to a single administrative group would have no effect on how the messaging infrastructure communicated.

The decentralized model is similar to how Exchange Server 5.5 sites were managed, where each site had its own administrative context (since message routing and administration were connected). Decentralized administration is most commonly used in larger organizations that have many branch locations operating independently of other locations, with their own local IT departments. In this type of model, you would have many administrative groups, perhaps one for each physical location.

The mixed model, as you would expect, uses a combination of centralized and decentralized administration. This model is most commonly used by larger organizations, where there is a need to centrally manage certain aspects of Exchange Server 2003, such as policies, while decentralizing administration of other aspects, such as the day-to-day Exchange server administration.

> **Tip**   It is worth repeating that administrative groups are in no way tied to the physical layout of the network, whereas routing groups are (routing groups are discussed in the next section). It is important to understand that administrative groups are a way to simplify the administration of the Exchange organization and are not related to the physical routing and communication between servers.

Once you have run ForestPrep and DomainPrep, you can gain access to the Exchange System Manager indirectly and create and modify administrative groups. Prior to the installation of Exchange (but after ForestPrep and DomainPrep are run), you can use the Active Directory Sites And Services console to modify the default administrative group. To create an administrative group after the installation of Exchange, use the Exchange System Manager utility, which is installed with Exchange Server 2003 and is located in the Microsoft Exchange program menu in the All Programs menu.

Routing Groups

Whereas administrative groups have no relationship to the physical network infrastructure, routing groups are directly related to the physical layout. You can think of routing groups as being much like Active Directory sites, which are used to group servers that share reliable, well-connected bandwidth. Routing groups come into play when you have multiple physical locations connected by slower wide area network (WAN) bandwidth, such as an Integrated Services Digital Network (ISDN) connection. Consider a scenario where you have two physical locations, Dallas and St. Louis, which have five servers running Exchange Server 2003 in each location. The two locations are physically connected by a 128K ISDN line. In this type of environment, you would create two routing groups, one for each location. This would map directly to the Active Directory site structure. Each routing group would contain its local servers, and a connector would be configured to connect the two routing groups. This could be either a routing group connector (the preferred way), an SMTP connector (for unreliable WAN connections), or an X.400 connector.

> **Exam Tip** Designing a routing group structure and configuring routing group connectors is not covered on this exam. However, understanding the concepts is imperative to being able to deploy Exchange Server 2003 successfully in a multi-location organization.

When you install the first Exchange Server 2003 server in an organization, a default routing group is created. You can rename this routing group to something more appropriate, and you can create additional routing groups using the Exchange System Manager utility. Creating routing groups is much like creating administrative groups, though a routing group is contained within an administrative group. As with administrative groups, by default, routing groups are not enabled. To enable routing groups, start Exchange System Manager, right-click on the organization name, click Properties, and select the check box to Display Routing Groups.

Subsequent Exchange servers are added to routing groups during the installation process, and if necessary, you can move servers between routing groups using Exchange System Manager. The only caveat is that in mixed mode, you cannot move servers between routing groups that belong to different administrative groups; you can only move servers between routing groups within the same administrative group. If you need to move a server to a routing group that is in a different administrative group, you must first move the server to the administrative group that contains the target routing group. Alternatively, you can move the entire routing group from one administrative group to another. This is a limitation of the default mixed mode operation, but once you convert to native mode, this limitation is lifted.

The other benefit that routing groups provide is a way of controlling message transfer. In this way, too, routing groups are very similar to Active Directory sites. With Active Directory, sites are used to define areas of well-connected bandwidth and areas of low bandwidth for the purpose of optimizing replication traffic. With routing groups, servers within a routing group are assumed to have high-speed, reliable bandwidth between them (such as on the same local area network [LAN]), and message transfer occurs immediately. Between routing groups, where bandwidth is assumed to be slow, a server in each group is designated as a *bridgehead server*, and traffic between routing groups is funneled through the bridgehead server in each group. This optimizes the flow of message traffic between routing groups and provides for a consistent, reliable flow of traffic.

Practice: Administrative and Routing Groups

In this practice, you will create an administrative and routing group structure based on a given scenario.

Exercise 1: Create Administrative Groups

You are the lead consultant of a team that is designing an Exchange Server 2003 infrastructure for Contoso, Ltd., a manufacturer of fine electric and acoustic guitars. The company has manufacturing plants in the United States, Mexico, Japan, and Germany, with world-wide headquarters in Dallas, Texas, and sales offices in Dallas, Boston, St. Louis, Los Angeles, Tokyo, Mexico City, and Berlin. You recommend a centralized administrative model for the United States and a decentralized model for the overseas locations. The proposal is accepted, and you begin to create the administrative groups after installing the first server running Exchange Server 2003 and creating the Contoso organization in Dallas.

1. From the Start menu, point to All Programs, then point to Microsoft Exchange, and then start the Exchange System Manager console.

2. Right-click the Contoso organization and click Properties.

3. When the Properties dialog box opens, select the check boxes to display both administrative and routing groups. Click OK to close the dialog box.

4. You are prompted to exit and re-start Exchange System Manager for the changes to take effect. Do so.

5. Expand the Administrative Groups node, and then right-click First Administrative Group and select Rename.

6. Type in **USA** for the name, since you'll later be installing the first server at the corporate headquarters in Dallas.

7. Right-click the Administrative Groups container, select New, and then click Administrative Group. Type **Germany** for the name and click OK. Notice that you have the USA administrative group that you modified previously in the Active Directory Sites And Services console.

8. Repeat the process and create administrative groups for Mexico and Japan.

Exercise 2: Create Routing Groups

This exercise uses the same scenario as Exercise 1, but this time you will be creating routing groups. Since the overseas offices have only a single location apiece, you will need to create a single routing group in each administrative group. In the USA administrative group, you will want to rename the default routing group and create routing groups for each location (Dallas, Boston, St. Louis, and Los Angeles).

1. Open the Exchange System Manager console if it isn't already open.

2. Expand the Administrative Groups node so you can see all of your administrative groups.

3. Expand the USA administrative group node, and then expand the Routing Groups node.

4. Notice that Exchange has configured a default First Routing Group. Right-click it and rename it **Dallas**.

5. Right-click the Routing Groups node in the USA administrative group node, select New, and then click Routing Group. Type **Boston** and click OK.

6. Repeat the process to create routing groups in the USA administrative group for St. Louis and Los Angeles.

7. Expand the Japan administrative group node. Repeat step 5 to create a routing group called Tokyo in the Japan administrative group.

8. Repeat the process to create routing groups called Mexico City and Berlin in the Mexico and Germany administrative groups, respectively.

Lesson Review

The following questions are intended to reinforce key information presented in this lesson. If you are unable to answer a question, review the lesson materials and then try the question again. You can find answers to the questions in the "Questions and Answers" section at the end of this chapter.

1. Describe when you would use multiple administrative groups in an Exchange Server 2003 organization and how administrative groups differ from routing groups.

   _____

   _____

2. Describe the differences between a centralized administrative model and a decentralized administrative model.

   _____

   _____

3. You are an Exchange administrator for an organization that has two physical locations in Dallas that are connected by an ISDN line. There is an Exchange administrator at the other location, as well, and you have two administrative groups so that each of you can manage your own Exchange server without the other interfering. There is a server running Exchange Server 2003 at each location, and the organization is running in mixed mode. Due to the changing economic

climate, your company closes the other office, consolidating all resources in the main office (and as a result, you are the only Exchange administrator). You bring all of the hardware back to the main office to set up. What do you need to do to move the Exchange server from the other office into the same routing group as the other Exchange server, since they are now located on the same LAN?

a. Use Exchange System Manager to move the server from one routing group to the other.

b. Use Exchange System Manager to first move the server into your administrative group, and then move it from the other routing group to your routing group.

c. Reinstall Exchange Server 2003 on the other server and place it into the correct routing group during the installation.

d. Reinstall Exchange Server 2003 on the other server and place it into the correct administrative group during installation, which will automatically place it in the routing group under that administrative group.

4. You are the senior Exchange administrator for the *contoso.com* domain, which has an Exchange Server 2003 organization that consists of two administrative groups: one for Contoso and one for Fabrikam, a subsidiary of Contoso. One of the divisions of Contoso is being consolidated with Fabrikam, and in the process, you are moving its server running Exchange Server 2003 from the First Routing Group in Contoso to the First Routing Group in Fabrikam. You try to drag and drop the server between routing groups but find that you are unable to. When you place the cursor over the routing group in Fabrikam, it shows a circle with a line through it, indicating you cannot move the server there. What would be preventing the move?

_____

_____

Lesson Summary

■ Administrative and routing groups are not enabled by default. You must enable them in Exchange System Manager to be able to view and manage them.

■ Administrative groups define the administrative topology of an Exchange organization, which can be different from or the same as the physical topology.

■ Routing groups define the physical topology of the Exchange organization and are contained within administrative groups.

- Servers cannot be directly moved between routing groups that are in different administrative groups in the default mixed mode. The server must be moved between administrative groups first, or the mode should be changed to native.

- The default First Administrative Group and First Routing Group can be renamed in the Active Directory Sites And Services console prior to installing Exchange Server 2003, after ForestPrep and DomainPrep have been run.

- After Exchange Server 2003 has been installed, administrative groups and routing groups are managed through Exchange System Manager.

- Administrative groups are created according to an administrative model: centralized, decentralized, or mixed.

Lesson 3: Mixed Mode and Native Mode

When planning your Exchange Server 2003 deployment, you'll need to consider in which mode your Exchange organization will operate. Since Exchange installs automatically in mixed mode, it's not critical that you make the decision initially; however, it is important particularly if you are currently supporting or migrating from an Exchange Server 5.5 environment.

After this lesson, you will be able to

- Understand the concepts behind mixed mode and native mode operation
- Identify the benefits and limitations of mixed mode
- Identify the benefits and limitations of native mode
- Understand when it is appropriate to convert from mixed mode to native mode

Estimated lesson time: 25 minutes

Mixed Mode and Native Mode Concepts

An Exchange Server 2003 organization can operate in one of two modes: native mode or mixed mode. Native mode offers full Exchange Server 2003 functionality, while mixed mode offers limited Exchange Server 2003 functionality but the benefit of interoperability between Exchange Server 2003 and Exchange Server 5.5. When you install Exchange Server 2003, your Exchange organization operates in mixed mode by default. This default setting ensures past and future interoperability with previous versions of Exchange. For example, you have the ability to install a server running Exchange Server 5.5 at a future date, even if no servers running Exchange Server 5.5 exist in the organization at the time of installation. You might encounter such a situation if your organization acquires another organization that is still running Exchange Server 5.5.

The concept of mixed mode and native mode organizations is similar to the concept of mixed mode and native mode domains in Active Directory. These are called *modes* in Windows 2000 Server and *functional levels* in Windows Server 2003, but the terms refer to the same thing. The similarity exists in terms of limiting new features that won't work on previous product versions versus exposing all of the new functionality. What mode you choose has tradeoffs between functionality and backwards compatibility. No direct relationship exists between the mode of the domain and the mode of an Exchange organization. With Exchange Server 2003, you can select native mode and mixed mode only at an organizational level.

Exam Tip   When an organization is in native mode, you only have servers running Exchange 2000 Server and Exchange Server 2003. Servers running Exchange 2000 Server and Exchange Server 2003 can coexist in native mode, so be aware of this when you come across scenarios where servers running Exchange 2000 Server are thrown into the mix.

A comparison of the benefits and limitations of each mode is useful in demonstrating the importance of the choice of mode for your Exchange Server 2003 organization. A particular benefit or limitation may be the deciding factor in your deployment plan, as to whether you need to convert to native mode as soon as possible in order to take advantage of native mode features, or whether you should stay in mixed mode to support previous versions of Exchange Server, previous applications, or connectors.

Mixed Mode Benefits and Limitations

The ability to operate an Exchange organization in mixed mode exists for backward compatibility with previous versions of Exchange Server and other software that relies on it. The differences between mixed mode and native mode are primarily concerned with the concept of administrative groups and routing groups. Mixed mode exists mainly to bridge the gap between Exchange Server 5.5 sites and Exchange 2000 Server and Exchange Server 2003 organizations by forcing Exchange 2000 Server and Exchange Server 2003 to operate within the boundaries of Exchange Server 5.5 sites. Administrative groups and routing groups cannot be managed independently in mixed mode. In other words, administrative groups and routing groups are mapped directly to sites and therefore do not have the flexibility that they have when the Exchange organization is operating in native mode.

Benefits of Mixed Mode

Running your Exchange organization in mixed mode ensures future interoperability between Exchange Server 2003 and previous versions of Exchange. The benefits of operating in mixed mode include the following:

- Interoperability between servers running Exchange Server 2003 and Exchange Server 5.5.
  - ❑ Routing between Exchange Server 2003 and Exchange Server 5.5 is seamless.
  - ❑ Exchange Server 2003 can use existing Exchange Server 5.5 connectors and gateways to connect to foreign e-mail systems and route e-mail messages.
  - ❑ Both Exchange Server 5.5 objects (users, custom recipients, and distribution lists) and Exchange Server 2003 objects (users, contacts, and groups) can be managed from Active Directory.

❑ Public folders replicated between Exchange Server 2003 and Exchange Server 5.5 can be securely accessed from clients on either system.

■ You have the option to install servers running Exchange Server 5.5 at a later date.

■ All Exchange Server 5.5 directory service objects such as servers and connectors are replicated to Exchange Server 2003 and are displayed in the Exchange System Manager console.

Limitations of Mixed Mode

When your Exchange organization is operating in mixed mode, there are limitations and issues you must consider, such as the following:

■ Exchange Server 5.5 sites are mapped directly to administrative groups.

■ Administrative groups are mapped directly to Exchange Server 5.5 sites, which means that you cannot create administrative groups independent of the routing infrastructure.

■ You can only move mailboxes between servers that are in the same administrative group.

■ Routing group membership must consist only of servers installed in the administrative group that is defined with the routing group.

■ You can move servers between routing groups, but all members of all routing groups must be members of the same administrative group.

■ Exchange 5.5 system objects present read-only properties when viewed from Exchange System Manager.

■ Some commands may not always function as you would expect them to due to interaction between older and newer components and management tools. For example, you cannot view the resource tables of an Exchange Server 5.5 server's database with Exchange System Manager.

Real World   Mixed Mode Administration

In an Exchange Server 5.5 site, not only are all servers managed as a single group, but all servers have reliable, high-speed connectivity for sending messages to one another. However, when an Exchange Server 2003 organization is in mixed mode and Exchange 5.x sites are mapped one-to-one with administrative groups, you can subdivide the routing structure for the servers running Exchange Server 2003 in the collection using routing groups. A server cannot belong to a routing group that is held under a different administrative group.

Because of the limitations of mixed mode, most organizations opt to convert to native mode unless they have a specific need to support Exchange Server 5.5 servers and sites.

Native Mode Advantages

Once an Exchange organization is converted from mixed mode to native mode, the organization is no longer interoperable with systems running Exchange Server 5.5. Exchange organizations operating in native mode can contain servers running both Exchange 2000 Server and Exchange Server 2003, and you can convert an Exchange organization to native mode only when all of the Exchange servers in it are running Exchange 2000 Server and Exchange Server 2003.

Convert your Exchange organization to native mode if the following apply:

- You do not have any servers running Exchange Server 5.5 in your organization (you've either migrated or decommissioned all of them or never had any to begin with).

- You have no plans to add servers running Exchange Server 5.5 to your organization in the future, such as a result of a merger or the acquisition of a company with servers running Exchange Server 5.5.

- Your organization will never require interoperability with servers running Exchange Server 5.5.

- Your organization does not use any connectors or gateway applications that run only on Exchange Server 5.5.

> **Important**   Once you convert from mixed mode to native mode, the organization is no longer interoperable with Exchange Server 5.5 systems. That isn't to say that you won't be able to send or receive e-mail with Exchange Server 5.5 servers, but you won't be able to have seamless integration in the same Exchange organization. It is important to note that converting to native mode is a one-time, one-way operation that cannot be reversed at a later date.

Advantages of Native Mode

Running an Exchange organization in native mode gives you the full functionality and flexibility of Exchange Server 2003 when you manage your messaging system.

- Greater flexibility for defining routing groups and administrative groups. Since administrative groups are not tied to Exchange Server 5.5 sites, you can utilize the full functionality of the administrative group model. (This issue is discussed further in Chapter 3, Lesson 3.)

- The ability to move mailboxes between servers in different administrative groups. (This issue is discussed further in Chapter 7, Lesson 3.)

- The ability to configure administrative and routing groups independent of each other since they are no longer connected to fit the site model. (This issue is discussed further in Chapter 3, Lesson 3.)

- Query-based distribution groups (QDGs) can be created only in a native-mode Exchange organization. (This issue is discussed further in Chapter 7, Lesson 2.)

- If routing bridgehead pairs are upgraded to Exchange Server 2003 in a native-mode organization, they will use 8BITMIME data transfers instead of converting down to 7-bit. This equates to considerably less traffic over WAN connections when compared to Routing Group Connectors. (This issue is discussed further in Chapter 5, Lesson 1.)

Converting to Native Mode

Converting to native mode is accomplished through Exchange System Manager, by right-clicking on the organization name at the top of the window and clicking Properties. This brings up the property sheet shown in Figure 3-2.

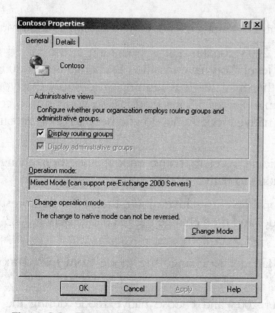

Figure 3-2   The organization's property sheet

As shown in Figure 3-2, there is a Change Mode button on the General tab. The button will be unavailable if you are in native mode, but if you are in the default mixed mode, you can click the button to change the mode. When you do, you will receive a warning message that advises you that once the operation is complete, you will not be able to convert back to mixed mode.

Lesson Review

The following questions are intended to reinforce key information presented in this lesson. If you are unable to answer a question, review the lesson materials and then try the question again. You can find answers to the questions in the "Questions and Answers" section at the end of this chapter.

1. Which of the following statements are true about an Exchange organization operating in mixed mode?

   a. Administrative groups are mapped to Exchange Server 5.5 sites.

   b. You can move mailboxes between servers in different administrative groups.

   c. You can move mailboxes between servers in the same administrative group.

   d. You can edit Exchange Server 5.5 system data from Exchange System Manager.

   e. You can install servers running Exchange Server 5.5 in your organization, even if you have only servers running Exchange Server 2003 presently.

   f. Servers running Exchange Server 5.5 and Exchange Server 2003 can route mail seamlessly.

   g. You can configure administrative groups independently of routing groups.

2. You have a Windows Server 2003 domain that is operating at the mixed mode domain and forest functional level. You have installed Exchange Server 2003 into the domain, which has no other mail services running. You know that you will never need to support Exchange Server 5.5 installations, so you want to convert the Exchange organization to native mode. What do you need to do to accomplish this?

   a. Raise the domain functional level to native mode, and then change the Exchange Server 2003 mode to native mode.

   b. Raise the domain functional level to native mode, then raise the forest functional level to native mode, and then change the Exchange Server 2003 mode to native.

   c. Use Exchange System Manager to change the mode from mixed mode to native mode.

   d. Reinstall Exchange Server 2003 and choose native mode during the Setup program.

   e. Use the Active Directory Sites And Services console to change the mode for the Microsoft Exchange service from mixed mode to native mode.

3. You are the senior Exchange administrator for *contoso.com*, which has an Exchange organization consisting of servers running Exchange Server 5.5, Exchange 2000 Server, and Exchange Server 2003. Due to a recent company reorganization, there is a need to decentralize much of the Exchange administration duties to local branch offices. This will require you to convert the organization to native mode in order to gain the flexibility necessary with administrative groups. What servers must you upgrade prior to converting to native mode?

_____

_____

4. You have been asked to give a technology presentation for IT management in your company. The topic of the presentation is why the company should upgrade its existing Exchange Server 5.5 infrastructure to Exchange Server 2003. Management is partially sold on the idea after hearing about administrative groups; they want to migrate Exchange Server 5.5 to Exchange Server 2003 in eight of the company's 12 locations and to install Exchange Server 2003 to coexist with the existing Exchange Server 5.5 servers in two other locations. They like the idea of administrative groups not being tied to the physical layout of the network since some locations do not have their own administrators, and in some cases, administrators are responsible for more than one location. After you describe how this works in native mode in Exchange Server 2003, they ask if you can set it up so that the eight administrative groups with only servers running Exchange Server 2003 can be converted to native mode right away, leaving the other administrative groups to be converted later once Exchange Server 5.5 is able to be fully replaced. What do you tell them?

_____

_____

Lesson Summary

■ Exchange Server 2003 installs in mixed mode by default. You must manually change the mode to native.

■ Mixed mode is used to provide backwards compatibility with Exchange Server 5.5 servers and sites, with a loss of full Exchange Server 2003 administrative and routing group flexibility and functionality.

■ Native mode allows administrative groups and routing groups to be configured independent of each other.

■ Changing the mode from mixed mode to native mode is a one-time, one-way process. Once complete, it cannot be reversed.

Lesson 4: Front-End and Back-End Servers

In a small organization, it is typical to install a server running Exchange Server 2003 and have it perform all of the Exchange-related tasks—host Internet virtual servers, host mailboxes, etc. In larger organizations with more complex network infrastructures, including the use of multiple firewalls, demilitarized zones (DMZs, also known as perimeter networks), and the sheer number of Exchange servers, it is often advantageous to split the roles of Exchange Server into a front-end and back-end configuration. The use of a front-end and back-end configuration needs to be carefully planned prior to installing Exchange Server 2003 servers into the organization. This is especially true when you are planning a large-scale deployment involving a number of Exchange Server 2003 servers and complex network and server access requirements from outside the firewall.

After this lesson, you will be able to

- Understand front-end and back-end server concepts
- Identify scenarios where you would use a front-end and back-end configuration

Estimated lesson time: 15 minutes

Front-End and Back-End Architecture

Having a front-end and back-end architecture allows you to manage Internet access protocols on a server that is separate from servers where mailbox and public folder stores are located. By splitting the functionality between servers, front-end servers handle incoming client connections while back-end servers are dedicated to running the mailbox and public folder stores.

All front-end and back-end servers must be in the same Active Directory forest. With Exchange 2000 Server, front-end servers were required to run the Enterprise Edition, but Exchange Server 2003, Standard Edition, supports configuration as a front-end server. A characteristic of, and in fact a requirement of, front-end servers is that they cannot host any mailboxes or public folders—in other words, no mailbox or public folder stores.

Benefits of Front-End and Back-End Architecture

Front-end and back-end architecture provides the following benefits:

- **Unified namespace** In a large organization with many Exchange servers, using front-end servers simplifies the administration. The primary advantage of front-end and back-end server architecture is the ability to have a single, consistent namespace through which users can access their mailboxes when there is more than one server (for example, *http://www.contoso.com/exchange* for Outlook Web Access). Users do not need to know the names of the servers that store their mailboxes, and if you want to move users' mailboxes from one server to another, there is no need to reconfigure the client computers.

- **Reduced overhead for SSL**   When connections are made using Secure Sockets Layer (SSL), information is encrypted and decrypted, which is processor-intensive and can negatively affect server performance. In a front-end and back-end configuration, the front-end server can process the encryption with the client, and the front-end server and back-end servers communicate without the overhead of SSL encryption. The result is improved performance and a greater number of users that can be supported than if you were using a single server.

- **Firewalls**   You can place the back-end server behind a firewall that is configured to allow only traffic from the front-end server. You can also place the front-end server on or behind an Internet firewall that is configured to allow Internet traffic only to the front-end server; the front-end server provides an additional layer of security because it does not contain user information. You can also configure the front-end server to authenticate requests before sending them to the back-end server; this configuration protects back-end servers from most denial of service (DoS) attacks.

The front-end server does not require much disk storage, but it should have a fast central processing unit (CPU) and a large amount of memory. If you enable SMTP on the front-end server, you should back up the hard disks because SMTP commits queued mail to the local disk. In addition, if the front-end server faces the Internet and accepts messages from Internet users, ensure that you have adequate virus scanning installed on the server.

> **Tip**   To increase performance, you can use an SSL accelerator card on the front-end server, or you can position an external SSL accelerator device between the clients and the front-end server. If you have a small number of front-end servers, an SSL accelerator card is simple and cost-effective. For a large number of servers, an external accelerator is more cost-effective because you need to store and configure an SSL certificate only once.

Front-End and Back-End Scenarios

The following are scenarios in which front-end and back-end architecture is commonly used.

Standard Front-End and Back-End Topology

To maintain a single namespace for e-mail servers while distributing users among several servers, you could designate a single server as a front-end server and have several back-end mailbox servers. In this scenario, you direct HTTP, POP3, and IMAP4 users to the front-end server and ensure that all virtual servers and virtual directories on the front-end server are configured identically on the back-end servers. By doing this, you could supply all external users with a common mail server name to access without having to worry about which server actually holds an individual's mailbox. The front-end server would communicate with the back-end server to find the appropriate mailbox and transfer message data as necessary.

> **See Also**   Internet Protocol virtual servers and virtual directories are discussed in Chapter 9, "Virtual Servers."

Front-End Server Behind the Firewall

One of the biggest benefits of a front-end and back-end architecture is with respect to making e-mail services available to Internet-based users. A common e-mail service that Exchange Server provides is Outlook Web Access (OWA), which integrates with IIS to make user mailboxes and public folders available to users by accessing them through a Web browser. To achieve security and still provide access to OWA, POP3, or IMAP4 from the Internet, you can place the Exchange organization behind the corporate firewall. At a minimum, the firewall must use port filtering to protect the front-end server from the Internet. If your firewall solution supports Internet Protocol (IP) address filtering, you should configure IP address filtering to accept requests that are directed to the front-end server and to block requests that are directed to other servers in the organization. By using this type of configuration, external users are unable to connect to anything except the specific mail ports on the front-end server and are unable to access the back-end servers (or other servers) directly. This provides an additional level of security over the standard front-end and back-end topology.

Load Balancing on the Front-End Server

To provide a single namespace through which users can access mailboxes while avoiding a bottleneck or single point of failure on the front-end server, use Network Load Balancing to spread the load over multiple front-end servers. The load-balancing solution you use should ensure that each user is always sent to the same front-end server for the duration of a session. Network Load Balancing requires the Enterprise Edition of Windows 2000 Server or Windows Server 2003.

> **See Also**   For more information on Network Load Balancing, see Chapter 6, "Microsoft Exchange Server 2003 and Clustered Environments." In this chapter, you will examine configuring Exchange Server 2003 as a front-end server and how you would manage the front-end and back architecture and troubleshoot problems related to them.

Lesson Review

The following questions are intended to reinforce key information presented in this lesson. If you are unable to answer a question, review the lesson materials and then try the question again. You can find answers to the questions in the "Questions and Answers" section at the end of this chapter.

1. Describe three reasons that you would want to use a front-end and back-end server architecture.

   _____

   _____

2. What versions of Exchange Server can be configured as front-end servers?

   a. Exchange Server 2000, Standard Edition

   b. Exchange Server 2000, Enterprise Edition

   c. Exchange Server 2003, Standard Edition

   d. Exchange Server 2003, Enterprise Edition

3. You are part of a team that is planning a large-scale Exchange Server 2003 deployment. Part of your role in the design is to research and recommend a solution to the problem of managing the remote access of mailboxes on 100 servers running Exchange Server 2003. Approximately 25,000 users will be accessing their mailboxes with connections coming into the network from the Internet, utilizing OWA and POP3. These connections from the Internet are not over a virtual private network (VPN), so they are unsecured. You know that you will recommend using front-end servers so the Exchange Server 2003 administration team will have an easier time managing remote access to the user mailboxes, but what type of configuration would be most appropriate for the needs of the organization?

   _____

   _____

4. You are a senior Exchange administrator for Contoso, Ltd., which has recently acquired Fabrikam, Inc. The companies have not yet fully merged and so are still two distinct Active Directory forests. You have been asked to begin to merge the Exchange Server 2003 organizations. You want to configure Contoso's front-end server infrastructure to support Fabrikam's servers running Exchange Server 2003. This would make remote user access consistent between organizations as everyone could use the same server addresses when configuring their mail clients. When you present your plan to the Exchange steering committee, consisting of senior Exchange administrators from both Contoso and Fabrikam, the plan is rejected. Why?

   _____

Lesson Summary

- Front-end and back-end server architecture is an effective means of simplifying mail and folder access to remote external users through a unified namespace.

- Front-end and back-end server architecture can be used to create a more secure Exchange environment by preventing external users from directly accessing servers that contain mailbox data.

- Front-end and back-end server architecture can reduce the burden on mailbox servers by allowing front-end servers to process SSL between the client and the front-end server.

Case Scenario Exercise

You are an Exchange Server systems consultant that has been contracted by Contoso, Ltd. to recommend an Exchange Server 2003 design for their company. Contoso has been in business since 1921 and over the years has grown into a global company. The company, headquartered in Dallas, currently has additional U.S. offices in Boston, St. Louis, Omaha, Los Angeles, Seattle, and Tampa. The company also has international offices in Tokyo, Seoul, Berlin, London, Mexico City, Lima, and Jakarta. Despite such an international presence and a forward-thinking business and manufacturing model, Contoso has been very slow to embrace technology and especially slow in developing an Internet presence. To date, the company has no Web site, though one is currently in development. The e-mail system, which is your concern, is an archaic menu-driven system that allows internal users to e-mail each other but has no Internet capabilities. Due to the changing economic climate and the need to operate more efficiently, Contoso is undergoing a significant infrastructure and process redesign, and a different consulting team from your firm has recently implemented Windows Server 2003 and Active Directory throughout the company.

Active Directory is laid out as a single forest with domains *contoso.com* (USA), *europe.contoso.com*, *asia.contoso.com*, and *sa.contoso.com*. Each location is configured as its own Active Directory site, and organizational units (OUs) are used to create the necessary administrative divisions for the company's decentralized administrative model (each site manages its own resources). The exception is the Enterprise Admins group, which consists of a handful of team members at the company's Dallas headquarters. This group oversees the Active Directory infrastructure, while the branch office administrators handle the day-to-day administration of their OUs. Exchange Server 2003 has been installed on one server in each domain to date.

- **Requirement 1**   You have been asked to deploy Exchange Server 2003 in a way that is consistent with the Active Directory administration model. You will need to plan an administrative and routing group topology to reflect the mixed centralized and decentralized model required by Contoso. The model needs to meet the following requirements:

  ❑ Dallas's Enterprise Admins group must be able to administer everything.

  ❑ Branch locations should be able to administer their Exchange servers on a day-to-day basis, including managing policies and configuring all server-specific options.

  ❑ Omaha does not have its own full-time IT staff, so it needs to be managed by the St. Louis office. As a result, its server should be in the St. Louis administrative group.

- **Requirement 2**   Because Contoso is installing Exchange Server 2003 for the first time, there is little in-house expertise in administering it. The IT director has identified seven systems administrators that will receive training and will perform various roles in the administration of Exchange. Two of the administrators will handle the modification of permissions, as necessary. Furthermore, the director wants the helpdesk managers in the network operations center to be able to view key Exchange Server 2003 data such as mail queues as part of handling calls from users. All administration will take place at the organization level. You need to delegate control as appropriate.

- **Requirement 3**   As part of Contoso's recent network infrastructure overhaul, all of the desktop computers have been replaced with new computers running Windows XP Professional and updated to SP2. Each of the seven administrators has a laptop running Windows 2000 Professional SP4. The IT director wants each of the Exchange Server 2003 administrators to be able to administer the Exchange organization from their own workstations, with the permissions appropriate to their administrative role.

Requirement 1

This requirement asks you to define an administrative model that will work for Contoso's Exchange organization.

1. Describe an appropriate administrative group structure for Contoso's Exchange organization given their requirements.

_____

_____

2. In a default Exchange Server 2003 organization, could you have Omaha's servers placed in the St. Louis administrative group?

_____

_____

Requirement 2

The second requirement involves delegating authority to the personnel who will be administering Exchange Server 2003.

1. Describe the type of administrative model that is best suited for Contoso, based on its organizational needs. Explain why it is the best choice.

_____

_____

2. How would you accommodate the needs of the help desk managers to be able to run the Exchange System Manager console to view message queue information while not allowing them to make changes or attempt to alter the message queues (such as forcing a delivery retry)?

_____

_____

3. Based on the information in the scenario, design a delegation of authority plan that would be the easiest to administer and update on a long-term basis, allow delegation of appropriate levels of permissions to different IT personnel, and meet the administrative model needs of Contoso.

_____

_____

Requirement 3

For this requirement, you need to ensure that all administrators can access Exchange System Manager from their own computers without having to use the server console itself.

1. Prior to installing Microsoft Exchange System Management Tools on the helpdesk managers' computers running Windows XP Professional SP2, which of the following components need to be installed on the computers? (Choose all that apply.)

   a. IIS

   b. Windows Server 2003 AdminPack

   c. WWW service

   d. IIS Manager

   e. SMTP service

2. Contoso's server environment is entirely Windows Server 2003–based, and the company never ran a prior server version of Windows (Windows Server 2003 replaced Novell NetWare 3.12). Given the nature of Contoso's migration to Windows Server 2003, identify a problem that must be addressed prior to installing Microsoft Exchange System Management Tools on the administrators' laptop computers running Windows 2000 Professional SP3.

   _____

   _____

Chapter Summary

- Exchange Server 2003 splits the Exchange Server 5.5 concept of sites into administrative groups and routing groups, which can be managed independently of each other when the organization is in native mode.

- Back-end servers contain mailboxes and front-end servers do not. By default, an Exchange Server 2003 server is both a front-end and a back-end server.

- Front-end servers can increase security by preventing remote users outside the firewall from connecting directly to servers that contain user data, such as mailboxes.

- Microsoft Exchange System Management Tools can be installed on non-Exchange servers to make administration more convenient. The operating systems that the tools can be run on are Windows XP Professional SP1 and above, Windows 2000 Professional and Server SP3 and above, and Windows Server 2003.

- Exchange Server 2003 components can be added or removed through the Microsoft Exchange Installation Wizard.

- After Setup completes, only the account used to run Setup has Exchange Full Administrator permissions. You must delegate control at either the organization or administrative group level for other security groups or user accounts that will have an administrative role in the organization.

Exam Highlights

Before taking the exam, review the key points and terms that are presented in this chapter. Return to the lessons for additional practice.

Key Points

- Delegate administrative control at the administrative group level for a decentralized administrative model, and delegate control at the organization level for a centralized administrative model. Create additional administrative groups as necessary.

- Knowing the Exchange Server 2003 service dependencies can be key in correctly diagnosing a problem.

- Use the Exchange View Only Administrator role to allow authorized personnel to monitor from Exchange System Manager without being able to make changes.

- Administrative groups and routing groups are mapped to Exchange Server 5.5 sites in mixed mode but can be managed independent of each other in native mode.

- Front-end servers should be upgraded prior to upgrading back-end servers.

Key Terms

site   An Exchange Server 5.5 concept that defines both the administration and message routing topologies of an Exchange organization. Exchange Server 2003 splits the site concept into administrative groups and routing groups that can be managed independent of each other (in native mode). In Active Directory, a site defines a collection of Active Directory resources that are connected by LAN speeds (10 MB or greater).

service dependency   Services often rely on other services running in order to be able to run. If a service that has a number of dependencies is stopped, intentionally or not, all dependent services will also stop.

administrative role   Exchange Server 2003 supports three administrative roles that can be delegated using the Exchange System Manager: Exchange Full Administrator, which can manage anything in the organization including permissions; Exchange Administrator, which can manage everything in the organization except permissions; and Exchange View Only Administrator, which has read-only administrative access to Exchange organization.

Questions and Answers

Page
3-10
Lesson 1 Review

1. You are the Exchange administrator for your organization. On Monday morning, users call to report that they are unable to open Microsoft Outlook; they receive an error message indicating that Exchange Server is unavailable. You check to see if the services are running and find that the Information Store service is stopped. You attempt to start it from Services and it fails, generating an error. Where do you begin troubleshooting?

Because the service fails to start, you would first check whether any services that the Information Store service is dependent on are in a stopped state. This would tell you if the problem is the Information Store service itself or one of the services on which it is dependent. The Information Store service is dependent on the Microsoft Exchange System Attendant and the EXIFS services. Failure of either one will cause the Information Store service to fail. In addition, you would verify the service account to ensure that it is not locked out and to check that its password was not changed by another administrator.

2. Which of the following Microsoft operating systems meet the minimum requirements to install Microsoft Exchange System Management Tools?

    a. Windows XP Home SP2

    b. Windows XP Professional

    c. Windows XP Professional SP1

    d. Windows 98 SE

    e. Windows NT Workstation 4.0 SP6a

    f. Windows 2000 Professional SP2

    g. Windows 2000 Professional SP3

    h. Windows Millennium (Windows Me)

The correct answers are c and g.

3. You have been assigned the task of designing a more streamlined administrative structure for your Exchange Server 2003 organization. Your organization currently consists of 15 administrators who have various levels of administrative control of Exchange, assigned individually at the administrative group level as well as the organizational level, in some cases. What would be your best approach to this task?

The best approach would be to start the Exchange Administration Delegation Of Control Wizard at both the organizational and administrative group levels and remove all individual user accounts other than the service account. You can then create security groups that match the Exchange Server 2003 administrative roles, with the plan to use those roles for delegating control at the organizational level. Then create additional security groups for each administrative group that has an administrator that should be restricted to only the administrative group level of authority. Then, assign the individual user accounts to the appropriate security groups, and from there you can delegate control, as required.

4. You are an Exchange administrator for an organization that has five Exchange administrators who perform various tasks. There are no additional Exchange administration roles delegated outside of the service account that Exchange Server 2003 was installed with. You are trying to convince the senior Exchange administrator, who is more management-oriented than IT-oriented, to delegate administrative control to the individual administrators or, at a minimum, to create security groups and delegate control to the groups, but he is reluctant. His reasoning is that it is more secure if only a single user account has the Exchange Full Administrator role for the organization. How would you counter his argument?

Having only a single account is actually *less* secure because all five Exchange administrators will share the same account. As a result, all the administrators will have access to Exchange Full Administrator rights whether they need them or not, and it will be nearly impossible to tell in the Security log which administrator performed a task because all events will have the same user account. Furthermore, having only a single account prevents limiting a particular administrator's rights to a specific administrative group or limiting their access to "view only."

Page
3-18
Lesson 2 Review

1. Describe when you would use multiple administrative groups in an Exchange Server 2003 organization and how administrative groups differ from routing groups.

You would use multiple administrative groups in order to create administrative boundaries in your organization. For example, if you need to have part of the organization administered by different personnel than the rest of the organization but you do not want to grant administrative permissions over the entire organization.

Routing groups are used to group servers by the physical topology of the network. Administrative groups are logical groupings not directly related to the physical layout of the network.

2. Describe the differences between a centralized administrative model and a decentralized administrative model.

A centralized administrative model involves a small number of administrative groups controlled by an IT department at one location, whereas a decentralized model uses many administrative groups to distribute the administration of the Exchange organization to IT personnel in different divisions or physical locations. A centralized model naturally works better in organizations where the IT department is centralized, and a decentralized model works best when branch offices have their own local IT personnel to manage the Exchange environment. A centralized model is used most commonly by smaller organizations, while a decentralized model is most commonly used by larger organizations.

3. You are an Exchange administrator for an organization that has two physical locations in Dallas that are connected by an ISDN line. There is an Exchange administrator at the other location, as well, and you have two administrative groups so that each of you can manage your own Exchange server without the

other interfering. There is a server running Exchange Server 2003 at each location, and the organization is running in mixed mode. Due to the changing economic climate, your company closes the other office, consolidating all resources in the main office (and as a result, you are the only Exchange administrator). You bring all of the hardware back to the main office to set up. What do you need to do to move the Exchange server from the other office into the same routing group as the other Exchange server, since they are now located on the same LAN?

    a. Use Exchange System Manager to move the server from one routing group to the other.

    b. Use Exchange System Manager to first move the server into your administrative group, and then move it from the other routing group to your routing group.

    c. Reinstall Exchange Server 2003 on the other server and place it into the correct routing group during the installation.

    d. Reinstall Exchange Server 2003 on the other server and place it into the correct administrative group during installation, which will automatically place it in the routing group under that administrative group.

The correct answer is b.

4. You are the senior Exchange administrator for the *contoso.com* domain, which has an Exchange Server 2003 organization that consists of two administrative groups: one for Contoso and one for Fabrikam, a subsidiary of Contoso. One of the divisions of Contoso is being consolidated with Fabrikam, and in the process, you are moving its server running Exchange Server 2003 from the First Routing Group in Contoso to the First Routing Group in Fabrikam. You try to drag and drop the server between routing groups but find that you are unable to. When you place the cursor over the routing group in Fabrikam, it shows a circle with a line through it, indicating you cannot move the server there. What would be preventing the move?

You can only move servers between routing groups that are in different administrative groups when the Exchange Server 2003 organization has been converted to native mode. By default, an organization is in mixed mode, which doesn't support this functionality.

Page
3-26

Lesson 3 Review

1. Which of the following statements are true about an Exchange organization operating in mixed mode?

    a. Administrative groups are mapped to Exchange Server 5.5 sites.

    b. You can move mailboxes between servers in different administrative groups.

    c. You can move mailboxes between servers in the same administrative group.

d. You can edit Exchange Server 5.5 system data from Exchange System Manager.

e. You can install servers running Exchange Server 5.5 in your organization, even if you have only servers running Exchange Server 2003 presently.

f. Servers running Exchange Server 5.5 and Exchange Server 2003 can route mail seamlessly.

g. You can configure administrative groups independently of routing groups.

The correct answers are a, c, e, and f.

2. You have a Windows Server 2003 domain that is operating at the mixed mode domain and forest functional level. You have installed Exchange Server 2003 into the domain, which has no other mail services running. You know that you will never need to support Exchange Server 5.5 installations, so you want to convert the Exchange organization to native mode. What do you need to do to accomplish this?

a. Raise the domain functional level to native mode, and then change the Exchange Server 2003 mode to native mode.

b. Raise the domain functional level to native mode, then raise the forest functional level to native mode, and then change the Exchange Server 2003 mode to native.

c. Use Exchange System Manager to change the mode from mixed mode to native mode.

d. Reinstall Exchange Server 2003 and choose native mode during the Setup program.

e. Use the Active Directory Sites And Services console to change the mode for the Microsoft Exchange service from mixed mode to native mode.

The correct answer is c.

3. You are the senior Exchange administrator for *contoso.com*, which has an Exchange organization consisting of servers running Exchange Server 5.5, Exchange 2000 Server, and Exchange Server 2003. Due to a recent company reorganization, there is a need to decentralize much of the Exchange administration duties to local branch offices. This will require you to convert the organization to native mode in order to gain the flexibility necessary with administrative groups. What servers must you upgrade prior to converting to native mode?

Native mode supports servers running Exchange 2000 Server and Exchange Server 2003, so you would need to upgrade or migrate the servers running Exchange Server 5.5 to one of these versions prior to converting to native mode. (It is easy to forget that native mode does not require Exchange Server 2003.)

4. You have been asked to give a technology presentation for IT management in your company. The topic of the presentation is why the company should upgrade its existing Exchange Server 5.5 infrastructure to Exchange Server 2003. Management is partially sold on the idea after hearing about administrative groups; they want to migrate Exchange Server 5.5 to Exchange Server 2003 in eight of the company's 12 locations and to install Exchange Server 2003 to coexist with the existing Exchange Server 5.5 servers in two other locations. They like the idea of administrative groups not being tied to the physical layout of the network since some locations do not have their own administrators, and in some cases, administrators are responsible for more than one location. After you describe how this works in native mode in Exchange Server 2003, they ask if you can set it up so that the eight administrative groups with only servers running Exchange Server 2003 can be converted to native mode right away, leaving the other administrative groups to be converted later once Exchange Server 5.5 is able to be fully replaced. What do you tell them?

Unfortunately, this scenario wouldn't work. The mode is configured at the organizational level, so mixed mode or native mode is all or nothing. You would have to keep the organization in mixed mode until all servers running Exchange Server 5.5 were migrated.

Page 3-31

Lesson 4 Review

1. Describe three reasons why you would want to use a front-end and back-end server architecture.

One benefit of using a front-end and back-end server architecture is enhanced security. External users accessing e-mail from the Internet through the HTTP, POP3, or IMAP4 protocols can be made to connect to a front-end server that authenticates them and processes client requests but does not contain the actual mailbox data.

A second benefit of using a front-end and back-end server configuration is being able to provide a unified namespace to external users. You might have many back-end servers hosting mailboxes, but with a front-end server, you would be able to supply all of your external users with the same server settings to access their e-mail remotely.

A third benefit is that using a front-end server can improve the processing time for SSL traffic and at the same time create less burden on the mailbox servers (the back-end servers) themselves. SSL can be negotiated and processed entirely by the front-end server, and traffic between the front-end and back-end servers can pass securely without the overhead of SSL.

2. What versions of Exchange Server can be configured as front-end servers?

a. Exchange Server 2000, Standard Edition

b. Exchange Server 2000, Enterprise Edition

c. Exchange Server 2003, Standard Edition

d. Exchange Server 2003, Enterprise Edition

The correct answers are b, c, and d.

3. You are part of a team that is planning a large-scale Exchange Server 2003 deployment. Part of your role in the design is to research and recommend a solution to the problem of managing the remote access of mailboxes on 100 servers running Exchange Server 2003. Approximately 25,000 users will be accessing their mailboxes with connections coming into the network from the Internet, utilizing OWA and POP3. These connections from the Internet are not over a virtual private network (VPN), so they are unsecured. You know that you will recommend using front-end servers so the Exchange Server 2003 administration team will have an easier time managing remote access to the user mailboxes, but what type of configuration would be most appropriate for the needs of the organization?

Because the remote users will not be accessing their mailboxes securely, it is recommended that you put the front-end server behind the firewall. You would only allow the specific ports required for POP3, SMTP, and OWA through the firewall to the front-end server, which would enhance the security of the configuration.

4. You are a senior Exchange administrator for Contoso, Ltd., which has recently acquired Fabrikam, Inc. The companies have not yet fully merged and so are still two distinct Active Directory forests. You have been asked to begin to merge the Exchange Server 2003 organizations. You want to configure Contoso's front-end server infrastructure to support Fabrikam's servers running Exchange Server 2003. This would make remote user access consistent between organizations as everyone could use the same server addresses when configuring their mail clients. When you present your plan to the Exchange steering committee, consisting of senior Exchange administrators from both Contoso and Fabrikam, the plan is rejected. Why?

The use of front-end and back-end architecture requires that both the front-end server and the back-end server be part of the same Active Directory forest. Therefore, your plan won't work until after *fabrikam.com* has been migrated into the *contoso.com* forest. Until that time, you would still have to maintain two separate namespaces.

Page
3-33
Case Scenario Exercise: Requirement 1

1. Describe an appropriate administrative group structure for Contoso's Exchange organization given their requirements.

Since day-to-day administration of Exchange is decentralized, you would want to create administrative groups for each location and delegate Exchange administrator permissions to the appropriate groups in each division. Omaha would be an exception as its servers are required to be placed in the St. Louis administrative group.

You would reserve Exchange Full Administrator permissions for the service account and the corporate Enterprise Admins group. By delegating control, you allow the local IT department to manage their local Exchange servers without having to grant them permissions that allow them to administer other locations' servers.

2. In a default Exchange Server 2003 organization, could you have Omaha's servers placed in the St. Louis administrative group?

You could, technically, but this wouldn't be the ideal configuration because in the default mixed mode, the administrative group model is tied to the routing model. By placing Omaha's servers in the St. Louis administrative group, you would be implying that they were on the same LAN, which could cause significant performance problems related to replication. The organization should therefore be converted to native mode first. Given that there are no servers running Exchange Server 5.5 nor are there ever likely to be, converting to native mode will be a simple process after installing the first server running Exchange Server 2003 into the organization.

Page
3-34

Case Scenario Exercise: Requirement 2

1. Describe the type of administrative model that is best suited for Contoso, based on its organizational needs. Explain why it is the best choice.

Because Contoso has decided to create an Exchange administration team at the organization level, you would want to build a centralized administrative model. This model can later be adapted, if necessary, when each of Contoso's individual locations has Exchange Server 2003 servers installed locally. Centralized administration fits best because the Exchange organizational infrastructure is centralized and managed from a single location, even though not all administrators have the same permissions.

2. How would you accommodate the needs of the help desk managers to be able to run the Exchange System Manager console to view message queue information while not allowing them to make changes or attempt to alter the message queues (such as forcing a delivery retry)?

The administrative role Exchange View Only Administrator exists for just such a purpose, so you can allow read-only access to Exchange data. You could assign this role to the help desk managers' user accounts directly or, even better, to a security group for Exchange View Only Administrators.

3. Based on the information in the scenario, design a delegation of authority plan that would be the easiest to administer and update on a long-term basis, allow delegation of appropriate levels of permissions to different IT personnel, and meet the administrative model needs of Contoso.

The best course of action would be to create security groups for each of the three Exchange Server 2003 administrative roles, assign the two administrators responsible for assigning permissions to the security group matching the Exchange Full Administrator role, and then assign the remaining five Exchange administrators to the security group matching the Exchange Administrator role. You would assign the helpdesk managers to the security group matching the Exchange View Only Administrator role so that they can use Exchange System Manager to monitor the message queues without being able to make modifications to any settings. After creating the security groups and adding the user accounts to the appropriate group, you would use Exchange System Manager to delegate control to each security group at the organization level, assigning the role that matches the security group membership.

Page
3-34 **Case Scenario Exercise: Requirement 3**

1. Prior to installing Microsoft Exchange System Management Tools on the helpdesk managers' computers running Windows XP Professional SP2, which of the following components need to be installed on the computers? (Choose all that apply.)

    a. IIS

    b. Windows Server 2003 AdminPack

    c. WWW service

    d. IIS Manager

    e. SMTP service

    The correct answers are a, b, and d.

2. Contoso's server environment is entirely Windows Server 2003–based, and the company never ran a prior server version of Windows (Windows Server 2003 replaced Novell NetWare 3.12). Given the nature of Contoso's migration to Windows Server 2003, identify a problem that must be addressed prior to installing Microsoft Exchange System Management Tools on the administrators' laptop computers running Windows 2000 Professional SP3.

    Windows 2000 Professional will require Adminpack.msi to be installed from the Windows 2000 Server installation CD. This could be an inconvenience initially for a company that has never had any computers running Windows 2000 Server and therefore likely doesn't have an installation CD for the program. They would need to obtain the Windows 2000 Server media through their Microsoft representative or download an evaluation version of Windows 2000 Server to install the AdminPack on the Windows 2000 Professional workstations. Neither would violate the licensing agreements.

4 Coexistence with Microsoft Exchange Server 5.5

Exam Objectives in this Chapter:

- Configure and troubleshoot Microsoft Exchange Server 2003 for coexistence with an existing Microsoft Exchange Server 5.5 organization
- Prepare the environment for the Exchange Server 2003 deployment
- Install, configure, and troubleshoot Exchange Server 2003
- Diagnose network connectivity problems

Why This Chapter Matters

When organizations install Exchange Server 2003, they do so in one of the following scenarios:

- Installing Exchange Server 2003 as a new installation in an organization with no previous mail system (most typical for a new organization).
- Migrating to Exchange Server 2003 from another mail system such as Lotus Notes or Novell GroupWise.
- Upgrading to Exchange Server 2003 from a previous version of Exchange Server.
- Installing Exchange Server 2003 to coexist with a previous version of Exchange Server.

The last three scenarios are the most common deployments of Exchange Server 2003 and are the focus of this chapter and of Chapter 5, "Migrating from Microsoft Exchange Server and Other Mail Systems."

This chapter focuses on preparing Exchange Server 5.5 to coexist with Exchange Server 2003 and installing Exchange Server 2003 into an existing Exchange Server 5.5 organization. Before you can install Exchange Server 2003 to coexist with Exchange Server 5.5, you must first connect Exchange Server 5.5 to Active Directory directory service. In this chapter, you will learn how to do that, as well as how to share information between Exchange Server 2003 and Exchange Server 5.5.

Lessons in this Chapter:

- Lesson 1: Connecting Exchange Server 5.5 to Active Directory 4-3
- Lesson 2: Installing Exchange Server 2003 into an Existing Exchange Server 5.5 Organization 4-23
- Lesson 3: Troubleshooting Connectivity Between Active Directory and Exchange Server 5.5 4-34

Before You Begin

To perform the exercises in this chapter, you will need the following:

- A server running Microsoft Windows 2000 Server SP3 or later and Exchange Server 5.5 SP3 or later. This server should be installed as Server01. The server should be a domain controller for the *litwareinc.com* domain. This chapter does not cover installing and configuring Exchange Server 5.5; it is assumed that you have already done this.

- A server running Windows Server 2003 installed into the *litwareinc.com* domain as a member server. This server should be installed as Server02.

Lesson 1: Connecting Exchange Server 5.5 to Active Directory

Exchange Server 5.5, designed before Active Directory came into existence, has some features similar to those in Active Directory. For example, Exchange Server 5.5 has a directory where it stores mailbox and configuration information. Exchange Server 5.5 was designed to run on Microsoft Windows NT 4, which was not a directory-aware network operating system. As a result, Windows NT account databases were separate from Exchange mailboxes, and there was no integration between the two. Exchange mailboxes were associated with Windows NT user accounts for authentication purposes, but any Windows NT account could be associated with any Exchange mailbox, and a Windows NT account could be associated with multiple Exchange mailboxes.

In contrast, Exchange Server 2003 tightly integrates with Active Directory, and there is a direct link between a user account and a mailbox. They are not two distinct objects as with Windows NT 4 and Exchange Server 5.5. The first task for achieving coexistence is to connect the Exchange Server 5.5 directory to Active Directory. Only then can you deploy Exchange Server 2003 into the existing Exchange Server 5.5 organization.

After this lesson, you will be able to

- Install the Active Directory Connector (ADC)
- Use ADC Tools
- Set up a connection agreement

Estimated lesson time: 75 minutes

Installing the Active Directory Connector

As stated previously, because Exchange Server 5.5 was designed to run in the non-directory Windows NT 4 environment, it has its own directory and no way of communicating with Active Directory. To solve this problem, Microsoft introduced the Active Directory Connector (ADC). Three versions of the ADC exist: the Windows 2000 Server version, the Exchange 2000 Server version, and the Exchange Server 2003 version. (In this chapter, the focus is on the Exchange Server 2003 version of the ADC.) The Windows 2000 Server version was limited in its functionality in that it could only synchronize the Site Naming context. While the ADC could synchronize account information between Exchange Server 5.5 and Active Directory, it could not synchronize the Configuration Naming context. As a result, it could not be used if you installed Exchange 2000 Server into an Exchange Server 5.5 organization.

The Exchange 2000 Server version of the ADC was more full-featured than the Windows 2000 Server version and allowed full connectivity between Active Directory and Exchange Server 5.5, but in the real world, it was cumbersome to work with since everything had to be configured manually. The Exchange Server 2003 version of the ADC improves on the Exchange 2000 Server version and offers a number of configuration wizards that help an administrator to configure ADC properties. Even though the wizards greatly simplify deployment of the ADC, it is still useful to be able to configure connection agreements and other settings manually.

A connection agreement defines one- or two-way communication between data sources. In this chapter, the emphasis in on the connection of the Exchange Server 5.5 directory with Active Directory. In this context, a connection agreement describes how information, such as mailboxes in an Exchange Server 5.5 organization, is replicated into Active Directory user accounts and vice versa.

Planning for an ADC Deployment

The ADC is implemented as a service in your Active Directory domain. Placement of the ADC is an important consideration because it can be a resource-intensive service. Generally, you will want to install the ADC on a member server in the same site as the server running Exchange Server 5.5. You don't want the server running the ADC and the server running Exchange Server 5.5 that is synchronizing with the ADC to be separated by slow bandwidth, if at all possible. Slow bandwidth is typically associated with wide area network (WAN) connections but can be viewed as anything less than 10 mega bits per second (Mbps).

The ADC uses an Active Directory global catalog server in a multidomain environment, so when configuring connection agreements after the installation, you should use an Active Directory domain controller that is a global catalog, preferably, or otherwise is on the same subnet as a global catalog.

There can be only a single instance of the ADC service on a given server, but you can install the ADC service on multiple servers in a domain if necessary (such as for redundancy). If you have multiple domains, you will need to install at least one instance of the ADC service in each domain. However, you can install as many instances of the ADC Management components as necessary to administer the organization.

ADC Installation

The account you use to install the ADC must be a member of the Schema Admins and the Enterprise Admins groups. In smaller Active Directory structures, there usually isn't a concern in using the domain Administrator account, but in large enterprise environments, the Administrator account in a given domain may not also be a member of the Schema Admins or the Enterprise Admins groups. This is because only the Administrator account in the forest root domain is a member of these groups by default. If you have child domains or additional domain trees in the forest, the Administrator account for those domains will not be a member of these groups by default.

You should run ForestPrep and DomainPrep prior to installing the ADC. The ADC Setup Wizard does extend the schema if it detects that ForestPrep has not been previously run, but you will run into problems later when configuring connection agreements if you have not run DomainPrep because the Setup Wizard creates two domain local groups: Exchange Services and Exchange Administrators.

Subsequent installations of the ADC in the same forest do not configure the Active Directory schema or create domain objects, so when performing subsequent installations, only Enterprise Admins membership is required of the installation account.

You will install the ADC as part of the practice at the end of this lesson.

Using the ADC Tools

Once you finish installing the ADC, you can configure it to synchronize between Active Directory and the Exchange Server 5.5 directory. You do this through the Active Directory Connector Services management console, which is accessed through the Start menu, in the Microsoft Exchange program menu. After starting the console, there are two options: Active Directory Connector (*servername*) and ADC Tools. The first option allows you to configure ADC connection agreements and settings manually. The second option, ADC Tools, provides configuration assistance through a series of wizards. Figure 4-1 shows the ADC Tools page.

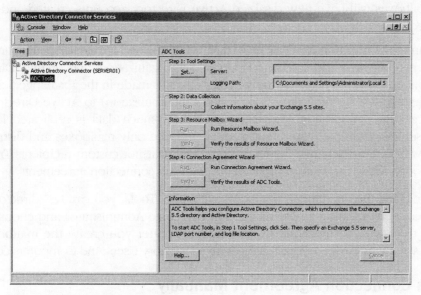

Figure 4-1   The ADC Tools page

Using ADC Tools is a four-step process:

1. Define the settings that will be used throughout. This consists of setting the Exchange Server 5.5 server and Lightweight Directory Access Protocol (LDAP) port to be used, as well as a directory to write log files created by ADC Tools to.

2. In the second step, you enter information about the Exchange Server 5.5 sites for use in later steps and identify user accounts that are associated with multiple mailboxes in the Exchange Server 5.5 organization, as well as Exchange Server 5.5 objects that do not match any objects in Active Directory and vice versa.

3. Run the Resource Mailbox Wizard. The wizard uses the data collected in Step 2 to allow you to manually resolve problems. For example, if you have a user account in Active Directory that is associated with multiple Exchange Server mailboxes, you can choose which mailbox will be the primary mailbox for the account and which mailboxes will be resource mailboxes. In Exchange Server 5.5, it was acceptable and common to have multiple mailboxes associated with a single Windows NT user account because there was no integration between the Windows NT accounts database and the Exchange Server 5.5 directory. With Exchange 2000 Server and Exchange Server 2003, which are tightly integrated with Active Directory, a one-to-one relationship between mailboxes and user accounts is required. As a result, there can be only one mailbox, which is defined as the primary mailbox here, associated with a user account, Mailboxes set as resource mailboxes will have new disabled Active Directory accounts created and associated with them.

4. Run the Connection Agreement Wizard, which is used to define connection agreements between the Exchange Server 5.5 organization and Active Directory. Connection agreements define whether changes made in the Exchange Server 5.5 directory will be replicated (also called synchronization) to Active Directory and vice versa. In addition, you can control how much data is replicated in some cases. For example, you might want to replicate only mailboxes and distribution lists from the Exchange Server 5.5 directory, but not custom recipients. You can choose what you want to replicate through the connection agreement.

After finishing the configuration process with ADC Tools, you can test directory synchronization by creating a new mailbox in Exchange Administrator and choosing the option to Create A New Windows NT Account. After you create the mailbox, you should see the new user account in the Active Directory Users And Computers console.

Setting Up a Connection Agreement Manually

While using ADC Tools is usually sufficient for configuring directory synchronization, there are times when you will want to configure connection agreements manually, especially in complex Exchange environments involving multiple sites. The Active

Directory Connector Services console is used for configuring connection agreements manually.

The environment into which you are deploying the ADC will dictate how you set up your connection agreement. For example, if you need mailboxes to be created automatically in Exchange Server 2003 for users created using the Active Directory Users And Computers console, you will have to replicate data from Windows to Exchange. Likewise, if you want the Active Directory user account to be deleted automatically when the associated mailbox is deleted, you must replicate data from Exchange to Active Directory.

When you begin to create a connection agreement manually, you should have a design plan in mind regarding what the connection agreement intends to accomplish and what servers will be involved. In a small organization, you may have only a single Exchange Server 5.5 server and a couple of domain controllers, which simplifies the configuration process. However, in a large organization, you have to plan more carefully. For example, when you create a new connection agreement, you must define a server that will manage the connection agreement. This can be any server in the organization that is running the ADC service. You must also choose whether directory replication will occur in one direction or whether there will be two-way replication back and forth between Active Directory and the Exchange Server directory.

In addition, you must also configure whether the connection agreement is the primary connection agreement for both the Windows domain and the Exchange organization. If this is the only connection agreement, configuration is simple because it will, of course, be the primary connection agreement for both. However, if you have multiple connection agreements that are replicating account and mailbox data, it is important that only one of them is configured as the primary connection agreement. The reason for this is that the primary connection agreement will take precedence when a conflict occurs in replication. If multiple primary connection agreements exist, you could easily end up with duplicate objects being created. The default configuration, on the Advanced tab of the connection agreement's properties, enables the connection as a primary connection agreement for both the Windows domain and the Exchange organization. You must clear the check boxes on the Advanced tab if you do not want the connection agreement enabled as the primary connection agreement.

Connection agreements are not limited only to intra-organization. You have the option to designate a connection agreement as an inter-organization connection agreement, which replicates data between an Exchange Server 5.5 organization and an Active Directory domain that contains a different organization. This is also configured on the Advanced tab of the connection agreement.

Two-way replication would be problematic if it simply began in both directions at once. As a result, the connection agreement defines which direction should begin replication. The default, set on the Advanced tab of the connection agreement's properties, is for replication to begin by synchronizing data from Exchange to Active Directory. This behavior can be changed by selecting From Windows from the drop-down list.

You can also delete connection agreements using the Active Directory Connector Services console. In fact, you must delete existing connection agreements prior to uninstalling the ADC. Deleting a connection agreement is a simple process. Right-click the connection agreement that you want to delete, and then click Delete from the context menu.

Replication occurs regularly according to the schedule configured for the connection agreement. However, there might be times when you want to replicate changes immediately and do not want to wait for the scheduled time or to reconfigure the schedule. You can initiate a manual replication on a connection agreement at any time by right-clicking the connection agreement in the Active Directory Connector Services console, and then clicking Replicate Now.

Practice: Connecting Exchange Server 5.5 to Active Directory

In this practice, you will create a number of Active Directory user accounts and Exchange Server 5.5 mailboxes. Once you install the ADC and use ADC Tools to configure directory synchronization, you will be able to see the effects of your configuration on the accounts and mailboxes by testing the configuration of your connection agreement. This will ensure synchronization is taking place.

This practice will use Server01 as outlined at the beginning of the chapter. Create the following Active Directory user accounts, and then create mailboxes in Exchange Server 5.5 and associate the mailboxes with the user accounts:

- Jenny Lysaker
- Bob Gage
- Nicole Holliday
- Amy Alberts
- Angela Barbariol
- Eli Bowen
- James Peters
- Karen Berge
- Jonathan Haas
- Mark Hassall
- Raymond Sam
- Sean Purcell

In addition, create the following security groups in Active Directory (you do not need to add users to the groups):

- MIS
- Marketing
- Sales
- Executive

Finally, create a mailbox named MIS in Exchange Server 5.5 and associate it with Nicole Holliday's user account. Create a mailbox named Executive and associate it with Mark Hassall's user account. Create mailboxes for Marketing and Sales and associate them with their respective Active Directory security groups. Create a user account for Nicole Carol, but do not create a mailbox for it.

Exercise 1: Install the ADC

1. Run ForestPrep and DomainPrep.
2. The ADC is located on the Exchange Server 2003 installation CD in a folder named ADC. For the purposes of this chapter, install the ADC on the Windows 2000 server running Exchange Server 5.5. From your CD-ROM drive, start \ADC\I386\Setup.exe.
3. The Active Directory Connector Setup Wizard starts. Click Next at the Welcome page.
4. The next page of the setup wizard is the EULA. Read through it, select the I Accept The Terms Of The License Agreement option, and then click Next.
5. On the Component Selection page, shown in Figure 4-2, choose which components to install. The first option is Microsoft Active Directory Connector Service Component, which is the actual service. The second option is Microsoft Active Directory Connector Management Components, which is the administrative tools used to manage the ADC service. Select both options, and then click Next.

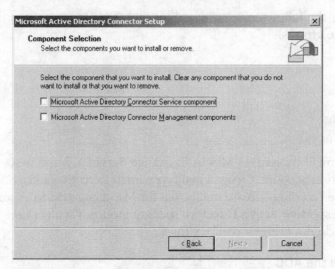

Figure 4-2   Selecting ADC components to install

6. The next page of the wizard prompts you to choose an installation location. You can accept the default location of \Program Files\MSADC or you can choose a different location. After selecting an installation location, click Next.

7. Next, you must supply a service account to be used by the ADC service. The Account Name will default to the account you are currently logged in with. If you created a service account for Exchange Server, use it instead. Enter the password as required, and then click Next.

8. Setup copies the required files to your server and configures its service. Click Finish when it is done. If a screen still appears prompting you to click Next when the installation is done, do so, and then click Finish.

Exercise 2: Prepare Exchange Server 5.5 for Directory Synchronization

1. On Server01, from the Start menu, point to Programs, point to Microsoft Exchange, and click Exchange Administrator.

2. Expand the Site container, and then expand the Configuration container. Click the Protocols container, and then double-click LDAP (Directory) Site Defaults.

3. Because Server01 is an Active Directory domain controller, the default LDAP port (389) is already in use and cannot be used by the ADC. You will need to change the LDAP port to something else that is not in use, so change the LDAP port number to 1389, and click OK.

4. From the Start menu, point to Programs, point to Administrative Tools, and click Services. Restart the Microsoft Exchange System Attendant service, and click Yes when prompted to restart all the services that depend on it. Close Services when done.

Exercise 3: Configure Directory Synchronization Using ADC Tools

To configure the ADC using ADC Tools, perform the following steps:

1. Click the ADC Tools link to the left of the Active Directory Connector Services console. Click Set. This will bring up the Tool Settings screen, shown in Figure 4-3.

Figure 4-3   Setting the server options for the ADC

There are a few things to note about this configuration step. First, the Server field is where you specify your Exchange Server 5.5 server. Second, the Port field refers to the LDAP port for communicating with the Exchange Server 5.5 server. The default LDAP port (389) must be changed if you installed the ADC on a domain controller. This is because Active Directory uses LDAP, and there will be contention for the port. Whatever you changed the port to in the previous lesson using the Exchange Server 5.5 (if you followed my recommendation, the port should be 1389) Administrator utility will need to be matched here. Finally, note the Logging Location for the log files. This path defaults to the My Documents folder of the user that is currently logged in, but you can change it to any folder.

> **Tip**   If you change the default LDAP port on the Exchange Server 5.5 server, you must restart the Microsoft Exchange services on the Exchange Server 5.5 server for the changes to take effect.

2. Click Run, which causes the wizard to collect information about your Exchange Server 5.5 site or sites. The Information field in ADC Tools displays information about the data collection—what was found and what steps will need to be performed to resolve any problems. The following is an example of output from this task:

```
Pass 1 of 4: Resource Mailbox Scan (objects processed: 14)
Warning: The Data Collection tool found objects that must be marked as resource
mailboxes before they can be replicated to Active Directory. Running the Resource
Mailbox Wizard in Step 3 will resolve these issues.
Pass 2 of 4: Active Directory Connector Object Replication Check (objects
processed: 19)
Warning: The Data Collection tool found objects that are not replicated from the
```

Exchange 5.5 directory to Active Directory. Running the Connection Agreement Wizard in Step 4 will resolve these issues.
Pass 3 of 4: Active Directory Object Replication Scan (objects processed: 0)
Active Directory Object Replication Scan completed. No unreplicated objects found.
Pass 4 of 4: Active Directory Unmarked Resource Mailbox Scan (objects processed: 0)
Active Directory Unmarked Resource Mailbox Scan completed. No problems found.
The Data Collection tool found objects that must be marked as resource mailboxes before they can be replicated to Active Directory. Running the Resource Mailbox Wizard in Step 3 will resolve these issues.
Finished Data Collection.

3. Next to Step 3, click Run. This will start the Resource Mailbox Wizard. This wizard helps to resolve any problems with Active Directory user accounts being mapped to multiple Exchange Server 5.5 mailboxes. As shown in Figure 4-4, you can choose the primary mailbox for each object found by the wizard. To set a resource, click the mailbox for the user, and then click Set As Primary (or Set As Resource if you are setting a resource mailbox). The reason for this is that there is a one-to-one relationship between Active Directory user accounts and Exchange Server mailboxes—a relationship that didn't exist under Windows NT 4 and Exchange Server 5.5. In the latter, it was common to have a resource mailbox, such as a mailbox called Payroll, associated with a user account. That user account might also be associated with a personal mailbox. To resolve this issue, when the wizard finds multiple mailboxes associated with a user account, you are prompted to define the mailbox as the primary mailbox for the user account, or as a resource mailbox. If you set it as a resource mailbox, a new disabled user account is created in Active Directory and is associated with the mailbox. When finished, click Next. Alternatively, you can export the list to a .csv file for further manipulation.

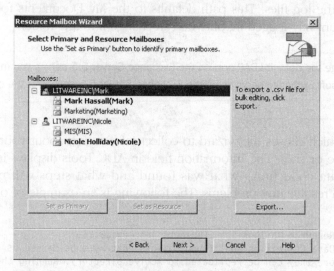

Figure 4-4 The Resource Mailbox Wizard

4. Next, you will set the site credentials. As shown in Figure 4-5, supply an administrative account and password for each Exchange Server 5.5 site. Note that if you have changed your default LDAP port, you will need to choose Specify A Server rather than Automatically Discover A Server. Click Next to continue.

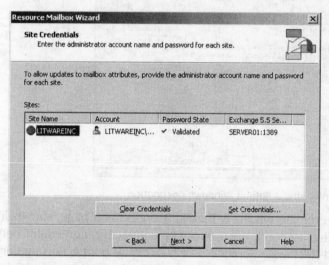

Figure 4-5   Establishing administrative credentials for each site

5. The last page of the Resource Mailbox Wizard is a summary of actions the wizard will take. Click Next, and the wizard completes. Click Finish when it is done to return to the ADC Tools page.

6. Next, verify the results of the Resource Mailbox Wizard. Click Verify to complete this step. You will see the wizard perform a verification step. When finished, you should see text that tells you that verification completed without a problem. If there are problems, the text advises you what you need to fix by re-running the Resource Mailbox Wizard.

7. After verification completes, click Run in Step 4 to start the Connection Agreement Wizard. The wizard uses the information collected in Step 1 to recommend connection agreement settings between the Exchange Server 5.5 organization and Active Directory.

8. After the Welcome page, the first configuration step is to select a Default Windows Destination, as shown in Figure 4-6. This is the container in Active Directory that will be used as the default location for new objects that are replicated with the Exchange Server 5.5 directory. Usually the built-in Users container is a good choice, but depending on your organizational unit (OU) structure, you may choose another container. Select a container, and then click Next.

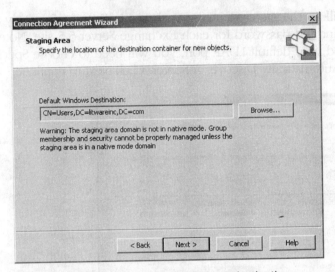

Figure 4-6   Configuring a default Windows destination

9. The next page of the wizard is the Site Connections page, shown in Figure 4-7. Choose whether to configure a two-way connection agreement between Active Directory and Exchange Server 5.5 or a one-way connection agreement. A two-way connection agreement replicates in both directions, which means that changes made in Active Directory are replicated to the Exchange directory and vice versa. A one-way connection agreement can be established in either direction, if desired. The default is a two-way connection agreement, which you should accept by clicking Next.

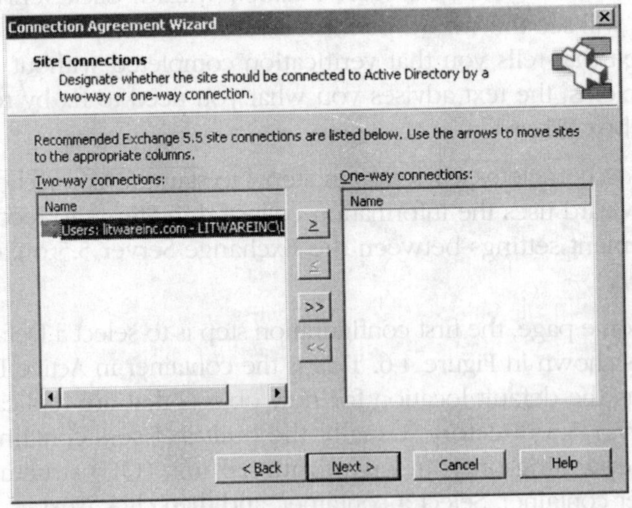

Figure 4-7   Configuring connection agreements

10. On the Site Credentials page, you must supply an administrative account and password for each Exchange Server 5.5 site. To do this, click the first Exchange Server 5.5 site and click Set Credentials. You can either type in the name of an administrative account or browse for one. Once you've entered an account, click OK to return to the Site Credentials page. Repeat the process for each Exchange Server 5.5 site, and then click Next to continue.

11. The next page of the wizard is the Domain Credentials page. Whereas site credentials validate your account in the Exchange Server 5.5 directory, domain credentials validate your account information in Active Directory. Click Set Credentials and enter the username and password for an account that has domain administrator permissions. Click OK, and then click Next to continue.

12. The wizard prompts you to choose what connection agreements to create. As shown in Figure 4-8, by default one agreement for users and mailboxes and one agreement for public folders are created. However, you can choose one or the other, if desired. After selecting the connection agreements, click Next.

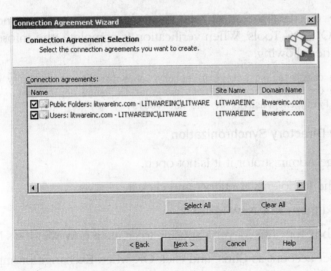

Figure 4-8   Configuring connection agreements

13. An installation summary similar to the one shown in Figure 4-9 lists the actions the wizard will perform. When you click Next, the connection agreements will be configured. When the process finishes, click Finish to return to the ADC Tools page.

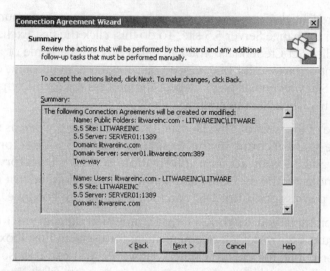

Figure 4-9   Connection agreement installation summary

14. Finally, verify the results of ADC Tools by clicking Verify in Step 4 next to Verify The Results Of ADC Tools. When verification is complete, the Information field will display the following:

```
ADC Tools are complete and Active Directory Connector is successfully configured.
Return to the Deployment Tools to continue your Exchange deployment.
Finished verifying the results of the ADC Tools.
```

Exercise 4: Verify Directory Synchronization

1. Start Exchange Administrator if it is not open.

2. Navigate to the Recipients container and click it.

3. Click File, and then click New Mailbox.

4. Create a mailbox for Chris Meyer, choosing to create a new Windows NT account.

5. Create the user account as Chris, and click OK when Exchange prompts you that the account will be created with a blank password.

6. Click OK to finish creating the mailbox.

7. Open Active Directory Users And Computers and navigate to the Users container.

8. Observe that there is a user account for Chris Meyer, which verifies that the connector works. Quit the program.

Exercise 5: Create a Connection Agreement Manually

1. Right-click the Active Directory Connector (*servername*) container in the console and point to New. You'll see that as in the ADC Tools Wizard, you can configure a Recipient Connection Agreement or a Public Folders Connection Agreement. Click Recipient Connection Agreement.

   First, assign a name to the connection agreement. It should be something descriptive since complex organizations might have multiple ADCs with many connection agreements configured. The replication direction dictates how the replication data will flow, and if you have multiple ADCs in your Exchange organization, you can choose which server will manage the connection. Once you have filled in this information, click the Connections tab, shown in Figure 4-10.

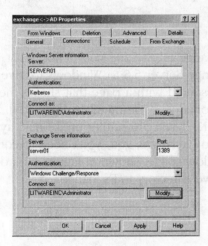

Figure 4-10   The Connections tab

2. On the Connections tab, fill in both sections for configuring two-way replication. You can also choose what authentication method to use. Note that on this tab, in the Exchange Server Information section, you can specify which port to use. This is for LDAP communication between the ADC and the Exchange Server 5.5 directory. If you need to change the port from the default 389, such as if the ADC is installed on a domain controller, you must match what you put here in the Exchange Server 5.5 directory.

3. The Schedule tab, shown in Figure 4-11, allows you to configure a schedule for replication. Depending on the size of your network and traffic patterns, you may want to alter the default schedule. Generally, you will not choose Always unless you are running on a small network or in a lab environment or if changes will not be made very regularly.

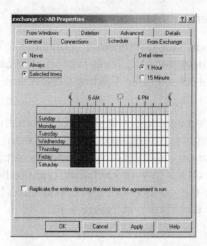

Figure 4-11 The connection agreement schedule

4. Figure 4-12 shows the From Exchange tab, where you define what information you want to replicate from Exchange Server 5.5 to Windows (Active Directory). When you click Add, you are presented with a page that shows the Recipients container and any other custom containers you might have created. Select what you want to replicate and click OK. If you are setting up a one-way agreement replicating from Active Directory to Exchange, you won't need to configure anything on this page. The From Windows page, shown in Figure 4-13, defines what information is replicated from Active Directory to Exchange.

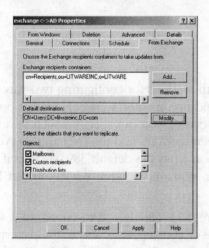

Figure 4-12 Configuring replication from Exchange to Active Directory

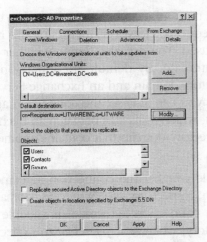

Figure 4-13   Configuring replication from Active Directory to Exchange

 Note   This is an example of the power of configuring a connection agreement manually rather than using the ADC Tools Wizard. Here, you can specify multiple Active Directory OUs from which to draw data, whereas you can choose only a single OU when using ADC Tools.

5. Figure 4-14 shows the Deletion tab of a Properties dialog box with the default settings. Here you are able to establish how deleted items are handled.

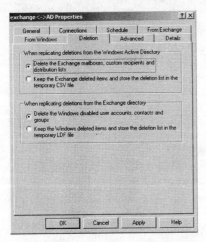

Figure 4-14   Configuring deleted item replication

6. The final configuration tab, the Advanced tab, is shown in Figure 4-15. There are a number of configuration options here. The first set of options is to define the page settings for Windows and Exchange replication. Paging groups together objects that will be replicated, resulting in better performance. Increasing the

default setting of 20 will result in more objects being replicated at once, which translates into fewer replication requests. However, increasing the number also increases the amount of memory used. You can also define whether the connection agreement is inter-site or intra-site. By default, a connection agreement replicates between an Active Directory domain and an Exchange Server organization within the domain. However, you can also set the connection agreement to be an inter-organization agreement, which replicates between an Exchange Server 5.5 organization and an Active Directory domain that contains another Exchange Server 5.5 organization.

Other configuration options include whether the connection agreement is a primary connection agreement with respect to the Windows domain and the Exchange organization. A primary connection agreement is capable of creating new objects in its respective directory, whereas if you clear this check box, only existing objects are replicated. If you have multiple connection agreements, only one should be set as the primary agreement; otherwise, you could end up with duplicate objects being created. Another configuration option on this tab is what action to take when mailboxes are replicated and there is no corresponding Active Directory user account. The default action is to create a new disabled user account, but you can also choose to create a new enabled user account (created with a blank password) or to create a contact in Active Directory.

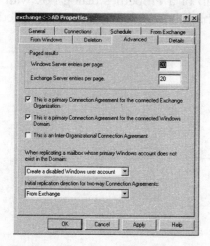

Figure 4-15   The Advanced tab

Lesson Review

The following questions are intended to reinforce key information presented in this lesson. If you are unable to answer a question, review the lesson materials and then try the question again. You can find answers to the questions in the "Questions and Answers" section at the end of this chapter.

1. You are the network administrator for Litware, Inc. Your network consists of the *litwareinc.com* domain, as well as *texas.litwareinc.com*, *dev.texas.litwareinc.com*, and *nebraska.litwareinc.com*. The *dev.texas.litwareinc.com* domain has its own administrator, who administers only that domain. The administrator calls you and explains that they are trying to connect their Exchange Server 5.5 site to Active Directory in order to migrate it to Exchange Server 2003. However, when he attempts to install the ADC on one of the Windows 2000 Server SP4 domain controllers, Setup fails with an error that he doesn't have enough permissions. He is unsure what to do because he is using the domain administrator account for the procedure. What is the problem and how do you fix it for him?

   _____

   _____

2. You have a mixed-mode Windows Server 2003 domain with a Windows NT 4 member server running Exchange Server 5.5. You want to migrate to Exchange Server 2003, so you upgrade the server to Windows 2000 Server and attempt to install the ADC. However, Setup fails. You verify that your account has membership in the Schema Admins, Enterprise Admins, and Domain Admins groups. Where else would you look to resolve the problem?

   _____

   _____

3. You are the administrator of an Exchange Server 5.5 site that is being migrated to Exchange Server 2003. You install the ADC on your Windows 2000 Server domain controller and use ADC Tools to set up the directory synchronization. When you run the Resource Mailbox Wizard portion of the configuration and try to verify the settings, an error is returned that the server cannot be contacted. Up to this point, everything worked fine. What step did you miss in the process?

   a. Setting the LDAP port in the Exchange Server 5.5 site

   b. Manually specifying a server rather that automatically discovering one

   c. Supplying the correct Exchange Server 5.5 site credentials

   d. Running ADC Tools with an Enterprise Admins user account

4. You are performing a migration from Exchange Server 5.5 to Exchange Server 2003 for your organization, which has Active Directory domains *contoso.com* and *fabrikam.com* located in the same forest. There is a single Exchange Server 5.5 server in the *contoso.com* domain that handles e-mail for both domains. You install and configure the ADC on a Windows 2000 Server member server in *contoso.com* and configure directory synchronization. Later, you test and find that synchronization is working in the *contoso.com* domain but not in the *fabrikam.com* domain, even though it is the same Exchange Server 5.5 site. Why is synchronization not working?

_____

_____

Lesson Summary

- The ADC is used to provide directory synchronization between Active Directory and Exchange Server 5.5.

- To install the ADC, both Windows 2000 Server and Exchange Server 5.5 must be running SP3 or later.

- The user account used to install the ADC must be a member of the Enterprise Admins group, as well as the Schema Admins and Domain Admins groups.

- ADC Tools provides a series of wizards to help you configure directory synchronization.

- Advanced connection agreements can be configured manually with the Active Directory Connector Services management console.

Lesson 2: Installing Exchange Server 2003 into an Existing Exchange Server 5.5 Organization

After directory synchronization has been established between Active Directory and the Exchange Server 5.5 site, the next phase of the Exchange Server 2003 deployment begins. There are two ways to deploy Exchange Server 2003: to upgrade one or more Exchange Server 5.5 servers directly to Exchange Server 2003, which is discussed in Lesson 1 of Chapter 5, "Migrating from Microsoft Exchange Server and Other Mail Systems," or to install Exchange Server 2003 as an additional server alongside existing Exchange Server 5.5 servers, which is the focus of this lesson.

After this lesson, you will be able to

- Install Exchange Server 2003 into an existing Exchange Server 5.5 organization
- Configure the Site Replication Service

Estimated lesson time: 120 minutes

Installing Exchange Server 2003 into an Exchange Server 5.5 Organization

Installing Exchange Server 2003 into an existing Exchange Server 5.5 organization is relatively easy once you have the ADC installed and synchronizing Active Directory with the Exchange Server 5.5 directory. In addition, there are deployment utilities on the Exchange Server 2003 installation CD that make installing Exchange Server 2003 even simpler. One such utility is Exchange Deployment Tools, which provides a number of configuration options to install Exchange Server 2003 into your existing environment. When you insert the CD and Autorun starts the Welcome page, you have the option to run Exchange Deployment Tools to guide you through installing Exchange Server 2003 in a number of scenarios, including installing Exchange Server 2003 into an existing Exchange Server 5.5 organization.

Note   Exchange Server 5.5 does not run on Windows Server 2003, but it is possible to have both Windows 2000 Server and Windows Server 2003 servers in your Active Directory domain. You can install Exchange Server 2003 into either operating system, with the caveat that Windows 2000 Server requires SP3 or later to support the Exchange Server 2003 installation.

Exchange Deployment Tools is a collection of tools that you can run either individually or in a series of steps in a wizard-like fashion. The latter is recommended unless you have a specific need to run the tools as individual components. The setup process for Exchange Server 2003 runs some of the tools automatically, and not all the tools are run for all installation types. For example, if you are running Setup to join an existing organization, only a subset of the tools is run. The full complement of Exchange Deployment Tools consists of the following:

- **DSConfigSum** Reports the total number of Exchange Server 5.5 sites and the total number of servers in each site.

- **DSObjectSum** Reports the total number of public folders, distribution lists, distribution lists with hidden membership, and contact objects.

- **UserCount** Reports the total number of users in each Exchange Server 5.5 site and the total number of users in the Exchange Server 5.5 directory.

- **VerCheck** Determines whether the organization contains the server versions required for upgrade to Exchange Server 2003.

- **OrgCheck** Performs the following functions:
  - ❑ Validates the schema extensions created by ForestPrep.
  - ❑ Ensures that the proper domain groups exist and are populated.
  - ❑ Ensures that the correct security descriptors are assigned.
  - ❑ Confirms that the Exchange configuration container exists.
  - ❑ Ensures that a global catalog server is available in a domain in which DomainPrep has been run.
  - ❑ Ensures that a global catalog server is available in the same site as the Exchange Server 2003 server or a site directly adjacent to the Exchange Server 2003 server's site.

- **PolCheck** Checks that all domain controllers in the local domain have the Manage auditing and security logs permission for the Exchange Enterprise Servers group and reports any domain controllers that do not have this permission.

- **OrgNameCheck** Checks for Exchange Server 5.5 organization and site names that do not comply with *RFC 2821*, which states the following:
  - ❑ All names may contain a maximum of 64 characters, with no leading or trailing spaces.
  - ❑ The LDAP display name must not contain the following characters: , = + < > # \ "
  - ❑ The display name (admin-display-name attribute) must not contain the following characters: ~ ! @ # $ % ^ & * ( ) _ + = { } [ ] | \ : ; " ' < , > . ? /

- **PubFoldCheck** Uses the Exchange Server 5.5 Directory Service/Information Store (DS/IS) consistency adjuster to ensure that the directory and the information store are synchronized. Inconsistencies between the directory and the information store occur when there is an entry for a public folder in the directory database without a corresponding entry in the information store, or vice versa.

- **ADCConfigCheck**   Ensures that Exchange Server 5.5 directory configuration objects were properly replicated from the Exchange Server 5.5 directory to Active Directory by searching Active Directory using the Exchange Server 5.5 object's ADCGlobalNames attribute. ADCConfigCheck lists any Exchange Server 5.5 configuration objects that are missing from Active Directory.

- **ADCObjectCheck**   Ensures that non-user, non-configuration objects in the Exchange Server 5.5 directory properly replicated to Active Directory. It confirms consistency of public folders, distribution lists, and contact objects between the Exchange Server 5.5 directory and Active Directory. If a public folder is not replicated to Active Directory, it recommends a public folder connection agreement. ADCObjectCheck also recommends custom recipient connection agreements and distribution list connection agreements.

- **ADCUserCheck**   Identifies the locations of user accounts and mailboxes and uses this information to recommend the connection agreements that you should set up. ADCUserCheck also uses the search process in Active Directory Connector to compare user objects in the Exchange Server 5.5 directory to objects in the Active Directory global catalog and reports any users in the Exchange Server 5.5 directory who are missing from Active Directory.

- **ADUserScan**   Verifies that mail-enabled users in Active Directory are replicated to the Exchange Server 5.5 directory. ADUserScan searches objects in Active Directory by targetaddress, emailaddress, proxyaddress, msExchHomeServerName, and legacyExchageDN. Then it searches the Exchange Server 5.5 directory for each object's counterpart using the legacy distinguished name (DN). If objects have not replicated from Active Directory to the Exchange Server 5.5 directory, ADUserScan recommends connection agreements.

- **ConfigDSInteg**   Runs configuration object checks that are designed to detect problems in Active Directory after Active Directory Connector has been running.

- **PrivFoldCheck**   Uses the Exchange Server 5.5 Directory Service/Information Store (DS/IS) consistency adjuster to ensure that the directory and the information store are synchronized. Inconsistencies between the directory and the information store occur when there is an entry for a mailbox in the directory database without a corresponding entry in the information store, or vice versa. PrivFoldCheck runs the DS/IS consistency adjuster with the following options:

  ❑ Synchronize with the directory and create new directory entries for mailboxes that do not have a corresponding directory entry. PrivFoldCheck creates an entry in the directory if a mailbox entry exists in the information store but not in the directory. PrivFoldCheck does not delete mailbox entries from the directory.

❑ Remove unknown user accounts. PrivFoldCheck removes users that are no longer valid from private information store folder permissions.

■ **RecipientDSInteg** Runs checks on each recipient object (User, Group, Contact, or Public Folder) in Active Directory. These checks are designed to detect problems in Active Directory after the Active Directory Connector has been running.

Later, when actually going through the graphical Exchange Deployment Tools utility, you will be able to see which tool is running during various stages of the process. This information is located under the column called Reference.

The Exchange Deployment Tools are executed by the exdeploy.exe command. By clicking on the link on the first Exchange Server 2003 installation screen, you start the graphical version of the utility.

> **Tip** Alternatively, you can run exdeploy.exe with commands from a command prompt if you need to automate some tasks through scripts. When you start \Support\Exdeploy\ Exdeploy.exe from a command prompt, you see a help screen similar to the one shown in Figure 4-16.

```
D:\support\ExDeploy>exdeploy
Usage:
exdeploy.exe [/s:<Exchange 5.5 server>[:port]|?] [/gc:<Global Catalog server>|?]
/c [/skip:<Tool1> [/skip:<Tool2>] ... ] [/site] [/p:<Log File Path>]
exdeploy.exe [/s:<Exchange 5.5 server>[:port]|?] [/gc:<Global Catalog server>|?]
/t:<Tool1> [/t:<Tool2>] ... ] [/site] [/p:<Log File Path>]
exdeploy.exe [/h|/?]

/s:<Exchange 5.5 server>[:port]|? Use <Exchange 5.5 server> as target server.  I
f specified, port is the TCP port used for LDAP connection.  Default port is 389
.
              ? means you will be prompted for a name of an Exchange 5.5 server.
         This is a required parameter for tools that use an Exchange 5.5 server.
/gc:<Global Catalog server>|? Use <Global Catalog server> as target server.
          ? means you will be prompted for a name of a Global Catalog server.
          This is an optional parameter. if not specified, exdeploy will discover
a Global Catalog.
/p:<Log File Path> Redirects progress output to <Log File Path>
/h, /? Display this help text.
/c <Comprehensive> Run all tools. Optionally, use with /skip: to skip specified
tools.
/skip:<Tool1> [/skip:<Tool2>] ... ] Skips specified tools or tool groups.
/t:<Tool1> [/t:<Tool2>] ... ] Runs all specified tools or tool groups.
/site Runs PrivFoldCheck on all servers in the same site as <Exchange 5.5 server
>.

Valid tools are:
     * DSConfigSum Runs Exchange 5.5 Directory Configuration Summary.
     * DSObjectSum Runs Exchange 5.5 Directory Object Summary.
     * UserCount Runs Exchange 5.5 Directory User Count.
     * VerCheck Runs Server Version Check.
     * ADCUserCheck Runs ADC User Replication Check.
     * NTDSNoMatch Runs NTDSNoMatch.
     * OrgNameCheck Runs Organization and Site Names Check.
     * ADCObjectCheck Runs ADC Object Replication Check.
     * ADUserScan Runs Active Directory User Replication Scan.
     * PolCheck Runs Policy Check.
     * OrgCheck Runs Organization Readiness Check.
     * PubFoldCheck Runs Public Folder DS/IS Check.
     * ADCConfigCheck Runs ADC Configuration Replication Check.
     * ConfigDSInteg Runs Exchange Server 2003 Configuration Object Check.
     * RecipientDSInteg Runs Exchange Server 2003 Recipient Object Check.
     * PrivFoldCheck Runs Private Folder DS/IS Check.
     * OrgReport Runs Existing Org Report.
     * GCVerCheck runs Global Catalog Server Version Check.

Valid tool groups are:
     * DSScopeScan is equivalent to DSConfigSum, DSObjectSum, UserCount, VerC
heck, OrgReport, and GCVerCheck.
     * UserPrep is equivalent to ADCUserCheck, NTDSNoMatch, VerCheck, and Org
NameCheck.
     * ADCCheck is equivalent to ADCUserCheck, ADCObjectCheck, and ADUserScan
.
     * OrgPrepCheck is equivalent to OrgCheck, PolCheck, and PubFoldCheck.

D:\support\ExDeploy>
```

Figure 4-16 The ExDeploy command-line utility

It is possible to run Setup directly, as you did in Chapter 2, "Planning a Microsoft Exchange Server 2003 Infrastructure," without using Exchange Deployment Tools. In simple single-site environments with only one or two servers, installing Exchange Server 2003 is relatively easy. However, the deployment tools are useful for providing a checklist of requirements and stepping you through the process so you don't overlook something.

Managing Mixed-Mode Servers

When you have a mixed-mode Exchange organization containing both Exchange Server 5.5 and Exchange Server 2003 servers, administration of the two types of servers remains separate. That is, you use Exchange Administrator to manage your Exchange Server 5.5 servers, and you use Exchange System Manager to administer your Exchange Server 2003 servers. While you can view properties of Exchange Server 5.5 servers in Exchange System Manager, you cannot perform any configuration tasks. The Exchange Administrator program will display Exchange Server 2003 servers because of the Site Replication Service, but you cannot manage Exchange Server 2003 servers this way. The reason for the incompatibility between versions is related to the significantly different architectures on which the products are based.

However, you can use the Active Directory Users And Computers console to manage mailboxes for users on both types of servers because of the synchronization provided by the ADC. Users will have Exchange attributes on their mailboxes relevant to what type of server their mailbox is stored on. Figure 4-17 shows the Exchange Features tab for a user stored on an Exchange Server 5.5 server in the Litwareinc organization, and Figure 4-18 shows the Exchange Features tab for a user stored on an Exchange Server 2003 server in the same organization.

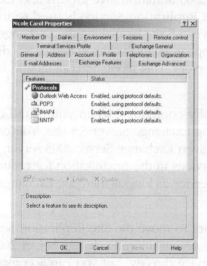

Figure 4-17   Exchange Features for an Exchange Server 5.5 mailbox

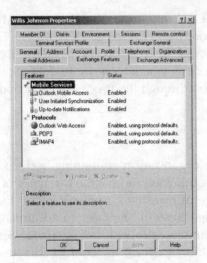

Figure 4-18   Exchange Features for an Exchange Server 2003 mailbox

If you want to make Exchange Server 2003 functionality available to users whose mailboxes are still on the Exchange Server 5.5 server, the only option is to move those mailboxes from the Exchange Server 5.5 server to the Exchange Server 2003 server.

Site Replication Service

The Site Replication Service is installed and configured automatically during Exchange Server 2003 setup. This service runs only in a mixed-mode Exchange environment where Exchange Server 5.5 servers coexist with Exchange 2000 Server and/or Exchange Server 2003 servers. The Site Replication Service provides mail-based directory replication between Exchange Server 2003 administrative groups and Exchange Server 5.5 sites. More specifically, the Site Replication Service is used to integrate Exchange Server 2003 into an Exchange Server 5.5 site by making the Exchange Server 2003 server running on Active Directory appear as an Exchange Server 5.5 directory service to the other Exchange Server 5.5 servers. This works in conjunction with the ADC to provide full integration.

The Site Replication Service is automatically configured when you install the first Exchange Server 2003 server into an existing Exchange Server 5.5 site. You can have only a single Site Replication Service on a given Exchange Server 2003 server, though you can install multiple Site Replication Services in the organization for redundancy. You cannot delete the last Site Replication Service as long as there are Exchange Server 5.5 servers in the organization.

There might be situations in which you want to move the Site Replication Service to another Exchange Server 2003 server in the organization. Exchange Server 2003 does not support moving the Site Replication Service directly, but you can accomplish the same task by installing and configuring the Site Replication Service on another Exchange Server 2003 server and then deleting the original.

To create a Site Replication Service on another Exchange Server 2003 server, perform the following steps:

1. Open Exchange System Manager and expand the Tools container.

2. Right-click Site Replication Service, point to New, and click Site Replication Service.

3. Click Yes at the prompt asking you to confirm your action, and then enter the required Exchange service account username and password. When finished, Exchange Server 2003 creates the Site Replication Service and automatically creates a configuration connection agreement.

Practice: Installing Exchange Server 2003 into an Existing Exchange Server 5.5 Organization

In this practice, you will install Exchange Server 2003 onto Server02 in the *litwareinc.com* domain. The server should have Windows Server 2003 installed, although configuring it as a domain controller is optional. Server01 must be online to complete the process.

Exercise 1: Install Exchange Server 2003 into an Existing Exchange Server 5.5 Organization

1. Complete the pre-installation tasks of installing ASP.NET, Simple Mail Transport Protocol (SMTP), Network News Transfer Protocol (NNTP), and the World Wide Web service on Server02. For more information on this, refer to Lesson 1 of Chapter 2.

2. Click the link for Exchange Deployment Tools, which will display the dialog box shown in Figure 4-19.

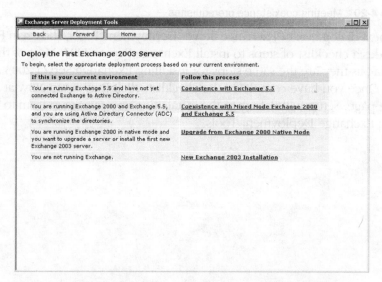

Figure 4-19   The graphical Exchange Server Deployment Tools

Here, you will find your current environment. Click the link that corresponds. In this instance, the second option describes the environment, where you have already connected Exchange Server 5.5 to Active Directory. Click the Coexistence With Mixed Mode Exchange 2000 And Exchange Server 5.5 link. The next dialog box of Exchange Server Deployment Tools, shown in Figure 4-20, describes what coexistence entails. Before installing Exchange Server 2003, you must first upgrade any ADCs to the Exchange Server 2003 version. This isn't an issue here, where the Exchange Server 2003 version of the ADC was used to connect Active Directory to Exchange Server 5.5, but in a real-world environment, it could be an issue if you have servers running Exchange Server 5.5 and Exchange 2000 Server on your network. Select the option to Install Or Upgrade The First Exchange Server.

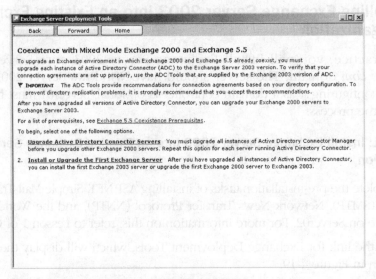

Figure 4-20   Meeting coexistence prerequisites

3. The next dialog box of Exchange Server Deployment Tools, shown in Figure 4-21, provides a checklist of steps to install Exchange Server 2003. Most of the steps are familiar, as they are the same steps for installing Exchange Server 2003 as in Chapter 2. Once you have completed the checklist, click Run Setup Now at the bottom of the page. Setup will default to the installation you ran Setup from to initially get to the Exchange Deployment Tools.

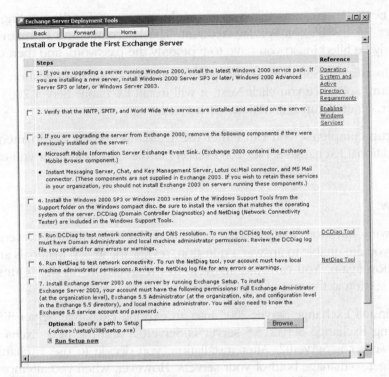

Figure 4-21 Exchange Server 2003 installation checklist

4. The Microsoft Exchange Installation Wizard starts. The installation process is similar to what you have performed previously, though there are some differences in the options you choose when installing Exchange Server 2003 into an existing Exchange Server 5.5 organization. Click Next to begin.

5. Click I Agree To Accept The EULA, and then click Next.

6. Click Custom Installation and install the Microsoft Exchange Server 5.5 Administrator. This makes administration more convenient since you can manage your Exchange Server 5.5 servers and Exchange Server 2003 servers from one system.

7. The Microsoft Exchange Installation Wizard will detect an existing Exchange Server 5.5 organization, and then you are prompted to choose whether to create a new organization or to join an existing one. Click Join An Existing Exchange Server 5.5 Organization, and then click Next.

8. Next, you must enter the name of an existing Exchange Server 5.5 server. The installation wizard advises you that it will test some prerequisite conditions and that it will take a few minutes. Click OK to continue.

9. Once the installation wizard resumes, you are prompted to accept the License Agreement. Do so, and then click Next.

10. The next step requires that you enter the password for the existing Exchange Server 5.5 Installation Service Account. The Username and Domain fields will already be filled in, so you have to type only the password, and then click Next.

11. The Installation Summary shows you the actions that the installation wizard will perform, and once you click Next, it will install Exchange Server 2003 onto your server. When Setup is complete, click Finish.

When Setup completes, you can either use Exchange Server Deployment Tools to install additional Exchange Server 2003 servers in the organization or you can exit the utility.

Lesson Review

The following questions are intended to reinforce key information presented in this lesson. If you are unable to answer a question, review the lesson materials and then try the question again. You can find answers to the questions in the "Questions and Answers" section at the end of this chapter.

1. You install Exchange Server 2003 into an existing Exchange Server 5.5 site. The existing Exchange Server 5.5 server is Server01, and the new Exchange Server 2003 server is Server02. After installation, you decide to use Exchange System Manager to manage both of your servers. However, when you attempt to configure settings for Server01, all the settings are unavailable. Why?

_____

_____

2. You have a mixed-mode Exchange organization that contains two Exchange Server 5.5 servers and three Exchange 2000 Server computers. Since directory synchronization is already in place between Active Directory and the Exchange Server 5.5 directory, you attempt to install an Exchange Server 2003 server into the organization by running Setup.exe from the installation CD. However, Setup fails and generates an error message that Exchange Server 2003 cannot be installed into the organization as it is presently configured. What configuration step do you need to perform prior to installing Exchange Server 2003?

_____

_____

3. You install Exchange Server 2003 into your existing Exchange Server 5.5 site and want to make some of the new features available to your existing users. Specifically, you want to enable some of the Mobile Information Services. Will you be able to make these features available to your Exchange Server 5.5–hosted mailboxes?

_____

_____

Lesson Summary

- The Exchange Server Deployment Tools utility provides a graphical interface that steps you through the process of installing Exchange Server 2003.

- Exchange Server Deployment Tools can also be run through the command-line exdeploy.exe utility.

- The Site Replication Service emulates an Exchange Server 5.5 directory service, working in conjunction with the ADC to provide seamless integration and connectivity between Exchange Server 2003 and Exchange Server 5.5.

- The Active Directory Users And Computers console can manage mailboxes for users on both Exchange Server 5.5 and Exchange Server 2003 servers, but Exchange System Manager can be used to administer only Exchange Server 2003, and Exchange Administrator can be used to administer only Exchange Server 5.5.

- The Site Replication Service can run only in a mixed-mode organization.

Lesson 3: Troubleshooting Connectivity Between Active Directory and Exchange Server 5.5

Ideally, following the planning and installation instructions will lead to a seamless Exchange Server 2003 deployment. Realistically, there might be times when you have problems, as an Exchange organization can be very complex when it includes multiple sites with multiple servers. Effectively troubleshooting connectivity between Exchange Server 2003 and Exchange Server 5.5 is essential to administering a mixed-mode organization.

After this lesson, you will be able to

- Merge duplicate accounts
- Troubleshoot the ADC
- Troubleshoot the Site Replication Service

Estimated lesson time: 20 minutes

Merging Duplicate Accounts

When you merge multiple directories, the possibility exists that you will encounter duplicate accounts. To handle this situation, Exchange Server 2003 comes with the Active Directory Account Cleanup Wizard (ADclean.exe). Duplicate accounts can result in performance problems with an Exchange organization and difficulty in authenticating users. However, handling duplicate accounts is not always as simple as deleting one account or the other that isn't needed. Sometimes both accounts contain information about the user that needs to be preserved. The Active Directory Account Cleanup Wizard solves this problem by allowing you to merge duplicate accounts, combining the settings from both.

The wizard attempts to identify duplicate accounts in Active Directory. You can have the wizard search Active Directory automatically and identify accounts, or you can manually specify accounts to be merged. You can also use a mixture of the two methods, by having the wizard do the bulk of the work by using its search capability, but manually specifying accounts that it does not recognize. Once the identification phase is complete, you have the ability to review and modify the merge operations that will take place. Once you are satisfied with the settings, you can either perform the actual merge operations or export the list of accounts to a .csv file to complete the merge process at a later time. This is useful if you are running the Active Directory Account Cleanup Wizard initially for informational purposes but do not want to have to redo the entire process later to perform the merge. At that time, you can import the .csv file into the wizard and complete the merge process.

There are a couple of scenarios in which you would most commonly run the Active Directory Account Cleanup Wizard. One scenario is after a migration from a Windows NT 4 domain, where you have some new disabled Active Directory user accounts that are duplicates of enabled Active Directory user accounts. You would run the wizard to merge the disabled and enabled accounts into a single account. Another scenario is to merge an Active Directory user account with a contact. You can do this provided that only one of the two being merged is mail-enabled, meaning it has an e-mail address associated with it.

You will use the Active Directory Account Cleanup Wizard to merge duplicate accounts in the practice at the end of this lesson.

Troubleshooting the ADC

Troubleshooting the ADC is usually related to replication issues. That is, objects configured in Exchange Server 5.5 are not being replicated to Active Directory and vice versa. There are a number of considerations when troubleshooting the ADC, both in a general sense and how it relates to Exchange Server 5.5 and Active Directory replication.

Basic ADC Troubleshooting

The following is a checklist to assist you in troubleshooting basic ADC problems.

- Is the ADC service running?
- Is a connection agreement configured between the Exchange Server computer and the Active Directory server?
- Is the container that you are replicating displayed in the Export Containers list or under any of the containers that are displayed in the Export Containers list?
- Is the Exchange Server 5.5 computer turned on and running? Is the Exchange Server 5.5 directory service running on the server?
- If there is only one Active Directory server, is it online?
- If you set up a connection agreement manually, did you select the object class that you are trying to replicate on both the From Windows and From Exchange tabs in the connection agreement properties?
- In the connection agreement properties, on the General tab, did you select the directions that you want to replicate information to and from? Is the connection agreement configured to replicate in the direction you need?
- Does the user account that you are using on the target directory have sufficient permissions to create or modify objects?

- Are any error messages logged in the server Application log (for example, messages that indicate incorrect credentials, that a server is down, or other errors)?

If your settings are configured properly, and there are no errors being generated in the Application log, check the following situations to determine why replication is not taking place in the direction you need.

Replication from Exchange Server 5.5 to Active Directory

The following list contains situations when an object does not replicate from Exchange Server 5.5 to Active Directory:

- Exchange object A matches Active Directory object B, but Active Directory object B was deleted.

- Exchange object A matches Active Directory object B, but Active Directory object B is not in a domain to which the ADC can write (for example, a different tree or domain in the same forest).

- The connection agreement is not an inter-organization connection agreement, and the ADC is matching a mailbox to a mail-enabled user. The ADC should match only to mailbox-enabled users.

- The connection agreement is not an inter-organization connection agreement, and the ADC is matching a custom recipient or a distribution list to a mailbox-enabled user.

- The server is not a bridgehead server for Active Directory, and the object could not be matched. In this case, the connection agreement does not create the object. To change this, open the properties of the connection agreement and, on the Advanced tab, select the This Is The Primary Connection Agreement For The Connected Windows Domain option.

Replication from Active Directory to Exchange Server 5.5

The following list contains scenarios in which an object does not replicate from Active Directory to Exchange Server 5.5.

- Active Directory object A matches Exchange Server 5.5 object B, but Exchange Server 5.5 object B was deleted.

- Active Directory object A matches Exchange Server 5.5 object B, but Exchange Server 5.5 object B is not in the same site as the Exchange Server 5.5 computer that is specified in the connection agreement.

- The connection agreement is not the primary connection agreement for the Exchange organization. In this case, the connection agreement does not create the object. To change this, open the connection agreement properties and, on the Advanced tab, select the This Is The Primary Connection Agreement For The Connected Exchange Organization option.

■ The object in Active Directory does not contain e-mail information. An object must contain at least one of the following attributes to replicate to Exchange: mail, legacyExchangeDN, textEncodedORAddress, proxyAddresses, or msExchHomeServerName. A group object may contain the mailNickname attribute, and users or contact objects may contain the targetAddress attribute.

Diagnostic Logging

Diagnostic logging is a useful tool for troubleshooting the ADC. You can log several categories of errors generated by the ADC. Figure 4-22 shows the Diagnostic Logging tab in the Active Directory Connector Services console. Right-click the ADC, then click Properties, and then click the Diagnostic Logging tab.

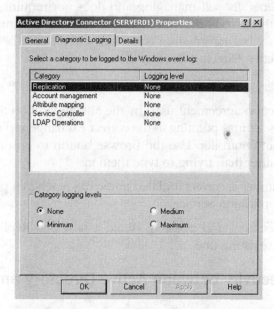

Figure 4-22   Active Directory Connector Diagnostics Logging

In general, you do not want to leave logging on, or at least not on very high levels. This is because logging will quickly fill up your Application log and make it difficult to find useful information in the Event Viewer. However, if you are troubleshooting, you can turn the logging up to maximum and then look at the Event Viewer to see the results. The logging categories are as follows:

■ **Replication**   Messages about events that occurred during replication

■ **Account Management**   Errors that occurred when writing or deleting objects during replication

- **Attribute Mapping** Errors that occurred when mapping attributes between Exchange Server 5.5 and Active Directory

- **Service Controller** Messages specifically related to services starting and stopping

- **LDAP Operations** Errors that occurred while making LDAP calls to access Active Directory

Exam Tip   For the exam, focus more on the actual configuration of connection agreements than on diagnostic logging.

Troubleshooting the Site Replication Service

The Site Replication Service is generally self-managing and does not require much administrative effort. The primary things to check when an ADC connection agreement is configured and working properly but information is not being replicated between the Site Replication Service and Active Directory are as follows:

- Ensure the Site Replication Service is running on an Exchange Server 2003 server.

- Ensure the Config_CA connection agreement used by the Site Replication Service is configured properly with its settings pointing to the correct Exchange server and to an Active Directory domain controller. Use the Browse button to ensure that you select the exact names rather than trying to type them in.

- Ensure that the LDAP port number is correct and that traffic can reach that port on the server running the Site Replication Service.

- Recreate the connection agreement and possibly create a new Site Replication Service, and then remove the existing one.

Practice: Troubleshooting Connectivity between Active Directory and Exchange Server 5.5

In this practice, you will run the Active Directory Account Cleanup Wizard and merge duplicate accounts. Before you begin, you must have completed the exercises in Lesson 1.

Exercise 1: Merge Duplicate Accounts

1. Start the Active Directory Account Cleanup Wizard on Server02. From the Start menu, point to All Programs, then point to Microsoft Exchange, then point to Deployment, and then click Active Directory Account Cleanup Wizard. When the wizard starts, click Next to bypass the Welcome page. The first step in cleaning up duplicate accounts is to identify them. Figure 4-23 shows the Identify Merging Accounts page of the wizard, which prompts you to select what containers to

search and the search behavior. You can either have the wizard search or import a .csv file of merging accounts, or both. On the Identify Merging Accounts page, choose to have the wizard search for existing accounts in the Users container in Active Directory.

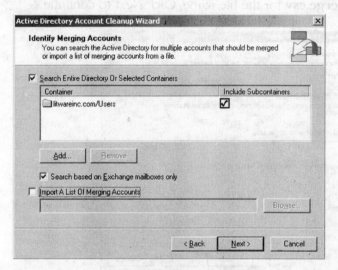

Figure 4-23   Identifying duplicate accounts

2. After identifying any duplicate accounts that exist, the wizard displays the Review Merging Accounts page, shown in Figure 4-24. If the wizard does not identify the accounts, click Add. Click Browse and find the user account for Nicole Carol as the Source Account and Nicole Holliday as the Target Account, as shown in Figure 4-24. Click OK, and then click Next.

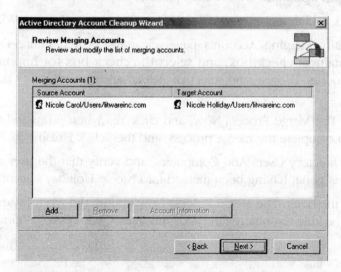

Figure 4-24   Reviewing accounts to be merged

3. Depending on your organization, you might have many user accounts that were found as duplicates. The wizard allows you to begin the actual merge process or to export the merge information to a .csv file for later review. This is shown in Figure 4-25. Select the option to Export The List Of Merge Accounts To A File, and type **c:\admerge.csv** for the file name. Click Next to continue.

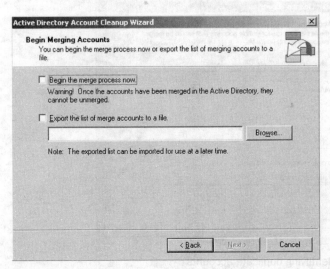

Figure 4-25   Choosing to begin the merge or to export to a .csv file

4. Click Next at the Summary page, and then click Finish.

5. Open the file C:\Admerge.csv in Microsoft Notepad to review the account information. After you review the file, you are able to start the Active Directory Account Cleanup Wizard again and choose the option to import a merge file.

6. Quit Notepad, and then start the Active Directory Account Cleanup Wizard again.

7. On the Identify Merging Accounts page, clear the Search Entire Directory or selected containers check box, and select the check box for Import A List Of Merging Accounts. Browse and select C:\Admerge.csv, then click OK, and then click Next.

8. Select Begin The Merge Process Now, and click Yes when prompted to confirm. Click Next to complete the merge process, and then click Finish.

9. Start Active Directory Users And Computers, and verify that the user account for Nicole Carol is gone, having been merged into Nicole Holliday's account.

10. If you chose the Begin The Merge Process Now option, the wizard warns you that you will not be able to unmerge the accounts later. Click Yes to confirm, and then click Next.

11. When finished, the wizard shows an Accounts Merge Results page. Review the statistics to determine whether any failures were reported. The page also has a configurable log file location where it will store the results. Click Next, and then click Finish.

Lesson Review

The following questions are intended to reinforce key information presented in this lesson. If you are unable to answer a question, review the lesson materials and then try the question again. You can find answers to the questions in the "Questions and Answers" section at the end of this chapter.

1. You recently completed installing an Exchange Server 2003 server into your existing Exchange Server 5.5 organization. After using this environment for a week, you notice that objects you create in Active Directory are being replicated to the Exchange Server 5.5 directory, but not the other way around. Where would you look to troubleshoot this problem?

   a. The Site Replication Service

   b. The Config_CA connection agreement in the ADC

   c. The Users:*domain* connection agreement

   d. Check that the ADC service is running

2. You are the Exchange Server administrator for a multidomain environment that has multiple Exchange Server 5.5 sites in the same organization. The company has approximately 20,000 employees located across North America. You installed ADCs as appropriate, and you installed an Exchange Server 2003 server in one of the sites. You run the Active Directory Account Cleanup Wizard, which identifies 225 duplicate accounts. What would be the best way to review these accounts prior to merging them?

   _____

   _____

3. You are the senior Exchange Server administrator for Contoso, Ltd., which has two Exchange Server 5.5 sites in the same organization. One site is named NAmerica, and the other site is named Europe. Both are in the same *contoso.com* domain. The Exchange Server 2003 ADC has been deployed on a server in the NAmerica site. You notice that replication is working between Active Directory and both sites, but a particular account is not replicating between Active Directory and the Europe site. What is causing replication to fail?

   a. The user account matches an Exchange mailbox, but the mailbox is in the NAmerica site rather than in the Europe site.

    b. A connection agreement must be configured between Active Directory and the Europe site.

    c. An ADC must be installed on a server in the Europe site.

    d. An instance of the Site Replication Service must be installed in the Europe site.

Lesson Summary

■ Use the Active Directory Account Cleanup Wizard to merge duplicate accounts identified during the process of merging multiple directories.

■ Duplicate accounts can be searched for or entered manually when using the Active Directory Account Cleanup Wizard.

■ Troubleshooting the ADC and Site Replication Service usually involves resolving replication problems and connection agreements.

Case Scenario Exercise

Litware, Inc., is a company that is in the process of migrating from Exchange Server 5.5 to Exchange Server 2003. The company has the following domains in its Windows Server 2003 Active Directory environment:

■ *litwareinc.com*

■ *dallas.litwareinc.com*

■ *boston.litwareinc.com*

■ *omaha.litwareinc.com*

The *litwareinc.com*, *dallas.litwareinc.com*, and *boston.litwareinc.com* domains each have their own Exchange Server 5.5 sites, and Exchange Server 5.5 SP2 runs on Windows 2000 Server member servers running SP4. Presently, there are no ADCs installed. The *omaha.litwareinc.com* domain, where the development group is based, is running a mixed-mode site of Exchange Server 5.5 and Exchange 2000 Server. The ADC has been installed and is replicating between Exchange 2000 Server and Active Directory in that domain.

The initial plan is to install Exchange Server 2003 on a Windows Server 2003 member server in each domain, establishing coexistence between Exchange Server 5.5 and Exchange Server 2003. After running in that environment for a period of time, the company will begin to migrate Exchange Server 5.5 computers to Exchange Server 2003. The company, for consistency, will also want to upgrade Exchange 2000 Server to Exchange Server 2003.

■ **Requirement 1**   Prior to connecting Exchange Server 5.5 to Active Directory, you must ensure that the environment meets the prerequisites. You will need to prepare for the Exchange Server 2003 installations by installing ADCs as required to support the installation.

■ **Requirement 2**   Once Exchange Server 5.5 is replicating with Active Directory, you will need to install Exchange Server 2003 on a new Windows Server 2003 server in each site.

Requirement 1

The first requirement involves ensuring that the environment meets all prerequisites.

1. Given the information provided, what is the one thing that will need upgrading in the *litwareinc.com*, *dallas.litwareinc.com*, and *boston.litwareinc.com* domains prior to installing the ADC?

   _____

   _____

2. Is there anything else that needs to be done in the *omaha.litwareinc.com* domain prior to configuring a new Windows Server 2003 server for the Exchange Server 2003 installation?

   _____

   _____

3. How many ADCs will you need to deploy to support this environment, and where will you need to install them?

   _____

   _____

Requirement 2

The second requirement involves installing Exchange Server 2003 in each domain.

1. You are installing Exchange Server 2003 on new Windows Server 2003 member servers. What do you need to install on the Windows Server 2003 servers prior to installing Exchange Server 2003?

   _____

   _____

2. After Exchange Server 2003 is installed, how will you enable the new functionality for existing Exchange Server 5.5 mailboxes?

_____

_____

Troubleshooting Lab

In this lab, you will create a connection agreement between Exchange Server 5.5 and Active Directory, but you will neglect to change the LDAP ports required when the ADC is installed on a domain controller. You will change the port settings, and then replication will succeed.

Before proceeding with this lab, you must have two servers installed as described at the beginning of this chapter. You must also install the ADC on Server01, the Windows 2000 Server domain controller.

Exercise 1: Configure a Connection Agreement

1. Start the Active Directory Connector Service console.

2. Right-click the Active Directory Connector (Server01), point to New, and then click Recipient Connection Agreement.

3. Create a two-way connection agreement to replicate between the Recipients and Users containers, both on Server01. Do not change any default values that are filled in. Complete the agreement.

4. Open Exchange Administrator and create a new mailbox. Click Create A New Windows NT Account and create a user account. Finish creating the mailbox.

5. Open Active Directory Users And Computers and navigate to the Users container. Observe that the user account does not exist in Active Directory.

Exercise 2: Change the LDAP Port

1. In the Active Directory Connector Service console, edit the connection agreement and change the LDAP port from 389 to 1389 on the Connections tab, under Exchange information.

2. In Exchange Administrator, expand the Configuration container and click the Protocols container. Click LDAP (Directory) Site Defaults, then click the File menu and click Properties.

3. Change the LDAP port to 1389 to match the ADC.

4. Start the Services console, and restart the Microsoft Exchange System Attendant, and click Yes when prompted to restart all the dependent services.

5. Once the services restart, right-click the connection agreement in the Active Directory Connector Service console, and click Replicate Now.

6. Refresh the view in Active Directory Users And Computers, and observe that the user account has now replicated.

Chapter Summary

- The ADC is used to synchronize the Exchange Server 5.5 directory with Active Directory.

- The Site Replication Service enables Exchange Server 2003 to appear as an Exchange Server 5.5 directory service for seamless integration.

- After installing Exchange Server 2003 into an existing Exchange Server 5.5 site, you still use Exchange Administrator to administer the Exchange Server 5.5 servers and use Exchange System Manager to administer the Exchange Server 2003 servers.

- Troubleshooting the ADC and Site Replication Service usually involves sorting out replication problems.

- You cannot move a Site Replication Service, but you can create a new one and then delete the old one.

Exam Highlights

Before taking the exam, review the key points and terms that are presented in this chapter. Return to the lessons for additional practice.

Key Points

- You must have an ADC installed in each domain that contains Exchange Server 5.5 servers.

- Exchange 2000 Server ADCs must be upgraded to the Exchange Server 2003 version prior to installing Exchange Server 2003.

- The Site Replication Service can run only in a mixed-mode Exchange organization.

- If the ADC is installed on a domain controller, you must change the LDAP port used by connection agreements.

Key Terms

connection agreement   A connection agreement defines what and how data will be replicated between the Exchange Server 5.5 directory and Active Directory. A connection agreement is part of an ADC, and an ADC can contain multiple connection agreements.

LDAP port   The Lightweight Directory Access Protocol (LDAP) is an industry standard protocol for accessing information in directories. Active Directory uses LDAP extensively, and if you install an ADC on an Active Directory domain controller, you must change the default LDAP port in your connection agreements.

replication   Replication is the process of synchronizing data between two or more directories or databases. Replication enables Active Directory and the standalone Exchange Server 5.5 directory to synchronize so that changes made in one directory are automatically reflected in the other.

Page
4-21
Lesson 1 Review

1. You are the network administrator for Litware, Inc. Your network consists of the *litwareinc.com* domain, as well as *texas.litwareinc.com*, *dev.texas.litwareinc.com*, and *nebraska.litwareinc.com*. The *dev.texas.litwareinc.com* domain has its own administrator, who administers only that domain. The administrator calls you and explains that they are trying to connect their Exchange Server 5.5 site to Active Directory in order to migrate it to Exchange Server 2003. However, when he attempts to install the ADC on one of the Windows 2000 Server SP4 domain controllers, Setup fails with an error that he doesn't have enough permissions. He is unsure what to do because he is using the domain administrator account for the procedure. What is the problem and how do you fix it for him?

   If ForestPrep and DomainPrep have not yet been run, the account that is used to install the ADC must be a member of the Schema Admins, Enterprise Admins, and Domain Admins security groups. While the administrator account for the *dev.texas.litwareinc.com* domain is in the Domain Admins group for that domain, it won't be in the Schema Admins or Enterprise Admins groups by default. As a result, the ADC will not be able to install properly. You must either grant the domain administrator account additional permissions, use the Run As command to run Setup under a different security context, or perform the installation for the other administrator.

2. You have a mixed-mode Windows Server 2003 domain with a Windows NT 4 member server running Exchange Server 5.5. You want to migrate to Exchange Server 2003, so you upgrade the server to Windows 2000 Server and attempt to install the ADC. However, Setup fails. You verify that your account has membership in the Schema Admins, Enterprise Admins, and Domain Admins groups. Where else would you look to resolve the problem?

   In order to install the ADC on Windows 2000 Server, the server must also be running SP3 or later and Exchange Server 5.5 SP3 or later. In this situation, Windows 2000 Server was installed but not the required service packs.

3. You are the administrator of an Exchange Server 5.5 site that is being migrated to Exchange Server 2003. You install the ADC on your Windows 2000 Server domain controller and use ADC Tools to set up the directory synchronization. When you run the Resource Mailbox Wizard portion of the configuration and try to verify the settings, an error is returned that the server cannot be contacted. Up to this point, everything worked fine. What step did you miss in the process?

   a. Setting the LDAP port in the Exchange Server 5.5 site

   b. Manually specifying a server rather that automatically discovering one

   c. Supplying the correct Exchange Server 5.5 site credentials

   d. Running ADC Tools with an Enterprise Admins user account

   The correct answer is b.

4. You are performing a migration from Exchange Server 5.5 to Exchange Server 2003 for your organization, which has Active Directory domains *contoso.com* and *fabrikam.com* located in the same forest. There is a single Exchange Server 5.5 server in the *contoso.com* domain that handles e-mail for both domains. You install and configure the ADC on a Windows 2000 Server member server in *contoso.com* and configure directory synchronization. Later, you test and find that synchronization is working in the *contoso.com* domain but not in the *fabrikam.com* domain, even though it is the same Exchange Server 5.5 site. Why is synchronization not working?

In order for directory synchronization to work, you must install the ADC in every domain that will participate in replication. In this case, even though *fabrikam.com* uses the same Exchange Server 5.5 site and server, its Active Directory database is separate from *contoso.com*. Therefore, you will need to install an instance of the ADC in *fabrikam.com* in order for synchronization to work.

Page
4-32

Lesson 2 Review

1. You install Exchange Server 2003 into an existing Exchange Server 5.5 site. The existing Exchange Server 5.5 server is Server01, and the new Exchange Server 2003 server is Server02. After installation, you decide to use Exchange System Manager to manage both of your servers. However, when you attempt to configure settings for Server01, all the settings are unavailable. Why?

Exchange System Manager provides read-only access to Exchange Server 5.5 servers, enabling you to view them but not to modify any settings.

2. You have a mixed-mode Exchange organization that contains two Exchange Server 5.5 servers and three Exchange 2000 Server computers. Since directory synchronization is already in place between Active Directory and the Exchange Server 5.5 directory, you attempt to install an Exchange Server 2003 server into the organization by running Setup.exe from the installation CD. However, Setup fails and generates an error message that Exchange Server 2003 cannot be installed into the organization as it is presently configured. What configuration step do you need to perform prior to installing Exchange Server 2003?

Prior to installing Exchange Server 2003, all existing ADCs must be upgraded from the Exchange 2000 Server version to the Exchange Server 2003 version. Without doing this prior to running Setup, the installation will fail.

3. You install Exchange Server 2003 into your existing Exchange Server 5.5 site and want to make some of the new features available to your existing users. Specifically, you want to enable some of the Mobile Information Services. Will you be able to make these features available to your Exchange Server 5.5–hosted mailboxes?

The only way you can make these features available is by moving the mailboxes from the Exchange Server 5.5 server to the Exchange Server 2003 server, which supports the new functionality. After moving the mailboxes, you will be able to configure them to use Exchange Server 2003–specific features.

Lesson 3 Review

1. You recently completed installing an Exchange Server 2003 server into your existing Exchange Server 5.5 organization. After using this environment for a week, you notice that objects you create in Active Directory are being replicated to the Exchange Server 5.5 directory, but not the other way around. Where would you look to troubleshoot this problem?

   a. The Site Replication Service

   b. The Config_CA connection agreement in the ADC

   c. The Users:*domain* connection agreement

   d. Check that the ADC service is running

   The correct answer is c.

2. You are the Exchange Server administrator for a multidomain environment that has multiple Exchange Server 5.5 sites in the same organization. The company has approximately 20,000 employees located across North America. You installed ADCs as appropriate, and you installed an Exchange Server 2003 server in one of the sites. You run the Active Directory Account Cleanup Wizard, which identifies 225 duplicate accounts. What would be the best way to review these accounts prior to merging them?

   When you have this many accounts to review, you likely do not want to review them within the Active Directory Account Cleanup Wizard. Instead, you can export the list to a .csv file, which can be opened in Notepad. There, you can easily review the account information and make modifications, as necessary. Once complete, you can run the wizard again and import the .csv file to complete the merge process.

3. You are the senior Exchange Server administrator for Contoso, Ltd., which has two Exchange Server 5.5 sites in the same organization. One site is named NAmerica, and the other site is named Europe. Both are in the same *contoso.com* domain. The Exchange Server 2003 ADC has been deployed on a server in the NAmerica site. You notice that replication is working between Active Directory and both sites, but a particular account is not replicating between Active Directory and the Europe site. What is causing replication to fail?

   a. The user account matches an Exchange mailbox, but the mailbox is in the NAmerica site rather than in the Europe site.

   b. A connection agreement must be configured between Active Directory and the Europe site.

   c. An ADC must be installed on a server in the Europe site.

   d. An instance of the Site Replication Service must be installed in the Europe site.

   The correct answer is a.

Page
4-43
Case Scenario Exercise: Requirement 1

1. Given the information provided, what is the one thing that will need upgrading in the *litwareinc.com, dallas.litwareinc.com,* and *boston.litwareinc.com* domains prior to installing the ADC?

   Exchange Server 5.5 requires a minimum of SP3 in order to replicate with Active Directory. Since the servers are running SP2 (which is not uncommon given the extensive changes made by SP3), they will need to be upgraded to SP3 or SP4 prior to installing the ADC.

2. Is there anything else that needs to be done in the *omaha.litwareinc.com* domain prior to configuring a new Windows Server 2003 server for the Exchange Server 2003 installation?

   Yes. Even though the domain is already running an ADC, the connector is the Exchange 2000 Server version. This ADC must be upgraded to the Exchange Server 2003 version prior to installing Exchange Server 2003 in the domain.

3. How many ADCs will you need to deploy to support this environment, and where will you need to install them?

   You will need to install a total of four ADCs, one for each domain. Even though the *omaha.litwareinc.com* domain already has an ADC, it will need to be upgraded to the Exchange Server 2003 version

Page
4-43
Case Scenario Exercise: Requirement 2

1. You are installing Exchange Server 2003 on new Windows Server 2003 member servers. What do you need to install on the Windows Server 2003 servers prior to installing Exchange Server 2003?

   Installing Exchange Server 2003 into an existing organization has the same requirements as installing it into a new organization. You must still install ASP.NET, SMTP, NNTP, and the World Wide Web service prior to installing Exchange Server 2003.

2. After Exchange Server 2003 is installed, how will you enable the new functionality for existing Exchange Server 5.5 mailboxes?

   In order to utilize the new features of Exchange Server 2003, you will need to move the desired mailboxes from the Exchange Server 5.5 server to the Exchange Server 2003 server in the site.

5 Migrating from Microsoft Exchange Server and Other Mail Systems

Exam Objectives in this Chapter:

- Migrate to Microsoft Exchange Server 2003 from other messaging systems
- Use the Microsoft Migration Wizard to migrate from foreign messaging systems
- Migrate from other Exchange organizations
- Upgrade from Exchange Server 5.5 to Exchange Server 2003
- Configure and troubleshoot Exchange Server 2003 for coexistence with other messaging systems
- Configure and troubleshoot Exchange Server 2003 for interoperability with other Simple Mail Transfer Protocol (SMTP) messaging systems

Why This Chapter Matters

With the constant evolution of technology and the marketplace competition to produce better products, companies continually evaluate their needs against their current technologies to determine whether it is necessary to update to a newer version of a product they are already running or to migrate to another vendor's competing product. This is especially true in the realm of messaging and collaboration—network services that are "mission critical" for most organizations. As a network or Exchange administrator, you will likely find yourself in a position of influence over technology purchases for upgrades and migrations, which are exceedingly common. Therefore, it is very important to know how to migrate other messaging systems to Exchange Server 2003 and to know how to configure Exchange Server 2003 to coexist with other messaging systems that an organization might use.

Lessons in this Chapter:

- Lesson 1: Upgrading from Exchange Server 5.5 and Exchange Server 2000 . . 5-3
- Lesson 2: Configuring Exchange Server 2003 to Coexist with Other Messaging Systems 5-26
- Lesson 3: Migrating from Other Messaging Systems 5-39

Before You Begin

To complete the exercises in this chapter, you will need to do the following:

- Complete the exercises in Chapter 3, "Configuring a Microsoft Exchange Server 2003 Infrastructure."

- Have Exchange Server 5.5 installed on the Microsoft Windows 2000 Server domain controller, Server01, in the *litware.com* domain and have Exchange Server 2003 installed on the Microsoft Windows Server 2003 server, Server02, in the same domain and Exchange organization.

To complete the migration process that began as coexistence in Chapter 4, "Coexistence with Previous Versions of Microsoft Exchange Server 2003," you will need:

- A domain controller running Windows 2000 Server SP3 or later installed as Server03 in the *fabrikam.com* domain. This server should be installed with Exchange 2000 Server in the Fabrikam organization.

Lesson 1: Upgrading from Exchange Server 5.5 and Exchange Server 2000

As an IT professional, and as an Exchange Server administrator, a common type of migration you'll be faced with is upgrading from a previous version of a product and migrating existing settings to the new environment. Depending on your environment, you might need to first migrate a Microsoft Windows NT 4 domain structure to Active Directory directory service as a precursor to migrating Exchange Server 5.5 to Exchange Server 2003. Or, you might have Active Directory already in place and need to upgrade or migrate an existing Exchange Server 5.5 or Exchange 2000 Server organization to Exchange Server 2003. Whatever the environment, it is important to be able to bring an existing Exchange Server organization up to the most current version.

> **Exam Tip**   Since these types of upgrades and migrations are very common in the real world, you can expect upgrading and migrating from previous versions of Exchange Server to be prominent on the exam.

After this lesson, you will be able to

- Upgrade and migrate an Exchange Server 5.5 organization to Exchange Server 2003
- Upgrade and migrate an Exchange Server 2000 organization to Exchange Server 2003

Estimated lesson time: 180 minutes

Upgrading and Migrating an Exchange Server 5.5 Organization to Exchange Server 2003

In Chapter 4, you configured Exchange Server 2003 to coexist in an existing Exchange Server 5.5 organization. One strategy for migrating to Exchange Server 2003 involves configuring Exchange Server 5.5 to synchronize with Active Directory. However, depending on how your Windows network and Exchange Server 5.5 organization are set up, there are two other migration scenarios you might face:

- Migrating Exchange Server 5.5 servers to new Exchange Server 2003 servers in the same organization
- Migrating user accounts and mailboxes to a new Active Directory domain and Exchange Server 2003 organization

Migrating Exchange Server 5.5 Servers to Exchange Server 2003 Servers in the Same Organization

Prior to migrating mailboxes from Exchange Server 5.5 to Exchange Server 2003, you must first migrate the user accounts from Windows NT 4 to Active Directory. The Active Directory environment can be Windows 2000 Server, Windows Server 2003, or a combination of the two network operating systems.

It is beyond the scope of this book to have an in-depth discussion of upgrading a Windows NT 4 domain to a Windows Server 2003 Active Directory domain, but there are some basic tenets to upgrading that must be observed. First, when upgrading a Windows NT 4 domain, you must first upgrade the primary domain controller (PDC) to Windows Server 2003. Once the PDC has been upgraded, Active Directory operates in Mixed mode, which supports both Windows Server 2003 and Windows NT 4 domain controllers. You are not required to upgrade any additional servers right away; however, the migration typically continues with upgrading Windows NT 4 backup domain controllers (BDCs) one at a time until all of the domain controllers have been upgraded. Once there are no longer any Windows NT 4 domain controllers in the domain, you can convert the domain to Windows 2000 Native mode or to the Windows Server 2003 functional level.

> **See Also**   Modes and functional levels are described in more detail in Chapter 3, "Configuring a Microsoft Exchange Server 2003 Infrastructure."

> **Tip**   Raising the functional level of the domain from Mixed mode will not preclude you from having Windows NT 4 member servers in your domain, only domain controllers.

The server that runs Exchange Server 5.5, however, cannot be upgraded from Windows NT 4 to Windows Server 2003, at least not right away. Exchange Server 2003 is the only version of Exchange Server that runs on Windows Server 2003. You will need to make the interim upgrade to Windows 2000 Server with SP3 or later on the server running Exchange Server 5.5, perform the upgrade to Exchange Server 2003, and then upgrade the operating system to Windows Server 2003.

In addition, performing an in-place upgrade of Exchange Server 5.5 to Exchange Server 2003 is not supported, which means that you cannot run the Setup program for Exchange Server 2003 on an existing Exchange Server 5.5 server, even if the server meets the prerequisites of having Windows 2000 Server with SP3 or later installed. In this situation, there are two options for upgrading: performing an in-place upgrade to Exchange 2000 Server first and migrating to a new server.

Interim Upgrade to Exchange 2000 Server   The first option is to perform an interim upgrade from Exchange Server 5.5 to Exchange 2000 Server. Exchange Server 2003 does support the in-place upgrade from Exchange 2000 Server, so you could upgrade Exchange Server 5.5 to Exchange 2000 Server and then immediately upgrade Exchange 2000 Server to Exchange Server 2003. This procedure would allow you to utilize your existing server hardware and avoid moving mailboxes to another server. Windows 2000 Server SP3 is a common platform supported by all three versions of Exchange Server and is the minimum supported service pack level, though you could also have SP4 installed.

In order to upgrade from Exchange Server 5.5 to Exchange 2000 Server, you must have the following in addition to the operating system requirement:

■ Exchange Server 5.5 SP3 or later.

■ Windows 2000 Server SMTP and Network News Transfer Protocol (NNTP) services installed in addition to the default Internet Information Services (IIS) components.

■ The user account for installing Exchange 2000 Server must have Schema Admins and Enterprise Admins permissions to run ForestPrep and Domain Admins permissions to run DomainPrep.

Installing Exchange 2000 Server is very similar to installing Exchange Server 2003 by using the Microsoft Exchange Installation Wizard. When you run the Setup program for Exchange 2000 Server, the installation wizard will identify the existing organization and give you the option either to create a new organization or to join or upgrade an existing organization. If you choose the upgrade option, you can proceed through the installation wizard and upgrade the installation of Exchange Server 5.5. However, during the initial upgrade, you cannot add components that were not installed with Exchange Server 5.5. After Setup is finished, you can re-run the installation wizard and add additional components, as necessary. Upgrading from Exchange 2000 Server to Exchange Server 2003 is discussed in Lesson 2 of this chapter.

Migrating Exchange Server 5.5 to Exchange Server 2003 on a Different Server   If you do not want to upgrade Exchange Server 5.5 to Exchange 2000 Server first in order to do an in-place upgrade, you have the option of migrating Exchange Server 5.5 directly to Exchange Server 2003 on a different server. In this case, you install a Windows 2000 Server or Windows Server 2003 Active Directory environment and connect the Exchange Server 5.5 organization to Active Directory using the Active Directory Connector (ADC). Once directory synchronization is achieved, install Exchange Server 2003 on a non-Exchange Server 5.5 server, joining the existing Exchange Server 5.5 organization. Once this is complete, you can use the Active Directory Users And Computers console to perform the Exchange task called Move Mailbox and move all of the mailboxes from the Exchange Server 5.5 server to the Exchange Server 2003 server in bulk.

Once all the mailboxes are moved, you have to move other resources from your Exchange Server 5.5 servers to the Exchange Server 2003 server, such as the public folder structure and any connectors in use. Then, you can remove the Exchange Server 5.5 server from the organization. If the Exchange Server 5.5 server was configured with an Internet Mail Connector to send and receive e-mail for the organization, you must configure an SMTP virtual server on the Exchange Server 2003 server and change the mail exchanger (MX) record in Domain Name System (DNS) to point to the new server. There will be a disruption in Internet mail delivery during this switchover process (typically 1–3 days for DNS to propagate across the Internet), and once you are sure all mail is flowing through your new SMTP virtual server, you can remove the Internet Mail Service (IMS) from the Exchange Server 5.5 server.

See Also   Configuring SMTP virtual servers is discussed in Chapter 10, "SMTP Protocol Configuration and Management." Configuring other types of virtual servers whose functions you might need to transfer from Exchange Server 5.5 to Exchange Server 2003, such as Outlook Web Access (OWA) and NNTP, are discussed in Chapter 9, "Virtual Servers."

When you are prepared to remove the last Exchange Server 5.5 server from the organization, perform the following steps:

1. Using the Services console, stop the Exchange Server 5.5 services, and then set the Microsoft Exchange System Attendant to Disabled.

2. From the Exchange Server 2003 server, start the Exchange 5.5 Administrator program, click File, and then click Connect To Server.

   You must use the Exchange Server 2003 version of the Exchange 5.5 Administrator program, which is installed through the Exchange Server 2003 Setup utility.

3. Connect to the Exchange Server 2003 server, and then delete the Exchange Server 5.5 server from the site.

4. Start the Active Directory Connector Services console. Right-click the Configuration Connection Agreement (Config_CA), and then click Replicate Now to force replication.

5. Open Exchange System Manager. Verify that the Exchange Server 5.5 server has been removed from the console, and then expand the Tools container. Delete the Site Replication Service. This procedure deletes the Config_CA connection agreement.

6. Delete any Recipient and Public Folder connection agreements that are configured in the Active Directory Connector Services console.

7. Use the Add/Remove Programs tool to uninstall the ADC.

8. You also have the option of switching the Exchange organization from Mixed mode to Native mode at this point. To do so, open Exchange System Manager, right-click the organization name, click Properties, and then click Change Mode.

Inter-Forest User Account Migration

In addition to being able to upgrade or migrate Exchange Server 5.5 within an organization, there are also times when it is necessary to migrate an Exchange Server 5.5 organization to a separate Exchange Server 2003 organization in another Active Directory forest. Conceptually, this is similar to migrating from a Windows NT 4 domain structure to an Active Directory domain in that you first have to deal with the user accounts, and only then can you migrate the mailboxes. Migrating from one organization to another has the following requirements:

- A two-way trust must be configured between the source and target domains.
- Administrative permissions in each of the following areas:
  - ❏ The source domain
  - ❏ The target domain and organizational unit (OU)
  - ❏ Each local computer whose security you migrate to the new domain

Migrating User Accounts with a Recipient Connection Agreement The biggest challenges in migrating Exchange Server from one organization to another are related to how mailboxes are tied to user accounts. Exchange 2000 Server and Exchange Server 2003 require a one-to-one relationship between user accounts and mailboxes. Therefore, a user account can only be associated with a single mailbox. Exchange Server 5.5 did not have that limitation since it maintained its own directory independent of Windows, so it was common to have a single Windows user account associated with multiple Exchange Server 5.5 mailboxes. This creates a potential problem when migrating Exchange Server 5.5 to Exchange Server 2003—one that must be resolved prior to or during the migration process. There are two different approaches to this problem: one uses the ADC and one uses the Active Directory Migration Tool.

You may recall from Chapter 4 that when configuring a Recipient Connection Agreement, you can have the ADC determine how to handle mailboxes that do not have a corresponding user account. By default, if the ADC cannot match a mailbox to an existing user account, it creates a new disabled user account. While this method will allow you to migrate your Exchange Server 5.5 mailboxes to a new Exchange Server 2003 organization, it is not the recommended way to do so. The newly created user accounts would have the disadvantage of having a different security identifier (SID) than the accounts currently in use in the source organization, which means they have no configured permissions and are not the mailbox owners for the corresponding mailboxes. In a large Exchange Server organization, there would be considerable work involved in manually enabling each account and then configuring each account individually to grant permissions to the associated mailbox.

Migrating User Accounts with the Active Directory Migration Tool   The simplest way to migrate user accounts from one domain to another is by using the Active Directory Migration Tool, which is included on the Windows Server 2003 installation CD, in the \I386\ADMT folder. The Active Directory Migration Tool makes it possible to perform both intra-forest migrations and inter-forest migrations, depending on your needs. Since Exchange Server supports only a single organization per Active Directory forest, when migrating Exchange Server 5.5 into a new Exchange Server 2003 organization, you would be performing an inter-forest migration using the Active Directory Migration Tool.

The most significant advantage of using the Active Directory Migration Tool is that it migrates the SID history of the user account, which enables accounts to retain their permissions after the migration. Version 2 of the Active Directory Migration Tool, which is the version included with Windows Server 2003, also allows for the migration of user account passwords (this functionality was not possible with version 1 of the Active Directory Migration Tool). This solves the common problem of having to manually set passwords or having to set a common password for all user accounts that the users have to change at first logon. However, with version 2, the installation of an additional dynamic link library (DLL) file is required. The idea behind this is that passwords are very sensitive, and manipulating them should be done as securely as possible. As a result, there is a process for exporting passwords, and the password list is protected by a secret key that you create using the command-line version of the Active Directory Migration Tool, Admt.exe.

> **See Also**   Two good sources of information detailing the use of the Active Directory
> Migration Tool are *Microsoft Knowledge Base articles 326480, "How to Use Active Directory
> Migration Tool Version 2 to Migrate from Windows 2000 to Windows Server 2003,"* and
> *325851, "HOW TO: Set Up ADMT for a Windows NT 4.0-to-Windows Server 2003 Migration."*

Migrating Exchange Server 5.5 to a New Exchange Server 2003 Organization

Once you have migrated the user accounts from the source domain in one Active Directory forest to the target domain in another Active Directory forest, you can begin the process of migrating the Exchange Server 5.5 mailboxes. To migrate an Exchange Server 5.5 organization to another organization, use the Exchange Migration Wizard. The Migration Wizard should be run on the target Exchange Server 2003 server. From the Start menu, point to All Programs, then point to Microsoft Exchange, then point to Deployment, and then click Migration Wizard.

The Migration Wizard attempts to match a mailbox in the source domain to an existing Active Directory user account in the target domain. If the mailboxes do not currently exist as users or contacts in Active Directory, the Migration Wizard creates new Active

Directory users. If an Exchange Server 5.5 mailbox already exists as a contact in Active Directory (for example, a contact that was created by the Inter-Organizational Connection Agreement), the Migration Wizard matches the Exchange Server 5.5 mailbox with the contact and then converts the contact to an Active Directory user account. After the Migration Wizard creates new users, it migrates mailbox data to Exchange mailbox stores. The success of the Migration Wizard in matching mailboxes to user accounts will depend on how you prepared Active Directory. If you have not created accounts in the new domain, the Migration Wizard will create new user accounts for each mailbox. If you have run the Active Directory Migration Tool and migrated the user accounts to the new domain, the Migration Wizard will be able to match each mailbox to its user account, creating a more seamless transition to the new domain and the new Exchange Server 2003 organization.

You will practice migrating the Exchange Server 5.5 organization you created in Chapter 3 to a new Exchange Server 2003 organization in another domain at the end of this lesson.

The following lists describe the tasks that are performed by the Exchange Migration Wizard, as well as the limitations of the wizard.

Tasks Performed by the Exchange Migration Wizard   The Exchange Migration Wizard is designed to perform the following tasks:

- Migrate all mailbox information to the new Exchange Server mailboxes, including the following data:
    - ❑ Inbox
    - ❑ Drafts
    - ❑ Sent Items
    - ❑ Calendar
    - ❑ Tasks
    - ❑ Custom folders created by the mailbox owner
    - ❑ Contacts
- Create new user accounts in Active Directory (if they do not already exist) based on the Exchange Server 5.5 accounts in the source organization.
- Migrate X.400, SMTP, cc:Mail, Microsoft Mail, and other e-mail addresses into the e-mail addresses attribute of the new user account in Active Directory.
- Convert Active Directory contacts to mail-enabled user accounts in Active Directory when you migrate from Exchange Server 5.5 (if the contacts were created by the ADC). If a contact has been manually created in the target Active Directory domain and a mailbox that has the same alias is migrated, a new

disabled user account with the number 1 appended to the name is created in Active Directory. The original contact remains unchanged. Only contacts that are created by the ADC are converted into mail-enabled user accounts by the Migration Wizard.

■ Update Exchange Server 2003 group membership when you migrate from Exchange Server 5.5. However, Exchange Server 5.5 distribution lists are not migrated. For example, if a distribution group in Active Directory contains contacts, during a migration procedure these contacts are converted to user accounts that are turned off, and the distribution group in Active Directory is updated to reflect this change.

Limitations of the Migration Wizard   The Migration Wizard does *not* perform the following tasks:

■ Clean up or remove mailboxes in the source organization. The original mailboxes in the source organization continue to receive messages after the migration process is complete. You must delete the original mailboxes and reconfigure user mail profiles (such as in Microsoft Outlook) to point to the new mailboxes that are hosted in the target Exchange Server organization.

■ Preserve access control lists (ACLs). The Migration Wizard does not preserve ACLs to other mailboxes or public folders other than the one associated with the user account. If a mailbox owner updates their mail profile to point to the new mailbox in the target Exchange organization after migration, they will no longer be able to connect to mail resources in the original (source) Exchange Server 5.5 organization.

■ Migrate mailboxes in the same organization. The source organization from which you migrate mailboxes must be different from the target organization.

■ Migrate personal mail archives or personal address books. Personal address books hold contact information, but they do so in a file that is stored outside of the server databases. This differs from the Contact folders that hold similar data within a user's server mailbox.

■ Migrate distribution lists. You can use either of the following methods to migrate Exchange Server 5.5 distribution lists:

   ❑ Convert the distribution list to a public folder, and then migrate the public folder.

   ❑ Export the distribution list, and then use the Ldifde or Csvde command-line utilities to convert them.

■ Migrate Inbox rules. After you use the Migration Wizard to migrate mailbox information, mailbox owners must recreate their Outlook Inbox rules.

■ Migrate public folders. You can migrate public folders by exporting them to .pst files or by using the Inter-organization Replication utility.

Once the migration is complete, the amount of administrative work you have to perform depends on whether you used the Active Directory Migration Tool to migrate Active Directory user accounts or whether new accounts were created by either the ADC or the Migration Wizard. If you used the Active Directory Migration Tool and migrated passwords as part of the process, users will simply need to log on to the new domain with the same username and password they used previously and create a new mail profile that points Outlook to the new Exchange Server 2003 server. Then they can open Outlook and resume work, except that they will need to reconfigure Inbox rules, .pst files, and personal address books.

If you did not use the Active Directory Migration Tool, you will need to configure the Active Directory user accounts by enabling them and connecting each of them individually to their corresponding mailbox. Then users can log on to the domain and reconfigure their mail profile to point to the new Exchange Server 2003 server.

> **Important**   When you migrate mailboxes using the Migration Wizard, the single instance storage feature of Exchange Server is lost. Typically, when a message is sent to multiple recipients in an organization, the message exists only once, and pointers are used internally to reference the single message to multiple mailboxes. This dramatically reduces the storage requirements of Exchange Server. When you migrate mailbox data to another organization, a message is duplicated in every mailbox that references it, as it loses its single instance. The end result is that the migrated information store can potentially be much larger than the source information store, so it is important to ensure there is adequate hard disk space on the destination drive prior to the migration.

Upgrading and Migrating an Exchange 2000 Server Organization to Exchange Server 2003

Upgrading from Exchange 2000 Server to Exchange Server 2003 is much simpler than upgrading from Exchange Server 5.5 because Exchange 2000 Server is Active Directory–aware. In fact, Microsoft supports an in-place upgrade of Exchange 2000 Server to Exchange Server 2003. This doesn't mean you can simply insert the Exchange Server 2003 installation CD and install the application over an existing Exchange 2000 Server installation without planning and meeting other requirements; however, once you do meet the requirements, you are able to install Exchange Server 2003 over an existing Exchange 2000 Server installation.

Prior to performing the upgrade, there are a number of issues to consider. One consideration is that Exchange Server 2003 does not provide support for certain features that existed in Exchange 2000 Server because some functionality has been moved from Exchange Server 2003 to other products, such as the Windows Server 2003 operating system and Microsoft Mobile Information Services. In the case of Lotus cc:Mail and Microsoft Mail, support for these connectors has been removed because the products are obsolete. If any of the following components are installed on the Exchange 2000 Server computer you are planning to upgrade, and if the components are still required, you must first move them to other servers and then remove them from the server being upgraded using the Exchange 2000 Server Setup program:

- Instant Messaging Service
- Microsoft Chat Service
- Key Management Service
- Microsoft Exchange Connector for Lotus cc:Mail
- Microsoft Mail Connector

In addition to removing components that Exchange Server 2003 does not support, you must meet the following operating system and Exchange 2000 Server requirements:

- You must have Exchange 2000 Server SP3 or later installed.
- You must have Windows 2000 Server SP3 or later installed.
- You must install Exchange Server 2003 in the same language version used by Exchange 2000 Server.
- You must upgrade front-end servers prior to upgrading the corresponding back-end servers.
- You must upgrade any ADCs to the Exchange Server 2003 version.

Once you have met the previous requirements, you will need to run ForestPrep and DomainPrep as you would when installing Exchange Server 2003 into a new organization or when joining an existing Exchange Server 5.5 organization. There are updates to the schema that must be made before Exchange 2000 Server can be upgraded to Exchange Server 2003. These schema updates are handled by ForestPrep. DomainPrep performs a number of tasks, including creating Exchange Domain Servers and Exchange Enterprise Servers security groups and creating the Microsoft Exchange System Objects container, which is used for mail-enabled public folders.

Since you are performing an in-place upgrade on your existing Exchange 2000 Server computer, there are additional pre-installation tasks that you will want to perform prior to installing Exchange Server 2003. Performing these tasks will ensure that your Exchange Server 2003 upgrade is smooth, and if for some reason you have problems, you will be able to recover from them.

- Delete the contents of the \Exchsrvr\Mailroot\vsi 1\BadMail folder. The Exchange Server 2003 Setup program re-stamps ACLs on all Exchange Server folders. If you have a lot of messages in your BadMail folder, Setup can take much longer than usual to complete.

- Audit and research any third-party Exchange Server add-on programs in use, such as antivirus software or spam filtering software. Verify that the programs are certified to work with Exchange Server 2003 or, at a minimum, that the vendor supports the product running on Exchange Server 2003.

- Make a full backup of Exchange and all its databases, and do a test restore to another server to ensure that the backup is good. If the in-place upgrade fails during the process, you will likely have to reinstall Exchange 2000 Server plus SP3 and then restore your databases from backup. It is worth noting that you can restore a database created under Exchange 2000 Server to Exchange Server 2003 because Exchange Server 2003 will simply patch the database to the newer version. However, the process does not work in reverse in that you cannot restore Exchange Server 2003 databases to a server running Exchange 2000 Server.

- Ensure that no Exchange Server–related programs, such as Exchange System Manager, are running at the time of the upgrade.

- Manually stop the services for third-party add-ons prior to running Setup.

After you have completed the pre-installation tasks, you can run Setup from the Exchange Server 2003 installation CD and choose the option to upgrade. Setup stops the core Exchange 2000 Server services during the upgrade, so naturally you must plan for down time. Exchange Server will be unavailable to users during the upgrade. When upgrading from Exchange 2000 Server to Exchange Server 2003, you cannot select additional components or customize the installation in any way. Exchange Server 2003 will be installed with the same Exchange 2000 Server components that are installed. After Setup completes, you can re-run it and add additional components, as necessary.

Migrating Exchange 2000 Server to a New Exchange Server 2003 Organization

To migrate an existing Exchange 2000 Server organization to a new Exchange Server 2003 organization, you use the Exchange Migration Wizard. The process is similar to migrating an Exchange Server 5.5 organization, but there are some differences. If you are not supporting Exchange Server 5.5 servers through ADCs, the migration of user accounts from one Active Directory domain to another is a little easier administratively. You still use the Active Directory Migration Tool, but you won't have to be concerned with the one-to-one relationship between Active Directory user accounts and Exchange Server mailboxes because Exchange 2000 Server imposes the same restriction that Exchange Server 2003 does.

Using the Active Directory Migration Tool is subject to many of the same requirements as when migrating an Exchange Server 5.5 organization. You must have administrative permissions in the source and target domains and a two-way trust must exist between domains. The combination of the Active Directory Migration Tool and the Migration Wizard allows you to first migrate the user accounts along with their SIDs and passwords and then migrate the mailbox data and have the mailboxes automatically associated with the correct user accounts.

The alternative way to migrate Exchange 2000 Server is to run only the Migration Wizard, which will create new disabled user accounts in the target domain if it cannot match an existing Active Directory user account to a mailbox. Then you manually enable the user accounts and configure them for use with the associated mailbox.

Practice: Upgrading from Exchange Server 5.5 and Exchange Server 2000

In this practice, you will use the Active Directory Migration Tool to migrate an existing Active Directory domain to a domain in a separate forest. Then, you will use the Exchange Migration Wizard to migrate an Exchange Server 5.5 organization to an Exchange Server 2003 organization in the other forest.

This practice builds on the exercises in Chapter 4, so you should have the following servers already in place:

- Server01 installed as a Windows 2000 Server domain controller in the *litwareinc.com* domain. This server should be running Exchange Server 5.5 in the Litwareinc organization and connected to Active Directory through an Exchange Server 2003 ADC.

- Server02 installed as a Windows Server 2003 server in the *litwareinc.com* domain. This server should be running Exchange Server 2003 in the Litwareinc organization and should have a Site Replication Service configured and replicating with Server01.

In addition, you will need:

- Server03 installed as a Windows Server 2003 domain controller in the *fabrikam.com* domain. Install Exchange Server 2003 into a new organization called Fabrikam.

Exercise 1: Configure a Trust Between Migrating Domains

1. On Server01, open the Active Directory Domains And Trusts console. Right-click *litwareinc.com*, and click Properties.

2. Click the Trusts tab. Next to Domains Trusted By This Domain, click Add.

3. Type **Fabrikam**, and then enter **123** as the password and confirm it.

4. Repeat steps 1–3 on Server03, but type **Litwareinc** for the domain.

5. On Server03, click Add next to Domains That Trust This Domain. Type **Litwareinc** and enter the password. Enter the security information for the Litwareinc Administrator account when prompted to verify the trust.

6. Repeat the process on Server01, configuring the Domains That Trust This Domain for Fabrikam.

7. On Server01, use the Active Directory Users And Computers console to add the Fabrikam\Administrator user account to the Schema Admins, Enterprise Admins, and Domain Admins security groups in the *litwareinc.com* domain.

8. On Server03, use Active Directory Users And Computers to add the Litwareinc Administrator user account to the same groups in the *fabrikam.com* domain.

Exercise 2: Migrate Active Directory User Accounts with the Active Directory Migration Tool

1. On Server02, start \I386\Admt\Admigration.msi from the Windows Server 2003 installation CD. Complete the installation wizard to install the Active Directory Migration Tool.

2. Insert a floppy disk into drive A. Start a command prompt and enter **admt key litwareinc a:**

   This will create a .pes file on the floppy disk for the purpose of migrating passwords along with the user account information.

3. Move the .pes file to the domain controller, Server01. Place it in the C:\Pes folder. Server01 is referred to as the Password Export Server.

4. Install the Password Migration DLL file on Server01 by running \I386\Admt \Pwdmig\Pwdmig.exe from the Windows Server 2003 installation CD.

5. When prompted, point the installation wizard to the .pes file in the C:\Pes folder.

6. The installation wizard will prompt you to restart the server when finished. Click Yes to restart.

7. After logging back in to Server01, start Regedit and modify the following registry key: HLM\System\CurrentControlSet\Control\LSA\AllowPasswordExport

Change the AllowPasswordExport DWORD value from 0 to 1 to allow the export, and then close the Registry Editor and restart Server01 again.

8. Start the Active Directory Migration Tool on Server02 by clicking Start and pointing to All Programs, then pointing to Administrative Tools, and then clicking Active Directory Migration Tool.

9. Right-click Active Directory Migration Tool in the console and click User Account Migration Wizard.

10. Choose Test The Migration And Migrate Later, and then click Next.

11. Choose Litwareinc for the source domain and Fabrikam for the target domain, as shown in Figure 5-1, and then click Next.

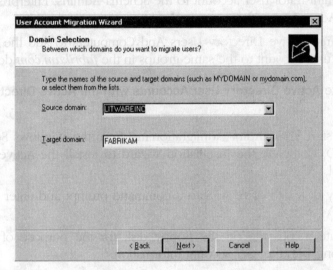

Figure 5-1   Choosing source and target domains for the migration

12. The next step is to add source user accounts to migrate to Active Directory. Click Add, which opens a standard Active Directory Find page. You can either type names in here or click Advanced and then click Find Now to generate a complete list of users, as shown in Figure 5-2. Once you select user accounts, click OK, and you will see a list of the users to be migrated, as in Figure 5-3.

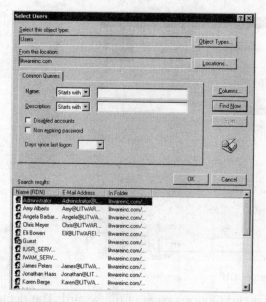

Figure 5-2 Listing all user accounts in the Users container in Active Directory

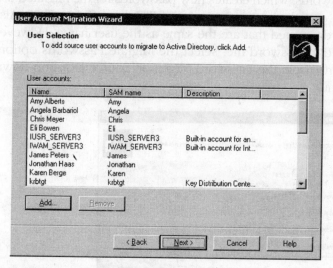

Figure 5-3 Adding user accounts to migrate

13. After selecting the user accounts to migrate, click OK, and then click Next. You will be prompted to specify the target OU for the migration. Probably you will want to use the Users container in the target domain, but you can specify any OU. For example, you may create a Litwareinc OU in the Fabrikam domain in which to place all the Litwareinc domain objects being migrated. Click Browse and select an OU, and then click OK. As shown in Figure 5-4, the wizard creates a Lightweight Directory Access Protocol (LDAP) path to the target OU. Click Next to continue.

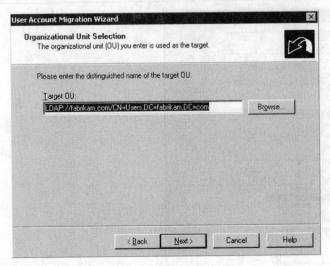

Figure 5-4 Specifying the target OU

14. Figure 5.5 shows the Password Options page of the wizard. The default setting is Complex Passwords, which creates new passwords for the migrated user accounts that meet the complexity requirements of Windows Server 2003. Also, you can have passwords created that are the same as the user name. However, since we have prepared a password file, select the Migrate Passwords option, and then choose Server01 from the Password Migration Source DC drop-down list. Click Next to continue.

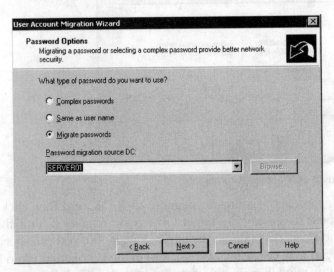

Figure 5-5 Migrating passwords

15. The Active Directory Migration Tool will test your migration settings and generate warning messages if it cannot continue. For example, if you set up your domain

to limit access to the Pre-Windows 2000 Compatible Access built-in group, the wizard will inform you that the Everyone group needs to be a member of this group. You can correct the problem and then try again.

16. The next step is to determine the account transition options, as shown in Figure 5-6. You can enable the target accounts in the target site because you are migrating the user accounts with their existing passwords. You choose to disable target accounts if you are not migrating passwords and want to leave the accounts disabled until you actually need them, or if you want to ensure that users do not log on before you migrate their mailboxes. The Target Same As Source option is useful if you want to maintain the same enabled or disabled state in the target domain as the user account had in the source domain. In other words, if it was enabled in the source domain, it will be enabled in the target domain.

You can also configure the source account options. Disabling source accounts is useful if you want users to immediately begin using their new accounts after the migration completes. You can also have the account expire after so many days to allow for a transition period.

The last option on this page is whether or not to migrate the user account's SID to the target domain. It is recommended that you do this if you are migrating passwords, in order to keep all of the account's ACL settings.

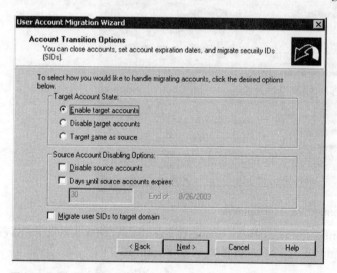

Figure 5-6 The Account Transition Options page

17. If you have not enabled auditing in the source domain, and you have selected the option to migrate user SIDs, the wizard will prompt you to enable auditing prior to continuing. Click Yes to continue. You may also have to click Yes to enable auditing for the target domain, as well.

18. A special local group in the format of *SourceDomain$$$* is required to migrate SIDs, as well. The wizard will prompt you that Litwareinc$$$ doesn't exist and ask if you want it to be automatically created. Click Yes.

19. The last setting that the wizard needs to set is the registry key *TCPipClientSupport* in the source domain. Click Yes to set this registry key. Server01 will need to be restarted at this point, so let the wizard restart the server before continuing.

20. The next step is to configure user options in the target domain, as shown in Figure 5-7. You can migrate a user's roaming profile, update their user rights, migrate associated user groups, and fix users' group memberships. You can also choose whether account names should be renamed and, if so, how. Click Next to continue.

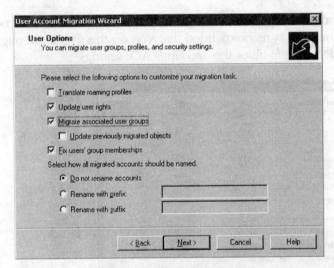

Figure 5-7 Configuring user options

21. Next, you configure any object property exclusions that you want to configure, as shown in Figure 5-8. Then click Next to continue.

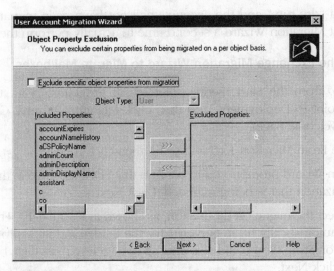

Figure 5-8   Configuring object property exclusions

22. The next step is to decide how naming conflicts will be handled during the migration. The Naming Conflicts page of the wizard is shown in Figure 5-9. You can choose to ignore conflicting accounts and not migrate them, to replace the target accounts with the source accounts, or to rename the source accounts in the target domain to resolve the conflict. Leave the default setting, and then click Next.

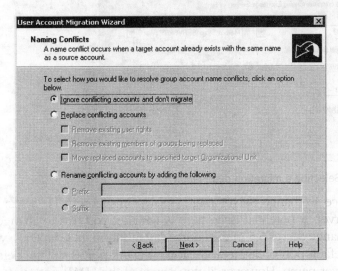

Figure 5-9   Configuring naming conflict settings

23. At this point, you have entered all of the information the wizard needs. Click Finish to see a Migration Status window showing real-time progress. When the migration completes, click View Log to view a text file log of what the wizard did. Since you chose to test the migration settings rather than perform the migration, this will be a "dry run," and the accounts will not have been migrated. Run the User Account Migration Wizard a second time to actually perform the migration.

Exercise 3: Use the Exchange Migration Wizard to Migrate Mailboxes

1. On Server03, from the Start menu, point to All Programs, point to Microsoft Exchange, point to Deployment, and then click Migration Wizard. Click Next to bypass the Welcome page.

2. Click Migrate From Microsoft Exchange, and then click Next.

3. The Migration Wizard prompts you to confirm that LDAP is active in the Exchange Server organization that is being migrated. Click Next.

4. You must select the migration destination, as shown in Figure 5-10. The Migration Wizard will automatically fill in Server03 for the Server and its Mailbox Store for the Information Store. You could also choose to migrate to .pst files, but leave the default and click Next.

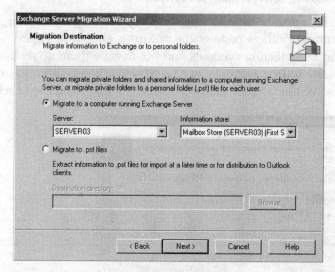

Figure 5-10   Selecting a migration destination

5. On the Source Exchange Server page, shown in Figure 5-11, select the source Exchange server. A potential issue here is whether you had to change the LDAP port for Exchange Server 5.5 in the source organization. In Chapter 4, we changed it from the default port of 389 to 1389. If your LDAP port is still the default, simply enter the server name. However, if you changed the LDAP port, you must put a colon and then the port number after the server name. Enter **Server01:1389**, and then enter the Administrator Account and Password and click Next.

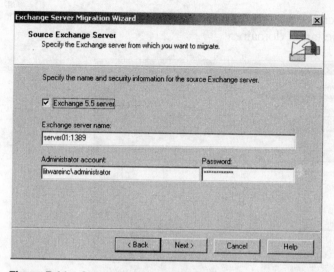

Figure 5-11   Specifying the source server

6. The Migration Information page is shown in Figure 5-12. Here you choose the information that you want to migrate. Select the option to Create/Modify Mailbox Accounts. Another option is to set a filter to migrate messages within a specified date range or to not migrate messages that contain specific subject lines. Click Next to continue.

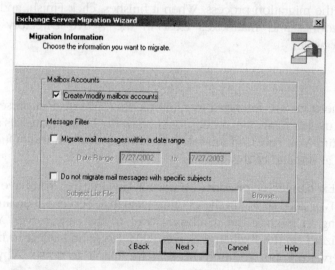

Figure 5-12   Configuring the message information to migrate

7. Next, you select the accounts you want to migrate on the Account Migration page, shown in Figure 5-13. Because you used the Active Directory Migration Tool to migrate the full user account information already, you do not need to migrate the accounts here. However, you still have to select the accounts because the mailboxes are tied to the accounts. Click Select All, and then click Next. The Migration

Wizard will create new accounts only if it does not match the mailbox to the account in the target domain.

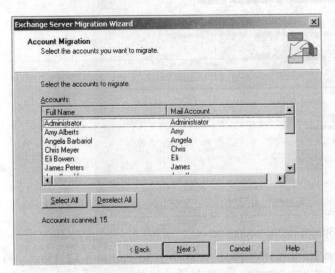

Figure 5-13   Configuring account migration options

8. Select the Users container for the target accounts, and click Next.

9. The Migration Wizard is now ready to perform the migration. Click Next to begin, and observe the migration process. When it finishes, click Finish, and then verify that the accounts and mailboxes exist in the Active Directory Users And Computers console.

Lesson Review

The following questions are intended to reinforce key information presented in this lesson. If you are unable to answer a question, review the lesson materials and then try the question again. You can find answers to the questions in the "Questions and Answers" section at the end of this chapter.

1. You are the Exchange Server administrator for Litware, Inc. You have installed an Exchange Server 2003 server in the existing Exchange Server 5.5 organization, and you are trying to migrate the mailboxes over to the new server. You run the Migration Wizard on the Exchange Server 2003 server and select to migrate from Exchange Server 5.5, but you find that you are unable to do so. Why would this happen?

2. You need to migrate a server from Exchange Server 5.5 to Exchange Server 2003, but you know that you cannot perform an in-place upgrade in this situation. Since Exchange Server 5.5 with SP4 is running on Windows 2000 Server with SP4, you decide to do an interim in-place upgrade from Exchange Server 5.5 to Exchange 2000 Server, and then you will upgrade Exchange 2000 Server directly to Exchange Server 2003. You install Exchange 2000 Server successfully and verify that users are able to log on and access mail, and then you immediately insert the Exchange Server 2003 installation CD and run Setup. However, Setup fails. What is the most likely cause?

_____

_____

3. You install a new Exchange Server 2003 server into your existing Exchange Server 5.5 organization. You successfully migrate all the mailboxes to the new server, and users are able to access their mail from the new server without any problems. One afternoon, you shut down the Exchange Server 5.5 server, planning to use the machine later for something else. The next day, you receive many complaints that e-mail is working within the company, but mail is not being sent to or received from the Internet. What is the problem?

_____

_____

Lesson Summary

- An in-place upgrade from Exchange Server 5.5 to Exchange Server 2003 cannot be performed. You must first upgrade to Exchange 2000 Server or install Exchange Server 2003 on a separate server and migrate all Exchange Server 5.5 resources to the new server.

- The Migration Wizard is not a full-featured migration tool, but you can use it in conjunction with the Active Directory Migration Tool to migrate existing user account settings and mailboxes.

- When migrating complex environments, you must upgrade front-end servers to Exchange Server 2003 prior to upgrading the corresponding back-end servers.

- Exchange 2000 Server functionality that isn't supported by Exchange Server 2003 (such as the Instant Messaging Service, Microsoft Chat Service, Key Management Service, and connectors for Microsoft Mail and Lotus cc:Mail) and that is still required must be removed from the server prior to upgrading.

Lesson 2: Configuring Exchange Server 2003 to Coexist with Other Messaging Systems

In addition to being able to coexist with previous versions of Exchange Server, Exchange Server 2003 can be configured to coexist with other non-Microsoft mail systems. This is very useful, for instance, if you have a UNIX environment that is being migrated to Windows and Active Directory, but you need to support the existing mail system until it can be fully migrated to Exchange Server 2003. You can use various connectors to connect Exchange Server 2003 to other mail systems to provide coexistence until you are ready to migrate.

After this lesson, you will be able to

■ Configure Exchange Server 2003 to coexist with Lotus Notes

■ Configure Exchange Server 2003 to coexist with X.400-compliant message systems

Estimated lesson time: 60 minutes

Configuring Exchange Server 2003 to Coexist with Lotus Notes

One of the more common non-Microsoft messaging systems in use is Lotus Notes. Exchange Server 2003 includes a Connector for Lotus Notes that allows synchronization between the two messaging systems. Conceptually, the connector is similar to the ADC, which is used to synchronize Active Directory with an Exchange Server 2003 directory. In this case, though, the Connector for Lotus Notes is used to synchronize Active Directory with the Lotus Notes directory.

Before you can use the Connector for Lotus Notes, you must first install it from the Exchange Server 2003 installation CD by performing the following steps:

1. On Server03, re-run Setup to start the Microsoft Exchange Installation Wizard.

2. Select Change on the Component Selection page for the Microsoft Exchange Messaging And Collaboration component.

3. Select Install for both the Connector For Lotus Notes and the Microsoft Exchange Calendar Connector.

4. Complete the wizard to install the components.

Once the Connector for Lotus Notes is installed, you can configure it using Exchange System Manager by performing the following steps:

1. On Server03, open Exchange System Manager. Navigating to the Connectors container will depend on whether you have Routing Groups displayed. If you do not have Routing Groups displayed, the Connectors container is off of the root of the

organization name. If you do have Routing Groups displayed, navigate to the Routing Groups container, and then expand the First Routing Group and click the Connectors container.

2. Right-click the Connector For Lotus Notes and click Properties.

3. To configure the Connector for Lotus Notes, you use a series of property tabs. The first is the General tab, shown in Figure 5-14. On this tab, you supply the Notes Server name, and you can configure the location of the Notes.ini file, the connector mailbox name, and how to handle Notes DocLinks. Once you enter the required server name, click the Address Space tab.

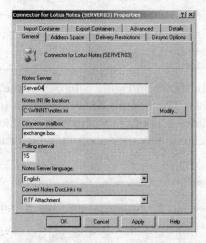

Figure 5-14   Configuring general settings

4. On the Address Space tab, you configure the common e-mail address space that will be used between Exchange Server 2003 and Lotus Notes. You can also configure whether the connector scope will apply to the entire organization or only to the specific routing group. This is only an issue if you have more than one routing group configured; otherwise, the scope is the same either way. Create an SMTP address space that applies to * (meaning everything), as shown in Figure 5-15.

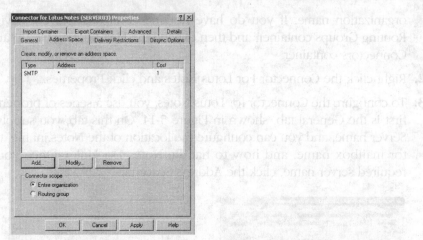

Figure 5-15   Configuring the address space

5. Next, click the Import Container tab, shown in Figure 5-16. Select the Users container for importing Notes accounts. The default behavior when importing a mailbox that doesn't have a Windows account is to create a contact in Active Directory. You can also select to create a new user account, which can be either enabled or disabled.

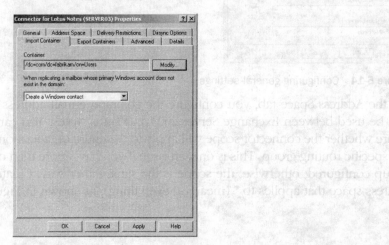

Figure 5-16   Configuring the import container

6. Next, click the Export Containers tab. You can configure Active Directory to export groups or contacts from any OU to the Notes directory, and you can export multiple containers. Add the Users container, as shown in Figure 5-17, and then click the Advanced tab.

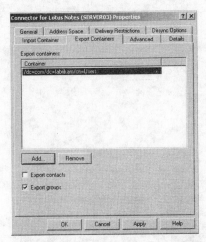

Figure 5-17 Configuring the export containers

7. On the Advanced tab, shown in Figure 5-18, you configure how mail is handled. You can configure message routing, which controls what domains are routable through the connector, as well as the router mailbox and the appearance of messages. You can also configure a message size limit here. Add *fabrikam.com* to the list of routable domains, and then click the Dirsync Options tab.

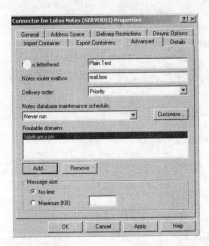

Figure 5-18 Configuring advanced options

8. On the Dirsync Options tab, shown in Figure 5-19, you configure a number of synchronization options, such as the schedule for synchronization, Address Book settings, and whether to initiate Exchange to Notes or Notes to Exchange synchronization immediately. You can immediately synchronize either a full reload of all data or an immediate update, which just overrides the schedule and immediately synchronizes any changes that have been made since the last synchronization.

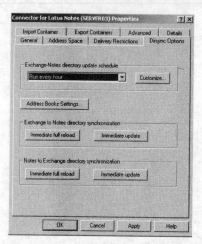

Figure 5-19   Configuring directory synchronization options

9. The last settings to configure are on the Delivery Restrictions tab, shown in Figure 5-20. Here, you can configure permissions for the connector, whether you want to allow everyone to send through it or to restrict access to certain users and groups. Click OK when you are done.

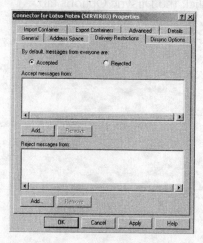

Figure 5-20   Configuring delivery restrictions

The Connector for Lotus Notes sets up directory synchronization of mail and account information, but it does not synchronize calendar information between Exchange Server and Notes. To do this, you must also configure the Microsoft Calendar Connector by performing the following steps:

1. Right-click the Calendar Connector in the Connectors container, and click Properties. The first tab is the General tab, shown in Figure 5-21. Select the connector used to import users into Active Directory. Click Modify and select the Connector

For Lotus Notes. On this tab, you can also change the default settings for the maximum number of days to maintain free and busy information, the maximum age in minutes of foreign free and busy information that can be used without querying the Notes calendar, and the maximum time in seconds to wait for queries to be answered. After configuring these settings, click the Calendar Connections tab.

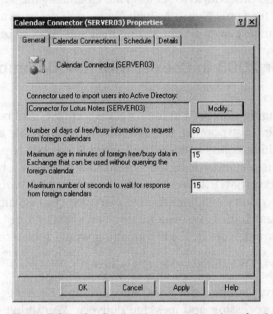

Figure 5-21   Configuring the general settings for the Calendar Connector

2. To create a new Calendar Connection, click Add, then click Lotus Notes, and then click OK.

3. As shown in Figure 5-22, you are required to identify the Notes server and the location of the Notes.ini configuration file. After supplying this information, click OK.

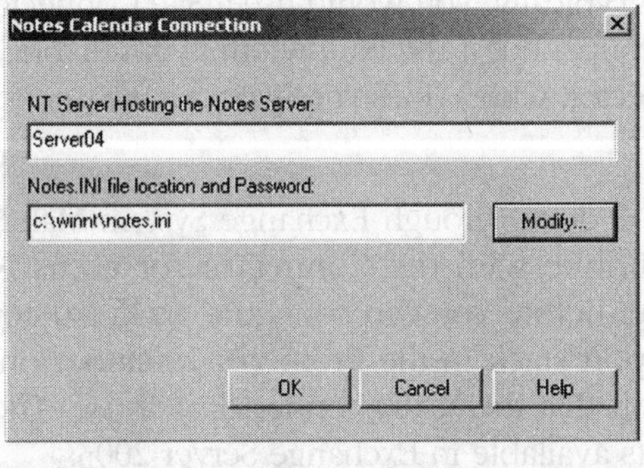

Figure 5-22   Configuring a Calendar Connection type

4. Click the Schedule tab. This is where you configure the schedule for synchronizing calendar information. This is a standard calendar like the one you configured for the ADC.

The Connector for Novell GroupWise is the other type of connector that comes with Exchange Server 2003, and the procedures to set it up are essentially the same as those for setting up the Connector for Lotus Notes. As with Notes, you do have to configure the Calendar Connector separately from synchronizing mail and account information.

Configuring Exchange Server 2003 to Coexist with X.400-Compliant Messaging Systems

There are two primary messaging standards in use for transporting e-mail between foreign messaging systems. The most popular is SMTP, which most people are familiar with. The other is X.400, which is less used in the United States but is prevalent in Europe and Canada. X.400 is a standards-based system that provides a hierarchical addressing structure. Whereas an SMTP address is in the format *host@domain*, an X.400 address is in the format "c=country;a=administrative management domain;p=private management domain;o=organization;s=surname;g=given (first) name". An SMTP address of *ChrisMeyer@Litwareinc.com* in X.400 formatting would look like this:

c=USA;a=;p=LITWAREINC;o=LITWAREINC;s=Meyer;g=Chris

All versions of Exchange Server support the X.400 standard, and Exchange Server 5.5 used X.400 for all internal processing and message delivery. You didn't even need SMTP addresses with Exchange Server 5.5 unless you were communicating with SMTP-based messaging systems, such as over the Internet.

In Exchange Server 2003, you can configure an X.400 connector to connect any X.400-compliant messaging system. There are two primary uses for the X.400 connector. One is to connect X.400 messaging systems that do not support any other common protocol to Exchange Server 2003. The other is to connect Exchange Server sites that are connected by unreliable bandwidth. Typically, you would use a Site Connector to connect Exchange Server 2003 routing groups, but if the bandwidth is unreliable, you can use the messaging-based X.400 connector, which doesn't rely on a consistent or permanent link for the connection.

Configuring an X.400 connector is done through Exchange System Manager. There is nothing additional to install, unlike with the Connector for Lotus Notes or the Connector for Novell GroupWise. Before you can configure an X.400 connector, you must first create an X.400 transport stack in the Protocols container on the desired server. This provides the transport that the X.400 connector will use. There are three different types of X.400 transports available in Exchange Server 2003:

- **TCP/IP X.400 Service Transport Stack**   Provides an interface for connecting X.400 messaging systems over the standard Transmission Control Protocol/Internet Protocol (TCP/IP) protocol.

- **X.25 X.400 Service Transport Stack**   Provides an interface for using X.25-compliant devices to connect X.400 systems.

- **RAS**   Provides an interface for using Remote Access Service (RAS) over a dial-up connection. This option will appear only if RAS is installed on the server.

After you configure the type of transport stack you want the X.400 connector to use, you can then configure the X.400 connector to use the transport stack. This is also done through Exchange System Manager, by right-clicking the Connectors container, pointing to New, and clicking the type of X.400 connector to create. To configure the X.400 connector, you use a series of property tabs, similar to configuring other connectors. If you are connecting to a non-Exchange Server X.400 system, you will need to obtain the necessary information about the destination end of the connector, and the administrator of the other system will need your information. You have to configure both ends of the connector for synchronization to work, so configuring an X.400 connector is usually a cooperative effort between mail system administrators.

Practice: Configuring Exchange Server 2003 to Coexist with Other Messaging Systems

In this practice, you will configure the local side of an X.400 connector that will be used to connect Exchange Server 2003 to a non-Exchange Server X.400 messaging system. Perform these tasks on Server03. Enable the display of Administrative Groups and Routing Groups, if they are not already enabled.

Exercise 1: Create an X.400 Transport Stack

1. Open Exchange System Manager, and navigate to Server03 in the console.

2. Expand Server03, and click the Protocols container.

3. Right-click X.400, point to New, and click TCP/IP X.400 Service Transport Stack.

4. The Properties dialog box, shown in Figure 5-23, appears and a default name is given. You do not need to configure the OSI Address Information, so click OK.

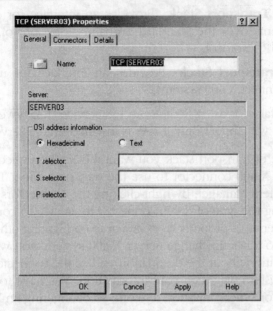

Figure 5-23   Configuring a new TCP/IP X.400 transport stack

5. Expand the Routing Groups container, and then expand First Routing Group. Right-click the Connectors container, point to New, and click TCP/IP X.400 Connector.

6. On the General tab, shown in Figure 5-24, provide a descriptive name for the connector. You also have to select the remote X.400 name. This information is provided by the administrator of the other X.400 system. When you click Modify, the Remote Connection Credentials screen, shown in Figure 5-25, appears, which prompts you to enter the name and password for the remote X.400 system. The password is used to prevent an unauthorized user from creating a connection to a system.

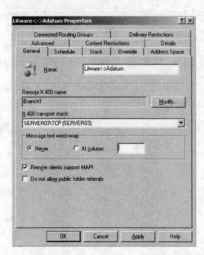

Figure 5-24   Configuring general settings for the X.400 connector

Figure 5-25   Configuring the remote X.400 name and entering its password

7. When you click the Schedule tab, you see a standard schedule screen. The default setting is Always Update, though you can schedule updating for different times if unreliable bandwidth, toll charges, or other reasons deem it necessary.

8. Next, click the Stack tab. You have the option of specifying either the DNS name of the remote X.400 host or the Internet Protocol (IP) address. This information is based on the X.400 transport stack configuration on the remote end and must match for the connection to work. Enter an IP address, and then click the Override tab.

9. The Override tab allows you to configure settings specific to the X.400 connector in a situation where you had multiple connections using the same X.400 transport stack. With only a single X.400 connector, there is nothing you need to configure, so continue by clicking the Address Space tab.

10. The Address Space tab is identical to the one used to configure the Connector for Lotus Notes. You add address spaces to define the type and format of addresses used through the connector. Create an address space that matches the remote end.

11. Click the Advanced tab. This tab, shown in Figure 5-26, allows you to configure link options and message settings. If the X.400 system on the other end is an Exchange Server system, use Allow Exchange Contents to send messages using the Exchange Server 2003 internal Message Database Encapsulated Format (MDBEF). If you are connecting to a non–Exchange Server X.400 system, clear the check box to send in the standard X.400 format.

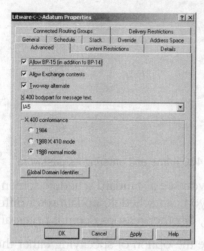

Figure 5-26   Configuring advanced message settings

12. Click the Content Restrictions tab. On this tab, shown in Figure 5-27, you can restrict the types of messages and the allowed size of messages that can pass through the connector. By default, there are no restrictions, but you can define restrictions, if necessary.

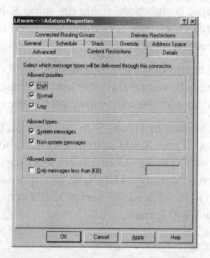

Figure 5-27   Configuring content restrictions

You are finished configuring this side of the X.400 connector. If you were connecting to another Exchange Server routing group, you would click the Connected Routing Groups tab and enter the information for the destination routing group or Exchange Server 5.5 site. Once the remote side of the X.400 connection is configured, you are able to transmit messages across the connector.

Lesson Review

The following questions are intended to reinforce key information presented in this lesson. If you are unable to answer a question, review the lesson materials and then try the question again. You can find answers to the questions in the "Questions and Answers" section at the end of this chapter.

1. You are trying to configure an X.400 connection between your Exchange Server 2003 organization and a remote X.400 messaging system running on a UNIX platform. After working with the administrator of the remote system to configure the connector, you test and find that your side of the connection receives messages fine, but on the remote end, the messages come out garbled. What do you need to do to fix the problem on your end?

   _____

   _____

2. You have set up directory synchronization between your Exchange Server 2003 organization and the Lotus Notes organization of a company that has recently merged with your company. E-mail is working fine and you are able to verify synchronization between Active Directory and Notes, but Outlook users are complaining that when they view the schedules of Notes users, the information is generally out of date. What can you do to correct the problem?

   _____

   _____

3. You are the administrator of two Exchange Server 2003 routing groups that have been connected by a T-1 line. Lately, the circuit has been very inconsistent, sometimes very slow, and sometimes dropping connection altogether. Message traffic is suffering as a result. What can you do to improve the reliability of the message transfer over the unreliable connection?

   _____

   _____

Lesson Summary

- Three connectors can be installed from the Exchange Server 2003 installation CD: Connector for Lotus Notes, Connector for Novell GroupWise, and the Microsoft Calendar Connector.

- The X.400 connector requires that an X.400 transport stack be configured beforehand.

- There are three types of X.400 transport stacks: TCP/IP, X.25, and RAS. You have only the option of RAS if the Remote Access Service is installed on the server.

- X.400 connectors can be used to connect Exchange Server routing groups when the bandwidth is too unreliable to use Site Connectors.

- The connectors for Lotus Notes and Novell GroupWise only synchronize mailbox and user account data. You must use the Calendar Connector in conjunction with the other connectors to synchronize calendar data.

Lesson 3: Migrating from Other Messaging Systems

While it is necessary to be able to migrate from previous versions of Exchange Server to Exchange Server 2003, it is equally important to be able to migrate from other messaging systems to Exchange Server 2003. There are a number of reasons why you would want to migrate from one product to another. One of the most common situations for migrating from one messaging system to another is a company merger or acquisition, and it is necessary to standardize on one platform rather than run two separate messaging platforms. Exchange Server 2003 makes it relatively easy to migrate from a number of other messaging systems.

After this lesson, you will be able to

■ Use the Migration Wizard to migrate from other messaging systems to Exchange Server 2003

Estimated lesson time: 45 minutes

Using the Migration Wizard to Migrate from Other Messaging Systems

In Lesson 1, you used the Migration Wizard to migrate an Exchange Server 5.5 organization to Exchange Server 2003. You can also use the Migration Wizard to migrate a number of other messaging systems. In fact, the Migration Wizard offers the following options:

■ **Import From Migration Files**   Use this option to import migration files created when you select Extract Migration Files only during migration.

■ **Migrate From Microsoft Mail for PC Networks**   Use this option to migrate Microsoft Mail for PC Networks users, mail, and schedule data directly from your Microsoft Mail post office.

■ **Migrate From Microsoft Exchange**   Use this option to migrate mailboxes from an Exchange 2000 Server or later organization or from an Exchange Server 5.5 site to an Exchange 2003 organization.

■ **Migrate From Lotus cc:Mail**   Use this option to migrate Lotus cc:Mail user mailboxes, messages, message drafts, attachments, folders, personal mail lists, and bulletin boards directly from your cc:Mail post office.

■ **Migrate From Lotus Notes**   Use this option to migrate users, mail, and schedule information from a Lotus Notes or Domino server.

■ **Migrate From Novell GroupWise 4.*x***   Use this option to migrate users, mail, and schedule information from your Novell GroupWise 4.*x* post office.

■ **Migrate From Novell GroupWise 5.*x***   Use this option to migrate users, mail, and schedule information from your Novell GroupWise 5.*x* post office.

- **Migrate From Internet Directory (LDAP through ADSI)**   Use this option to migrate mail account information from an LDAP-compliant Internet directory to Active Directory.

- **Migrate From Internet Mail (IMAP4)**   Use this option to migrate messages from an IMAP4-compliant messaging system to users' Exchange mailboxes.

Using the Migration Wizard to migrate any messaging system follows the same basic principles used when migrating Exchange Server 5.5 to Exchange Server 2003. You must adequately plan for the migration by ensuring that the account being used to perform the migration has administrative permissions in both the source and target domains, that DNS is configured properly so all servers involved can effectively communicate, and that you have mapped out the target containers for the account migration in advance.

When migrating user accounts, it is important to plan for how they will be handled in the target domain. When migrating from a Windows NT 4 or Active Directory domain to another Active Directory domain, you can plan to migrate user accounts, existing passwords, and SIDs. This simplifies the mailbox portion of the migration. When you migrate entirely through the Migration Wizard, you must plan for how you will configure passwords in the target domain, since passwords cannot be migrated through the Migration Wizard.

Probably the most important aspect of any migration is preparing the user community and setting expectations. A migration can be performed flawlessly from a technical standpoint, but if you fail to adequately communicate with the user community, you will have problems afterward with frustrated users who can't access their e-mail the way they expect to. Therefore, you will want to ensure that your migration project plan includes provisions for preparing users for the downtime and for handling concerns that may arise.

Most of the migration process is planning, but once you are ready to make the switch from one messaging system to another, use the Migration Wizard to walk through the process. Do a test run first, which allows you to see if the migration will work correctly without errors, and if errors do occur, you can correct the problems before performing the real migration. Once the test migration is running without errors, schedule the migration for a time when it will least affect users, and complete the migration to Exchange Server 2003.

Lesson Review

The following questions are intended to reinforce key information presented in this lesson. If you are unable to answer a question, review the lesson materials and then try the question again. You can find answers to the questions in the "Questions and Answers" section at the end of this chapter.

1. Which of the following messaging systems is *not* supported by the Migration Wizard?

   a. Lotus cc:Mail

   b. SendMail

   c. Microsoft Mail

   d. Internet Mail

2. You are trying to migrate a Lotus Notes server in the domain *adatum.com* to an Exchange Server 2003 organization in the *fabrikam.com* domain. You are performing a test migration using the Migration Wizard, and the wizard asks you to specify the name of your Lotus Notes server. After you do, you receive an error that the server cannot be contacted. You verify that the Notes server is running, and users in the *adatum.com* domain are not complaining about being unable to access e-mail. How would you troubleshoot this problem?

   _____

   _____

3. You are involved in a migration of mail systems between two companies. Litware, Inc., which runs Exchange Server 2003, has acquired Contoso, which runs Novell GroupWise on the NetWare operating system. What type of information will you be able to migrate to Exchange Server 2003, and how will user accounts be handled?

   _____

   _____

Lesson Summary

- The Migration Wizard can be used to migrate from a number of third-party messaging systems.

- Whatever the supported platform you are migrating to, use the Migration Wizard and follow the same basic procedures for identifying the type of system to migrate, the destination server, and the source accounts, and for defining how accounts and messages will be handled in the target domain, for excluding or limiting migrated content, and for selecting the target location for the migrated accounts.

■ You should perform a test migration using the Migration Wizard prior to performing a live migration.

Case Scenario Exercise

Litware, Inc. is a fast-growing software development company. It has acquired several smaller companies over the last year but has been struggling to merge the various messaging platforms of the different companies. Litware, Inc. is running Exchange Server 5.5, but management wants to upgrade to Exchange Server 2003. The Litware, Inc. organization consists of two Exchange Server 5.5 servers, one at each of their two locations. The *litwareinc.com* domain is running Windows 2000 Server SP2 on all its servers. Exchange Server 5.5 is not connected to Active Directory. The primary Exchange Server system, Server05, has approximately 500 mailboxes and is located at the corporate office. The second server, Server06, has approximately 250 mailboxes and is located at their branch office. Server07 has recently been deployed with Windows 2000 Server SP4 and has been designated as the server to consolidate all mailboxes to.

There is a pressing need to migrate one of the acquired companies, Contoso, Ltd., to the *litwareinc.com* domain as quickly as possible. Contoso, Ltd. runs Exchange 2000 Server SP3 on Windows 2000 Server SP4 computers in the *contoso.com* domain. Management wants to eliminate the *contoso.com* domain altogether.

■ **Requirement 1**   The first requirement is to upgrade Litware, Inc. to Exchange Server 2003. You need to connect Exchange Server 5.5 to Active Directory, install Exchange Server 2003 into the existing Exchange Server 5.5 organization, and move all of the mailboxes to the new Exchange Server 2003 server. Management also wants all Windows 2000 Server systems upgraded to Windows Server 2003.

■ **Requirement 2**   The second requirement is to migrate Contoso to the *litwareinc.com* domain and Exchange Server organization. You must migrate both the user accounts and the mailboxes and then eliminate the *contoso.com* domain.

Requirement 1

The first requirement involves upgrading the Litware, Inc. Exchange Server 5.5 organization to Exchange Server 2003.

1.   Installing the Exchange Server 2003 version of the ADC requires a minimum of Windows 2000 Server SP3, but all servers except the new Server07 are running SP2. Before installing the ADC, should you update the service pack level to SP4 or

simply upgrade to Windows Server 2003, since management wants to upgrade anyway? What influences your decision?

_____

_____

2. Describe the process for upgrading Exchange Server 5.5 to Exchange Server 2003 at the corporate office.

_____

_____

Requirement 2

The second requirement is to migrate Contoso's user accounts and mailboxes to the *litwareinc.com* domain and the Litware, Inc. Exchange Server organization and then eliminate the *contoso.com* domain.

1. What tool do you use to retain the SIDs while migrating Contoso's user accounts to Litware, Inc., and what do you need to do to migrate the existing user passwords?

_____

_____

2. After successfully migrating Contoso's existing user accounts to the *litwareinc.com* domain, what do you need to do prior to running Dcpromo, removing the *contoso.com* domain, and joining Contoso's servers to the *litwareinc.com* domain?

_____

_____

Troubleshooting Lab

In this lab, you will attempt to use the Migration Wizard to migrate mailboxes from Server01 to Server02 in the Litware, Inc. organization. The procedure will fail because the wizard can only migrate between organizations, not within an organization. You will then use the Active Directory Users And Computers console to move the mailboxes.

Before proceeding with this lab, you must have the system requirements as outlined at the beginning of this chapter.

Exercise 1: Attempt to Migrate Mailboxes with the Migration Wizard

1. On Server02, start the Migration Wizard. From the Start menu, point to All Programs, Microsoft Exchange, and Deployment, and then click Migration Wizard.

2. Click Next to bypass the Welcome page.

3. Select to Migrate From Microsoft Exchange and click Next.

4. Click Next on the following page, which advises you about migrating from another Exchange Server organization.

5. On the Migration Destination page, note that the information for Server02 is automatically filled in. Click Next.

6. On the Source Exchange Server page, type **Server01:1389** and enter the Administrator account information. Click Next.

7. Note the error, "Unable to perform the migration. Please enter a source Exchange server outside of the target Exchange organization." Quit the Migration Wizard.

Exercise 2: Migrate Mailboxes with Active Directory Users And Computers

1. Open the Active Directory Users And Computers console on Server01.

2. Click the Users container to see a list of user accounts.

3. Highlight to select Amy Alberts, Chris Meyer, and Eli Bowen. Right-click Eli Bowen and click Exchange Tasks.

4. Select Move Mailbox from the list of Exchange Tasks, and click Next.

5. Move the mailboxes to Server02.

Chapter Summary

- Exchange Server 5.5 cannot be upgraded in-place; you must first upgrade to Exchange 2000 Server and then to Exchange Server 2003, or install Exchange Server 2003 on a different server and move the Exchange Server 5.5 resources to the new server.

- Exchange 2000 Server can be upgraded directly to Exchange Server 2003 if the Windows 2000 Server level is SP3 or later.

- If you upgrade Exchange 2000 Server to Exchange Server 2003, you must run ForestPrep and DomainPrep again with Exchange Server 2003. The same permissions requirements apply as when installing Exchange Server 2003 in a new organization.

- The Migration Wizard can only migrate an Exchange Server organization to another organization. It cannot be used to migrate accounts and mailboxes within an organization.

- X.400 connectors can connect other Exchange Server organizations, other Exchange Server routing groups in the same organization, or non–Exchange Server X.400-compliant messaging systems.

- The Migration Wizard can migrate previous versions of Exchange Server in other organizations to an Exchange Server 2003 organization, and it can also migrate popular third-party messaging systems, such as Lotus Notes and Novell GroupWise.

- Exchange Server 2003 can be configured to synchronize directories with Lotus Notes and Novell GroupWise with connectors that can be installed from the Exchange Server 2003 installation CD.

Exam Highlights

Before taking the exam, review the key points and terms that are presented in this chapter. Return to the lessons for additional practice.

Key Points

- Site Connectors are used to connect routing groups when there is reliable bandwidth. X.400 connectors are used to connect routing groups when bandwidth is unreliable.

- The Migration Wizard cannot migrate existing account information. You must use the Active Directory Migration Tool to retain existing settings.

- To configure an X.400 connector, you must first create an X.400 transport stack.

- Synchronizing with Lotus Notes and Novell GroupWise is a two-part process. Configuring the Connector for Lotus Notes or the Connector for Novell GroupWise synchronizes account and message data, but you must also configure a Calendar Connector in order to synchronize calendar data.

Key Terms

security identifier (SID)   A SID is an attribute of a user account that uniquely identifies it in a Windows domain. A SID is unique and is used only once, so if you delete and recreate an account with all the same data, the operating system sees them as two different accounts. Because SIDs are unique, if you migrate a user account using the Migration Wizard and a new account is created in the target domain, you will have to recreate all the security settings manually.

X.400   A standards-based messaging system that is most commonly used outside of the United States. Exchange Server 2003 is X.400-compliant and can communicate with any X.400-compliant messaging system.

access control list (ACL)   ACLs define the security settings that are attached to an object in Active Directory. Every object has an ACL, which is used to determine what objects have permissions to the object and what level of permissions they have. The Migration Wizard is not able to migrate ACL settings.

source domain and target domain   When you use either the Active Directory Migration Tool or the Migration Wizard, you define a source domain that contains the accounts and mailboxes you are migrating and a target domain that is the destination for the migration.

Questions and Answers

Page
5-24
Lesson 1 Review

1. You are the Exchange Server administrator for Litware, Inc. You have installed an Exchange Server 2003 server in the existing Exchange Server 5.5 organization, and you are trying to migrate the mailboxes over to the new server. You run the Migration Wizard on the Exchange Server 2003 server and select to migrate from Exchange Server 5.5, but you find that you are unable to do so. Why would this happen?

   The Migration Wizard is able to move mailboxes only between servers in different organizations. It cannot be used to move mailboxes between servers within the same organization. To accomplish this, you would use the Active Directory Users And Computers console and select Move Mailbox from the Exchange Tasks menu of the user accounts with the mailboxes you want moved.

2. You need to migrate a server from Exchange Server 5.5 to Exchange Server 2003, but you know that you cannot perform an in-place upgrade in this situation. Since Exchange Server 5.5 with SP4 is running on Windows 2000 Server with SP4, you decide to do an interim in-place upgrade from Exchange Server 5.5 to Exchange 2000 Server, and then you will upgrade Exchange 2000 Server directly to Exchange Server 2003. You install Exchange 2000 Server successfully and verify that users are able to log on and access mail, and then you immediately insert the Exchange Server 2003 installation CD and run Setup. However, Setup fails. What is the most likely cause?

   Upgrading from Exchange 2000 Server requires SP3. In this instance, you successfully upgraded Exchange Server 5.5, so there are no permissions problems, and the version of Windows supports Exchange Server 2003. Once you install the latest service pack for Exchange 2000 Server, you will be able to perform the in-place upgrade.

3. You install a new Exchange Server 2003 server into your existing Exchange Server 5.5 organization. You successfully migrate all the mailboxes to the new server, and users are able to access their mail from the new server without any problems. One afternoon, you shut down the Exchange Server 5.5 server, planning to use the machine later for something else. The next day, you receive many complaints that e-mail is working within the company, but mail is not being sent to or received from the Internet. What is the problem?

   In addition to moving mailboxes, you must also transfer any connectors that are in use. In this instance, the Internet Mail Service is still on the Exchange Server 5.5 server. First, you need to start the server back up, and then you need to configure an SMTP virtual server on the new Exchange Server 2003 server and schedule the time to switch the MX record in DNS to the new server when the downtime will have the least impact.

Page
5-37
Lesson 2 Review

1. You are trying to configure an X.400 connection between your Exchange Server 2003 organization and a remote X.400 messaging system running on a UNIX platform. After working with the administrator of the remote system to configure the connector, you test and find that your side of the connection receives messages fine, but on the remote end, the messages come out garbled. What do you need to do to fix the problem on your end?

By default, Allow Exchange Contents is enabled, which sends messages in Exchange's internal format. This works when the destination system is an Exchange Server system, but when it is a non-Exchange Server system, you have to clear the option in order for messages to be sent in the standard X.400 format.

2. You have set up directory synchronization between your Exchange Server 2003 organization and the Lotus Notes organization of a company that has recently merged with your company. E-mail is working fine and you are able to verify synchronization between Active Directory and Notes, but Outlook users are complaining that when they view the schedules of Notes users, the information is generally out of date. What can you do to correct the problem?

The Schedule tab of the Calendar Connector's properties must be configured to synchronize calendar data. The default setting is Never, which does not synchronize calendar data, and depending on what schedule you create, your data may become out of date before it synchronizes again.

3. You are the administrator of two Exchange Server 2003 routing groups that have been connected by a T-1 line. Lately, the circuit has been very inconsistent, sometimes very slow, and sometimes dropping connection altogether. Message traffic is suffering as a result. What can you do to improve the reliability of the message transfer over the unreliable connection?

When bandwidth is reliable, you typically use Site Connectors to connect Exchange Server 2003 routing groups. However, X.400 connectors can be used to connect Exchange Server routing groups, as well, and they are useful when bandwidth is unreliable. This is because the X.400 connector uses messaging-based data transfer rather than remote procedure call (RPC), which requires a reliable connection. By implementing an X.400 connector, you can improve message transfer reliability in this situation.

Page
5-41
Lesson 3 Review

1. Which of the following messaging systems is *not* supported by the Migration Wizard?

   a. Lotus cc:Mail

   b. SendMail

   c. Microsoft Mail

   d. Internet Mail

The correct answer is b.

2. You are trying to migrate a Lotus Notes server in the domain *adatum.com* to an Exchange Server 2003 organization in the *fabrikam.com* domain. You are performing a test migration using the Migration Wizard, and the wizard asks you to specify the name of your Lotus Notes server. After you do, you receive an error that the server cannot be contacted. You verify that the Notes server is running, and users in the *adatum.com* domain are not complaining about being unable to access e-mail. How would you troubleshoot this problem?

One of the most common problems when migrating across domains is having DNS set up incorrectly. You should first verify that you have connectivity and name resolution between the two domains by attempting to ping the Notes server by DNS name from the Exchange Server 2003 server. If you are able to resolve the DNS problem, you should be able to connect to the Notes server with the Migration Wizard.

3. You are involved in a migration of mail systems between two companies. Litware, Inc., which runs Exchange Server 2003, has acquired Contoso, which runs Novell GroupWise on the NetWare operating system. What type of information will you be able to migrate to Exchange Server 2003, and how will user accounts be handled?

The Migration Wizard will be able to effectively migrate all user mailbox data, but it will not be able to migrate NetWare user accounts intact. The Migration Wizard will create new user accounts for the NetWare users in Active Directory and then associate the migrated mailboxes with the new user accounts.

Page
5-42

Case Scenario Exercise: Requirement 1

1. Installing the Exchange Server 2003 version of the ADC requires a minimum of Windows 2000 Server SP3, but all servers except the new Server07 are running SP2. Before installing the ADC, should you update the service pack level to SP4 or simply upgrade to Windows Server 2003, since management wants to upgrade anyway? What influences your decision?

You will need to install SP3 or SP4 for Windows 2000 Server rather than upgrade to Windows Server 2003. Only Exchange Server 2003 is supported on Windows Server 2003, so upgrading your Windows 2000 Server systems to Windows Server 2003 will cause your Exchange Server 5.5 organization to fail.

2. Describe the process for upgrading Exchange Server 5.5 to Exchange Server 2003 at the corporate office.

First you need to connect the existing Exchange Server 5.5 organization to Active Directory and have a two-way Recipient Connection Agreement configured. But before doing so, you need to install SP3 or SP4 for Windows 2000 Server on at least the server hosting the Active Directory Connector Service. Once you have the two directories replicating, you can install Exchange Server 2003 onto Server07 and have it join the existing Exchange Server 5.5 organization. After the Exchange Server 2003 server is installed and the Site Replication Service is configured, you can begin moving mailboxes from the Exchange Server 5.5 server to the Exchange Server 2003 server by using the Active Directory Users And Computers console.

You should schedule the mailbox moves because users will need to update their Outlook profiles to point to the new server. After the mailboxes are moved, you would move any connectors from the Exchange Server 5.5 server, as well as any public folder stores and other resources being hosted on the Exchange Server 5.5 server. Once all of the resources are reallocated to Server07, shut down Server05. Then repeat the process to move resources from Server06 to Server07.

Page
5-43

Case Scenario Exercise: Requirement 2

1. What tool do you use to retain the SIDs while migrating Contoso's user accounts to Litware, Inc., and what do you need to do to migrate the existing user passwords?

   The Active Directory Migration Tool is designed to migrate user account data while retaining SID history and ACL settings. The Migration Wizard is not a full-featured account migration tool; it is unable to migrate existing account information. It can only create new accounts in the target domain or match mailboxes to existing accounts. In order to migrate passwords, you have to install the password migration DLL file using Pwdmig.exe from the Windows Server 2003 installation CD and then create a .pes file to be used during the password migration.

2. After successfully migrating Contoso's existing user accounts to the *litwareinc.com* domain, what do you need to do prior to running Dcpromo, removing the *contoso.com* domain, and joining Contoso's servers to the *litwareinc.com* domain?

   Migrating the user accounts with the Active Directory Migration Tool does not migrate the Exchange mailboxes. The mailboxes are still associated with Contoso user accounts, so you need to run the Migration Wizard to migrate the mailboxes to the Litware, Inc. Exchange Server organization and have the mailboxes associated with the migrated user accounts in the *litwareinc.com* domain. After running the Migration Wizard, users will need to log on to the *litwareinc.com* domain with their user accounts and edit their mail profiles to point to the new mail server.

6 Installing Microsoft Exchange Server 2003 Clusters and Front-End and Back-End Servers

Exam Objectives in this Chapter:

- Prepare the environment for the Microsoft Exchange Server 2003 deployment
- Install, configure, and troubleshoot Exchange Server 2003 in a clustered environment
- Manage, monitor, and troubleshoot Exchange Server clusters
- Manage and troubleshoot front-end and back-end servers
- Monitor, manage, and troubleshoot infrastructure performance

Why This Chapter Matters

Messaging systems are often a "mission critical" network service within an organization. Therefore, minimizing the downtime of the e-mail servers is one of the top priorities of a network administrator. For companies that require the ultimate in performance and reliability, Exchange Server 2003 supports being installed on network load balanced and clustered servers, which use redundant hardware resources to ensure that there is not a single point of failure and that the applications that run on them have as close to 100 percent uptime as possible. Another performance-maximizing benefit of Exchange Server 2003 is that it supports front-end and back-end architecture, which was introduced in Chapter 3, "Configuring a Microsoft Exchange Server 2003 Infrastructure."

This chapter focuses on Exchange Server organizations designed to support thousands of users with a server architecture that is more advanced than has been previously discussed. It is important to be just as comfortable working with Exchange Server 2003 in an enterprise clustered environment supporting thousands of users as in a small single-server environment supporting a few dozen users.

Lessons in this Chapter:

- Lesson 1: Installing Exchange Server 2003 in a Clustered Environment 6-3

- Lesson 2: Managing an Exchange Server 2003 Cluster. 6-19

- Lesson 3: Installing Exchange Server 2003 in a Front-End and
  Back-End Configuration. 6-29

Before You Begin

In order to complete the exercises in this chapter, you will need the following hardware and software:

- Two Microsoft Windows Server 2003 servers installed into the *tailspintoys.com* Active Directory domain. Server01 should be a domain controller, and Server02 should be a member server. Server01 must have two network cards.

- Exchange Server 2003, Enterprise Edition

Lesson 1: Installing Exchange Server 2003 in a Clustered Environment

Clustering servers is one of the most common techniques for providing hardware and software redundancy for an application such as Exchange Server 2003. By creating a cluster, you ensure that there is no single point of failure with your server hardware that would result in e-mail services going offline. Clustering also allows you to take one node offline for maintenance (for example, to reboot after installing a service pack or to upgrade hardware) while allowing the other nodes to continue servicing client computer requests.

Clustering does not protect against poor network administration practices and poorly configured software, nor does it help if you have a catastrophic event, such as a flood or tornado, physically destroy the servers. However, a properly implemented cluster of Windows Server 2003 servers can result in significantly improved uptime for the Exchange Server services.

After this lesson, you will be able to

- Understand the basics of Network Load Balancing and Microsoft Cluster Service
- Understand how Exchange Server 2003 is supported on the Microsoft Cluster Service
- Install Exchange Server 2003 on a Windows Server 2003 server cluster

Estimated lesson time: 90 minutes

Network Load Balancing and Microsoft Cluster Service

Note   This lesson provides an overview of clustering technologies as they relate to deploying Exchange Server 2003, but it is not intended to be an exhaustive planning and deployment guide. Clustering on a real-world network requires careful resource planning and is more involved than this lesson covers. It is recommended that you consult additional resources, such as the Microsoft Windows Server 2003 Resource Kit, prior to deploying clustering technology in a production environment.

Microsoft supports two types of clustering with its clustering technologies, Network Load Balancing and Microsoft Cluster Service. This can cause confusion for IT professionals who are not familiar with the specific aspects of each technology. The goal of the technologies is to ensure that the failure of one physical server does not result in a network service or application becoming unavailable to client computers, but the two clustering services achieve this goal in fundamentally different ways.

Network Load Balancing

The first clustering technology is Network Load Balancing, which is available with any version of Windows Server 2003. Network Load Balancing is configured through the Network Load Balancing Manager, which is located in the Administrative Tools program menu. Network Load Balancing runs as a driver in Microsoft Windows and distributes incoming requests across each node in the cluster. A cluster using Network Load Balancing can contain as few as two nodes and up to 32 nodes. The primary purpose of Network Load Balancing is to load balance by distributing Transmission Control Protocol/Internet Protocol (TCP/IP) traffic among each server node in a cluster. To client computers, the cluster is seen as a single resource and is addressed by a single Internet Protocol (IP) address (though each node also retains its own unique IP address). However, even though the cluster is seen as a single resource, applications are installed individually on each node. For example, if you have a cluster consisting of four servers running Exchange Server 2003, each server node would have Exchange Server 2003 installed on it. For applications that are load balancing–aware, such as Exchange Server 2003, when one of the nodes fails or goes offline, the load is automatically distributed to other nodes in the cluster. When the server node is brought back online, it automatically resumes functioning in the cluster without any additional intervention.

Note   It is worth noting that Network Load Balancing is not "clustering" in the traditional sense of the word, though it is considered a clustering technology. A traditional cluster, discussed later in this chapter, involves multiple systems acting as a single unit with complete failover capabilities.

Note   Network Load Balancing is also supported on Windows 2000 Advanced Server, Windows 2000 Datacenter Server, and Windows NT 4 Advanced Server. There are some differences in the functionality of Network Load Balancing among previous versions of Windows and Windows Server 2003 server versions. In this chapter, we will focus exclusively on clustering in Windows Server 2003.

Because of its design and function, Network Load Balancing is well suited to scaling Web and FTP types of applications, where the application service being provided should always be available and able to handle heavy traffic loads.

Network Load Balancing by default operates in Unicast mode, which means that the cluster is seen as one physical IP host on the network, and each node shares a common network Media Access Control (MAC) address. You can also configure Network Load Balancing to operate in Multicast mode, which allows each cluster node to be seen by its own MAC and IP addresses on the network. There are advantages and disadvantages of each mode, depending on your network environment and specific needs.

An advantage that Network Load Balancing has over Microsoft Cluster Service is that no special hardware is required to support a multiple-node cluster. In the next section of this chapter, you will learn about Microsoft Cluster Service, which requires that special shared resources are used in a multi-node arrangement. A cluster using Network Load Balancing can consist of typical servers, with one or more network adapters in each. In addition, you can have a cluster using Network Load Balancing that includes multiple Windows Server operating systems, for example, one node running Windows 2000 Advanced Server and another node running Windows Server 2003, Enterprise Edition.

Another advantage of Network Load Balancing is that the servers are not required to be members of a domain, which makes Network Load Balancing particularly well suited for use on perimeter networks as front-end servers, relaying communications to back-end servers inside of a firewall.

Network Load Balancing can work with servers containing only one network card, but there are advantages to using two network cards. Not only does it increase the fault tolerance of the individual server, but it allows for communication between cluster nodes in the default Unicast mode. Since cluster nodes share a common IP address and MAC address, they are normally unable to communicate with each other. A second network adapter allows you to configure a private network between cluster nodes, thus enabling communication.

Network Load Balancing works by using a concept called *heartbeats*, which are network packets emitted every second by each node in a cluster. When a node in a cluster goes offline, the heartbeats stop. By default, after five seconds (which equates to five heartbeats) the remaining nodes in the cluster begin a process called *convergence* to remove the unresponsive server. The process also redirects incoming client requests to other nodes for handling. The downside to this method is that the Network Load Balancing service cannot detect when a specific service is offline on a server; it only detects when the server itself is unresponsive. This can cause traffic to be directed to a server that is unable to service the request.

Another disadvantage to using Network Load Balancing is that it works only with TCP/IP, which is not a problem with most networks but can be something to consider with networks that employ other protocols, such as NWLink.

Microsoft Cluster Service

Microsoft Cluster Service is the second type of clustering technology provided by Windows Server 2003. Conceptually, it is similar in some ways to Network Load Balancing. Specifically, the Cluster Service uses heartbeats to monitor the status of nodes in a cluster, and a cluster appears as a single network resource to client computers. Where the Cluster Service differs significantly from Network Load Balancing is that the Cluster Service is application service–aware, meaning it can monitor the "health" of an application and not only the server itself. The cluster storage device has specific requirements. It cannot consist of any of the following:

- IDE disks
- Software RAID
- Dynamic volumes
- Mount points/mounted volumes
- Encrypting File System
- Remote Storage

Server clusters using the Clustering Service can be set up as one of three different cluster configurations:

- **Single Node server clusters**   Can be configured with or without external cluster storage devices. For Single Node server clusters without an external cluster storage device, the local disk is configured as the cluster storage device.

- **Single Quorum Device server clusters**   Have two or more nodes and are configured so that every node is attached to one or more shared storage devices, such as an external array of Small Computer System Interface (SCSI) disks. The cluster configuration data is stored on a single cluster storage device, known as the *quorum* device.

- **Majority Node Set server clusters**   Have two or more nodes but the nodes may or may not be attached to one or more cluster storage devices. The cluster configuration data is stored on multiple disks across the cluster, and the Cluster Service makes sure that this data is kept consistent across the different disks.

For Single Quorum Device and Majority Node Set server clusters, there are different ways in which you can configure the Cluster Service. How you set up the cluster will depend on your specific needs for *failover*, which is the process in which application services are moved to another node in the cluster. *Failback* defines how application services are moved back to the original server node once it is back online. The available modes of operation in Windows Server 2003 are:

- **N-node Failover Pairs**   Applications in this mode are configured to failover only between two specified server pairs.

- **N+I Hot-Standby Server**   Commonly referred to as Active/Passive mode. In a two-node cluster in this mode, one active node handles all client requests, while the passive node monitors the active node. If the active node fails, the cluster fails over to the passive node, which begins servicing client requests. N+I refers to scaling the model to larger node clusters and having N number of active nodes and I number of passive nodes. This model tends to be less popular with management because of the perceived waste of resources having server resources sitting idle and being utilized only when another server fails. However, it is the most scalable and reliable.

- **Failover Ring**   An implementation also commonly referred to as Active/Active mode. In this model, all server nodes are active and servicing client requests. When a node fails, the cluster fails over the service to another active node. In a failover ring, the order of failover is predetermined by the configuration defined by the administrator.

- **Random Failover**   This model is similar to the failover ring in that it is an Active/Active implementation, except in this model, when a node fails it is randomly failed over to another active node. By randomly failing over to another active node, the administrative burden of having to define a failover ring is removed.

The Cluster Service requires Windows Server 2003, Enterprise Edition or Windows Server 2003, Datacenter Edition. Up to eight-node clusters are supported, with the caveat that beyond two nodes, each node in the cluster must be running the same operating system version. Unlike with Network Load Balancing, you cannot mix operating system versions in a cluster. However, a two-node cluster can use a combination of Windows 2000 Advanced Server, Windows 2000 Datacenter Server, Windows Server 2003, Enterprise Edition, and Windows Server 2003, Datacenter Edition.

Unlike Network Load Balancing, the Cluster Service is application- and service-aware, which means it can monitor at the service level rather than only being able to test for general server responsiveness. This makes the Cluster Service well suited to database applications such as Microsoft SQL Server and Exchange Server.

Server nodes running the Cluster Service are required to be members of a domain. This requirement makes them better suited to functioning as back-end servers inside a firewall than as front-end servers on a perimeter network.

Setting up the networking side of the Cluster Service has stricter requirements than Network Load Balancing. Cluster Service nodes are required to have two or more network adapters and to be connected to a minimum of two local area networks (LANs). This is to prevent a network failure from being a single point of failure for the cluster and also because the Cluster Service uses an internal private network to communicate between nodes of the cluster and an external public network to communicate with client computers that the cluster services. You can also have a mixed network that carries public and private network traffic. A common configuration of network adapters is *teaming*, where multiple adapters are joined through software to function as a single unit, with a single MAC address and a single IP address. If multiple network adapters are configured in a teaming configuration, at least one nonteamed network adapter must be configured for the private network that the server nodes communicate on. Furthermore, all server nodes in the cluster must belong to the same IP subnet, both the private and public networks. It is recommended that all server nodes in a cluster use identical make and model of network adapters.

Server nodes using the Cluster Service can be either domain controllers or member servers, but they must all belong to the same domain. In addition, the Cluster Service requires a minimum of two Domain Name System (DNS) servers in a domain for use. If you create a two-node cluster and those are the only two servers in the domain, you must make both DNS servers and configure each node to use itself for the primary DNS server and use the other node as the secondary DNS server.

Exchange Server 2003 and Clustering

It is clear that both Network Load Balancing and Microsoft Cluster Service provide the ability to create highly available servers that are much more reliable than a typical single-server configuration. However, since the technologies serve different purposes, it is important to choose the best technology for an Exchange Server 2003 cluster.

> **Important** Clustering requires Exchange Server 2003, Enterprise Edition. You cannot configure Exchange Server 2003, Standard Edition, to use Windows clustering technologies. This can be confusing because Windows Server 2003, Standard Edition, supports up to four-node clustering.

The primary factor in favor of using Network Load Balancing is that it does not require any special hardware; you do not need an external shared storage device for the cluster. The primary factor in favor of using the Cluster Service is that it is application service–aware, so you can failover when a service fails and not only when a server fails to respond with heartbeats. This typically becomes the deciding factor because for organizations large enough to implement clustering technology, the need to be able to failover when one of the Exchange Server services stops is greater than the associated cost of the shared external storage device. Therefore, the Cluster Service is recommended for Exchange Server 2003 clusters rather than Network Load Balancing.

It is important to note that the Cluster Service does not load balance applications as Network Load Balancing does, because the Cluster Service is designed to serve a different purpose. Clusters using the Cluster Service failover their application services when a node fails. Clusters using Network Load Balancing don't failover but simply redirect the flow of traffic to an active node when one node fails. In addition, the Cluster Service is designed with clustering database–driven applications such as SQL Server and Exchange Server in mind. The logistics of trying to have a mailbox store, for example, partitioned across multiple cluster nodes are impossible given the structure of Exchange Server. You can manually load balance by placing services on different cluster nodes, but services are single instance with the Cluster Service.

Active/Active and Active/Passive Exchange Server 2003 Clusters

There are additional considerations when using the Cluster Service with Exchange Server 2003. It is recommended that you use an active/passive model for your cluster because active/active clusters are limited to two nodes with Exchange Server 2003. Another limitation of active/active clusters is that they can only support a maximum of 1900 concurrent client connections. Active/passive clusters scale better in that they can consist of up to eight nodes, and therefore they scale to significantly higher numbers than a two-node active/active cluster. In addition, active/passive clusters are generally more reliable because when a failover occurs, it goes to an idle node rather than to a node that is already servicing client requests.

Exchange Server 2003 supports an active/active configuration for all of its components, with one exception—the Message Transfer Agent (MTA). The MTA is an Exchange Server 2003 service that serves a couple of purposes. The first purpose is to manage connections between Exchange Server 2003 and X.400-based messaging systems. The second purpose is to manage connections and gateways built from the Exchange Development Kit. The MTA is always active/passive; there can be only one MTA running at a given time on a cluster. The MTA is created on the first server node of a cluster, and subsequent server nodes depend on that MTA. If the server node running the MTA fails, the service fails over to another node.

Exchange Server 2003 Clustering Components

Exchange Server 2003 is a clustering-aware application, and as such, it configures its components to use a cluster when it is installed on one. A resource dynamic-link library (DLL) file, Exres.dll, is installed and communicates with the Cluster Service. Exchange Server 2003 uses Windows Server 2003 cluster groups, which contain cluster resources such as IP addresses and other network settings. An Exchange Server 2003 virtual server is installed, which contains cluster resources such as an IP address, physical disk resources, and the Exchange System Attendant service, which in turn installs other required Exchange Server 2003 services.

Note   A "virtual server" on a cluster is not the same as an IP virtual server, which provides services, such as Post Office Protocol 3 (POP3), Simple Mail Transport Protocol (SMTP), Hypertext Transfer Protocol (HTTP), Outlook Web Access (OWA), and so on, through Exchange Server 2003. IP virtual servers are the focus of Chapter 9, "Virtual Servers." With respect to clustering, a virtual server is an instance of the application configured on a node of the cluster, using the cluster resources listed in the previous paragraph.

Network Components A typical installation of a two-node Exchange Server 2003 cluster includes a public network used by clients to connect to Exchange Server 2003 virtual servers and a private network for server node communication within the cluster. A typical two-node cluster has, at a minimum, seven IP addresses and five NetBIOS names and assumes the following configuration:

- Each server node of the cluster has two static IP addresses (the public and private network connection IP addresses of each physical member server) and one NetBIOS name.

- The cluster itself has a static IP address and a NetBIOS name.

- Each Exchange Server 2003 virtual server has a static IP address and a NetBIOS name.

> **Important** It is strongly recommended that you use a private cluster network and static IP addresses in any Exchange Server 2003 cluster deployment. While it is possible to deploy clustering using only a public network or Dynamic Host Configuration Protocol (DHCP) to assign and renew cluster node IP addresses, this is not recommended. Using DHCP creates a point of failure because if your DHCP server is unable to renew the public IP addresses, clients will not be able to connect to the cluster. This would result in the entire cluster failing. Also, if your public network fails, your server nodes cannot communicate with each other, and as a result, in the case of a server node failing, cluster resources would not be able to failover to another node.

Disk Components The most important disk in the cluster is the disk designated as the quorum disk resource. The quorum disk resource maintains configuration data about the cluster and also provides persistent physical storage across system failures. Because the cluster configuration is stored on this disk, all nodes in the cluster must be able to communicate with the node that owns it. In order to meet these requirements, the disk must be a shared external resource, where each node can be physically connected to it. The shared external disk resource used by the cluster for the quorum disk must be physically attached to a shared bus and must be accessible from all nodes in the cluster.

The quorum disk stores the most current version of the cluster configuration database in the form of recovery logs and registry checkpoint files. These files contain node-independent storage of cluster configuration and state data. When a node joins or forms a cluster, the Cluster Service updates the node's private copy of the configuration database. When a node joins an existing cluster, the Cluster Service retrieves the configuration data from the other active nodes. The Cluster Service uses the quorum disk resource recovery logs to

■ Guarantee that only one set of active, communicating nodes is allowed to operate as a cluster.

■ Enable a node to form a cluster only if it can gain control of the quorum disk resource.

■ Allow a node to join or remain in an existing cluster only if it can communicate with the node that controls the quorum resource.

Permissions

In order to create an Exchange Server 2003 cluster, the user account used to create the cluster must have certain permissions. First, the user account must have the ability to administer the cluster, which means it must be a member of the local Administrators group on the server nodes of the cluster that will host Exchange Server 2003. In order to create the first Exchange Server 2003 virtual server, the user account must have Exchange Full Administrator permissions at the organizational level. To create additional Exchange Server 2003 virtual servers, the user account must have Exchange Full Administrator permissions at the administrative group level that the server nodes belong to.

Storage Groups

Storage groups (discussed in detail in Chapter 7, "Managing Recipient Objects and Address Lists") are used in Exchange Server 2003 to create multiple mailbox stores and public folder stores for specific administrative purposes. Mailbox stores are databases that contain mailboxes, and public folder stores are databases that contain public folders. Exchange Server 2003, Enterprise Edition, supports a maximum of four storage groups on a server. This is a consideration when using clustering because if a server node fails, the node that its services failover to must be able to handle all its resources. For example, if Server01 has three storage groups and Server02 has two storage groups, and Server01 fails, Server02 will not be able to mount all of Server01's storage groups because it would exceed the limit of four. Therefore, in a two-node cluster, you will want to limit each Exchange Server 2003 virtual server to no more than two storage groups, even though each can support four.

Installing Exchange Server 2003 on a Windows Server 2003 Cluster

Installing Exchange Server 2003 on a cluster is similar to other installation processes with which you are now familiar. However, you must prepare the Windows Server 2003 cluster servers prior to installing Exchange Server 2003. Also, after installing Exchange Server 2003 on the nodes of the cluster, there are additional steps which are necessary to create the Exchange Server 2003 virtual servers.

Once the Windows Server 2003 cluster is configured, you must run ForestPrep and DomainPrep, as if you were installing on a single server, including the level of permissions required. Then, you install Exchange Server 2003 on each node of the cluster. When the installation is complete, you use the Cluster Administrator console to configure the Exchange Server 2003 virtual servers. In the practice at the end of this lesson, you will set up a cluster, install Exchange Server 2003 on the first node, and use Cluster Administrator to configure the Exchange Server 2003 virtual server.

To upgrade to Exchange Server 2003 on an existing cluster, you use a method known as a *rolling upgrade*. In this method, one server node is manually failed over to another node and upgraded, and then after the upgrade, the services are failed back. Upgrading in this manner, the cluster is never completely offline during the upgrade and continues to service client requests. Nodes are upgraded one at a time rather than all at once. Upgrading a previous version of Exchange Server to Exchange Server 2003 has all of the requirements that exist when upgrading single servers, as discussed in Chapter 5, "Migrating from Microsoft Exchange Server and Other Mail Systems."

Practice: Installing Exchange Server 2003 in a Clustered Environment

In this practice, you will configure a single-node Windows Server 2003 cluster and then install Exchange Server 2003 onto the cluster. This allows you to install Exchange Server 2003 on a cluster using a single server without the requirement of having the external shared disk resource. In the real world, this type of configuration is useful for testing cluster-aware applications prior to deploying them in a production environment.

Exercise 1: Configure a Windows Server 2003 Cluster

Before you begin, you will need to assign the two network adapters in Server01 to two different IP subnets. If you are installing Server01 onto an existing network, use an IP address on that network for the network adapter on the public network. Use a separate private IP address range for the private network address of the cluster node, such as 192.168.1.0/24, 176.16.1.0/24, or 10.1.1.0/24. Server01 will also need to have a second physical disk installed, formatted as NTFS and empty. This will become the quorum disk.

1. To start the Cluster Administrator console, click Start, point to Administrative Tools, and click Cluster Administrator. The Cluster Service is automatically installed on Windows Server 2003, but by default it is not configured.

2. When the Cluster Administrator console opens, it prompts you to choose a cluster connection to open. Since no cluster exists, click the drop-down list and click Create New Cluster. Click OK.

3. The New Server Cluster Wizard starts, and the Welcome page, shown in Figure 6-1, identifies the information you need in order to create the cluster. Click Next to continue.

Figure 6-1   Creating a new cluster

4. All nodes of a cluster must belong to the same domain, and the domain that the server you are running Cluster Administrator on is automatically selected. You must enter a name for the cluster on the Cluster Name And Domain page, shown in Figure 6-2, and then click Next to continue.

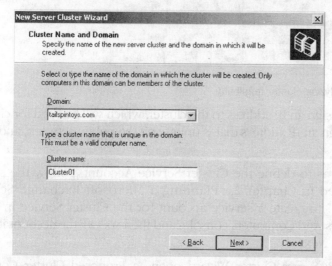

Figure 6-2   Specifying the name and domain of the cluster

5. The next step is to identify the server that will be the first node in the cluster. It will default to the server you are currently on, but you can choose another server,

if necessary. Click Advanced, and you will see that by default the new cluster will be created with a Typical (Full) configuration, but you have the option to select an Advanced (Minimum) configuration. Cancel this page and click Next to continue creating the cluster.

6. The next page is the Analyzing Configuration page, shown in Figure 6-3. The wizard analyzes the configuration of the server to determine cluster feasibility. A check mark next to an item indicates a successful configuration. A caution symbol indicates potential problems to be addressed. In this instance, the caution symbols represent the inability of the wizard to locate an external shared disk device for the quorum, which means a local (single-node) quorum disk will be used. You can click View Log or Details to get additional information about the analysis and even re-analyze if you correct a problem without exiting the wizard. Click Next to continue.

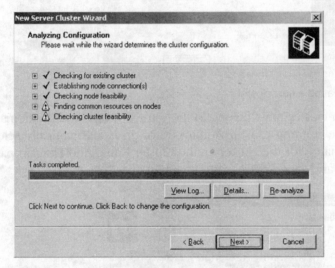

Figure 6-3   Analyzing cluster feasibility

7. You have to assign an IP address to the cluster, which will be used for cluster management. Assign an IP address that is unique on the public network, and then click Next.

8. The next step is to define the Cluster Service Account. Follow the same practices discussed in Chapter 2, "Planning a Microsoft Exchange Server 2003 Infrastructure," to create a service account for the Cluster Service in the Active Directory Users And Computers console, and then specify the account information here and click Next.

9. Next, the New Server Cluster Wizard opens a Proposed Cluster Configuration page, shown in Figure 6-4. You can click Quorum to see the type of quorum configuration that will be created, and you can click View Log to view detailed information. Click Next.

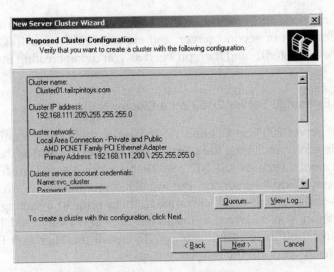

Figure 6-4   The Proposed Cluster Configuration page

10. The wizard will begin to create the new cluster. You can monitor its progress, and then click Next when it is complete.

11. When the Completing The New Server Cluster Wizard page appears, you have successfully configured the first server node in the cluster. You can click View Log to see detailed information about the creation process or click Finish to exit. After you click Finish, Cluster Administrator will automatically connect to the new cluster, as shown in Figure 6-5.

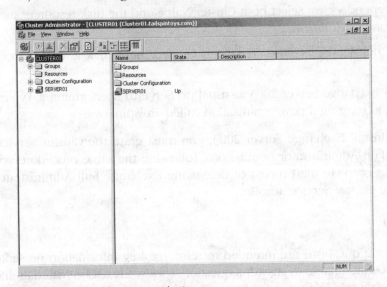

Figure 6-5   The new server cluster

To Create the second node in the cluster, you complete a very similar process. Start Cluster Administrator on your second server, and choose Add Nodes To Cluster. You can browse and select Cluster01, and then proceed as you did in creating the first node in the cluster.

Exercise 2: Install Exchange Server 2003 on a Cluster Node

Installing Exchange Server 2003 on a cluster node has the same basic requirements as installing on a single server, including the permissions required as well as the Windows Server 2003 components, such as ASP.NET, SMTP, Network News Transfer Protocol (NNTP), and the World Wide Web service. Pre-installation requirements are covered in detail in Chapter 2 and you will need to complete them prior to installing Exchange Server 2003. In addition, you will need to install the Microsoft Distributed Transaction Coordinator by using the Cluster Administrator. To install the Microsoft Distributed Transaction Coordinator, perform the following steps:

1. Start the Cluster Administrator console, if it is not already started.

2. Expand the Groups container, right-click Cluster Group, point to New, and then click Resource.

3. For the name, type **MSDTC**, and select Distributed Transaction Coordinator from the Resource Type list. Click Next to continue.

4. On the Possible Owners page, Server01 should already be selected. Click Next to continue.

5. For Dependencies, select both Cluster Name and the disk resource, such as Local Quorum. Click Finish.

6. After the MSDTC resource has been created, right-click it, and then click Bring Online.

7. Install Exchange Server 2003 as usual on Server01, performing a Typical installation and creating a new organization called TailspinToys.

After you install Exchange Server 2003, you must grant the Cluster Service account Exchange Full Administrator permissions, following the same procedure you used in Chapter 3. Complete the process of delegating Exchange Full Administrator permissions to the Cluster Service account.

Lesson Review

The following questions are intended to reinforce key information presented in this lesson. If you are unable to answer a question, review the lesson materials and then try the question again. You can find answers to the questions in the "Questions and Answers" section at the end of this chapter.

1. You are a senior network administrator for a fast-growing company that wants to implement a clustering technology in order to ensure the continued availability of a Web application if one of the Web servers fails and, more importantly, to handle the increased traffic that is expected in the future. You are asked whether you should deploy Network Load Balancing or the Cluster Service for this application, and why you would choose one over the other.

_____

_____

2. You are setting up an Exchange Server 2003 virtual server on the Cluster Service, using a two-node active/active configuration. As you read through a planning checklist, you identify how the services will failover. Which Exchange Server 2003 service cannot be set to an active/active configuration like the other services?

   a. Microsoft Exchange Information Store

   b. Microsoft Exchange System Attendant

   c. Microsoft Exchange Message Transfer Agent

   d. Microsoft Exchange Routing Service

3. You are the administrator of an Exchange Server 2003 cluster that consists of Server01 and Server02 in a two-node active/passive configuration. The servers have the following TCP/IP configuration:

   Server01 (active)

   ❑ Local Area Connection 1 (Public) — IP Address — 10.1.1.250, DHCP

   ❑ Local Area Connection 2 (Private) — IP Address — 192.168.254.1, static

   Server02 (passive)

   ❑ Local Area Connection 1 (Public) — IP Address — 10.1.1.251, DHCP

   ❑ Local Area Connection 2 (Private) — IP Address — 192.168.254.2, static

   Over a holiday weekend, a Windows Server 2003 domain controller fails due to a faulty hard drive. On Tuesday morning, you order a hard drive for the server, and it is scheduled for delivery on Wednesday. Tuesday afternoon, users begin to report that e-mail is down. You check the cluster, and it appears at first glance to be functioning properly internally. You manually fail over the cluster to the second node, but the problem is not corrected. Where should you look next to troubleshoot the problem?

_____

_____

Lesson Summary

- Exchange Server 2003, Enterprise Edition, is required in order to use clustering technologies.

- Two clustering technologies exist in Windows Server 2003: Network Load Balancing and the Cluster Service.

- Network Load Balancing is used primarily to scale applications by providing load balancing functionality.

- The Cluster Service does not provide load balancing but instead provides continual application service availability through failover and failback functions.

- Exchange Server 2003 supports two-node active/active clusters and up to eight-node active/passive clusters with at least one passive node.

Lesson 2: Managing an Exchange Server 2003 Cluster

Once you have installed Exchange Server 2003 on a Windows Server 2003 cluster, there are additional administrative tasks to perform in order to create the Exchange Server 2003 virtual server. Even after you have set up the Exchange Server 2003 virtual server, you can manage details about the cluster and the services that run on it. Some of the settings include how long a service will be unresponsive before restarting, the time-frame after which to allow a failover, and whether to allow automatic or manual failback.

After this lesson, you will be able to

- Create an Exchange Server 2003 virtual server
- Manage Exchange Server 2003 clustered services

Estimated lesson time: 60 minutes

Creating an Exchange Server 2003 Virtual Server

The final step in configuring Exchange Server 2003 to run on a Windows Server 2003 cluster is to create the Exchange Server 2003 virtual servers. The number of Exchange Server 2003 virtual servers you need to create depends on whether you are creating an active/passive or an active/active cluster. If you are setting up a two-node active/passive Exchange Server 2003 cluster, you will be setting up one Exchange Server 2003 virtual server. If you are setting up a two-node active/active Exchange Server 2003 cluster, you will set up two Exchange Server 2003 virtual servers, since both server nodes will be active. You must repeat this step for each active node that will run an Exchange Server 2003 virtual server. In the practice at the end of this lesson, you will create an Exchange Server 2003 virtual server on Server01.

Each Exchange Server 2003 virtual server consists of a static IP address, a unique network name, a shared physical disk, and an Exchange System Attendant resource. You create each resource individually, in turn, in Cluster Administrator. Using Cluster Administrator, first you create the network and disk resources, and then you create the Exchange System Attendant resource. After you successfully create the Exchange System Attendant resource, Exchange System Attendant automatically creates all the other resources for the Exchange Server 2003 virtual server. The Exchange System Attendant resource creates the following resources, which are shown in the Cluster Administrator window in Figure 6-6:

- Exchange Message Transfer Agent Instance
- Exchange Information Store Instance
- Exchange Routing Service Instance
- Exchange MS Search Instance

- SMTP Virtual Server Instance

- Exchange HTTP Virtual Service Instance

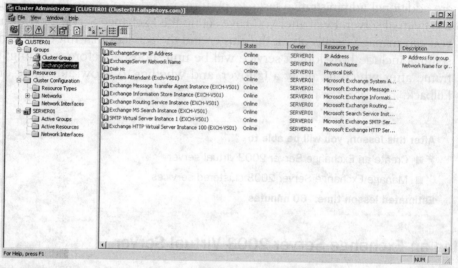

Figure 6-6   An Exchange Server 2003 virtual server configuration

The Message Transfer Agent Instance resource is created only in the first Exchange Server 2003 virtual server added to a cluster. All Exchange Server 2003 virtual servers in the cluster share the single Message Transfer Agent Instance resource.

Managing Exchange Server 2003 Clustered Services

After creating the Exchange Server 2003 virtual server, there are additional configuration options for determining how the cluster handles the Exchange Server services. These configuration options are managed in Cluster Administrator. In most cases, the default settings are adequate, but should you need to change a setting, you can.

One set of settings you might configure is how the group fails over and fails back. Figures 6-7 and 6-8 show the Failover and Failback property dialog boxes for the Exchange Server 2003 virtual server. On the Failover page, you can configure the number of times the node is allowed to failover (Threshold) during the period, which is defined in hours. If the node exceeds the threshold, it is taken offline and the Cluster Service does not attempt to bring the server back online. On the Failback dialog box, you see that the default behavior is to not allow automatic failback when the server node returns to online operation. If no failback policy is configured, the group will run on the alternate node until another failover situation occurs that causes the group to failover to the original node. In order to have resources fail back, you must configure a policy. When you configure a failback policy, you have the option to fail back immediately or only between certain hours. Immediate failback can be undesirable because it could occur in the middle of the business day. During a failback, the active services are taken offline while they are failed back to the original node, at which point they will be brought back online. The failback process can take up to 15 minutes, which will result in a disruption of service. Therefore, it is generally better to configure a failback period after business hours or during a slow time on the network. To set the time on the policy, use the twenty-four-hour system of expressing time, with 0 being 12:00 A.M. and 23 being 11:00 P.M.

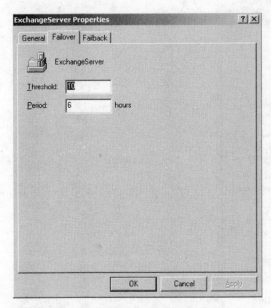

Figure 6-7   Server node failover properties

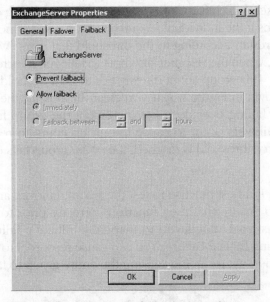

Figure 6-8   Server node failback properties

You can also right-click any of the resources listed in Cluster Administrator (such as those shown in Figure 6-6) and click Properties to access property tabs, which allow you to configure dependencies if you need to make changes for a resource. If you click the Advanced tab in the properties of any resource, you will see a dialog box like that in Figure 6-9.

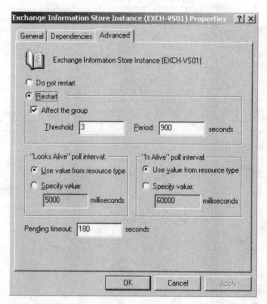

Figure 6-9   Advanced resource properties

On the Advanced tab, you configure settings for only the specific resource. In this example, the properties of the Exchange Information Store Instance are being edited. Here, you can define what happens if the individual resource fails on a server node. By default, resources will attempt to restart according to the threshold that is set. With the Affect The Group option selected, when the resource attempts to failover, it increments the group's failover count by one. This group count directly ties to the threshold set on the group's failover policy, as shown in Figure 6-7. If you clear the box for the Affect The Group option, the resource failing over does not increment the group failover count. When enough resource failovers occur to cause the group count to reach its threshold, or the individual resource threshold is reached, the entire group fails over to another node on the cluster.

When you first deploy a cluster, it is a best practice to test the restart, failover, and fail-back policies. This allows you to ensure that they function correctly prior to a real failure occurring. Cluster Administrator allows you to manually initiate a failure by right-clicking a resource and clicking Initiate Failure. You can cause resources to restart according to their restart policy this way, including causing the entire group to failover to another node.

Another way to test the failover policy is by manually stopping the cluster service on a server node. To do this, click the node you want to failover in the Cluster Administrator console, and then click the File menu and click Stop Cluster Service. This will cause an immediate node failure and cause the configured failover to occur. You can then start the service again and test the failback policy, if one is configured.

Practice: Managing an Exchange Server 2003 Cluster

In this practice, you will create an Exchange Server 2003 virtual server and, in the process, create the necessary IP address resource, network name resource, disk resource, and System Attendant resource.

Exercise 1: Create an Exchange Server 2003 Virtual Server

The first task is to create a new group for the Exchange Server 2003 resources. While you could use the existing Cluster Group set up by Windows, it is recommended that you store application resources in their own groups.

1. On the first node of the cluster, from the Start menu, point to Administrative Tools, and then click Cluster Administrator. Right-click the Groups container, point to New, and then click Group.

2. The New Group Wizard starts. In the Name field, type **ExchangeServer** for the name of this Exchange Server 2003 cluster group.

3. On the Preferred Owners page, verify that there is either one or no cluster nodes listed in the Preferred Owners box, and then click Finish. The new Exchange Server 2003 virtual server (cluster group) is displayed under Groups.

> **Note**   If the Preferred Owners page contains both nodes in the cluster, configure the order of the list on the second server node as the opposite of the list on the first node. For example, if the Preferred Owners list on the first node lists Server01 and then Server02, configure the second node to list Server02 and then Server01.

Exercise 2: Create an IP Address Resource

1. Right-click the Exchange Server 2003 virtual server, point to New, and then click Resource.

2. The New Resource Wizard starts. On the New Resource page, type **ExchangeServer IP Address**.

3. From the Resource Type drop-down list, select IP Address. Verify that the Group box contains the name of your cluster group, as shown in Figure 6-10, and then click Next.

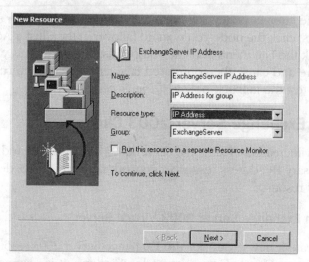

Figure 6-10   Configuring the resource type

4. On the Possible Owners page, verify that Server01, which has Exchange Server 2003 installed on it, appears in the Possible Owners list, and then click Next.

5. On the Dependencies page, verify that no resources appear in the Resource Dependencies list, and then click Next.

6. On the TCP/IP Address Parameters page, in the Address box, type the static IP address of the Exchange Server 2003 virtual server. This should be an address that works on your public network, yet is unique to any other already assigned to the physical server or to the cluster.

7. Verify that the subnet mask for the Exchange Server 2003 virtual server is correct and that the LAN connection to the public network is selected, and then click Finish.

Exercise 3: Create a Network Name Resource

1. Right-click the Exchange Server 2003 virtual server, point to New, and then click Resource.

2. The New Resource Wizard launches. On the New Resource page, type **ExchangeServer Network Name**.

3. In the Resource Type list, click Network Name, and then click Next.

4. On the Possible Owners page, verify that Server01 appears in the Possible Owners box, and then click Next.

5. On the Dependencies page, click the IP Address resource for this Exchange Server 2003 virtual server in the Available Resources list, and then click Add. Click Next.

6. On the Network Name Parameters page, shown in Figure 6-11, in the Name field, type a name, such as **Exch-VS01** (Exchange Virtual Server 01), for the Exchange Server 2003 virtual server. This name is the network name that identifies the Exchange Server 2003 virtual server on your network. Click Finish when done.

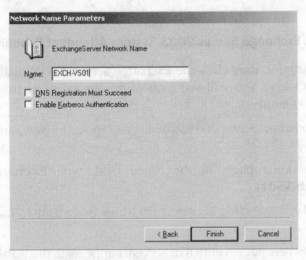

Figure 6-11   Configuring the network name

Exercise 4: Add a Disk Resource to the Exchange Server 2003 Virtual Server

In this exercise, you will create a new disk resource. You must create a disk resource for each disk that you want to associate with the Exchange Server 2003 virtual server. Disk resources must be SCSI disks and connected through SCSI or Fibre channel. If you attempt to use an Integrated Device Electronics (IDE) disk, you will be able to create the resource but not to bring it online later. If the resource you want to add already exists in another group, you can move it from the other group. If the disk resource you want to add does not yet exist, you must create it.

1. Right-click the Exchange Server 2003 virtual server, point to New, and then click Resource.

2. On the New Resource page, type **Disk <*drive letter*>**, where *drive letter* is a logical drive on the disk. For the description, use something descriptive, such as **Disk F: Log Files** (substitute the drive letter you use).

3. In the Resource Type list, click Physical Disk, and then click Next.

4. On the Possible Owners page, verify that Server01 appears in the Possible Owners list, and then click Next.

5. On the Dependencies page, verify that no resources appear in the Resource Dependencies list, and then click Next.

6. On the Disk Parameters page, select the disk you want. If the disk does not appear here, it means that either another cluster group already has defined a resource for it or it was not successfully installed.

7. Click Finish. The disk resource appears as a resource of the Exchange Server 2003 virtual server.

Exercise 5: Create an Exchange Server 2003 System Attendant Resource

1. In Cluster Administrator, right-click the Exchange Server 2003 virtual server, and then click Bring Online. You will see each of the resources go from Offline to Online Pending to Online.

2. Right-click the Exchange Server 2003 virtual server, point to New, and then click Resource.

3. On the New Resource page, in the Name field, type **Exchange System Attendant - (Exch-VS01)**.

4. In the Resource Type list, click Microsoft Exchange System Attendant, and then click Next.

5. On the Possible Owners page, verify that Server01 appears in the Possible Owners list, and then click Next.

6. On the Dependencies page, select both the Network Name and Physical Disk resources for this Exchange Server 2003 virtual server in the Available Resources list, and then click Add. Click Next.

7. On the Data Directory page, verify the data directory location. You must verify that this location points to the shared physical disk resource assigned to this Exchange Server 2003 virtual server. Exchange Server 2003 will use the drive you select in this step for storing the transaction log files, the default public store files, and the mailbox store files (Pub1.edb, Pub1.stm, Priv1.edb, and Priv1.stm). Click Finish.

8. Right-click the Exchange Server 2003 virtual server, and then click Bring Online.

If you are creating an active/active cluster, you must repeat these exercises again on the second node, such as Server02. In an active/passive configuration, you must repeat the processes on each server node in the cluster that will be active. If you are creating a two-node active/passive Exchange Server 2003 cluster, you are done. If you start Exchange System Manager and expand the Servers container, you will see the new Exchange Server 2003 virtual server, Exch-VS01, as shown in Figure 6-12.

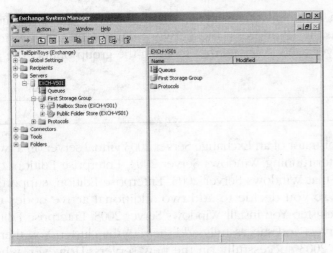

Figure 6-12   The new Exchange Server 2003 virtual server

Lesson Review

The following questions are intended to reinforce key information presented in this lesson. If you are unable to answer a question, review the lesson materials and then try the question again. You can find answers to the questions in the "Questions and Answers" section at the end of this chapter.

1. You are the administrator of a two-node active/passive Exchange Server 2003 cluster that is currently not in production but is being tested prior to being put into production. You are testing your failover policies, so you initiate failures on several resources until the group failure threshold is reached. The server successfully fails over the group to the formerly passive node, and the previously active node becomes passive. You want the group to fail back to the original service, but after an hour of waiting, the group is still running on the second node. It is late in the day so you decide to go home and deal with it the next day, since the cluster is not yet in production. The next morning, you notice that the cluster is still running on the second node, and you can't find a command in the Cluster Administrator GUI to initiate a failback. What can you do to get the group back on the original server node?

_____

_____

2. You are setting up a test server to practice with the cluster service as a prelude to a later cluster deployment. You don't have any real servers available, but you know that you can use a single system and a local quorum disk resource for testing purposes. You set up a desktop workstation class machine that has a SCSI C drive and an IDE D drive and 512 MB of RAM with Windows Server 2003,

Enterprise Edition, and then you install the clustering service and Exchange Server 2003. You create the IP address, the network name, and the physical disk resources. However, when you attempt to bring the group online, the process fails. Why?

_____

_____

3. You are the administrator of an Exchange Server 2003 virtual server on a two-node active/active cluster running Windows Server 2003, Enterprise Edition, on each node. You know that Windows Server 2003, Enterprise Edition, supports eight-node clustering, so you decide to add two additional active nodes to your Exchange Server cluster. You install Windows Server 2003, Enterprise Edition, on two additional servers and successfully add them to the cluster. You then install Exchange Server 2003 successfully on the new servers. However, when you attempt to create the virtual servers, you find that you are unable to, even though you have the correct permissions to do so. What is the problem, and how can you solve it?

_____

_____

Lesson Summary

- By default, cluster groups that failover to another node do not automatically fail back.

- In order for cluster groups to fail back, you must create a failback policy.

- An Exchange Server 2003 cluster group consists of an IP address resource, a network name resource, a physical disk resource, and an Exchange System Attendant resource.

- The Exchange System Attendant resource installs all the additional Exchange Server resources.

Lesson 3: Installing Exchange Server 2003 in a Front-End and Back-End Configuration

Front-end and back-end server configurations were introduced in Chapter 3, where the basic concepts and benefits of the architecture were discussed. In this lesson, you will learn how to install and configure Exchange Server 2003 in a front-end and back-end configuration and how to use clustering to maximize the benefits of the front-end and back-end architecture.

> **After this lesson, you will be able to**
> - Configure Exchange Server 2003 as a front-end server
> - Understand how to incorporate Network Load Balancing and the Cluster Service to create highly scalable and highly available Exchange Server 2003 organizations
>
> **Estimated lesson time: 45 minutes**

Configuring Exchange Server 2003 as a Front-End Server

Both Exchange Server 2003, Standard Edition, and Exchange Server 2003, Enterprise Edition, support configuration as front-end servers, which do not host user mailbox and public folder stores. One of the primary benefits of using a front-end server is that it allows you to publish a single external server address to Internet-based clients, regardless of what physical back-end server actually hosts a particular mailbox or public folder replica. In addition, there is a security benefit of having a front-end server outside of a firewall that communicates with Internet-based client computers and communicates securely with the back-end servers. This prevents Internet-based traffic from communicating directly with Exchange Server 2003 servers that host user data.

There are a number of potential configuration changes to be made prior to configuring an Exchange Server 2003 server as a front-end server because front-end servers, by design, only relay traffic from the Internet to back-end servers on the internal network. First, the server cannot host a Recipient Update Service. If it does, you will have to delete or move the Recipient Update Service to another server using Exchange System Manager. Next, the Exchange Server 2003 server cannot host offline address lists. If it does, you must remove them from the server using Exchange System Manager. The Mailbox Management service, which starts and stops the mailbox cleanup agent, cannot be run on a front-end server either and must be removed. Finally, the free and busy service, which tracks the free and busy status of user calendars, does not run on front-end servers. Once you remove these services, you will be able to configure the server as a front-end server. In the practice at the end of this lesson, you will configure a front-end server.

There are several additional considerations when creating front-end servers.

- If the front-end server accepts SMTP mail from Internet-based clients, you must start the Microsoft Exchange Information Store service and mount at least one mailbox store. In certain situations, such as generating nondelivery reports, the SMTP service requires the store to perform a conversion. If a mailbox store is not mounted, messages that have to be converted are stuck in the local delivery queue. For security reasons, make sure that user mailboxes are not stored in the mailbox store of a front-end server. If there are servers that are running Exchange Server 5.5 in the same site or routing group, the Microsoft Exchange MTA Stacks service must run on the front-end server. By doing so, the MTAs can bind and transfer mail by using remote procedure call (RPC), which was the method of internal message transport in Exchange Server 5.5 (Exchange Server 2003 uses SMTP).

- If you must change the configuration by using Internet Services Manager, such as for changing the Secure Sockets Layer (SSL) configuration, leave the mailbox store intact on the front-end server.

- When you create a front-end server, do not delete the First Storage Group object in Exchange System Manager. The Microsoft Exchange Information Store service (and its related services) depends on the First Storage Group object.

If you are installing Exchange Server 2003 into an existing Exchange 2000 Server front-end and back-end configuration, you must first upgrade all the front-end servers and then upgrade the back-end servers.

As a general guideline, use one front-end server for every four back-end servers. However, this number is only a guideline; it is not a rule. Front-end servers do not need large or particularly fast disk storage, but they should have fast central processing units (CPUs) and a large amount of memory. There is no need to back up the disks on the front-end server unless you choose to enable SMTP. SMTP must be backed up because it writes queued mail to the local disk. For POP3, Internet Message Access Protocol 4 (IMAP4), and HTTP (OWA), no user data is stored on the drives of the front-end server.

Front-End and Back-End Servers and Clustering

The front-end and back-end architecture scales well with the use of Network Load Balancing and the Cluster Service. Since front-end servers do not host user data, they are more akin to Web servers than a typical Exchange Server configuration. As a result, front-end servers are well suited for using Network Load Balancing. In this type of configuration, you can scale up to 32 nodes in a cluster using Network Load Balancing, having the cluster service Internet-based clients connecting through OWA, POP3, or IMAP4. The cluster functions as a single entity to client requests and relays traffic back and forth between the client computer and the back-end server.

Back-end servers are better suited for the Cluster Service. A common highly scalable and highly available Exchange Server 2003 configuration is to create a cluster using Network Load Balancing, configure all the Exchange Server 2003 server nodes on the cluster as front-end servers, and have them connect to a back-end Exchange Server 2003 active/passive cluster running the Cluster Service.

When you have front-end servers, it is necessary to modify settings using both Cluster Administrator and Exchange System Manager. To configure a clustered back-end server using the Cluster Service, you must map each front-end server to all server nodes of the back-end Cluster Service cluster so that any node can accept proxy requests from any front-end server. Proxy requests are requests for messaging services from client computers running OWA, POP3, or IMAP4 that are sent to the back-end cluster through the front-end servers. All communication between front-end and back-end servers goes through TCP port 80, regardless of the port used for communication between the client computer and the front-end server.

Exchange Server 2003 uses the concept of virtual servers to refer to instances of IP services that it provides. By default, there are a number of different services that Exchange Server 2003 is configured with to support different types of messaging clients. For example, there are virtual servers for HTTP access to Exchange Server 2003, as well as for POP3, IMAP4, NNTP, and SMTP access. They are *virtual* servers because each service runs within the context of the Exchange Server 2003 server, not as truly separate servers. However, at the same time, each virtual server can be configured independently with its own IP address, security settings, and port numbers. But these IP virtual servers are not the same as a virtual server running on the Cluster Service. An HTTP virtual server on a Cluster Service cluster defines the resources that make an IP HTTP virtual server available through Exchange Server 2003 on a cluster.

There are a few steps to configure HTTP virtual server resources for an Exchange Server 2003 virtual server functioning as a back-end server. First, you must create the HTTP virtual servers in Exchange System Manager. Next, you must create virtual directories to match the directories configured on the front-end server. Finally, you must add new HTTP virtual server resources to the Exchange virtual server. However, you do not need to perform this configuration if you are only making the default HTTP virtual server available, servicing a single domain. The default configuration of Exchange Server 2003 and the Exchange Server 2003 virtual server already has the HTTP virtual server, virtual directory, and HTTP virtual server cluster resource configured. However, if you are supporting multiple domain names through HTTP, you must create separate HTTP virtual servers for each domain. For example, if Contoso, Ltd., acquires Fabrikam, Inc., and after merging, it is necessary for users to access mailboxes in both *contoso.com* and *fabrikam.com*. By default, there is an IP virtual server for *contoso.com*, but you will need to create an additional one for *fabrikam.com*. Creating virtual servers and virtual directories is the focus of Chapter 9.

Practice: Installing Exchange Server 2003 in a Front-End and Back-End Configuration

In this practice, you will configure Server02 in the *tailspintoys.com* domain as a front-end server, connecting to the Exch-VS01 back-end virtual server that you created earlier in this chapter. Before completing these exercises, you must complete the exercises in Lessons 1 and 2 of this chapter.

Exercise 1: Configure Exchange Server 2003 as a Front-end Server

1. Make sure that Server01 is online and that the Exchange Server 2003 virtual server Exch-VS01 is running. On Server02, install Exchange Server 2003 as a typical installation, which will have it join the Tailspintoys organization.

2. After installing Exchange Server 2003, reboot if prompted.

3. Start Exchange System Manager and expand the Recipients container. Click the Recipient Update Services container.

4. There should be two Recipient Update Services that reference Server02. Right-click the one that has (TAILSPINTOYS) in the name, and then click Delete. Right-click the one that has (Enterprise Configuration) in the name, and then click Properties. Next to Windows Domain Controller, click Browse, and then enter **Server01** for the name. This will move the Recipient Update Service off of Server02. Click OK, and then click OK again.

5. Click the Offline Address Lists container. You should have offline address lists for both Exch-VS01 and Server02. Right-click the Default Offline Address List for Server02, and then click Delete.

6. Expand the Servers container. Right-click Server02 and click Properties. Select the check box for This Is A Front-End Server, and click OK. You will see a warning message similar to Figure 6-13. Click OK to continue.

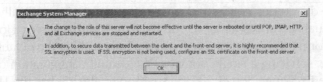

Figure 6-13 Confirming the conversion to a front-end server

7. Restart all the Exchange Server services, as well as the World Wide Web Publishing Service.

In a simple front-end and back-end topology, no additional configuration is required on the front-end servers. However, if you are hosting multiple domains, you must configure virtual servers and virtual directories for each of the domains you will be hosting.

Lesson Review

The following questions are intended to reinforce key information presented in this lesson. If you are unable to answer a question, review the lesson materials and then try the question again. You can find answers to the questions in the "Questions and Answers" section at the end of this chapter.

1. You are the Exchange Server administrator for TailspinToys, which recently acquired WingtipToys. TailspinToys uses a front-end server outside of its firewall that connects to a back-end server cluster. You have migrated the mailboxes for WingtipToys employees onto the Exchange Server 2003 cluster. In order to support Internet-based client computers connecting to WingtipToys resources, you configure a new HTTP virtual server and virtual directory on the front-end server for *wingtiptoys.com* and mimic it on the Exchange Server 2003 virtual server. However, mail traffic fails to flow properly, even though it works fine for TailspinToys. You verify the network settings, and they are all correct. What else might you be missing?

_____

_____

2. You install Exchange Server 2003 clean onto a new server, with the plan to make it a front-end server in an existing Exchange Server 2003 organization. After a successful installation, you start Exchange System Manager and expand the Servers container, then right-click the server and then click Properties. You select the check box for This Is A Front-End Server and click OK, but you receive an error. What did you do wrong?

_____

_____

3. You are the Exchange Server administrator for an organization that has an existing Exchange 2000 Server front-end and back-end server architecture. There are four non-load-balanced front-end servers servicing 15 non-clustered back-end servers. You want to upgrade to Exchange Server 2003 on all servers. In what order would you upgrade?

a. Upgrade a front-end server and then each of its corresponding back-end servers, and then repeat the process with the next front-end server.

b. Upgrade all the back-end servers, and then upgrade all the front-end servers.

c. Upgrade back-end servers, then upgrade the corresponding front-end server, and then repeat the process with the next set of back-end servers.

d. Upgrade all the front-end servers, and then upgrade all the back-end servers.

Lesson Summary

- Front-end servers work best with Network Load Balancing, and back-end servers work best with the Cluster Service.

- A general guideline is to use one front-end server for every four back-end servers.

- Recipient Update Services, Offline Address Lists, the Mailbox Management service, and the free and busy service are not supported on front-end servers.

- Front-end servers should have a mailbox store defined but should not host user mailboxes.

- You must duplicate the virtual server and virtual directory configuration between the front-end and back-end servers.

Case Scenario Exercise

TailspinToys is an innovative and fast-growing toy manufacturing company that has recently signed an exclusive contract to produce the action figures, spaceships, and other miscellaneous toys for an upcoming blockbuster movie. As a result of their involvement with the movie, the marketing department forecasts a 5000 percent increase in traffic to the company Web site and a 500 percent increase in the amount of Web-based orders, which are delivered through to their Exchange Server 2003 server. The mail server currently processes about 7500 e-mail messages a day, of which approximately 1500 are customer-driven messages. Management is extremely concerned about the ability of the network infrastructure to handle the increased load and fears that not being able to fill Internet orders properly will result in a loss of immediate business and a poor customer service reputation and that it will have a long-term effect by causing the movie studio to use a different manufacturer to produce the toys for the sequel.

Because the problem is deemed critical in nature, you, as the network manager, have been given a lot of latitude in designing an infrastructure for e-mail and Web services that will scale to meet the requirements of the network traffic and that will be very reliable.

In addition, management has decided that it will label toys destined for the fast food restaurant market with its WingtipToys brand. Therefore, the Web ordering system will need to process orders for both *tailspintoys.com* and *wingtiptoys.com*. Also, sales people in the field will need to access e-mail using OWA for both e-mail domains.

- **Requirement 1** After researching the problem, you decide to maintain your existing Exchange Server 2003 server for internal employee e-mail and to set up a clustered Exchange Server 2003 server configuration for storing and processing customer e-mail. You need to configure the cluster so that it will provide the most reliability against failure.

■ **Requirement 2**   You decide to use a front-end and back-end architecture for the configuration, but you need to ensure that it can handle e-mail for both domain names, which will go to mailboxes and public folders both on the Exchange Server 2003 server hosting employee mailboxes and on the new Exchange Server 2003 cluster. You also need to ensure that e-mail access through the front-end servers, which sit outside of the firewall, is always available.

Requirement 1

The first requirement involves adding an Exchange Server 2003 cluster to an existing Exchange Server 2003 organization.

1. You determine that you will need to use the Cluster Service rather than Network Load Balancing to ensure the availability of the Exchange Server services. You plan to start with a two-node cluster, given the amount of e-mail traffic you expect the cluster to handle. Should you use an active/active model or an active/passive model? Why?

   _____

   _____

2. Describe the process that you will use to set up this cluster using Windows Server 2003 and Exchange Server 2003, Enterprise Edition.

   _____

   _____

Requirement 2

The second requirement involves configuring the front-end and back-end architecture to support multiple domains and to provide constant availability to Internet-based OWA users.

1. For the back-end server, you used the Cluster Service. Should you also use it on the front-end server? Why or why not?

   _____

   _____

2. How will the server nodes in the cluster using Network Load Balancing handle one of the servers going offline?

   _____

   _____

3. After configuring the Exchange Server 2003 two-node active/passive cluster and setting a two-node network load balanced cluster as front-end servers in Exchange System Manager, what additional step must you take so that the *tailspintoys.com* domain can also receive e-mail on the cluster through the front-end servers for *wingtiptoys.com*?

Chapter Summary

- Network Load Balancing and the Cluster Service both increase the availability of application services but in different ways.

- Network Load Balancing scales to 32 servers, and the Cluster Service scales to 8 servers.

- The Cluster Service requires two network adapters: one for the public network and one for private intra-node communication.

- Network Load Balancing does not require special hardware, whereas the Cluster Service requires an external shared disk resource for a multi-node cluster.

- A cluster service account should be configured prior to creating the cluster and granted the Exchange Full Administrator role after installing Exchange Server 2003.

- Exchange Server 2003, Enterprise Edition, is required for clustering.

- Typically, front-end cluster servers use Network Load Balancing, while back-end clusters use the Cluster Service.

- The recommended use of Exchange Server 2003 in a clustered environment is in an active/passive configuration.

Exam Highlights

Before taking the exam, review the key points and terms that are presented in this chapter. Return to the lessons for additional practice.

Key Points

- Use static IP addressing for cluster network adapters. This prevents DHCP from being a point of failure.

- Cluster nodes brought back online do not fail back unless a failback policy is configured.

- Network Load Balancing cannot monitor application services.

- The Cluster Service cannot load balance.

- Exchange Server 2003 supports only two-node active/active clusters.

Key Terms

cluster group   A cluster group is a collection of cluster resources and is used to define the settings that make up a virtual server on a cluster. When a failover occurs on a node of the cluster, it is the cluster group that fails over to another node.

cluster resource   A cluster resource is an individual component of a cluster virtual server, such as an IP address, a network name, or a physical disk. Cluster resources are collected into groups. When a resource fails, it restarts according to a configurable policy. If a resource exceeds its restart threshold, it can force a failover of the entire group it belongs to.

virtual server   A virtual server is a configured server resource that exists through a set of software resources and settings. A virtual server is a way of mapping a collection of services and resources to physical resources and having them appear to client computers as distinct physical servers.

quorum disk   The Cluster Service uses a quorum disk to maintain the master copy of the configuration data for all server nodes in a cluster. The quorum disk in a multi-node cluster must be on a shared disk resource accessible by all members of the cluster.

node   A server that is a member of a cluster.

Questions and Answers

Page
6-16

Lesson 1 Review

1. You are a senior network administrator for a fast-growing company that wants to implement a clustering technology in order to ensure the continued availability of a Web application if one of the Web servers fails and, more importantly, to handle the increased traffic that is expected in the future. You are asked whether you should deploy Network Load Balancing or the Cluster Service for this application, and why you would choose one over the other.

   You should choose to deploy Network Load Balancing in this situation. The Cluster Service is designed to provide high availability of application resources, but it does not load balance in any way. This makes it less suitable than Network Load Balancing for scaling applications to handle increased traffic. While Network Load Balancing cannot monitor at the service level like the Cluster Service, the primary goal is to handle the increased traffic.

2. You are setting up an Exchange Server 2003 virtual server on the Cluster Service, using a two-node active/active configuration. As you read through a planning checklist, you identify how the services will failover. Which Exchange Server 2003 service cannot be set to an active/active configuration like the other services?

   a. Microsoft Exchange Information Store

   b. Microsoft Exchange System Attendant

   c. Microsoft Exchange Message Transfer Agent

   d. Microsoft Exchange Routing Service

   The correct answer is c.

3. You are the administrator of an Exchange Server 2003 cluster that consists of Server01 and Server02 in a two-node active/passive configuration. The servers have the following TCP/IP configuration:

   Server01 (active)

   ❑ Local Area Connection 1 (Public) — IP Address — 10.1.1.250, DHCP

   ❑ Local Area Connection 2 (Private) — IP Address — 192.168.254.1, static

   Server02 (passive)

   ❑ Local Area Connection 1 (Public) — IP Address — 10.1.1.251, DHCP

   ❑ Local Area Connection 2 (Private) — IP Address — 192.168.254.2, static

   Over a holiday weekend, a Windows Server 2003 domain controller fails due to a faulty hard drive. On Tuesday morning, you order a hard drive for the server, and it is scheduled for delivery on Wednesday. Tuesday afternoon, users begin to report that e-mail is down. You check the cluster, and it appears at first glance to be functioning properly internally. You manually failover the cluster to the second node, but the problem is not corrected. Where should you look next to troubleshoot the problem?

The next place to check is actually the first place you should check, which is basic network connectivity. All too often, network administrators make a high-level change such as failing over a cluster node without first determining where the problem really lies. In this instance, the domain controller that failed was likely the DHCP server, and the cluster was unable to renew its IP addresses and therefore released them. While clusters can use dynamic IP addressing on the public network, it is recommended to use static addressing to avoid this type of problem. To fix the problem, you can either assign static IP addresses to the network adapters connected to the public network or bring the DHCP server back online. Since you're waiting on a hard drive, you should configure static IP addressing and then register those addresses in DNS. Then clients will be able to connect again.

Page
6-27
Lesson 2 Review

1. You are the administrator of a two-node active/passive Exchange Server 2003 cluster that is currently not in production but is being tested prior to being put into production. You are testing your failover policies, so you initiate failures on several resources until the group failure threshold is reached. The server successfully fails over the group to the formerly passive node, and the previously active node becomes passive. You want the group to fail back to the original service, but after an hour of waiting, the group is still running on the second node. It is late in the day so you decide to go home and deal with it the next day, since the cluster is not yet in production. The next morning, you notice that the cluster is still running on the second node, and you can't find a command in the Cluster Administrator GUI to initiate a failback. What can you do to get the group back on the original server node?

   Failback is controlled through a policy that is defined at the group level. You need to right-click the group, then click Properties, and then click the Failback tab. The default setting is to not fail back, but you can configure the group to fail back immediately when the original node returns to service or to fail back only during certain hours. In this situation, you could set the policy to Immediately, which would cause the group to fail back after you click OK.

2. You are setting up a test server to practice with the cluster service as a prelude to a later cluster deployment. You don't have any real servers available, but you know that you can use a single system and a local quorum disk resource for testing purposes. You set up a desktop workstation class machine that has a SCSI C drive and an IDE D drive and 512 MB of RAM with Windows Server 2003, Enterprise Edition, and then you install the clustering service and Exchange Server 2003. You create the IP address, the network name, and the physical disk resources. However, when you attempt to bring the group online, the process fails. Why?

When you create a physical disk resource, it will allow you to select an available IDE hard drive; however, you won't be able to bring the resource online. Only SCSI disks are supported as physical disk resources. In this case, the SCSI C drive is already in use as the local quorum disk, so it cannot be used as the physical disk resource for the Exchange Server 2003 virtual server. You must add another SCSI drive in order to proceed.

3. You are the administrator of an Exchange Server 2003 virtual server on a two-node active/active cluster running Windows Server 2003, Enterprise Edition, on each node. You know that Windows Server 2003, Enterprise Edition, supports eight-node clustering, so you decide to add two additional active nodes to your Exchange Server cluster. You install Windows Server 2003, Enterprise Edition, on two additional servers and successfully add them to the cluster. You then install Exchange Server 2003 successfully on the new servers. However, when you attempt to create the virtual servers, you find that you are unable to, even though you have the correct permissions to do so. What is the problem, and how can you solve it?

Exchange Server 2003 supports only active/active configurations on two-node clusters. In this situation, you cannot add two additional active nodes without changing the configuration to an active/passive model with at least one passive node. You could configure three active nodes and one passive node, or add a fifth server and have four active nodes and one passive node. Exchange Server 2003, Enterprise Edition, supports the full eight-node clustering of Windows Server 2003, Enterprise Edition, but only with at least one passive node.

Page 6-33 **Lesson 3 Review**

1. You are the Exchange Server administrator for TailspinToys, which recently acquired WingtipToys. TailspinToys uses a front-end server outside of its firewall that connects to a back-end server cluster. You have migrated the mailboxes for WingtipToys employees onto the Exchange Server 2003 cluster. In order to support Internet-based client computers connecting to WingtipToys resources, you configure a new HTTP virtual server and virtual directory on the front-end server for *wingtiptoys.com* and mimic it on the Exchange Server 2003 virtual server. However, mail traffic fails to flow properly, even though it works fine for TailspinToys. You verify the network settings, and they are all correct. What else might you be missing?

Since you are running the back-end server as an Exchange Server 2003 virtual server on a cluster, you must create an HTTP virtual server resource in the Exchange Server cluster group in addition to creating the virtual servers and virtual directories. Once you set this up, mail traffic should flow properly. If you were not using a cluster, this additional step would not be required.

2. You install Exchange Server 2003 clean onto a new server, with the plan to make it a front-end server in an existing Exchange Server 2003 organization. After a successful installation, you start Exchange System Manager and expand the Servers container, then right-click the server and then click Properties. You select the check box for This Is A Front-End Server and click OK, but you receive an error. What did you do wrong?

Prior to configuring a server as a front-end server, you must remove any services from it that are not supported on front-end servers. By default, Exchange Server 2003 configures servers with a Recipient Update Service and a Default Offline Address List. Neither are supported on front-end servers and must be removed before Exchange System Manager will allow you to designate a server as a front-end server.

3. You are the Exchange Server administrator for an organization that has an existing Exchange 2000 Server front-end and back-end server architecture. There are four non-load-balanced front-end servers servicing 15 non-clustered back-end servers. You want to upgrade to Exchange Server 2003 on all servers. In what order would you upgrade?

   a. Upgrade a front-end server and then each of its corresponding back-end servers, and then repeat the process with the next front-end server.

   b. Upgrade all the back-end servers, and then upgrade all the front-end servers.

   c. Upgrade back-end servers, then upgrade the corresponding front-end server, and then repeat the process with the next set of back-end servers.

   d. Upgrade all the front-end servers, and then upgrade all the back-end servers.

   The correct answer is d.

Case Scenario Exercise: Requirement 1

Page 6-35

1. You determine that you will need to use the Cluster Service rather than Network Load Balancing to ensure the availability of the Exchange Server services. You plan to start with a two-node cluster, given the amount of e-mail traffic you expect the cluster to handle. Should you use an active/active model or an active/passive model? Why?

Microsoft recommends an active/passive configuration for most applications, which is appropriate for this situation. The e-mail traffic is less of a concern than the Web traffic with respect to quantity, and it can easily be handled by a higher-end server. By configuring a cluster with an active node and a passive node, you can ensure that if the active node fails, the passive node will come online to service client requests. In addition, the active/passive model is scalable up to eight nodes, so you can add additional active nodes later, if necessary.

2. Describe the process that you will use to set up this cluster using Windows Server 2003 and Exchange Server 2003, Enterprise Edition.

First you will install the Windows Server 2003 operating system on the server that will become the first node in the cluster. After the operating system is configured and a service account for the cluster is created, you start Cluster Administrator and choose to create a new cluster using the New Server Cluster Wizard. Then, you will install Exchange Server 2003 on the server, joining the existing organization. After the installation, you will delegate the cluster service account the Exchange Full Administrator role in Exchange System Manager. Then you will use

Cluster Administrator to create a cluster group for the Exchange Server 2003 virtual server, and then create cluster resources for IP address, network name, physical disk, and Exchange System Attendant. The Exchange System Attendant will install the other Exchange Server resources, which you will bring online when the cluster is complete.

Page
6-35

Case Scenario Exercise: Requirement 2

1. For the back-end server, you used the Cluster Service. Should you also use it on the front-end server? Why or why not?

The Cluster Service is inappropriate for the front-end server cluster. The Cluster Service does not load balance, which makes it less suited for use on front-end servers. You do want clustering technology in place but would be better off using Network Load Balancing for this part of the configuration. Network Load Balancing can load balance client connections and it can be used to provide a unified namespace to Internet-based clients. These users and Web applications can use a single Uniform Resource Locator (URL) for each e-mail domain, regardless of which back-end server hosts the mailbox or public folder that is being accessed.

2. How will the server nodes in the cluster using Network Load Balancing handle one of the servers going offline?

Network Load Balancing cannot monitor at the application service level, but if a server goes offline, the other servers in the cluster will perform convergence to assume the load previously handled by the offline server and mark it as offline.

3. After configuring the Exchange Server 2003 two-node active/passive cluster and setting a two-node network load balanced cluster as front-end servers in Exchange System Manager, what additional step must you take so that the *tailspintoys.com* domain can also receive e-mail on the cluster through the front-end servers for *wingtiptoys.com*?

In order to support multiple domains, you must configure a second HTTP virtual server for the *wingtiptoys.com* domain. You must create this virtual server on both front-end servers and on the active node of the back-end cluster (since only the active node has Exchange Server 2003 installed on it), and then create an HTTP virtual server cluster resource for the *wingtiptoys.com* domain in the Exchange Server cluster group in Cluster Administrator. Default HTTP virtual servers already exist in these three places, so the primary domain *tailspintoys.com* is already configured.

7 Managing Recipient Objects and Address Lists

Exam Objectives in this Chapter:

- Manage recipient policies
- Manage user objects
- Manage distribution and security groups
- Manage contacts
- Manage address lists

Why This Chapter Matters

After installing Microsoft Exchange Server 2003 and creating an organization, the next logical step is to configure the recipient objects that will use the Exchange server. As an Exchange administrator in the real world, you will find that the majority of your day-to-day administrative work will involve managing recipients.

Administering recipient objects is more complex than simply creating user objects and distribution lists. A good Exchange administrator is one who can make her users more efficient in how they work and, therefore, more productive. In this chapter, you will gain the skills necessary to master this testing domain and to add value to your organization by exceeding basic user administration.

Lessons in this Chapter:

- Lesson 1: Configuring Recipient Objects 7-3
- Lesson 2: Configuring Information Stores. 7-46
- Lesson 3: Creating and Managing Address Lists and Recipient Policies 7-58

Before You Begin

In order to complete the exercises and examples in this chapter, you need to have the following:

- Two servers running Microsoft Windows Server 2003 installed and configured as Server01 and Server02 in the *contoso.com* domain.

- Exchange Server 2003, Enterprise Edition, installed on both servers.

- Microsoft Outlook 2003 installed on a workstation in the domain or, alternatively, on one of the servers.

Lesson 1: Configuring Recipient Objects

As an administrator who has previously managed a Microsoft Exchange Server 5.5 environment, one of the biggest changes you will notice when administering Exchange Server 2003 is recipient management because Exchange Server 5.5 maintained its own directory independent of Microsoft Windows. Exchange Server 2003 tightly integrates with Active Directory directory service objects (such as domain user accounts). One difference between Exchange Server 5.5 and Exchange Server 2003 is that you use the Active Directory Users And Computers console to manage Exchange mailboxes rather than a standalone Exchange Administrator utility. Another difference is that there is a one-to-one relationship between Active Directory objects and Exchange mailboxes. With Exchange Server 5.5, it was common to create generic mailboxes, such as *sales@contoso.com*, and associate those mailboxes with a Windows security group. It was also common for more than one mailbox to be associated with a given domain user account. Exchange Server 2003 does not allow you to work in the same one-to-many way as Exchange Server 5.5; however, there are ways to accomplish the same tasks.

After this lesson, you will be able to

- Identify the Exchange Server 2003 recipient types
- Manage Exchange mailboxes
- Manage mail-enabled groups

Estimated lesson time: 120 minutes

Recipient Types

Exchange Server 2003 supports different types of recipients depending on how you need to send e-mail to a recipient and where that recipient is located in relation to your Exchange organization. Recipient objects can be categorized into four different types: user, contact, group, and public folder. The first three types are configured and managed through the Active Directory Users And Computers console, while public folders are created using the Outlook client.

User Recipients

User recipients are the recipient objects that represent employees and contractors who work for your organization, and they are tied to Active Directory user accounts. They can have e-mail addresses as part of the organization, such as *@contoso.com*, or they can have e-mail addresses external to the organization. These recipient objects are configured through the Active Directory Users And Computers console because they are user accounts in the Active Directory domain. User recipients can be either mailbox-enabled or mail-enabled, depending on your needs.

A *mailbox-enabled user* is a user account that has a mailbox in the Exchange organization and, as a result, can send and receive e-mail through the Exchange Server 2003 infrastructure. This type of user is typically a corporate employee who logs on to the Active Directory domain with his domain user account and accesses the Exchange Server 2003 server holding his mailbox through the Outlook client (though there are other means by which a mailbox can be accessed, such as with Outlook Web Access [OWA], Internet Message Access Protocol 4 [IMAP4], and Post Office Protocol 3 [POP3]). Mailbox-enabled users are the most common type of recipient object in an Exchange organization.

Mail-enabled users are similar to mailbox-enabled users in that they have domain user accounts in the Active Directory domain. However, in contrast to a mailbox-enabled user, a mail-enabled user does not have a mailbox in the Exchange organization. Instead, a mail-enabled user has only an e-mail address. In certain scenarios, you would want to make a user account mail-enabled rather than mailbox-enabled. One such scenario is if you have a contractor working onsite for your company who needs access to the network (a domain user account) but does not need a corporate e-mail account. In this situation, you could create a user account for the contractor and mail-enable it, using the contractor's personal e-mail address through their Internet service provider (ISP). For example, if there is a user account named Willis in the *contoso.com* domain, but his personal e-mail address is *willis@proseware.com*, you would mail-enable the user account and assign the *willis@proseware.com* address to the account. This allows Willis to appear in the Global Address List (GAL) so he can be easily located by other employees and contractors and added to distribution lists, and yet have his e-mail sent to his personal account.

Another scenario in which you would want to use mail-enabled users rather than mailbox-enabled users is when you have offsite contractors working for you who need to have corporate e-mail addresses but do not need access to the network. For example, a publisher wants customers to be able to send e-mail messages to an author at a corporate e-mail address, but the author doesn't work onsite for the company and never accesses the corporate network. For instance, Lucerne Publishing employs freelance writers for various contract assignments for its print and online magazines. The company wants readers to be able to send e-mail to each writer at e-mail addresses in the *@lucernepublishing.com* domain. The freelance writers all have personal e-mail accounts, and none have Active Directory user accounts for Lucerne. To solve the problem of needing to have mail accounts for users that do not have user accounts, the Exchange administrator at Lucerne would create mail-enabled user accounts for each writer, disable the account (since it won't be used to access the network), and then forward the *@lucernepublishing.com* e-mail address to the personal address of the writer. Essentially, this configuration allows the writer to have an e-mail address in the *@lucernepublishing.com* domain that would be displayed publicly, yet e-mail addressed to the account would be redirected to the writer's personal account, such as one with *hotmail.com*.

Contact Recipients

A *contact recipient* is similar to a mail-enabled user in that the e-mail address points to a mailbox that is not a part of the Exchange organization. However, contacts do not have user accounts in the Active Directory domain like mail-enabled users do. You would typically use contact recipients when users in your organization need to send mail to a particular address outside the organization on a regular basis, and you want to provide the convenience of making the address available in the GAL or available for use in other Exchange Server address lists and distribution lists. Contact recipients are similar to contacts stored in a user's individual Contacts folder. The difference is that with Exchange Server 2003, you can make contacts available to the entire organization.

A common scenario for using contact recipients is when two companies merge but have separate Active Directory forests and Exchange organizations. In this situation, it is necessary for employees in both organizations to communicate with each other on a regular basis. For instance, if *contoso.com* and *adatum.com* merged, you could configure all of the users in *adatum.com* as contact recipients in the GAL of *contoso.com* and vice versa. This allows users in both Exchange organizations to communicate quickly and efficiently.

If you are migrating from Exchange Server 5.5 to Exchange Server 2003, contact recipients map directly to custom recipients in Exchange Server 5.5.

Group Recipients

Group recipients closely resemble mail-enabled users in that they can have e-mail addresses that are a part of the Exchange organization, but they do not have mailboxes that store e-mail. Where group recipients differ is that when an e-mail message is sent to an address associated with the group, everyone in the group receives the message. From a functionality standpoint, this is the same as a distribution list in Exchange Server 5.5.

Because of the integration with Active Directory, Exchange Server 2003 supports mail-enabling both of the group types that Active Directory supports: security groups and distribution groups. *Security groups*, as the name implies, are used for assigning permissions to resources. These are the domain local, global, and universal groups you use to manage access to Active Directory resources. *Distribution groups* have no relation to security or accessing resources and thus cannot be assigned permissions. However, distribution groups are useful for grouping users into a list related to some common purpose. For example, you might have a distribution group that represents all your company's sales employees nationwide, a scenario where you typically would have a number of security groups that contain all these users. Say you are administering *wideworldimporters.com* and you have offices in 20 U.S. cities, and each location is a separate Active Directory site. You might have security groups for each location in order to assign permissions. You can mail-enable each security group, and e-mail *bostonsales@wideworldimporters.com* and *dallassales@wideworldimporters.com*, and so on. If you want to send e-mail to all sales groups in a single message, your options are to create another security group that contains all the other groups (which would be unnecessary if you do not need to assign security permissions to that national sales group) or to create a distribution group that exists for e-mail purposes only, which is the better choice.

Another situation in which you would use distribution groups involves inter-departmental groups or projects that require sending e-mail to groups of people who don't fit neatly into one or two security groups. By creating distribution groups, you can easily group the users as desired without having to consider network resource security issues.

Public Folder Recipients

Public folder recipients are different from other recipient objects in that they are not individual users or groups of users but rather a mail-enabled folder in an Exchange organization. Users can be granted access to the public folder through standard security permissions (individual or group) and can access the public folder through the Outlook client by navigating through the public folder hierarchy. Managing public folders is the focus of Chapter 8, "Public Folders."

Public folder recipients are used for a number of purposes, including discussion forums, newsgroup postings, and creating a repository for customer feedback e-mail. For example, you are the administrator for Contoso. Ltd., a company that has just launched a new product line. As part of the launch, marketing wants to be able to receive customer feedback. While you can set up a distribution group, which will result in incoming messages being sent to everyone in the group, a more ideal solution is to mail-enable a public folder. This will result in all customer e-mail sent to *feedback@contoso.com* being posted to the folder, a single location where anyone who has been granted permission to the folder can view the messages. This is especially useful when people such as executive managers want to monitor feedback but do not want to receive every customer e-mail in their personal mailboxes.

Creating Recipient Objects

When you install Exchange Server 2003, by default all Active Directory user accounts have mailboxes created in the Exchange organization. However, if you have an existing user that doesn't have a mailbox, you can still mailbox-enable the user after the fact. The Exchange Task Wizard is used to mailbox-enable and to mail-enable users and groups.

When you install Exchange Server 2003, Setup extends the Active Directory Users And Computers management console to support Exchange Server functionality. One way it does this is by adding another step to the process of creating a user account. This step prompts you to create a mailbox for the user, as shown in Figure 7-1.

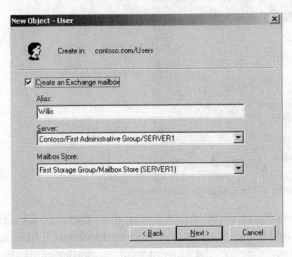

Figure 7-1   Creating a mailbox

By default, the check box to create the mailbox is selected. If you want the user to be mail-enabled instead, simply clear the box and finish the user creation process as usual. If you do want to create the mailbox, leave the box selected and verify that the default settings for Server and Mailbox Store are correct. For Server, you can select any Exchange server in your Exchange organization from the drop-down list. Exchange Server 2003, Enterprise Edition, supports creating multiple storage groups (which hold mailbox stores) on a server, which is why you have the option to select an alternate mailbox store. (Storage groups are discussed in Lesson 2 of this chapter.) Once you make your selections, finish creating the user account as usual.

Mail-enabling an existing user account, group, or contact is accomplished using a procedure similar to mailbox-enabling an account. Right-click the target user, group, or contact in the Active Directory Users And Computers console and select Exchange Tasks from the shortcut menu. The Exchange Task Wizard starts. Depending on what you have previously configured for the object, you'll have a number of task choices, such as those shown in Figure 7-2.

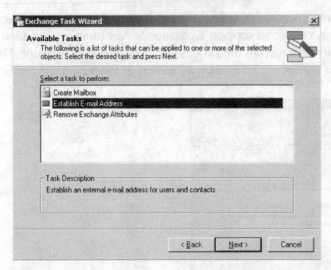

Figure 7-2 The Available Tasks page of the Exchange Task Wizard

To mail-enable an object, select Establish E-Mail Address from the task list, and then click Next to continue. The next page of the wizard is the Establish E-Mail Address page, shown in Figure 7-3, which displays the current mail properties of the object.

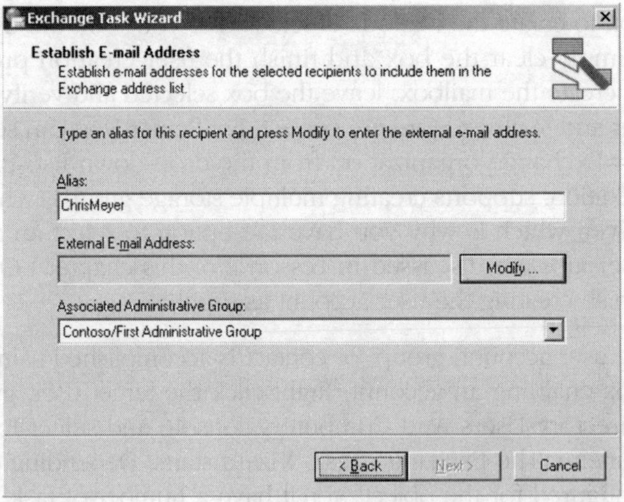

Figure 7-3 The mail properties of the selected object

If you click Modify, you will be prompted to choose the type of e-mail address you want to create in the New E-Mail Address page, shown in Figure 7-4.

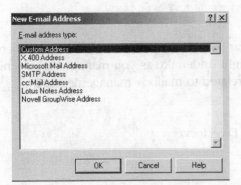

Figure 7-4   Choosing an e-mail address type

Your selection here will determine which configuration page will appear next. Figure 7-5 shows an example of configuring a Simple Mail Transfer Protocol (SMTP) address.

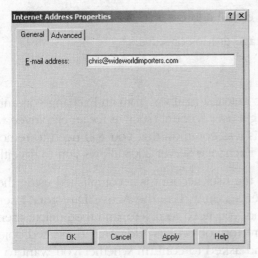

Figure 7-5   Configuring an SMTP address for a mail-enabled object

After you configure an address, the object will appear in the GAL for the Exchange organization.

Managing Mailboxes

Once you've created an Exchange organization of mailbox-enabled users, there are a number of administrative tasks you might undertake as you manage the organization. Some of the common Exchange tasks related to mailbox management are

- Deleting a mailbox
- Reconnecting a mailbox in Active Directory
- Hiding mailboxes from the GAL
- Modifying e-mail addresses
- Configuring storage limits
- Configuring permissions on mailboxes
- Configuring delivery restrictions
- Forwarding mailboxes to other e-mail addresses
- Moving mailboxes to other storage groups or servers

Deleting a Mailbox

There are times when you'll need to delete a mailbox from an Exchange organization, usually in conjunction with removing a user account (such as for an employee who no longer works for the company). It is less common that you will need to remove the mailbox but keep the user account. Exchange Server 2003 allows you to do either.

Deleting a mailbox while removing the user account is accomplished using the same procedure you use to delete a user account. Use the Active Directory Users And Computers console to select the users you need to delete, and then delete them. You will be prompted that the Active Directory object has additional associated objects (in this case an Exchange mailbox) and asked to confirm whether you want to delete them.

Alternatively, you can remove only the mailbox from an existing user account without deleting the account itself. To do this, use the Exchange Task Wizard in Exchange System Manager. To reach the wizard in Exchange System Manager, navigate to the Mailboxes folder in the mailbox store of the server that contains the account, right-click the mailbox, point to Exchange Tasks, and then click Delete Mailbox. This is shown in Figure 7-6.

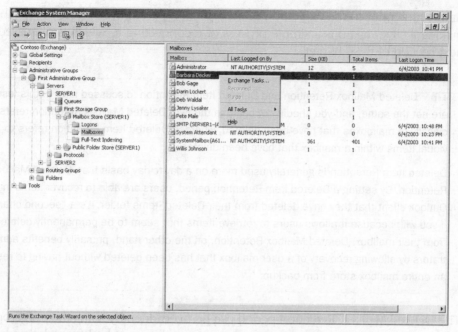

Figure 7-6   Deleting a mailbox by using the Exchange Task Wizard

Deleted Mailbox Retention   The Deleted Mailbox Retention period is a feature of Exchange Server 2003 that is enabled by default. When you delete a mailbox, Exchange Server 2003 will mark it for deletion, but the mailbox will not be permanently deleted for 30 days. The retention period is a configurable length of time and is set at the mailbox store level, as shown in Figure 7-7. Access the mailbox store properties by right-clicking the desired mailbox store (note the navigation path in Figure 7-6) and clicking Properties from the shortcut menu.

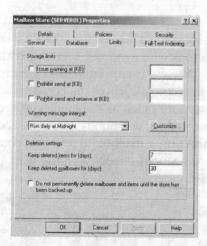

Figure 7-7   Configuring the Deleted Mailbox Retention period

At any time prior to the expiration of the retention period, recovering the mailbox and making it "live" again is a simple process of reconnecting it, which is discussed in the next section of this chapter.

> **Tip** Deleted Mailbox Retention and Deleted Item Retention (discussed later in this lesson) are not the same, and you should not confuse the two. Deleted Mailbox Retention refers specifically to mailboxes that have been deleted, whereas Deleted Item Retention refers to individual items within a mailbox that have been deleted.
>
> Deleted Item Retention is generally used more on a day-to-day basis than Deleted Mailbox Retention. By setting a Deleted Item Retention period, users are able to recover items in their Outlook client that they have deleted from their Deleted Items folder. It's a "second chance," if you will, because it allows users to retrieve items that seem to be permanently deleted from their mailbox. Deleted Mailbox Retention, on the other hand, primarily benefits administrators by allowing recovery of a user mailbox that has been deleted without having to restore an entire mailbox store from backup.

The Deleted Mailbox Retention period can be overridden by using the *purge* option in Exchange System Manager. You can purge a mailbox marked for deletion by right-clicking it in the Mailboxes folder of the mailbox store and then clicking Purge from the shortcut menu. This option is useful if you know you no longer need a mailbox and are trying to free up space.

> **Important** Once you purge deleted mailboxes, the only way to recover them is from backup. This is also true of mailboxes whose retention period has expired.

Reconnecting a Mailbox in Active Directory

Reconnecting a mailbox is the process of associating a mailbox marked for deletion with a live user account. There are a few situations when you will need to perform this task. One such situation is if you accidentally delete a user account and their mailbox from Active Directory. Another situation is if an employee leaves the company and you need to assign the mailbox to another user account (such as the employee's replacement). The task of reconnecting a mailbox marked for deletion is accomplished using Exchange System Manager. If you are reconnecting a mailbox to a user account that was accidentally deleted, make sure you have restored or recreated the user account first.

> **Note**   If you perform this task in a lab environment, you may find the option for Reconnect unavailable (dimmed). This happens when the Exchange Cleanup Agent hasn't run and updated Active Directory to reflect the deletion. You can force the Exchange Cleanup Agent to run immediately by right-clicking Mailboxes in your mailbox store and selecting Run Cleanup Agent from the shortcut menu. After you refresh, you should see the mailbox you deleted marked with a red X.

1. Open Exchange System Manager and navigate to the Mailboxes folder in the mailbox store on your Exchange server. When you click the Mailboxes folder, you will see all the mailboxes in that mailbox store listed in the contents pane of the console window.

> **Important**   If you create mailbox-enabled user accounts for your lab in the Active Directory Users And Computers console, you might be puzzled if the mailboxes for the user accounts do not appear here. Once you create a mailbox-enabled user, you must *initialize* the mailbox by sending a message to it before it will appear and be available to manage through the Mailboxes folder.

2. Right-click the mailbox that has been deleted and that you want to reconnect, and then select Reconnect from the shortcut menu. You will be prompted to select a new user for the mailbox, as shown in Figure 7-8.

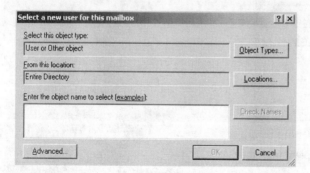

Figure 7-8   Reconnecting a user account to a mailbox

3. You can either type in a name or search for a name in Active Directory using this dialog box. Once you have selected the desired user account, click OK to complete the task. Exchange will notify you that the task completed successfully, and you will see that the red X on the mailbox in Exchange System Manager disappears.

Hiding Mailboxes and Addresses from the GAL

As an Exchange administrator, you will create mailboxes that are designed for a specific purpose but that are not intended to be used by internal employees, such as a mailbox to receive notifications from your antivirus software. Or, if an employee leaves the company, but her mailbox needs to remain active for a period of time after her departure in order to receive any important messages. In either of these situations, it is unlikely that you would want to have the e-mail address appear in the GAL. First, you don't want internal users to mistakenly send messages to those addresses. Second, the GAL can become cluttered with these addresses and make it less efficient for users to work with.

To deal with this issue, Exchange Server 2003 allows you to hide recipient objects from the GAL on an as-needed basis. To hide an object from the GAL, open the Active Directory Users And Computers console and navigate to the desired recipient object. Right-click it, and then click Properties. Click the Exchange Advanced tab, shown in Figure 7-9.

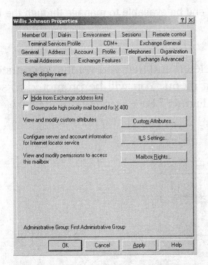

Figure 7-9 Hiding a recipient from the GAL

To hide a mailbox from the GAL, select the option to Hide From Exchange Address Lists. This will prevent the object from appearing in the GAL and other Exchange address lists but will not prevent those objects from receiving e-mail sent to them.

> **Real World   Hiding and Deleting Mailboxes**
>
> It is often tempting to delete mailboxes for users who leave a company. However, usually you will find that it is necessary to maintain an employee's e-mail account for a period of time, particularly when the employee worked directly with customers and clients. By hiding the mailbox rather than deleting it, you ensure that the mailbox will still receive messages and can be accessed as necessary but won't appear in Exchange address lists. In addition, you will save yourself some work when management requests to review the former employee's mailbox a couple of months after he left, and the Deleted Mailbox Retention period has expired. A good practice is to hide the mailbox for 30 to 90 days before deleting it, unless you're specifically advised to keep it longer.

Modifying E-Mail Addresses

Occasionally, you will need to change the e-mail address for a user or otherwise add an alias for a user, for example, when an employee gets married and changes her last name. In this situation, you want to create an alias so the user can gradually migrate to the new address. For example, if the employee Nicole Caron changes her name to Nicole Holliday, and her e-mail address is *ncaron@contoso.com*, you can simply change her e-mail address to *nholliday@contoso.com* and she will receive e-mail at her new address. However, anyone who tries to send e-mail to her at her previous address will receive a non-delivery report (NDR). Therefore, the best option is to create a second SMTP address for Nicole and set *nholliday@contoso.com* as the default. This approach will make the new address live and make it the default reply address but still allow her to receive e-mail sent to *ncaron@contoso.com* with no additional configuration or action necessary.

To create an alias, perform the following steps:

1. Open the Active Directory Users And Computers console and edit the properties of the target user account.

2. Find and click the E-Mail Addresses tab. You will see the currently configured e-mail addresses for the user.

3. Click New to open the New E-Mail Address dialog box, shown in Figure 7-10, which lists the types of new e-mail addresses that you can configure.

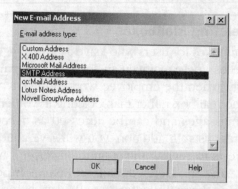

Figure 7-10   Configuring e-mail address types

4. Select SMTP Address and click OK. Then type the new e-mail address and click OK.

5. As shown in Figure 7-11, there are now two SMTP addresses listed for the user. The address shown in bold is the *primary address*, which means it will be the address that is used when e-mail is sent using that interface (in this case SMTP). The address in regular type is an alias (known as a *secondary address*), which means the user will receive e-mail sent to that address but it will not be the default address that recipients will see when e-mail is sent.

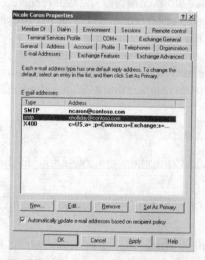

Figure 7-11   Configured e-mail addresses for a recipient object

If necessary, you can have more than one secondary address, but only one address of each type can be primary at any given time. For example, you may have three SMTP addresses and two X.400 addresses, but only one SMTP address and one X.400 address can be primary. To set the primary address, highlight the address you want to make primary and click Set As Primary. You will see the address become boldface and the previous primary address change from bold to regular type.

Configuring Storage Limits

An aspect of administering Exchange Server 2003 that tends to result in tension between users and the administrator is storage limits. With the general corporate emphasis on productivity and the amount of e-mail the average user receives daily, more often than not mailboxes become full of unnecessary items because users find it difficult to set aside time to manage their mailboxes (or they haven't been trained how to do so). In a large organization, this can result in dramatically increased backup and restore times. In small to medium-sized companies, mailbox management could be the difference between being able to run Exchange Server 2003, Standard Edition (which supports a maximum mailbox store size of 16 gigabytes [GB]) and having to use the more expensive (albeit more featured) Exchange Server 2003, Enterprise Edition.

There is flexibility in configuring storage limits in Exchange Server 2003. You can apply the same restrictions to the entire mailbox store or to specific mailbox-enabled users. Likewise, you can override the global settings configured at the store level for individuals that need to have different limits. This is useful if you have a particular mailbox-enabled user that regularly receives e-mail with file attachments and you don't want the same limitations imposed as on standard mailboxes. There are three ways that you can configure storage limits:

- Individual mailbox
- Individual mailbox store
- Mailbox store policy

Configuring Storage Limits for Individual Mailboxes   You configure storage limits for individual mailboxes using the properties of the user account in the Active Directory Users And Computers console.

1. From the Active Directory Users And Computer console, right-click the user account that you want to set storage limits on, and then click Properties.

2. Click the Exchange General tab, and then click Storage Limits to open the Storage Limits dialog box, shown in Figure 7-12.

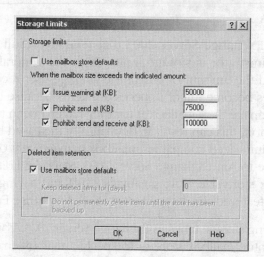

Figure 7-12   Overriding the default storage limits

3. To override the mailbox store settings, clear the box for the Use Mailbox Store Defaults option. Select the check boxes for the settings you wish to configure and enter the values as desired. You can configure the following storage limit settings:

❑ Issue Warning At (KB): When a user's mailbox reaches this threshold, the user receives an automated message from the system administrator warning that they are over their storage limit. Included in the e-mail are details regarding their storage limit and their current mailbox size. The frequency of the automated messages is configurable in Exchange System Manager and by default runs each night at midnight.

❑ Prohibit Send At (KB): Some users become complacent about the warning messages, particularly if they usually keep their mailbox size close to their storage limit. You can configure a threshold that, once crossed, forces the user to clean up their mailbox before they can send any more e-mail.

❑ Prohibit Send And Receive At (KB): Once this threshold is passed, the mailbox will be unable to send or receive e-mail until the size of the mailbox is reduced below the threshold. This setting should be used with caution, particularly when the mailbox belongs to a user that communicates with customers or clients. However, it can be useful to configure a limit so that a mailbox cannot receive any more e-mail, for example, to prevent a malicious person from flooding an unmonitored mailbox with large file attachments and causing the mailbox store size to increase until it fills the available disk space. If you employ this setting, you should configure it significantly higher than the warning in order to reduce the risk of preventing legitimate e-mail from arriving.

❑ Deleted Item Retention: Deleted Item Retention refers to the period of time an item is kept after it has been deleted from the Deleted Items folder in a mailbox. By default, Exchange Server 2003 is configured to keep deleted items for seven days. Within that time frame, an item that has been emptied from the Deleted Items folder can be recovered by the user in the Outlook client by clicking the Tools menu and selecting Recover Deleted Items. You can choose to override the mailbox store's setting for Deleted Item Retention, though usually there is no need to as a common global setting works best. However, you might want to configure it to a larger setting than normal, for example, if you have a user that habitually deletes items and then later decides they want the items back, and you want to save yourself time restoring from backups.

Exam Tip   In previous versions of Exchange Server, the default Deleted Item Retention period was zero days, meaning once items were removed from the Deleted Items folder, they were gone. Administrators were required to manually configure a Deleted Item Retention period for one to exist. Only Exchange Server 2003 has a Deleted Item Retention configured by default.

Configuring Storage Limits for Individual Mailbox Stores   Configuring storage limits for individual mailbox stores is done through Exchange System Manager, by navigating to the mailbox store you want to configure and editing its properties, and then selecting the Limits tab. The configuration dialog box, shown in Figure 7-13, has some elements similar to those in Figure 7-12 but also some important differences.

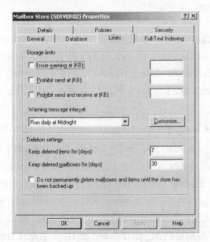

Figure 7-13   Configuring storage limits at the mailbox store level

Figure 7-13 shows the default settings for an Exchange Server 2003 installation. Note that in addition to configuring the storage limits for every mailbox in the mailbox store, you can also configure the Deletion settings for the mailbox store. Here you decide how long deleted mailboxes are kept before being purged and how long deleted items within a mailbox are kept before being purged. Configuring these settings makes Exchange administration easier in recovering from unintended deletions, whether of user mailboxes or when users want to restore deleted e-mail.

This dialog box is also where you configure the schedule that Exchange Server 2003 uses to send out warning messages to mailboxes that have crossed their storage limit thresholds. By default, warnings are sent daily at midnight. By clicking the drop-down list, you can select from a number of predefined schedules or create a custom schedule to match your needs (such as if you want to send out warnings multiple times per day or at a time not provided as an option in the predefined list).

Configuring Storage Limits with Mailbox Store Policies   Configuring storage limits at the mailbox store level simplifies Exchange administration in that you do not have to configure limits for every individual mailbox. But what if you have a large Exchange organization with 50 mailbox stores worldwide, and you need to make the same storage limit changes to all of them? Fortunately, you do not have to configure each individual mailbox store. Exchange Server 2003 allows you to simplify the administration of multiple mailbox stores by using policies.

Mailbox store policies allow you to configure a single policy and then assign it to all the mailbox stores that exist within the administrative group. You can also copy the policy to other administrative groups rather than duplicate the administrative effort of configuring storage limit settings. To create a mailbox store policy, perform the following steps:

1. Open Exchange System Manager. By default, there is no container for system policies in an administrative group, so if you haven't previously created a policy, you probably don't have a policy folder. To create one, right-click the administrative group container that contains your server and select New, and then click System Policy Container.

2. Next, right-click the System Policies folder and select New, and then click Mailbox Store Policy. This will open the dialog box shown in Figure 7-14, which prompts you to choose which property pages you want to have available in the policy. You might wonder why you wouldn't have every property page available. However, since you create policies for specific purposes, it makes sense to select only the pages that you need for your policy. With the flexibility of policies, it is recommended that you create a policy for a specific purpose rather than trying to account for everything in one policy. This is especially true in large organizations, where you may need multiple policies to manage different needs. Select the Limits page and click OK.

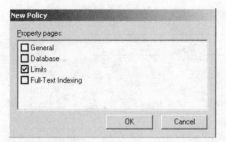

Figure 7-14   Choosing which pages display for a policy

3. The new policy is opened and ready for configuration. The General tab prompts you to name the policy. Give it a descriptive name, such as Storage Limits.

4. When you click the Limits (Policy) tab, you will notice that the page is the same as the dialog box for the individual mailbox store, shown in Figure 7-13. The settings are not the same if you have configured individual mailbox store storage limits, but all the options are the same. After you configure your policy and click OK, you are returned to Exchange System Manager, and you can see your new policy in the System Policies container.

5. Right-click the policy and select Add Mailbox Store. (Even though you've created a new mailbox store policy, at this point it doesn't apply to anything. You have to assign the policy to the desired mailbox stores.)

6. The Select The Items To Place Under The Control Of This Policy dialog box, shown in Figure 7-15, appears next and prompts you to enter a mailbox store name that you want to apply the policy to. If you know the name of the mailbox store, you can type it in, but in a large Exchange organization, you may not want to type in every mailbox store name. A quick way to view all of the available mailbox stores for the policy is to click Advanced, which opens the dialog box shown in Figure 7-16.

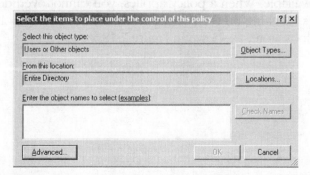

Figure 7-15   Assigning a mailbox store policy

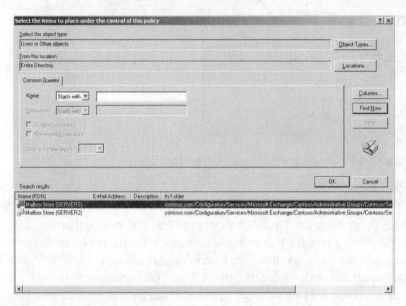

Figure 7-16   Searching Active Directory for mailbox stores

7. The easiest way to search is to not enter anything but simply to click Find Now. This will return all the mailbox stores in your administrative group, similar to what is shown in Figure 7-16. Select the mailbox stores you want the policy to apply to, and click OK. Exchange Server 2003 will confirm that you want to add the mailbox store to the policy.

8. Once you've finished adding the mailbox stores to the policy, you'll see them in the contents pane of the Storage Limits policy container. Double-clicking a mailbox store will allow you to see the effects of the policy. For example, notice in Figure 7-17 that because a mailbox store policy that configures storage limits has been applied to Server2, all the options on the Limits page for the individual mailbox store are unavailable. When a policy applies, you cannot override the policy with local settings. Clicking on the Policies tab shows you what policies are in effect on this mailbox store, as shown in Figure 7-18.

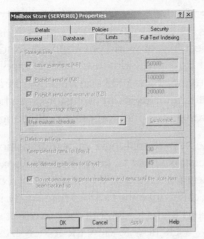

Figure 7-17   Policy effects on local settings

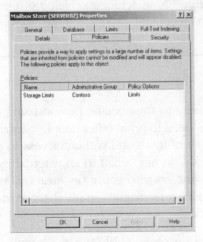

Figure 7-18   The Policies tab

9. The final step after configuring the policy is to apply the policy, which hasn't yet been done even though you selected the mailbox stores that the policy should apply to. To apply the policy, right-click it in Exchange System Manager and select Apply Now. This will cause your policy settings to be applied as you have configured them. Manually applying the policy prevents unintended changes from taking effect immediately.

Once you have created a policy, you do not have to re-create it under every administrative group that you want to apply the same settings to. Using Exchange System Manager, you can simply right-click and drag the policy from the System Policies container in one administrative group to the System Policies container in another administrative group, and then choose Copy from the shortcut menu. Apply the policy in the destination administrative group, and you are finished.

Real World   Storage Limits

Storage limits are often a touchy subject in real-world environments and can be a source of tension between users and Exchange administrators. Storage limits are best put in place when the Exchange Server 2003 organization is deployed because trying to implement limits later, after users are accustomed to not having limits, is likely to be met with great resistance and corporate politicking.

Education and communication are the keys to making a smooth transition to storage limits and helping users to understand how to keep their mailboxes below their storage limits and why it is important to do so. When trying to reduce their mailbox size, users often get frustrated because they may delete many items and even remove the items from the Deleted Items folder, but they may not see much of a change in the mailbox size. Show users how to view the folder sizes through Outlook, and teach them that often the problem is not the number of e-mail messages but a small number of very large file attachments. Helping users to help themselves will reduce their frustration level and also reduce the amount of stress on you.

Configuring Mailbox Permissions

While a mailbox is typically assigned only to the specific person using it, there are times when there is a legitimate business need to grant other people permissions to the mailbox. For example, if a manager is out of town and without access to the network and needs her assistant to send a proposal on her behalf to an external user. Or, if an account manager is working on a deal just prior to going on vacation, and the sales director needs to monitor the account manager's mailbox in his absence in case a message comes in related to the proposed deal.

Mailbox permissions fall into two categories: being able to send e-mail on behalf of someone and being able to access a mailbox in order to view, edit, or create items. Granting Send On Behalf permissions can be done by the administrator in the user's properties in the Active Directory Users And Computers console or by the user himself in the Outlook client. Both methods accomplish the same thing, and when viewing the properties in either location, you see the same settings. To grant Send On Behalf permissions using the Active Directory Users And Computers console, open the console and perform the following steps:

1. Edit the user's properties and click the Exchange General tab.
2. Click Delivery Options, which displays the dialog box shown in Figure 7-19.

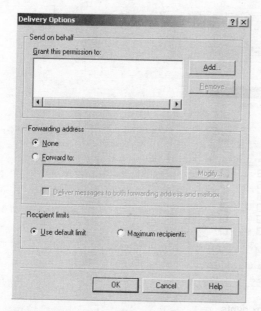

Figure 7-19 Granting Send On Behalf permissions

3. When you click Add, you are presented with the standard Active Directory object selection dialog box, like that shown in Figure 7-15. Type in the name of the user you want to grant Send On Behalf permission to, and click OK. You will see that user's name in the Grant This Permission To field.

Granting mailbox rights can also be performed by the administrator in the Active Directory Users And Computers console or by the user himself through the Outlook client. However, rights granted through the Active Directory Users And Computers console do not have the same level of granularity that rights granted through Outlook have. Through Outlook, mailbox rights can be granted to a specific folder. For example, if an assistant needs to set appointments in her manager's calendar, you do not have to give her permissions that would let her view the manager's Inbox. Through the Active Directory Users And Computers console, the rights you can apply relate only to being able to view or modify permissions or to grant full mailbox access to a user account.

To grant mailbox rights using the Active Directory Users And Computers console, open the console and perform the following steps:

1. Edit the user's properties and click the Exchange Advanced tab.

2. Click Mailbox Rights, which displays the dialog box shown in Figure 7-20.

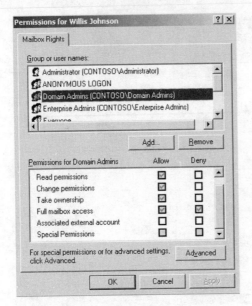

Figure 7-20 Granting mailbox rights

3. You can modify rights or add additional users and grant them rights. Permission check boxes that are unavailable are inherited permissions that cannot be modified here.

Granting permissions in Outlook is a straightforward process, as follows:

1. Right-click the folder you want to grant permission to, such as your calendar, and click Properties.

2. Click the Permissions tab, which displays a dialog box similar to that shown in Figure 7-21.

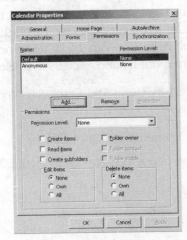

Figure 7-21 Granting permissions to a user folder in Outlook

3. When you click Add, you are presented with the GAL, from which you can select all of the users who you want to have permission to this folder. Once you select them and click OK, you will see them appear in the permissions list.

4. Users are given the permission level equal to what is initially set for default, and you then configure the permissions on an individual basis. This is another instance when it can make sense to utilize group permissions rather than multiple individuals.

> **Exam Tip**   If a user grants permissions to a folder in Outlook, there are two ways that folder can be opened. The first way is by clicking File, selecting Open, and then selecting Other User's Folder. The second way is to add the mailbox to the profile from the Tools menu and selecting E-Mail Accounts. If the user needs to add the other user's mailbox to their profile in order to view a folder, such as a calendar, it is required that they have full permission at the mailbox level and then the designated permissions at the folder level. If the user is granted permissions only at the folder level, they will be able to add the mailbox to their profile but they won't be able to navigate to the folder.

Configuring Delivery Restrictions

More often than not, you will configure delivery restriction settings at the virtual server level rather than at the mailbox level, but there are times when it is appropriate to specify delivery restrictions for a specific mailbox or group of mailboxes that are different from the settings at the server level. Delivery restrictions can apply to the size of messages sent from the mailbox, the size of messages sent to the mailbox, and from whom the mailbox is allowed to receive messages. To configure delivery restrictions for a mailbox, edit the user's properties in the Active Directory Users And Computers console and click the Exchange General tab, and then click Delivery Restrictions. Figure 7-22 shows the configuration options available.

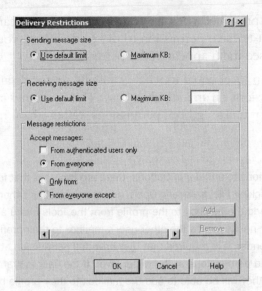

Figure 7-22   Configuring delivery restrictions for a mailbox

You might need to configure a specific delivery restriction on a mailbox if you have a customer feedback mailbox, and you know it should be receiving only text messages. You could prevent messages greater than 50 kilobytes (KB) from being delivered to that mailbox, which would prevent the flooding of the mailbox by a malicious user with messages containing large attachments. Or you might need to set a delivery restriction if you have a mailbox configured to send out automatic responses to messages it receives. You could configure a restriction of the sent message size to prevent the mailbox from being used inappropriately to send other types of messages.

Forwarding Mailboxes to Other E-Mail Addresses

While you can grant permissions to a mailbox for another user, sometimes it makes more sense to forward a mailbox rather than have a user monitor two separate mailboxes. For instance, if an employee leaves the company and his mailbox needs to remain active for a period of time, you can grant another user rights to that mailbox. However, a simpler method is to forward the mailbox to the designated user. Then all messages that come in to the mailbox are automatically forwarded to the designated mailbox, so that user gets both her messages and the forwarded messages in one location (you can tell them apart by looking at whom the e-mail is addressed to). Another example of when you would want to forward a mailbox is when a manager needs an assistant to keep track of her e-mail while she is out of town and without access to the network. The assistant can be granted permissions to the manager's Inbox, but then the assistant will have access to all past messages, too, which is undesirable. Instead, you can forward the mailbox to the assistant while also having the messages delivered to the manager's mailbox, which accomplishes the goal of allowing the assistant to monitor the manager's e-mail without being able to see past e-mails. When the manager returns, you simply turn off the forwarding of the mailbox.

To configure mailbox forwarding, perform the following steps:

1. Open the Active Directory Users And Computers console and edit the properties of the user account.

2. Next, click the Exchange General tab, and then click Delivery Options.

3. Under Forwarding Address, click Forward To, and then click Modify and enter the name of the user who should receive the messages (or browse Active Directory). Click OK.

4. The check box for Deliver Messages To Both Forwarding Address And Mailbox determines the behavior of the forwarding. If you select it, both mailboxes will receive new messages as they arrive. If you do not select it, only the forwarding mailbox will receive new messages.

Moving Mailboxes to Other Servers and Mailbox Stores

As your organization grows and changes, employees will change divisions or locations. Depending on the size and complexity of your Exchange organization, an employee move can result in a situation where he needs to have his mailbox in a different mailbox store or even on a different server. Exchange Server 2003 makes it easy to accommodate mailbox moves, and there are a couple of different ways to accomplish the task.

Moving Mailboxes with the Exchange Task Wizard   If you need to move only a few mailboxes within the same organization, you can use the Exchange Task Wizard and choose the Move Mailbox option, which will open the Move Mailbox page, shown in Figure 7-23.

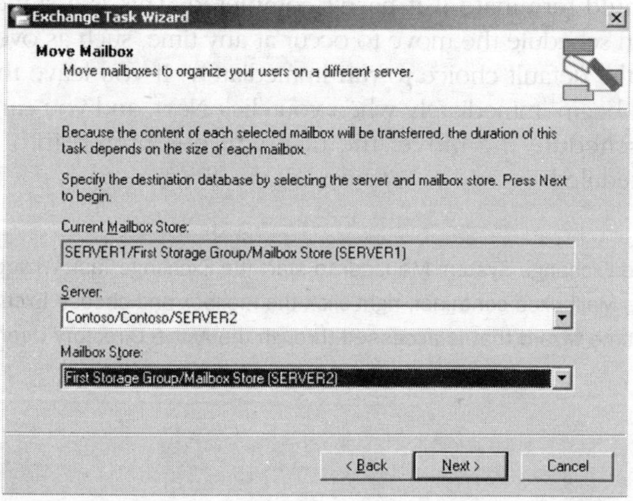

Figure 7-23   Using the Exchange Task Wizard to move a mailbox

In Figure 7-23, you see the current location of the mailbox. The Server and Mailbox Store drop-down lists provide the available options of where to move the mailbox. In Figure 7-23, the mailbox is being moved from the first mailbox store on Server1 to the first mailbox store on Server2. Once you click Next on this page, you are prompted to determine how to handle corrupted messages found during the move, as shown in Figure 7-24.

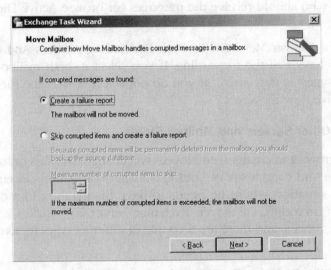

Figure 7-24   Determining how to handle corrupted messages

The default is simply to cancel the mailbox move and generate a report. You may decide that the move should continue anyway and skip the corrupted messages. When you click Next on this page, you are able to determine when the move will take place and when the task should terminate if it hasn't completed. This is a standard task scheduler page. You can schedule the move to occur at any time, such as overnight or at a later date, or take the default choice to run immediately. If you leave the default setting, the process will begin immediately when you click Next, and you can monitor the progress. If you schedule the move, the task will be entered into the Task Scheduler to run as scheduled.

Note   You can also use Exchange System Manager to start the Exchange Task Wizard. From the mailbox store, in the Mailboxes container, right-click the mailbox and choose Exchange Tasks. This starts the same wizard that is accessed through the Active Directory Users And Computers console.

> **Exam Tip**   There are limitations when moving mailboxes with the Exchange Task Wizard. You cannot move mailboxes between administrative groups unless your Exchange organization is in Native mode. You also cannot move mailboxes between Exchange organizations. However, you can do either using the Microsoft Exchange Mailbox Merge Wizard, even if your organization is still in Mixed mode.

Moving Mailboxes with the Microsoft Exchange Mailbox Merge Wizard   The Exchange Task Wizard is useful for moving a small number of mailboxes within the same organization, but it isn't designed to move mailboxes in bulk or to move mailboxes across Exchange organizations. For these tasks, use the Microsoft Exchange Mailbox Merge Wizard.

The Microsoft Exchange Mailbox Merge Wizard is not installed by default with Exchange Server 2003. You must copy Exmerge.exe and Exmerge.ini from the installation CD to the \Exchsrvr\Bin folder on your Exchange server. Once you do this, start Exmerge.exe. When you start the wizard and pass the Welcome page, you are given the choice of a one-step or a two-step merge process, as shown in Figure 7-25.

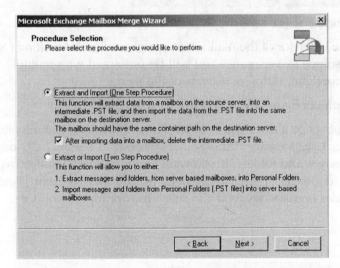

Figure 7-25   The Microsoft Exchange Mailbox Merge Wizard

There are some considerations when using the Mailbox Merge Wizard. The process exports mailbox data out to personal storage files (.pst files), then imports them into the same mailboxes on another server. In the process, the Single Instance Storage feature of Exchange, where a message is stored once and referenced by pointers to as many mailboxes as contain the message, is lost. Each migrated mailbox will have a copy of every message it contained, which can increase the size of the mailbox store considerably.

1. Select the Extract And Import (One-Step Procedure) option, and click Next to continue.

2. Next, you are prompted to select a Source Server, as shown in Figure 7-26.

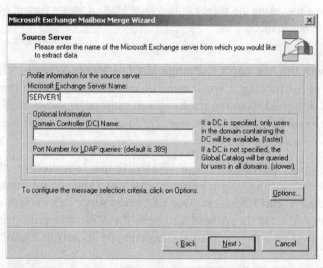

Figure 7-26   Selecting the source server

3. You can control the behavior of the mailbox merge procedure by clicking Options after entering the source server name. You will be presented with multiple pages that allow you to configure different aspects of the merge.

4. The options you can configure are as follows:

   ❑ *Data*—The Data page allows you to control how much data you migrate. The default setting, User Messages And Folders, shown in Figure 7-27, migrates only user messages and folders. If you want to migrate additional items, such as the user's dumpster items (items held by the Deleted Item Retention period) or folder permissions, you can select the appropriate options.

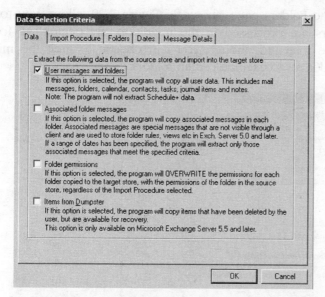

Figure 7-27 The Data page

❑ *Import Procedure*—The Import Procedure page, shown in Figure 7-28, allows you to define how the data should be written to the destination mailbox store. You can copy the data to the target store (which could create duplicate items), merge the data, replace existing data, or archive the data (deletes it from the source store after copying).

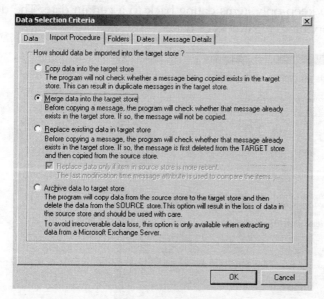

Figure 7-28 The Import Procedure page

❑ *Folders*—The Folders page, shown in Figure 7-29, allows you to configure what folders are processed in the migration. By default, all folders in a mailbox are migrated, though you can choose to limit the migration to specific folders or to exclude certain folders.

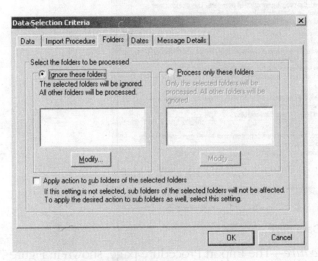

Figure 7-29   The Folders page

❑ *Dates*—On the Dates page, shown in Figure 7-30, you can select messages between specific dates and times to be migrated. This is useful if you have users who have years worth of e-mail, tasks, and calendar items saved, and you wish to keep only items dating back to a certain date. The default is to migrate everything, regardless of date.

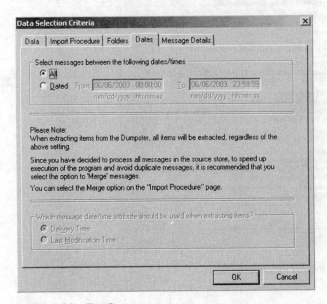

Figure 7-30   The Dates page

❑ *Message Details*—The Message Details page, shown in Figure 7-31, allows you to extract items based on message subjects or attachment names. This is especially useful if you are working with a very large mailbox, and you want to extract only specific types of messages.

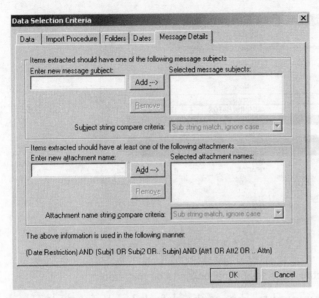

Figure 7-31   The Message Details page

5. After configuring your options, click OK, and then click Next to continue the wizard. This brings you to the Destination Server page, shown in Figure 7-32.

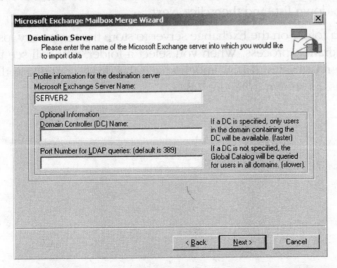

Figure 7-32   Selecting the destination server for the migrated mailboxes

6. Type the name of the destination server for the migration, and then click Next to continue the wizard. The Mailbox Selection page, shown in Figure 7-33, opens, and you can choose the mailboxes you want to migrate. Select the mailboxes you want to migrate, and then click Next.

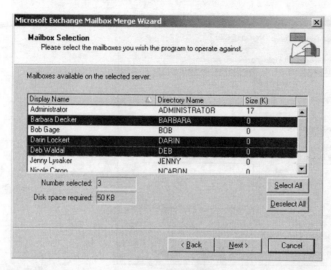

Figure 7-33   Selecting the specific mailboxes to be migrated

7. Next, you are prompted to choose the default locale for the target mailboxes. If your destination is in the same country, such as the United States, then you probably have only a single locale in your Exchange organization. If you are moving the mailboxes to a server in a different locale, select the one that is appropriate from the drop-down list, and then click Next.

8. Next, choose a folder on the Exchange server to store the temporary .pst files used during the migration process. When you select a folder, you will see the amount of disk space required and how much space the drive containing the selected folder contains, as shown in Figure 7-34.

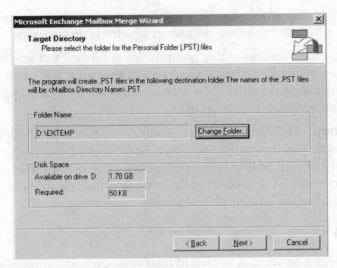

Figure 7-34   Selecting a folder to store the temporary .pst files used in the migration

9. Before the migration process begins, you will have the option to save the settings for use at a later date. This is useful if you want to run the migration later as part of a batch and not have to redefine all the settings. After you decide whether to save your settings, click Next to start the migration. A Process Status window will display, showing you vital statistics about the migration, including the elapsed time and how many successes and failures have occurred. When the operation completes, you can click Finish to exit. If there were any errors, an ExMerge.log file will be created in your \Exchsrvr\Bin folder. You can view it to see what went wrong in the process.

Managing Mail-Enabled Groups

As discussed earlier in this chapter, mail-enabled groups are typically Active Directory security and distribution groups that have been assigned an e-mail address, and when mail is sent to the group address, it is routed automatically to each member of the group. Mail-enabling an existing group is done through the Exchange Task Wizard by choosing the Create An E-Mail Address task from the list. Mail-enabling a new group as you create it adds one extra step, as Exchange extends the New Object creation wizard to prompt you with the option to create an e-mail address and assign the object to an administrative group.

Before mail-enabling Active Directory groups, you should have a clear understanding of the effects of group scope on the Exchange Server messaging capability of these groups. There are three scopes for groups: domain local, global, and universal.

- **Domain local group** Membership of this group is not published to the global catalog server. This means that Exchange Server users cannot view full membership of a mail-enabled domain local group when their user accounts are located in domains other than the domain in which the group exists.

■ **Global group**   Membership of this group is not published to the global catalog server. This means that Exchange Server users cannot view full membership of a mail-enabled global group when their user accounts are located in domains other than the domain in which the group exists.

■ **Universal group**   Membership of this group is published to all global catalog servers in a forest. This means that Exchange Server users in any domain can view full membership of mail-enabled universal groups. If you have multiple domains in your environment, it is recommended that you mail-enable only universal groups and not domain local or global groups.

Expansion Servers

An *expansion server* is a server that is used to resolve or expand the membership of a mail-enabled group whenever a message is sent to that group. Because of the limited scopes of a domain local group or a global group, Exchange users in one domain are not able to view the membership of groups defined in another domain. Exchange is unable to deliver messages sent by users in one domain to groups defined in another domain. To resolve group membership, you must use an expansion server when mail-enabling domain local groups or global groups in environments that have multiple domains. The expansion server that you choose must exist in the same domain as the mail-enabled group. Expansion servers are identified on a group-by-group basis by editing the properties of the group in the Active Directory Users And Computers console and then clicking the Exchange Advanced tab. The default setting is to use any server in the organization, but you can click the drop-down list and choose a specific server.

Query-Based Distribution Groups

A *query-based distribution group* is a new type of distribution group introduced in Exchange Server 2003. A query-based distribution group provides essentially the same functionality as a standard distribution group; however, instead of specifying static user memberships, a query-based distribution group enables you to use a Lightweight Directory Access Protocol (LDAP) query to specify membership in the distribution group dynamically (for example, all employees in an accounting department or all employees in a particular office building). Therefore, adding a user account in the accounting department would result in their automatic membership in a query-based distribution list for the accounting department. The use of query-based distribution groups can considerably lower the administrative overhead in maintaining certain distribution groups, especially those that have memberships that undergo frequent changes.

Query-based distribution groups are not without disadvantages though. They place more of a performance load on server resources. Every time an e-mail message is sent to a query-based distribution group, an LDAP query is executed against Active Directory to determine the membership of the query-based distribution group. In addition, a query-based distribution group can only be created in an organization that is running Exchange Server 2003 or later and that has been switched to Native mode.

To create a query-based distribution group, perform the following steps:

1. Start the Active Directory Users And Computers console, then right-click the Users container and select New, and then click Query-Based Distribution Group.

2. The New Object wizard starts, and the first page prompts you for the name of the group and an alias for it (by default the alias will be the same as the name). Complete the two fields, and then click Next to continue.

3. The next step is to build the LDAP query by filtering the types of addresses you want to include in the query. You can also specify what Active Directory container the query should begin at (all subcontainers will be included), shown in Figure 7-35. Select the address types, and then click Next to continue.

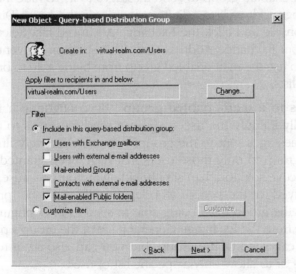

Figure 7-35   Selecting the address types that the LDAP query should filter for

4. The wizard will prompt you to confirm your selections and then will create the group when you click Finish.

You can preview the results of the query-based distribution group by editing the properties of the group in Active Directory Users And Computers and going to the Preview tab. The preview will show you the contents of the group, as well as the syntax of the LDAP query that is being run. If the results are not what you intended, you can simply click the General tab and modify the query, then preview it again to see if the changes corrected the problem.

Limiting Access to Mail-Enabled Groups

In certain situations, you might want to limit access to your mail-enabled groups to only members of the group. For example, if you have a mail-enabled group that is intended for a particular purpose, such as receiving customer feedback from external customers, you might want to limit the amount of unwanted internal messages sent to this group. Similarly, you might want to prevent users from sending messages to a mail-enabled group if it contains sensitive information, as in the case of a mail-enabled group that is reserved for management.

There are two ways to limit access to a mail-enabled group: hiding the mail-enabled group and restricting access to the mail-enabled group.

- **Hiding a mail-enabled group**   When you hide a mail-enabled group, it will not appear in Exchange address lists, so users will not be able to look up the mail-enabled group and send e-mail to it. However, users can still use the SMTP address of the mail-enabled group to send messages to it. To hide a mail-enabled group from Exchange address lists, edit its properties in the Active Directory Users And Computers console and click the Exchange Advanced tab. Select the option to Hide Group From Exchange Address Lists. This solution prevents users who legitimately need to use the mail-enabled group from being able to browse to it in Exchange address lists.

- **Restricting access to a mail-enabled group**   By configuring a mail-enabled group to specifically identify the users who can send messages to the group or who can receive messages sent to the group, you can effectively limit who uses the mail-enabled group to only those users that have been granted permission. This is a more effective solution than simply hiding a group because it allows the group to be displayed for the people who legitimately use it but prevents users who shouldn't use the group from being able to send to it. Configuring message restrictions is done from the Exchange General page of the group's properties. By default, everyone can send to the group, but you can also set it to allow only authenticated users or to allow only a specific list of users.

Note   Groups exist to provide a convenient way to send e-mail to a number of users simultaneously, but they do not preclude users from simply selecting all of the individual members they wish to send to. Therefore, while restricting group access can limit the convenience factor of sending e-mail, it cannot prevent a determined user from selecting every individual user in the GAL to get around the restriction.

Practice: Configuring Recipient Objects

In this practice, you will create four mailbox-enabled users, two mail-enabled groups, configure properties for the objects, and move a mailbox from one server to another.

Exercise 1: Create Recipient Objects

1. Using the Active Directory Users And Computers console, create mailbox-enabled accounts for the following users, placing them in the mailbox store on Server01:

   ❏ Chris Preston

   ❏ Kim Akers

   ❏ Alan Shen

   ❏ Willis Johnson

2. Create the following mail-enabled distribution groups in Active Directory Users And Computers, placing them in the mailbox store on Server02:

   ❏ Engineering

   ❏ Marketing

3. Add Chris Preston and Kim Akers to the Engineering group, and add Alan Shen and Willis Johnson to the Marketing group.

4. Open Outlook and send an e-mail to each user you created in order to initialize his or her mailbox.

5. Verify the presence of the mailboxes in Exchange System Manager by opening the Mailboxes folder in the mailbox store containing the mailboxes.

Exercise 2: Delete and Reconnect a Mailbox

1. In the Active Directory Users And Computers console, right-click Chris Preston and select Exchange Tasks to start the Exchange Task Wizard.

2. From the list of tasks, choose Delete Mailbox and follow the wizard to delete Chris's mailbox.

3. Open Exchange System Manager and navigate to the Mailboxes folder in the mailbox store that holds the mailboxes.

4. If Chris Preston's mailbox does not have a red X on it, right-click the Mailboxes folder and select Run Cleanup Agent, and then refresh the view.

5. Right-click the mailbox for Chris Preston and choose Reconnect. Follow the prompts to reconnect the mailbox to Chris Preston's user account.

Exercise 3: Forward a Mailbox

Alan Shen has left his position at Contoso, Ltd. Before he left, he was working on a marketing proposal with multiple clients. Willis Johnson will be taking over those accounts, and he needs to ensure that if anyone sends an e-mail to Alan's mailbox, it goes to him instead.

1. Open the Active Directory Users And Computers console and edit the properties of Alan Shen's user account.

2. Click on the Exchange General tab, and then click Delivery Options.

3. Under Forwarding Address, select Forward To: and click Modify to add an address.

4. Type in **Willis Johnson**, and then click Check Names. Active Directory should identify the user account and underline it. Click OK.

5. Leave the check box cleared to Deliver Messages Both To Forwarding Address And Mailbox. Since Alan no longer works for Contoso, there's no need for his mailbox to receive the new messages.

6. Click OK to exit the properties of Alan Shen's account.

7. From Outlook, send an e-mail from yourself to Alan Shen.

8. Open Willis Johnson's Inbox by clicking File, then clicking Open, and then selecting Other User's Folder. Note that the e-mail you sent to Alan Shen is in Willis Johnson's Inbox. Open Alan Shen's Inbox and confirm that the message was not delivered there.

Exercise 4: Move a Mailbox

To reduce the load on Server01, you decide to move some users to Server02.

1. Open Exchange System Manager and navigate to the Mailboxes folder in the mailbox store on Server01.

2. Select both Willis Johnson and Kim Akers, then right-click and choose Exchange Tasks.

3. From the task list, choose Move Mailbox.

4. Select Server02 from the drop-down list for the server, and note that the mailbox store changes to the store on Server02.

5. Complete the wizard, monitoring the progress of the mailbox moves.

6. Verify by clicking the Mailboxes folder on Server02 that its mailbox store now contains the two mailboxes (you may have to refresh the view manually).

Exercise 5: Restrict Access to a Mail-Enabled Group

1. In the Active Directory Users And Computers console, edit the properties of the Engineering group.

2. Click on the Exchange General tab.

3. Under Message Restrictions, select Accept Messages: From Everyone Except: and add Alan Shen.

4. Create Outlook mail profiles for Alan Shen, Willis Johnson, and Kim Akers.

5. Log on to Outlook as Kim Akers and send an e-mail to the Engineering distribution group. Since Kim is a member of the Engineering group, she will receive the message sent to the group address in her Inbox.

6. Close Outlook, change profiles to Willis Johnson, and then log on to Outlook as him. Send an e-mail to the Engineering distribution group. Close Outlook and then reopen it using Kim's profile. Note that she received the e-mail sent from Willis.

7. Close Outlook and then reopen it using Alan Shen's profile. Send an e-mail to the Engineering distribution group. Note that Alan will almost immediately receive a non-delivery report from System Administrator, and the error will inform him that he does not have permission to send to that address.

Lesson Review

The following questions are intended to reinforce key information presented in this lesson. If you are unable to answer a question, review the lesson materials and then try the question again. You can find answers to the questions in the "Questions and Answers" section at the end of this chapter.

1. You are the Exchange Server administrator for Contoso, Ltd. You have just finished creating a new mailbox-enabled user for a new employee named Jenny who will start work next week, but shortly after you are done, you realize that you put the mailbox on the wrong server. You open Exchange System Manager and navigate to the Mailboxes folder on the server that currently holds her mailbox but find that the mailbox is not listed, even after refreshing the view. You check the mailbox store on the other server and it is not there either. Why might this be happening?

_____

_____

2. You are an Exchange Server administrator responsible for 25 servers running Exchange Server 2003, Standard Edition, and approximately 10,000 mailboxes contained within a single administrative group. Several of your servers are close to the 16 GB mailbox store limit, and rather than incur the expense of upgrading to Exchange Server 2003, Enterprise Edition, management has approved implementing storage limits on mailboxes across the board. What is the most efficient approach to configuring storage limits for this environment?

   _____

   _____

3. The CEO of your company calls you and informs you that she is going out of town for two weeks and needs to have her assistant check her e-mail while she is gone. However, she doesn't want the assistant to be able to access e-mail that is already in the mailbox because it contains confidential information. What is the best way to set it up so the assistant can check the CEO's e-mail while she is out of town?

   _____

   _____

4. You configure the assistant's address as the forwarding address for the CEO's mailbox, and when the CEO leaves town, e-mail addressed to her goes to the assistant, as planned. However, when the CEO returns from her trip, she is dismayed to find that she has not received any e-mail since she left. What happened?

   _____

   _____

5. You are the Exchange Server administrator for Contoso, Ltd. You have been asked to create a distribution group for a new interdepartmental task force that is being created for special projects. The members of the group are likely to change frequently depending on the project. What type of group should you create so that ongoing administration is as easy as possible?

   a. A security group

   b. A distribution group

   c. A query-based distribution group

   d. A universal group

Lesson Summary

- Recipient objects in Exchange Server 2003 can be mailbox-enabled users, mail-enabled groups, mail-enabled contacts, and mail-enabled public folders.

- The Exchange Task Wizard, accessible from both Exchange System Manager and Active Directory Users And Computers, is used for many common tasks such as creating and deleting mailboxes and e-mail addresses, and moving mailboxes.

- Mailboxes must be initialized before they will appear in the Mailboxes folder of a mailbox store.

- Query-based distribution groups are used to define group membership dynamically by using an LDAP query each time the group is sent an e-mail message.

- Exchange extends the Active Directory Users And Computers console to include Exchange-specific pages. These pages allow you to configure many settings on an individual user basis, such as storage limits, message restrictions, forwarding addresses, and mailbox rights.

- System policies can be used to quickly and easily configure settings, such as storage limits, for a large number of mailbox stores and users.

Lesson 2: Configuring Information Stores

Mailbox stores are only a portion of what can be contained within a storage group. The information store service of Exchange Server 2003 manages all the storage groups on a server, which can contain public folder stores as well as mailbox stores. Storage groups are one of the most significant advantages Exchange Server 2003, Enterprise Edition, has over Exchange Server 2003, Standard Edition. Exchange Server 2003, Standard Edition, supports having only a single storage group per server, containing one mailbox store and one public folder store. Exchange Server 2003, Enterprise Edition, can support up to four storage groups per server, with each storage group containing up to five databases (combinations of mailbox stores and public folder stores).

After this lesson, you will be able to

- Understand storage group architecture
- Understand the use of multiple databases and storage groups
- Add storage groups and databases
- Move Exchange Server 2003 storage groups and databases

Estimated lesson time: 30 minutes

Understanding Storage Group Architecture

The Exchange Server 2003 storage architecture consists of databases (also known as information stores) that are grouped together within a storage group. Each database is comprised of two files: the rich text file (.edb file) and the streaming file (.stm file). These files are managed as a single unit by the Microsoft Exchange Information Store service. There are additional files, as well, that are common to the entire storage group.

- **E00.chk**   The checkpoint file, which is used to mark which transactions in the transaction log have been committed to the database. E00 indicates the first storage group on a server. When you create additional storage groups, the file name that is created will be incremented to E01, E02, and so on.

- **E00.log**   The current transaction log. Exchange Server 2003 first writes data to a transaction log rather than to the database itself, which allows for better performance and scalability.

- *Mailbox*.**edb**   The rich text file. While the extension will always be .edb, the name of the file is defined at the time the storage group is created. By default, it will be named the same as the storage group.

- *Mailbox*.**stm**   The streaming file. As with the rich text file, the name of the streaming file is defined at the time the storage group is created.

- **Res1.log** The first of two reserved transaction logs. The reserved logs are used to reserve a portion of disk space for use by Exchange Server 2003 in case the hard disk runs out of space. This allows the Exchange Server 2003 services to shut down normally rather than crashing when the disk becomes full.

- **Res2.log** The second reserved transaction log. Each transaction log is 5 megabytes (MB) in size.

- **Tmp.edb** A temporary transaction log used by Exchange Server 2003.

- **E00tmp.log** When the E00.log file reaches 5 MB in size, it is renamed, and another E00.log file is created. This E00tmp.log file is used to bridge the gap by storing transactions that occur while the process of renaming E00.log takes place.

There are .edb and .stm files for each database in a storage group but only one set of log files for all databases within a storage group.

Understanding the Use of Multiple Databases and Storage Groups

Multiple storage groups can be used for a number of purposes in an Exchange Server 2003 organization. One of the most common purposes is related to backup and restore. Even in small companies, it is not uncommon to have over 20 GB in e-mail, particularly if storage limits are not used. In large organizations, 100 GB or greater in e-mail is often stored on the e-mail servers. With Exchange Server 5.5 and earlier, only a single mailbox store (called the private information store) is possible. As a result, all the e-mail is stored in a single database file. That poses a significant problem when it comes to backing up and restoring data. The problem isn't so much with backing up the database as it is with restoring it. A restore typically takes twice as long as a backup, so if you have a 100-GB mailbox store that takes eight hours to back up to tape, you can expect it to take roughly 16 hours to restore the database in the event of a disaster. Because e-mail is such a vital corporate application, that length of downtime is unacceptable in most cases. That time frame doesn't even include the time it takes to replace any faulty hardware and reinstall or restore Windows prior to restoring Exchange.

By using multiple databases, you can reduce the individual mailbox store size, making backup and restore easier to manage. However, a limitation is that you cannot schedule backups for individual databases within a storage group if you want them to run at different times. Backup scheduling applies at the storage group level. So, to get around that, you would instead use multiple storage groups, which would allow you the flexibility of different backup schedules for each storage group.

In addition, you can restore mailbox stores individually, in the order you choose, in case of a disaster recovery. For example, while you are restoring Exchange Server 2003, the executive management group requests that getting their e-mail online be the highest priority. If you had the executives in their own mailbox store, you could restore that database first and get the executives' e-mail online, then work on restoring the rest of the company's e-mail. Using multiple databases also allows the flexibility of taking one database offline for maintenance, or restoring an individual database, without affecting the other databases. This results in limiting downtime to a subset of users rather than to all of them.

Another advantage to using multiple storage groups is that you can configure circular logging settings independent of each other. *Circular logging* is a process that saves disk space usage by reusing the same set of log files, overwriting older transactions with newer ones. This differs from the process described earlier where the transaction log is renamed when it reaches 5 MB in size and a new log is created. This is the default behavior and can result in significant disk usage if backups are not performed regularly. Naturally, backups should always be run on a regular basis, generally at least once a day. When a backup is run, transactions are committed to the database and the unnecessary log files are deleted. With circular logging, only full backups can be run. Incremental or differential backups cannot be used because of the way circular logging works. As a result, if you have to restore a database, you can restore only to your last full backup.

> **Caution**   This characteristic of circular logging is a very important and significant limitation. Therefore, the use of circular logging is strongly discouraged unless you have no other choice, such as a short-term workaround with a failed tape backup drive and insufficient disk resources to hold the growing log files until the tape drive is replaced.

By default, circular logging is not enabled. However, if you do enable it, the setting applies to all databases in a storage group. So, if you want to have circular logging on a particular database but you don't want other databases to use circular logging, you would use a separate storage group to house the database that needs circular logging and configure it in the properties of the storage group.

> **See Also**   Exchange Server 2003 also supports Recovery Storage Groups, which are a special type of storage group used specifically for recovering databases. Recovery Storage Groups are discussed in more detail in Chapter 12, "Backup and Restore," which discusses backup and restore of Exchange Server 2003.

Adding Storage Groups and Databases

Prior to adding more storage groups and databases, you should adequately plan for them because they increase the complexity of administering Exchange Server 2003. Planning involves determining the business needs for the storage group infrastructure, which usually relates to backup and restore needs and to administrative requirements.

To add a storage group, use Exchange System Manager. Each server running Exchange Server 2003 can host up to four storage groups. (However, remember that if you are using Exchange Server 2003 on a Cluster Service cluster, you need to ensure that a storage group can hold the databases from another node in the case of a failover.) Navigate to the server on which you want to create the new storage group. Then, right-click the server, point to New, and then click Storage Group. This opens a Properties page for the new storage group. The first task is to name the storage group. As soon as you start typing a name, Exchange Server 2003 will automatically fill in the paths to its installation directory and use the name for the location of the transaction logs and system path. This is shown in Figure 7-36.

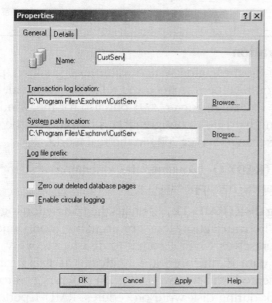

Figure 7-36   Storage group properties

You can change the paths, and you probably should. Exchange Server 2003, like previous versions of Exchange Server, performs best when the transaction logs and the databases are on separate physical drives. This approach is also highly recommended for improved recovery since, if a hard drive fails, it will not take out both the transaction logs and the databases.

> **Important**   If the partition that the transaction logs are located on completely fills up, the Information Store service will stop in order to prevent data corruption. You can correct the problem by freeing up disk space and then restarting the service.

On the Properties page, the Transaction Log Location defines the path to the transaction log files. The System Path Location sets the location for the storage of temporary and recovered files. The Log File Prefix is not user-configurable, but after you create the storage group, you will be able to view the prefix, such as E01, E02, and so on. The Zero Out Deleted Database Pages setting clears deleted data from the hard drive, at the expense of system performance. The last configuration option, Enable Circular Logging, reduces disk usage by reusing a single transaction log rather than creating a new one each time the 5 MB size limit is reached.

> **Exam Tip** Transaction log files are always 5 MB in size. Exchange Server 2003 creates an empty 5 MB file and then fills it with data. When the 5 MB size limit is reached, a new file is created. A transaction log file that is not 5 MB in size is almost certainly corrupted.

> ### Real World   Disk Configuration
>
> Because of the critical nature of the messaging system within a corporation, planning a server configuration for optimal performance and reliability is crucial. This includes not only planning for Exchange Server 2003 but also for the Windows operating system. The following hard disk configuration is considered the best practice for a server running Exchange Server 2003 in the real world:
>
> - **Mirrored system disk (RAID-1)** Contains the operating system and Exchange Server 2003 binaries (the application itself).
>
> - **Mirrored transaction log disk (RAID-1)** Contains the transaction logs for Exchange Server 2003. The transaction logs are arguably more important than the databases themselves when it comes to disaster recovery, and RAID-1 is ideal because data is mirrored automatically as it is written. RAID-1 should be implemented with the two drives on different controllers so as to avoid a bottleneck during disk write procedures. RAID-1 performs better than RAID-5, which is better suited to write-once and read-many type of operations.
>
> - **RAID-5 database disk partition** Contains the storage group and its database. RAID-5, which provides disk striping with parity, scales well (requires a minimum of three disks and can have up to 32) and, with the use of a hot spare (another powered drive that isn't presently part of the RAID set), up to two drives can fail before data is lost. RAID-5 is well suited for storing the databases because it is reliable and performs best when data is read more often than it is written. Another good option is RAID-0+1, which is a combination of disk striping (without parity) and disk mirroring. A RAID-0 stripe set is created, and then the stripe set is mirrored. This overcomes the primary limitation of RAID-1, which is that it can utilize only two drives. However, RAID-0+1 is costly in terms of disk hardware because even though it scales well, the mirroring function results in only half of the total disk space being available for data.

This type of configuration should be scaled as the number of storage groups and databases grows. For each storage group, which contains its own set of transaction logs, you should have a separate mirrored disk set for the logs. Likewise, each database should go on its own RAID-5 disk partition, or RAID-0+1 if cost is not a concern. This ensures the optimal level of server performance and the greatest level of reliability. In addition, if there is a performance difference between hard disks in your server, you will want to place the transaction logs on the fastest disks.

It may not be practical from a cost standpoint to have such an extensive disk configuration in all environments, but the goal is to provide the best possible performance and reliability.

Once you create a storage group, you will likely want to add a database to it. Databases can be either mailbox stores or public stores. To add a database, right-click the storage group in Exchange System Manager and point to New, and then click Mailbox Store. As you can see in Figure 7-37, Exchange Server 2003 displays a Properties dialog box.

See Also   Creating and managing public stores and public folders is the topic of Chapter 8, "Public Folders."

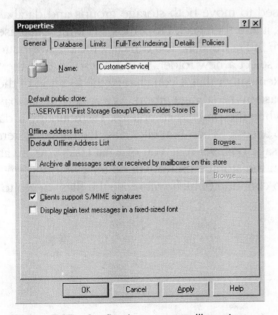

Figure 7-37   Configuring a new mailbox store

Some of the properties to configure for the mailbox store have already been discussed in this chapter, such as Limits and Policies. Options on the General page that you might configure are the path for the default public store for the database, the offline address list that should be used by users in this mailbox store, and whether to archive all messages sent or received by mailboxes on the server. If you choose to do this, log files will be created that record all incoming and outgoing e-mail messages.

Once you have added a new database to your storage group, you can manage it just like any other database. Likewise, if you add a mailbox store, you will have the ability to move users to the new mailbox store.

Moving Exchange Server 2003 Storage Groups and Databases

When Exchange Server 2003 is first installed, it places the first storage group and databases it creates in the Mdbdata folder underneath the installation path (for example, C:\Program files\Exchsrvr\Mdbdata). While this works, it does not allow for the optimal level of performance and reliability. Exchange Server 2003 performs best when its transaction logs and database files are on separate physical disks (or disk arrays). With Exchange Server 5.5 and earlier, there was a utility called Performance Optimizer that analyzed your server and made recommendations as to where to place the transaction logs and database files (storage groups did not exist, so that wasn't an option). You had the option to accept the recommendations, to override them by choosing the locations yourself, or to do nothing at all. Performance Optimizer is not included with Exchange Server 2003, but you can still move databases.

Exchange System Manager is used to move both storage groups and databases. To move a storage group, right-click it and then click Properties. Click the Database tab to open a dialog box like that shown in Figure 7-38. You can click the Browse button next to Transaction Log Location and select a new folder. You can also change the System Path Location in the same way. Remember that if you change the location of the transaction logs, it affects every database in the storage group. As a result, all databases will be dismounted (taken offline) while the process completes. Dismounting a database makes it unavailable for users to access. When you click OK, Exchange System Manager will prompt you with a message box, warning you of what tasks you are about to perform and that all databases in the storage group will be temporarily dismounted. You are prompted to click Yes to continue (which will move the files) or No to return to the Properties dialog box.

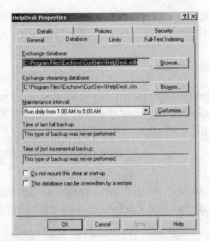

Figure 7-38   Database properties

Moving a database is similar to moving a storage group. Using Exchange System Manager, right-click the database that you want to move and click Properties. Next, click the Database tab. For a database, you have the option of moving the Exchange Database (.edb file) and the Exchange Streaming Database (.stm file). Generally, there is no advantage in separating these files, so it makes sense to keep them located in the same folder. After choosing new folder locations and clicking OK, Exchange System Manager will prompt you to confirm, as shown in Figure 7-39.

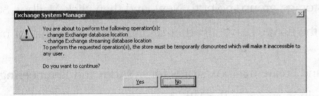

Figure 7-39   Confirming the database move

When moving a storage group or database, you can move the log files and database files to any folder that you want to create. When you move log and database files, it is recommended that you create the \Exchsrvr\Mdbdata file structure on the destination disk partition for consistency, but you are not required to do so.

If you move data to another partition, you must grant the following default permissions to the new Mdbdata folder that contains the log files and database files:

- Administrators: Full Control
- Authenticated Users: Read and Execute, List Folder Contents, Read
- Creator Owner: None
- Server Operators: Modify, Read and Execute, List Folder Contents, Read, Write
- System: Full Control

Moving log files or database files invalidates all existing incremental and differential backups, so it is recommended that you perform a full backup after the move.

Practice: Configuring Information Stores

In this practice, you will create a new storage group and mailbox stores. You will then move the storage group to a new location, observing how the change affects the databases within the storage group and the creation of new databases.

Exercise 1: Create a Storage Group

1. To start Exchange System Manager, from the Start menu, point to All Programs, then point to Microsoft Exchange, and then click Exchange System Manager.

2. Navigate to the Exchange Server 2003 server that you will be adding the storage group to. Right-click the server, point to New, and then click Storage Group.

3. Type **MIS** for the name. Leave all settings at their default for now, but observe that the paths for the transaction logs are the installation root of Exchange Server 2003 plus the name of the storage group, such as C:\Program files\Exchsrvr\Mis. Click OK.

4. The new storage group should have been created on the server.

Exercise 2: Add Mailbox Stores

1. Right-click the MIS storage group, point to New, and then click Mailbox Store.

2. Type **HelpDesk** for the name. Leave all other settings at their default for now and click OK.

3. Repeat the process and create mailbox stores for SysAdm and Engineering.

4. Observe the new mailbox stores in the MIS storage group.

Exercise 3: Move a Storage Group

1. If you have a D hard disk partition, create a folder structure for D:\Exchsrvr\Mis. If you have only a C partition, create a folder structure such as C:\Exchsrvr\Mis to complete this exercise. This exercise assumes two physical disk drives configured as C and D.

2. Right-click on the MIS storage group in Exchange System Manager and click Properties.

3. Because the transaction logs and database files should be on separate physical disks, you will only need to move one or the other. The databases tend to consume more disk space than the transaction logs, so change the System Path

Location. To do this, click Browse and select D:\Exchsrvr\Mis, and then click OK twice. When prompted to continue, click Yes. All databases in the storage group will be temporarily dismounted while the process completes.

Exercise 4: Move a Database

1. Right-click the HelpDesk mailbox store and click Properties. Click the Database tab. Observe that even though you moved the System Path Location for the storage group, the databases themselves do not move automatically and still reflect their original location.

2. Click Browse next to Exchange Database and select D:\Exchsrvr\Mis\Helpdesk for the new path. Click OK.

3. Click Browse next to Exchange Streaming Database and select D:\Exchsrvr\Mis\Helpdesk for the new path. Click OK twice, and then click Yes when prompted to continue. The database will be temporarily dismounted while the process completes, but no other databases in the storage group will be affected.

4. Repeat the process and move the SysAdm and Engineering mailbox stores.

5. Right-click the MIS storage group, point to New, and then click Mailbox Store. Type **Development** for the name. Click the Database tab. Observe that the default location of the Exchange Database and Exchange Streaming Database has changed to reflect the move of the System Path Location for the storage group.

Lesson Review

The following questions are intended to reinforce key information presented in this lesson. If you are unable to answer a question, review the lesson materials and then try the question again. You can find answers to the questions in the "Questions and Answers" section at the end of this chapter.

1. You are the Exchange Server administrator for Contoso, Ltd. Because of the high level of interactivity between the Sales group and Contoso's customer base, executive management is concerned that if e-mail went down, it would take too long to get the Sales staff back online. The CIO researches Exchange Server 2003 and asks you about segregating the e-mail for Sales into its own group outside the general mailbox store so that Sales could be restored first in case of a disaster recover. He also does not want Sales to have the mailbox limits that everyone else has. Furthermore, whereas the general mailbox store is backed up nightly, the CIO wants the Sales group e-mail to be backed up twice a day in order to minimize potential data loss. How would you meet these requirements?

2. You are a network administrator who has been asked to define the specifications for a new server running Exchange Server 2003 that will be purchased to replace an existing server. The server will host three storage groups that each contain 2 to 5 databases, as follows:

Storage Group	Database
General	General Mailbox Store
	General Public Store
Executive	Executive Mailbox Store
	Executive Public Store
Support	SysAdm Mailbox Store
	Development Mailbox Store
	HelpDesk Mailbox Store
	Engineering Mailbox Store
	Support Public Store

Because of the existing server's previous reliability problems, you have been told that cost is not a consideration and that performance and reliability are the deciding factors. Design a disk configuration for the new server that will maximize the performance and reliability of the new server, as well as give the best flexibility in administering information stores.

_____

_____

3. You are the network and Exchange Server administrator for a small company that uses Exchange Server 2003. The server running Exchange Server 2003 has only two hard disks, so you have moved the single storage group and its two databases to the second disk (D), leaving the transaction logs on C. Your company does most of its communication with customers and clients by e-mail. After about six months, you occasionally run into a problem where the Information Store service shuts down toward the end of the day. This usually happens on days when one or more mass e-mails have been sent to customers. You find that after the nightly full backup runs, you are able to restart the Information Store service successfully. Management is concerned about the Exchange server going down too often and wants to know what the problem is and how you can fix it.

_____

_____

Lesson Summary

- Exchange Server 2003 uses a combination of database files and transaction logs to manage data. Information is first written to a transaction log and later committed to the database.

- Transaction logs are always 5 MB in size. Exchange Server 2003 creates an empty 5 MB file and then fills it up with data. Once the log file is full, a new empty 5 MB file is created, and the process repeats.

- Exchange Server 2003, Enterprise Edition, supports up to four storage groups. Each storage group can contain up to five databases, which can be any combination of mailbox stores and public stores.

- Exchange System Manager is used to create storage groups and databases and to change the folder locations for them.

- Circular logging reduces the disk space usage by transaction logs but at the expense of being able to perform incremental or differential backups.

Lesson 3: Creating and Managing Address Lists and Recipient Policies

In Exchange Server 2003, there is a single GAL for the entire Exchange organization, by default. In organizations with thousands of Exchange users, the GAL can be very cumbersome to navigate, making it difficult for users to find the recipients they are looking for. Exchange Server 2003 allows the administrator to create additional custom address lists to meet the needs of the organization, including offline address lists that are available when users are not connected to the network. Address lists are simply a collection of Active Directory objects that have been grouped by one or more common attributes (such as department name). An address list can contain users, contacts, public folders, and groups.

After this lesson, you will be able to

■ Create and modify address lists

■ Administer address lists .

■ Manage a Recipient Update Service

■ Work with offline address lists

■ Create and apply recipient policies

Estimated lesson time: 60 minutes

Creating and Modifying Address Lists

Address lists are a convenient way of filtering the GAL into more manageable groupings. Address lists are different from distribution groups in that there is no "membership" in an address list like there is in a group. Address lists are formed through LDAP queries that filter the display of the Exchange organization based on criteria you define. You primarily find address lists used in large Exchange organizations that contain thousands of users and many physical locations. For example, *contoso.com* has 10,000 entries in the GAL (mailbox-enabled users, mail-enabled users, contacts, and groups). The company has 20 physical locations with roughly 500 employees and contractors at each location. Most users communicate only with users at their own location. Rather than a user having to navigate the 10,000-entry GAL, you could use address lists to filter the GAL to only the users in a given location. That would considerably reduce the number of entries displayed to a user, making the address list more efficient to use.

Another situation in which you would use an address list is when you want to be able to locate users quickly by their group membership but where a distribution list wouldn't be appropriate. An example is an address list that filters all of the Sales staff globally for Contoso into a single list. This would allow the vice president of Sales and others to access a complete list of salespeople throughout Contoso without having to e-mail an entire distribution list.

Creating an Address List

Address lists are created using the Exchange System Manager. When you start Exchange System Manager, click the Recipients container. There are three subcontainers related to address lists: All Address Lists, All Global Address Lists, and Offline Address Lists. When Exchange Server 2003 is installed and an organization is created, the following default address lists are created:

- All Address Lists
  - ❏ All Contacts
  - ❏ All Groups
  - ❏ All Users
  - ❏ Public Folders
- All Global Address Lists
  - ❏ Default Global Address List
- Offline Address Lists
  - ❏ Default Offline Address List

For small to medium-sized Exchange Server 2003 organizations, these default lists are often sufficient. Large organizations will likely need additional address lists to address specific needs. Creating an address list begins by determining what type of address list it will be and therefore which of the three address list containers to place it in. The process of creating an address list in the All Address Lists container is as follows:

1. Right-click All Address Lists, point to New, and click Address List.

2. Type in a name for the address list that describes its function.

3. Click Filter Rules to open the Find Exchange Recipients dialog box.

4. By default, all Exchange recipients will be included in the filter, so click the Advanced tab to narrow the criteria.

5. Click the Field menu, and then select a recipient type (User, Contact, Public Folder, or Group) and the attribute you want to filter by (such as Department).

6. Type a value for the attribute. For example, if you chose Department, you could type **sales**.

7. Click Add to add the attribute to the Condition list. Click OK, and then click Finish to create the address list.

Another option you can filter for is related to mailbox-enabled users. By clicking the Storage tab on the Find Exchange Recipients dialog box, you can select whether to include mailboxes on all servers in the Exchange organization, only mailboxes on a specific server, or only mailboxes in a specific mailbox store.

After you create the address list, you will see it in the container in Exchange System Manager. Right-click the address lists and click Properties. This opens a Properties dialog box, like the one shown in Figure 7-40, which shows you the LDAP query being used to generate the address list.

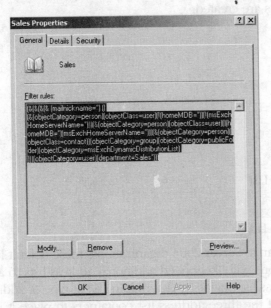

Figure 7-40   The LDAP query for an address list

In this example, the address list is filtering for all users that have a Department attribute of *sales*. By clicking Preview, you can see how the address list will appear when a user selects it in Outlook. Figure 7-41 shows an example of a previewed address list.

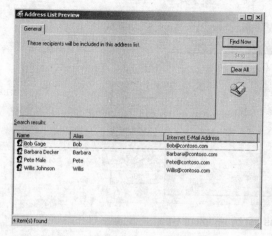

Figure 7-41   Previewing an address list

Modifying an Address List

There are times when you will need to modify an address list. Perhaps you previewed the address list you just created, and the results were not what you intended. Or you may have an existing list that you need to modify to be more or less inclusive, such as a situation where you had an address list that included users as well as contacts, and now you want it to include only users. Rather than having to delete the address list and recreate it from scratch, Exchange Server 2003 allows you to modify an address list and make changes.

To modify an address list, perform the following steps:

1. Right-click it in Exchange System Manager and click Properties. This opens the Properties dialog box, like the one in Figure 7-40.

2. Click Modify. This opens the same Find Exchange Recipients dialog box that you used in creating the address list. Figure 7-42 shows the General tab, where you can limit the types of recipients you want to include in the filter. This is useful if you want to exclude certain types, such as contacts. Figure 7-43 shows the Advanced tab, where you can specify the attributes and values that you want to filter for.

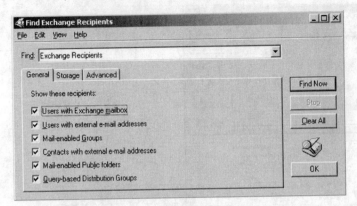

Figure 7-42   Filtering an address list by recipient type

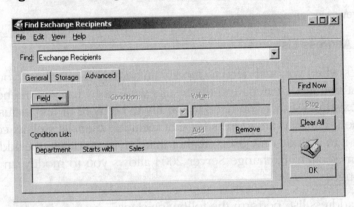

Figure 7-43   Filtering an address list by attributes

Once you modify an address, you can preview it again to ensure that the results are what you intended.

Administering Address Lists

Creating and modifying address lists is the majority of the administrative work involved in managing address lists. However, you can perform additional administrative tasks to administer an address list. One is to configure access permissions for an address list, and another is to override address list update scheduling by forcing an immediate update.

Setting Permissions on Address Lists

By default, all users in an organization can access all address lists (the Authenticated Users group has List Contents permission). There might be situations where you want to restrict access to a particular address list, such as to keep users from using an executive management address list to e-mail all executives easily. Denying access to an address list does not prevent users from e-mailing the recipients in the address list by other means, such as selecting them from the GAL, but it does prevent them from see-ing a particular address list when they are using Outlook.

To set permissions for an address list, perform the following steps:

1. Right-click the address list in Exchange System Manager and click Properties.

2. Click the Security tab, shown in Figure 7-44, which shows the users and groups with configured permissions and what those permissions are.

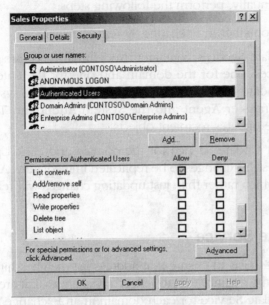

Figure 7-44   The security properties of an address list

3. A gray check box means that the permissions have been inherited from a higher level object, in this case the All Address Lists container. You can add users and groups and configure their permissions or change the permissions for existing users and groups that are listed.

Setting permissions must be done carefully because group membership can cause unintended results. This is especially true when you use the explicit Deny permission rather than unselecting Allow.

> **Important**   If the address list is part of an offline address list that a user has permission to download, they will be able to access the address list offline. This is true even if they have been explicitly denied permission online.

Updating an Address List Manually

Normally when you make changes to an address list, the changes are replicated to other Exchange servers in the organization by the Recipient Update Service. This replication occurs on a configurable schedule. There are times when you do not want to wait until the next scheduled update takes place, so Exchange Server 2003 allows you to force an immediate update manually.

To update an address list manually, perform the following steps:

1. Expand the Recipients container in Exchange System Manager.

2. Click the Recipient Update Services container. Notice that there are two default Recipient Update Services: one for the domain and one for the enterprise. The enterprise Recipient Update Service is responsible for updating system objects such as the Message Transfer Agent and the System Attendant. The domain Recipient Update Service updates recipient objects.

3. Right-click the Recipient Update Service for the domain and click Update Now. This will force any address list changes to be replicated immediately. Alternatively, you can click Rebuild, which rather than just updating changes will rebuild all the address lists.

Managing a Recipient Update Service

The Recipient Update Service exists to ensure that address list memberships are accurate by updating them across the organization to reflect any changes that are made. You need to have a Recipient Update Service for each domain in an Exchange Server 2003 organization. However, that is the minimum requirement. You can have multiple Recipient Update Services in a domain, and it is useful to do so if you have a domain that spans multiple Active Directory sites. Whether you are creating a new Recipient Update Service or modifying an existing one, the configuration options are similar. Figure 7-45 shows what the Recipient Update Services Properties dialog box looks like. To reach this dialog box, expand the Recipient Update Services container in Exchange System Manager, and then right-click Recipient Update Service in the contents pane and click Properties.

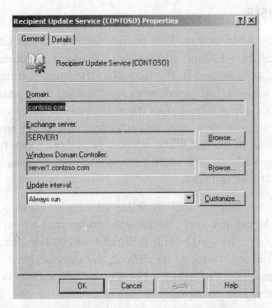

Figure 7-45   The Recipient Update Service Properties

The options you can configure are as follows:

- **Domain**   The domain that the Recipient Update Service is responsible for.

- **Exchange Server**   The Exchange server that the Recipient Update Service runs on.

- **Windows Domain Controller**   The domain controller that the Recipient Update Service will contact and communicate with when making updates to Active Directory.

- **Update Interval**   The schedule that the Recipient Update Service will use to update address lists. The default setting is Always Run, which means that whenever a change is made, the Recipient Update Service will make the update immediately. You can click the drop-down menu to choose a different interval or click Customize to create a custom schedule. The Always Run setting can create a lot of network traffic if frequent changes are made to address lists, which can have undesirable effects on performance.

A Recipient Update Service is created automatically in a domain when Exchange Server 2003 is installed, if there isn't one already. In domains where there are no Exchange Server 2003 servers but there are Exchange Server 5.5 servers that are part of the organization, you must create a Recipient Update Service for that domain. To do so, you must first run DomainPrep in the domain. Then start Exchange System Manager, right-click Recipient Update Services, point to New, and then click Recipient Update Service. Select the destination domain for the Recipient Update Service and complete the other fields previously listed, as required.

Working with Offline Address Lists

Offline address lists are not unique address lists. That is, they are not different address lists than the regular online address lists. Offline address lists are used to make address lists available to users who are not connected to the network. The most common scenario in which they are used is with mobile users who synchronize their mailboxes remotely, such as over a hotel phone line. These users then disconnect and work with Outlook offline in order to save toll charges, only reconnecting when they are done and ready to transmit their e-mail all at once. Offline address lists allow these types of users to have the benefit of using address lists when composing e-mail, even though they are not connected online with the network.

An offline address list does not necessarily parallel an online address list. That is, it isn't a case of simply selecting an address list and checking a box to make it available offline. Exchange Server 2003 configures a Default Offline Address List during the installation of the first server in the organization. By default, the only address list that is made available offline is the Default Global Address List. Figure 7-46 shows the properties of the Default Offline Address List.

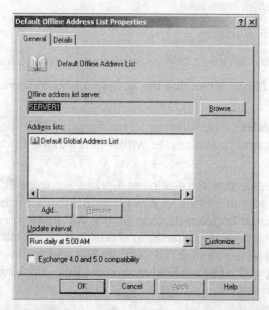

Figure 7-46 The Default Offline Address List properties

The properties that you can configure include the following:

- **Offline Address List Server** The server that holds the offline address list. You can place it on any Exchange Server 2003 server in the organization.

- **Address Lists** The address lists that are associated with this offline address list. You can add or remove address lists by using the Add and Remove buttons.

- **Update Interval**   The schedule used by the Recipient Update Service to update address list changes in Active Directory.

- **Exchange 4.0 and 5.0 Compatibility**   Some features of Exchange Server 2003 address lists are compatible only with Exchange Server 5.5 and later. You can enable compatibility with earlier versions of Exchange Server by selecting this check box.

Offline address lists are flexible because they can be configured at the mailbox store level. Remember that in the properties of a mailbox store, one of the fields is for the offline address list for the database. Because you can apply different offline address lists to different mailbox stores, it is sometimes advantageous to create additional offline address lists to meet the specific needs of a mailbox store. Creating an offline address list is similar to creating a regular address list.

1. Right-click the Offline Address Lists container, point to New, and then click Offline Address List. You will be prompted to name the list and choose a server in the organization to store it.

2. After selecting the server, click Next. You will need to select address lists to add to the new offline address list. The Default Global Address List is included by default, but you can remove it and add other address lists.

3. Click Next. Exchange Server 2003 will inform you that the offline address list will be created during the next maintenance period. Click Next again, and then click Finish.

To apply the new offline address list to a mailbox store, right-click the desired mailbox store in Exchange System Manager and then click Properties. Next to the Offline Address List field, click Browse, and then either type the name of the offline address list or search Active Directory for it. Once you click OK to select the offline address list and then click OK again to apply it, all mailboxes in that mailbox store will use the new offline address list.

Creating and Applying Recipient Policies

Recipient policies are a quick and effective way of defining different e-mail addresses for different users in your organization. For example, Contoso, Ltd. acquires Fabrikam, Inc., a company that has 5000 employees. Contoso has migrated Fabrikam's Exchange Server 2003 organization into Contoso's Exchange Server 2003 organization, but Fabrikam needs to maintain its old e-mail addresses in addition to its new *@contoso.com* addresses so any e-mail that comes from customers is not returned as undeliverable.

In this situation, it would be very inefficient to edit the properties of each Fabrikam user and configure the primary and secondary e-mail addresses. Instead, you could use a recipient policy to do all the work for you. You would create a policy that defines

@contoso.com as the primary SMTP address and *@fabrikam.com* as the secondary SMTP address for all users who have a user attribute of Company defined with the value Fabrikam. The Recipient Update Service would then update all users matching the filter with the new e-mail address configuration.

To create a recipient policy, perform the following steps:

1. Right-click the Recipient Policies container underneath the Recipients container in Exchange System Manager, point to New, and then click Recipient Policy.

2. You are prompted to choose which property pages to include. You can add or remove property pages after the policy is created, so for now select both E-Mail Addresses and Mailbox Manager Settings, and click OK. Realistically, you would probably want to configure separate recipient policies if you need to manage both types of properties. As when configuring other types of policies, while you can consolidate both types of policies into a single policy, the real power is in the flexibility of being able to create multiple policies to serve different needs within an enterprise organization.

3. Next, you must type a name for your recipient policy. The name should be something descriptive so you know from the name what function the policy performs.

4. After naming the policy, click the E-Mail Addresses (Policy) tab. At this point, the addresses listed are the same as what is in the Default Policy. Using the Contoso and Fabrikam example, you would add an SMTP address of *@fabrikam.com* and leave it as a secondary address, with *@contoso.com* being the primary SMTP address.

5. Once you've defined your e-mail addresses, click the General tab and then click Modify to define the LDAP query. This opens the same Find Exchange Recipients dialog box that you previously used when creating an address list. The procedure is the same in filtering the policy membership by using attributes and values. For example, if you want the policy to apply to everyone who has the Company attribute for their user account set to Fabrikam, you specify that on the Advanced tab of this dialog box.

6. Once you define the filter, click OK. Exchange Server 2003 will inform you that if you made changes that cause recipient objects to no longer be under the control of this policy, their membership may not be re-evaluated (meaning their addresses may stay the same). Click OK twice to finish creating the policy. Exchange Server 2003 will prompt you to confirm that you want to apply the policy to all users that match the filter. Click Yes to confirm.

7. The policy will be applied at the next update interval by the Recipient Update Service, but you can force the immediate updating of user accounts by right-clicking the recipient policy you created and clicking Apply This Policy Now.

When you create multiple recipient policies, there is one more configuration option to set. Recipient policies are applied in the order listed, with higher policies having a higher priority level than lower policies. You can right-click a policy and click Move Up or Move Down to increase or decrease its priority in relation to other policies. The Default Policy always has the lowest priority, and it cannot be moved up in relation to other policies.

Practice: Creating and Managing Address Lists and Recipient Policies

In this practice, you will prepare your Exchange Server 2003 organization's user accounts and then create address lists that filter based on user attributes. You will then create an offline address list, add the address lists you created to it, and assign it to a mailbox store.

Exercise 1: Prepare the Exchange Server 2003 Environment

Start the Active Directory Users And Computers console. Create the following user accounts with the associated user attributes:

User	Office	Department	Company
Nicole Caron	Dallas	Sales	Contoso
Willis Johnson	Dallas	Marketing	Contoso
Jenny Lysaker	St. Louis	Sales	Fabrikam
Pete Male	St. Louis	Marketing	Fabrikam
Sheela Word	Boston	Sales	Contoso
Bob Gage	Boston	Sales	Fabrikam
Darin Lockert	Boston	Marketing	Contoso
Deb Waldal	Boston	Marketing	Fabrikam
Chris Meyer	Omaha	Sales	Contoso

Exercise 2: Create Address Lists

1. Start Exchange System Manager. Expand the Recipients container to view the address list containers.

2. Right-click All Address Lists, point to New, and then click Address List.

3. For the Address List Name, type **Sales**.

4. Click Filter Rules, and then click the Advanced tab.

5. From the Field menu, point to User, and then click Department.

6. Under the Condition field, select Is (Exactly) from the menu.

7. For the value, type **Sales**. Click Add.

8. Click OK, and then click Finish.

9. Right-click the Sales address list in the All Address Lists container, and then click Properties.

10. Click Preview. Observe that the group membership consists of each user that has a Department attribute of Sales.

11. Repeat the process to create address lists for Marketing, Dallas, St. Louis, Boston, Omaha, Contoso, and Fabrikam. Use the Office and Company user attributes as required to filter the address list based on those values.

Exercise 3: Create an Offline Address List

1. Right-click Offline Address Lists in the Recipients container, point to New, and then click Offline Address List.

2. Type **Company Offline** for the name, and click Browse to select a server. Choose Server02 to host the offline address list.

3. After clicking Next, remove the Default Global Address List from the list of Address Lists. Click Add and add the Contoso and Fabrikam address lists to the offline address list.

4. Click Next, and then click Next again when Exchange Server 2003 informs you that the list will be created during the next maintenance period. Click Finish to complete creating the offline address list.

Exercise 4: Assign an Offline Address List to a Mailbox Store

1. In Exchange System Manager, navigate to the Support storage group that you created earlier in this chapter.

2. Right-click the HelpDesk mailbox store in the Support storage group, and then click Properties.

3. Click Browse next to the Offline Address List field.

4. Type **Company Offline**, and then click Check Names. The name of the address list should become underlined.

5. Click OK, and then click OK again to apply the offline address list to the mailbox store.

Lesson Review

The following questions are intended to reinforce key information presented in this lesson. If you are unable to answer a question, review the lesson materials and then try the question again. You can find answers to the questions in the "Questions and Answers" section at the end of this chapter.

1. You are the Exchange Server administrator for Contoso, Ltd. The vice president of Sales calls you with some changes to the Sales address list that he wants to be made immediately. You make the changes and e-mail him confirmation that the changes have been made. A few minutes later, he calls you back and is upset because he doesn't see any difference in the Sales address list. Why can't he see the changes, and what can you do to correct the problem as quickly as possible?

---

2. You are the Exchange Server administrator for Fabrikam, Inc. The CIO calls you and asks you to set up an address list for a special internal auditing task force the company is putting together. Since the list membership is sensitive, management does not want the user community to be able to view the list membership and ideally not even be able to see that the list exists. You create the address list and are now editing the security settings for the list. How should you configure the security settings to meet the requirements of management?

---

3. You are the Exchange Server administrator for Contoso, Ltd., a company that uses offline address lists to support a mobile sales staff and an executive management team that travels extensively between office locations. Separate address lists exist for Executive Management and for Sales, among other lists, and both are made available offline in the Mobile Offline Address List that you have created. Company policy is that no one except executive management has access to their address list, and you have configured the security settings on the Executive Address List so that only the Executive security group can view and use the list.

One afternoon, you receive a call from the CEO. She is at a remote site working on a large proposal with a member of the Sales team, and she saw that when the salesperson went to e-mail the proposal, he was able to see the Executive Address List. Also, when the salesperson left the room, the CEO attempted to pull up the Executive Address List on the salesperson's laptop and was able to do so. She is upset that people are able to access this address list despite a company policy against it, and she wants to know what you are going to do to fix the problem immediately. Why can the salesperson access the list, and what can you do to fix the problem?

Lesson Summary

- Address lists can be created to filter the GAL into logical groupings based on organizational need.

- Address lists differ from distribution groups in that membership is only for display purposes; no e-mail address is associated with an address list.

- Offline address lists are used to make one or more address lists available when a user is not connected to the network.

- If a user has permission to download an address list as part of an offline address list, then they will be able to access the list offline even if they have been denied permission to the list online.

- Offline address lists are assigned at the mailbox store level.

- The Recipient Update Service is responsible for updating address list changes in Active Directory. It can be scheduled to always run or configured to run at scheduled intervals.

Case Scenario Exercise

You have been hired as an Exchange Server consultant by Fabrikam, Inc., which has a single Exchange Server 2003 server that supports its 1000 users. The server was installed and configured by the former network administrator, who installed Exchange Server 2003 with all the default settings, including the default installation paths. The server has been very unreliable of late, and the new network administrator does not know Exchange Server 2003 well enough to correct the problems. You have been asked to analyze the current server, make changes based on the requirements of management, recommend further optimizations to improve performance and reliability, and implement those optimizations after management approves them. As part of your recommendations, you are asked to consult with the company's users to determine their needs.

You analyze the server and the Exchange Server 2003 environment and find the following:

- The server is a Quad processor system running relatively recent Intel Xeon processors, with 4 GB of random access memory (RAM), and an external Small Computer System Interface (SCSI) hard disk tower with twelve 18.2-GB hard disks. Presently, there is a single 18.2-GB disk configured as the C partition, and the rest is a RAID-5 D partition.

- The server operating system is Windows Server 2003, Standard Edition. The Exchange version is Exchange Server 2003, Standard Edition.

- The single storage group contains a mailbox store that is roughly 15 GB in size.

- Strict storage limits are placed on the mailboxes in the store. Users are warned that their mailboxes are over the limit at 10 MB, and at 15 MB, they cannot send e-mail until they reduce their mailbox size.

- Delivery restrictions prevent messages greater than 1 MB from being sent or received.

- Circular logging has been enabled on the mailbox store.

- Full backups are run on Fridays, with differential backups being performed Monday through Thursday. A couple of times in the past, restores have needed to be done from tape, and both times they were only able to recover to the previous Friday. Management was also frustrated at the length of time it took for the restore and wants to know if next time they can restore e-mail for Sales and Executive Management first, then restore everyone else's e-mail. They would also like the e-mail for these two groups to be backed up twice a day rather than nightly like everyone else.

After talking to users in several business units, you find that the severe mailbox storage limits are causing users to spend a lot of their time managing their mailboxes in an effort to stay under their limits. The delivery restrictions also pose a significant problem for the sales and marketing staffs, which need to have a convenient way to send and receive proposals and ads that are being worked on with clients.

Another common complaint from both the user community and management is that the GAL is inefficient to use with so many entries. They wish there was a way to view the GAL by department.

- **Requirement 1**   The first requirement is to deal with the server reliability and backup and restore problems. You need to reconfigure the server as necessary for optimal performance and reliability. To accomplish this, you need to make sure you address the problems of the disk configuration, the Exchange Server 2003 software configuration, and the backup plan.

- **Requirement 2**   You discuss the storage limits complaint with the project manager. She advises you that while management would like to see the limits relaxed so users do not have to continually manage their storage space, they want to keep reasonable limits in place to keep e-mail from getting unmanageable. However, they would like the Sales and Marketing groups to have no storage limits.

■ **Requirement 3**   Because the GAL is currently very inefficient to use, you will need to plan and implement address lists. These will allow users to filter the GAL into more manageable, logical groupings.

Requirement 1

The first requirement involves reconfiguring the server for better performance and reliability, as well as for better backup and recovery.

1. In order to meet management's backup and restore requirements, what part of the current server configuration must be upgraded or reconfigured?

   a. Windows Server 2003

   b. Exchange Server 2003

   c. The C partition

   d. The D partition

2. In order to meet the backup and restore requirements, describe how you would reconfigure the storage groups.

   _____

   _____

3. Describe the disk configuration for the server that would allow for the optimal level of performance and reliability.

   _____

   _____

4. Explain why the backup and restore process is not working as intended and what you can do to correct it.

   _____

   _____

Requirement 2

The second requirement involves configuring different storage limits for the Sales and Marketing groups than for everyone else.

1. Of the 1000 users in the Fabrikam organization, 250 are sales and marketing users. How would you configure the same storage limits for each of the sales and marketing users as efficiently as possible?

   _____

   _____

Requirement 3

For this requirement, you will need to create address lists for Executive, Sales, Marketing, MIS, HR, Financial Services, and Development.

1. Describe the process that you will use to create the required address lists.

   _____

   _____

2. There is an existing Executive distribution group in the Exchange organization, and it is configured not to allow anyone except members of the Executive group to send e-mail to it. Management does not want users to be able to use the Executive Address List to circumvent the restriction. How do you prevent users from accessing it?

   _____

   _____

   _____

Troubleshooting Lab

In this lab, you will configure a recipient policy to add a secondary e-mail address and then troubleshoot why the policy change does not take effect.

Before proceeding with this lab, you must have completed the previous exercises in this chapter and have configured the user accounts with their Department, Office, and Company attributes as previously defined.

Exercise 1: Create a Recipient Policy

1. Start Exchange System Manager. Expand the Recipients container, right-click Recipient Policies, point to New, and then click Recipient Policy.

2. Create a recipient policy that will apply a second SMTP address of *@fabrikam.com*. Set it to be the primary address, which will cause the *@contoso.com* address to become the secondary SMTP address.

3. Filter the recipient policy to all users who have the Company attribute of Fabrikam. Click Find Now to view the results of the query and observe some of the names of users. Click OK to save the changes.

4. Confirm all the Exchange Server 2003 prompts, and return to Exchange System Manager after finishing the creation of the recipient policy.

5. Start the Active Directory Users And Computers console. Edit the properties of Bob Gage, and then click the E-Mail Addresses tab. Observe that his settings have not been updated, despite having the Automatically Update E-Mail Addresses Based On Recipient Policy option selected. Quit the user's properties.

Exercise 2: Apply the Recipient Policy

1. Return to Exchange System Manager. Right-click the recipient policy you just created and click Apply This Policy Now.

2. If prompted by Exchange System Manager, confirm that you want to apply the policy.

3. Return to Active Directory Users And Computers. Edit the properties of Bob Gage again, and then click the E-Mail Addresses tab. Observe that his e-mail addresses have been updated to reflect the changes made by the recipient policy. Quit the user's properties.

Chapter Summary

- Exchange Server 2003 recipients can be mailbox-enabled users, or mail-enabled users, contacts, public folders, or groups.

- Deleted Mailbox Retention and Deleted Item Retention are used to provide extra protection against inadvertent deletions, keeping you from having to restore from backup.

- Storage limits can be configured on individual mailboxes, on individual mailbox stores, or by mailbox store policies that can be applied to multiple mailbox stores.

- Access to distribution groups and address lists can be limited through permissions.

- Multiple storage groups can be used to implement different backup schedules.

- A storage group can contain five mailbox or public stores, and a single server can contain up to four storage groups.

- Recipient policies are used to apply e-mail addresses to the users that match the filter.

- A single offline address list can make multiple address lists available offline, and a storage group uses the same offline address list for every mailbox store in the group.

- A single set of transaction logs exists for all mailbox stores in a storage group, but each mailbox store has its own database files.

Exam Highlights

Before taking the exam, review the key points and terms that are presented in this chapter. Return to the lessons for additional practice.

Key Points

- If circular logging is enabled, incremental and differential backups cannot be used.

- Transaction logs and database files should be placed on different physical disks (not just on different partitions). Transaction log paths are configured at the storage group level, and database paths are configured at the mailbox store level.

- Deleted mailboxes can be reconnected to an Active Directory user account in Exchange System Manager if the Deleted Mailbox Retention period has not expired.

- If you have a domain in an Exchange organization that has only servers running Exchange Server 5.5, you must install a Recipient Update Service into that domain to update address lists.

Key Terms

circular logging   A process by which transaction log files are reused in order to conserve disk space. With circular logging enabled, neither incremental nor full backups can be performed, and in case of disaster, it is only possible to restore the Exchange data to the point of the last full backup.

transaction log   Exchange Server 2003 first writes data to a transaction log file, and the data is later committed to the actual database. This process significantly improves the performance of Exchange Server 2003 because the database is not faced with the same level of read/write requests it would otherwise have if the data was written directly to the database.

storage group   Storage groups contain Exchange Server 2003 databases, which can be either mailbox stores or public stores. Exchange Server 2003, Standard Edition, supports only a single storage group on a server. Exchange Server 2003, Enterprise Edition, supports up to four storage groups, with each containing up to five databases.

Recipient Update Service   The Recipient Update Service is responsible for ensuring that address list membership is updated and replicated throughout the Exchange Server 2003 organization. An instance of the Recipient Update Service must exist in each domain that has Exchange servers of any version participating in the organization.

Page
7-43

Lesson 1 Review

1. You are the Exchange Server administrator for Contoso, Ltd. You have just finished creating a new mailbox-enabled user for a new employee named Jenny who will start work next week, but shortly after you are done, you realize that you put the mailbox on the wrong server. You open Exchange System Manager and navigate to the Mailboxes folder on the server that currently holds her mailbox but find that the mailbox is not listed, even after refreshing the view. You check the mailbox store on the other server and it is not there either. Why might this be happening?

A mailbox must be initialized before it will display in the Mailboxes folder. One way the mailbox can be initialized is when the user logs in to it the first time, such as through Outlook. However, in this case, the user doesn't start work until the following week, so the mailbox hasn't been used. The quickest way to initialize the mailbox is to send a message to it from your own account. Once you do this and refresh the view, you will be able to see the mailbox in Exchange System Manager.

Alternatively, you would still be able to use the Exchange Task Wizard from the user's account in Active Directory Users And Computers to move the mailbox, even if the mailbox has not been initialized.

2. You are an Exchange Server administrator responsible for 25 servers running Exchange Server 2003, Standard Edition, and approximately 10,000 mailboxes contained within a single administrative group. Several of your servers are close to the 16 GB mailbox store limit, and rather than incur the expense of upgrading to Exchange Server 2003, Enterprise Edition, management has approved implementing storage limits on mailboxes across the board. What is the most efficient approach to configuring storage limits for this environment?

There are two levels at which you can configure storage limits: the individual mailbox level and the mailbox store level. The prospect of configuring limits on 10,000 individual mailboxes is daunting and highly impractical (it could take weeks to complete). The best option is to configure limits at the mailbox store level. There are two ways to accomplish this. You could edit the mailbox store on each server and configure the settings. With 25 servers, this would involve performing the configuration steps 25 times, which would likely take several hours. Or, you could use a mailbox store policy, which allows you to configure the settings a single time and add all of the servers and mailbox stores to the administrative group that the policy should apply to. Using this method, you could accomplish the task at hand in less than five minutes.

3. The CEO of your company calls you and informs you that she is going out of town for two weeks and needs to have her assistant check her e-mail while she is gone. However, she doesn't want the assistant to be able to access e-mail that is already in the mailbox because it contains confidential information. What is the best way to set it up so the assistant can check the CEO's e-mail while she is out of town?

In this situation, you should configure the CEO's mailbox to forward to the assistant while she is out of town. This way, the assistant will receive the e-mail that arrives during the CEO's absence without being able to access other items in the mailbox.

4. You configure the assistant's address as the forwarding address for the CEO's mailbox, and when the CEO leaves town, e-mail addressed to her goes to the assistant, as planned. However, when the CEO returns from her trip, she is dismayed to find that she has not received any e-mail since she left. What happened?

You forgot to select the option to Deliver Messages To Both Forwarding Address And Mailbox. As a result, all new e-mails were forwarded to the assistant, but they were not delivered to the CEO's mailbox. Unfortunately, all you can do at this point is to have the assistant manually forward all the CEO's e-mail between the time she left and the time she returned to her mailbox.

5. You are the Exchange Server administrator for Contoso, Ltd. You have been asked to create a distribution group for a new interdepartmental task force that is being created for special projects. The members of the group are likely to change frequently depending on the project. What type of group should you create so that ongoing administration is as easy as possible?

    a. A security group

    b. A distribution group

    c. A query-based distribution group

    d. A universal group

The correct answer is c.

Page
7-55
Lesson 2 Review

1. You are the Exchange Server administrator for Contoso, Ltd. Because of the high level of interactivity between the Sales group and Contoso's customer base, executive management is concerned that if e-mail went down, it would take too long to get the Sales staff back online. The CIO researches Exchange Server 2003 and asks you about segregating the e-mail for Sales into its own group outside the general mailbox store so that Sales could be restored first in case of a disaster recover. He also does not want Sales to have the mailbox limits that everyone else has. Furthermore, whereas the general mailbox store is backed up nightly, the CIO wants the Sales group e-mail to be backed up twice a day in order to minimize potential data loss. How would you meet these requirements?

In order to meet the requirements, you need to create a new storage group and place the new mailbox store inside this storage group. The primary reason for this is that backup schedules are set at the storage group level, not at the individual database level. As a result, the only way to configure a different backup schedule for Sales is for it to have its own storage group. Mailbox limits can be set at the mailbox store level, so limits would not force a decision either way, and neither would the need to restore the Sales mailbox store prior to restoring the general mailbox store.

2. You are a network administrator who has been asked to define the specifications for a new server running Exchange Server 2003 that will be purchased to replace an existing server. The server will host three storage groups that each contain 2 to 5 databases, as follows:

Storage Group	Database
General	General Mailbox Store
	General Public Store
Executive	Executive Mailbox Store
	Executive Public Store
Support	SysAdm Mailbox Store
	Development Mailbox Store
	HelpDesk Mailbox Store
	Engineering Mailbox Store
	Support Public Store

Because of the existing server's previous reliability problems, you have been told that cost is not a consideration and that performance and reliability are the deciding factors. Design a disk configuration for the new server that will maximize the performance and reliability of the new server, as well as give the best flexibility in administering information stores.

Since cost is not a factor, you have the ability to use the best configuration possible for your new server. This involves having a mirrored system partition that holds the operating system and Exchange Server 2003 binaries, a mirrored disk partition for each storage group's transaction logs, and a RAID-5 disk partition for each storage group's databases. A possible disk configuration would look like the following:

C — mirrored partition (operating system and Exchange Server 2003)

D — CD-ROM drive

E — mirrored partition (General storage group's transaction logs)

F — mirrored partition (Executive storage group's transaction logs)

G — mirrored partition (Support storage group's transaction logs)

H — RAID-5 partition (General Mailbox Store and General Public Store)

I — RAID-5 partition (Executive Mailbox Store and Executive Public Store)

J — RAID-5 partition (SysAdm Mailbox Store, HelpDesk Mailbox Store, and Support Public Store)

K — RAID-5 partition (Engineering Mailbox Store and Development Mailbox Store)

This type of configuration would provide a great level of performance, administrative flexibility, and reliability.

3. You are the network and Exchange Server administrator for a small company that uses Exchange Server 2003. The server running Exchange Server 2003 has only two hard disks, so you have moved the single storage group and its two databases to the second disk (D), leaving the transaction logs on C. Your company does most of its communication with customers and clients by e-mail. After about six months, you occasionally run into a problem where the Information Store service shuts down toward the end of the day. This usually happens on days when one or more mass e-mails have been sent to customers. You find that after the nightly full backup runs, you are able to restart the Information Store service successfully. Management is concerned about the Exchange server going down too often and wants to know what the problem is and how you can fix it.

The Information Store service shuts down automatically when the partition that holds the transaction logs fills up. Each transaction log is 5 MB in size, and a new one is created whenever the 5 MB limit is reached. In this situation, where e-mail is being used extensively and mass e-mails are being sent, it is likely that the C partition is not large enough for Exchange Server 2003. As a result, the partition is filling up with log files throughout the day, culminating with the Information Store service stopping when the partition reaches capacity.

When a full backup is run, it purges the transaction logs, so the disk space is returned. This is why the Information Store service is able to restart and Exchange Server 2003 works again.

The best solution would be to add at least one new disk to the server and move the transaction logs to the new drive. This would alleviate the problem. An alternative would be to enable circular logging on the storage group. This would result in the same transaction log set being reused rather than a new log file being created every 5 MB. Since full backups are being run nightly, this would be possible because you can't perform incremental or differential backups when circular logging is enabled. The caveat to this solution is that you will only be able to restore a database back to the last full backup; any data created during the time between the backup and the failure would be lost.

Page 7–71

Lesson 3 Review

1. You are the Exchange Server administrator for Contoso, Ltd. The vice president of Sales calls you with some changes to the Sales address list that he wants to be made immediately. You make the changes and e-mail him confirmation that the changes have been made. A few minutes later, he calls you back and is upset because he doesn't see any difference in the Sales address list. Why can't he see the changes, and what can you do to correct the problem as quickly as possible?

The Recipient Update Service is responsible for updating Active Directory with changes that are made to address lists. If the Recipient Update Service is set to run on a schedule rather than set to Always Run, changes will not be reflected until the next maintenance interval. However, you can force an immediate update by right-clicking the Recipient Update Service in the domain that contains the vice president's user account and clicking either Update Now or Rebuild. The former will update the changes in the address lists, while the latter will completely rebuild the address lists based on the LDAP queries.

2. You are the Exchange Server administrator for Fabrikam, Inc. The CIO calls you and asks you to set up an address list for a special internal auditing task force the company is putting together. Since the list membership is sensitive, management does not want the user community to be able to view the list membership and ideally not even be able to see that the list exists. You create the address list and are now editing the security settings for the list. How should you configure the security settings to meet the requirements of management?

You would first configure a security group for the task force and for the executive management team, if one did not already exist. Next, right-click the address list in Exchange System Manager, click Properties, and then click the Security tab. Add the security groups for the task force and the executive team to the list of users and groups with permissions, and configure them to have the same permissions as the Authenticated Users group. Finish configuring the permissions by removing the Everyone, Authenticated Users, and Anonymous Logon groups from the list.

3. You are the Exchange Server administrator for Contoso, Ltd., a company that uses offline address lists to support a mobile sales staff and an executive management team that travels extensively between office locations. Separate address lists exist for Executive Management and for Sales, among other lists, and both are made available offline in the Mobile Offline Address List that you have created. Company policy is that no one except executive management has access to their address list, and you have configured the security settings on the Executive Address List so that only the Executive security group can view and use the list.

One afternoon, you receive a call from the CEO. She is at a remote site working on a large proposal with a member of the Sales team, and she saw that when the salesperson went to e-mail the proposal, he was able to see the Executive Address List. Also, when the salesperson left the room, the CEO attempted to pull up the Executive Address List on the salesperson's laptop and was able to do so. She is upset that people are able to access this address list despite a company policy against it, and she wants to know what you are going to do to fix the problem immediately. Why can the salesperson access the list, and what can you do to fix the problem?

Once an offline address list is downloaded, the security settings no longer apply. So, if a user has permission to download an address list and part of an offline address list, they will be able to access the address list offline, even if they do not have permission to it online. Therefore, the solution in this situation is to not include both address lists as part of the same offline address list. You could create a separate mailbox store for the Executive group and assign an offline address list to that mailbox store that included all the address lists, including the Executive Address List. Then, in the offline address list that was assigned to the mailbox store containing the Sales group, remove the Executive Address List from the list of Address Lists.

Case Scenario Exercise: Requirement 1

1. In order to meet management's backup and restore requirements, what part of the current server configuration must be upgraded or reconfigured?

   a. Windows Server 2003

   b. Exchange Server 2003

   c. The C partition

   d. The D partition

   The correct answer is b. Exchange Server 2003, Standard Edition, supports only a single storage group with one mailbox store and one public store. In addition, the size of the mailbox store database cannot exceed 16 GB. To meet the requirements, you will need to first upgrade to Exchange Server 2003, Enterprise Edition. Windows Server 2003, Standard Edition, supports all of the requirements for this scenario; you do not need Windows Server 2003, Enterprise Edition, in order to run Exchange Server 2003, Enterprise Edition.

2. In order to meet the backup and restore requirements, describe how you would reconfigure the storage groups.

   Because management wants a different backup schedule for the Sales and Executive groups than for everyone else, you will need to place them in a separate storage group. Backup schedules are set at the storage group level rather than at the mailbox store level, so simply creating additional mailbox stores in the same storage group will not work. Since the Executive and Sales groups will have the same backup schedule, you can create one storage group for both of them and create two mailbox stores in the new storage group.

3. Describe the disk configuration for the server that would allow for the optimal level of performance and reliability.

   In this scenario, you want to completely reconfigure the disks. For best performance and reliability, mirror the C partition, using two of the 18.2-GB disks in the process. Then install Windows Server 2003 and Exchange Server 2003, Enterprise Edition, on this mirrored partition.

   The next step would be to use four more of the disks to create two mirrored partitions: D and E. On these partitions, you will later place the transaction logs for the Executive and Sales storage groups, and the General storage group.

   With the last six disks, create two RAID-5 partitions: F and G (each consisting of three disks). On these partitions, you will later place the database files for the Executive and Sales mailbox stores (F), and the General mailbox store (G). This will not be completely ideal since in a perfect world you would be able to put the Executive and Sales mailbox stores on their own individual partitions. However, with the number of disks you have in this situation, this configuration is the best choice.

4. Explain why the backup and restore process is not working as intended and what you can do to correct it.

Circular logging had been enabled on the mailbox store in order to conserve disk space on the 18.2-GB C partition, which was near capacity with a 15-GB database, over 1 GB for Windows Server 2003, plus other files and folders. A limitation of circular logging is that incremental and differential backups do not work; only full backups can be run. As a result, the only good backup of Exchange in a week was the Friday full backup. Therefore, whenever they had to restore, they could only recover back to the previous Friday. The two options here are to change the backup schedule so that full backups are always done (no differentials) or to disable circular logging. With the new disk configuration, disk space will not be the issue it was previously, so disabling circular logging is the better choice.

Page
7-74

Case Scenario Exercise: Requirement 2

1. Of the 1000 users in the Fabrikam organization, 250 are sales and marketing users. How would you configure the same storage limits for each of the sales and marketing users as efficiently as possible?

Storage limits can be configured in one of three ways: by mailbox store policy, at the individual mailbox store level, or at the individual user level. In this situation, there is already a mailbox store for the Sales group, but there is not one for the Marketing group. It would still be much more efficient to create a mailbox store for Marketing and move everyone in the marketing department into the new mailbox store. Since the Marketing group does not need the same backup schedule as the Executive and Sales groups, you can create Marketing's mailbox store in the general First Storage Group.

To identify all of the marketing users quickly, use the Find command against the Users container in Active Directory Users And Computers to find every user account that has their Department attribute set to Marketing. Then, use the Exchange Task Wizard to move all the mailboxes to the new Marketing mailbox store.

By default, there are no storage limits on a mailbox store, so the Sales and Marketing groups do not have limits. Neither does the Executive Mailbox Store, which is supposed to have the same limits as the default Mailbox Store that contains all other users. Create a mailbox store policy in Exchange System Manager by right-clicking the System Policies container in the First Administrative Group, pointing to New, and clicking Mailbox Store Policy. Configure the Limits page to reflect a 50-MB warning limit and a 100-MB "cannot send" limit. Add the Mailbox Store and Executive Mailbox Store to the policy. This will override the existing limit policies on both mailbox stores.

Page
7-75

Case Scenario Exercise: Requirement 3

1. Describe the process that you will use to create the required address lists.

Exchange System Manager is used to create and modify address lists. Expand the Recipients container, right-click All Address Lists, point to New, and then click Address List. After naming the address list, click Filter Rules to configure the LDAP query that will define the list membership. You can use the Find Exchange Recipients dialog box to find users based on their department, which is most appropriate for this situation. Then repeat the process for each list that needs to be created.

2. There is an existing Executive distribution group in the Exchange organization, and it is configured not to allow anyone except members of the Executive group to send e-mail to it. Management does not want users to be able to use the Executive Address List to circumvent the restriction. How do you prevent users from accessing it?

By default, all users can access all address lists. However, when necessary, you can set the permissions on an address list to control access to it. This is done by right-clicking the address list, clicking Properties, and then clicking the Security tab. In this situation, add the Executive security group to the permissions list and grant the group the same permissions currently held by the Authenticated Users group. Then remove the Everyone, Anonymous Logon, and Authenticated Users groups from the list of users and groups with permissions.

8 Public Folders

Exam Objectives in this Chapter:

- Manage and troubleshoot public folders
- Manage and troubleshoot permissions
- Monitor, manage, and troubleshoot infrastructure performance

Why This Chapter Matters

When people think of Microsoft Exchange Server, typically the first thing that comes to mind is e-mail. However, e-mail is only part of the functionality of Exchange Server. Public folders provide a powerful means of collaboration, enabling users to easily share many different types of data within an Exchange organization. In addition, public folders can be used as a common repository for data that is accessed by multiple users, such as a customer feedback e-mail address. A well-designed public folder infrastructure enables the user community to work more efficiently, resulting in a smoother workflow and increased productivity.

Lessons in this Chapter:

- Lesson 1: Creating Public Folders. 8-2
- Lesson 2: Administering Public Folders. 8-13
- Lesson 3: Public Folder Security. 8-26

Before You Begin

In order to complete the exercises in this chapter, you will need to have the following hardware and software:

- Two computers running Microsoft Windows Server 2003 installed into the same Active Directory domain. (Whether the second computer is also a domain controller is purely optional; it won't affect Setup either way.)

- Microsoft Outlook 2000 or Outlook 2003 installed on one of the servers or on another workstation that is part of the domain.

Lesson 1: Creating Public Folders

Public folders provide a way to store information that can be shared by users in an Exchange Server 2003 organization. When you use public folders in combination with customized Outlook forms, they become the repository for collaboration applications such as bulletin boards, discussion groups, customer tracking systems, and so on. Users can access public folders in different ways. One way is by using Outlook. Public folders can also be accessed with Network News Transfer Protocol (NNTP) and Hypertext Transfer Protocol (HTTP) clients, which are popular methods of allowing public folder access to users outside the organization, such as customers.

After this lesson, you will be able to

- Understand the uses of public folders
- Create public folders
- Create a new public folder tree

Estimated lesson time: 45 minutes

Using Public Folders

Public folders are contained in public folder stores. The public folder listing that is viewed by the client software, such as Outlook, is arranged in a tree structure that is called a public folder tree (also known as a hierarchy). Any public folder that contains subfolders is referred to as a parent folder, and a parent folder can contain child folders that exist as subfolders. Public folders that are created at the root of a public folder tree are referred to as top-level folders.

Public folders provide a number of benefits, including the following:

- Allowing messages to be sent to public folders using e-mail addresses that are stored in Active Directory directory service instead of posting messages to the folders.

- Allowing users both internal to the Exchange Server 2003 organization and external to the organization to collaborate.

- Making newsgroups available to users.

- Allowing Web browsers to gain access to public folders by specifying a Uniform Resource Locater (URL) to that folder.

- Performing full-text index searches on public folder contents.

- Allowing users to gain access to any public folder in the organization. By default, Exchange Server 2003 enables public folder referrals between routing groups.

There are other uses for public folders, as well. Public folders are very flexible in that they are able to hold almost any kind of data you might want to store and make that data available to other users. Public folders are often used to provide a customer feedback e-mail address. If you used a standard user mailbox in this situation, you would have messages being sent to a single individual. If you used a distribution list for the feedback e-mail address, everyone in the list would receive every e-mail sent to the address, which might not be desirable, particularly if an executive manager wanted to be able to monitor the feedback e-mail periodically but without having to receive all of the messages in his or her own mailbox. By using a public folder arrangement, feedback e-mails from customers could be posted to the public folder and permissions granted to the folder for everyone who needed access. This would create a central repository for the e-mail messages.

Another common scenario for using public folders is to create group or departmental shared calendars. These calendars can be used for tracking sales appointments for a sales staff, maintaining an employee vacation schedule, listing employee birthdays or anniversary dates, and so on.

Creating Public Folders

There are two ways to create public folders. The most common way is by using Outlook because users can easily create their own public folders inside of top-level folders to which they have been granted permission. This eases the administrative burden since the administrator does not have to create every public folder that is required. With the Exchange Server 2003 version of Outlook Web Access (OWA), you can use and create public folders. This is a significant upgrade from the Exchange Server 5.5 version of OWA, which had no support for public folders. The other method used to create public folders is to use Exchange System Manager. This method accomplishes the same thing as creating public folders in Outlook, but this method is used exclusively by Exchange administrators.

Creating Public Folders in Outlook

By default, all users in an Exchange organization can create public folders under the All Public Folders top-level folder. This default behavior can be modified; this topic is discussed in Lesson 3 of this chapter. To create a public folder in Outlook 2003, perform the following steps:

1. Expand the Public Folders container in the Folder List, and then expand the All Public Folders container to see the list of current public folders.

2. Right-click All Public Folders, and then click New Folder. This will open the Create New Folder dialog box, shown in Figure 8-1.

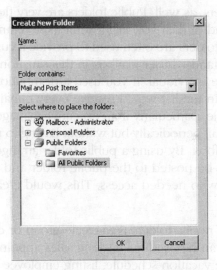

Figure 8-1   Creating a new public folder

3. Type a name for the folder. The name should be descriptive and identify the purpose of the folder.

4. The default type of items for a new public folder is Mail And Post Items. However, you can click the drop-down list to select one of the following:

   ❑ Calendar Items

   ❑ Contact Items

   ❑ Journal Items

   ❑ Note Items

   ❑ Task Items

   Choose the type of items you want the folder to contain. Each public folder can contain only one of the above item types.

5. The last configuration option is Select Where To Place The Folder. It will default to the folder you were in when you chose to create a new folder, in this case All Public Folders. You can easily navigate to a different folder, if desired, and folders can be nested inside one another. Once you select a location, click OK to create the public folder.

Creating Public Folders in OWA

Creating a public folder using OWA is very similar to creating a public folder using Outlook and can be done as follows:

1. Log on to OWA, then click the Public Folders link from the navigation menu.

2. A new browser window will open with Public Folders as the root container. This view maps directly to the All Public Folders container you saw in Outlook, and you will see a list of public folders under the Public Folders container.

3. Right-click Public Folders, and then click New Folder. The Create New Folder–Web Page Dialog dialog box, shown in Figure 8-2, opens.

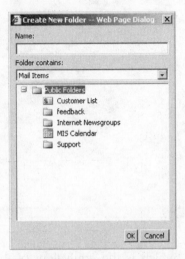

Figure 8-2   Creating a public folder in OWA

4. Enter the information to create a new public folder.

Creating Public Folders in Exchange System Manager

Exchange Server 2003 administrators can create public folders using Exchange System Manager. This is especially useful for creating a hierarchy of top-level folders for users and then assigning permissions so users can only create subfolders in specific top-level folders. This allows the administrator to control the amount of top-level folders and to keep the public folder hierarchy from getting too cluttered and inefficient to use.

1. Open Exchange System Manager and navigate to an administrative group, and then expand the Folders container to view the public folder trees, as shown in Figure 8-3.

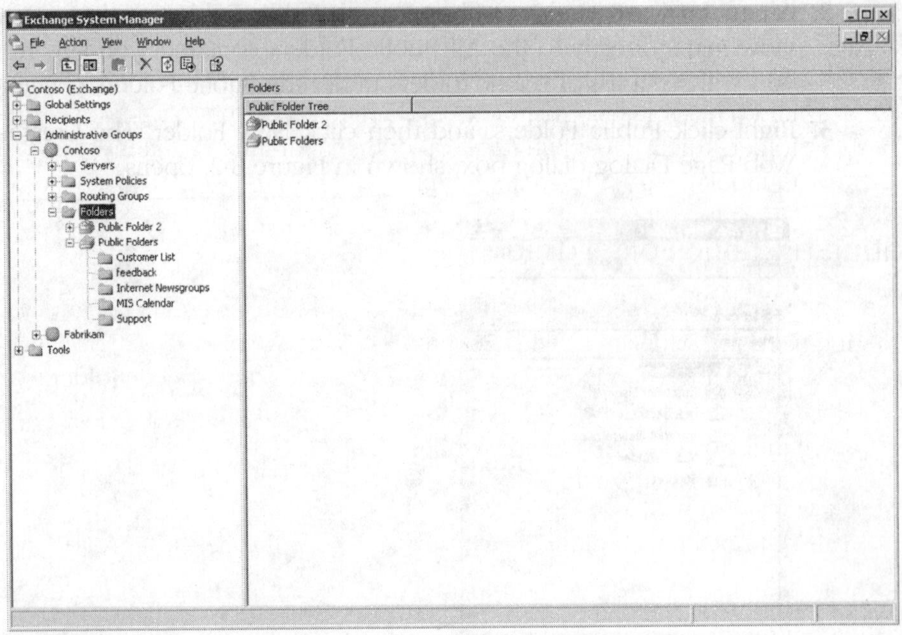

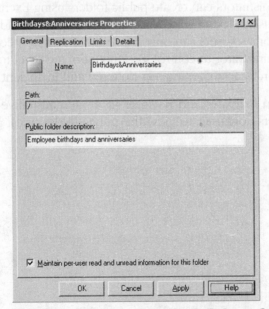

Figure 8-3   The Folders container

2. Expand the Public Folders container, which is the equivalent of the All Public Folders container that displays in Outlook. This will show you the current folders in your public folder tree.

3. Right-click the Public Folders container, point to New, and then click Public Folder. You will see a dialog box similar to the one shown in Figure 8-4.

Figure 8-4   Creating a public folder in Exchange System Manager

4. Fill in the information to identify the folder. Note that there is no option to configure the type of items the public folder will contain. The folder will contain Mail And Post Items, which cannot be changed. These folders can also be used to contain other folders, which can hold any type of items. If you need to create public folders that will contain items other than Mail And Post Items, you will need to use Outlook or OWA to create them.

Creating a Public Folder Tree

When you view public folders through the All Public Folders container, you are viewing a public folder tree, which is also known as a hierarchy. There are two types of public folder trees in Exchange Server 2003: the Default public folder tree and General Purpose public folder trees. There can be only a single Default public folder tree in an Exchange Server 2003 organization; however, you can create as many General Purpose trees as your organization requires.

The Default Public Folder Tree

The Default public folder tree is automatically created by the Setup program when you install the first Exchange Server 2003 server and create your organization. The Default public folder tree is listed in Exchange System Manager as Public Folders and is displayed in Outlook as All Public Folders. The tree contains the list of all public folders within the tree.

The Default public folder tree is replicated to each Exchange server that contains a public folder store that is associated with that tree. As a result, users can easily browse the public folder hierarchy. By default, this public folder tree exists on every public folder server in an Exchange Server 2003 organization.

General Purpose Public Folder Trees

General Purpose public folder trees are additional public folder trees that you can create. Similar to the Default public folder tree, a General Purpose public folder tree is replicated to each server running Exchange 2000 Server (or a later version) that contains a public folder store associated with that tree. As a result, you can create additional public folder trees that are replicated to selected public folder servers in the Exchange organization.

General Purpose public folder trees do not support Messaging Application Programming Interface (MAPI) clients, so the General Purpose public folder tree that you create will not be visible or accessible to Outlook users. Instead, General Purpose trees are accessible only by NNTP and HTTP clients. In addition, to allow users to access a General Purpose public folder tree from a Web browser, you will need to implement an HTTP virtual server in your Exchange Server 2003 organization.

See Also   Virtual servers, including HTTP, are discussed in Chapter 9, "Virtual Servers." What you need to know in order to complete the exercises in this chapter will be provided.

A common use for General Purpose public folder trees is to store custom applications. You can use separate General Purpose public folder trees to store custom collaboration applications according to the functional, business, or geographic requirements of your users. For example, you can use one tree to store personnel department applications and use another tree to store accounting applications or research and development applications.

Another common use of General Purpose public folder trees is to make public folder data available to users outside of the organization, such as business partners and customers. By using a separate public folder tree, you can keep this type of data separate from the folder content in the Default tree, as well as apply different security settings. Multiple public folder trees provide similar benefits to using multiple storage groups in that they offer greater backup and restore flexibility in addition to the security benefits.

How to Create General Purpose Public Folder Trees

You can create as many General Purpose public folder trees as necessary, though you must associate a public folder tree with a public folder store in order to use it. Therefore, you are generally limited in adding public folder trees to the number of public stores that the organization has. A public folder tree can have only one public store on a given server associated with it. You must first create the public folder tree using Exchange System Manager and then create a public store and associate it with the tree.

Practice: Creating Public Folders

In this practice, you will create a new public folder tree and then create a new public store and associate it with the tree you create. Then, you will create a public folder in the new public folder tree. You will then create a new HTTP virtual server for the public folder tree and verify that you can access the public folder tree through a Web browser.

Exercise 1: Create a Public Folder Tree and Public Store

1. Open Exchange System Manager and navigate to your administrative group. Right-click the Folders container in the administrative group, point to New, and then click Public Folder Tree.

2. Name the tree **CustomerForum** and click OK.

3. Navigate to your server in Exchange System Manager and expand the container node. Right-click a storage group on the server, point to New, and then click Public Store.

4. Name the public store **Forums**, and then click Browse to associate the store with a public folder tree.

5. Click the new public folder tree you just created from the list of Available Public Folder Trees, and then click OK.

6. Click OK to finish creating the public store, and then click Yes to mount the database.

Exercise 2: Create Public Folders

1. In Exchange System Manager, navigate to the CustomerForum public folder tree that you created.

2. Right-click CustomerForum, point to New, and then click Public Folder.

3. Name the folder **Setup Support**, and then click OK.

4. Repeat the process to create public folders for Announcements and Features Wishlist.

5. Verify the existence of the new public folders in the list under the CustomerForum public folder tree.

Exercise 3: Create a Virtual Directory

1. In Exchange System Manager, navigate to the administrative group and to your server, and then expand the Protocols container.

2. Expand the HTTP container to view Exchange Virtual Server, and then expand it to view the containers below.

3. Right-click Exchange Virtual Server, point to New, and then click Virtual Directory. This opens a Properties dialog box, as shown in Figure 8-5.

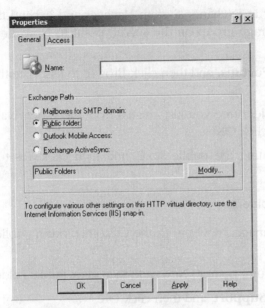

Figure 8-5   Configuring a virtual directory

4. Name the virtual directory **Forums** and then click Modify to change the Exchange path from the default Public Folders.

5. In the Choose A Public Folder dialog box, click CustomerForum, and then click OK.

6. Click OK again to finish creating the virtual directory.

Exercise 4: Access the Public Folder Tree through HTTP

1. Wait about two minutes for the configuration to complete in the Exchange organization, and then open Microsoft Internet Explorer.

2. Enter the URL to your public folder tree, which is in the format of *http://servername/virtualdirectory*. If your server is Server01 in this exercise, you would type **http://Server01/Forums**. Then you will see a browser window like that in Figure 8-6.

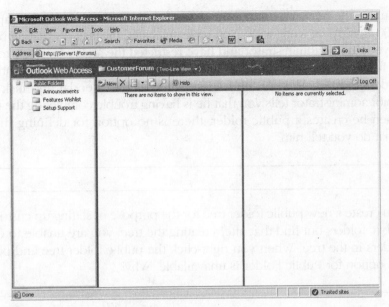

Figure 8-6   Browsing the public folder tree

3. Note the public folder structure you created. Close Internet Explorer.

Lesson Review

The following questions are intended to reinforce key information presented in this lesson. If you are unable to answer a question, review the lesson materials and then try the question again. You can find answers to the questions in the "Questions and Answers" section at the end of this chapter.

1. You are the Exchange Server administrator for Litware, Inc. You create a new public folder tree to support customer forums, and you explain to users that they will not be able to use Outlook to access these folders but will have to use Internet Explorer instead. A couple of days later, you receive a call from a user who says that they are using Internet Explorer, but they see only the same folders they see in Outlook. They don't see the customer forums. What are they doing wrong?

2. You are the network administrator for Fabrikam, Inc., which has approximately 1500 employees worldwide. You have delegated the task of creating public folders to your junior administrator and have restricted the ability for users to create public folders. The sales director puts in a work order to have a number of public folders created. Most of the folders will contain calendar and task items. Your junior administrator tells you that he is having trouble completing the task and that when he creates a public folder, there is no option for defining the item type. What do you tell him?

_____

_____

3. You create a new public folder tree for the purpose of setting up customer support public folders but find that after creating the tree, you are unable to create public folders in the tree. When you right-click the public folder tree and point to New, the option for Public Folder is unavailable. Why?

_____

_____

Lesson Summary

- There are two types of public folder trees: the Default public folder tree and General Purpose public folder trees.

- There is only a single Default public folder tree in an Exchange organization. You can configure as many General Purpose public folder trees as necessary.

- A public folder tree must be associated with a public store for it to be usable.

- Public folders in the Default public folder tree can be created using Exchange System Manager, Outlook, or OWA.

Lesson 2: Administering Public Folders

To have an effective and efficient public folder infrastructure, you must be able to administer public folders. Public folder administration includes tasks such as managing e-mail properties, storage limits, folder location, and replication.

After this lesson, you will be able to

■ Manage e-mail properties for public folders

■ Set storage limits on public folders

■ Move public folders

■ Control public folder replication and referrals

Estimated lesson time: 60 minutes

Managing E-Mail Properties for Public Folders

Public folders created natively in Exchange Server 2003 using Exchange System Manager are not mail-enabled by default. This differs from folders that have been migrated from Exchange Server 5.5, which are all mail-enabled during the migration. Therefore, after creating a public folder in Exchange Server 2003, you must mail-enable the folder if you want it to be able to receive e-mail. Mail-enabling a public folder is done through Exchange System Manager.

1. In Exchange System Manager, navigate to the public folder you want to mail-enable.

2. Right-click the folder, point to All Tasks, and then click Mail Enable.

Mail-enabling a public folder by default creates e-mail addresses for X.400 and SMTP. You can view these e-mail addresses or add additional addresses, if necessary. If you right-click the public folder that you mail-enabled and click Properties, you will see that there are additional tabs, as follows:

■ E-Mail Addresses

■ Exchange General

■ Exchange Advanced

■ Member Of

E-Mail Addresses Tab

On the E-Mail Addresses tab, you view and create e-mail addresses to be associated with the public folder.

1. Click the E-Mail Addresses tab.

2. Click New, and then select SMTP Address from the list of e-mail address types. Click OK.

3. Type an e-mail address for the folder and click OK.

4. View the new address on the E-Mail Addresses tab, shown in Figure 8-7.

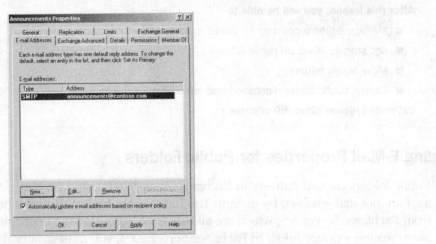

Figure 8-7   Configuring e-mail addresses for public folders

You can configure alternate e-mail addresses, as well, though there can be only a single primary address.

Exchange General Tab

On the Exchange General tab, you configure properties for the public folder that are similar to what you would configure for a user mailbox. When you click the Exchange General tab, you first see the public folder tree that the folder belongs to, as well as the alias for the folder. Generally, the alias is the same as the folder name, though you can choose to make it different, which is useful if the folder name is long.

> **Real World   E-Mail Addresses and Aliases**
>
> Unless there is a compelling reason to have an alias different from the e-mail address, you should leave it the same. The following is a real-world scenario that illustrates this policy.
>
> The company Fabrikam, Inc. has had the address *fabrikam.com* for about a year; prior to that, its address was *contoso.com*. Whenever the administrator set up a new user, his SMTP address always defaulted to *@contoso.com*, and the administrator would have to change the SMTP address manually to *@fabrikam.com*. The administrator found the global Recipient Policy setting for defining e-mail addresses and changed the SMTP address policy from *contoso.com* to *fabrikam.com*.

When Exchange Server updated everyone's e-mail addresses based on the new policy, it used the Alias field to regenerate SMTP addresses. Approximately 20 percent of mailboxes, distribution lists, and public folders had matching aliases and SMTP addresses (for example, an employee named Jenny Lysaker had both her SMTP address and alias as *Jenny*) and were unaffected by the update. However, approximately 80 percent had different aliases and SMTP addresses (for example, an employee named Bob Gage had an alias of *BobG* and an SMTP address of *Bob*). In these cases, Exchange overwrote the existing SMTP address with the new one and drew from the Alias field to create the new one. As a result, most employees, distribution lists, and public folders were unavailable to users outside of the organization because their addresses were no longer correct. Faced with the prospect of restoring from backup or manually editing each SMTP address and correcting it (about 750 addresses total), the company chose the latter.

The restoration would be a tedious process, and one that could be avoided by having the aliases match the SMTP address. The administrator caused the problem by having Exchange update all existing addresses, but the inconsistency in naming aliases and e-mail addresses contributed to the seriousness of the problem.

Figure 8-8 shows the Delivery Restrictions dialog box that opens when you click the Delivery Restrictions button on the Exchange General tab.

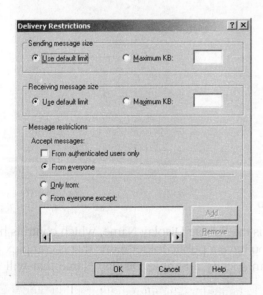

Figure 8-8   Configuring delivery restrictions for a public folder

The delivery restrictions are similar to what you would configure for a user mailbox. If you have folders both send and receive e-mail, you can set limits on the size of the messages. Under Message Restrictions, you have the option of limiting who can send e-mails to the folder. This is useful when you have a folder being used by an application or by a limited group of users and you want to prevent others from sending messages to it. You can also prevent only specific users from sending to the folder.

On the Exchange General tab, click Delivery Options to configure Send On Behalf permissions for the folder and to configure forwarding addresses. If you are using a public folder to support a customer base, such as for receiving feedback e-mail, you might want to allow employees to reply to a customer as the address associated with the folder (such as *feedback@contoso.com*) rather than using their personal address. You would use a forwarding address if you wanted an additional e-mail address to receive the messages, as well. For example, you might want the main support person for a customer forum to receive the e-mails in their own mailbox in addition to having the messages reside in the public folder.

Exchange Advanced Tab

When you click the Exchange Advanced tab, the options shown in Figure 8-9 are available.

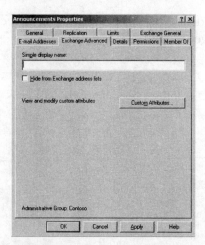

Figure 8-9 The Exchange Advanced tab

The first setting you can configure is the Simple Display Name, which controls how the folder appears in address lists. If you have a public folder name that is complex or contains non-ANSI characters, you can specify a Simple Display Name that will appear instead in your address lists.

Often, public folders are created for a specific application or purpose and are not intended to be used by users in the organization. It is useful to hide these folders from address lists so users do not even see them. The Hide From Exchange Address Lists option controls whether these folders are visible in address lists. A hidden folder still functions and can receive messages, but it is not visible when browsing the list of recipients in the Global Address List (GAL).

There is also the option of defining custom attributes for public folders. When configuring recipient objects (typically user mailboxes), Exchange Server 2003 provides fields for defining a number of attributes for the recipient, such as department, title, phone extension, and so on. The list of attributes is not exhaustive, so Exchange Server 2003 allows you to define custom attributes. With public folders, by default you don't have the option of defining many of the common attributes, but you can click Custom Attributes on the Exchange Advanced tab and define additional attributes for the folder, as required.

Finally, the Exchange Advanced tab informs you of the administrative group in which the public folder resides.

Member Of Tab

The Member Of tab is used to add the public folder to Active Directory groups so that you can make the public folder part of a distribution list. When a public folder belongs to a security or distribution group, it receives all messages sent to the e-mail address associated with the group. The Member Of tab is shown in Figure 8-10.

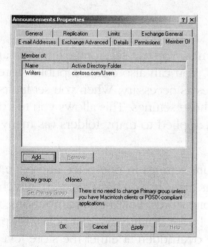

Figure 8-10   The Member Of tab

Since you cannot log on as a folder, putting a public folder in a security group does not allow it to authenticate for accessing any resources. However, security groups can be mail-enabled like distribution groups, so it may be useful to add a public folder to a security group for e-mail alone.

Setting Storage Limits on Public Folders

Public folders are largely unlimited in the type of data they can hold. They are also used to make resources available to users outside of the organization, such as customers. Therefore, the size of public folders can grow quickly. Delivery restrictions can help to keep the size of individual items in the public folder within a defined size, but they do not prevent the folder from growing in size until it fills the hard disk. In order to control the size of the public folder itself, you implement storage limits. The Limits tab of a public folder is shown in Figure 8-11.

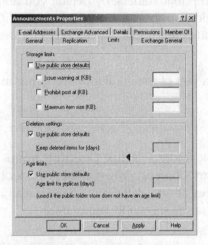

Figure 8-11   The Limits tab

There are three ways to configure storage limits. You can set storage limits on an entire public store or on individual public folders. You can also create a public store policy and apply the policy to as many public stores as necessary. When you set limits on the public store, all folders in the store inherit those settings. This allows you to configure settings in one place and have the settings applied to many folders (as many as you have in the store).

A public store policy allows you to configure settings in one place and have the settings apply to multiple public stores (up to as many as you have created), which in turn apply to all of the public folders in the public stores. For large organizations, policies greatly simplify the administration of public folder storage. When a policy is applied to a public store, the storage limits cannot be overridden at either the store level or the individual public folder level. However, if you configure storage limits on a public store, you can override the limits on an individual public folder basis. This allows you to make exceptions to the limit settings configured at the store level.

Configuring public store policies, public store limits, and public folder limits is identical to the process of configuring mailbox stores and mailboxes, which was discussed in

Chapter 7, "Managing Recipient Objects and Address Lists." Refer to Chapter 7 for step-by-step instructions on configuring store policies and storage limits.

Age Limits

One important feature of storage limits for public folders is the ability to set age limits, which is the amount of time a folder will retain items before automatically deleting them. This feature is disabled by default, but it is very commonly used when public folders are used to host Internet newsgroups, which often generate thousands of messages and gigabytes of content daily. Setting an age limit on this type of content allows you to keep public folders from being cost-prohibitive to maintain in terms of disk space requirements.

Moving Public Folders

Part of the administration of public folders is maintaining the organization of the public folder tree. Depending on who has permissions to create folders, you might find the structure of the tree becoming inefficient and nonintuitive over the course of time as users work with public folders. Exchange Server 2003 allows you to move public folders within a tree so you can maintain a public folder structure that works well for your organization. You can also copy public folders and paste them into other folders in the public folder tree.

> **Exam Tip**   Public folders can only be moved within a public folder tree. You cannot move or copy a folder between trees.

Exchange System Manager is used to move and copy public folders. The easiest way to move a public folder is to drag and drop it from one location to the other. You can also right-click the folder you want to move and click Cut from the menu, and then right-click the destination folder and click Paste. Copying a folder follows a similar format. Right-click the folder that you want to copy and click Copy, and then right-click the destination folder and click Paste.

Public Folder Replication

In a large organization, it is usually inefficient and, at times, even costly for remote sites to access public folders in other sites separated by slower wide area network (WAN) bandwidth. This is especially true when there are toll charges for bandwidth usage. Exchange Server 2003 supports replication of public folders, which places replicas of folders in other public stores. A replica can be placed in a public store on a server in another site and the content replicated back and forth on a schedule (such as after business hours).

Every server in an organization has a Default public store that is associated with the Default public store tree. In order to set up replication for public folders you have created in additional public folder trees, you must first create a public store on the server that will hold the replica. When you configure a public store, you associate it with a particular public folder tree. Even though you associate the store with an existing tree, this by itself does not enable replication. Once you have a public store on a destination server, you can configure a public folder to replicate to the other server.

To replicate a public folder, perform the following steps:

1. In Exchange System Manager, navigate to the Folders container and expand the list of public folder trees. Expand the tree that contains the folder you want to replicate.

2. Right-click the desired public folder, and then click Properties.

3. Click the Replication tab, shown in Figure 8-12.

Figure 8-12   Configuring replication properties

4. Click Add. This will open a dialog box that lists the servers with an available public store. Select a public store and click OK.

5. Typically, there is no need to change the Public Folder Replication Interval, which is the schedule, or the Replication Message Priority. However, you can change their configuration here, if necessary. Once done, click OK to complete the process.

Tip   You can also remove a replica using a similar process, in which you choose to remove rather than to add a replica.

You might change the replication schedule if you have content that needs to be replicated more or less often than normal. For example, you might want a folder that contains important project information to replicate whenever a change occurs. You could configure that folder to replicate on a different schedule than the rest of the folders. Likewise, you can configure a replication schedule at the public store level and have it apply to all public folders in the store. In addition, you can use a public store policy to configure replication settings, just as you did in setting storage limits.

Exchange Server 2003 uses a multimaster replication model, which means that all replicas of a public folder are equal and contain the exact same content. A replica copied from one server to another is a separate instance of a public folder and its content. There is no master replica, which means that modifications to any replica are replicated to other replicas equally.

Depending on the nature of the public folder, you may not want to replicate a particular public folder. For example, you may have a public folder that contains critical customer data that the users in your organization rely on to make business decisions. To ensure that the information contained in the public folder is completely up-to-date, you should consider not replicating that particular public folder.

When considering replicating a public folder, you should also weigh network traffic against client traffic. A folder that contains constantly changing information, such as a newsgroup downloaded from an external site, is probably not a good candidate for replication because replicating such a public folder could result in more network traffic than simply allowing users to access it across the WAN.

Manual Replication

While replication usually occurs according to the defined schedule, there are times when you might need to manually initiate replication rather than waiting for the replication interval to elapse. An example would be when you have just created a new public folder tree or public folder and want to make it available to other servers immediately. You can initiate manual replication on both public folder trees and public folders. To replicate a public folder tree manually, perform the following steps:

1. Right-click the public folder tree in Exchange System Manager and click Send Hierarchy. The Send Hierarchy dialog box, shown in Figure 8-13, opens.

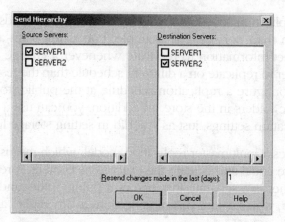

Figure 8-13   Manually replicating a public folder tree

2. Select the server that you want to replicate from (the source server), and choose one or more servers that you want to replicate to (destination servers). You can choose to resend only changes that have been made since a specified number of days ago.

3. Click OK, and when Exchange System Manager prompts you that a large amount of network traffic can be generated by this procedure, click Yes to continue.

Manually replicating a public folder is similar to the previous procedure. In step 1, right-click the public folder and then click Send Contents. Steps 2 and 3 are the same.

Public Folder Referrals

When a user connects to a public folder store and the store does not contain a copy of the content the user is requesting, Exchange Server 2003 automatically redirects the user to a server that does contain the content. This occurs behind the scenes with no intervention required by the user and is known as a referral. In the default configuration, Exchange Server 2003 will attempt to refer the user to another server within the routing group and then use the routing group structure to go to a server in another routing group, if necessary. Exchange Server 2003 allows you to configure specific servers to which referrals are allowed and to assign costs to each server in order to prioritize the list of referral servers. To customize the list of referral servers, perform the following steps:

1. Right-click the desired server in Exchange System Manager and click Properties.

2. Click the Public Folder Referrals tab, shown in Figure 8-14.

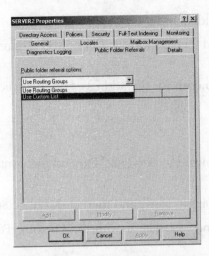

Figure 8-14   Configuring public folder referrals

3. The default setting is to use routing groups. Click the drop-down list under Public Folder Referral Options, and click Use Custom List.

4. Click Add and then select the servers you want to configure as referral servers. Click OK when done, and then click OK again to save the new configuration.

Practice: Administering Public Folders

In this practice, you will mail-enable a public folder on Server01 and configure it with an e-mail address. Then, you will configure a public store on Server02 and configure the public folder you created on Server01 to replicate to Server02.

Before you begin, you must have two Exchange Server 2003 systems installed as Server01 and Server02 in the same Exchange organization in the *contoso.com* domain, and you must have completed the exercises in Lesson 1 of this chapter.

Exercise 1: Mail-Enable a Public Folder

1. On Server01, open Exchange System Manager. Navigate to the Folders container in your administrative group.

2. Expand the Folders container to see your public folder trees, and then expand the CustomerForum tree.

3. Right-click the Announcements folder, point to All Tasks, and then click Mail Enable.

4. Right-click the Announcements folder, and then click Properties.

5. Click the E-Mail Addresses tab, and then click New. Click SMTP Address, and then click OK.

6. Type **Announcements@Contoso.com** for the address, and then click OK. Click OK again to finish.

Exercise 2: Replicate a Public Folder

1. In Exchange System Manager, navigate to Server02. Expand the container to see the storage groups.

2. Right-click First Storage Group, point to New, and then click Public Store.

3. Name the public store **Forums** and associate it with the CustomerForum public folder tree. Click OK to finish.

4. Navigate to the CustomerForum public folder tree. Right-click the Announcements public folder and click Properties.

5. Click the Replication tab, and then click Add. Click Server02 in the list, and then click OK. Click OK again to create the replica.

Exercise 3: Initiate Manual Replication

1. Right-click the Announcements public folder, and then click Send Contents.

2. Click Server01 in the Source Server column, and then click Server in the Destination Server column. Click OK, and then click Yes in response to the warning that appears.

Lesson Review

The following questions are intended to reinforce key information presented in this lesson. If you are unable to answer a question, review the lesson materials and then try the question again. You can find answers to the questions in the "Questions and Answers" section at the end of this chapter.

1. You are the Exchange Server administrator for Litware, Inc. The VP of marketing has requested that an e-mail folder be set up for customer feedback. He wants a way to monitor the messages that are coming in, and he wants new messages to be forwarded to everyone in the marketing department except for himself. He wants two designated people to be able to reply to messages using the *feedback@litwareinc.com* address. Would a distribution group or a public folder be the best choice for this situation, and why?

_____

_____

2. You are the Exchange Server administrator for Contoso, Ltd., a company that has recently merged with Fabrikam, Inc. Management wants to move several customer support forums from Fabrikam into Contoso. The forums are public folders that exist in different public folder trees on different servers. The two Exchange organizations have already been merged, with the structure being that Fabrikam and Contoso are in separate administrative groups. How would you move the folders?

    a. Drag and drop the folders in Exchange System Manager from the current public folder tree to the destination tree.

    b. Cut the public folders from the current public folder tree and paste them into the destination tree.

    c. Create a replica of the desired folders in the destination tree, and delete the original folders after the contents have replicated.

    d. Create new public folders in the destination tree. Back up the folders in the Fabrikam public folder tree and restore the contents to the folders in the Contoso public folder tree.

3. You attempt to configure storage limits on a public folder that needs to have a greater limit than it currently has, but you find that all of the limit properties are unavailable when you attempt to edit the properties of the folder. Why is this happening?

    _____

    _____

Lesson Summary

- Public folders can be mail-enabled to receive e-mail, as well as added to security and distribution groups.

- Storage limits can be placed on public folders to limit the size of individual messages as well as the size of the folder itself.

- Storage limits and replication settings can be configured through a public store policy, through an individual public store, or through individual public folders.

- Public folders can only be moved within a public folder tree, not between trees.

Lesson 3: Public Folder Security

You configure public folder security to define and control the level of access users have to a public folder. You can grant or deny permissions to different aspects of a public folder, enabling you to ensure that users can access the content they need but not the content that they shouldn't have access to.

After this lesson, you will be able to

- Understand inherited permissions and assigned permissions
- Configure client permissions, directory rights, and administrative rights

Estimated lesson time: 45 minutes

Inherited and Assigned Permissions

Permissions control the creation, management, and use of public folders and their contents and are either granted by inheritance or assigned. A public folder inherits its permissions from parent objects. For example, a top-level folder will inherit permissions from the administrative group and from the Exchange organization. Similarly, a child folder will inherit permissions from its parent folder in the public folder tree. When you create a public folder, you need to assign permissions that specify the individuals or groups that will have the rights to perform designated activities in that folder. You can assign both client access permissions and administrative rights to the folder.

Child folders inherit parent folder settings only at the time they are created. By default, any changes that you later make to a parent folder will not automatically be inherited by child folders. However, you can have the permission changes that you make to a parent folder applied to every child folder. To do this, perform the following steps:

1. Right-click the parent folder whose permissions you want to propagate, point to All Tasks, and then click Propagate Settings. The Propagate Folder Settings dialog box is shown in Figure 8-15.

Figure 8-15   Propagating public folder permissions

2. While you can propagate a number of settings, here you only want to click Folder Rights. Click OK to finish.

Important   Any changes you make specifically to a child folder will be lost if you choose to propagate those settings from the parent folder.

Permission Categories

There are three categories of permissions for public folders in Exchange, as shown in Table 8-1.

Table 8-1   Public Folder Permission Categories

Permission	Description
Client permissions	Enables you to control the permissions of the users who are accessing the public folder. For example, you can control who has read and write permissions on a public folder.
Directory rights	Enables you to control which users can manipulate a mail-enabled public folder object that is stored in Active Directory.
Administrative rights	Enables you to assign specific administrative permissions to specific administrators. For example, you might want to grant only three of the 10 administrators at your company the rights to replicate certain sensitive public folders. Administrative rights are inherited by child folders from their administrative group. Administrative rights applied to a folder are not inherited by child folders by default but can be propagated to child folders.

Configuring Permissions

Client permissions are the type of permissions an administrator most commonly works with, and there are two ways to configure them. The first way is by using Exchange System Manager. Right-click a public folder, click Properties, then click the Permissions tab, and then click Client Permissions to open a dialog box similar to the one shown in Figure 8-16.

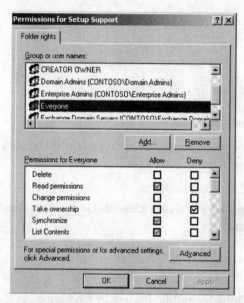

Figure 8-16   Configuring client permissions in Exchange System Manager

Here, you can add users and groups and configure a granular level of access to the folder. You can also configure advanced Folder Rights by clicking Advanced. By default, everyone can read and write to public folders that are created.

The easier way to configure client permissions is by using Outlook, which uses roles-based permissions rather than the more detailed Folder Rights.

1. Open Outlook, expand the Public Folders node in the folder list, and then expand All Public Folders.

2. Right-click a public folder and click Properties, and then click the Permissions tab, shown in Figure 8-17.

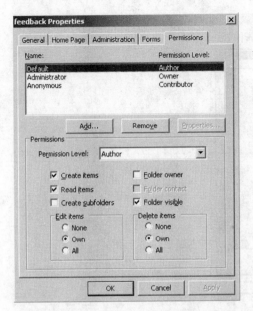

Figure 8-17   Configuring client permissions in Outlook

3. By default, everyone has the Author permission level, which gives them the right to read and create items and to edit and delete their own items.

Tip   The Permissions tab is available only to users and groups that have been configured with the Folder Owner permission role. Non-owners cannot manipulate permissions.

4. To add users and groups, click Add and then assign each the desired role.

Exam Tip   Because Outlook can see only public folders in the Default public folder tree, it cannot be used to configure permissions for public folders that reside in General Purpose trees. You will have to use Exchange System Manager to configure those permissions.

More client security settings can be configured by clicking the Administration tab, shown in Figure 8-18, in the public folder's properties.

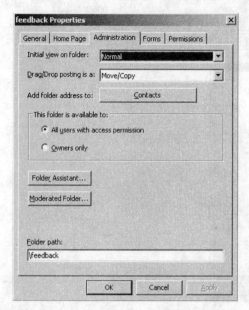

Figure 8-18   Configuring additional security settings

The settings on this tab that are related to security are This Folder Is Available To and Moderated Folder. You can choose whether all users with access permission can use the folder (the default) or whether only users and groups assigned the Folder Owner role can use the folder. A moderated folder is one that requires a moderator to approve all messages that get posted to the folder. This is often used in customer mailing lists or forums where it is highly desirable to limit the amount of off-topic traffic that gets posted. When you click Moderated Folder, the Moderated Folder dialog box, shown in Figure 8-19, opens.

To configure a moderated folder, you must first select the check box to make the folder a moderated folder. Next, you need to assign a user or group to which new messages to the folder should be forwarded. These users will view a message for content and decide if it should be posted. Finally, you assign moderators that have the authority to move the messages into the folder upon approval. You can also have an automatically generated e-mail sent in reply to new messages to explain to the sender that the folder is moderated and that they will not see their post until it is approved. You can use a standard response or create your own custom response.

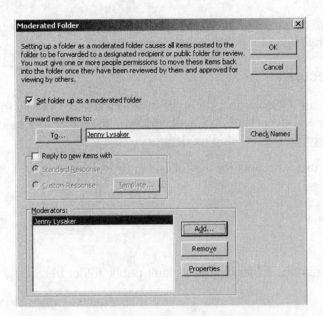

Figure 8-19   Configuring moderated folder settings

Configuring Directory Rights

Directory rights control what users and groups have permission to change e-mail-related attributes of a mail-enabled public folder. By default, only the Administrator account and members of the Administrators, Enterprise Admins, Exchange Domain Servers, and Exchange Enterprise Servers groups have these permissions. Authenticated Users are able to read permissions but not to do anything else. Generally, these settings are sufficient and don't need to be changed. To change the directory rights, perform the following steps:

1. Right-click the public folder in Exchange System Manager and click Properties.

2. Click the Permissions tab, and then click Directory Rights.

3. Add users or groups as desired and configure the permissions you want them to have.

4. Click OK when you are done, and then click OK again to finish.

Configuring Administrative Rights

Administrative rights control the users and groups that can use Exchange System Manager, a custom Microsoft Management Console (MMC) console, or any other administrative utility to change the replication, storage limits, and other settings for a public folder. By default, only administrators in the Active Directory domain and enterprise have administrative rights to a public folder.

Configuring administrative rights is similar to configuring directory rights. Both are configured on the Permissions page of a public folder's properties.

Practice: Public Folder Security

In this practice, you will use Outlook to assign permission roles to a public folder to two Active Directory user accounts. Then, you will configure the folder as a moderated folder and assign a forwarding address and moderators to the folder.

Before you begin, create user accounts for the following users:

■ Jenny Lysaker

■ Bob Gage

■ Chris Meyer

Also, create the following public folders in the Default public folder tree:

■ Feedback

■ Support

Exercise 1: Assign Client Permission Roles

1. Open Outlook and expand the Folders container, and then expand All Public Folders.

2. Right-click the Feedback public folder, and then click Properties. Click the Permissions tab.

3. Click Add, and then add Jenny Lysaker, Bob Gage, and Chris Meyer. Assign Jenny the Folder Owner permission, assign Bob the Publishing Editor role, and assign Chris the Editor role. Note the differences in permissions each role has.

4. Click OK to finish.

Exercise 2: Configure a Moderated Public Folder

1. Right-click the Support public folder, and then click Properties. Click the Administration tab.

2. Click Moderated Folder.

3. Select the check box to Set Folder Up As A Moderated Folder.

4. Assign Jenny Lysaker to Forward New Replies To.

5. Add Jenny Lysaker and Bob Gage as moderators to the folder.

6. Click OK to finish.

Lesson Review

The following questions are intended to reinforce key information presented in this lesson. If you are unable to answer a question, review the lesson materials and then try the question again. You can find answers to the questions in the "Questions and Answers" section at the end of this chapter.

1. You are the senior Exchange Server administrator for Litware, Inc. You receive a call from the customer support manager, who is concerned because customers are calling to say that their e-mail messages sent to *support@litwareinc.com* are being returned as undeliverable. That address is associated with a public folder, so you check the folder properties and find that the e-mail address has been changed to *litwaresupport@litwareinc.com*. After investigating, you determine that the address was changed by your junior administrator, who normally is responsible only for setting up e-mail addresses for new users. How would you restrict him from being able to edit public folder e-mail addresses in the future?

   _____

   _____

2. You are the Exchange Server administrator for Contoso, Inc. The company has a CustomerSupport public folder that functions as a discussion forum. The folder resides in the Default public folder tree. The customer service manager, Bob, says he needs to have administrator permissions to the folder in order to configure settings such as limits, as needed, and to assign permissions to other support techs. However, you have concerns about giving a non-administrator administrator access. What permissions should you give Bob to ensure that he can do his job, but not give him too much authority?

   _____

   _____

3. You are the senior Exchange Server administrator for Litware, Inc., a software development company that sells a number of productivity applications. You have a General Purpose public folder tree for your Customer Support forums. There is a top-level folder called Support, which contains child folders named for each product your company sells. Those folders contain child folders for different versions of each product. Support personnel regularly interact in these folders with customers who post questions. Because each support tech works only on a particular product, each one is given permission to access only the parent folder and child folders of the product he or she supports. You have a junior administrator who configures the permissions to the folders for the support staff as required.

One afternoon, you receive a call from the department manager, who states that none of his support staff can access any of the public forums. You ask your junior administrator, and he tells you he made a permission change on the top-level folder but nowhere else. What did he do that is causing this problem?

_____

_____

Lesson Summary

- Client permissions can be configured through Exchange System Manager for any public folder and through Outlook for public folders that are in the Default public folder tree.

- Directory rights control the permissions to configure e-mail-related properties for mail-enabled public folders.

- Administrative rights control the permissions to run administrative utilities, such as Exchange System Manager, to configure public folder settings such as limits and replication.

Case Scenario Exercise

You are the Exchange Server administrator for Litware, Inc., a software development company that specializes in productivity software. Litware employs approximately 500 people worldwide and has an extensive network of clients and resellers. The Exchange organization consists of five Exchange Server 2003 computers located in different routing groups for sites throughout the world. The company is growing rapidly, and an aspect of the growing pains has been that communication between internal sales and support, and clients and resellers, has deteriorated. E-mail is not as effective as it once was because often there is a need for multiple people to be involved in a project or situation, with each communicating with a group of people. As a result, tracking progress is difficult.

You believe a public folder infrastructure would be better suited for the type of communication that needs to take place, and you propose such a solution to management. They agree that public folders have the potential to solve many of the problems, but they have some requirements that they feel must be met before you can proceed.

- **Requirement 1**   Management wants to ensure that the public folders for the clients do not get mixed up with the folders used internally. Ideally, they don't want internal users even to be able to see the client public folders.

- **Requirement 2**   Marketing is concerned about negative press and feedback, so it wants posts to the Customer Support forum to be screened by a support manager prior to being posted. They also do not want the Announcements folder to be cluttered with irrelevant messages; it should have only announcements posted to it.

- **Requirement 3**   Accounting wants public folders set up for each client so they can post a client's account information, such as their aging reports. It is important that this information always be available, even if one of the Exchange Server 2003 servers goes offline.

Requirement 1

The first requirement involves ensuring that client public folders do not get mixed up with the company's internal folders.

1. What is the ideal way to configure the client public folders so they will not be confused with Litware's internal folders?

   a. Hide the public folders from the address lists.

   b. Use a unique identifier as part of the name for each client folder so they are easily identifiable.

   c. Configure a separate public folder tree for the client folders.

   d. Configure a separate public store for the client folders.

2. Explain why the correct answer to question 1 is the best choice.

   _____

   _____

3. Which of the following software programs would be able to access the client folders? Select all that apply.

   a. Outlook Express

   b. OWA

   c. Outlook

   d. Internet Explorer

Requirement 2

The second requirement involves limiting who can post messages in certain public folders.

1. The Marketing department wants to ensure that the Announcements folder does not get cluttered with off-topic posts. What is the best way to configure this public folder?

_____

_____

2. What is the best way to configure the Customer Support public folder?

_____

_____

Requirement 3

For this requirement, the Accounting department wants to be able to post confidential customer account information and ensure that the data will always be available.

1. Because the Accounting department wants to post confidential information for clients to see in public folders, what will you recommend for the solution?

_____

_____

2. Accounting decides to use a public folder to post nonconfidential client files, and they need to ensure that the data is always available. How will you accomplish this?

_____

_____

_____

Troubleshooting Lab

In this lab, you will mail-enable a public folder and attempt to send an e-mail message to it. When it fails, you will correct the problem by configuring an e-mail address for the folder and then verifying it works.

Before proceeding with this lab, you must have met the requirements that were outlined at the beginning of the chapter, and you must have mailbox-enabled the Administrator account. Outlook must be installed and configured with a mail profile for the Administrator account.

Exercise 1: Create a Public Folder and Test E-Mail

1. Open Exchange System Manager and navigate to the Folders container. Expand the Folders container.

2. Expand Public Folders. Create a public folder called Feedback in the Default public folder tree.

3. Minimize Exchange System Manager and open Outlook. Send an e-mail message to the public folder *feedback@contoso.com*.

4. You will get a non-delivery report (NDR) almost immediately. Minimize Outlook when you do.

Exercise 2: Mail-Enable and Create an Additional E-Mail Address for a Public Folder

1. Maximize Exchange System Manager. Right-click the Feedback folder, point to All Tasks, and then click Mail Enable.

2. Wait a couple of minutes, then right-click the Feedback folder and click Properties.

3. Click the E-Mail Address tab, and then click New. Click SMTP Address, and then click OK.

4. Type **customerfeedback@contoso.com** for the address. Click OK, and then click OK again to finish (leaving *feedback@contoso.com* as the primary address). Minimize Exchange System Manager.

5. Maximize Outlook. Send another e-mail to *feedback@contoso.com*. You should not get an NDR this time.

6. Send a second e-mail to *customerfeedback@contoso.com*.

7. Verify that the messages arrived in the public folder by navigating to the Feedback public folder in the All Public Folders container in the Folder List. There should be two unread messages in the folder—the ones you just sent.

Chapter Summary

■ Public folders must be mail-enabled before they can receive e-mail.

■ Public folders can be moved or copied within a public folder tree but not outside of the tree.

■ Only the Default public folder tree is available to Outlook users.

■ General Purpose public folder trees can be accessed by NNTP and HTTP clients but not by MAPI (Outlook and OWA) clients.

- Client permissions for public folders can be configured in Exchange System Manager, or in Outlook for folders that are in the Default public folder tree.

- Permissions in Exchange System Manager are rights-based, whereas permissions configured in Outlook are roles-based (though they accomplish the same thing).

- A public folder store must be associated with a public folder tree. An unassociated public folder tree cannot be used, even though you can create public folders in it.

Exam Highlights

Before taking the exam, review the key points and terms that are presented in this chapter. Return to the lessons for additional practice.

Key Points

- General Purpose public folder trees are not available to MAPI (Outlook and OWA) clients.

- Public folder replicas are all equal. There is no "master replica." Replication works on a multimaster model like Active Directory.

- Public folders cannot be moved or copied between public folder trees under any circumstances.

- Public store policies can be used to configure settings for storage limits and replication settings and can be used to apply one set of settings to as many public stores as you assign the policy to. Each public store receiving the policy will by default pass those settings on to all public folders in the store.

Key Terms

replica   A copy of a public folder that is placed in a public store on another server. Replicas are used to provide fault tolerance, allowing public folders to remain available even if one server goes offline. Replicas are also used to help control bandwidth usage by creating local copies of folders that otherwise would reside on a remote server.

referral   When a user attempts to access a public folder on a public folder server and the server does not contain the content the user is looking for, a referral is made to another public folder server. Referral servers are configured by default to use routing group membership, but an administrator can also configure a custom referral list to be used.

top-level folder   In an Exchange Server 2003 public folder hierarchy, a top-level folder is the highest level folder in the tree. By default, users can create top-level folders, but a common security practice is to remove this permission so that only administrators can create top-level folders and users can create subfolders.

public folder tree   A public folder tree is a container that creates a hierarchy of public folders. Exchange Server 2003 supports two types of public folder trees: the Default public folder tree and General Purpose public folder trees. You can have only a single Default public folder tree in an organization, but you can have as many General Purpose trees as necessary.

Questions and Answers

Page
8-11

Lesson 1 Review

1. You are the Exchange Server administrator for Litware, Inc. You create a new public folder tree to support customer forums, and you explain to users that they will not be able to use Outlook to access these folders but will have to use Internet Explorer instead. A couple of days later, you receive a call from a user who says that they are using Internet Explorer, but they see only the same folders they see in Outlook. They don't see the customer forums. What are they doing wrong?

   The user misunderstood what you meant when you said to access the customer forums using Internet Explorer. The user has logged in through OWA, which is still treated like a MAPI client and unable to see anything but the Default public folder tree. The user must use the specific URL that goes to the customer forums folder tree.

2. You are the network administrator for Fabrikam, Inc., which has approximately 1,500 employees worldwide. You have delegated the task of creating public folders to your junior administrator and have restricted the ability for users to create public folders. The sales director puts in a work order to have a number of public folders created. Most of the folders will contain calendar and task items. Your junior administrator tells you that he is having trouble completing the task and that when he creates a public folder, there is no option for defining the item type. What do you tell him?

   He needs to use Outlook to create the public folders rather than Exchange System Manager. When you create a folder in Exchange System Manager, it always defaults to holding Mail And Post Items, and this cannot be changed. When you create a public folder in Outlook, you have the option of defining the item type for the folder.

3. You create a new public folder tree for the purpose of setting up customer support public folders but find that after creating the tree, you are unable to create public folders in the tree. When you right-click the public folder tree and point to New, the option for Public Folder is unavailable. Why?

   Before you can create public folders in a public folder tree, you must first associate the tree with a public store. The public store is where the public folder is held, so until you create the store and associate it with the tree, you will be unable to create public folders in that tree.

Page
8-24

Lesson 2 Review

1. You are the Exchange administrator for Litware, Inc. The VP of marketing has requested that an e-mail folder be set up for customer feedback. He wants a way to monitor the messages that are coming in, and he wants new messages to be forwarded to everyone in the marketing department except for himself. He wants two designated people to be able to reply to messages using the

feedback@litwareinc.com address. Would a distribution group or a public folder be the best choice for this situation, and why?

You would need to use a public folder in order to meet the requirements of this scenario. By using a public folder, the messages would be contained in a single location so the VP could view the folder at his leisure to monitor feedback. This would keep the messages separate from his personal e-mail, which is what he wants. In addition, you can configure a forwarding address on the public folder to forward to designated marketing personnel. You could also assign Send On Behalf permissions to the folder to the users that need to be able to reply to customers using the feedback address.

2. You are the Exchange administrator for Contoso, Ltd., a company that has recently merged with Fabrikam, Inc. Management wants to move several customer support forums from Fabrikam into Contoso. The forums are public folders that exist in different public folder trees on different servers. The two Exchange organizations have already been merged, with the structure being that Fabrikam and Contoso are in separate administrative groups. How would you move the folders?

   a. Drag and drop the folders in Exchange System Manager from the current public folder tree to the destination tree.

   b. Cut the public folders from the current public folder tree and paste them into the destination tree.

   c. Create a replica of the desired folders in the destination tree, and delete the original folders after the contents have replicated.

   d. Create new public folders in the destination tree. Back up the folders in the Fabrikam public folder tree and restore the contents to the folders in the Contoso public folder tree.

   The correct answer is d.

3. You attempt to configure storage limits on a public folder that needs to have a greater limit than it currently has, but you find that all of the limit properties are unavailable when you attempt to edit the properties of the folder. Why is this happening?

   There is a public store policy applied to the public store to which the public folder belongs. When a policy applies, you cannot override it manually.

Lesson 3 Review

1. You are the senior Exchange Server administrator for Litware, Inc. You receive a call from the customer support manager, who is concerned because customers are calling to say that their e-mail messages sent to *support@litwareinc.com* are being returned as undeliverable. That address is associated with a public folder, so you check the folder properties and find that the e-mail address has been changed to *litwaresupport@litwareinc.com*. After investigating, you determine that the address was changed by your junior administrator, who normally is responsible

only for setting up e-mail addresses for new users. How would you restrict him from being able to edit public folder e-mail addresses in the future?

By configuring the directory rights on the public folders, you can limit who is able to edit e-mail properties for a public folder. This would allow you to ensure that the junior administrator would not edit the e-mail address again.

2. You are the Exchange Server administrator for Contoso, Inc. The company has a CustomerSupport public folder that functions as a discussion forum. The folder resides in the Default public folder tree. The customer service manager, Bob, says he needs to have administrator permissions to the folder in order to configure settings such as limits, as needed, and to assign permissions to other support techs. However, you have concerns about giving a non-administrator administrator access. What permissions should you give Bob to ensure that he can do his job, but not give him too much authority?

Because Bob needs to be able to configure administrative settings such as limits, you will need to give him administrative rights to the CustomerSupport public folder. It would make sense to also give him Folder Owner client permissions, but that permission by itself will not allow Bob to administer settings for the folder. Administrative rights are assigned on a per-folder basis, so the folder being in the Default public folder tree will not affect the situation.

3. You are the senior Exchange Server administrator for Litware, Inc., a software development company that sells a number of productivity applications. You have a General Purpose public folder tree for your Customer Support forums. There is a top-level folder called Support, which contains child folders named for each product your company sells. Those folders contain child folders for different versions of each product. Support personnel regularly interact in these folders with customers who post questions. Because each support tech works only on a particular product, each one is given permission to access only the parent folder and child folders of the product he or she supports. You have a junior administrator who configures the permissions to the folders for the support staff as required.

One afternoon, you receive a call from the department manager, who states that none of his support staff can access any of the public forums. You ask your junior administrator, and he tells you he made a permission change on the top-level folder but nowhere else. What did he do that is causing this problem?

The junior administrator propagated the changes. When you choose to propagate changes, the permissions you configure on a parent folder will overwrite the permissions on a child folder. The propagation is not cumulative, meaning the permissions do not add to what is already there. Instead, the parent permissions replace the child permissions. As a result, the support techs, who did not have permissions to the top-level folder, are now unable to access their own folders.

Page
8-35

Case Scenario Exercise: Requirement 1

1. What is the ideal way to configure the client public folders so they will not be confused with Litware's internal folders?

   a. Hide the public folders from the address lists.

   b. Use a unique identifier as part of the name for each client folder so they are easily identifiable.

   c. Configure a separate public folder tree for the client folders.

   d. Configure a separate public store for the client folders.

   The correct answer is c.

2. Explain why the correct answer to question 1 is the best choice.

   Configuring a separate public folder tree for the client folders will prevent Outlook users from seeing the folders since only folders in the Default public folder tree are available to Outlook users. This immediately accomplishes the goal of keeping the client folders separate. An additional step is to create a public store to associate with the new public folder tree, but that answer in and of itself does not solve the problem. A separate public store can be created, but if no new public folder tree exists, the new public store will be associated with the Default public folder tree automatically. Using some sort of designation in the name of client folders could help, but it isn't the best solution. Hiding the client folders from address lists will only affect mail-enabled public folders and will only keep the folders from appearing in address lists. It will not prevent the folders from appearing when a user browses the folder list in Outlook.

3. Which of the following software programs would be able to access the client folders? Select all that apply.

   a. Outlook Express

   b. OWA

   c. Outlook

   d. Internet Explorer

   The correct answers are a and d.

Page
8-35

Case Scenario Exercise: Requirement 2

1. The Marketing department wants to ensure that the Announcements folder does not get cluttered with off-topic posts. What is the best way to configure this public folder?

   You want to limit who can post to the Announcements public folder. This folder does not need to be a moderated folder because there is no indication that anyone other than specific individuals should be able to post to it. Therefore, the best course of action is to change the default client permissions from read and write permissions to read-only. Then, use Exchange System Manager to add the users or groups that will be posting announcements and give them the required read and write permissions.

2. What is the best way to configure the Customer Support public folder?

In this instance, you expect that people outside the company will be posting messages on a regular basis. Therefore, removing their write permission is not an effective solution. However, you still want to control the content that gets posted. To do this, configure the Customer Support forum as a moderated folder. This way, new messages to the folder can be properly scanned and edited if necessary by a support manager prior to the messages posting in the folder. This meets the Marketing department's requirement of limiting negative feedback by allowing the support manager to remove any potentially offensive content while leaving the actual question intact.

Page
8-36

Case Scenario Exercise: Requirement 3

1. Because the Accounting department wants to post confidential information for clients to see in public folders, what will you recommend for the solution?

There is not a viable solution to this problem. What Accounting wants in this situation is more akin to a File Transfer Protocol (FTP) site, which public folders are not designed to mimic. With an FTP site, you can put the FTP service on a standalone server and create local user accounts for each client. That way, clients can log in and access a folder that you have configured and given their account permission to access. With public folders, the basic premise is that they are *public*. In addition, servers running Exchange Server 2003 must belong to an Active Directory domain, which means they cannot be standalone servers. As a result, you would have to configure Active Directory user accounts in your domain for clients, which poses other security risks. Using public folders for this task is not appropriate.

2. Accounting decides to use a public folder to post nonconfidential client files, and they need to ensure that the data is always available. How will you accomplish this?

You will want to create a replica of the folder on at least one other Exchange Server 2003 server in the organization. This will provide fault tolerance so that even if one server goes offline, the content will still be available on another public folder server.

9 Virtual Servers

Exam Objectives in this Chapter:

- Configure and troubleshoot Microsoft Exchange Server 2003 for coexistence with other messaging systems
- Manage and troubleshoot Internet protocol virtual servers
- Manage user objects

Why This Chapter Matters

In a clustering environment, Exchange Server 2003 runs as a virtual server because any node in a cluster can assume control of a virtual server. If the node running the Exchange virtual server experiences problems, the virtual server goes offline for a brief period until another node takes control. Exchange Server 2003 installs as a virtual server in both Microsoft Windows clusters and load balancing clusters. Load balancing and failover protection are important features of any e-mail system.

Exchange Server 2003 Internet protocol virtual servers provide Simple Mail Transport Protocol (SMTP) resources that handle relay and e-mail delivery, Hypertext Transport Protocol (HTTP) resources that provide Web-based access to Exchange mailboxes and public folders, and Network News Transfer Protocol (NNTP) virtual servers that provide access to newsfeeds. Virtual servers can also be configured to provide access to e-mail messages for Internet Message Access Protocol version 4 (IMAP4) and Post Office Protocol version 3 (POP3) clients.

Virtual servers carry out essential functions within an Exchange organization and are likely to be tested extensively in Exam 70-284.

Lessons in this Chapter:

- Lesson 1: Overview of Exchange Server 2003 Virtual Servers 9-3
- Lesson 2: Configuring Virtual Server Settings 9-20
- Lesson 3: Configuring Authentication. 9-41
- Lesson 4: Maintaining Virtual Servers. 9-52

Before You Begin

To perform the exercises in this chapter, you need the following hardware and software:

- Two Microsoft Windows Server 2003, Enterprise Edition, servers installed in the *tailspintoys.com* Active Directory directory service domain. Server01 should be a domain controller, and Server02 should be a member server. Server01 should be multihomed. Local Area Connection implements a connection to the internal network (that is, it is on the same network as Server02). Local Area Connection 2 simulates a connection to an external network but does not physically need to be connected to anything.

- Server01 should be an enterprise root certification authority (CA) server.

- Exchange Server 2003, Enterprise Edition, should be installed on both servers. Server01 and Server02 should be back-end and front-end servers, respectively.

- A Domain Name System (DNS) server needs to be available. Typically, DNS is installed on the domain controller.

Lesson 1: Overview of Exchange Server 2003 Virtual Servers

In Chapter 6, "Installing Microsoft Exchange Server 2003 Clusters and Front-End and Back-End Servers," you created a Windows cluster group and a load balancing cluster group and installed Exchange Server 2003 on cluster nodes. Exchange Server 2003 installs on a cluster node as a logical virtual server. Default HTTP and SMTP virtual servers install and are enabled as part of the Exchange Server 2003 installation process. POP3, IMAP4, and NNTP virtual servers also install but are disabled by default.

After this lesson, you will be able to

■ Explain how virtual servers are used in a clustered environment

■ Explain the functions of POP3, IMAP4, NNTP, HTTP, and SMTP virtual servers

■ Describe the default configurations of POP3, IMAP4, NNTP, HTTP, and SMTP virtual servers

Estimated lesson time: 45 minutes

Virtual Servers in a Windows Clustering Environment

Exchange virtual servers use the Windows clustering services, which are included in Windows Server 2003, Enterprise Edition, and Windows Server 2003, Datacenter Edition. These services control all aspects of Windows clustering. Back-end servers require failover support and are typically configured in a Windows clustering environment. Exchange Server 2003 uses the following Windows clustering features:

■ **Resource DLL**   This allows Exchange Server 2003 to communicate with the Windows clustering services and customizes Exchange to provide Windows clustering functionality.

■ **Groups**   An Exchange virtual server in a cluster is defined as a Windows cluster group containing cluster resources, such as an Internet Protocol (IP) address and Exchange Server 2003 System Attendant.

■ **Resources**   Exchange virtual servers include the Windows clustering services, such as IP address resources, network name resources, and physical disk resources. Exchange virtual servers also include their own Exchange-specific resources.

■ **Shared nothing architecture**   Although all nodes in the cluster can access shared data, they cannot access it at the same time. For example, if two physical disk resources are assigned to node 1 of a two-node cluster, node 2 cannot access these disk resources until node 1 fails or is taken offline, or until the disk resource is moved to node 2 manually. This feature prohibits dynamic load balancing in Windows clusters.

Virtual Servers in a Network Load Balancing Environment

Windows Server 2003 servers can be clustered to provide network load balancing. This is typically implemented on front-end servers, where load balancing is a requirement. You implement network load balancing by creating identical redundant virtual servers on all front-end servers that are part of the network load balancing cluster. In this case, the configuration of every server in the network load balancing cluster must be the same; otherwise, clients may experience different behavior depending on the server to which they are routed.

Note   Windows clustering and network load balancing were discussed in depth in Chapter 6. They are mentioned only briefly here, as part of an overview of virtual servers.

Exchange Virtual Server Requirements

An Exchange virtual server requires, at a minimum, the following resources:

- A static IP address
- A network name
- One or more dedicated physical disks for shared storage
- An Exchange 2003 Server System Attendant resource (this installs other Exchange resources)

Client computers connect to an Exchange virtual server the same way that they connect to a standalone computer running Exchange Server 2003. Windows Server 2003 provides the IP address resource, the network name resource, and the disk resources. Exchange Server 2003 provides the System Attendant resource and other required resources. When you create the System Attendant resource, all other required and dependant resources are installed.

Table 9-1 lists the Exchange Server 2003 components and their dependencies.

Table 9-1   Exchange Server 2003 Virtual Server Resources and Dependencies

Component	Description	Dependency
System Attendant	Controls the creation and deletion of all the resources in the virtual server.	Network name Shared disk
Exchange store	Provides mailbox and public folder storage for Exchange Server.	System Attendant
SMTP	Handles relay and delivery of e-mail.	System Attendant
IMAP4	Provides access to e-mail messages for IMAP4 clients (optional).	System Attendant

Table 9-1   Exchange Server 2003 Virtual Server Resources and Dependencies

Component	Description	Dependency
POP3	Provides access to e-mail messages for POP3 clients (optional).	System Attendant
HTTP	Provides access to Exchange mailboxes and public folders via HTTP—for example, Microsoft Outlook 2003 Web Access (OWA).	System Attendant
Exchange MS Search Instance	Provides content indexing for the virtual server.	System Attendant
Message transfer agent (MTA)	Responsible for communication with X.400 systems and for interoperation with Exchange Server 5.5.	System Attendant
Routing service	Builds the link state tables.	System Attendant

> **Note**   There can be only one MTA per cluster. The MTA is created on the first Exchange virtual server. All additional Exchange virtual servers are dependent on this MTA.

Overview of POP3 Virtual Servers

POP3 allows a client to retrieve a specific user's mail from the server. POP3 clients can access only their server inboxes; they cannot access other public or private folders. POP3 does not provide full manipulation of mail on the server. Messages can be left on the server if required, but typically, mail is downloaded to the client and then deleted. POP3 does not send e-mail—SMTP handles this.

You can configure a POP3 virtual server to grant or deny access to specific computers, groups of computers, or domains. You can grant or deny access to a single computer based on an IP address or by overriding POP3 access on a per-user basis. A group of computers can be denied or granted access based on their subnet address and mask. You can also control access to an entire domain by specifying a domain name.

You can view a list of currently connected users. You can immediately disconnect a single user from this list without disrupting the service of other connected users or denying new connection requests.

Installing Exchange Server 2003 automatically installs a default POP3 virtual server. You need to ensure that the default server supports the needs of your specific POP3 clients.

> **Note**   The Microsoft Windows Server 2003 POP3 service is not installed on an Exchange Server 2003 server. If you want to install Exchange Server 2003, then you need to uninstall the Microsoft Windows Server 2003 POP3 service and POP3 Web Administration (if installed). Exchange uses its own Microsoft Exchange POP3 service to support POP3 clients. You need to enable this service on your Exchange server before POP3 virtual servers can start.

POP3 Virtual Server Configuration

Exchange creates the default POP3 virtual server with an IP address of (All Unassigned). As a result, the Exchange server's IP address identifies the POP3 service on the network. By default, incoming connections use TCP port 110, and Secure Sockets Layer (SSL) connections use port 995. You can use the default IP address, TCP port, and SSL port, or you can assign a different IP address from any available network card. If you have more than one POP3 virtual server on an Exchange server, then each virtual server must have a unique combination of TCP port, SSL port, and IP address.

> **Note**   To enable SSL on the POP3 virtual server, you must request and install a certificate.

By default, any POP3 client that supports basic authentication can access a POP3 virtual server. You can use selective authentication methods to restrict access, or you can list only specific computers that are allowed to use the service. To further enhance security, you can include or exclude single computers, subnets, and entire domains from accessing a POP3 virtual server. The detailed procedures for securing a POP3 virtual server using encryption, authentication, and access control are discussed later in this chapter.

By default, a POP3 virtual server can accept an unlimited number of inbound connections. In practice, there are limitations imposed by the finite resources of the Exchange Server 2003 server. To prevent a server from becoming overloaded, you can limit the number of connections made to the POP3 resource.

Messages sent by an Internet client are stored in an Internet format, and no message conversion occurs when a POP3 client reads the message. Messages sent by a Messaging Application Programming Interface (MAPI) client are converted from Microsoft Rich Text Format (RTF) to Multipurpose Internet Mail Extensions (MIME) when read by a POP3 client. If POP3 clients use UNIX to UNIX encoding (uuencode), then you can use uuencode instead of MIME when messages are converted.

Before a POP3 client can connect to a server, a mailbox-enabled user must be created in Active Directory for the client. The POP3 client will also need to be configured with account information that is necessary to allow the client to connect to the POP3 virtual server. Overriding server defaults at the user level allows you to support clients with different needs that are accessing the same POP3 virtual server. This is discussed in detail in Chapter 10, "SMTP Protocol Configuration and Management."

Overview of IMAP4 Virtual Servers

Like POP3, IMAP4 allows a client to retrieve a specific user's mail from the server. Also, IMAP4 can only retrieve e-mail from a user's mailbox, and SMTP is used to send e-mail. There are strong similarities in the ways that POP3 and IMAP4 virtual servers are configured and managed. However, there are significant differences, and this chapter therefore covers IMAP4 in full, at the risk of appearing to duplicate much of what it says about POP3.

> ### IMAP4 vs. POP3
> IMAP4 and POP3 are both Internet messaging protocols that allow users to access e-mail. Neither can send e-mail; SMTP is used for this purpose. The protocols differ in where users manipulate their messages. POP3 allows clients to download mail from their inboxes on a server to the client computer where messages are managed. IMAP4 allows clients to access and manage their mail on the server. Unlike POP3 users, IMAP4 users can access other public and private folders on the server if they have permission to do so.

You can configure an IMAP4 virtual server to grant or deny access to specific computers, groups of computers, or domains. You can grant or deny access to a single computer based on an IP address or by overriding IMAP4 access on a per-user basis. A group of computers can be denied or granted access based on their subnet address and mask. You can also control access to an entire domain by specifying a domain name.

You can view a list of currently connected users. You can immediately disconnect a single user from this list without disrupting the service of other connected users or denying new connection requests. You can configure an IMAP4 virtual server to list all public folders. If you disable this feature, Exchange lists only the client's private folders.

Installing Exchange Server 2003 automatically installs a default IMAP4 virtual server. You need to ensure that the default server supports the needs of your specific IMAP4 clients.

> **Note**   Exchange uses its own Microsoft Exchange IMAP4 service to support IMAP4 clients. You need to enable this service on your Exchange server before IMAP4 virtual servers can start.

IMAP4 Virtual Server Configuration

Exchange creates the default IMAP4 virtual server with an IP address of (All Unassigned). As a result, the Exchange server's IP address identifies the IMAP4 service on the network. By default, incoming connections use TCP port 143, and SSL connections use port 993. You can use the default IP address, TCP port, and SSL port, or you can assign a different IP address from any available network card. If you have more than one IMAP4 virtual server on an Exchange server, then each virtual server must have a unique combination of TCP port and IP address.

> **Note**   To enable SSL on the IMAP4 virtual server, you must request and install a certificate. If you need more information on SSL, refer to the Windows Server 2003 help files.

By default, any IMAP4 client that supports basic authentication can access an IMAP4 virtual server. You can use selective authentication methods to restrict access, or you can list only specific computers that are allowed to use the service. To further enhance security, you can include or exclude single computers, subnets, and entire domains from accessing an IMAP4 virtual server. The detailed procedures for securing an IMAP4 virtual server using encryption, authentication, and access control are discussed later in this chapter.

By default, an IMAP4 virtual server can accept an unlimited number of inbound connections. In practice, there are limitations imposed by the finite resources of the Exchange Server 2003 server. To prevent a server from becoming overloaded, you can limit the number of connections made to the IMAP4 resource.

Messages sent by Internet clients are stored in MIME format, and no message conversion takes place when IMAP4 clients read the messages. Messages sent by MAPI clients are converted from RTF to MIME when read by IMAP4 clients.

Before an IMAP4 client can connect to a server, a mailbox-enabled user must be created in Active Directory for the client. The IMAP4 client will also need to be configured with account information that is necessary to allow the client to connect to the IMAP4 virtual server. Overriding server defaults at the user level allows you to support clients with different needs that are accessing the same IMAP4 virtual server. Chapter 10 discusses this in detail.

Overview of NNTP Virtual Servers

NNTP defines a set of client and server commands used to access *newsgroups*. Exchange Server 2003 uses NNTP virtual servers to enable Outlook users to participate in online discussions over the Internet. You can also enable users running client applications that support NNTP to access newsgroup public folders on computers running Exchange.

Users can read and post items to NNTP newsgroups, which are implemented in Exchange as public folders. Items in newsgroups can be replicated to Usenet host computers through *newsfeeds*. You can assign a moderator to a newsgroup to ensure that only approved articles are posted.

Exchange Server 2003 does not implement NNTP virtual servers by using a built-in Exchange service (unlike POP3 and IMAP4). Instead it uses the Windows Server 2003 (or Windows 2000 Server) NNTP service. This service is designed to support a stand-alone newsgroup server, and this makes it easy to create group discussions. When you install Exchange Server 2003, the NNTP service is enhanced. This enables the NNTP virtual server to interface with other news servers through newsfeeds.

Using an NNTP virtual server, you can administer newsgroup services from a centralized location and control authentication and client connections. You can create additional NNTP virtual servers to host multiple domains on a single Exchange server.

You can create both public and private virtual servers and configure different authentication requirements on each. A public news server can be used, for example, to give users quick and easy access to technical support information.

NNTP virtual servers can be used in a master/subordinate configuration. To create a master server, you use the New NNTP Feed Wizard to define a remote server as a subordinate server, rather than directly defining the server as a master server.

In Windows 2000 Server, the NNTP service starts automatically. This is not the case in Windows Server 2003, where you need to configure and start the service manually. You can customize the default NNTP virtual server settings and create and configure additional NNTP virtual servers.

You can cancel a posting, create a new newsgroup, and remove a newsgroup by sending *control messages*. Control messages are received by the NNTP service and posted to one of the special newsgroups that are automatically created to manage control messages. These are the *control.cancel*, *control.newgroup*, and *control.rmgroup* newsgroups.

NNTP Virtual Server Configuration

Exchange creates the default NNTP virtual server with an IP address of (All Unassigned). As a result, the Exchange server's IP address identifies the NNTP service on the network. By default, incoming connections use TCP port 119, and SSL connections use port 563. You can use the default IP address, TCP port, and SSL port, or you can assign a different IP address from any available network card. If you have more than one NNTP virtual server on an Exchange server, then each virtual server must have a unique combination of TCP port, SSL port, and IP address.

By default, an NNTP virtual server can accept an unlimited number of inbound connections. In practice, there are limitations imposed by the finite resources of the Exchange Server 2003 server. To prevent a server from becoming overloaded, you can limit the number of connections made to the NNTP resource. You can also limit the length of time idle connections remain logged on to the server. By default, Exchange disconnects idle sessions after 10 minutes. You can also control the size of individual articles that a user can post, or you can limit the total size of articles that a user can post during a single connection.

You can define expiration policies to limit how long articles are stored on a newsgroup's NNTP virtual server. An expiration policy can apply to a single newsgroup or to all newsgroups on the virtual server.

You have a number of ways of controlling access to an NNTP virtual server. You can specify whether users can connect anonymously or whether they need to supply valid usernames and passwords. If users connect over a public network, you can encrypt the connection using SSL, assuming you have obtained the necessary certificate. You can explicitly grant or deny access based on the IP address of the client, and you can include or exclude single computers, subnets, and entire domains. You can also specify the users who are permitted to administer a virtual server by restricting access to administrative tasks on the NNTP server by specifying the accounts that are authorized to modify server settings.

By default, Exchange enables basic authentication on NNTP virtual servers. To enhance security, you can use SSL with basic authentication to encrypt all information. If you use basic authentication on NNTP virtual servers, anonymous authentication is disabled. If you want to use both anonymous and basic authentication, then you need to create additional NNTP servers. Integrated Windows authentication is also available but is not a practical option in some newsgroup scenarios.

You create a new newsgroup by using the Use New Newsgroup Wizard. The NNTP service creates the directory for the newsgroup automatically, and you have the option of specifying a moderated newsgroup. You can use *newsfeeds* to distribute articles among multiple computers. Newsfeeds can distribute newsgroup articles between servers within your organization, and between your organization and the Internet through a Usenet host. You can use master, subordinate, and peer newsfeeds to distribute the newsgroup load among servers. A server can have both a subordinate feed and a peer feed.

A *virtual directory* is a public folder store that enables you to store newsgroup files on multiple disk drives. This can improve the performance of a heavily used drive and can provide more storage. Virtual directories also enable you to change the physical location of the directory without changing the name of the newsgroup.

Overview of HTTP Virtual Servers

The World Wide Web uses the HTTP protocol to define how messages are formatted and transmitted and the actions Web servers and browsers take in response to HTTP commands. Web Distributed Authoring and Versioning (WebDAV) is an extension of the HTTP version 1.1 protocol that allows an HTTP client to retrieve and manipulate information held in the Information Store.

Exchange Server 2003 supports HTTP virtual servers and WebDAV to provide the following functions:

- **Document access**   HTTP and WebDAV support a collaborative environment in which users can edit documents, protect data, collect resources in a common folder, and move or copy files.

- **E-mail access**   HTTP and WebDAV can be used to access mailboxes and messages, notify users that new e-mail has arrived, and allow users to move, copy, or delete e-mail on the server.

- **Application access**   HTTP and WebDAV are standards-based application layer protocols that allow access to mailboxes and public folders through a unique Uniform Resource Locator (URL). This allows custom applications to retrieve data directly from the Information Store.

Exchange provides support for WebDAV through HTTP virtual servers. Internet Information Services (IIS) converts the folder contents displayed by the HTTP virtual server displays into Web pages and sends them to a user's browser. The default HTTP virtual server (known as the Exchange virtual server) is created by IIS, and you must administer this server using IIS Manager. However, if you create additional HTTP virtual servers in Exchange, then you should administer them using Exchange System Manager.

A default HTTP virtual server is automatically installed, configured, and enabled when you install Exchange Server 2003. It provides users with access to public and private folders. Users can access data by using *http://server_name/public* to access to public folders and *http://server_name/exchange/mailbox_name* to access mailboxes.

HTTP Virtual Server Configuration

Exchange creates the Exchange virtual server with an IP address of (All Unassigned). As a result, the Exchange Server 2003 server's IP address identifies the HTTP service on the network. By default, incoming connections use TCP port 80, and SSL connections use port 443. You can use the default IP address, TCP port, and SSL port, or you can assign a different IP address from any available network card. If you have more than one HTTP virtual server on an Exchange server, then each virtual server must have a unique combination of TCP port, SSL port, and IP address.

The default HTTP virtual server authentication settings vary between server roles, depending on whether the Exchange server is a front-end server or a back-end server. For example, Integrated Windows Authentication is enabled by default on a back-end, but not on a front-end, additional HTTP virtual server. Basic authentication is enabled by default on both back-end and front-end servers, and anonymous access is disabled. If you enable anonymous connections, this allows HTTP clients to access resources without specifying a Windows user account. You can also configure an HTTP virtual server to use SSL encryption, provided you first obtain and install the required certificate.

To prevent a server from becoming overloaded, you can limit the number of connections the HTTP virtual server accepts. You can also limit the length of time that idle connections remain logged on to the server. By default, Exchange Server 2003 limits the number of incoming connections to 1,000 and disconnects idle sessions after 60 seconds.

Creating Additional HHTP Virtual Servers and Virtual Directories

You can create additional HTTP virtual servers to provide for a number of different collaboration scenarios. For example, you might want to use Integrated Windows Authentication on the default virtual server, but also to provide users outside your organization with information about your company. In this situation, you can enable anonymous access on a separate HTTP virtual server.

You can use additional HTTP virtual servers to supplement access to folders that the default Web site in IIS provides. For each virtual server that you create, you must define one virtual directory as the root of the server for publishing content. You can create additional virtual directories to publish content that is not contained within the server's own directory structure. For example, the virtual directory can provide access to a public folder (or to a mailbox) on a remote domain.

When you create a new HTTP virtual server, you must provide access to a public folder or public folder tree, and to an SMTP mailbox domain in order to configure the server's root. You can change the default e-mail domain of the HTTP virtual server, or you can create additional virtual directories to provide access to mailboxes in multiple domains.

When you create a virtual directory, you provide users with access to the contents of a public folder through a URL that takes the form *http://virtualserver/public*, where *virtualserver* is the DNS name of the virtual server. You can also access a published directory through Microsoft Internet Explorer or through any client that supports the industry standard HTTP and WebDAV protocols. You can use Microsoft Office to create and save documents directly into an HTTP directory through a feature called Web Folders that lets you work with files and folders that are on a Web server, just as you would with files and folders in My Computer or Windows Explorer.

Controlling Access to an HTTP Virtual Server

HTTP virtual servers allow you to support a *collaborative authoring environment*. When you collaborate on confidential material, you need to control access to the data. You may, however, also want users outside of your organization to access public information. In this case, you can use separate HTTP virtual servers and specify different access settings on each.

You can configure read, write, and browse permissions on a virtual directory. When you set these permissions, all users are granted the same permissions to access the folders or mailboxes that the virtual directory specifies. Virtual directory settings are general restrictions imposed by IIS and do not override permissions set on the user's account to access mailboxes and public folders.

By default, users can access private mailboxes using a URL in the form of *http://server_name/exchange/mailbox_name* after a standard Exchange installation and setup is complete. If you create a new mailbox store, a different URL is automatically assigned to it. This URL is based on the virtual directory name.

OWA

A default HTTP virtual server is installed and configured during the Exchange Server 2003 installation process to support OWA. You can use OWA to configure Exchange so users can access e-mail, calendar information, shared applications, and any content in the public information store by using a Web browser. To enable your users to access OWA from the Internet, your Exchange Server 2003 server must have an Internet connection, a public IP address, and a registered domain name.

> **Real World   Do You Need a Registered Domain Name?**
>
> In theory, you do not need a registered domain name because OWA users can access their e-mail using an IP address. In the real world, however, this leads to a lot of problems for the administrator and a lot of very unhappy users.

OWA can be disabled for the Exchange organization by stopping the HTTP virtual server. It can also be disabled on a per-user basis. Per-user settings are discussed in detail in Chapter 10.

> **Exam Tip**   Bear in mind that OWA is an application, not a protocol. An HTTP virtual server manages OWA. There is not a specific OWA virtual server.

Overview of SMTP Virtual Servers

SMTP is the Internet standard for transporting and delivering electronic messages. Exchange Server 2003 expands the SMTP service to give administrators greater control over the routing and delivery of messages and to provide secure access and channels for managing the service.

When Exchange Server 2003 is installed, it automatically installs, configures, and enables a default SMTP virtual server. You can alter settings on this server to configure security options, message delivery options, and message filtering. You can configure the SMTP virtual server and the SMTP Connector to support other messaging systems and to relay mail for IMAP4 and POP3 clients.

SMTP works closely with DNS, and you can add Mail Exchanger (MX) records in DNS to support your SMTP virtual servers. You can configure SMTP to pull e-mail, which is queued at your Internet Service Provider (ISP), through a dial-up connection.

Detailed SMTP configuration is discussed in Chapter 10; therefore, this chapter contains only an overview of the SMTP virtual server. Domain administration is not performed on the SMTP virtual server. You manage local domains through Recipient policies, and you implement most of the configuration you require for sending e-mail to remote domains at the SMTP Connector.

If you have different groups of users with varying security requirements or message-size needs, then you may want to create additional SMTP virtual servers. You can also, for example, configure one virtual server to handle Internet e-mail, while another handles internal e-mail. Where you support POP3 and IMAP4 clients, you need to permit open relaying for these clients. You do not want to permit open relaying for your entire Exchange organization because this permits the propagation of junk mail. While you can use discretionary access control lists (DACLs) on a single SMTP virtual server to manage this situation, it is often safer and easier to create an additional virtual server for clients that require relaying. Chapter 10 discusses this in detail.

Configuring an SMTP Virtual Server

The display name (for example, Default SMTP Virtual Server) and the IP address and TCP port combination identify an SMTP virtual server. You can also select the IP address that will be associated with the virtual server; by default, this is (All Unassigned). The default SMTP port is TCP port 25. Multiple virtual servers can use port 25, but you must assign a different IP address to each virtual server.

You can configure the SMTP virtual server to authenticate incoming connections and also to provide the authentication credentials required by a receiving server. Three authentication methods are available: anonymous access, basic authentication, and Integrated Windows Authentication. You can choose to use one, two, or all three methods. The default setting deactivates anonymous access on SMTP virtual servers. To allow anonymous access, you must manually disable authentication on the virtual server.

If basic authentication is enabled, you can require that all clients use *Transport Layer Security (TLS)* encryption to connect to an SMTP virtual server. TLS is developed from, and is similar to, SSL. This option secures the connection and encrypts the clear-text password sent by the basic authentication method. However, TLS is intended for a point-to-point SMTP connection where both parties know that the other supports TLS. It should not be used if clients access through the Internet. You need to obtain a certificate to implement TLS encryption.

You can grant or deny access to an SMTP virtual server to specific users or groups. By default, all IP addresses can access an SMTP virtual server. You can set restrictions by specifying a single IP address, a group of addresses using a subnet mask, or a Windows domain name.

> **Caution**   If you grant or deny access based on domain name, you need to configure reverse DNS lookup on each connection. Reverse DNS lookup is resource-intensive and can degrade performance.

You can configure an SMTP virtual server to limit the number of messages sent in a single connection. You can improve system performance by allowing the use of multiple connections to deliver messages. You can also configure message size limits and limit the number of message recipients.

Practice: Enabling and Starting the POP3, IMAP4, and NNTP Services

In this practice, you enable and start the services that are disabled by default. You then check the status of the corresponding virtual servers and start them, if required.

Exercise 1: Start the Disabled Services

By default, the default POP3, IMAP4, and NNTP virtual servers are disabled. To enable them, you need to start the relevant services. You can choose the automatic startup type if you want the service to start any time you restart the Exchange server. Choosing the manual startup type lets you decide when you want the service to start. Typically, the manual setting is used for troubleshooting. In this practice, we configure all three services on Server01 to start automatically.

> **Note** On your practice, two-computer network, you perform this exercise on Server01 while logged on as a domain administrator. In a production network, the *Principle of Least Privilege* mandates that you should use the runas utility while logged on as an ordinary user to a client computer that has the appropriate administrator tools installed.

To enable and start the disabled service, perform the following steps:

1. Open the Services console on Server01.
2. Right-click Microsoft Exchange POP3 and click Properties. The Properties dialog box for the service is shown in Figure 9-1.

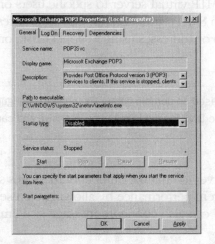

Figure 9-1 The Microsoft Exchange POP3 service Properties dialog box

3. In the Startup Type drop-down list, select Automatic.
4. Click Apply.
5. Click Start.
6. Click OK.
7. Repeat the same procedure for the Microsoft Exchange IMAP4 service and the Network News Transport Protocol (NNTP) service.

Exercise 2: Start the POP3, IMAP4, and NNTP Virtual Servers

You cannot assume that the virtual servers will start when you enable and start the services. You must check the servers and start them as necessary.

Tip   It is wise to check that virtual servers have started any time that you restart the Exchange server. Even when the services are set to start automatically, the virtual servers do not always start on reboot.

To start the POP3, IMAP4, and NNTP virtual servers, perform the following steps:

1. Start Exchange System Manager.

2. Navigate to Administrative Groups\First Administrative Group\Servers\Server01 \Protocols\NNTP.

Note   If Exchange System Manager is not configured to display Administrative Groups, right-click TailSpinToys (Exchange), click Properties, select the check boxes beside Routing Groups and Administrative Groups, and then click OK.

3. Right-click Default NNTP Virtual Server. If Start is unavailable (but Stop is not), then the server has started. If not, then click Start.

4. Expand IMAP4 and POP3 on the console pane, and repeat the same procedure for Default IMAP4 Virtual Server and Default POP3 Virtual Server.

Note   You can also determine whether or not a virtual server has started by examining its icon. If you see a white X inside a red circle, then the server is stopped. If you see two black bars inside a white circle, then the service is paused.

Exercise 3: Assign IP Addresses to Virtual Servers

In Lesson 2 of this chapter, you create and configure additional virtual servers. Before you do this, you need to assign the IP address for Local Area Connection to the default virtual servers. You can then assign the IP address for Local Area Connection 2 to the additional virtual servers in a later exercise. This exercise assumes that all the default virtual servers are started.

To assign IP addresses, perform the following steps:

1. Start Exchange System Manager.

2. Navigate to Administrative Groups\First Administrative Group\Servers\Server01 \Protocols\IMAP4.

3. Right-click Default IMAP4 Virtual Server. Click Pause.

4. Right-click Default IMAP4 Virtual Server again. Click Properties.

5. On the General tab, in the IP Address drop-down list, select the IP address of Local Area Connection.

6. Click Advanced to view the virtual server configuration, as shown in Figure 9-2. Click OK.

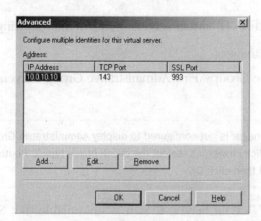

Figure 9-2 Configuring the default IMAP4 virtual server

7. Click OK to close the Properties dialog box.

8. Right-click Default IMAP4 Virtual Server. Click Pause.

9. Repeat the same procedure for the POP3, NNTP, and SMTP virtual servers.

Exam Tip If you try to use the same procedure to configure the default HTTP virtual server (the Exchange virtual server), it will not work. Remember that the default HTTP virtual server was created using IIS, and you must use IIS Manager to configure it.

10. Open the Internet Information Services (IIS) Manager console.

11. Expand Server01\Web Sites, right-click Default Web Site, and click Properties.

12. On the Web Site tab, in the IP Address drop-down list, select the IP address of Local Area Connection.

13. Click OK to close the Properties dialog box.

Lesson Review

The following questions are intended to reinforce key information presented in this lesson. If you are unable to answer a question, review the lesson materials and then try the question again. You can find answers to the questions in the "Questions and Answers" section at the end of this chapter.

1. What is the default port configuration of a POP3, an IMAP4, and an NNTP virtual server?

   _____

   _____

2. Which protocol services associated with Exchange Server 2003 virtual servers are disabled by default?

   _____

   _____

3. The default HTTP virtual server is known as the Exchange virtual server. What additional feature distinguishes it from all other virtual servers?

   _____

   _____

Lesson Summary

- Exchange back-end servers typically use Windows clustering for failover support.
- Exchange front-end servers typically use Network Load Balancing clusters.
- HTTP, NNTP, POP3, IMAP4, and SMTP virtual servers are available on an Exchange Server 2003 server.
- POP3 and IMAP4 retrieve but do not send e-mail. SMTP is used to send mail.
- POP3 manages e-mail on the client. IMAP4 manages it on the server. Messages sent by a MAPI client are converted from RTF to either MIME or uuencode when read by a POP3 client. IMAP4 does not support uuencode.
- NNTP virtual servers enable Outlook users to participate in online discussions over the Internet. They also enable users running client applications that support NNTP to access newsgroup public folders on computers running Exchange.
- HTTP virtual servers support WebDAV and OWA.
- SMTP virtual servers can be configured to support other messaging systems and to relay mail for IMAP4 and POP3 clients.

Lesson 2: Configuring Virtual Server Settings

In this lesson, you create additional Internet protocol virtual servers and configure these servers. It is possible to configure the default virtual servers, but typically the default settings (other than specifying an IP address) can be left unaltered to support normal Exchange operations. You create an additional virtual server for a specific purpose and configure it accordingly.

After this lesson, you will be able to

- Create and configure an additional HTTP virtual server
- Create and configure an additional NNTP virtual server
- Create and configure an additional POP3 virtual server
- Create and configure an additional IMAP4 virtual server
- Create and configure an additional SMTP virtual server

Estimated lesson time: 120 minutes

Creating Additional Virtual Servers

In this lesson, you create default virtual servers on Server01, which is a multihomed back-end server. In general, you create a new virtual server if you require different levels of authentication for different groups of users, or different access criteria, or if you want some, but not all, traffic to be encrypted. Additional virtual servers can also provide the following facilities that are specific to the server protocol:

- **HTTP** You can create additional HTTP virtual servers to provide for a number of different collaboration scenarios where different levels of authentication and access control are required. You can use additional HTTP virtual servers to supplement access to folders that the default Web site provides. When you create an additional HTTP virtual server, you also create an additional virtual directory. You can use additional virtual directories to publish content that is not contained within the server's own directory structure.

- **NNTP** You can create additional NNTP virtual servers to host multiple domains on a single Exchange server. You can, for example, use the default virtual server to access public newsgroups and implement public newsfeeds and to create an additional virtual server for internal newsgroups.

- **POP3 and IMAP4** You create additional POP3 and IMAP4 virtual servers if you have groups of clients with differing requirements. For example, you might have one group of POP3 clients that can understand messages in MIME format while another group uses uuencode. Where there are sufficient numbers in both groups, you would create an additional virtual server. If there were only a few users in the second group, you would configure per-user settings.

■ **SMTP**   You can create an additional SMTP virtual server and configure one virtual server to handle Internet e-mail while the other handles internal e-mail. You can also create an additional virtual server to support open relaying for POP3 and IMAP4 clients. Often, however, configuration is best implemented on an SMTP connector rather than on a virtual server. Chapter 10 discusses this in detail.

Configuring Virtual Server Settings

When you create virtual servers, you assign identities to them and specify parameters, such as IP address and, if necessary, TCP and SSL port numbers. You can configure additional settings on a new virtual server when you create it, or you can create it and configure it later. If you want to change the configuration on a running virtual server, then you should pause the server before making the configuration change and restart it afterwards.

Configuring an HTTP Virtual Server

When you create a new HTTP virtual server, you need to assign a unique identity—that is, a unique combination of IP address, TCP port, SSL port, and host name. You also need to configure the server's virtual directory by providing access to a public folder and to a mailbox. When you have created a new virtual server, you can configure it using Exchange System Manager. (Remember that the default HTTP virtual server—the Exchange virtual server- -is configured using IIS.) You can do any or all of the following:

■ Limit the number of concurrent connections to the virtual server and configure the number of seconds that must elapse before an unsuccessful connection times out.

■ Control access to the server by setting connection limits, configuring read, write, and browse permissions, setting script and executable access, and editing authentication methods (allowing anonymous access, if required).

■ Create additional virtual directories to publish content not contained within the server's own directory structure. Virtual directories appear to client browsers as though they are part of the virtual server's directory tree. You can also set a default document.

Configuring POP3 and IMAP4 Virtual Servers

The procedures to create and configure POP3 and IMAP4 virtual servers are almost identical. When you create a new POP3 virtual server, you complete the New POP3 Virtual Server Wizard to specify the server's IP address and TCP port. When you create a new IMAP4 virtual server, you complete the New IMAP4 Virtual Server Wizard to specify the server's IP address and TCP port. After you complete the appropriate wizard, you can configure the settings using Exchange System Manager. You can do any or all of the following:

- Control access to the server by editing the authentication methods. If you want to enable SSL encryption, you need to obtain, install, and associate a certificate.

- Secure access by IP address, subnet, or domain name.

- Limit the number of connections that can be made to the virtual server at any one time and the length of time that idle connections remain logged on to the server. By default, Exchange disconnects idle sessions after 30 minutes.

- Configure client support by specifying message formats. On POP3 virtual servers, you can specify uuencode and support Macintosh clients by specifying BinHex for Macintosh.

- Disable complete public folder listings to improve the performance of clients that have difficulty with a large number of folders (IMAP4 only).

- Enable fast message retrieval to improve performance for clients that do not require exact message sizes (IMAP4 only).

Configuring NNTP Virtual Servers

You create additional NNTP virtual servers by completing the New NNTP Virtual Server Wizard. This lets you specify the IP address and TCP port. You also need to specify the path to internal files, the storage medium, and the path to the virtual directory that stores the news content. After you complete the wizard, you can configure the settings using Exchange System Manager. You can do any or all of the following:

- Set connection and posting limits.

- Control access to the server by editing the authentication methods. If you want to enable SSL encryption, you need to obtain, install, and associate a certificate. You can also secure access by IP address, subnet, or domain name.

- Create a newsgroup and a newsgroup expiration policy. If you create a moderated newsgroup, you need to specify the path to the directory that stores articles until moderators approve them. You should specify the path to the pickup directory of the SMTP virtual server that is used for moderated groups. Normally, this is the default SMTP virtual server and the path is \Inetpub\Mailroot\Pickup.

- Create a newsfeed in either a master/subordinate or peer configuration.

Configuring SMTP Virtual Servers

You create additional SMTP virtual servers by completing the New SMTP Virtual Server Wizard. This lets you specify the IP address. If you want to change the default settings for the TCP port and the SSL port, you can do so by using Exchange System Manager. You can also use Exchange System Manager to do any or all of the following:

- Configure incoming and outgoing connections.

- Specify authentication settings for incoming connections and for outbound messages. If required, you can also set up the virtual server to resolve anonymous e-mail. Take care with this setting. If you configure an SMTP virtual server to resolve anonymous e-mails, it is possible for unauthorized users to send e-mail by using the forged address of legitimate users.

- Specify TLS encryption, if you have obtained the necessary certificate.

- Set IP address and domain name restrictions, and grant or deny submit permissions to users or groups. You can also configure filtering.

- Configure relaying. Be careful to restrict this as severely as possible; open relaying can increase the risk of your Exchange organization being used for junk mail propagation.

- Specify limits for message size, number of recipients, and the number of messages per connection. You can also change the location of the SMTP queue.

- Specify a storage location for copies of non-delivery report (NDR) messages and configure a masquerade domain to replace the actual identity of that storage location in the outgoing message heading.

- Configure message delivery by specifying retry intervals and message hop count. You can also specify fully qualified domain name (FQDN) and configure the server either as a smart host or to forward outgoing e-mail to a smart host. You can enable reverse DNS lookup and create a reverse DNS list.

> **Exam Tip** A *masquerade domain* on an SMTP virtual server replaces the local domain name used in Mail From lines in the protocol. The replacement occurs on the first hop only and refers to the SMTP message heading information. The From line displayed by e-mail clients is in the message body. The masquerade domain name does not change this.

As you can see from the above list, you have many configuration options on a virtual SMTP server. You can also configure connections (such as a dial-up connection to an ISP) using the Routing And Remote Access console, and you need to configure DNS support. Also, it is often good practice to configure settings on an SMTP connector that uses a virtual server as a bridgehead, rather than on the server itself. For these reasons, this chapter only gives a summary. Chapter 10 discusses SMTP in detail.

Front-End and Back-End Configuration

You can manage Internet access protocols on a separate server from the one on which the message store runs by deploying a front-end and back-end configuration. A front-end server does not store mailboxes or other sensitive information and can therefore interface more securely with the Internet and with external sectors of a large intranet or extranet. A front-end and back-end configuration provides a unified namespace and a reduction of overhead for SSL encryption.

Internet protocol virtual servers on front-end Exchange Server 2003 servers handle incoming client connections, while the back-end virtual servers are dedicated to running the databases. You need to create a virtual HTTP server on each back-end server to handle front-end requests.

In topologies that contain Exchange Server 2003 front-end and back-end servers, the implementation of authentication settings varies between server roles. On front-end servers, the type of authentication used by IMAP4 and POP3 virtual servers is set to basic authentication and cannot be changed (although you can specify SSL encryption). On POP3 and IMAP4 back-end servers, you can select basic authentication or Integrated Windows Authentication. You have the option to specify encryption if you use basic authentication on back-end servers, but typically you would not do so. Integrated Windows Authentication cannot be specified on front-end additional HTTP virtual servers.

The implementation of the connection time-out setting varies between server roles. On back-end servers, the connection time-out setting limits the length of time for which a client is permitted to remain connected to the server without performing any activity. On front-end servers, the connection time-out setting limits the total length of the client's session, regardless of client activity. You should therefore configure this setting on your front-end servers so that your users can download the maximum message size permitted over the slowest supported connection speed. This ensures that your clients are not disconnected while downloading messages.

> **Exam Tip**   Scenario-type exam questions may present you with a situation where configuration settings are not having the expected effect. If a question states that user connections are timing out during large downloads, then look for a configuration on a front-end server that specifies an idle time rather than a total session value.

If POP3 clients use calendaring, then you need to configure the POP3 clients to keep copies of their messages on the server. If the POP3 client is configured to delete mail from the server after it has been downloaded to the client, clicking the URL within the meeting request will result in an HTTP 404 error, indicating that the OWA meeting request is not available.

> **Caution**   If your Exchange Server 2003 organization uses front-end and back-end servers, you should configure the URL your users use to access calendaring information on the Calendaring tab of the POP3 and IMAP4 virtual servers on your back-end server. Exchange does not recognize any URL settings configured on the Calendaring tab of your front-end servers.

Practice: Creating and Configuring Virtual Servers

In this practice, you create and configure virtual servers for all the supported Internet protocols. Before you do this, however, you need to create mailbox-enabled users to associate with the virtual servers.

Exercise 1: Create Mailbox-Enabled Users

The Active Directory Users And Computers console manages user objects such as mailboxes. When Exchange System Manager is installed on a Windows Server 2003 server, a set of extensions is added to the standard console. This allows you to create an Exchange mailbox for user accounts.

You need to create mailbox-enabled users for IMAP4 and POP3 clients. You also need user accounts that can send e-mail to each other for testing purposes. You use the normal procedure for creating a user in Active Directory. When Exchange System Manager is installed, new users are mailbox-enabled by default.

To create mailbox-enabled users, perform the following steps:

1. Access the Active Directory Users And Computers console.

2. In the console tree, double-click the domain node, right-click the Users folder, point to New, and then click User.

3. Type **Don Hall** in the Full Name box and type **d.hall** in the User Logon Name box. Click Next.

4. Clear the User Must Change Password At Next Logon check box. Select the User Cannot Change Password and Password Never Expires boxes. Specify the password as **password&2**. Click Next.

5. Confirm that the Create An Exchange Mailbox box is selected by default. Click Next.

6. Click Finish.

7. Use the same procedure to add the users listed in Table 9-2. If you want to send or retrieve mail as one of these users, then use the runas utility.

Table 9-2   Mailbox-Enabled Users

Full name	User logon name	Password
Kim Akers	k.akers	password&2
Michelle Alexander	m.alexander	password&2
Sean Alexander	s.alexander	password&2
Michael Allen	m.allen	password&2
Nancy Anderson	n.anderson	password&2

Exercise 2: Create an HTTP Virtual Server

In this exercise, you create an additional HTTP virtual server on Server01. Typically, you create an HTTP virtual server on a back-end server to support each of your front-end servers. Authentication and encryption settings are configured in Lesson 3. In this and subsequent exercises, you define the server's unique identity, set its Exchange path, limit the number of concurrent connections, specify the number of seconds that must elapse before an unsuccessful connection times out, set read, write, and browse permissions on the virtual directory, and set script and executable access. You also enable forms-based authentication and configure compression settings for OWA.

An HTTP virtual server is identified on the network by a unique combination of IP address, host name, TCP port, and, if encryption is enabled, SSL port. For each virtual server that you create, you must define one virtual directory as the root of the server for publishing content. If you want to set the virtual server's Exchange path to a public folder store, you need to create a public folder for this purpose. Chapter 8, "Public Folders," described this procedure.

To create a new HTTP virtual server, perform the following steps:

1. Start Exchange System Manager.

2. Navigate to Administrative Groups\First Administrative Group\Servers\Server01 \Protocols\HTTP.

3. In the console tree, right-click HTTP, point to New, and then click HTTP Virtual Server.

4. On the General tab, type **HTTP_server1** in the Name box.

5. In the IP Address drop-down list, select the IP address of Local Area Connection 2.

6. To assign a unique identity, click Advanced, and then click Add.

7. In the Host Name box, type **virtual**, as shown in Figure 9-3, and then click OK.

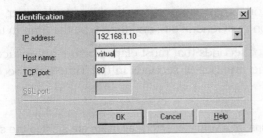

Figure 9-3   Assigning a unique identity

8. Click OK to close the Advanced dialog box, and then click Apply on the General tab.

> **Note**   You can differentiate a virtual server by IP address, TCP port number, host name, or any combination of the three. If, however, you differentiate by host name only, you need additional entries in DNS to direct the browser to access a specific virtual server. Microsoft recommends that you avoid differentiating by host name only.

9. To provide access to a public folder, select Public Folder under Exchange Path on the General tab.

10. Click Modify, select a folder from the tree, and then click OK.

11. To provide access to an SMTP mailbox domain and configure the virtual server's route, select Mailboxes For under Exchange Path on the General tab. If you want to provide access to mailboxes for an SMTP domain other than the one listed, click Modify, select an SMTP domain, and then click OK.

12. Click OK to close the virtual server Properties dialog box. Check whether the new HTTP virtual server has started. If not, start it.

Exercise 3: Configure an HTTP Virtual Server

In this lesson, you configure the additional HTTP virtual server that you created in the previous lesson. Because this is not the default HTTP virtual server, it can be configured using Exchange System Manager. As stated previously, authentication and encryption settings are described in Lesson 3.

To configure the additional HTTP virtual server, perform the following steps:

1. Start Exchange System Manager.

2. Navigate to Administrative Groups\First Administrative Group\Servers\Server01 \Protocols\HTTP.

3. Right-click HTTP_server1, and then click Pause.

4. Right-click HTTP_server1, and then click Properties.

5. To limit the number of concurrent connections to the virtual server, select Limit Number Of Connections on the General tab, and then type the limit in the text box.

6. To configure the number of seconds that must elapse before an unsuccessful connection times out, type the number of seconds in the Time-Out (Secs) text box. The default is 900.

> **Note**   When you set permissions on a virtual directory, all users are granted the same permissions to access the folders or mailboxes the virtual directory specifies. Virtual server settings do not override permission to access mailboxes and public folders set on the user's account.

7. To configure read, write, and browse permissions on the virtual server's root directory, click the Access tab.

8. Use the check boxes to grant or deny all users the ability to read, write, or browse directories, as shown in Figure 9-4.

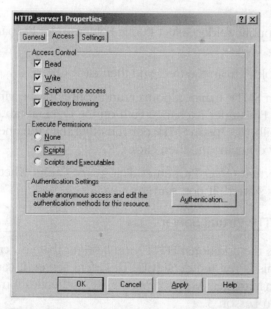

Figure 9-4   Configuring read, write, and browse permissions

> **Note**   This procedure sets permissions on the root directory. If you want to set permissions on additional virtual directories, expand the HTTP virtual server in Exchange System Manager, right-click a virtual directory, and then click Properties.

9. When you grant script access or enable scripts to run, you allow all connected users to view the source of the scripts and to run the scripts. You set script and executable access on the Access tab as follows:

   ❑ Allow users to view the script code by selecting the Script Source Access check box in the Access Control section, if it is not already selected.

   ❑ Restrict all users from running scripts by selecting None in the Execute Permissions section.

   ❑ Allow all users to execute scripts but not executables by selecting Scripts in the Execute Permissions section.

   ❑ Allow all users to execute both scripts and executables by selecting Scripts And Executables in the Execute Permissions section.

10. Click OK to close the virtual server Properties dialog box.

11. Right-click the virtual server, and then click Pause to restart it.

Exercise 4: Configure Forms-Based Authentication

You can use Exchange System Manager to configure OWA settings for both the default HTTP virtual server and any additional HTTP virtual servers you create. *Forms-based authentication* provides additional security for OWA users. When you enable forms-based authentication, a new logon page for OWA will store the user's user name and password in an in-memory session cookie instead of in the browser. When a user closes the browser, the cookie is cleared. It is also cleared automatically after a period of inactivity. If you enable forms-based authentication, then you have the option of enabling *compression*. The low compression setting will compress static files only; the high compression setting will compress both static and dynamic files.

To enable forms-based authentication and set compression, perform the following steps:

1. Start Exchange System Manager.

2. Navigate to Administrative Groups\First Administrative Group\Servers\Server01 \Protocols\HTTP.

3. Right-click the virtual server that you want to configure, and then click Pause.

4. Right-click the paused server, and then click Properties.

5. Click the Settings tab.

6. Select the Enable Forms Based Authentication check box on the Outlook Web Access pane.

7. Select a compression level from the Compression drop-down menu.

8. Click OK to close the virtual server Properties dialog box.

9. Right-click the paused server. Click Pause again to restart it.

Exercise 5: Create a POP3 Virtual Server

In this exercise, you create an additional virtual server to support POP3 clients and then, in the next exercise, you configure the virtual server. You can use the same procedures to configure the default virtual server. When you create a new POP3 virtual server, it is disabled by default, so there is no need to pause it for configuration. If you configure it correctly, then it should start automatically. If you want to alter the configuration on a running server, you should pause it first.

You can create additional virtual servers on a single computer to handle multiple local mail domains and provide administration for several messaging scenarios. In this exercise, you create an additional virtual server on the back-end Exchange server, Server01.

To create a POP3 virtual server, perform the following steps:

1. Start Exchange System Manager.
2. Navigate to Administrative Groups\First Administrative Group\Servers\Server01 \Protocols\POP3.
3. In the console tree, right-click POP3, point to New, and then select POP3 Virtual Server.
4. The New POP3 Virtual Server Wizard starts. In the Name box, type **POP3_server1**, and then click Next.
5. In the Select The IP Address For This Virtual Server drop-down menu, select the IP address of Local Area Connection 2.
6. Click Finish. The wizard closes and a disabled virtual server is created. You can now configure this virtual server.

Exercise 6: Configure a POP3 Virtual Server

In this exercise, you configure the new POP3 virtual server that you created. Authentication and encryption settings are configured in Lesson 3. In this exercise, you configure connection settings, restrict access by IP address, subnet, or domain, specify message format, and examine the calendaring settings.

To configure the new POP3 virtual server, perform the following steps:

1. Start Exchange System Manager.
2. Navigate to Administrative Groups\First Administrative Group\Servers\Server01 \Protocols\POP3.
3. Right-click POP3_server1, and then click Properties.
4. On the General tab, click Advanced. If you want to, you can alter the settings for the IP address, TCP port, and SSL port by clicking Add. You do not need to do so at this point, so click Cancel.

5. You can limit the number of connections to prevent the POP3 virtual server from becoming overloaded. Click Limit Number Of Connections To on the General tab, and then type an integer between 1 and 1,999,999,999.

6. To limit the length of time idle connections remain logged on to the server, specify the maximum time in the Connection Time-Out (Minutes) box.

7. To selectively include or exclude single computers, subnets, and domains from accessing a POP3 virtual server, select the Access tab and click Connection.

8. To allow only specified computers, groups of computers, or domains to access the virtual server, select Only The List Below, and then click Add. You can then specify one of the following:

   ❑ The static address of a single computer

   ❑ A group of computers with contiguous IP addresses, defined by the subnet address and mask

   ❑ A domain, defined by the complete domain name

> **Note**   If you want more practice in using a network address and a subnet mask to specify a range of IP addresses, there are many excellent tutorials on the Internet, for example, at *http://learntosubnet.com*.

9. Click OK to return to the Connection dialog box.

10. To restrict specified computers, groups of computers, or domains from accessing the virtual server, select All Except The List Below, and then click Add. As before, you can specify a single IP address, a subnet, or a domain. Figure 9-5 shows a subnet specification.

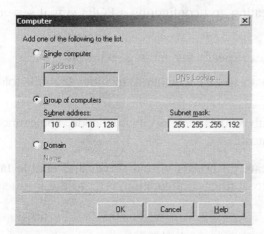

Figure 9-5   Specifying a subnet

11. Click OK to return to the Connection dialog box.

12. Click OK to close the Connection dialog box.

13. To specify the message format that your POP3 clients support, click the Message Format tab.

14. If your clients support MIME encoding, then select MIME. You can then specify one of the following:

    ❑ Use RTF. You specify this by selecting the Use Exchange Rich-Text Format check box. This disables the other MIME options. (You can also specify RTF if your clients use uuencode.)

    ❑ Provide Message Body As Plain Text

    ❑ Provide Message Body As HTML

    ❑ Both

15. If your clients support uuencode, then select UUEncode; if you are supporting Macintosh clients, then select Use Binhex For Macintosh.

16. If multiple character sets exist for one code page, then Exchange uses the character setting specified on the Message Format tab. You can select a character set in the Character Set drop-down menu.

17. To configure the OWA server that POP3 clients access when they download meeting requests, click the Calendaring tab. By default, the back-end Exchange server is specified. You can specify a front-end server if you need to do so.

18. Click OK to close the virtual server Properties dialog box.

Exercise 7: Create and Configure an IMAP4 Virtual Server

This is almost identical to creating and configuring a POP3 virtual server. There are three differences:

■ On the General tab, you can specify fast message retrieval.

■ On the General tab, you can specify whether to include all public folders when a folder list is requested.

■ On the Message Format tab, you cannot specify uuencode. You cannot, therefore, specify BinHex for Macintosh.

In this practice, you will create an IMAP4 virtual server and enable fast message retrieval. If you want to do any further configuration, refer to the instructions for the POP3 virtual server.

To create and configure an IMAP4 virtual server, perform the following steps:

1. Start Exchange System Manager.

2. Navigate to Administrative Groups\First Administrative Group\Servers\Server01 \Protocols\IMAP4.

3. In the console tree, right-click IMAP4, point to New, and then select IMAP4 Virtual Server.

4. The New IMAP4 Virtual Server Wizard starts. In the Name box, type **IMAP4_server1**, and then click Next.

5. From the Select The IP Address For This Virtual Server drop-down menu, select the IP address of Local Area Connection 2.

6. Click Finish. The wizard closes, and a disabled virtual server is created.

7. Right-click the new IMAP4 virtual server, and then click Properties.

8. On the General tab, select the Enable Fast Message Retrieval check box.

9. Click OK to close the virtual server Properties dialog box.

Exercise 8: Create an NNTP Virtual Server

In this exercise, you create an additional NNTP virtual server. You need to create folders to store NNTP files and newsgroups, and you can do this either before you start or while you are creating the virtual server. When you have created the new virtual server, you can add new newsgroups, feeds, expiration policies, and virtual directories. Exchange System Manager provides wizards for these tasks, and this exercise and the following one are limited to creating and configuring the virtual server. Authentication and encryption are covered in Lesson 3.

You can create additional NNTP virtual servers to host multiple domains on a single server or to implement separate public and private servers. Each virtual server must have a unique IP address and TCP port combination. Microsoft recommends assigning different IP addresses and using the standard NNTP TCP port, 119.

Note   When you create an NNTP virtual server, you are asked to specify two directory paths: a path for internal files and a path for newsgroup files. In the exercise, these are both on the same partition. In a production system, put these two files on different disk partitions. Keeping the files on separate disk partitions reduces the chance of corruption if the partition runs out of disk space.

To create an NNTP virtual server, perform the following steps:

1. Start Exchange System Manager.

2. Navigate to Administrative Groups\First Administrative Group\Servers\Server01\Protocols\NNTP.

3. In the console tree, right-click NNTP, point to New, and then select NNTP Virtual Server.

4. The New NNTP Virtual Server Wizard starts. In the Name box, type **NNTP_server1**, and then click Next.

5. Select the IP address of Local Area Connection 2, enter TCP port **119**, and then click Next.

6. Enter **C:\NNTP_files\filegroup** as the path to internal server files. If you are prompted to create this folder, then click OK. Click Next.

7. Specify File System as your storage medium. (You also have the option of specifying a public folder database or a share on a remote computer at this stage.) Click Next.

8. Enter **C:\NNTP_news\newsgroup** as the path to store the news content. If you are prompted to create this folder, then click OK. Click Finish.

9. The new NNTP virtual server is created. Unlike IMAP4 and POP3 virtual servers, new NNTP virtual servers are enabled on creation.

Exercise 9: Configure an NNTP Virtual Server

To configure the new NNTP virtual server, perform the following steps:

1. Start Exchange System Manager.

2. Navigate to Administrative Groups\First Administrative Group\Servers\Server01\Protocols\NNTP.

3. Right-click NNTP_server1, and then click Pause.

4. Right-click NNTP_server1, and then click Properties.

5. On the General tab, click Advanced. If you want to, you can alter the settings for the IP address, TCP port, and SSL port by clicking Add. However, you do not need to do this in this instance, so click Cancel.

6. You can limit the number of connections to prevent the NNTP virtual server from becoming overloaded. Select the Limit Number Of Connections To option on the General tab, and then type an integer between 1 and 1,999,999,999.

7. To limit the length of time idle connections remain logged on to the server, specify the maximum time in the Connection Time-Out (Minutes) box.

8. To selectively include or exclude single computers, subnets, and domains from accessing an NNTP virtual server, click the Access tab, and then click Connection.

9. To allow only specified computers, groups of computers, or domains to access the virtual server, select Only The List Below, and then click Add. You can then specify one of the following:

   ❏ The static address of a single computer

   ❏ A group of computers with contiguous IP addresses, defined by the subnet address and mask

   ❏ A domain, defined by the complete domain name

10. Click OK to return to the Connection dialog box.

11. To restrict specified computers, groups of computers, or domains from accessing the virtual server, select All Except The List Below, and then click Add. As before, you can specify a single IP address, a subnet, or a domain. Figure 9-5, on page 9-32, shows a subnet specification.

12. Click OK to return to the Connection dialog box.

13. Click OK to close the Connection dialog box.

14. To control the size of individual articles that a user can post, or to limit the total size of articles a user can post during a single connection, click the Settings tab.

15. Ensure that the Allow Client Posting check box is selected.

16. To limit the size of a single article that a user can post, click Limit Post Size (KB), and then select a value.

17. To limit the amount of data that a user can post to a newsgroup during a single connection, click Limit Connection Size (MB), and then select a value.

18. Ensure that the Allow Feed Posting check box is selected.

19. To limit the size of a single article a user can post to a newsfeed, click Limit Post Size (KB), and then select a value.

20. To limit the amount of data that a user can post to a newsfeed during a single connection, click Limit Connection Size (MB), and then select a value.

21. In addition, you can allow other servers to pull news articles from this server, allow or disallow control messages, and specify the SMTP server for moderated groups, the default moderator domain, and the administrator e-mail account. The Settings tab is shown in Figure 9-6.

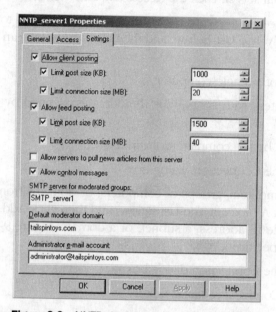

Figure 9-6   NNTP virtual server settings

Exercise 10: Create an SMTP Virtual Server

SMTP configuration is described in detail in Chapter 10. In this chapter, you create an SMTP virtual server and perform a limited configuration. You need to create an additional SMTP virtual server to carry out the practices in Chapter 10.

To create an additional SMTP virtual server, perform the following steps:

1. Start Exchange System Manager.

2. Navigate to Administrative Groups\First Administrative Group\Servers\Server01 \Protocols\SMTP.

3. In the console tree, right-click SMTP, point to New, and then select SMTP Virtual Server.

4. The New SMTP Virtual Server Wizard starts. In the Name box, type **SMTP_server1**, and then click Next.

5. From the Select The IP Address For This Virtual Server drop-down menu, select the IP address of Local Area Connection 2.

6. Click Finish. The wizard closes and a disabled virtual server is created.

Exercise 11: Configure an SMTP Virtual Server

To configure the new SMTP virtual server, perform the following steps:

1. Start Exchange System Manager.

2. Navigate to Administrative Groups\First Administrative Group\Servers\Server01 \Protocols\SMTP.

3. Right-click SMTP_server1, and then click Properties.

4. On the General tab, click Advanced. You can use the Advanced dialog box to alter the settings for the IP address and TCP port and to add a filter. Do not change any of these settings in this exercise. Click Cancel.

5. You can limit the number of connections to prevent the SMTP virtual server from becoming overloaded. Click Limit Number Of Connections To on the General tab, and then type an integer between 1 and 1,999,999,999.

6. To limit the length of time idle connections remain logged on to the server, specify the maximum time in the Connection Time-Out (Minutes) box.

7. To selectively include or exclude single computers, subnets, and domains from accessing an SMTP virtual server, click the Access tab, and then click Connection.

8. To allow only specified computers, groups of computers, or domains to access the virtual server, select Only The List Below, and then click Add. You can then specify one of the following:

   ❑ The static address of a single computer

   ❑ A group of computers with contiguous IP addresses, defined by the subnet address and mask

   ❑ A domain, defined by the complete domain name

9. Click OK to return to the Connection dialog box.

10. To restrict specified computers, groups of computers, or domains from accessing the virtual server, select All Except The List Below, and then click Add. As before, you can specify a single IP address, a subnet, or a domain.

11. Click OK to return to the Connection dialog box.

12. Click OK to close the Connection dialog box.

13. Click the Messages and Delivery tabs, shown in Figures 9-7 and 9-8, respectively. The configuration settings shown on these tabs are straightforward. More advanced configurations are described in Chapter 10.

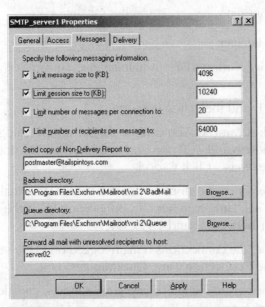

Figure 9-7 SMTP virtual server messages settings

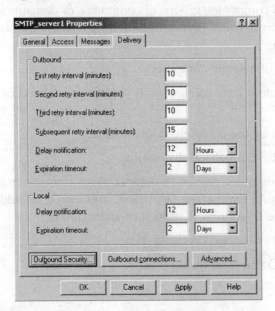

Figure 9-8 SMTP virtual server delivery settings

14. Click OK to close the virtual server Properties dialog box.

Lesson Review

The following questions are intended to reinforce key information presented in this lesson. If you are unable to answer a question, review the lesson materials and then try the question again. You can find answers to the questions in the "Questions and Answers" section at the end of this chapter.

1. What function do virtual servers on front-end Exchange Server 2003 servers perform, and what function do virtual servers on back-end Exchange Server 2003 servers perform? What do you need to install on each back-end server to handle front-end requests?

   _____

   _____

2. How does the implementation of the connection time-out setting differ between server roles?

   _____

   _____

3. You want to limit access to a virtual server. You want to ensure that only hosts with IP addresses 10.0.10.129 through 10.0.10.191 can access the server. You click the Access tab of the virtual server's Property box and then click Connection. Then you select Only The List Below. What parameters do you add?

   a. Network address 10.0.10.129, subnet mask 255.255.255.192

   b. Network address 10.0.10.128, subnet mask 255.255.255.192

   c. Network address 10.0.10.129, subnet mask 255.255.255.128

   d. Network address 10.0.10.128, subnet mask 255.255.255.128

Lesson Summary

- You can create additional HTTP, IMAP4, POP3, NNTP, and SMTP virtual servers on both front-end and back-end Exchange Server 2003 servers.

- Virtual servers supporting the same Exchange server should either have different IP addresses or different TCP port numbers. You can distinguish virtual servers by hostname, but this causes problems in DNS.

- You can limit the number of concurrent connections to a virtual server and configure the number of seconds that must elapse before an unsuccessful connection times out.

- You can control access by using authentication.

- You can encrypt e-mails, including authentication information, if you obtain, install, and associate a certificate.

- You can control client access by IP number, subnet, or domain name.

- POP3 servers can convert RTF to MIME or uuencode format and support BinHex for Macintosh. IMAP4 virtual servers do not support uuencode or BinHex for Macintosh.

- IMAP4 supports fast message retrieval.

- SMTP virtual servers can be configured to relay e-mail for POP3 and IMAP4 clients.

Lesson 3: Configuring Authentication

This lesson looks at the authentication methods configurable on Internet protocol virtual servers and at certificate-based encryption. The lesson also introduces client configuration, which is discussed in detail in Chapter 10.

After this lesson, you will be able to

- Obtain, install, and associate a certificate to enable SSL encryption on HTTP, NNTP, IMAP4, and POP3 virtual servers, and TLS encryption on SMTP virtual servers
- List the encryption methods available on all supported Internet protocol virtual servers and both back-end and front-end Exchange servers
- Distinguish between the various authentication methods available
- Configure the appropriate levels of authentication on virtual servers

Estimated lesson time: 45 minutes

Configuring Virtual Server Authentication Methods

Authentication ensures that the user is who he or she claims to be. More powerful authentication methods such as Kerberos ensure that the e-mail server is authenticated in addition to the user. Encryption ensures that only the recipient for whom a message is intended can read it.

Authentication Exchange supports three methods of user authentication. These are anonymous authentication, basic authentication, and Integrated Windows Authentication.

Anonymous Authentication This is the most common method used for Internet communication and provides limited access to specific public folders and directory information. Anonymous authentication is supported by all clients and is used to allow users to access unsecured content in public folders.

Basic Authentication Exchange performs simple challenge and response authentication by requiring that users enter their user name, domain name, and password to gain access to mailbox data. Most client computers support basic authentication. This method provides the simplest level of security.

> **Important** Basic authentication sends a user's name and password as clear text. Therefore, it is insecure. Basic authentication should not be used unless there is no alternative or unless the entire TCP/IP session is encrypted.

Integrated Windows Authentication   This method offers security, efficient communication, and transparency. You can use Integrated Windows Authentication when you have Windows-based clients that do not use encryption. This method uses Kerberos for clients running Windows 2000 Server or later, and new technology local area network (LAN) manager (NTLM) for Windows clients that are not running Active Directory. When you use Integrated Windows Authentication, the password is sent as an encrypted value.

Encryption

Encryption scrambles the contents of an e-mail message into a code that can only be read by the person who has the key to decode it on his or her computer. Authentication does not encrypt message data. Therefore, to make your data truly secure, you should encrypt e-mail messages transferred between the client and the server. Because TLS and SSL encrypt the entire TCP/IP session between the client and the server, the session is secure even if you chose a logon authentication method, such as basic authentication, that does not encrypt the user name and password.

HTTP, POP3, IMAP4, and NNTP virtual servers can use SSL encryption. SMTP virtual servers use TLS, which is a development of SSL. To use encryption, a virtual server must have a certificate issued by a trusted CA.

> **Exam Tip**   Remember that encryption scrambles the message. It is not an authentication method and does not authenticate the user. Remember also that encryption can be specified on a virtual server only if basic authentication is enabled. Finally, remember that encryption can be implemented only if a certificate is obtained. Some dialog boxes let you check the encryption setting before you obtain the certificate, but this has no effect until the certificate is installed.

Other Authentication Methods

Some POP3 and IMAP4 clients use *Simple Authentication and Security Layer (SASL)* authentication. This authentication method uses Kerberos or NTLM to authenticate hosts. SASL can be specified on POP3 and IMAP4 virtual servers on back-end Exchange Server 2003 servers.

You can specify digest authentication on HTTP virtual servers. This authenticates Windows domain servers rather than users. The settings on the Exchange virtual server (the default HTTP virtual server) also let you specify Microsoft .NET Passport authentication.

Supported Authentication Methods

Available authentication methods can vary, depending both upon the type of virtual server and upon whether the Exchange server is configured as a back-end or a front-end server. Table 9-3 gives the details.

Table 9-3   Supported Authentication Methods

Virtual server protocol	Exchange server configuration	Supported authentication methods
POP3 and IMAP4	Back-end	Basic SASL
HTTP	Back-end	Anonymous Basic Digest Integrated Windows Authentication .NET Password (Exchange virtual server only)
NNTP and SMTP	Back-end and front-end	Anonymous Basic Integrated Windows Authentication
POP3 and IMAP4	Front-end	Basic (cannot be changed)
HTTP	Front-end	Anonymous Basic Digest .NET Password (Exchange virtual server only) Integrated Windows Authentication (Exchange virtual server only)

Encryption can be configured on virtual servers on both back-end and front-end Exchange servers. Typically, encryption is configured on front-end servers that connect to the Internet. TLS encryption can be used on SMTP virtual servers, and SSL encryption on all other types of virtual servers. Both types of encryption require a certificate.

Configuring Client Access to Virtual Server Protocols

Exchange Server 2003 supports HTTP and WebDAV to provide enhanced functionality for HTTP clients retrieving and manipulating information in Web storage systems. You can also configure an HTTP virtual server to support OWA and allow clients to access e-mail, calendar information, shared applications, and any content in the public folder store, simply and efficiently by using a Web browser.

IMAP4 clients can access mail in an Exchange mailbox without downloading the entire mailbox to a specific computer. Exchange uses NNTP to enable Outlook users to participate in online discussions over the Internet. Exchange also enables users running client applications that support NNTP to access newsgroup public folders on computers running Exchange.

Exchange allows POP3 clients to access user inboxes on Exchange. However, POP3 users cannot access other public or private folders. POP3 is not intended to provide full manipulation of mail on the server. Although messages can be left on the server, mail is usually downloaded to a user's computer and then deleted.

To configure POP3 and IMAP4 clients, you need to create a mailbox-enabled user, specify account information on the client, and set per-user options. These procedures are described in detail in Chapter 10.

Practice: Obtaining, Installing, and Associating a Certificate for an IMAP4 Virtual Server on a Front-End Exchange Server

This procedure is used to obtain, associate, and install an encryption certificate on the default IMAP4 virtual server on the front-end Exchange server, Server02. The same procedure can be used to obtain, install, and associate a certificate on the following virtual servers:

- An IMAP4 virtual server on a back-end Exchange server
- A POP3 virtual server on either a front-end or a back-end Exchange server
- An NNTP virtual server on either a front-end or a back-end Exchange server
- An SMTP virtual server on either a front-end or a back-end Exchange server

To obtain, install, and associate a certificate on an HTTP virtual server on either a front-end or a back-end Exchange server, you need to access the Web Server Certificate Wizard by using the IIS Manager console rather than Exchange System Manager.

If you have not already done so, you need to start the Exchange IMAP4 service on Server02 as described in Lesson 1. This procedure assumes that this service and the default virtual server are running.

To obtain, install, and associate a certificate, perform the following ssteps:

1. Start Exchange System Manager.

2. Navigate to Administrative Groups\First Administrative Group\Servers\Server02\Protocols\IMAP4.

3. Right-click Default IMAP4 Virtual Server, and then click Pause.

4. Right-click Default IMAP4 Virtual Server, and then click Properties.

5. On the Access tab, click Certificate.

6. To request a new certificate, complete the Web Server Certificate Wizard. When prompted, select the Create A New Certificate option. Because there is a CA in your domain, you can obtain the certificate immediately.

7. Click Apply to save your settings.

8. To install the certificate, click Certificate again.

9. Complete the Web Server Certificate Wizard again. This time, select Assign An Existing Certificate when prompted.

10. To associate the certificate and require a secure channel, click Communication on the Access tab.

11. Click Require Secure Channel.

12. If 128-bit encryption is supported on the computer hosting the IMAP4 virtual server, click Require 128-bit Encryption.

13. Click OK to close the virtual server Properties dialog box.

14. Restart the virtual server.

> **Note**   You do not need to obtain a certificate every time you want to enable encryption on a virtual server. If you have obtained a certificate for one virtual server on your Exchange server, you can use the Web Server Certificate Wizard to assign it to other virtual servers.

Practice: Configuring Authentication

This procedure is the same for all virtual servers, except for the options that can be set. For the HTTP default virtual server, you use the IIS Manager console to access the Authentication sheet through the Directory Security tab of the Exchange Properties box, but otherwise the procedure is identical.

Exercise 1: Configure Authentication on Virtual Servers on a Back-End Exchange Server

To configure authentication, perform the following steps:

1. Start Exchange System Manager.

2. Navigate to Administrative Groups\First Administrative Group\Servers\Server01 \Protocols.

3. Expand HTTP, NTTP, POP3, IMAP4, and SMTP.

4. Right-click any virtual server except the Exchange virtual server (the HTTP default virtual server), and then click Pause.

5. Right-click the paused virtual server, and then click Properties.

6. On the Access tab, click Authentication.

7. Specify the authentication settings. Figures 9-9 through 9-12 show the available options.

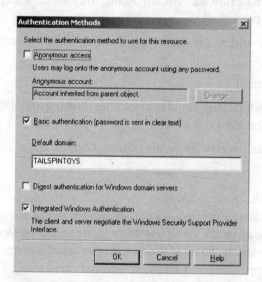

Figure 9-9   Authentication options for an additional HTTP virtual server on a back-end Exchange server

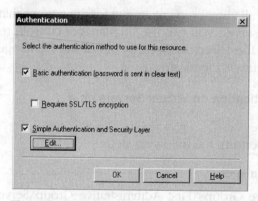

Figure 9-10   Authentication options for POP3 and IMAP4 virtual servers on a back-end Exchange server

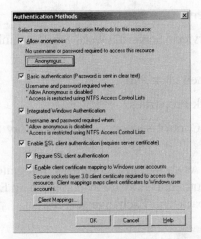

Figure 9-11   Authentication options for an NNTP virtual server

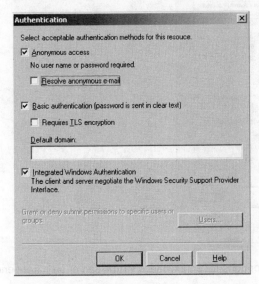

Figure 9-12   Authentication options for an SMTP virtual server

8. Click OK to close the virtual server Properties dialog box.

9. Restart the virtual server.

Exercise 2: Configure Authentication on the Default HTTP Virtual Server on a Front-End Exchange Server

The purpose of this exercise is to describe the use of the IIS Manager console to configure authentication settings on a default HTTP virtual server. The procedure also illustrates the difference between HTTP virtual servers on a back-end and on a front-end Exchange server.

1. Start the IIS Manager console on Server02.

2. Expand Internet Information Services\Server02\Web Sites\Default Web Site \Exchange.

3. Right-click Default Web Site, and then click Pause.

4. Right-click Exchange, and then click Properties.

5. In the Authentication And Access Control section on the Directory Security tab, click Edit.

6. Configure the settings as required. As shown in Figure 9-13, Integrated Windows Authentication and .NET Passport authentication are available on an Exchange virtual server on both front-end and back-end Exchange servers.

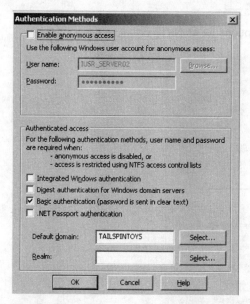

Figure 9-13 Authentication options for an Exchange virtual server on a front-end or back-end Exchange server

However, on an additional HTTP server on a front-end Exchange server, these options are not available. Figure 9-14 shows the authentication settings available in this case.

Figure 9-14   Authentication options for an additional HTTP virtual server on a front-end Exchange server

7. Click OK to close the Authentication dialog box.

8. Click OK to close the Exchange Properties dialog box.

9. Restart the default Web site.

Exercise 3: Examine Authentication Settings on a POP3 Virtual Server on a Front-End Exchange Server

The purpose of this exercise is to examine the Authentication dialog box on a POP3 virtual server on a front-end Exchange server. The Authentication dialog box on an IMAP4 virtual server on a front-end Exchange server looks exactly the same.

To examine authentication settings, perform the following steps:

1. Start Exchange System Manager.

2. Navigate to Administrative Groups\First Administrative Group\Servers\Server02 \Protocols\POP3.

3. Right-click Default POP3 Virtual Server, and then click Properties.

4. On the Access tab, click Authentication.

5. The Authentication dialog box is shown in Figure 9-15. Note that on a front-end server, basic authentication is specified and cannot be changed. The only configuration possible is to enable encryption.

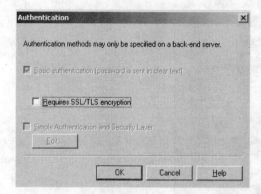

Figure 9-15   Authentication dialog box for a POP3 virtual server on a front-end Exchange server

6. Click OK to close the virtual server dialog box.

Lesson Review

The following questions are intended to reinforce key information presented in this lesson. If you are unable to answer a question, review the lesson materials and then try the question again. You can find answers to the questions in the "Questions and Answers" section at the end of this chapter.

1. Which additional Internet protocol virtual servers support Integrated Windows Authentication? (Select all that apply.)

    a. HTTP, back-end

    b. HTTP, front-end

    c. NNTP, back-end

    d. NNTP, front-end

    e. POP3, back-end

    f. POP3, front-end

    g. IMAP4, back-end

    h. IMAP4, front-end

    i. SMTP, back-end

    j. SMTP, front-end

2. On which types of virtual servers is the authentication method fixed and not configurable?

    _____

    _____

3. Why is basic authentication considered a security risk?

_____

_____

Lesson Summary

- There are three methods of user authentication: anonymous, basic, and Integrated Windows Authentication.

- Encryption can be configured if basic authentication is used and a certificate is obtained and installed.

- Available authentication methods can vary depending on whether the virtual server is on a back-end or a front-end Exchange server.

- The authentication method on IMAP4 and POP3 virtual servers on front-end Exchange servers cannot be changed.

- You configure the default HTTP virtual server (the Exchange server) using the IIS Manager console. You use Exchange System Manager to configure all other virtual servers.

Lesson 4: Maintaining Virtual Servers

This lesson looks at the procedures for viewing connected users on a virtual server and terminating connections. The lesson also discusses diagnostic logging. Chapter 14, "Troubleshooting Microsoft Exchange Server 2003," discusses detailed troubleshooting procedures. Also, Chapter 13, "Monitoring Microsoft Exchange Server 2003," describes diagnostic logging in more detail.

After this lesson, you will be able to

- Start, stop, pause, and restart a virtual server
- View all connected users on a virtual server
- Disconnect a single user connection or all user connections
- Set the level for diagnostic logging
- View the events generated by diagnostic logging

Estimated lesson time: 30 minutes

Virtual Server Status

You can stop, start, pause, and restart an Internet protocol virtual server by right-clicking the appropriate server in the console pane of Exchange System Manager and clicking the appropriate command. If the virtual server is paused, then clicking on Pause again will restart it. If all options are unavailable, then the server is disabled. This happens, for example, if a POP3 virtual server has just been created and has not been configured. If a virtual server cannot be started, then either the required protocol service is not running or the server does not have a unique combination of TCP port and IP address.

You can determine the status of a virtual server by examining the console pane in Exchange System Manager. If the virtual server is running, the server's folder displays an open mailbox in the console tree. If the virtual server is stopped, the console displays a red circle with a white X inside it. If the virtual server is paused, the console displays a white circle with two black bars inside it. If the server is disabled, there is no symbol inside the white circle.

Viewing Connected Users and Terminating Connections

If you pause a virtual server, you do not disconnect any currently connected users, but no additional users can connect until you restart the server. If you stop a virtual server, then this disconnects all user sessions. You can also terminate selected user connections without disturbing other connections. Before you stop or pause a virtual server, or carry out any reconfiguration, you should view the list of connected users. It is good practice to pause a server and wait for users to disconnect before you make any changes, or to send messages to connected users warning them that they will be disconnected after a specified time period.

Diagnostic Logging

You can use diagnostic logging to record significant events relating to authentication, connections, and client actions. The Windows Server 2003 event log on the Exchange server that hosts the virtual server records the diagnostic logging events. You set the level of logging on the host server (not on the protocol virtual server). The default logging level is None. This logging level records critical and error events only.

Practice: Viewing and Managing Connected Users on an IMAP4 Virtual Server

In this practice, you view the list of connected users on an IMAP4 virtual server. The procedure also describes how to disconnect a single user and how you can disconnect all users without stopping the virtual server. This practice describes the procedure on an IMAP4 virtual server. The same procedure can be used on any Internet protocol virtual servers except for HTTP virtual servers.

Exercise 1: Viewing and Managing Connected Users on an IMAP4 Virtual Server

To view and manage connections on an IMAP4 virtual server, perform the following steps:

1. Open Exchange System Manager.

2. Navigate to Administrative Groups\First Administrative Group\Servers\Server01 \Protocols\IMAP4.

3. Double-click IMAP4_server1.

4. To populate the details pane with information about connected users, click Current Sessions in the console tree.

5. To disconnect a single user, right-click the user in the details pane, and then click Terminate. If no users are currently connected, then you cannot perform this step.

6. To disconnect all users, right-click anywhere on the details pane, and then click Terminate All.

Lesson Review

The following questions are intended to reinforce key information presented in this lesson. If you are unable to answer a question, review the lesson materials and then try the question again. You can find answers to the questions in the "Questions and Answers" section at the end of this chapter.

1. What symbol indicates that a virtual server is stopped, and what symbol indicates that it is paused?

   _____

   _____

2. When would you pause a virtual server rather than stopping it?

   _____

   _____

3. What diagnostic logging level logs high-level events by logging a single entry for each major task performed by the service?

   a. None

   b. Minimum

   c. Medium

   d. Maximum

Lesson Summary

- You can start, stop, pause, and restart a virtual server by right-clicking it in Exchange System Manager and then clicking the appropriate command.

- You can view connected sessions, disconnect any session, and disconnect all sessions.

- You can set the level of diagnostic logging by using Exchange System Manager and view the results of this logging by using Event Viewer.

Case Scenario Exercise

You are the Exchange 2003 administrator for Coho Winery. The employees at your company use a variety of client computers including IMAP4 and POP3 clients. All employees need to be able to send and receive Internet e-mail. Coho Winery is involved in a number of collaboration projects with Coho Vineyard. Some of the data is confidential.

Coho Winery's marketing employees mostly use Apple Macintosh clients. They frequently send and receive e-mails with large attachments. They report that sometimes their client connections time out when downloading these attachments and that at other times the e-mail messages are difficult to read.

Users who have IMAP4 clients are experiencing a wide range of problems. Your chief information officer (CIO) states that the budget does not permit client upgrades, and she wants you to get the Exchange Server 2003 organization working with the clients that are currently available.

- **Requirement 1**   Management is concerned that members of the public who browse to the company Web site may be able to access the private collaboration information. You are required to ensure that this cannot happen.

- **Requirement 2**   Users in the marketing department need to be able to download large attachments. They also need to be able to read all their e-mails without formatting-related problems.

- **Requirement 3**   You need to ensure that IMAP4 clients receive an acceptable level of service.

Requirement 1

You need to prevent users outside the company from accessing private collaboration information.

1. Management requires assurance that confidential collaboration information is not made available to casual browsers and the general public. How do you set up your Exchange Server 2003 organization to meet this concern?

_____

_____

2. You have delegated the task of configuring the Exchange virtual server to an assistant administrator. You have configured all the appropriate rights and permissions. Your assistant reports that when she attempts to configure HTTP virtual servers (particularly the Exchange virtual server) using Exchange System Manager, most of the controls she wants are dimmed. What do you tell her?

_____

_____

Requirement 2

You need to set up the e-mail system so that members of the Marketing department can read all their e-mail, including messages with large attachments.

1. Your assistant has configured the timeout settings on the POP3 virtual servers on your front-end Exchange Server 2003 servers. Users complain that connections are timing out before they can download large attachments. What is the most likely reason for this?

   _____

   _____

2. Some of your users who log on to Apple Macintosh computers report difficulties in reading e-mails. What is the most likely reason for this problem?

   _____

   _____

Requirement 3

IMAP4 clients must receive an acceptable level of service.

1. Users logged on to IMAP4 clients in Coho Winery report poor e-mail performance. Users on other clients are not experiencing the same problems. You inspect the Application log on Event Viewer, but there is insufficient detail for you to diagnose the problem. You decide that you need to monitor IMAPSvc events more closely. In particular, you need more detail when a fault occurs. How do you meet this requirement?

   _____

   _____

Troubleshooting Lab

Coho Winery employees who are logged on to IMAP4 clients report problems with mail retrieval. In order to diagnose these problems, you reconfigure the diagnostic level for IMAP4 virtual servers so that the Application log in Event Viewer records entries for each step taken to run a task, and the level of logging gives more detail once the location of the problem is found. (You can use the same procedure for POP3 virtual servers by selecting the POP3Svc service.)

Before proceeding with this lab, ensure that you have two Exchange Server 2003 servers configured as described in the "Before You Begin" section at the start of this chapter. Ensure that the Microsoft Exchange IMAP4 service is started. You also need to have created the additional IMAP4 virtual server IMAP4_server1 as described in this chapter.

Exercise 1: Set a Diagnostic Level and Read the Resulting Entries in the Event Log

To set a diagnostic level and read the event log, perform the following steps:

1. Open Exchange System Manager.

2. Navigate to Administrative Groups\First Administrative Group\Servers\Server01.

3. Right-click Server01, and then click Properties.

4. Click the Diagnostics Logging tab, and then click IMAP4Svc in the Services section.

5. Click an item in Category. The dialog box shown in Figure 9-16 appears.

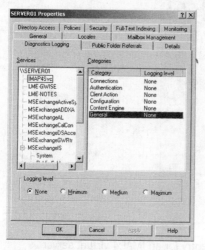

Figure 9-16   Setting a diagnostic logging level

The appropriate section in the dialog box now becomes active and you can select a Logging Level:

❑ *None*—This level logs only critical and error events.

❑ *Minimum*—This level logs high-level events by logging a single entry for each major task performed by the service. This level of logging can help identify where a problem might be occurring.

❑ *Medium*—This level records entries for each step taken to run a task. This level of logging gives more detail once the location of the problem is found.

❏ *Maximum*—This level records entries for each line of code in the service, providing a complete trail of the operation of a service and logging all events. This level of logging can affect server performance and should be used only when detailed debugging is required.

6. Select Medium, and then click OK.

7. Pause, and restart Default IMAP4 Virtual Server and IMAP4_server1.

8. Open Event Viewer on Server01.

9. In Event Viewer, in the application log, double-click an event of type IMAP4SVC. Figure 9-17 shows a typical event log entry.

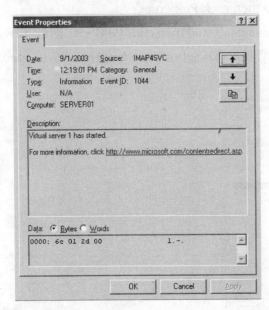

Figure 9-17   An Application event log entry for an IMAP4 virtual server

10. Click OK to close the Event Properties box.

11. Close Event Viewer and Exchange System Manager.

Chapter Summary

1. Exchange back-end servers typically use the Microsoft Cluster Service for failover support. Exchange front-end servers typically use load balancing clusters.

2. HTTP, NNTP, POP3, IMAP4, and SMTP virtual servers are available on an Exchange Server 2003 server. The Default HTTP virtual server is called the Exchange server. POP3 and IMAP4 retrieve but do not send e-mail. SMTP is used to send mail. HTTP virtual servers support WebDAV and OWA.

3. You can control access by using anonymous authentication, basic authentication, and Integrated Windows Authentication. You can encrypt e-mails, including authentication information, if you obtain, install, and associate a certificate, and you can control client access by IP address, subnet, or domain name.

4. You can set the level of diagnostic logging by using Exchange System Manager and view the results of this logging by using Event Viewer.

Exam Highlights

Before taking the exam, review the key points and terms that are presented in this chapter. Return to the lessons for additional practice.

Key Points

- You need Exchange Server 2003, Enterprise Edition, to implement the Microsoft Cluster Service. However, you can implement the Network Load Balancing service. The Microsoft Cluster Service is for failover protection and does not provide load balancing.

- The Default HTTP virtual server is called the Exchange virtual server and must be configured using IIS Manager rather than Exchange System Manager. POP3 and IMAP4 do not send e-mail; SMTP is used for this purpose. HTTP virtual servers support WebDAV and OWA. There is not a specific WebDAV or OWA virtual server.

- Unless you encrypt the entire TCP/IP session using SSL or TLS, using basic authentication will transmit passwords over a network in clear text. You can control client access by IP address, subnet, or domain name, or by using authentication.

- POP3 manages e-mail on the client. IMAP4 manages it on the server. IMAP4 supports fast message retrieval, but does not support uuencode or BinHex for MacIntosh. SMTP virtual servers can be configured to relay mail for IMAP4 and POP3 clients.

Key Terms

Internet protocol virtual server   Exchange Server 2003 uses virtual servers to handle e-mail messages that use the various Internet protocols. Exchange Server 2003 HTTP, SMTP, NNTP, IMAP4, and POP3 virtual servers.

Exchange virtual server   The Exchange virtual server is the default HTTP virtual server. It manages the default Web page. By default, it manages OWA and WebDAV access. The Exchange virtual server is configured using IIS Manager rather than Exchange System Manager.

diagnostics logging   Diagnostics logging is a feature of Exchange System Manager that lets you define the level at which the events written to the application log in Event Viewer are logged.

Questions and Answers

Page
9-19
Lesson 1 Review

1. What is the default port configuration of a POP3, an IMAP4, and an NNTP virtual server?

   Incoming POP3 connections use TCP port 110, and POP3 SSL connections use port 995. Incoming IMAP4 connections use TCP port 143, and SSL connections use port 993. Incoming NNTP connections use TCP port 119, and SSL connections use port 563.

2. Which protocol services associated with Exchange Server 2003 virtual servers are disabled by default?

   The NNTP service, the Exchange POP3 service, and the Exchange IMAP4 service.

3. The default HTTP virtual server is known as the Exchange virtual server. What additional feature distinguishes it from all other virtual servers?

   It is configured using IIS Manager rather than Exchange System Manager.

Page
9-39
Lesson 2 Review

1. What function do virtual servers on front-end Exchange Server 2003 servers perform, and what function do virtual servers on back-end Exchange Server 2003 servers perform? What do you need to install on each back-end server to handle front-end requests?

   Internet protocol virtual servers on front-end Exchange Server 2003 servers handle incoming client connections, while the back-end virtual servers are dedicated to running the databases. You need to create a virtual HTTP server on each back-end server to handle front-end requests.

2. How does the implementation of the connection time-out setting differ between server roles?

   On back-end servers, the connection time-out setting limits the length of time for which a client is permitted to remain connected to the server without performing any activity. On front-end servers, the connection time-out setting limits the total length of the client's session, regardless of client activity.

3. You want to limit access to a virtual server. You want to ensure that only hosts with IP addresses 10.0.10.129 through 10.0.10.191 can access the server. You click the Access tab of the virtual server's Property box and then click Connection. Then you select Only The List Below. What parameters do you add?

   a. Network address 10.0.10.129, subnet mask 255.255.255.192

   b. Network address 10.0.10.128, subnet mask 255.255.255.192

   c. Network address 10.0.10.129, subnet mask 255.255.255.128

   d. Network address 10.0.10.128, subnet mask 255.255.255.128

   The correct answer is b.

Page
9-50

Lesson 3 Review

1. Which additional Internet protocol virtual servers support Integrated Windows Authentication? (Select all that apply.)

   a. HTTP, back-end

   b. HTTP, front-end

   c. NNTP, back-end

   d. NNTP, front-end

   e. POP3, back-end

   f. POP3, front-end

   g. IMAP4, back-end

   h. IMAP4, front-end

   i. SMTP, back-end

   j. SMTP, front-end

   The correct answers are a, c, d, i, and j.

2. On which types of virtual servers is the authentication method fixed and not configurable?

   IMAP4 and POP3 virtual servers on front-end Exchange servers.

3. Why is basic authentication considered a security risk?

   The user's password is sent in clear-text.

Page
9-53

Lesson 4 Review

1. What symbol indicates that a virtual server is stopped, and what symbol indicates that it is paused?

   If the virtual server is stopped, the console displays a red circle with a white X inside it. If the virtual server is paused, the console displays a white circle with two black bars inside it.

2. When would you pause a virtual server rather than stopping it?

   When you do not want to disconnect current user sessions but want to prevent any more users from connecting.

3. What diagnostic logging level logs high-level events by logging a single entry for each major task performed by the service?

   a. None

   b. Minimum

   c. Medium

   d. Maximum

   The correct answer is b.

Page
9-55

Case Scenario Exercise: Requirement 1

1. Management requires assurance that confidential collaboration information is not made available to casual browsers and the general public. How do you set up your Exchange Server 2003 organization to meet this concern?

   Although you can meet the HTTP requirements by implementing a secure virtual directory for WebDAV collaboration, Management will probably be more at ease if you create an additional HTTP virtual server. You can allow anonymous access to the virtual server that manages your company Web site, and configure filtering, authentication, and encryption on the virtual server that manages the WebDAV collaboration.

2. You have delegated the task of configuring the Exchange virtual server to an assistant administrator. You have configured all the appropriate rights and permissions. Your assistant reports that when she attempts to configure HTTP virtual servers (particularly the Exchange virtual server) using Exchange System Manager, most of the controls she wants are dimmed. What do you tell her?

   The Exchange virtual server, or the Default HTTP virtual server, is administered using the IIS Manager console, not the Exchange System Manager console.

Page
9-56

Case Scenario Exercise: Requirement 2

1. Your assistant has configured the timeout settings on the POP3 virtual servers on your front-end Exchange Server 2003 servers. Users complain that connections are timing out before they can download large attachments. What is the most likely reason for this?

   This setting on a back-end server will cause a timeout after a period of inactivity. On a front-end server, the same setting causes a timeout whether there has been activity or not. It is possible that your assistant has used the same setting on back-end and front-end servers.

2. Some of your users who log on to Apple Macintosh computers report difficulties in reading e-mails. What is the most likely reason for this problem?

   Macintosh clients understand uuencode and BinHex for Macintosh. If a POP3 client uses uuencode rather than Multipurpose Internet Mail Extensions (MIME), and requires BinHex for Macintosh, then you or your assistant needs to configure this type of encoding for those clients. This could involve either creating an additional POP3 virtual server or setting per-client options.

Page
9-56

Case Scenario Exercise: Requirement 3

1. Users logged on to IMAP4 clients in Coho Winery report poor e-mail performance. Users on other clients are not experiencing the same problems. You inspect the Application log on Event Viewer, but there is insufficient detail for you to diagnose the problem. You decide that you need to monitor IMAPSvc events more closely. In particular, you need more detail when a fault occurs. How do you meet this requirement?

   You need to increase your diagnostic logging level. You do this by using the application log in Event Viewer to view the logs. You use Exchange System Manager to change the diagnostic logging level.

10 SMTP Protocol Configuration and Management

Lessons in this Chapter:

- Configure and troubleshoot for interoperability with other Simple Mail Transfer Protocol (SMTP) messaging systems
- Manage and troubleshoot connectivity
- Diagnose network connectivity problems

Why This Chapter Matters

SMTP is the standard protocol for transporting messages between Transmission Control Protocol/Internet Protocol (TCP/IP) hosts; in other words, it transfers e-mail over the Internet and most intranets. The protocol comprises a series of plain-text commands used to transfer messages between hosts. A Microsoft Exchange Server 2003 administrator needs a sound understanding of how SMTP transfers messages, how it is configured, and how SMTP communication is secured.

Extended SMTP (ESMTP) extends SMTP functionality to support advanced messaging commands that are used, for example, for host authentication and encryption. Most e-mail messaging systems support SMTP, and many systems also support ESMTP. For the examination, you need to know how to configure SMTP, how to resolve SMTP connectivity problems, how to configure SMTP outbound security, and how to ensure SMTP interoperability.

 Note This chapter focuses on managing and configuring SMTP. Security, monitoring, and troubleshooting will be covered when appropriate, but these topics are discussed in more depth in Chapter 11, "Microsoft Exchange Server 2003 Security," Chapter 13, "Monitoring Microsoft Exchange Server 2003," and Chapter 14, "Troubleshooting Microsoft Exchange Server 2003."

Lessons in this Chapter:

- Lesson 1: Managing SMTP Message Transfer Support 10-3
- Lesson 2: Configuring SMTP Security and Advanced Options 10-21
- Lesson 3: Configuring Interoperability with Other SMTP
  Messaging Systems 10-36

Before You Begin

To perform the exercises in this chapter, you need the following hardware and software:

- Two Microsoft Windows Server 2003, Enterprise Edition, servers installed in the *tailspintoys.com* Active Directory directory service domain. Server01 should be a domain controller, and Server02 should be a member server.

> **Note** Provided that Server01 and Server02 are configured as described above, the actual domain name does not matter. If your domain name is not *tailspintoys.com*, there is no need to change it.

- Server01 should be an enterprise root certification authority (CA) server. (If you are unsure of how to install Certificate Services, please refer to the Windows Server 2003 help files.)
- Exchange Server 2003, Enterprise Edition, should be installed on both servers. Server01 and Server02 should be back-end and front-end servers, respectively.
- Preferably, a modem should be installed on Server02. This is not essential.
- A Domain Name System (DNS) server needs to be available. Typically, DNS is installed on the domain controller.
- You need to have created and configured an additional SMTP server. This is one of the practices in Chapter 9, "Virtual Servers."

Real World   Experimentation with Third-Party Servers and Client

Experienced users often want to expand their networks so they can carry out further experiments. In this chapter, for example, you might find it valuable to install additional client hosts (such as UNIX hosts) and to use messaging systems other than Exchange Server 2003. In this case (and given that most of us have limited budgets), you should consider the use of products such as Connectix Virtual PC (*www.connectix.com*) or VMWare (*www.vmware.com*).

Lesson 1: Managing SMTP Message Transfer Support

SMTP uses SMTP connectors and virtual servers to implement connections, and you can configure SMTP for a variety of environments. SMTP recipients can have a single SMTP address or multiple SMTP addresses. Exchange Server 2003 can segregate recipients into *virtual organizations*, each with its own SMTP address space.

After this lesson, you will be able to

- Explain how an SMTP connection works
- Describe common SMTP commands and reply codes
- Explain how an ESMTP connection works
- Describe common ESMTP commands
- Configure DNS to support SMTP
- Configure an SMTP connector
- Identify methods of troubleshooting SMTP connectivity

Estimated lesson time: 90 minutes

How SMTP Implements a Connection

Note   This lesson gives an overview of SMTP and ESMTP commands but does not describe the contents of SMTP and ESMTP network packets in detail. For more information, refer to Requests for Comments (RFCs) 821, 822, and 1869. RFCs can be found at *www.rfc-editor.org/rfc.html*.

When an Exchange Server 2003 host communicates with another host, it does so using standard SMTP commands and numerical reply codes over TCP port 25. This communication uses an *asymmetric request-response* protocol, which simply means that one host sends a command, waits for a reply, and then sends the next command. Suppose that an SMTP client (Host01) sends a message to an SMTP server (Server01). The procedure is as follows:

1. Host01 initiates a TCP connection to Server01. Server01 returns response 220 (ready), which indicates that it has opened a connection.

2. Host01 sends a helo command. This requests that an SMTP session be initiated. Server01 returns response 250, which indicates that the requested action is okay and has been completed.

3. Host01 identifies the sender of the message using the mail from: command. Server01 returns response 250.

4. Host01 identifies Server01 as the recipient using the rcpt to: command. Server01 returns response 250.

5. Host01 indicates that it is ready to send the message using the data command. Server01 returns a 354 response, which indicates that the message should start.

6. Host01 sends the message.

7. Host01 indicates the end of the session using the quit command. Server01 returns a 221 response, indicating that the SMTP service is closing the connection.

Common SMTP Commands

The SMTP commands define the mail transfer or the mail system function requested by the user. The commands consist of alphabetic character strings terminated by the carriage return/line feed character (<CRLF>). If a command code has parameters, then it is followed by a space character (<SP>), the parameters, and then <CRLF>. Table 10-1 lists the common SMTP commands. This list is not comprehensive. A full list of commands can be found in the RFCs.

Table 10-1   Common SMTP Commands

Command	Description
helo	Requests an SMTP session and identifies the sending SMTP host to the receiving SMTP host. The argument field contains the fully qualified domain name (FQDN) of the sending host.
mail from:	Identifies the sender of the message. This is not necessarily the same as the sending SMTP host; for example, the sending host could be acting as a relay.
rcpt to:	Identifies the message recipient. If there are several recipients, then the command is used for each recipient.
data	Indicates that the sending host is ready to transmit the message.
quit	Indicates the end of the SMTP session.
rset	Aborts the current mail transaction.
quit	Disconnects the TCP session.
vrfy	Allows the sending host to verify that the recipient is valid before sending the message.
turn	Triggers the recipient server to send queued messages destined for the sending server. This command is used in a dial-up environment to poll a host for queued messages.

Common SMTP Reply Codes

Table 10-2 lists the common SMTP reply codes. The commands are text strings, whereas the replies are numbers. However, reply codes 220 and 221 include the FQDN of the receiving host as a parameter. As before, this list is not comprehensive.

Table 10-2   Common SMTP Reply Codes

Reply code	Description
220	Indicates that the SMTP service is ready.
221	Indicates that the SMTP service is closing the transmission channel.
250	Indicates that the requested action is okay and has been completed.
354	Indicates to the sending host that the message should be transmitted.
450	Indicates that the requested action has not been taken because the mailbox is busy.
451	Indicates that the requested action has been aborted due to a local error in processing.
452	Indicates that the requested action has not been taken because there is insufficient system storage.
500	Indicates a syntax error or unrecognized command.
550	Indicates that the requested action has not been taken because the mailbox is unavailable or not found.
552	Indicates that the requested action has been aborted because the storage allocation was exceeded.
554	Indicates that the transaction failed.

How ESMTP Implements a Connection

ESMTP uses the standard SMTP commands and response codes over TCP port 25 but also provides additional capabilities such as delivery notification. ESMTP communication can be made more secure by means of advanced messaging commands that support host authentication and encryption. If an ESMTP host initiates a session with a host that does not support the protocol, then it will use normal SMTP.

Windows 2000 and Windows 2003 operating systems support ESMTP by default. There are also ESMTP clients available for UNIX and Apple Macintosh operating systems.

Let us again suppose that an ESMTP client (Host01) sends a message to an SMTP server (Server01). The procedure is as follows:

1. Host01 initiates a TCP connection to Server01. Server01 returns response 220 (ready), which indicates that it has opened a connection.

2. Host01 sends an ehlo command (rather than a helo command). This requests that an ESMTP session be initiated. If Server01 supports ESMTP, then it returns response 250, which indicates that the requested action is okay and has been completed. If, however, Server01 does not support ESMTP, then it returns response 500, indicating that it does not recognize the command.

3. If Host01 receives response 250, then it continues with the ESMTP session. This is similar to an SMTP session except that the extended commands are available. If, on the other hand, Host01 receives response 500, then it sends an SMTP helo command and starts a normal SMTP session.

Common ESMTP Commands

ESMTP uses the standard SMTP commands (with the exception of helo) and also uses some additional commands. Table 10-3 lists some common ESMTP commands. A more detailed list of ESMTP commands is available in RFC 1869. Further details are given in the additional RFCs listed in the table.

Table 10-3   Common ESMTP Commands

Command	Description
atrn	An authenticated turn command (refer to Table 10-1) that runs only if the session has been authenticated. It is described in RFC 2645.
etrn	This command is similar to turn, but it specifies the remote host to which the mail is to be delivered. It is described in RFC 1985.
pipelining	Allows SMTP commands to be sent in batches without waiting for a response from the receiving host.
chunking	Makes the sending of large Multipurpose Internet Mail Extensions (MIME) messages more efficient by "chunking" data together as it is transported between SMTP hosts.
starttls	Provides a Secure Sockets Layer (SSL) connection between the SMTP client and server by initiating a Transport Layer Security (TLS) connection. The client system must initiate the TLS connection.
auth	Provides a form of Simple Authentication and Security Layer (SASL) SMTP authentication that uses Kerberos and Microsoft's new technology local area network (LAN) manager (NTLM) protocol to authenticate SMTP hosts. The SASL mechanism used is specified in the command parameter.
auth=login	Provides a form of SASL for clients such as Netscape and Exchange Server 5.5 that require basic SMTP authentication.
help	Outputs a list of the commands supported by the SMTP host. It is described in RFC 821.
vrfy	Determines whether an e-mail account exists and whether the account is disabled by default. It is described in RFC 821.

Table 10-3   Common ESMTP Commands

Command	Description
dsn	Generates and sends a delivery status notification to the sending host if there is a delivery failure. The command is considered an improvement on the non-delivery report (NDR) mechanism. It is described in RFC 1891.
size	Determines the size of a message prior to its acceptance. In standard SMTP, a message must be transmitted to the receiving system in whole or in part before it can be rejected for exceeding a size limitation. The command is described in RFC 1870.
x-eps gssapi ntlm login	Uses an authentication mechanism that supports Kerberos and NTLM. It supports the same authentication mechanisms as auth.
x-exps=login	Uses an Exchange Server 5.5–specific authentication mechanism that supports NTLM and provides compatibility with Exchange Server 5.5.
x-link2state	Specifies support for the Exchange 2000 Server link state command verb. For example, it can be used to advertise the fact that a server is capable of exchanging link state information.
xexch50	Used when establishing a connection with another server running Exchange. It is used to transfer Exchange-specific content in messages.

Real World   Hazards of Using the vrfy Command

In real-world systems, the vrfy command is often disabled. Many administrators consider it a security risk because it could help a malicious third party determine the identity of enabled e-mail accounts.

Testing an ESMTP Connection

The ehlo command may be used to test connectivity between your Exchange Server 2003 server and a remote SMTP host. If the remote host recognizes the command, then you can authenticate sending and receiving hosts and use encryption. You first establish a connection over TCP port 25 using the telnet utility. On establishing the connection, telnet will indicate whether the remote host supports ESMTP. However, this is not sufficient to indicate that an ESMTP connection can be established. It is possible, for example, that the recipient host is an Exchange server with the System Attendant service stopped. To test ESMTP connectivity, you must then issue the elho command. If you are testing the connection while logged on at another computer (which should be the case in a production network), then you need to follow the command with the FQDN of your server. If the remote host responds with a 250 reply, then it supports ESMTP commands. Figure 10-1 illustrates this technique.

```
Telnet server01.tailspintoys.com                              _ □ ×
220 Server01.TailSpinToys.com Microsoft ESMIP MAIL Service
ready at  Mon, 25 Aug 2003 09:32:54 -0700
EHLO
250-Server01.TailSpinToys.com Hello [10.0.10.100]
250-TURN
250-SIZE
250-ETRN
250-PIPELINING
250-DSN
250-ENHANCEDSTATUSCODES
250-8bitmine
250-BINARYMIME
250-CHUNKING
250-VRFY
250-X-EXPS GSSAPI NTLM LOGIN
250-X-EXPS=LOGIN
250-AUTH GSSAPI NTLM LOGIN
250-AUTH=LOGIN
250-X-LINK2STATE
250-XEXCH50
250 OK
-
◄                                                           ►
```

Figure 10-1   Testing ESMTP connectivity

You can use the same technique to test standard SMTP connectivity between your server and a remote host. In this case, you should use the helo command rather than the ehlo command.

Exam Tip   You should know that ESMTP is required for facilities such as authentication, encryption, and delivery notification (but not for NDRs), and you should be able to distinguish between the helo and ehlo commands. You should also be able to recognize commands as SMTP or ESMTP and summarize their functions.

SMTP Folders

SMTP uses three system folders to temporarily store messages in transit. By default, these folders are created on an Exchange Server 2003 server in C:\Program Files\Exchsrvr\Mailroot\vsi 1. The folders are as follows:

- **Pickup**   SMTP delivers any SMTP formatted messages that are placed in the Pickup folder. Exchange Server 2003 does not use this folder.

- **Queue**   SMTP stores inbound SMTP messages in this folder when they are received. Internet Information Services (IIS) then processes these messages for delivery.

- **Bad Mail**   SMTP stores undeliverable messages that cannot be returned to the sender in this folder.

If you want to change the location of these folders, you need to make the change in the configuration partition of Active Directory. Otherwise the changes will be overwritten. Use the Adsiedit.exe tool for this purpose.

Configuring DNS to Support SMTP

Having a well-designed DNS service is critical to the operation of an Exchange Server 2003 organization. In a production network, you should ensure that DNS does not constitute a single point of failure by the use of secondary DNS servers, Active Directory Integrated DNS, or both. When an SMTP host sends an e-mail message to another SMTP host, DNS resolves the SMTP domain name of the receiving host to its IP address. SMTP domain names and host addresses are held in DNS Mail Exchanger (MX) records.

Typically, an organization registers multiple MX records in DNS to provide fault tolerance if an SMTP host becomes unavailable. If the recipient SMTP host is unavailable, then the sending SMTP host retrieves all MX records for the receiving domain from DNS and resolves the lowest-preference SMTP host name to an IP address. If the SMTP host with the lowest preference is not available, the SMTP host with the second-lowest preference is used. When an available SMTP host's IP address is resolved, an SMTP session is established with that host.

Exchange recipients can have a single SMTP address or multiple SMTP addresses. Exchange can segregate recipients into multiple *virtual organizations*, each with its own SMTP address space and domain name. You can configure DNS to support multiple Exchange servers within your organization and implement a single or multiple domain namespaces. Your DNS configuration also depends on how your Exchange organization is connected to the Internet and whether your DNS records are managed internally or by your Internet service provider (ISP).

MX Records for an Organization that Manages Its Own DNS

Table 10-4 shows how you could configure MX records if your organization manages its own DNS and has a single namespace. Host (A) records should exist for Server01, Server02, and Server03.

Table 10-4   MX Records for a Single Namespace

Record	Preference	SMTP host
MX	10	*server01.tailspintoys.com*
MX	20	*server02.tailspintoys.com*
MX	30	*server03.tailspintoys.com*

Tables 10-5 and 10-6 show how you could configure MX records if your organization manages its own DNS and has multiple namespaces. Host (A) records should exist for Server01 and Server02 in both the *tailspintoys.com* and *nwtraders.com* namespaces.

Table 10-5   MX Records Added to the tailspintoys.com Namespace

Record	Preference	SMTP host
MX	10	*server01.tailspintoys.com*
MX	20	*server02.tailspintoys.com*

Table 10-6   MX Records Added to the nwtraders.com Namespace

Record	Preference	SMTP host
MX	10	*server01.nwtraders.com*
MX	20	*server02.nwtraders.com*

MX Records for an Organization Whose ISP Manages Its DNS

Table 10-7 shows how your ISP could configure MX records if your organization has a dial-up connection to the Internet and the ISP manages your organization's DNS. Notice that the ISP's smart hosts are in a load-sharing configuration and have equal preference. Host (A) records for Smarthost01 and Smarthost02 must exist in the ISP's namespace.

Table 10-7   MX Records in an ISP's Namespace for a Dial-Up Connection

Record	Preference	SMTP host
MX	10	*smarthost01.yourisp.com*
MX	10	*smarthost02.yourisp.com*

Table 10-8 shows how your ISP could configure MX records if your organization has a permanent connection to the Internet and the ISP manages your organization's DNS. In this configuration, messages will be delivered to the ISP's smart hosts if the connection goes down, and you can retrieve them when the connection is re-established. Host (A) records for Smarthost01 and Smarthost02 must exist in the ISP's namespace, as must a Host (A) record for *server01.tailspintoys.com*.

Table 10-8   MX Records in an ISP's Namespace for a Permanent Connection

Record	Preference	SMTP host
MX	10	*server01.tailspintoys.com*
MX	20	*smarthost01.yourisp.com*
MX	20	*smarthost02.yourisp.com*

Configuring Internet Connectivity

If you want to change how messages flow in and out of your Exchange organization, you have several options that allow you to control and configure Internet connectivity. These include the following:

- Creating and configuring an additional SMTP virtual server and configuring an SMTP connector to use this virtual server as a bridgehead.

- Limiting the scope of the SMTP connector to the routing group.

- Configuring the credentials on the SMTP connector.

- Configuring the SMTP connector only to receive e-mail or only to send e-mail.

- Configuring Internet message formats and message delivery parameters.

> **Exam Tip**   You do not *need* to configure an SMTP connector for e-mail to function. Nor do you need to connect an Exchange server either to other servers in an organization or to the Internet. The default SMTP virtual server manages all these connections. Beware of exam questions that ask what you need to do to implement Exchange Server 2003 connectivity to the Internet. Exchange Server 2003 can connect to the Internet by default.

Creating an Additional SMTP Virtual Server

You can use the default virtual server to configure control filters, relay restrictions, message formats, outbound security, and smart host options. However, if you want to control these items domain by domain, you should create an additional virtual server and then configure an SMTP connector to use the virtual server as a bridgehead server.

When you configure the virtual server in this way, the SMTP connector overrides any settings that the SMTP virtual server and SMTP connector share. You can, for example, create an SMTP connector with an address space for a specific e-mail domain and configure that connector to use a virtual server that does not have any filters configured. This setup can be used for sending messages across an extranet to one of your organization's associate companies. You create and configure an SMTP connector later in this lesson. You should have created an additional SMTP virtual server in Chapter 9.

Limiting the Scope of an SMTP Connector

You can limit the scope of an SMTP connector to a specific routing group. You would do this if you did not want messages from other routing groups to be delivered by the SMTP connector. However, if you want the SMTP connector to act as a backup to other similarly configured SMTP connectors in other routing groups, then you should accept the default scope setting, which is Entire Organization.

Configuring the Credentials on an SMTP Connector

You would configure the credentials on an SMTP connector if, for example, the connector is configured to deliver messages to a domain, and the SMTP server in that domain requires authentication. Configuring connector credentials does not affect the virtual server, which could, for example, be configured with no outbound security. Clients could then connect to other domains anonymously, while authentication is required to connect to the domain where it is specified.

Configuring an SMTP Connector Only to Receive E-Mail or Only to Send E-Mail

Suppose, for example, that your Exchange Server 2003 server cannot perform DNS lookups for Internet addresses, and you want to designate this server as your gateway to the Internet. In this case, you can configure an SMTP connector and then designate a bridgehead server for the connector to use. You also need to configure the connector scope, message routing, and address space.

Configuring Internet Message Formats and Message Delivery Parameters

Internet message formats enable you to configure the encoding, format, and type of messages (such as out-of-office or NDRs) that you send to a specific domain. The domain can then reference a specific destination, such as *nwtraders.com*. Alternatively, you can use a wildcard, for example *.edu, to reference a large group of destinations. You can define the message format for all SMTP domains or for specific domains.

> **Note**   You can also use the Internet Mail Wizard to create an SMTP connector and to configure an Exchange Server 2003 server to send and receive Internet mail. This wizard is intended primarily for small to medium-sized companies with less complex environments than large enterprise companies. Internet Mail Wizard creates the SMTP connector for outgoing Internet e-mail and then configures the SMTP virtual server to accept incoming e-mail. However, if you have already set up SMTP connectors or created additional SMTP virtual servers on your Exchange Server 2003 server, then you cannot run the wizard unless you reset your server configuration to its default state.

Configuring SMTP Relays

Relaying occurs when one SMTP host forwards SMTP e-mail to another SMTP host without resolving the recipient addresses. You can use an SMTP connector to relay e-mail messages between Exchange Server 2003 and other SMTP-compatible messaging systems such as UNIX Sendmail (see *www.sendmail.org*) or to other SMTP hosts on the Internet. The bridgehead server or servers defined on SMTP connectors will relay e-mail messages directly to a smart host or to a remote server on which recipient addresses are stored.

There are six different ways to configure SMTP relays in Exchange Server 2003:

- Configuring an SMTP virtual server to use a smart host
- Configuring an SMTP virtual server to forward unresolved messages to a smart host
- Configuring an SMTP virtual server as a relay host
- Configuring an SMTP virtual server to limit the servers that can relay e-mail messages
- Configuring an SMTP connector to use a smart host
- Configuring the domains to which you want to relay messages

Configuring an SMTP Virtual Server to Use a Smart Host

An SMTP virtual server, by default, uses DNS to resolve the recipient's SMTP address. You can instead configure the virtual servers in your organization to forward all outbound mail to a *smart host*. The virtual server does not then attempt to resolve the SMTP domain name through DNS but instead sends the message to the smart host for delivery. Reasons for using a smart host include

- It provides an entry and an exit point for all Internet messages or messages to a foreign messaging system. This allows you to manage Internet message traffic.
- It provides dial-up solutions. Clients can use a dial-up connection to send messages to and receive messages from the permanently connected SMTP smart host. This reduces connection time because the clients do not need permanent connections to the Exchange server.

You identify the smart host by an FQDN or by an IP address. However, if you use the latter method and then change the IP address, then you need to change that IP address on every virtual server. If you use an IP address, then you must enclose it in square brackets. Exchange checks first for a server name and then for an IP address. The brackets identify a value as an IP address, and Exchange bypasses the DNS lookup. You configure a virtual server to use a smart host by entering the smart host's identity in the Smart Host box in the virtual server's Advanced Delivery dialog box.

Configuring an SMTP Virtual Server to Forward Unresolved Messages to a Smart Host

Where an organization has other SMTP messaging systems in addition to Exchange, you can forward all unresolved SMTP messages from Exchange to a smart host. If the smart host cannot resolve the recipient's name, then the message is returned with an NDR. You configure an SMTP virtual server to forward unresolved messages to a smart host by entering the smart host's identity in the Forward All Mail With Unresolved

Recipients To Host box on the virtual server's Messages tab.

Configuring an SMTP Virtual Server as a Relay Host

If you configure an SMTP virtual server as an inbound relay host, this gives Exchange Server 2003 smart host capabilities. You can then configure other SMTP servers to use the Exchange virtual server as their smart host and forward all outbound messages to the virtual server. The virtual server then resolves the recipient's SMTP domain name through DNS and delivers the messages. You configure a virtual server as a relay host by configuring Relay Restrictions on the virtual server's Access tab.

Configuring an SMTP Virtual Server to Limit the Servers That Can Relay E-Mail Messages

You can prevent unwanted SMTP hosts from using your SMTP host as a relay agent for bulk unsolicited commercial e-mail. You do this by specifying who or what can relay e-mail messages through your organization. You can specify which computers, groups of computers, or domains should be allowed to relay e-mail messages by configuring the SMTP virtual server. You configure the SMTP virtual server to specify which servers can relay e-mail messages through your organization by configuring Relay Restrictions on the virtual server's Access tab.

Configuring an SMTP Connector to Use a Smart Host

An SMTP connector, by default, uses DNS to resolve the recipient's SMTP address. You can instead configure the connector to forward all outbound mail to a *smart host*. You configure an SMTP connector to use a smart host by entering the smart host's identity in the Forward All Mail Through This Connector To The Following Smart Hosts box on the General tab of the SMTP connector's Properties dialog box.

> **Note** You can configure smart hosts on both SMTP virtual servers and SMTP connectors. Microsoft recommends that you configure smart hosts on the connector because connectors can handle message delivery on a per-domain basis.

Configuring the Domains to Which You Want to Relay Messages

You may want to limit the domains to which you relay messages rather than the domains from which you relay messages. This can be useful when your organization has multiple SMTP messaging systems that operate under different SMTP domain names. You may want your SMTP host to accept messages from any domain but then forward them only to specific domains, such as the other domains in your organization. You can specify the domains to which you want to relay messages on an SMTP connector's Address Space tab.

Practice: Creating MX Records and Configuring an SMTP Connector

In this practice, you configure DNS to support your Exchange Server 2003 organization and then create and configure an SMTP connector. These are the typical administrative tasks that you carry out when setting up SMTP in an Exchange organization.

Exercise 1: Create MX Records for Your Exchange Server 2003 Servers

In this exercise, you will create MX records for Server01 and Server02. The exercise assumes that both servers are configured as Exchange Server 2003 servers and that the domain controller, Server01, is the primary DNS server (either standard primary or Active Directory Integrated). The MX records will be configured so that an SMTP connection to your organization will first access Server01 and will access Server02 if Server01 is unavailable. After creating the MX records, you use the Command console to verify them.

To create MX records for Server01 and Server02, perform the following steps:

1. Open the DNS console.
2. In the console tree, expand Server01, expand Forward Lookup Zones, and then expand *tailspintoys.com*.
3. In the console tree, right-click *tailspintoys.com*, and then click New Mail Exchanger (MX).
4. In the New Resource Record dialog box, in the Fully Qualified Domain Name (FQDN) Of Mail Server box, type **Server01.tailspintoys.com**. In the Mail Server Priority box, type **10**, and then click OK.
5. Verify that a new record of type Mail Exchanger (MX) exists for *server01.tailspintoys.com*.
6. In the console tree, right-click *tailspintoys.com*, and then click New Mail Exchanger (MX).
7. In the New Resource Record dialog box, in the Fully Qualified Domain Name (FQDN) Of Mail Server box, type **Server02.tailspintoys.com**. In the Mail Server Priority box, type **20**, and then click OK.
8. Verify that a new record of type Mail Exchanger (MX) exists for *server01.tailspintoys.com*. At this point, your screen should look like Figure 10-2.

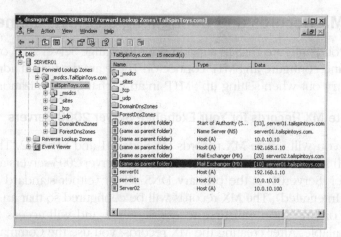

Figure 10-2 Verifying that MX records exist

9. To verify that the record for Server01 is resolvable, open the Command console on Server02.

10. At the command prompt, type **nslookup -querytype=mx Server01** and then press ENTER. Information about the primary name server *server01.tailspintoys.com* DNS settings should be returned, as shown in Figure 10-3.

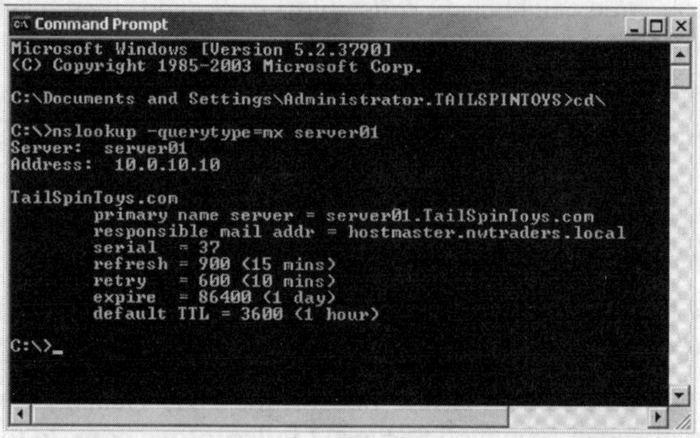

Figure 10-3 Verifying that the MX record for Server01 can be resolved

11. Close the Command and the DNS consoles.

Exercise 2: Create and Configure an SMTP Connector

In this exercise, you create and configure an SMTP connector and specify the default SMTP virtual server on Server02 as the bridgehead server. You must complete this exercise to complete subsequent practices in this chapter.

1. Open Exchange System Manager and browse to Administrative Groups\First Administrative Group\Routing Groups\First Routing Group\Connectors.

2. Right-click Connectors, point to New, and then click SMTP Connector.

3. In the Properties dialog box, in the Local Bridgeheads pane, click Add.

4. In the Add Bridgehead dialog box, click SERVER02 Default SMTP Virtual Server, and then click OK.

5. In the Properties dialog box, in the Name box, type **General SMTP Connector**.

6. Select the Address Space tab, and then click Add.

7. In the Add Address Space dialog box, click SMTP, and then click OK.

8. In the Internet Address Space Properties dialog box, verify that E-Mail Domain is set to * to indicate that all outbound SMTP e-mail uses this connector, and then click OK.

9. Click OK in the General SMTP Connector Properties dialog box.

10. Verify that the General SMTP Connector object exists in the First Routing Group\Connectors container, as shown in Figure 10-4.

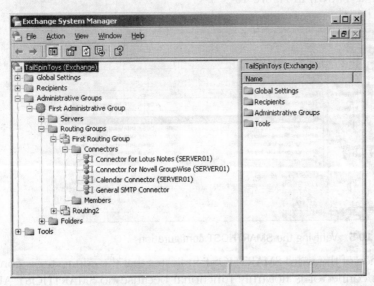

Figure 10-4   The General SMTP Connector object

Practice: Configuring an SMTP Connector to Use a Relay Host for Outbound SMTP

In this practice, you will configure your SMTP connector to use a relay host for outbound SMTP. To complete this practice, an SMTP connector must exist in your organization. If an SMTP connector does not exist, you must create one by completing Exercise 2 of the previous practice, "Create and Configure an SMTP Connector."

To configure Exchange to use an SMTP relay host, perform the following steps:

1. Open Exchange System Manager, browse to Administrative Groups\First Administrative Group\Routing Groups\First Routing Group\Connectors, and then expand Connectors.

2. In the console tree, right-click General SMTP Connector, and then click Properties.

3. In the General SMTP Connector Properties dialog box, on the General tab, click Forward All Mail Through This Connector To The Following Smart Hosts, type **SMARTHOST** and then click OK. (Note that the SMARTHOST computer does not exist. It is merely a name specified for testing purposes.)

4. To verify that the SMARTHOST configuration is set properly, send a test message from Outlook Web Access (OWA) to *d.hall@tailspintoys666.com*, and then check the Queues object located in Exchange System Manager at Administrative Groups\First Administrative Group\Servers\Server02\Queues. Verify the existence of the General SMTP Connector - SMARTHOST (SMTP Connector) object, as shown in Figure 10-5.

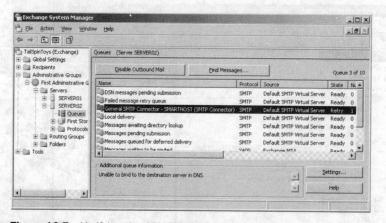

Figure 10-5   Verifying the SMARTHOST configuration

The presence of the word SMARTHOST indicates that the connector is configured correctly. The connector is not truly functional because no SMARTHOST AU computer and no network connectivity exist outside the computers on your test network.

Lesson Review

The following questions are intended to reinforce key information presented in this lesson. If you are unable to answer a question, review the lesson materials and then try the question again. You can find answers to the questions in the "Questions and Answers" section at the end of this chapter.

1. You are a network administrator, and you want to test connectivity between a host on your network and a new Exchange Server 2003 server that has just been configured. You want to ensure that e-mail messages to that server can be encrypted. You can ping the server by host name. You connect to port 25 on the server. What command should you use?

   a. atrn

   b. etrn

   c. elho

   d. helo

2. You are the administrator of the Contoso ISP. You have two SMTP servers configured as smart hosts: *smart1.contoso.com* and *smart2.contoso.com*. Your ISP manages DNS records for Northwind Traders, whose Exchange Server 2003 server has the FQDN *mailserv.nwtraders.com*. Northwind Traders has a permanent connection to your ISP. How should you configure the MX records for this setup in DNS?

   a. MX 10 *smart1.contoso.com*

   MX 10 *smart2.contoso.com*

   MX 20 *mailserv.nwtraders.com*

   b. MX 10 *mailserv.contoso.com*

   MX 20 *smart1.contoso.com*

   MX 20 *smart2.nwtraders.com*

   c. MX 10 *smart1.contoso.com*

   MX 20 *smart2.contoso.com*

   MX 30 *mailserv.nwtraders.com*

   d. MX 10 *mailserv.contoso.com*

   MX 10 *smart1.contoso.com*

   MX 10 *smart2.nwtraders.com*

3. You administer your company's Exchange Server 2003 organization. Your company has two e-mail domains. You want to control filters, relay restrictions, message formats, outbound security, and smart host options separately for each domain. What technique would you use?

   a. Create an additional virtual server and configure an SMTP connector to use it as a bridgehead.

   b. Configure all these items on the default SMTP virtual server.

   c. Configure Internet message formats and delivery parameters for each domain.

   d. Limit the scope of the SMTP connector to a specific routing group.

4. You administer an Exchange Server 2003 server. You want this server to act as a smart host. Your organization has a single SMTP domain. How do you configure your server?

   a. Configure an SMTP connector to forward all outbound mail.

   b. Configure the default SMTP virtual server as a relay host.

   c. Configure the default SMTP virtual server to forward all unresolved messages.

   d. Configure the default SMTP virtual server to specify which servers can relay e-mail.

5. You want your Exchange Server 2003 organization to have smart host capability. How should you configure a virtual server to provide such capability, and how is the configuration implemented?

   _____

   _____

Lesson Summary

- SMTP transfers e-mail messages using a series of plain-text commands that are passed from a sending host to a receiving host. The receiving host responds using numerical codes. ESMTP extends SMTP functionality.

- DNS uses MX records to identify e-mail servers and to resolve their IP addresses.

- You can control Internet access by creating and configuring additional SMTP virtual server and SMTP connectors.

- When one SMTP host forwards e-mail to another SMTP host without resolving the recipient address, the process is called relaying.

- You can configure SMTP relays to restrict relay traffic, to interface with foreign messaging systems, and to set up your Exchange Server 2003 server as a smart host.

Lesson 2: Configuring SMTP Security and Advanced Options

Chapter 11 discusses Exchange Server 2003 security in detail. In this lesson, we restrict our discussion to securing SMTP traffic by using authentication, encryption, and reverse DNS lookup. We also consider when to use—and when to restrict or prevent—open relaying and how to restrict user accounts from sending Internet e-mail. In addition, this lesson covers the use of the Routing and Remote Access service to connect Exchange servers to the Internet and to retrieve e-mail from an ISP by configuring advanced options, such as specifying the use of the etrn command. Finally, this lesson discusses methods of troubleshooting a problematic e-mail connection.

After this lesson, you will be able to

- Configure inbound and outbound connections on an SMTP virtual server
- Explain and distinguish between various authentication methods
- Configure inbound authentication and encryption on an SMTP virtual server
- Explain how reverse DNS lookup can be used to prevent IP spoofing attacks
- Configure delivery restrictions so that only selected users can send and receive Internet e-mail
- Restrict or prevent the propagation of unsolicited commercial (junk) e-mail
- Retrieve e-mail from an ISP over a dial-up connection

Estimated lesson time: 60 minutes

Configuring Connections

A connection is initiated whenever a message is sent to or received from a remote server. You can configure both incoming and outgoing connections on your SMTP virtual server.

Configuring Incoming Connections

You configure incoming connections on an SMTP virtual server in the virtual server's Properties dialog box. On the General tab, you can specify the options listed in Table 10-9.

Table 10-9   Incoming Connection Options

Option	Description
Limit Number Of Connections To	Specifies the number of concurrent connections for incoming message delivery. If the check box is not selected, no limit is imposed. When the check box is selected, the minimum is one connection.
Connection Time-Out (Minutes)	Specifies the time allowed before an inactive connection is closed. The default is 10 minutes.

Configuring Outgoing Connections

You also use the Properties dialog box to configure the outgoing connections used by your virtual server to deliver messages. In this case, the settings are in Outbound Connections on the Delivery tab. These settings can help you monitor system resources by limiting inactive connections and connections to remote domains. They are listed in Table 10-10.

Table 10-10   Outgoing Connection Options

Option	Description
Limit Connections To	Specifies the total number of simultaneous outbound connections to all remote domains that can exist at one time. The default is 1,000 connections. The minimum is one connection. This setting can be used to improve system performance in conjunction with the Limit Number Of Messages Per Connection To option on the Messages tab. If you do not select the check box, no limit is imposed.
Time-Out (Minutes)	Specifies the time allowed before an inactive connection closes. The default is 10 minutes.
Limit Connections Per Domain To	Limits connections to any single remote domain. The default is 100 connections. This number should be less than or equal to the value for the Limit Connections To option. If you do not select the check box, no limit is imposed.
TCP Port	Allocates the TCP port on SMTP remote servers to which the SMTP virtual server connects. The default is port 25. The outgoing port setting can be the same as the port setting for incoming transmissions.

Securing SMTP Traffic

You can secure SMTP traffic by using authentication, encryption, and reverse DNS lookup. *Authentication* ensures that the user is who he or she claims to be. More powerful authentication methods such as Kerberos ensure that the e-mail server is authenticated in addition to the user. *Encryption* ensures that only the recipient for whom a message is intended can read it. *Reverse DNS lookup* is used to prevent *spoofing*, where an attacker impersonates a trusted host by using its IP address in an attempt to gain unauthorized access.

Authentication

Exchange supports three authentication methods: anonymous authentication, basic authentication, and Integrated Windows Authentication. The method that you choose for SMTP depends on your environment.

Anonymous Authentication   This is the most common method used for Internet communication and provides limited access to specific public folders and directory information. Anonymous authentication is supported by all clients and is used to allow users to access unsecured content in public folders. To enable users to connect anonymously, you create a user account in IIS.

Basic Authentication   Exchange performs simple challenge and response authentication by requiring users to enter their user name, domain name, and password to gain access to mailbox data. Most client computers support basic authentication. This method provides the simplest level of security.

> **Important**   Basic authentication sends a user's name and password as clear text. It is therefore insecure. Basic authentication should not be used unless there is no alternative or unless the entire TCP/IP session is encrypted.

Integrated Windows Authentication   This method offers security, efficient communication, and transparency. You can use Integrated Windows Authentication when you have Windows-based clients that do not use TLS. This method uses Kerberos for clients running Windows 2000 or later and NTLM for Windows clients that are not running Active Directory. When you use Integrated Windows Authentication, the password is sent as an encrypted value.

Encryption

Encryption scrambles (or *hashes*) the contents of an e-mail message into a code that can be read only by the person who has the key to decode it on his or her computer. Authentication does not encrypt message data. Therefore, to make your data truly secure, you should use TLS to encrypt e-mail messages transferred between the client and the server. Because TLS encrypts the entire TCP/IP session between the client and the server, the session is secure even if you chose a logon authentication method, such as basic authentication, that does not encrypt the user name and password. To use TLS, the server must have an X.509 SSL certificate issued by a trusted CA. For more information about TLS, refer to RFC 2487.

Reverse DNS Lookup

IP spoofing is an attack on a network in which an attacker impersonates a trusted host by using its IP address in an attempt to gain unauthorized access to a computer network. Enabling reverse DNS lookup helps to prevent IP spoofing. Reverse DNS lookup resolves an IP address to a hostname or FQDN. In this application, DNS uses reverse lookup to confirm that the IP address of the sending host is from the network that is specified by the sender's registered SMTP domain name. The result of the reverse lookup is written into the SMTP header of the message, indicating whether the lookup matched.

> **Caution**   Reverse DNS lookup can degrade message transfer performance and prevent the relaying of messages through multiple hops.

Restricting Internet E-Mail

Your organization could have a large number of employees but allow only a few of them to send and receive Internet e-mail. Some companies, for example, restrict Internet e-mail access to full-time employees only, or a school might allow staff to receive and send Internet e-mail, but not students.

You can configure the SMTP connector so that only specific users or groups can send e-mail outside of the company and control how messages are sent from a specific recipient to specific connectors. You can use the options on the Delivery Restrictions tab of a connector's properties to accept or reject e-mail messages from any sender listed in the directory. If, for example, you add the address of a sender to the Reject Messages From list, any messages from that sender that access the connecter are returned.

By default, a connector accepts all messages from all senders. Delivery restrictions are optional and you must configure them if you want them to be used. You restrict user accounts from sending Internet e-mail by navigating to Connectors in Exchange System Manager, right-clicking the connector that you want to restrict, clicking Properties, and then specifying the name of the sender or senders in the Accept Messages From or

Reject Messages From pane on the Delivery Restrictions tab. Detailed steps for restricting user accounts from sending Internet e-mail are included in a practice later in this lesson.

Preventing or Restricting Junk E-Mail Propagation

If your Exchange organization is connected to the Internet and uses *open relaying*—that is, you do not restrict or prevent relaying—then your Exchange servers are vulnerable to an attack called *mail relaying*. This is a practice in which unauthorized users send e-mail messages from the e-mail server of an organization that is not their own. This enables them to use the resources of the organization or to make it appear that the messages originated from that organization. This practice is often used to send unsolicited commercial e-mail, commonly referred to as junk mail or spam. When an unauthorized user uses your Exchange server to send out junk e-mail, the following events happen:

- The unauthorized user sends a single e-mail message to your SMTP server and addresses multiple recipients in the message. These recipients have e-mail addresses that are in domains external to your Exchange organization.

- Because SMTP servers use anonymous authentication by default, your server accepts the inbound message.

- After the message is accepted, your SMTP server recognizes that the message recipients belong to external domains, so it delivers the messages.

The unauthorized user needs to send only one junk e-mail message to your SMTP server, which could then deliver the message to thousands of recipients. This distribution slows down your Exchange server, congests your queues, and upsets people who receive the junk e-mail message. It may also cause other legitimate servers to block e-mail from your Exchange server.

By default, relaying is not permitted on virtual SMTP servers. There are times, however, when relaying is required. For example, you may have Post Office Protocol 3 (POP3) and Internet Message Access Protocol 4 (IMAP4) clients who rely on SMTP for message delivery and who have legitimate reasons for sending e-mail messages to external domains. In this case, you should not allow, or should seriously restrict, open relaying on any Exchange server connected to the Internet. You should then create an additional SMTP virtual server that is dedicated to receiving e-mail messages from POP3 and IMAP4 clients. This additional SMTP virtual server can use authentication combined with SSL-based encryption and can be configured to allow relaying for authenticated clients.

You prevent unauthorized users from propagating junk e-mail through your Exchange organization by preventing or restricting open relaying. You can prevent open relaying by not granting relay permissions to any other hosts. You can restrict relaying to a limited number of users or groups by using a Discretionary Access Control List (DACL) to specify the groups of users who can relay e-mail messages through an SMTP virtual server. The latter technique is useful if you have a group of users who should be allowed to relay e-mail messages to the Internet, but you want to prevent anyone else from doing so. You can also grant relay permission to an IP address, domain, and subnet in Exchange.

Practices later in this chapter provide detailed instructions on how to prevent and restrict open relaying and how to override relay restrictions on an SMTP virtual server.

Retrieving E-Mail from an ISP Over a Dial-Up Connection

If your organization connects to the Internet via a dial-up connection to an ISP, and if you configure Exchange to receive Internet e-mail messages using SMTP, then any e-mail message that is sent while your connection is not active can be lost. In this situation, you should connect your Exchange servers to the Internet by using the Routing and Remote Access service. You need to configure the on-demand dial-up connection in Routing and Remote Access, and then configure a smart host for the Exchange SMTP virtual server or SMTP connector.

A *pull relationship* is a relationship in which one computer queues messages and the other computer pulls them by using the turn or etrn commands. You can use an SMTP connector when you require a pull relationship between servers and configure this connector to retrieve e-mail in a queue from a remote SMTP server at specified intervals. This means that a remote domain—typically at an ISP—can receive and hold e-mail on behalf of a destination domain. Messages sent to the remote domain are held until the SMTP etrn or turn command is received from an authorized account on your Exchange server.

You can configure Exchange to use etrn commands to pull e-mail for a specific routing group by browsing to the Connectors container for that routing group in Exchange System Manager, right-clicking the SMTP connector, and then clicking Properties. In the Properties dialog box, click Advanced, and then click Request ETRN/TURN When Sending Messages. If you need to, specify the times at which you want the SMTP connector to contact the remote domain and trigger the delivery of queued e-mail, and then select the Additionally Request Mail At Specified Times check box.

The detailed procedures for creating a demand-dial interface and configuring an SMTP connector to pull e-mail from an ISP are described in a practice later in this lesson.

Identifying Message Delivery Failures

When a message is delivered from one host to another, a failure may occur at several points. The first step in troubleshooting the problem is to identify where the failure occurred. You can use the telnet and nslookup utilities to tackle the problem.

- **telnet**   In the previous lesson, you learned how telnet can be used to test an ESMTP connection. If an SMTP host is unable to deliver messages, you can use telnet to check whether a TCP port can be opened to a receiving host and whether the receiving host is responding. You can use the telnet fully_qualified_domain_name 25 command to specify the TCP port (port 25 for SMTP) to open to a destination host and either the ehlo or helo commands to test the SMTP connection.

- **nslookup**   You can use the nslookup command to query DNS to confirm that DNS is working properly and that MX and A (host) records exist for a particular SMTP domain. You can, for example, use the nslookup –querytype=mx tailspintoys.com command to return all the DNS MX records for the domain *tailspintoys.com*.

Practice: Configuring SMTP Security and Demand-Dial Communications

In this practice, you configure authentication and encryption, restrict selected user accounts from sending Internet e-mail, and configure relaying. You have the option to prevent open relaying in Exchange, restrict open relaying permission to selected users, or override relay settings on an SMTP virtual server. Finally, you configure your SMTP virtual server to pull mail that is queued on another server.

Exercise 1: Configure Authentication for Incoming Messages

In this exercise, you configure authentication on the additional virtual server that you created in Chapter 9. The same procedure can be used to configure authentication on the default virtual server. You can perform this task while logged on at either Server01 or Server02 as a domain or exchange administrator.

> **Real World**   **Keeping It Secure with Runas**
>
> On a production network, the *Principle of Least Privilege* requires that you perform administrative tasks by using the runas utility while logged on at a client computer (with the appropriate tools installed) as an ordinary user.

To configure authentication for incoming messages, perform the following steps:

1. Open Exchange System Manager.

2. Navigate to Administrative Groups\First Administrative Group\Servers\Server01 \Protocols\SMTP.

3. Right-click SMTP_server1, and then click Properties. (Note that the additional virtual server SMTP_server1 was created in a practice in Chapter 9.)

4. On the Access tab, under Access Control, click Authentication.

5. You can now select the authentication method or methods. If you select Basic Authentication, then you can specify a Windows domain name or accept the default. This default domain differs from the SMTP virtual server default domain. Do not select the Requires TLS Encryption check box unless you have obtained the necessary certificate and configured encryption as described in the next exercise. Figure 10-6 shows the Authentication page.

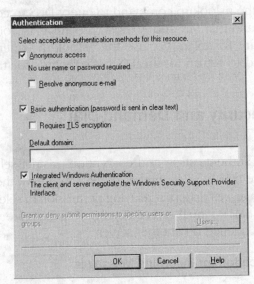

Figure 10-6   The Authentication page

6. Click OK. Click OK again to close the SMTP_server1 Properties box.

Exercise 2: Configure TLS Encryption

To require TLS encryption on a virtual service, you need to obtain the appropriate certificates and specify TLS Encryption. You then have the option to configure the encryption strength.

> **Note**   You can require that all clients use TLS encryption to connect to an SMTP virtual server. This option secures the connection, but it is not used for authentication. To enable TLS encryption on a virtual server, you must create key pairs and configure key certificates on the Exchange server running the SMTP service. This can be done through IIS. Clients can then use TLS to encrypt the session with Exchange, and thus all messages are sent. Exchange can also use TLS to encrypt sessions with remote servers. If your virtual server is on the Internet, requiring TLS encryption on inbound connections is not recommended. Very few of these connections will support TLS, and users will not be able to connect to your server. In most cases, you should encrypt mail messages instead of the SMTP channel. TLS is intended for an intranet and extranet point-to-point SMTP connection where both parties know the other supports TLS.

Secure Sockets Layer and Transport Layer Security

SSL is a communications protocol that provides public key cryptography services to ensure privacy over public networks. It was designed to establish a secure communications channel to encrypt critical information, such as credit card numbers. The Internet Engineering Task Force (IETF) has now combined SSL with other protocols and authentication methods to create a new protocol known as Transport Layer Security (TLS).

To enable, specify, and configure TLS encryption, perform the following steps:

1. Access Exchange System Manager.

2. Navigate to Administrative Groups\First Administrative Group\Servers\Server01 \Protocols\SMTP.

3. Right-click SMTP_server1, and then click Properties.

4. To set up new key certificates and manage installed key certificates for the SMTP virtual server, click Certificate on the Access tab, under Secure Communication.

5. Complete the Web Server Certificate Wizard.

> **Note**   You can complete the wizard and obtain the certificate immediately only if Server01 is configured as an enterprise root CA. Otherwise, you save the request to a file that you need to submit to a CA to obtain the certificate.

6. On the Access tab of the SMTP_server1 Properties box, click Authentication.

7. Select the Requires TLS Encryption box. You can select the box only if you have specified Basic Authentication.

8. Click OK.

9. Under Secure Communication, click Communication.

10. In Security, select the Require Secure Channel check box.

11. Select the Require 128-bit Encryption check box if you require this level of encryption. Figure 10-7 shows the Security page.

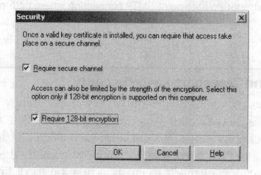

Figure 10-7   The Security page

12. Click OK.

13. Click OK again to close the SMTP_server1 Properties box.

Exercise 3: Restrict User Accounts from Sending Internet E-Mail

In this exercise, you will specify the users who are prohibited from sending Internet e-mail. You can specify groups in addition to, or instead of, individual users.

> **Important**   To complete this practice, an Internet mail connector must exist in your organization. If an Internet mail connector does not exist, you must create one by completing the exercise titled "Create and Configure an SMTP Connector" earlier in this lesson.

1. Open Exchange System Manager and browse to Administrative Groups\First Administrative Group\Routing Groups\First Routing Group\Connectors.

2. In the details pane, right-click General SMTP Connector, and then click Properties.

3. Click Delivery Restrictions on the General tab on the SMTP Connector Properties dialog box.

4. On the Delivery Restrictions tab, in the Reject Messages From pane, click Add.

5. In the Select Recipient box, type the usernames of the prohibited users. Use a semicolon to separate the usernames—for example, m.alexander; s.alexander; m.allen; n.anderson. Click OK.

6. Click OK in the SMTP Connector Properties dialog box.

Figure 10-8 shows the usernames being added.

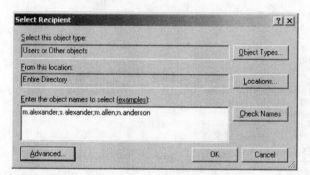

Figure 10-8   Adding prohibited users

> **Note**   The next three exercises for configuring open relaying specify the additional SMTP virtual server that you created in Chapter 9. However, they can also be carried on the default SMTP server on either Server01 or Server02.

Exercise 4: Prevent Open Relaying

Open relaying is disabled by default. However, a situation could exist where it has previously been enabled, and you now need to disable it.

1. Access Exchange System Manager.

2. Navigate to Administrative Groups\First Administrative Group\Servers\Server01 \Protocols\SMTP.

3. Right-click SMTP_server1, and then click Properties.

4. Click Relay on the Access tab. This displays the Access Control options.

5. On the Relay Restrictions dialog box, ensure that the selection for those computers that may relay e-mail messages is set to Only The List Below, and that the list is blank.

6. Clear the Allow All Computers Which Successfully Authenticate To Relay, Regardless Of The List Above check box. This box should always be cleared unless you are using POP3 and IMAP4 clients with this virtual server. Figure 10-9 shows the Relay Restrictions dialog box.

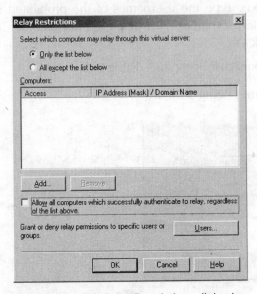

Figure 10-9   The Relay Restrictions dialog box

7. Click OK.

8. Click OK again to close the SMTP_server1 Properties dialog box.

> **Caution**   If you configure All Except The List Below, and anonymous access is allowed as an authentication method, any computer on the Internet that is not on the list can relay e-mail messages through the virtual server. This condition is called *anonymous relay* and can result in unauthorized users relaying junk e-mail or other unwanted messages through your server. In addition, operating an anonymous relay may be in violation of your ISP's terms of service.

Exercise 5: Configure the SMTP Connector to Override Relay Settings on the SMTP Virtual Server

In this exercise, you configure Exchange to allow SMTP relaying for both authenticated and unauthenticated users. You do this by configuring the SMTP connector to override relay settings on the SMTP virtual server.

Important   To complete this exercise, an Internet mail connector must exist in your organization. If an Internet mail connector does not exist, you must create one by completing the exercise titled "Create and Configure an SMTP Connector" earlier in this lesson.

1. Open Exchange System Manager, browse to Administrative Groups\First Administrative Group\Routing Groups\First Routing Group\Connectors, and then expand Connectors.

2. In the console tree, right-click General SMTP Connector and click Properties.

3. On the Address Space tab, select the Allow Messages To Be Relayed To These Domains check box, and then click OK. Click OK when warned that this overrides the default restrictions for relaying on the SMTP virtual server.

Note   In the next two exercises, you simulate the situation where you connect your Exchange organization to your ISP by means of a demand-dial connection and configure your Exchange Server 2003 server to pull e-mail from your ISP's server. If you want to test this setup "for real," you need two Exchange Server 2003 servers with modems that are in different domains and are linked by a telephone line. You can, however, complete the exercises as described without this setup.

Exercise 6: Connect to the Internet by Using Routing and Remote Access

In this exercise, you configure a demand-dial connection on Server02. For security reasons, you would normally use a front-end server to access the Internet. You cannot complete this exercise unless you have a modem installed on Server02. If you do not have a modem installed, then you can complete Exercise 7 as a practice, but you will not be able to pull mail across a demand-dial connection.

1. Open the Routing and Remote Access console on Server02, expand Server02, and right-click Ports. A modem installed on Server02 should be displayed as a port.

2. Right-click the port, and then click Properties.

3. On the Port Properties dialog box, click Configure, select the Demand-Dial Routing Connections (Inbound And Outbound) check box, and then click OK.

4. To create a demand-dial interface and configure it to use the modem to dial up to the ISP, you need to perform two actions:

   ❑ Right-click the server, make sure that the router flag is on and that LAN and Demand Dial Routing is selected, and then click OK.

   ❑ Right-click Routing Interfaces, and then click New Demand Dial Interface.

5. Add a default network route that uses the newly created demand-dial interface.

Exercise 7: Configure Exchange Server 2003 to Pull Queued E-Mail from Another Server by Using the Etrn Command

In this exercise, you will configure Server02 to pull e-mail messages from another server.

> **Important**   To complete this exercise, an Internet e-mail connector must exist in your organization. If an Internet e-mail connector does not exist, you must create one by completing the exercise titled "Create and Configure an SMTP Connector" earlier in this lesson.

1. Open Exchange System Manager, browse to Administrative Groups\First Administrative Group\Routing Groups\First Routing Group\Connectors, and then expand Connectors.

2. In the console tree, right-click General SMTP Connector and click Properties.

3. On the Advanced tab, click Request ETRN/TURN From Different Server. In the Server box, type **ISPSERVER**, and then click OK.

4. Restart Server02.

Lesson Review

The following questions are intended to reinforce key information presented in this lesson. If you are unable to answer a question, review the lesson materials and then try the question again. You can find answers to the questions in the "Questions and Answers" section at the end of this chapter.

1. You administer an Exchange Server 2003 server with a dial-up connection to an ISP. You want your ISP to hold your e-mail until your Exchange server connects. You then want all queued e-mail to be delivered to your Exchange server. How do you configure this?

   _____

   _____

2. You want your Exchange Server 2003 organization to have smart host capability. How should you configure a virtual server to provide such capability, and how is the configuration implemented?

   _____

   _____

3. You administer an Exchange Server 2003 organization in a school. Staff members are permitted to send Internet e-mail, but students are not. How do you prevent students from receiving and sending Internet e-mail?

_____

_____

4. How do you prevent unauthorized users from propagating junk e-mail through your Exchange organization?

   a. By configuring reverse DNS lookup

   b. By permitting anonymous authentication

   c. By preventing open relaying

   d. By preventing IMAP4 and POP3 clients from accessing your organization

Lesson Summary

- You can configure both incoming and outgoing connections on your SMTP virtual server.

- You can secure SMTP traffic by using authentication, encryption, and reverse DNS lookup.

- Basic authentication transmits the user's password in clear text.

- TLS encrypts the message body in addition to the username and password.

- Reverse DNS lookup can help prevent spoofing.

- To prevent your Exchange Server 2003 organization from being used to forward junk mail, you prevent or restrict open relaying.

- You can configure an SMTP connector to restrict specific users and groups from sending and receiving Internet mail.

- In a pull relationship, one computer queues messages and the other computer pulls them by using the turn or etrn commands.

- You can use an SMTP connector when you require a pull relationship between servers, and configure this connector to retrieve e-mail in a queue from a remote SMTP server at specified intervals.

- You can use the nslookup and telnet utilities to identify where a message delivery failure occurred.

Lesson 3: Configuring Interoperability with Other SMTP Messaging Systems

Exchange Server 2003 can be configured to work with other messaging systems that use SMTP for mail delivery. If you want to configure Exchange Server 2003 to coexist with messaging systems for which connectors are not provided, then you need to obtain third-party gateways for these systems. Alternatively, if your organization already implements Exchange Server 5.5, and an Exchange Server 5.5 connector exists, you can create a mixed mode Exchange organization.

In the case of Microsoft Mail, you can use Exchange System Manager in Exchange Server 2003 to configure a server running Exchange 2000 Server in your organization as a directory synchronization requestor or server for directory synchronization.

Exchange Server 2003 integrates with IIS to provide an efficient and secure environment that allows users running Internet clients to access Exchange data locally and remotely. This feature enables you to configure Exchange interoperability with messaging systems that use SMTP for mail delivery. You can configure global settings to customize default formatting configurations and message size limits that are applied across every mailbox and virtual server in your organization.

Exchange Server 2003 supports Hypertext Transfer Protocol (HTTP) and Web Distributed Authoring and Versioning (WebDAV) to provide enhanced functionality for HTTP clients retrieving and manipulating information in Web storage systems. You can also configure an HTTP virtual server to support OWA, and allow users to access e-mail, calendar information, shared applications, and any content in the public folder store simply and efficiently by using a Web browser.

Users with an IMAP4 client can access mail in their Exchange mailbox without downloading the entire mailbox to a specific computer. Exchange uses Network News Transfer Protocol (NNTP) to enable Microsoft Outlook users to participate in online discussions over the Internet. Exchange also enables users running client applications that support NNTP to access newsgroup public folders on computers running Exchange.

Exchange supports POP3 to allow POP3 users to access their private inboxes on Exchange. However, the limitations of POP3 do not allow POP3 users to access other public or private folders, and POP3 is not intended to provide full manipulation of mail on the server. Although messages can be left on the server, mail is usually downloaded to a user's computer and then deleted.

IMAP4 and POP3 clients use SMTP for mail delivery. As discussed in the previous lesson, Exchange Server 2003 can be configured to relay mail for these clients.

After this lesson, you will be able to

- Configure system-wide global settings in Exchange Server 2003
- Explain how SMTP works with an HTTP virtual server to provide Web storage implementations
- Describe how Exchange Server 2003 supports OWA
- Explain how NNTP is configured to implement online discussions and access newsgroup public folders
- Describe how Exchange Server 2003 supports IMAP4 and POP3 clients

Estimated lesson time: 60 minutes

Note   This lesson explains how Exchange Server 2003 supports HTTP, IMAP4, NNTP, POP3, and OWA clients. It does not describe the detailed installation and configuration of the relevant virtual servers, which was covered in depth in Chapter 9.

Configuring Global Settings

The Exchange Server 2003 global settings feature allows you to configure system-wide settings. This facility is useful, for example, when a majority of your users may have similar message conversion needs or the same delivery restrictions. You can define default formatting configurations and message size limits that can be applied across every mailbox and virtual server in your organization.

You can override global settings for special messaging situations by configuring the individual Exchange objects with different settings. Global settings are applied only when no configurations have been made at the virtual server level or at the individual mailbox level.

An SMTP virtual server will not accept a message from a client or another server if the message exceeds its message size limit. When a message is accepted, the SMTP virtual server will try to deliver it to all recipient mailboxes. Only then do global restrictions apply. All recipient mailboxes whose limits are not exceeded then accept the message (mailbox limits can be set globally or on a per-user basis).

Internet formats are used when messages are sent to, or are received from, an Internet recipient. When Messaging Application Programming Interface (MAPI) clients send messages, these messages are converted from Microsoft Rich Text Format (RTF) to MIME. Adding the MIME types of media or content that users send or receive through e-mail to the list of MIME types helps recipients open and display the attachment correctly.

A domain node allows you to create a set of guidelines for SMTP to use when sending messages to a specific remote domain. For example, if you have MAPI clients that send messages to an associate company on a regular basis, you can create a policy for SMTP to use when sending messages to your associate's domain. The policy allows you to specify the format that your associate needs to use to view your messages. When you add a domain node, you create a new set of SMTP guidelines to use with a remote domain. This does not create a new domain in your organization.

When you create a domain node, you can specify the message format that SMTP should use when sending e-mail. You can, for example, choose to use UNIX to UNIX encoding (uuencode) instead of MIME.

Setting Message Defaults

Messages sent by Internet clients are stored in MIME format, and no message conversion takes place when clients read the messages. SMTP converts messages sent by MAPI clients from RTF to MIME. You specify how SMTP converts outbound messages sent by a MAPI client to an Internet client. You can associate MIME content types with an extension to ensure that messages convert correctly. You can also specify how all messages sent to a specific domain are converted.

To set Internet message defaults, you associate MIME types with an extension and configure message defaults by creating a new SMTP policy, specifying message formats, and setting advanced options, such as allowing out of office responses, automatic replies, and delivery reports. These procedures are described in detail later in this lesson.

Setting Mailbox Defaults

You can set message size and recipient limits globally on the mailboxes in your organization by accessing the Defaults tab in Exchange System Manager. Limiting message size conserves system resources because larger messages are more difficult to process and more likely to cause bottlenecks in the Exchange routing engine. A message with many recipients can also tax your system with directory lookups and delivery connections. Message size limits can apply to inbound or outbound messages, or to both. Recipient limits apply to all messages.

 Important   All global delivery restriction settings can be overridden by per-user settings made on individual mailboxes.

You may also want to designate a mailbox as the SMTP *postmaster account*. This is the account that will appear in the From line of all NDRs sent out by your organization.

Therefore, whenever someone replies to an NDR, either to report the delivery failure or to seek help in diagnosing the situation, this is the account that will be contacted.

The Postmaster account uses an alias that will proxy replies to a valid SMTP e-mail address, such as *postmaster@domain.com*. You select the account of the user that has this responsibility in Active Directory Users And Computers and select the E-Mail Addresses tab in the user account's Properties dialog box. You then click New, click SMTP Address, and specify the alias in the E-Mail Address box on the Internet Address Properties sheet.

Supporting HTTP Clients

HTTP is the protocol used by the World Wide Web to define how messages are formatted and transmitted and what actions Web servers and browsers take in response to various commands. WebDAV is an extension to the HTTP version 1.1 protocol. WebDAV allows an HTTP client to retrieve and manipulate information held in the Information Store.

Exchange Server 2003 supports HTTP and WebDAV to provide the following functions for general data access:

- **Document access**   HTTP and WebDAV support a collaborative environment in which users can edit documents, protect data, collect resources in a common folder, move or copy files, and modify file information.

- **E-mail access**   HTTP and WebDAV can be used to access mailboxes and messages, to notify users that new e-mail has arrived, and to allow users to move, copy, or delete e-mail on the server.

- **Application access**   HTTP and WebDAV are standards-based application layer protocols. Mailboxes and public folders are accessed through a unique Uniform Resource Locator (URL). This allows custom applications to retrieve data directly from the Information Store.

> **Note**   The default HTTP virtual server is created by IIS, and you must administer this server using IIS. However, if you create additional HTTP virtual servers in Exchange then you can (and should) administer them using Exchange System Manager.

You can create additional HTTP virtual servers to provide for a number of different collaboration scenarios. For example, you might want to use Integrated Windows Authentication on the default virtual server, but also to provide users outside your organization with information about your company. In this situation, you can enable anonymous access on a separate HTTP virtual server.

By default, users can access private mailboxes using a URL in the form of *http:// server_name/exchange/mailbox_name* after a standard Exchange installation and setup is complete. If you create a new mailbox store, a different URL is automatically assigned to it. This URL is based on the virtual directory name.

Virtual Directories

Virtual directories provide users connecting to a virtual HTTP server with access to public folders or mailboxes. For each virtual server you create, you must define one virtual directory as the root of the server. The virtual directory is used for publishing a public folder or mailboxes in an SMTP domain. You can create additional virtual directories to publish content not contained within the server's own directory structure. The virtual directory can provide users with access to a public folder or mailbox on a local or remote domain.

When you create a virtual directory, you provide users with access to the contents of a public folder through a URL that takes the form *http://virtualserver/public*, where *virtualserver* is the DNS name of the virtual server. You can also access a published directory through Microsoft Internet Explorer or through any client that supports the industry standard HTTP and WebDAV protocols. You can use Microsoft Office to create and save documents directly into an HTTP directory through a feature called Web Folders that lets you work with files and folders that are on a Web server, just as you would with files and folders in My Computer or Windows Explorer.

Outlook Web Access

An HTTP virtual server is installed and configured during the Exchange Server 2003 installation process to support OWA. You can use OWA to configure Exchange so that users can access e-mail, calendar information, shared applications, and any content in the public information store by using a Web browser. To enable your users to access OWA from the Internet, your Exchange Server 2003 server must have an Internet connection, a public IP address, and a registered domain name.

OWA can be disabled for the Exchange organization by stopping the HTTP virtual server. It can also be disabled on a per-user basis by accessing the user's Properties dialog box in the Active Directory Users And Computers console. On the Exchange Features tab, you select Outlook Web Access, and then click Disable as shown in Figure 10-10.

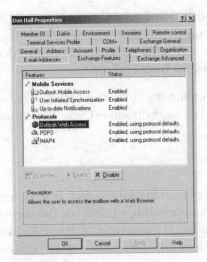

Figure 10-10   Disabling OWA for an individual user

Supporting IMAP4 Clients

IMAP4 allows a client to access messages in private and public folders. IMAP4 clients can access mail in their Exchange mailbox without downloading the entire mailbox to a specific computer. A single client can access multiple mailboxes to retrieve specific messages or message portions, such as attachments. IMAP4 clients can also search a mailbox and store flags to identify messages that have been read.

> **Exam Tip**   IMAP4 and POP3 access but do not send e-mail. This functionality is handled by SMTP. Therefore, you can discard any answer in the exam that specifies IMAP4 or POP3 as an e-mail delivery method.

You can create multiple IMAP4 virtual servers on a single computer to handle multiple local mail domains and provide administration for a number of different messaging scenarios. You can configure your IMAP4 server to grant or deny access to specific computers, groups of computers, or domains. You can grant or deny access to a single computer either based on an IP address or by overriding IMAP4 access on a per-user basis. A group of computers can be either denied or granted access based upon subnet address and mask. You can also control access to an entire domain by specifying a domain name.

Configuring IMAP4 Clients

Before an IMAP4 client can connect to a server, you need to create a mailbox-enabled user for the client in Active Directory. You also need to configure the IMAP4 client with the account information it needs to allow it to connect to the IMAP4 virtual server.

In topologies that contain Exchange front-end and back-end servers, you must configure the URL your users use to access calendaring information on the Calendaring tab of an IMAP4 virtual server's Properties box on your back-end server. Exchange does not recognize any URL settings you configure on your front-end servers.

To configure IMAP4 clients, you need to create a mailbox-enabled user, specify account information on the client, and set per-user options. These procedures are described in detail later in this lesson.

Supporting POP3 Clients

POP3 allows a client to retrieve a specific user's mail from the server. POP3 clients can access only their server inboxes and cannot access other public or private folders. POP3 is not intended to provide full manipulation of mail on the server. Typically, mail is only downloaded and then deleted. POP3 does not send e-mail; SMTP performs this function.

Both POP3 and IMAP4 allow clients to access their mail. The difference between these protocols is where clients manipulate their messages. IMAP4 allows a client to access and manage mail on a server. POP3 allows a client to download mail from an inbox on a server to the client computer.

You can configure a POP3 virtual server to grant or deny access to specific computers, groups of computers, or domains. You can grant or deny access to a single computer based on an IP address or by overriding POP3 access on a per-user basis. A group of computers can be denied or granted access based on their subnet IP address and subnet mask. You can also control access to an entire domain by specifying a domain name.

When a POP3 client reads messages sent by a MAPI client, it converts them from RTF to MIME or uuencode.

You can view a list of currently connected users. You can immediately disconnect a single user from this list without disrupting the service of other connected users or denying new connection requests.

Configuring POP3 Clients

Before a POP3 client can connect to a server, you need to create a mailbox-enabled user for that client in Active Directory. You also need to configure account information on the POP3 client that allows the client to connect to the POP3 virtual server.

> **Note** In topologies that contain Exchange front-end and back-end servers, you configure the URL that your users use to access calendaring information on the Calendaring tab of a POP3 virtual server's Properties dialog box on your back-end server. Exchange does not recognize any URL settings you configure on your front-end servers. If you use calendaring with POP3 clients, then you must configure the POP3 client to keep a copy of the message on the server.

To configure POP3 clients, you need to create a mailbox-enabled user and specify account information for that user on the POP3 client. If necessary, you can then configure user-specific settings. A detailed description of these procedures is given later in this chapter.

Allowing Clients to Send Mail

An SMTP virtual server transfers data between Exchange servers. To allow IMAP4 or POP3 clients to send messages using SMTP, you need to configure an SMTP virtual server to relay messages for these clients. This procedure is described in Lesson 2 of this chapter.

Supporting NNTP Clients

NNTP defines a set of client and server commands used to access newsgroups. Exchange Server 2003 uses NNTP to enable Outlook users to participate in online discussions over the Internet. Users running client applications that support NNTP can also access newsgroup public folders on computers running Exchange, and read and post items, such as messages and documents. Items in newsgroups can be replicated to Usenet host computers through newsfeeds.

The Windows 2003 NNTP service is designed to support a standalone newsgroup server, making it easy to create group discussions. When you install Exchange Server 2003, the NNTP service is enhanced with the capability to interface with other news servers through newsfeeds. The NNTP service communicates with external NNTP servers to make popular Usenet groups available to your users.

An NNTP virtual server allows you to administer newsgroup services by controlling authentication and client connections from a centralized location. You can create additional virtual servers to host multiple domains on a single server, or you can create a public and private virtual server and keep them separate for authentication purposes.

You can control which articles are posted to a newsgroup by assigning a moderator to the newsgroup. Articles submitted to a moderated newsgroup are not posted until the moderator approves them.

> **Note**   The NNTP default virtual server and the NNTP service are disabled by default. If you want to configure the default server, create an additional server, configure newsfeeds, and define subordinate servers. Then you must first enable and start the NNTP service in the Services console.

Practice: Message and Client Configuration

In this practice, you configure the format of message extensions, create a policy for SMTP to use when sending messages, and configure IMAP4 and POP3 clients. In order to configure clients, you need to create mailbox-enabled users. This exercise is therefore included for your convenience, although users have been created in practices in previous chapters.

Exercise 1: Associate MIME Types with Extensions

When SMTP sends a MAPI message to an Internet client, it assigns a content type to attachments based on the extension of the attachment file. You can map a new file extension to a specific type of content. You can also define your own MIME types.

To associate a MIME type with an extension, perform the following steps:

1. Open Exchange System Manager.
2. In the console tree, double-click Global Settings.
3. Right-click Internet Message Formats, and then click Properties.
4. On the General tab, double-click a content type.
5. To change the content type, select a new content type in the Type drop-down list.
6. To change the extension, enter a new file extension in the Associated Extension box. You do not need to include the "." before the extension.
7. To map a new content type to an extension, select a new content type in the Type drop-down list, and then enter a new file extension in the Associated Extension box. You do not need to include the "." before the extension.
8. Click OK. Click OK again to close the Properties dialog box.

Exercise 2: Configure Message Defaults

You can create a policy for SMTP to use when sending messages to a specific domain. The policy allows you to specify the format used by recipients in that domain to view messages.

To set message defaults for a domain, you need to create a new SMTP policy, and then specify message formats and advanced options for that policy.

To create a new SMTP policy for a domain, perform the following steps:

1. Access Exchange System Manager.

2. In the console tree, double-click Global Settings.

3. Right-click Internet Message Formats, point to New, and then click Domain.

4. On the General tab, in Name, type a descriptive name for the policy, and then in SMTP Domain, type the DNS name of the domain.

5. On the Message Format tab, in the Message Encoding section, select either MIME or UUEncode.

   ❑ If you select MIME, you can define how the message is formatted. To display text only and replace graphics and active links with textual representations, select Provide Message Body As Plain Text. To display graphics and links to other documents, select Provide Message Body As HTML. If you are not sure which format the client can read, select Both to provide both plaintext and HTML.

   ❑ If you select UUEncode, you can specify that you support Macintosh clients. To use BinHex, which is an encoding scheme similar to uuencode but is a more common format for Macintosh files, select Use BinHex For Macintosh.

6. To support multilingual messages, choose a code page from the MIME and Non-MIME messages drop-down lists in the Character Sets section. Windows 2003 uses code pages to read messages containing international character sets. Figure 10-11 shows this dialog box.

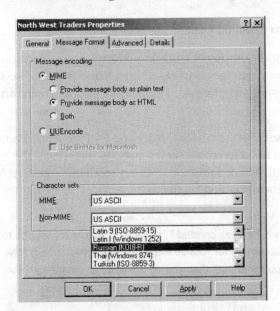

Figure 10-11 Configuring multilingual support

7. Access the Advanced tab.

8. If you want to send all messages in RTF, then select Always Use. If, however, you want to encode messages in MIME with HTML, then select Never Use.

9. If you want to send text in the original format without forcing line breaks, then select Never Use in Message Text Word Wrap. If, however, your recipients have a limited area to display messages, or if you want to reformat line breaks so that text flows no further than a specific column, then select Use At Column, and type the number of the column.

10. Select Allow Out Of Office Responses to notify the sender that the recipient is out of the office.

11. Select Allow Automatic Replies to notify the sender that the message was received.

12. Select Allow Automatic Forward to deliver a duplicate message to a different recipient.

13. Select Allow Delivery Reports to allow senders in the specified SMTP domain to receive delivery reports when they send mail to your Exchange organization.

14. Select Allow Non-Delivery Reports to allow senders in the specified SMTP domain to receive NDRs from your Exchange organization.

15. To display the sender's name as it appears in the Address Book, instead of the shortened alias name used to route the message, select Preserve Sender's Display Name On Message.

16. Click OK.

Exercise 3: Create a Mailbox-Enabled User

The Active Directory Users And Computers console manages user objects such as mailboxes. When Exchange System Manager is installed on a Windows 2003 server, a set of extensions is added to the standard console. This allows you to create an Exchange mailbox for user accounts.

You need to create mailbox-enabled users for IMAP4 and POP3 clients. You should use this procedure each time you need to create such a user. In fact, this is the normal procedure for creating a user in Active Directory. When Exchange System Manager is installed, new users are mailbox-enabled by default.

Note   Mailbox-enabled users have been created in previous chapters for various testing purposes. The procedure is repeated here for your convenience, but if you already have mailbox-enabled user accounts that you could use, then you do not need to create any more.

To create a mailbox-enabled user, perform the following steps:

1. Open the Active Directory Users And Computers console.

2. In the console tree, double-click the domain node, right-click the Users folder, point to New, and then click User.

3. To create a user account, complete the New Object-User Wizard. Notice that Create An Exchange Mailbox is selected by default.

Exercise 4: Configure an IMAP4 Client

You use the previous procedure to create a mailbox-enabled user account that the IMAP4 clients can use. When you have done that, you configure the IMAP4 client with account information so that these users can log on to that client. You then configure per-user options for any accounts for which the server settings are not appropriate.

When you have created a place to store user messages (that is, a user mailbox), you need to direct the client to the appropriate server and configure the account information so the user can log on. Because IMAP4 clients vary, the process differs for each client; however, all clients must specify the same type of information, as follows:

- **An IMAP4 account name**   This is the user's alias in Active Directory, for example, d.hall.

- **An IMAP4 e-mail address**   This is the user's Internet address and includes the alias followed by the domain name, for example, *d.hall@tailspintoys.com.*

- **An IMAP4 server name**   Use the name of the Exchange computer hosting the IMAP4 virtual server or the DNS entry of the front-end IMAP4 server.

- **An SMTP server name**   Because every Exchange server contains a default SMTP server, you can use the same computer name as the IMAP4 virtual server host.

You may need to override server defaults for specific clients. Suppose, for example, that the majority of your IMAP4 clients can interpret HTML. Therefore, you set the server to provide message bodies in HTML by default. However, a few IMAP4 clients cannot interpret HTML. To provide plain text messages for those clients, you configure their IMAP4 options on a per-user basis.

Note   You can also create additional virtual servers on a single computer to provide administration for several messaging scenarios. This solution is best suited for a large number of clients with varying needs.

To configure an IMAP4 client and set per-user options, perform the following steps:

1. Open the Active Directory Users And Computers console.

2. In the console tree, click Users.

3. Right-click a mailbox-enabled user in the details pane, and then click Properties.

4. On the Exchange Features tab, click IMAP4.

5. Click Properties. Figure 10-12 shows the Properties control.

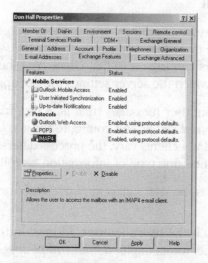

Figure 10-12   Accessing per-user properties for an IMAP4 user

6. Click Use Protocol Defaults to clear the check box and configure client settings.

7. You can now configure options for the specific user. Table 10-11 describes the available settings.

8. Click OK, and then click OK again to close the user Properties dialog box.

Table 10-11   Per-User IMAP4 Settings

Setting	Description
MIME Encoding	MIME provides a way to describe a message consisting of different parts. By definition, all IMAP4 clients are MIME-aware. Options include: ■ Provide message body as plain text ■ Provide message body as HTML ■ Both

Table 10-11   Per-User IMAP4 Settings

Setting	Description
Default Character Set	Exchange supports multilingual messages using Windows code pages instead of Internet character sets. Most languages have a one-to-one correspondence between the character set and code page. If multiple character sets exist for one code page, then Exchange uses the character setting specified on the Message Format tab.
Use Microsoft Exchange Rich Text Format	If this setting is enabled, then IMAP4 clients receive messages in RTF. All IMAP4 clients receive the information as an attachment. If the IMAP4 client understands RTF, the attachment opens and displays as a normal message. If the IMAP4 client does not understand Exchange RTF, then the recipient needs to open the attachment manually.
Enable Fast Message Retrieval	By default, Exchange calculates the exact size of a message. To increase the speed of message retrieval for clients that do not require exact message size reports, you can enable the server to use approximate message sizes.
Include All Public Folders When A Folder List Is Requested	By default, Exchange lists all public folders in response to the IMAP4 list ""* command. To improve performance for clients that have problems listing a large number of folders, you can set this option to list only the client's private folders.

Exercise 5: Configure a POP3 Client

A POP3 client also stores messages in users' mailboxes, and mailbox-enabled user accounts need to be created. When you have done that, you configure the POP3 client with account information so that these users can log on to that client. You then configure per-user options for any accounts for which the server settings are not appropriate.

> **Note**   This exercise is very similar to configuring an IMAP4 client. However, there are significant differences in the per-user settings, and therefore the instructions are given in full.

When you have created a place to store user messages (that is, a user mailbox), you need to direct the client to the appropriate server and configure the account information so the user can log on. Because POP3 clients vary, the process differs for each client; however, all clients must specify the same type of information.

- **A POP3 account name**   This is the user's alias in Active Directory, for example, k.akers.

- **A POP3 e-mail address** This is the user's Internet address and includes the alias followed by the domain name, for example, *k.akers@tailspintoys.com*.

- **A POP3 server name** Use the name of the Exchange computer hosting the POP3 virtual server or the DNS entry of the front-end POP3 server.

- **An SMTP server name** Because every Exchange server contains a default SMTP server, you can use the same computer name as the POP3 virtual server host.

You may need to override server defaults for specific clients. Suppose, for example, that the majority of your POP3 clients can interpret HTML. You therefore set the server to provide message bodies in HTML by default. However, a few POP3 clients cannot interpret HTML. To provide plain text messages for those clients, you configure their POP3 options on a per-user basis.

To configure a POP3 client and per-user options, perform the following steps:

1. Open the Active Directory Users And Computers console.

2. In the console tree, click Users.

3. In the details pane, right-click a mailbox-enabled user, and then click Properties.

4. On the Exchange Features tab, click POP3.

5. Click Properties.

6. Click Use Protocol Defaults to clear the check box and configure client settings.

7. You can now configure options for the specific user. Table 10-12 describes the available settings.

8. Click OK, and then click OK again to close the user Properties dialog box.

Table 10-12   Per-User POP3 Settings

Setting	Description
MIME Encoding	MIME provides a way to describe a message consisting of different parts. Options include: ■ Provide message body as plain text ■ Provide message body as HTML ■ Both
UUEncode	Uuencode converts a binary file into printable 7-bit ASCII characters without loss of information. If you select uuencode, then you have the option of specifying BinHex for Macintosh.
Default Character Set	If multiple character sets can be used to convert a message, then a default character set is selected.

Table 10-12   Per-User POP3 Settings

Setting	Description
Use Microsoft Exchange Rich Text Format	If this is enabled, then POP3 clients receive messages in RTF. All POP3 clients receive the information as an attachment. If the client can interpret RTF, the attachment opens and displays as a normal message. Clients who cannot interpret RTF need to open the attachment manually.

Lesson Review

The following questions are intended to reinforce key information presented in this lesson. If you are unable to answer a question, review the lesson materials and then try the question again. You can find answers to the questions in the "Questions and Answers" section at the end of this chapter.

1. In what format does an Internet client send a message, and how does SMTP convert it? In what format does a MAPI send a message, and how does SMTP convert it?

   _____

   _____

2. What type of virtual server does Exchange Server 2003 use to support WebDAV?

   a. HTTP virtual server

   b. SMTP virtual server

   c. POP3 virtual server

   d. IMAP4 virtual server

3. In what ways are POP3 and IMAP4 similar, and how do they differ?

   _____

   _____

Lesson Summary

- Exchange Server 2003 supports connectivity to other SMTP systems through the configuration of an SMTP connector as an Internet mail connector and the configuration of global defaults.

- Per-user settings override global defaults for specific users.

- Exchange Server 2003 supports NNTP newsgroups and newsfeeds.

- Exchange Server 2003 supports WebDAV and OWA by using the default HTTP virtual server.

- POP3 and IMAP4 clients can retrieve mail from Exchange Server 2003 mailboxes. These clients use SMTP to send mail.

Case Scenario Exercise

You are the domain and Exchange administrator at the Baldwin Museum of Science. The museum is a much-respected and highly reputable organization that does not condone spam or junk mail. Due to its high public profile, the museum has been subjected to attacks from the Internet. In particular, viruses have been sent to museum staff in e-mail attachments.

All the servers in your domain have recently been upgraded and have Windows Server 2003, Enterprise Edition installed. However, museum employees use a wide variety of workstations, including POP3 and IMAP4 clients. Currently the museum's ISP handles its external DNS resolution requirements. This can sometimes lead to delays due to slow name resolution, even though the museum has a permanent connection to the ISP.

Management has asked you to bring these problems under control.

Requirement 1   E-mails containing viruses have caused problems in the past because they were sent to staff members who did not have the knowledge required to deal with them. You have obtained and installed antivirus software. Nevertheless, management requires that you restrict the ability to send and receive Internet e-mail to a small group of users.

Requirement 2   Some staff members who need to send and receive Internet e-mail use POP3 or IMAP4 clients. You are required to ensure that these staff members have full e-mail functionality. At the same time you need to ensure that the museum's domain cannot be used to relay junk mail.

Requirement 3   You are asked to implement a DNS solution that enables the museum to handle its own external DNS resolution. Currently the museum uses Active Directory integrated DNS installed on its domain controllers to handle internal DNS name resolution, but it forwards external name resolution requests to its ISP.

Requirement 1

The first requirement stipulates that you restrict Internet e-mail access to a select group of users.

1. Management has given you a list of all the staff members that are allowed to send and receive Internet mail. How do you now ensure that these employees, and only these employees, can send and receive external e-mail, without restricting the ability of all employees to send and receive internal e-mail?

   _____

   _____

2. You are currently training an assistant administrator. She asks you why you configured delivery restrictions on an SMTP connector and not on an SMTP virtual server. What do you tell her?

   _____

   _____

Requirement 2

You must set up the e-mail system so that staff members who use use POP3 or IMAP4 clients have full e-mail functionality, while ensuring that the museum's domain cannot be used to relay junk e-mail.

1. You send an e-mail message to Kim Akers, an Exchange Full Administrator at Consolidated Messenger. Kim does not get the message. The message is short and has no attachments. You receive an NDR saying that your message was rejected because it came from an unsafe source. You need to send mail to Kim. How do you solve the problem?

   _____

   _____

2. You have disabled relaying on your default virtual server, but this has not solved your open relaying problem. What else do you need to check?

   _____

   _____

Requirement 3

You must implement a DNS solution that enables the museum to handle its own external DNS resolution.

1. You are asked to amend your DNS configuration so that name resolution over the Internet is handled by your DNS servers and not by the ISP. What DNS records do you need to change?

_____

_____

Troubleshooting Lab

A junk e-mail sender is using your organization to relay unsolicited commercial e-mail. You need to restrict relaying and allow relaying permission only to security groups that contain users of IMAP4 or POP3 clients.

The lab requires that you have a global security group called IMAP4users and one called POP3users. You also need to have a test network that is set up as described in the "Before You Begin" section at the start of this chapter.

To do this, proceed as follows:

1. Open Exchange System Manager.
2. Navigate to Organizational Groups\First Organizational Group\Servers\Server01\ Protocols\SMTP, right-click Default SMTP Virtual Server and then click Properties.
3. On the Access tab, in the Relay Restrictions pane, click Relay.
4. Ensure that the Allow All Computers Which Successfully Authenticate To Relay Regardless Of The List Above check box is cleared. Having this box checked is almost certainly the cause of your problem.
5. Click Users.
6. Remove any users or groups that should not be allowed to submit or relay mail through the server. Allowing these permissions to groups that should not have them could also be contributing to your problem.

Note   You should remove a group rather than checking Deny beside a permission. If you deny Submit or Relay Permissions to, for example, Authenticated Users, then allowing them for other groups will not be effective.

7. Click Add, and type POP3users in the Enter The Object Names To Select box. Click Check Names to confirm the group exists, and then click OK.

8. Click Add, and type IMAP4users in the Enter The Object Names To Select box. Click Check Names to confirm the group exists, and then click OK.

Tip   Click the Examples link to view the acceptable formats for your entries, as shown in Figure 10-13.

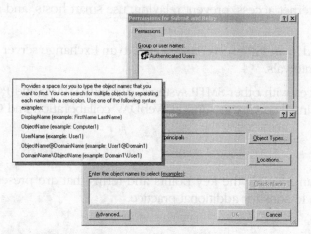

Figure 10-13   Displaying valid entry formats

9. In the Permissions For Submit And Relay dialog box, grant Relay Permission to POP3users and to IMAP4users.

10. In the Permissions For Submit And Relay dialog box, grant Submit Permission to POP3users and to IMAP4users.

Note   You must allow Submit Permissions if you want to allow Relay Permissions.

11. Click OK.

12. Click OK again to close the Relay Restrictions dialog box. Click OK again to close the SMTP_server1 Properties dialog box.

Chapter Summary

- SMTP makes a connection and sends e-mail across that connection. ESMTP extends the functionality of SMTP to enable authentication, encryption, and message delivery information.

- DNS supports Exchange Server 2003 by using MX records to identify e-mail servers and resolve their IP addresses.

- You can create and configure additional SMTP virtual servers and SMTP connectors to control Internet access, prevent relaying, use smart hosts, and act as smart hosts.

- E-mail can be held in an ISP's server and pulled to an Exchange server on demand or at scheduled intervals.

- Exchange interfaces with other SMTP systems, supports IMAP4 and POP3 clients, and uses HTTP virtual servers to support WebDAV collaboration and OWA.

Exam Highlights

Before taking the exam, review the key points and terms that are presented in this chapter. Return to the lessons for additional practice.

Key Points

- SMTP transfers e-mail messages using a series of plain-text commands that are passed from a sending host to a receiving host. The receiving host responds using numerical codes. ESMTP extends SMTP functionality.

- You can control Internet access by creating and configuring additional SMTP virtual server and SMTP connectors. You can use these to configure incoming and outgoing connections, to control relaying, and to configure security settings.

- You can use an SMTP connector when you require a pull relationship between servers, and configure this connector to retrieve e-mail in a queue from a remote SMTP server at specified intervals.

- Exchange Server 2003 supports connectivity to other SMTP systems through the configuration of an SMTP connector as an Internet mail connector and the configuration of global defaults.

- POP3 and IMAP4 clients can retrieve mail from Exchange Server 2003 mailboxes. These clients use SMTP to send mail. Per-user settings override global defaults for specific users.

Key Terms

Extended Simple Mail Transfer Protocol (ESMTP)   An extension of the basic Simple Mail Transfer Protocol (SMTP) that provides additional commands for server communication.

Internet Message Access Protocol version 4 (IMAP4)   An Internet messaging protocol that enables a client to access mail on a server rather than downloading it to the user's computer.

Post Office Protocol version 3 (POP3)   An Internet protocol that allows a user to download mail from their inbox on a server to the client computer where messages are managed.

Simple Mail Transfer Protocol (SMTP)   An Internet standard for transporting and delivering electronic messages. SMTP is the default transport for Exchange Server 2003.

Questions and Answers

Page
10-19 **Lesson 1 Review**

1. You are a network administrator, and you want to test connectivity between a host on your network and a new Exchange Server 2003 server that has just been configured. You want to ensure that e-mail messages to that server can be encrypted. You can ping the server by host name. You connect to port 25 on the server. What command should you use?

   a. atrn

   b. etrn

   c. elho

   d. helo

   The correct answer is c.

2. You are the administrator of the Contoso ISP. You have two SMTP servers configured as smart hosts: *smart1.contoso.com* and *smart2.contoso.com*. Your ISP manages DNS records for Northwind Traders, whose Exchange Server 2003 server has the FQDN *mailserv.nwtraders.com*. Northwind Traders has a permanent connection to your ISP. How should you configure the MX records for this setup in DNS?

   a. MX 10 *smart1.contoso.com*

        MX 10 *smart2.contoso.com*

        MX 20 *mailserv.nwtraders.com*

   b. MX 10 *mailserv.contoso.com*

        MX 20 *smart1.contoso.com*

        MX 20 *smart2.nwtraders.com*

   c. MX 10 *smart1.contoso.com*

        MX 20 *smart2.contoso.com*

        MX 30 *mailserv.nwtraders.com*

   d. MX 10 *mailserv.contoso.com*

        MX 10 *smart1.contoso.com*

        MX 10 *smart2.nwtraders.com*

   The correct answer is b.

3. You administer your company's Exchange Server 2003 organization. Your company has two e-mail domains. You want to control filters, relay restrictions, message formats, outbound security, and smart host options separately for each domain. What technique would you use?

    a. Create an additional virtual server and configure an SMTP connector to use it as a bridgehead.

    b. Configure all these items on the default SMTP virtual server.

    c. Configure Internet message formats and delivery parameters for each domain.

    d. Limit the scope of the SMTP connector to a specific routing group.

    The correct answer is a.

4. You administer an Exchange Server 2003 server. You want this server to act as a smart host. Your organization has a single SMTP domain. How do you configure your server?

    a. Configure an SMTP connector to forward all outbound mail.

    b. Configure the default SMTP virtual server as a relay host.

    c. Configure the default SMTP virtual server to forward all unresolved messages.

    d. Configure the default SMTP virtual server to specify which servers can relay e-mail.

    The correct answer is b.

5. You want your Exchange Server 2003 organization to have smart host capability. How should you configure a virtual server to provide such capability, and how is the configuration implemented?

    You configure the SMTP virtual server as an inbound relay host. You can then configure other SMTP servers to use the Exchange virtual server as their smart host and forward all outbound messages to the virtual server. You implement this by configuring Relay Restrictions on the virtual server's Access tab.

Page 10-34

Lesson 2 Review

1. You administer an Exchange Server 2003 server with a dial-up connection to an ISP. You want your ISP to hold your e-mail until your Exchange server connects. You then want all queued e-mail to be delivered to your Exchange server. How do you configure this?

    You configure your SMTP connector to request ETRN/TURN from the ISP server. This will cause your Exchange server to send the etrn command to the ISP on connection. The etrn command pulls queued e-mail from the server that holds it.

2. You want your Exchange Server 2003 organization to have smart host capability. How should you configure a virtual server to provide such capability, and how is the configuration implemented?

    You configure the SMTP virtual server as an inbound relay host. You can then configure other SMTP servers to use the Exchange virtual server as their smart host and forward all outbound messages to the virtual server. You implement this by configuring Relay Restrictions on the virtual server's Access tab.

3. You administer an Exchange Server 2003 organization in a school. Staff members are permitted to send Internet e-mail, but students are not. How do you prevent students from receiving and sending Internet e-mail?

    You configure the SMTP connector so that only approved users or groups can send e-mail outside of the school. You restrict user accounts from sending Internet e-mail by navigating to Connectors in Exchange System Manager, right-clicking the connector that you want to restrict, clicking Properties, and specifying the name of the sender or senders in the Accept Messages From or Reject Messages From area on the Delivery Restrictions tab. In this case, the connector is configured to accept messages from staff users and to reject messages from student users.

4. How do you prevent unauthorized users from propagating junk e-mail through your Exchange organization?

    a. By configuring reverse DNS lookup

    b. By permitting anonymous authentication

    c. By preventing open relaying

    d. By preventing IMAP4 and POP3 clients from accessing your organization

    The correct answer is c.

Page
10-51

Lesson 3 Review

1. In what format does an Internet client send a message, and how does SMTP convert it? In what format does a MAPI send a message, and how does SMTP convert it?

    Messages sent by Internet clients are sent in MIME format, and no message conversion takes place. Messages sent by MAPI clients are sent in RTF, and SMTP converts this to MIME format.

2. What type of virtual server does Exchange Server 2003 use to support WebDAV?

    a. HTTP virtual server

    b. SMTP virtual server

    c. POP3 virtual server

    d. IMAP4 virtual server

    The correct answer is a.

3. In what ways are POP3 and IMAP4 similar, and how do they differ?

Both POP3 and IMAP4 allow clients to access their mail. Neither can send mail; this function is implemented by SMTP. The difference between these protocols is where clients manipulate their messages. IMAP4 allows a client to access and manage mail on a server. POP3 allows a client to download mail from an inbox on a server to the client computer.

Page
10-53

Case Scenario Exercise: Requirement 1

1. Management has given you a list of all the staff members that are allowed to send and receive Internet mail. How do you now ensure that these employees, and only these employees, can send and receive external e-mail, without restricting the ability of all employees to send and receive internal e-mail?

If you have not already done so, you first need to create an SMTP connector and configure it to use your default SMTP virtual server as a bridgehead. You navigate to this SMTP connector in Exchange System Manager. In the Properties dialog box, you access the Delivery Restrictions tab, specify that messages from everyone are rejected, and then add the individual user accounts of the users that are permitted to send and receive external e-mail in the Accept Messages From box. You cannot add security groups to this box, but you may want to put these users in a global security group for other reasons, such as auditing.

2. You are currently training an assistant administrator. She asks you why you configured delivery restrictions on an SMTP connector and not on an SMTP virtual server. What do you tell her?

You can configure user-based delivery restrictions on an SMTP connector and computer-based delivery restrictions on an SMTP virtual server. If you configure restrictions based on computer accounts, then the users who should be able to use external e-mail might not have that facility if they logged on at another computer.

Page
10-53

Case Scenario Exercise: Requirement 2

1. You send an e-mail message to Kim Akers, an Exchange Full Administrator at Consolidated Messenger. Kim does not get the message. The message is short and has no attachments. You receive an NDR saying that your message was rejected because it came from an unsafe source. You need to send mail to Kim. How do you solve the problem?

Your problem goes further than not being able to send mail to Kim. An organization can appear on an e-mail block list because other, less reputable organizations are relaying junk e-mail through it. In the short term, you can ask Kim to place the Baldwin Museum of Science's domain on an exception list so you can e-mail her, but you need to sort out the relaying problem, otherwise other organizations will also add your domain to their block lists.

Because you have IMAP4 or POP3 clients, you cannot disable relaying. However, you need to ensure that only these clients can relay, and nobody else. You can configure relaying on your default SMTP virtual server so that only users with IMAP4 and POP3 clients can relay. Alternatively you can disable relaying on your default SMTP virtual server, create an additional SMTP virtual server, permit relaying on that virtual server, and permit only IMAP4 and POP3 clients to access that server.

2. You have disabled relaying on your default virtual server, but this has not solved your open relaying problem. What else do you need to check?

If an SMTP connector permits relaying, then this overrides the settings on its bridgehead server. Access the SMTP connector's Properties dialog box. On the Address Space tab, uncheck Allow Messages To Be Relayed To These Domains.

Page
10-54

Case Scenario Exercise: Requirement 3

1. You are asked to amend your DNS configuration so that name resolution over the Internet is handled by your DNS servers and not by the ISP. What DNS records do you need to change?

Because your DNS servers already perform internal name resolution, there should already be MX records for all your Exchange Server 2003 servers in your DNS zone file. Because you have a permanent connection to your ISP, your ISP's DNS zone file will contain an MX record for your bridgehead Exchange Server 2003 server. You need to inform your ISP and request that this record be removed. (You also need to configure a stand-alone DNS server with a standard primary zone in your DMZ and alter your root hints files, but this information is not required by the question.)

Before You Begin

vity Across Firewalls

To perform the exercises in this c software:

■ Two Microsoft Windows Server *tailspintoys.com* Active Directory domain controller, and Server02 multihomed. Local Area Connec as Local Area Connection on Ser ulates an external network and c want, you could use it for your

Note   If your Active Directory domain i rename it. Instead, use your domain na mentioned in the chapter exercises.

■ Server01 should be an enterprise

■ Exchange Server 2003, Enterpri Server01 and Server02 should be

■ A Domain Name System (DNS) installed on the domain controll

■ Microsoft Outlook 2003 shoul purposes.

■ At least one computer on your te to download sample virus prote

■ A modem should be installed c some steps in one of the exercis is installed.

zed users from accessing private networks that ically, a firewall prevents external users from rk from the Internet. All e-mail messages that the firewall, which blocks messages that do not

fy the ports that can be shut down

a Messaging Application Programming Interface when separated by a firewall r connecting a MAPI client to an Exchange server

remote procedure call (RPC) over Hypertext

ewing each data packet that enters or leaves the ts based on source address, destination address, es (if the appropriate software is installed) and ves your network. A firewall can act as a *proxy* nd filtering out packets that contain inappropri-

es external networks should be protected by a that contain private stores need strong protec- ire weaker protection and more functionality. nent light (or no) firewall protection between l, and strong firewall protection to protect back- the intranet. The front-end servers are then said lso known as a perimeter network.

specific proxy server that understands mail pro- ta is corrupted or from an unacceptable source. u do not need a separate proxy server.

TCP Port Filtering

Transmission Control Protocol (TCP) enables two hosts to establish a connection and exchange data. A TCP port provides a specific (abstract) location for the delivery of the TCP segments. TCP ports are identified for a specific application or service that uses TCP. For example, the HTTP service uses TCP port 80, and Simple Mail Transfer Protocol (SMTP) uses TCP port 25.

You can secure network applications and services by restricting connections to their associated ports. TCP port filtering enables you to control the type of network traffic that reaches your Exchange servers and network devices.

You can use a firewall to allow only essential Internet traffic to pass through specified TCP ports. You could, in theory, configure your network to allow only SMTP traffic to pass through your firewall on port 25. In practice, Exchange traffic requires additional ports to be opened to allow remote clients and servers to communicate with your network. You can, however, filter traffic through these ports (for example, by source address or domain name) and prohibit traffic through ports that you are not using. Table 11-1 lists TCP ports and their associated services.

Table 11-1   Exchange Server 2003 Ports and Services

Port	Service
25	SMTP
80	HTTP
88	Kerberos
102	Message Transfer Agent (MTA) - X.400 connector over TCP/IP
110	Post Office Protocol version 3 (POP3)
119	Network News Transfer Protocol (NNTP)
135	Client/server communication RPC Exchange administration
143	Internet Message Access Protocol version 4 (IMAP4)
389	Lightweight Directory Application Protocol (LDAP)
443	HTTP using Secure Sockets Layer (SSL)
563	NNTP using SSL
636	LDAP using SSL
993	IMAP4 using SSL
995	POP3 using SSL
3268 and 3269	Global catalog lookups

> **Important**   Table 11-1 lists all the ports that Exchange Server 2003 uses for all modes of operation. However, this does not imply that you should open all these ports in your firewall. For example, if you do not support IMAP4 or POP3 clients, the corresponding ports should be closed. In general, open as few ports as necessary.

MAPI Client Connection Through a Firewall

You can allow messages sent by a MAPI client (such as Outlook) to connect to an Exchange Server 2003 server through a firewall by configuring RPC over HTTP. You can also configure static port assignments for the Information Store (IS) by adding entries to the Windows registry or configure Microsoft Internet Security and Acceleration (ISA) Server to route all Internet traffic, but the recommended option is to configure RPC over HTTP. This eliminates the need for a virtual private network (VPN) connection when a user is accessing Exchange information. Users running Outlook can connect directly to an Exchange server over the Internet by using HTTP, even if both the Exchange server and Outlook are behind firewalls and located on different networks.

When you deploy RPC over HTTP, you configure your Exchange front-end server as an RPC proxy server. The RPC proxy server specifies what ports the RPC client uses to communicate with domain controllers, global catalog servers, and the Exchange servers. You can locate the RPC proxy inside the firewall or on the DMZ.

Inside the Firewall   You can deploy ISA Server in the DMZ and configure the RPC proxy server on an Exchange front-end server inside the firewall. This eliminates the need to open the ports for the RPC proxy server to communicate with other computers because the ISA server is responsible for routing RPC over HTTP requests to the Exchange front-end server. When you choose this option, you can configure the RPC proxy server to use all the ports it needs within the specified range.

On the DMZ   You can configure the RPC proxy server on an Exchange Server 2003 front-end server located on your DMZ. When using this option, you should limit the number of ports that the RPC proxy server uses.

Practice: Configuring Exchange Server 2003 to Use RPC Over HTTP

To configure Exchange Server 2003 to use RPC over HTTP, you need to complete the following steps:

- Configure your Exchange front-end server (Server02) as an RPC proxy server.
- Configure basic authentication in the RPC virtual directory in Internet Information Services (IIS).

- Modify the registry on the Exchange back-end server (Server01) that communicates with the proxy server to use a specified number of ports.
- Open the specific ports on the internal firewall on the back-end server.
- Create an Outlook profile for your users to use with RPC over HTTP.

Exercise 1: Configure a Front-End Server to Use RPC Over HTTP

To configure your Exchange front-end server to use RPC over HTTP, perform the following steps:

1. Ensure that your Windows 2003 Server installation CD is in the CD-ROM drive on Server02.
2. On Server02, double-click Add Or Remove Programs on the Control Panel.
3. Click the Add/Remove Windows Components icon.
4. In the Windows Components dialog box that appears, select Networking Services, and then click Details.
5. In the Networking Services Component dialog box, select RPC Over HTTP Proxy, and then click OK.
6. In the Windows Components dialog box, click Next to install the RPC over HTTP Proxy Windows component. Follow the steps in the Configure Components Wizard. Click Finish to close the wizard.

Exercise 2: Configure the RPC Virtual Directory

To configure the RPC virtual directory on the RPC proxy server (Server02), perform the following steps:

1. On Server02, open the IIS Manager console.
2. Navigate to Server02\Web Sites, expand Default Web Site, right-click Rpc, and then click Properties.
3. Click the Directory Security tab on the Rpc Properties page, and then click Edit in the Authentication And Access Control pane.
4. Disable Anonymous Access and select Basic Authentication in the Authentication Methods window. If a warning box appears, then click Yes to close it. Click OK.
5. Click OK to close the IIS Manager console.

Exercise 3: Configure the RPC Proxy Server to Use Specific Ports

In this exercise, you configure the RPC proxy server (Server02) to use specified ports. In your test network, you can configure the same ports on Server01. In a real-world scenario, you need to repeat the configuration on all the servers with which your front-end server communicates.

To configure the RPC proxy server to use a specified number of ports for RPC over HTTP, perform the following steps:

1. On Server02, from the Start menu, click Run, type **regedit** in the Run box, and then click OK.

> **Caution**   Take care when editing the registry. Incorrect registry changes can damage your operating system.

2. Navigate to the registry key HKEY_LOCAL_MACHINE\Software\Microsoft\Rpc\ RpcProxy.

3. Right-click the Valid Ports registry key and click Modify.

   In the Edit String window, in the box under Value Data, enter the following information: **Server01:593;Server01:6001-6004**

> **Note**   Server01 is also the domain controller and catalog server on your test network. In a production network, you need to include all the domain controllers (including the global catalog server) and back-end Exchange servers with which your RPC proxy server communicates.

4. Close the registry editor on Server02.

5. To configure the back-end Exchange server (Server01) to use specified ports for RPC over HTTP requests, start the registry editor on that server.

6. Navigate to the registry key HKEY_LOCAL_MACHINE\SYSTEM\ CurrentControlSet\Services\MSExchangeSA\Parameters.

7. Right-click Rpc/HTTP NSPI Port, and then click Modify.

> **Note**   If Rpc/HTTP NSPI Port does not exist, then you need to create it. In this case, click Edit, click New, and then select DWORD Value.

8. In the Base window, select Decimal.

9. In the Value Data field, enter **6003**, as shown in Figure 11-1, and then click OK.

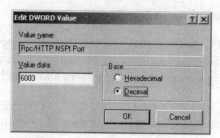

Figure 11-1 The Rpc/HTTP NSPI port setting

10. To set the port for DS Referral, right-click HTTP Port, and then click Modify.

11. As before, select Decimal in the Base window, type **6003** in the Value Data field, and then click OK.

12. To use the Exchange Store, navigate to HKEY_LOCAL_MACHINE\SYSTEM\CurrentControlSet\Services\MSExchangeIS\ParametersSystem.

13. Right-click RPC/HTTP Port, and then click Modify.

14. Select Decimal in the Base window, type **6001** in the Value Data field, and then click OK.

15. Close the registry editor on Server01.

> **Note** The above exercise is a simplified procedure to illustrate this technique on a test network. For more details about configuring RPC over HTTP, search *www.microsoft.com* for the Microsoft Exchange Titanium Getting Started Guide.

Exercise 4: Create an Outlook Profile to Use with RPC Over HTTP

For users to use RPC over HTTP from their client computers, they need an Outlook profile that is set to use RPC over HTTP. This is normally done on a client computer. If you want to practice the technique on your test network, you can perform the steps on Server01. However, unless you have a modem installed as specified at the start of this chapter, you will not be able to perform steps 12 through 17.

> **Note** Server01 is a domain controller. On a production network, you would be unlikely to install a modem on a domain controller or to use it as a client. Here you are using a two-computer network for learning purposes only.

To create an Outlook profile to use RPC over HTTP, perform the following steps:

1. On Server01, from the Start menu, click Control Panel.

2. If you are using Category View in Control Panel, then click Other Control Panel Options in the See Also pane, and then select Mail.

3. If you are using Classic View in Control Panel, then select Mail.

4. Click Show Profiles.

5. In the Mail dialog box, click Add.

6. In the New Profile dialog box, enter a name for this profile in the Profile Name box—for example, **RPC over HTTP**.

7. In the New E-Mail Accounts Wizard, select Add A New E-Mail Account, and then click Next.

8. On the Server Type page, select Microsoft Exchange Server, and then click Next.

9. In the Exchange Server Settings dialog box, shown in Figure 11-2, enter **Server01** and the account user name where appropriate. Click Check Name. Click OK.

Figure 11-2   The Exchange Server Settings dialog box

10. Click More Settings.

11. On the Connection tab, in the Connection pane, select Connect Using Internet Explorer's Or A 3rd Party Dialer.

12. In the Modem pane, select Connect To My Exchange Mailbox Using HTTP.

13. Click Exchange Proxy Settings.

14. On the Exchange Proxy Settings page, in the Connections Settings window, enter **server01.tailspintoys.com** in the Use This URL To Connect To My Proxy Server For Exchange box.

15. Select Connect Using SSL Only.

16. Select Mutually Authenticate The Session When Connecting With SSL.

17. Enter **msstd:server02.tailspintoys.com** in the Principal Name For Proxy Server box.

18. On the Exchange Proxy Settings page, in the Proxy Authentication Settings window, select Basic Authentication from the Use This Authentication When Connecting To My Proxy Server For Exchange drop-down menu.

19. Click OK.

20. Click Finish.

Exercise 5: Configure an Internet Connection Firewall

You may choose to use a hardware firewall supplied by a manufacturer such as Cisco or SonicWALL. In that case, refer to the manufacturer's instructions for configuration. However, you may choose to configure Microsoft Internet Connection Firewall (ICF) that is supplied with Windows 2003 Server.

To enable and configure ICF, perform the following steps:

1. On Server01, access the local area connection that connects to Server02.

2. Right-click the connection icon and click Properties.

3. On the Advanced tab, select the Protect My Computer And Network By Limiting Or Preventing Access To This Computer From The Internet check box, and then click Settings.

4. On the Services tab of the Advanced Settings dialog box, select the services that you want to pass through the firewall. This dialog box is shown in Figure 11-3. You can add services and specify ports by clicking Add.

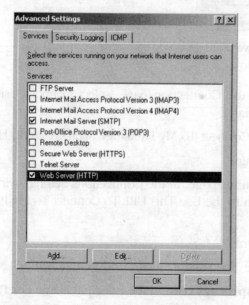

Figure 11-3   Configuring the ICF Advanced Settings

5. Click OK.

6. Click OK to close the Local Area Connection Properties box.

Lesson Review

The following questions are intended to reinforce key information presented in this lesson. If you are unable to answer a question, review the lesson materials and then try the question again. You can find answers to the questions in the "Questions and Answers" section at the end of this chapter.

1. What is the advantage of using RPC over HTTP to allow a MAPI client such as Outlook to connect to Exchange through a firewall?

_____

_____

2. What TCP ports do you need to open on a firewall to allow HTTP, SMTP, and HTTP over SSL traffic? (Select all that apply.)

    a. Port 21

    b. Port 25

    c. Port 80

    d. Port 110

    e. Port 119

    f. Port 143

    g. Port 443

    h. Port 563

Lesson Summary

- A firewall protects your network by blocking traffic through unwanted TCP ports and by filtering traffic through permitted ports.

- Exchange back-end servers require strong firewall protection. Exchange front-end servers can be in the DMZ.

- A MAPI client such as Outlook can use RPC over HTTP to communicate with Exchange through a firewall.

Lesson 2: Protecting Against Computer Viruses

In this lesson, you will learn about viruses, worms, and Trojan horses, investigate what they do, and look at methods of protecting against them. Although worms and Trojan horses are not viruses, technical literature often categorizes all three types of threat as virus attacks, and this lesson takes the same approach.

A key to combating viruses is to understand the processes by which they spread in an Exchange organization. You can then take sensible precautions.

Real World   Taking Precautions

The key phrase here is "sensible precautions." There is no such thing as perfect security, and security always needs to be balanced against usability. You must always be aware of fresh threats, and your organization should present as small a target as possible to an attacker. It must also be a moving target; what is secure today is not secure tomorrow. Security is not just a case of purchasing a good firewall and reputable antivirus software and then forgetting about it.

After this lesson, you will be able to

- Explain what computer viruses are
- Distinguish between viruses, worms, and Trojan horses
- Describe how viruses are spread
- Prepare an antivirus strategy
- Choose antivirus software
- Explain what virus-clean policies and procedures are and create such policies and procedures
- Explain why security updates are necessary and locate and download such updates

Estimated lesson time: 45 minutes

Viruses, Worms, and Trojan Horses

A computer *virus* is a piece of executable code that can attach itself to files or programs. The virus then replicates and spreads its infected files over the network, from one computer to another. A virus requires a *host* program to work—that is, the virus must be run before it can replicate and infect other computers.

Viruses often deliver a *payload*. This is an action that a virus carries out in addition to replication. While some viruses simply replicate, tying up resources but causing very little damage otherwise, the more unpleasant strains can drop payloads that can corrupt software or data. Even if a virus does not deliver a payload, replication can cause problems by consuming storage space, memory, and bandwidth, and degrading the performance of the infected computer and the network to which the computer is attached.

A *worm* is a program that can replicate itself in the same way as a virus. However, a worm does not require a host program and can replicate itself automatically whenever an application or the operating system transfers or copies files.

A *Trojan horse* is a program that pretends to be one thing (usually something benign, such as a computer game or a utility) but does damage when it is run. A Trojan horse cannot replicate itself. It relies on users to spread the program through e-mail.

Virus Transmission

Viruses are typically transmitted in e-mail attachments or in programs downloaded from the Internet. A user activates the virus by opening the e-mail message or by starting the program. The virus then loads itself into a legitimate program's memory space and searches for other programs. If the virus finds another suitable program, it modifies that program by adding its virus code. The next time the program is run, it infects other programs, and the virus spreads. If a virus infects a messaging system, it spreads quickly because e-mail clients send messages to other clients and also provide access to software such as address book programs.

A virus can infect secure resources, such as files, applications, and operating system source files. Therefore, you should always install and configure new computers while they are disconnected from an external network. Before you reconnect to the network, you can apply software upgrades, and then install antivirus software and run a manual scan of the software by using the latest signature files.

Preparing an Antivirus Strategy

You need to prepare an antivirus strategy to protect your messaging system. This strategy should include educating users about viruses, installing antivirus software in the appropriate locations, and ensuring that the antivirus software is current.

You educate users by making them aware of current virus threats and the importance of keeping their computer systems up to date with the latest signature files and security updates. If users are aware of viruses, they may be able to help stop the spread of a virus that is attacking the system. For example, users should know not to open attachments that they receive from any application (including e-mail clients and instant messaging applications) unless they know the sender and they are expecting the attachment.

Important   Many users believe it is sufficient to install antivirus software and to regularly update virus signatures. It is not. Users also need to download and install operating system updates that include security patches to fix known *holes*, or security weaknesses. You need to make users aware of this, and whenever possible, encourage them to take advantage of the various auto-patching functionalities made available by Microsoft, such as Windows updates.

You can use a variety of methods to alert users of an e-mail virus threat, including e-mail messages explaining what attachments not to open and information about current virus threats, known viruses, and how to combat them.

Blocking Downloads

Your advice on this topic needs to be reasonable and sensible. You cannot advocate blocking the download of all attachments if, for example, you work for a publishing company that frequently receives work from authors by this method. You should instead inform users (and management) about known exploitable file types, such as .bat, .com, .scr, .vbs, and embedded Hypertext Markup Language (HTML) scripts. Some organizations prohibit the download of any executable code from the Internet. These organizations can still be attacked but will not have downloaded up-to-date virus signature files or security updates.

Installing Antivirus Software

Your antivirus strategy should include plans for installing antivirus software. This can be installed on client computers, servers, and firewalls.

Client-Side Antivirus Software   Viruses are activated when users open infected attachments. Therefore, you should install client-side antivirus software on all the clients that connect to your network, including remote clients. Client-side antivirus software installs file system filters that check files for the signatures of known viruses as these files are written to disk. Some antivirus software searches e-mail attachments for virus code on the e-mail client. If a virus is detected, then the software deletes the attachment or copies the attachment to the local hard disk and disinfects the file.

Note   This system is not perfect. Sometimes useful and required attachments are detected as viruses. If you send zipped files as self-extracting executable (.exe) packages, some filters may block them.

Server-Side Antivirus Software   Server-side antivirus software scans mailbox and public folder stores, and some server-side antivirus software can also scan transports and eliminate any virus that it finds before that virus enters your network.

Antivirus software that you install on an Exchange Server 2003 server must be developed specifically for Exchange, because Exchange has a large database and the antivirus software must differentiate between the signature of a known virus and a random string of bytes that matches a virus signature.

You should install server-side antivirus software on every Exchange server in your organization. This helps to prevent viruses from spreading to users who are not using client-side antivirus software.

Firewall Antivirus Software   A firewall protects your network from unauthorized access and can also provide virus protection. Antivirus software on a firewall scans files as they enter the firewall and filters out the viruses before they reach your network. It also destroys any viruses exiting from your network. This last is an important consideration. Security systems need to protect against the malicious or careless insider as much as against external attack.

Typically, firewall antivirus software enables you to specify how viruses are processed. You can configure firewall antivirus software to remove an attachment, to send e-mail to an administrator, or to hold the suspect message in a queue for later review.

Keeping Your Protection Current

New computer viruses, or new strains of old viruses, constantly appear. You need to ensure that your antivirus software is up to date and that you have downloaded signature files for the latest viruses. You must configure every component in your organization in which virus protection is implemented to receive updates automatically. Automatic updates do not require administrator or user intervention and are particularly important on client computers because users often do not regularly update their software or definitions.

> **Caution**   Virus protection updates can introduce new code. If you configure systems for automatic updates, then you do not have a chance to test the code in your environment and therefore cannot tell in advance if the new code causes problems with your software. This is not a reason for failing to implement automatic updates, but it is something you should be aware of.

Choosing Antivirus Software

Microsoft does not currently distribute an antivirus package, and you need to choose software from a third-party vendor. You need to take a number of factors into account when you choose antivirus software, including the following:

- Does the software integrate with Exchange Server 2003 and with other services in your environment?

- Does the software significantly degrade Exchange Server performance?

- Does the vendor support the software for use with Exchange Server?

- Does the software guard against viruses, worms, Trojan horses, and other malicious code?

- Does the software support automated deployment of client-based software?

- Do mechanisms exist for monitoring clients from a single, central location?

- Does the software provide the same level of security for remote systems as it does for locally connected computers?

- Does the software scan both inbound and outbound e-mail?

- Does the software support automated updates?

- How often does the vendor release product updates—especially in the event of a virus attack—and does the vendor guarantee that the product will be updated to detect new viruses as required?

- Does the software provide virus scanning at the Exchange Server client, the Exchange Server IS, Exchange Server transport, and firewall level?

- Is the vendor TruSecure International Customer Service Association (ICSA) Lab or CheckMark certified?

Tip To obtain more information about security software vendor specifications, access *http://trusecure.com*, *http://www.icsa.com*, and *http://www.check-mark.com*.

Virus-Clean Policies and Procedures

Virus attacks can still occur, even after you have prepared an antivirus policy and installed antivirus software. Your security strategy should include virus-clean policies and procedures that will help to prevent such attacks. You also need to plan what to do when a virus does attack your system.

These policies and procedures should be in position before a virus attack occurs. They should help you to:

- Understand the extent and source of an attack
- Protect sensitive data
- Protect systems and networks
- Recover infected systems
- Enable your organization to continue operating
- Collect information about the attack
- Prevent further damage
- Support legal investigations

Real World   Virus-Clean Policies

The list of policies and procedures in the main text gives a number of good reasons for implementing virus-clean policies. In the real world, their major advantage is that you have a policy in place that you can follow in a difficult situation. The stress, and sometimes panic, that occurs when your organization is under serious attack is not conducive to cool and coherent strategy planning.

If a virus attack occurs that could cause extensive damage, then your planned procedures should enable you to isolate the affected systems by taking them offline. If your antivirus software does not then completely remove the virus from the affected system, you must restore the system to its original state by using backup data that has not been compromised. You may also need to reinstall the operating system and all of the applications by using source disks.

Tip   If a virus-infected e-mail message spreads to a user mailbox, you may be able to remove the virus from the mailbox by using the Exmerge.exe tool. Exmerge.exe usually exists in the C:\Program Files\Exchsrvr\bin subdirectory. If not, it can be downloaded from *http:// www.microsoft.com/exchange/2003/updates*. For more information on this utility, search the *http://support.microsoft.com* site for article Q265441.

When you restore a system, you must ensure that it is functioning normally by using *historical baselines*. Historical baselines allow you to compare the current performance for items such as message delivery rates to those of your system before the system was restored. You must also monitor your system for repeat virus outbreaks.

Spam Masquerading as an Administrator Alert

A recent method of attack that bypasses most firewalls and filters that block unsolicited advertisements (otherwise known as *spam*) makes use of the Messenger service on User Datagram Protocol (UDP) port 135. This service is used by administrators to send messages to users and should not be confused with Microsoft's MSN chat client that is installed on Microsoft Windows 2000, Windows NT, and Windows XP clients. To date, some companies have this advertising method, known as *NetBIOS spam*, to market firewall and virus protection software. Neither the companies nor their products appear on any recommended lists issued by reputable software suppliers such as Microsoft. However, a method that sends spam today could be used to send worms tomorrow. Unless the Messenger service is required (and it seldom is on client computers that access the Internet), it should be disabled.

Security Updates

Security updates are product updates that eliminate known security vulnerabilities. When a security update becomes available, you should immediately evaluate your system to determine if the update is relevant to your current situation. Suppliers release security updates for client software such as Web browsers, for client operating systems, and for server software and operating systems such as Windows Server 2003 and Exchange Server 2003. If the Windows operating system is vulnerable, then Exchange is also vulnerable.

You can download security updates from software companies' Web sites. You can find Exchange updates at *http://www.microsoft.com/exchange/downloads* and *http://support.microsoft.com*. Depending on the configuration of your operating system, you may automatically be prompted to download Windows updates. You can access the Windows update site by clicking Start and then Windows Update.

You can also access bulletins and utilities to keep you informed about the latest security issues and fixes. Table 11-2 gives details of the available bulletin services.

Table 11-2   Bulletin Services

Service	Location
Microsoft Security Notification Service	http://www.microsoft.com/technet/security/bulletin/notify.asp
Microsoft Security Web site	*http://www.microsoft.com/security*
Microsoft Windows Update	*http://v4.windowsupdate.microsoft.com/en/default.asp*

Table 11-3 lists the utilities that can assist in keeping your system secure.

Table 11-3   Security Utilities

Utility	Function	Download location
Microsoft Baseline Security Analyzer (MBSA)	Checks for missing patches, blank or weak passwords, and vulnerabilities on servers running Windows 2000 or later, Microsoft Internet Information Services (IIS), Microsoft SQL Server, and Microsoft Internet Explorer 5.01 or later.	*http://www.microsoft.com/technet*
Microsoft Software Update Services (SUS)	Helps keep Windows-based computers and servers up to date with the latest critical updates.	*http://www.microsoft.com/windows2000/ windowsupdate/sus/default.asp*
Microsoft Systems Management Server (SMS)	Automates the distribution and installation of the recommended security fixes for large companies with multiple locations.	*http://www.microsoft.com/catalog*

Virus Signatures

You need to keep your software and operating system up to date. If you install third-party virus detection software, this must also be kept up to date. However, the task that needs to be done most often is to download virus signatures (or definitions) for the new threats that appear regularly on the Internet. Virus signatures identify viruses, worms, and Trojan horses, and allow virus detection software to detect and eliminate them.

Your virus protection is only as good as your signature list, and this too must be kept up to date. Virus signatures should be downloaded regularly. If a new and serious attack occurs, the virus signature needs to be downloaded as soon as it is available. When you purchase antivirus software, you may also need to purchase a subscription to a professional virus signature update service. Check with your vendor to determine their policies and procedures.

> **Caution**   A virus attack can re-occur some time after you believe the virus was eradicated. A user returning from a vacation or leave of absence can open the attachment to an old e-mail message and re-introduce the problem.

Practice: Downloading Antivirus Software

You can usually download evaluation antivirus software from the Internet before you decide on a purchase. You first need to check that the software supports Exchange. Microsoft publishes a list of approved antivirus software suppliers, as this practice illustrates.

Exercise 1: Download Antivirus Software

To download antivirus software, perform the following steps:

1. Access *http://www.microsoft.com/exchange/partners/antivirus.asp*.

2. Read the disclaimer. Microsoft makes no warranties or representations with regard to these products or services.

3. Select a supplier (for example, Symantec) and click the hyperlink.

4. Access the fact sheet and any other resource that assists you in evaluating the product's suitability.

5. Access the evaluation software (typically called Trialware).

6. Follow the prompts and complete the necessary forms. Download the evaluation software installation packet to a shared folder on a server and install it on all computers on your trial network.

7. Obtain details of cost and service contracts. Check out the frequency of virus definition downloads. Apply the criteria listed under "Choosing Antivirus Software" in this lesson.

8. Repeat the process for other listed suppliers.

Lesson Review

The following questions are intended to reinforce key information presented in this lesson. If you are unable to answer a question, review the lesson materials and then try the question again. You can find answers to the questions in the "Questions and Answers" section at the end of this chapter.

1. What is the difference between a virus and a worm?

   _____

   _____

2. How does a Trojan horse spread?

_____

_____

3. Which Microsoft utility checks for missing patches, blank or weak passwords, and operating system vulnerabilities?

   a. SMS

   b. SUS

   c. MBSA

   d. Security Notification Service

Lesson Summary

- Viruses, worms, and Trojan horses can attack your e-mail system through the Internet.

- You need to keep your operating systems, applications, antivirus software, and virus signature files up to date.

- Antivirus software can run on a client, a server, and a firewall.

- Virus-clean policies need to be in place before a virus attack occurs.

Lesson 3: Securing Mailboxes

Securing mailboxes is a critical task because user mailboxes, mailbox features, and mailbox content are often one of the greatest security risks within any company.

After this lesson, you will be able to

- List and evaluate the guidelines for securing mailboxes
- Explain how message filtering can be used to reduce junk e-mail
- Configure the junk e-mail feature in Outlook
- Explain recipient and sender filtering
- Apply and configure recipient and sender filtering

Estimated lesson time: 45 minutes

Message Filtering

Unsolicited commercial e-mail, or junk e-mail, wastes users' time, uses memory resources, and consumes network bandwidth. Although you probably cannot entirely eliminate junk e-mail, you can use *message filtering* to reduce the amount that your users receive. The purpose of message filtering is to eliminate junk e-mail without restricting legitimate e-mail.

> **Note**   Junk e-mail is sometimes known as spam. Technically, spam is any type of unsolicited advertisement. Spam can appear as e-mail, as pop-up boxes on Web sites, and even as surface mail. Junk e-mail is spam, but not all spam is junk e-mail.

Message filtering examines e-mail headers and message bodies and matches them against established junk e-mail rules. Outlook 2003 and Outlook Web Access (OWA) include a set of built-in message filters, collectively referred to as the Junk E-Mail feature, to identify unsolicited commercial e-mail. The Junk E-Mail feature enables users to configure Trusted Senders, Trusted Recipients, and Junk Senders lists. If, for example, a sender is listed on the Junk Senders list, the message is moved into the Junk E-Mail folder or deleted. In Outlook 2003, the Junk E-Mail feature is enabled by default, and Microsoft provides updates for the built-in message filters. Outlook and OWA also enable you to block external content, such as malicious code, in HTML messages.

Exchange Server 2003 filtering examines e-mail headers and checks them against established filter rules. To use the Exchange filtering features, you must first configure the properties of the global Message Delivery object to create global filters. Then you need to configure SMTP virtual servers to use these global filters.

Block Lists

A block list is a list of domain names and Internet Protocol (IP) addresses that are known junk e-mail sources. You can develop a block list for your company by routinely updating your Global Accept and Deny List configuration, or you can subscribe to a Realtime Blackhole List or Relay Blocking List (RBL) maintained by a third-party company, such as Mail Abuse Prevention System (MAPS).

 See Also For more information about MAPS, see *http://www.mail-abuse.org*.

Block lists cannot completely prevent unsolicited e-mail because senders use a variety of tactics, such as spoofing (or forging) subject headers or using third-party servers to send the mail. Block lists can also block legitimate e-mail because some domains may be incorrectly listed in the block list, possibly because junk e-mail senders use them as relays, as discussed in Chapter 10, "SMTP Protocol Configuration and Management."

Connection Filtering

Connection filtering enables you to check the IP address of the connecting SMTP server against an RBL. If a match is found, Exchange Server 2003 rejects every intended message recipient except for any defined as an exception. Exchange Server 2003 connection filtering also enables you to configure multiple connection filter rules and specify the order in which they are applied. Creating multiple rules permits you to use the same IP address with different sets of rules—for example, when you subscribe to two different RBL providers. You can also configure exceptions to allow e-mail messages to be delivered to specific recipients, or from a specific sender, regardless of block list entries.

When you configure connection filtering, you establish a rule that SMTP uses to perform a DNS lookup on an RBL. When an e-mail message is sent to your organization, Exchange contacts the RBL provider. The provider then checks for the existence of a host record in DNS and issues one of two responses:

- **127.0.0.X status code** This indicates that the IP address was found on the block list, and it also lists the type of offense, such as known source of unsolicited e-mail or known relay server.

- **Host not found** This indicates that the IP address was not found on the block list.

Evaluating E-Mail

If Outlook receives an unauthenticated e-mail message from an external source, it evaluates the source IP address against the Accept and Deny lists and rejects the message if a match is found on the Deny list. If the IP address is not on the Accept or Deny list, Outlook evaluates the message against an RBL. If a match is found on the RBL, then Outlook stops the message at the protocol level.

Otherwise, Outlook evaluates messages against any third-party, anti-junk e-mail products or plug-ins configured at the transport layer. The third-party product analyzes the message and assigns it a *Spam Confidence Level (SCL)* value that indicates the degree to which the message can be considered unsolicited commercial e-mail. The SCL value is from 1 through 10—the lower the value, the higher the probability that the message is junk mail.

Outlook moves the e-mail message into the information store and, based on the SCL value and Outlook's user settings, it either delivers the message to a folder or deletes it. If you set Outlook's filter to Low, it sends any message ranked below 4 to the Junk E-Mail folder. If you set the filter to High, Outlook sends any message ranked below 7 to the Junk E-Mail folder.

Guidelines for Securing Mailboxes

When developing a strategy for securing Exchange Server 2003 mailboxes, you should consider the following guidelines:

- **Prevent users outside your Exchange organization from receiving out-of-office e-mail messages**   You can configure the default SMTP policy, or create SMTP policies on a domain-by-domain basis, that do not reply to out-of-office messages or forward such messages to the Internet.

- **Prevent users from receiving e-mail from unidentified domains or from predetermined domains**   You can configure virtual servers to deny messages from unidentified domains or from any domain that you select.

- **Limit access to e-mail content by digitally signing and encrypting e-mail messages**   You can ensure that only the intended recipient views the message content by using digital signatures and encryption.

- **Prohibit unauthorized users from using distribution lists**   You can configure distribution lists to accept e-mail from authenticated users only.

- **Filter unsolicited e-mail**   You can create a message filter and then apply that filter to each applicable virtual server. You can filter a message by sender, recipient, or domain.

- **Prevent junk e-mail**   You can search incoming and outgoing e-mail for specific words, phrases, and senders. You can configure OWA and Outlook 2003 to determine how junk e-mail should be handled.

Recipient and Sender Filtering

You can block unwanted e-mail based on IP addresses, sender e-mail address, recipient e-mail addresses, or e-mail domain. You block e-mail by configuring Accept and Deny lists, which can be configured through the global Message Delivery object and then applied to individual virtual servers.

Recipient Filtering   You can use recipient filtering to reduce junk e-mail. You can filter e-mail that is addressed to users who are not found in Active Directory or to whom the sender does not have permissions to send e-mail. Exchange Server 2003 rejects any incoming e-mail that matches the defined criteria at the protocol level and returns a 550 error. You can also use recipient filtering to filter messages that are sent to well-defined recipients, such as *root@domain* and *inet@domain*. This practice is indicative of unsolicited commercial e-mail.

> **Note**   Recipient filtering rules apply only to anonymous connections. Authenticated users and other Exchange servers bypass these rules.

Sender filtering   Sender filtering reduces junk e-mail by enabling you to create filters based on the sender of the message. You can, for example, filter messages that are sent by specific users or messages that are sent without sender addresses. You can archive filtered messages, or you can drop the connection if the sender's address matches the filter criterion.

Practice: Configuring the Junk E-Mail Feature in Outlook 2003 and Enabling Connection Filtering

In this practice, you configure the level of junk e-mail protection that you require in Outlook 2003 and enable and configure connection filtering on your front-end server.

Exercise 1: Configure the Junk E-Mail Feature in Outlook 2003

To configure the Junk E-Mail feature in Outlook 2003, perform the following steps:

1. Start Outlook.
2. On the Tools menu, click Options.

3. On the Preferences tab, click Junk E-Mail.

4. Configure the required level of protection (No Protection, Low, High, or Safe Lists Only).

5. If you want to delete junk e-mail instead of moving it to a folder, you can select the relevant check box.

6. Add entries to the Trusted Senders, Trusted Recipients, and Junk Senders lists by selecting the relevant tabs. You can also import lists from, and export them to, a text file.

7. Click OK.

Exercise 2: Enable Connection Filtering

In this exercise, you configure Exchange Server 2003 to enable connection filtering on Server02 and then block mail from a malicious user and a junk mail sender. Note that fictitious names are used for the block list provider, the malicious user, and the junk mail sender.

To enable connection filtering, perform the following steps:

1. Open Exchange System Manager and click Global Settings.

2. In the details pane, right-click Message Delivery, and then click Properties.

3. Select the Connection Filtering tab.

4. Click Add.

5. In the Connection Filtering Rule dialog box, in the Display Name box, type **Blocklist Provider**. In the DNS Suffix Of Provider box, type **contosoblocklists .com**, and then click OK.

6. Click OK to close the Message Delivery Properties dialog box.

7. Read the message in the Exchange System Manager dialog box, and then click OK.

8. In Exchange System Manager, navigate to Administrative Groups\First Administrative Group\Servers\Server02\Protocols\SMTP.

9. Right-click Default SMTP Virtual Server, and then click Properties.

10. Click Advanced on the General tab of the Default SMTP Virtual Server Properties dialog box.

11. In the Advanced dialog box, click Edit.

12. In the Identification dialog box, select the Apply Connection Filter check box as shown in Figure 11-4, and then click OK.

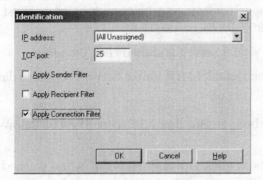

Figure 11-4 Setting connection filtering

13. In the Advanced dialog box, verify that Filter Enabled is set to Yes, and then click OK.

14. Click OK to close the Default SMTP Virtual Server Properties dialog box.

Exercise 3: Block an E-Mail Address and a Domain

To block a specific e-mail address and the domain of a known junk mail sender, perform the following steps:

1. Open Exchange System Manager.

2. In the console tree, click Global Settings.

3. In the details pane, right-click Message Delivery, and then click Properties.

4. Access the Sender Filtering tab in the Message Delivery Properties dialog box.

5. Click Add.

6. In the Add Sender dialog box, type **donhall@nwtraders.com**, as shown in Figure 11-5, and then click OK.

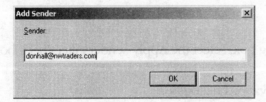

Figure 11-5 Blocking e-mail from a specific user

7. In the Message Delivery Properties dialog box, ensure that the Drop Connection If Address Matches Filter check box is selected, and then click OK.

8. In the Warning dialog box, click OK to acknowledge that this filter must be enabled on the virtual server.

9. In Exchange System Manager, navigate to Administrative Groups\First Administrative Group\Servers\Server02\Protocols\SMTP.

10. Right-click Default SMTP Virtual Server, and then click Properties.

11. Select the Access tab in the Default SMTP Virtual Server Properties dialog box.

12. Click Connection.

13. In the Connection dialog box, ensure that All Except The List Below is selected, and then click Add.

14. In the Computer dialog box, click Domain, click OK when warned that this is a resource intensive configuration, type **treyresearch.com,** as shown in Figure 11-6, and then click OK.

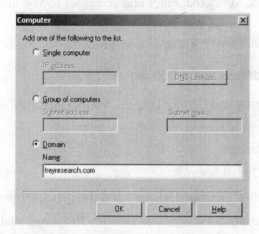

Figure 11-6   Blocking e-mail from a domain

15. In the Connection dialog box, click OK.

16. Select the General tab in the Default SMTP Virtual Server Properties dialog box, and then click Advanced.

17. Click Edit.

18. In the Identification dialog box, select the Apply Sender Filter check box, and then click OK.

19. Click OK to close the Advanced dialog box.

20. Click OK to close the Default SMTP Virtual Server Properties dialog box.

Lesson Review

The following questions are intended to reinforce key information presented in this lesson. If you are unable to answer a question, review the lesson materials and then try the question again. You can find answers to the questions in the "Questions and Answers" section at the end of this chapter.

1. How does Exchange Server 2003 filtering work, and what do you need to configure in order to use it?

_____

_____

2. An e-mail message has an SCL value of 3. Which of the following statements is true?

  a. The sender was found on the Deny list.

  b. The sender was found on the Accept list.

  c. The message probably is not junk e-mail.

  d. The message probably is junk e-mail.

Lesson Summary

- Outlook 2003, OWA, and Exchange Server 2003 can filter junk e-mail.
- E-mail can be accepted or rejected based on the address of a single sender or on a domain name.
- E-mail from an external source can be rejected based on the recipient address.
- A Realtime Blackhole List or Relay Blocking List (RBL) provides a third-party solution to the junk e-mail problem.

Lesson 4: Implementing Digital Signature and Encryption Capabilities

This lesson describes digital signatures and encryption and then explains how these capabilities enhance Exchange Server 2003 security. The lesson explains how public key infrastructure (PKI) is used to send digitally signed and encrypted e-mail messages. It also describes PKI components. Finally, the lesson describes how the enrollment process enables digital signature and encryption capabilities.

After this lesson, you will be able to

- Explain what digital signature and encryption capabilities are
- Explain what a PKI is
- Describe the PKI components that enable digital signature and encryption capabilities
- Describe how the enrollment process enables digital signature and encryption capabilities
- Describe the process of creating and deploying digital signature and encryption certificates
- Configure Outlook digital signature and encryption capabilities

Estimated lesson time: 30 minutes

Digital Signature and Encryption

Digital signature and encryption enable you to secure your messaging system by protecting e-mail messages from modification and inspection by malicious third parties as they are transmitted from the sender to the receiver.

A *digital signature* is a code attached to an e-mail message that ensures that the individual who is sending the message is really who he or she claims to be. The code is linked to the message content so that any modification of the content of the message during transit will result in an invalid signature.

You can protect e-mail messages against inspection by using *encryption*. Encryption is a cryptographic technique that translates the contents of an e-mail message into an unreadable format. There are many different types of encryption. Exchange implements *public key encryption*, which uses a public key that is known to everyone and a private key that is known only to the recipient of the message.

For example, when Don Hall wants to send a secure message to Kim Akers, Don uses Kim's public key to encrypt the message. Kim then uses her private key, known only by her, to decrypt Don's message. If a public key is used to encrypt messages, only the corresponding private key can be used to decrypt those messages. It is almost impossible to deduce a private key, even if you know the public key.

Real World   Private Keys

The function of real-world security is to make it very difficult for an attacker to breach the system. Remember that there is no known limit to human ingenuity and no system is perfect. Remember also that a private key is effective only if no third party knows it. The longer a private key exists, the more likely it is to be cracked.

Exchange Server 2003 and Outlook 2003 implement digital signature and encryption capabilities by using Secure Multi-Purpose Internet Mail Extensions (S/MIME), which is the version of the MIME protocol that supports encryption.

Public Key Infrastructure

A PKI is a policy that is used to establish a secure method for exchanging information. It is also an integrated set of services and administrative tools for creating, deploying, and managing public key–based applications. It includes cryptographic methods and a system for managing the process that enables you to identify users and securely exchange data.

PKI signature and encryption capabilities enable you to strengthen the security of your Exchange Server 2003 organization by protecting e-mail from being read by anyone other than the intended recipient or from being altered by anyone other than the sender while the message is in transit, or while the message is stored either on the client in a .pst file or on the Exchange server in the mailbox store.

A PKI includes components that enable digital signature and encryption capabilities. A PKI contains the components listed in Table 11-4.

Table 11-4   PKI Components

PKI component	Description
Digital certificate	Authenticates users and computers.
Certificate template	Defines the content and purpose of a certificate. Typically one certificate template is created for digital signatures and another is created for encryption. However, a single certificate template can be created for both purposes.
Certificate revocation list (CRL)	Lists the certificates that are revoked by a CA before the certificates reach their scheduled expiration date.
Certificate authority (CA)	Issues certificates to users, computers, and services, and then manages these certificates.

Table 11-4   PKI Components

PKI component	Description
Certificate publication points and CRL distribution points	Provide locations where certificates and CRLs are made publicly available. Certificates and CRLs can be made available through a directory service, such as X.500, LDAP, or through directories that are specific to the operating system and Web servers.
Certificate and CA management tools	Manage issued certificates, publish CA certificates and CRLs, configure CAs, import and export certificates and keys, and recover archived private keys.
Applications and services that are enabled by public keys	Use certificates for e-commerce and secure network access by using digital signature and encryption capabilities.
Certificate servers	Enable you to create, issue, and manage certificates by using Microsoft Certificate Services. Using Certificate Services on Windows Server 2003 with Exchange Server 2003 integrates all of the certificate functionality into a single service, rather than relying on multiple services, such as Microsoft Key Management Service (KMS), which was required in previous versions of Exchange. The benefits of certificate servers include the following: ■ Issuing certificates from a single, archived location. ■ Maintaining a copy of all the private keys on the server, thus allowing users to retrieve their private key information if they are unable to access the information locally. ■ Enabling automatic certificate deployment to users with valid credentials. ■ Importing archived private keys and certificates into a CA.

Tip   When a PKI is checking the validity of a certificate, one of the first things it does is to check it against a CRL. If no CRL exists, an error may be returned. Therefore, you may need to issue a certificate and then revoke it to create a CRL before a PKI will operate correctly.

Practice: Deploying Digital Signature and Encryption Certificates

Using a certificate for digital signatures or encryption requires that you deploy the certificate in Exchange Server 2003 by using auto-enrollment settings and that you verify the Outlook configuration. Before starting this practice, you need to obtain a certificate, if you have not already done so. To do this, open Internet Explorer, access *http:// Server01/Certsrv* and complete the wizard. If Server01 is not a CA, you need to obtain a certificate over the Internet from an external CA, such as VeriSign.

Exercise 1: Implement Digital Signature and Encryption Capabilities on Exchange Server 2003

To configure Exchange Server 2003 to allow users to digitally sign and encrypt messages, perform the following steps:

1. Open the Certification Authority console on Server01.

2. Expand Tailspintoys.

3. Right-click Certificate Templates, point to New, and then click Certificate Template To Issue.

4. In the Enable Certificate Templates dialog box, click Exchange User, and then click OK.

5. In the Certification Authority console, right-click Certificate Templates, and then click Manage.

6. Right-click Exchange User in the details pane of the Certificate Templates console, and then click Properties.

7. Select the Security tab in the Exchange User Properties dialog box.

8. Click Authenticated Users in the Group Or User Names box.

9. In the Permissions For Authenticated Users box, select the Allow check box for the Enroll permission, as shown in Figure 11-7, and then click OK.

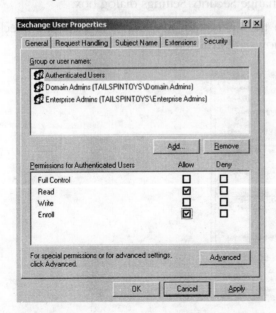

Figure 11-7   Allowing Authenticated Users Enroll permission so they can digitally sign and encrypt e-mail

10. Close the Certificate Templates management list and the Certification Authority console.

Exercise 2: Configure Digital Signature and Encryption Capabilities on Outlook 2003

After you deploy the digital signing and encryption certificates, you can then configure Outlook to use the certificates to enable digital signature and encryption capabilities. This would normally be done on a client workstation. On your test network, you can do it on Server01.

To configure digital signature and encryption capabilities on Outlook, perform the following steps:

1. Open Outlook on Server01.

2. On the Tools menu, click Options.

3. On the Security tab of the Options dialog box, click Settings.

4. Type a name for the e-mail digital certificate (for example, **mail-certificate**) in the Security Settings Name box, or accept the default.

5. In Certificates and Algorithms in the Signing Certificate pane, click Choose beside Signing Certificate, select a signing certificate, and then in the Hash Algorithm box, select an algorithm.

6. In Certificates and Algorithms in the Signing Certificate pane, click Choose beside Encryption Certificate, select an encryption certificate, and then in the Hash Algorithm box, select an algorithm.

7. Click OK to close the Change Security Settings dialog box.

8. On the Security tab, in the Encrypted box, select or clear the check boxes as required. Figure 11-8 shows the available options.

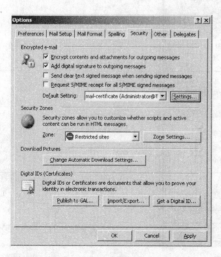

Figure 11-8   Encryption and signature options

9. Click OK to close the Options dialog box.

Tip   If the CA issues you a multipurpose certificate, you can designate the same certificate in both the Signing Certificate box and the Encryption Certificate box.

Lesson Review

The following questions are intended to reinforce key information presented in this lesson. If you are unable to answer a question, review the lesson materials and then try the question again. You can find answers to the questions in the "Questions and Answers" section at the end of this chapter.

1. Which PKI component defines the content and purpose of a certificate?

   a. Certificate template

   b. CA

   c. CRL

   d. Certificate publication point

2. Don Hall sends an encrypted message to Kim Akers. How does Don encrypt it, and how does Kim read it?

   _____

   _____

3. Kim Akers wants to send a message to Don Hall, but Don needs to be certain that the message really is from Kim. How can he verify this?

   _____

   _____

Lesson Summary

- Encryption ensures that only the person for whom a message is intended can read it.

- A digital signature proves the sender's identity and gives an assurance that the message has not been altered in transit.

- Encryption and digital signatures are implemented using private and public key pairs, which are issued as certificates. Exchange Server 2003 supports this process by using a PKI.

Lesson 5: Configuring Administrative Permissions

This lesson presents an overview of administrative groups and how to create them. The lesson then explains how to configure administrative permissions by using the Exchange Administration Delegation Wizard.

After this lesson, you will be able to

- Explain the function and purpose of administrative groups
- Explain where a new computer running Exchange Server is added
- Create an administrative group
- Grant Exchange Server administrative permissions by using the Exchange Administration Delegation Wizard
- Configure advanced security permissions

Estimated lesson time: 45 minutes

Administrative Groups

An administrative group is a collection of Exchange Server 2003 objects that are grouped together for the purpose of managing and delegating permissions. An administrative group can contain servers, routing groups, policies, and public folder hierarchies. If, for example, your organization has two administrators, and each one manages a group of Exchange Server 2003 servers, then you can create two administrative groups. You can then delegate permissions to each administrator.

You can create administrative groups to support the various administrative models (centralized, decentralized, or mixed). Note that an administrative group is not a group of administrators. Rather, it is a group of objects to administer. These objects include the following:

- System policy objects
- Routing group objects
- Public folder tree objects
- Server objects

Adding an Exchange Administrative Group

When you set up an Exchange Server 2003 organization, you automatically create the First Administrative Group container, and the Exchange Server 2003 server is added to this group. If you then add a new computer running Exchange Server 2003 to your Exchange organization, the computer is added to this administrative group.

If, however, you create additional administrative groups before adding further servers, then Setup prompts you to select the administrative group to which any additional server should be added. You use the Administrative Groups container to create an administrative group in a practice later in this lesson.

> **Note**   The Administrative Groups container is not displayed by default in Exchange Server 2003. To display this container, you need to open Exchange System Manager and enable Display Administrative Groups in the Organization object's Properties box. This was done in a practice in an earlier chapter and is usually one of the first tasks an Exchange Server 2003 administrator performs. It is therefore easy to forget that before you can create a new administrative group, you must first display this container.

The Exchange Administration Delegation Wizard

Exchange administrative permissions enable administrators to perform tasks in Exchange Server 2003. You use the Exchange Administration Delegation Wizard to select users or groups and grant them administrative permission to objects in your Exchange organization. This makes administration more secure because you can specify who can gain access to which Exchange objects.

You can start the Exchange Administration Delegation Wizard from the Organization object or from an administrative group object. If you start the wizard from the Organization object, then the permissions you assign propagate down the hierarchy to all the objects in the organization. If, on the other hand, you start the wizard from an administrative group object, then the permissions you assign propagate to all the objects in that administrative group. However, in the latter case, read-only permissions are also granted from the administrative group object, *up* the hierarchy. This enables an administrator to view the hierarchy. To use the Exchange Administration Delegation Wizard, you must have Exchange Full Administrator permissions at the organization level.

> **Tip**   The read-only permission does not appear in Exchange System Manager. You can view it by using the Adsiedit.exe utility.

Roles and Associated Permissions

The Exchange Administration Delegation Wizard supports the following roles:

- **Exchange Full Administrator**   Exchange Full Administrators can administer Exchange system information. They can add, delete, and rename objects, and modify permissions. You should delegate this role to administrators who need to configure and control access to your Exchange e-mail system.

- **Exchange Administrator** Exchange Administrators can fully administer Exchange system information but cannot modify permissions. You should delegate this role to users or groups who are responsible for day-to-day administration tasks such as adding, deleting, and renaming objects.

- **Exchange View Only Administrator** An Exchange View Only Administrator can view Exchange configuration information. You should delegate this role to administrators who do not need to modify Exchange objects.

> **Exam Tip** It is common (if somewhat sloppy) usage to refer to Exchange Full Administrators as Exchange administrators. If an exam question states that someone is an Exchange administrator, it will mean just that. The person will not have an Exchange Full Administrator role.

In addition to the roles supported by the Exchange Administration Delegation Wizard, other Windows Server 2003 group memberships are required to manage Exchange. If, for example, you want to assign write permission to an administrator for objects in an organization or administrative group, then that administrator must be a local administrator on each Exchange Server 2003 server that he or she needs to manage.

When you create an Exchange Server 2003 organization, the Exchange Domain Servers group and the Exchange Enterprise Servers group are created automatically. These two groups are assigned permissions that allow Exchange servers to gain access to Exchange configuration and recipient information in Active Directory. These are system groups for use by Exchange only, and you should not use them to give administrative privileges to users or groups.

Advanced Security Permissions

A child object in Exchange Server 2003 inherits permissions from its parent object by default. Advanced security permissions enable you to provide additional administrative control by enabling you to modify or prevent inherited permissions. When, for example, you create a new routing group, that group inherits the permissions from the administrative group in which it was created. If you want different permissions applied to the new routing group object, then you can access the object's Properties box and use the Advanced option on the Security tab to block permission inheritance.

You can also prevent inherited permissions from propagating to child objects by modifying the access control settings. You can specify, for each access control setting, whether the permissions should apply only to the object, or to the object and to its child objects.

If you remove inherited permissions and specify that permissions must be applied to the parent object only, the child objects are left with no permissions (an implicit Deny permission). Removing permissions prevents access to Exchange objects in Exchange System Manager. However, you can restore the permissions by using the Adsiedit.exe utility.

The Adsiedit.exe Utility

You can use the Active Directory Services Interface (ADSI) Edit Microsoft Management Console (MMC) snap-in, otherwise known as the Adsiedit.exe utility, to grant advanced security permissions that cannot be granted by using Exchange System Manager or Active Directory Users And Computers. For example, the utility enables you to grant permissions on the Administrative Groups container that are propagated to the new child administrative groups.

Practice: Creating and Using an Administrative Group

In this practice, you create an additional administrative group and delegate control of that group to a user named Don Hall. An account for Don Hall should have been created in Chapter 9, "Virtual Servers." If this account does not exist, create it before you start.

Exercise 1: Create an Administrative Group

In this exercise, you create an administrative group. This group is required to complete subsequent exercises in this practice.

To create an administrative group, perform the following steps:

1. Open Exchange System Manager.
2. Right-click Administrative Groups, click New, and then click Administrative Group.
3. In the Properties dialog box, type **NewAdmin**, and then click OK.
4. In the console tree, expand Administrative Groups, right-click NewAdmin, click New, and then click System Policy Container.
5. Expand NewAdmin and verify that a System Policies container exists.
6. Right-click the System Policies container under NewAdmin, click New, and then select Mailbox Store Policy.
7. Enable all four Property pages in the New Policy dialog box, and then click OK.
8. Enter a name for the policy, for example, **NewMail**.
9. Configure the Properties box tabs as required. Figure 11-9 shows a possible, if rather strict, configuration of the Limits (Policy) tab.

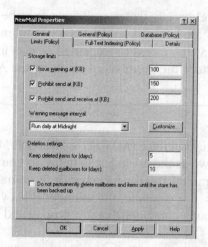

Figure 11-9   Configuring a limits policy

10. Click OK when you have configured the Mailbox policy.

11. Use the same technique to create a Public Store policy and a Server policy.

Tip This procedure created new policies from scratch. If policies already exist, for example in the First Administrative Group's System Policies container, you can paste them into the new System Policies container and edit them as required.

Exercise 2: Delegate Control of an Administrative Group

In this exercise, you delegate control of the NewAdmin administrative group to Don Hall. You grant Don the Exchange Administrator role, but not the Exchange Full Administrator role, for that administrative group. If the NewAdmin administrative group does not exist, then you need to create it by completing the previous exercise. You cannot delegate control if you have only one administrative group.

To delegate control of an administrative group, perform the following steps:

1. Open Exchange System Manager and expand Administrative Groups.

2. In the console tree, right-click NewAdmin, and then click Delegate Control.

3. The Exchange Administration Delegation Wizard opens. On the Welcome page, click Next.

4. On the Users Or Groups page, click Add.

5. In the Delegate Control dialog box, click Browse.

6. In the Select Users, Computers Or Groups dialog box, type **Don Hall**. Click Check Names to verify that Don Hall's account exists, as shown in Figure 11-10, and then click OK.

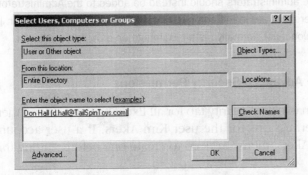

Figure 11-10   Delegating control to Don Hall

7. In the Delegate Control dialog box, in the Role box, click Exchange Administrator, and then click OK.

8. On the Users Or Groups page, click Next.

9. Click Finish.

10. In the Exchange System Manager dialog box, read the warning, and then click OK.

> **Exam Tip**   Remember this warning. An Exchange administrator must also be a member of the local machine administrator group on any Exchange Server 2003 server that he or she administers. Watch out for the omission of this step in procedures described in exam scenarios.

11. Open Active Directory Users And Computers on Server01.

12. Expand the domain name and click Users. In the details pane, right-click Don Hall, and then click Properties.

13. In the Don Hall Properties dialog box, click Member Of.

14. On the Member Of tab, click Add.

15. In the Select Groups dialog box, type **Administrators**. Click Check Names to confirm the group exists, and then click OK.

16. In the Don Hall Properties dialog box, click OK.

Note   Because of the restrictions of your two-computer test network, Don Hall has been added to the Administrators group on a domain controller. You would not do this on a production network. Exchange administrators should instead be added to the Administrators groups on the Exchange servers that are in the administration group that they administer. In a production network, you would not normally install Exchange on a domain controller.

Exercise 3: Configure Advanced Security Permissions

In this exercise, you enable the Security tab for all Exchange objects and then configure advanced security permissions for the user Kim Akers. If a user account does not already exist for Kim Akers, then you need to create one before starting this practice.

Note   The ADSI support tool is not installed by default. To complete this practice, you need to install the Windows Server 2003 support tools. The installation file is in Support/Tools on the Windows Server 2003 installation CD.

To configure advanced security permissions, perform the following steps:

1. On Server01, from the Start menu, click Run, type **regedit**, and then click OK.

2. Navigate to HKEY_CURRENT_USER\Software\Microsoft\Exchange.

3. Expand Exchange, right-click EXAdmin, click New, and then click DWORD Value.

4. Change New Value #1 to **ShowSecurityPage**, and then press Enter.

5. Double-click ShowSecurityPage. In the Edit DWORD Value dialog box, in the Value Data box, type **1**, as shown in Figure 11-11, and then click OK.

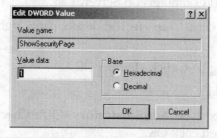

Figure 11-11   Creating the ShowSecurityPage registry entry

6. Close the Registry Editor.

7. From the Start menu, click Run, type **mmc**, and then click OK.

8. In the MMC console, click File, and then click Add/Remove Snap-In.

9. In the Add/Remove Snap-In dialog box, click Add.

10. In the Add Standalone Snap-In dialog box, click ADSI Edit, click Add, and then click Close.

11. In the Add/Remove Snap-In dialog box, click OK.

12. Right-click ADSI Edit, and then click Connect To.

13. In the Connection Settings dialog box, in the Select A Well Known Naming Context box, select Configuration, and then click OK.

14. Navigate to ADSI Edit\Configuration\CN=Configuration,DC=Tailspintoys,DC=com\CN=Services\CN=Microsoft Exchange\CN=Tailspintoys. Right-click CN=Administrative Groups, and then click Properties.

15. On the Security tab, click Add.

16. In the Select Users, Computers, Or Groups dialog box, type **Kim Akers** and then click OK.

17. In the CN=Administrative Groups Properties dialog box, click Advanced.

18. In the Advanced Security Settings For Administrative Groups dialog box, in the Permission Entries list, click the entry for Kim Akers, and then click Edit.

19. In the Permission Entry For Administrative Groups dialog box, in the Apply Onto drop-down list, click This Object And All Child Objects. The dialog box is shown in Figure 11-12. Click OK.

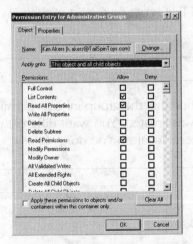

Figure 11-12   Granting Kim Akers permissions on all administrative groups

20. In the Advanced Security Settings For Administrative Groups dialog box, clear the Allow Inheritable Permissions From The Parent To Propagate To This Object And All Child Objects. Include These With All Entries Explicitly Defined Here check box, and then click OK.

21. In the CN=Administrative Groups Properties dialog box, click OK.

22. To verify that permissions are configured correctly, right-click any administrative group in Exchange System Manager, select Properties, and access the Security tab. Verify that Kim Akers has permissions on the administrative group.

Lesson Review

The following questions are intended to reinforce key information presented in this lesson. If you are unable to answer a question, review the lesson materials and then try the question again. You can find answers to the questions in the "Questions and Answers" section at the end of this chapter.

1. You use Exchange System Manager to delegate control of an administration group to Don Hall. The administration group contains three Exchange Server 2003 servers called Server A, Server B, and Server C. You give Don the Exchange Administrator role. Don reports that he is unable to carry out any administration on the servers. What do you need to do?

   _____

   _____

2. You want to grant advanced permissions on an administration group. You make the necessary registry changes, then try to add the ASDI edit snap-in to the Microsoft Management Console. ASDI Edit is not on the list of snap-ins. What have you forgotten to do?

   _____

   _____

3. You create a new routing group and find that the group inherits permissions from the administrative group in which it was created. You want different permissions applied to the new routing group object. What do you do?

   _____

   _____

Lesson Summary

- An administrative group is a group of Exchange objects that can be administered. You can delegate various levels of administrative control over an administrative group to users and security groups.

- If you delegate administrator roles to users and groups to enable them to manage the servers in an administration group, you also need to grant local administrator rights on the servers to these users and groups.

- Objects in an administrative group inherit their property settings from objects higher up in the hierarchy. You can block properties inheritance.

- You can use the Asdiedit.exe support tool to configure advanced administrative settings.

Lesson 6: Disabling Services and Protocol Logging

This lesson discusses the services that are used by Exchange Server 2003, explains service dependencies, and explains which services can be disabled to provide enhanced Exchange security. The lesson also discusses protocol logging and how this can be used to audit access on the various Exchange Server 2003 protocol virtual servers.

> **After this lesson, you will be able to**
>
> ■ Describe the services that Exchange Server 2003 uses
>
> ■ Explain why you should allow only required services to run on Exchange Server 2003
>
> ■ Identify the required services on an Exchange front-end server
>
> ■ Identify the required services on an Exchange back-end server
>
> ■ Manage protocol logging on HTTP virtual servers including the Exchange virtual server
>
> ■ Manage protocol logging on NNTP and SMTP virtual servers
>
> **Estimated lesson time: 30 minutes**

Services Used by Exchange Server 2003

Exchange Server 2003 comprises a number of processes, components, and services that communicate with each other on local and remote computers. Exchange servers must communicate with other Exchange servers, domain controllers, and several different types of client. Depending on the role an Exchange server plays and the clients it supports, some of these services are not necessary and may be disabled. Disabling a service increases security because the port that the service uses is no longer available for port-based attacks.

Security Alert   Disabling unused services increases security. If, however, any port is not used, you should preferably block it at the firewall as well as stop any service that uses it. Your firewall is your main method of protection. Where a server is in a DMZ, it may not always be possible to block a port, and in this case, it is particularly important to disable unused services.

When evaluating whether to disable a particular service, you need to consider what other services, processes, and components depend on it. Sometimes a service may not be essential to the core operation of an Exchange server, but disabling the service may reduce the functionality by disabling some useful peripheral services.

Role-Independent Services

The Exchange Server 2003 services that you require mainly depend on the role that your Exchange server provides in your environment. However, some Exchange services are required for Setup to run, for administration to be performed, and for routing and indexing to function, as well as interoperability with previous versions of the product.

Setup Reinstall and Upgrade   For Exchange Server 2003 Setup to run, you must install and enable, but not necessarily start, the following services:

- NNTP

- SMTP

- World Wide Web Publishing Service

- IIS Admin Service

> **Note**   Exchange Server 2003 installs (but does not enable) its own IMAP4 and POP3 services during setup. It will not install on a Windows 2003 server unless the Windows POP3 service (if present) is uninstalled.

Exchange Server 2003 Setup disables a number of services by default. However, if these services are subsequently enabled, their current state is preserved during reinstalls or upgrades. These services are as follows:

- NNTP

- Microsoft Exchange IMAP4

- Microsoft Exchange POP3

Administration   The following services are required to administer Exchange Server 2003:

- Microsoft Exchange System Attendant

- Microsoft Exchange Management

- Windows Management Instrumentation

Routing   The following services are required to enable Exchange Server 2003 to route messages:

- Microsoft Exchange Routing Engine

- IIS Admin Service

- SMTP

Compatibility   The following services are required to provide compatibility with earlier versions of Exchange:

- Microsoft Exchange Event Service

- Microsoft Exchange Site Replication Service

- Exchange MTA Stacks (Exchange Server 5.5 compatibility only)

Additional Features   The following services provide additional features for Exchange Server 2003:

- Microsoft Search

- World Wide Web Publishing Service

Services on an Exchange Front-End Server

An Exchange front-end server accepts requests from clients and then forwards those requests to the appropriate back-end server for processing. Therefore, you can disable many of the Exchange services that are installed by default.

> **Exam Tip**   Do not try to memorize which services can or cannot be disabled on a back-end or a front-end Exchange server. Instead, read and understand the reasons why a service is or is not essential. Questions on this topic can often be answered by applying reasoning and common sense.

The following are required services on a front-end server:

- **Microsoft Exchange Routing Engine**   You require this service to enable Exchange routing functionality.

- **IPSEC Services**   This service provides end-to-end security between clients and servers on Transmission Control Protocol/Internet Protocol (TCP/IP) networks. You require this service if you want to configure an Internet Protocol security (IPSec) filter on OWA servers.

- **IIS Admin Service**   This service is dependent on the MSExchange routing engine. You require this service to allow Exchange routing functionality.

- **World Wide Web Publishing Service**   You require this service if you want client computers to communicate with OWA or Outlook Mobile Access front-end servers.

The following services can be disabled on a front-end server:

- **Microsoft Exchange IMAP4**   You require this service only if the server is configured for IMAP4 clients.

- **Microsoft Exchange Information Store**   You require this service only if there are user mailboxes or public folders. It can therefore be disabled because front-end servers do not contain user data.

- **Microsoft Exchange POP3**   You require this service only if the server is configured for POP3 clients.

- **NNTP**   You require this service only for installation and if newsgroup functionality is specified.

The following services could optionally be disabled on a front-end server:

- **Microsoft Exchange System Attendant**   System Attendant can be disabled because it is required on a front-end server only if you plan to make configuration changes to Exchange Server. However, the justification for disabling this service is, at best, debatable. If you do decide to disable it, make sure that it is definitely not needed.

- **Microsoft Exchange Management**   This service allows you to specify, through the user interface (UI), which domain controller or global catalog server Exchange Server 2003 will use when accessing the directory. The service is also required for message tracking. You can disable this service without affecting the core functionality of Exchange. However, you may need Message Tracking to audit Exchange functionality.

- **SMTP**   You need to enable the SMTP service only if you have configured your front-end server to receive SMTP mail, either as a gateway or as a front-end server for IMAP4 or POP3. If the server is an SMTP gateway, the Information Store and System Attendant services are also required. As with System Attendant, the advantages of disabling this service are debatable. In practice, it is unusual for the SMTP service to be disabled on any Exchange Server 2003 server.

- **Outlook Mobile Access**   This service provides mobile access to users. If you are not using Outlook Mobile Access, you can disable it globally. This makes the application inaccessible, and no requests can be made to the back-end server.

 Note   ForestPrep disables Outlook Mobile Access by default.

If your front-end server is used to establish POP3, IMAP4, or SMTP connections, do not enable the World Wide Web Publishing Service, and enable the Microsoft Exchange POP3 or IMAP4 service, as appropriate. If you enable POP3, IMAP4, or SMTP, then you also need to enable the Exchange Information Store service (MSExchangeIS) and the Microsoft Exchange System Attendant service (MSExchangeSA).

Services on an Exchange Back-End Server

The function of an Exchange back-end server is to store user mailboxes. In a front-end and back-end configuration, you can disable several of the Exchange services that are installed by default.

The following are required services on a back-end server:

- **Microsoft Exchange Information**   Back-end servers contain user mailboxes and public folders. You require this service to enable the information store services.

- **Microsoft Exchange Management**   You require this service if you want to provide message tracking and to audit message flow.

- **Windows Management Instrumentation (WMI)**   You need to ensure this service is enabled. It is dependent on Microsoft Exchange Management.

- **Microsoft Exchange MTA Stacks**   You require this service if you need compatibility with previous versions of Exchange or if there are X.400 connectors.

- **Microsoft Exchange System Attendant**   You require this service if you want to perform Exchange administration and for Exchange maintenance to run.

- **Microsoft Exchange Routing Engine**   You require this service if you want to coordinate message transfer between Exchange servers.

- **1PSEC Services**   You require this service if you want to implement an IPSec policy on the back-end server.

- **IIS Admin Service**   The MSExchange routing engine requires this service.

- **NTLM Security Support Provider**   You need to ensure that this service is enabled. It is dependent on System Attendant.

- **Microsoft Exchange SMTP**   Exchange requires this service to transfer messages.

- **World Wide Web Publishing Service**   You require this service if you want to provide communication with OWA and Outlook Mobile Access front-end servers.

The following services can be disabled on a back-end server:

- **Microsoft Exchange IMAP4**   You can disable this service unless you have configured a corresponding front-end server for IMAP4 access.

- **Microsoft Exchange POP3**   You can disable this service unless you have configured a corresponding front-end server for POP3 access.

- **Microsoft Search**   You can disable this service unless you need to implement full-text indexing of mailbox or public folder stores.

- **Microsoft Exchange Event Service**   You can disable this service unless you require compatibility with previous versions of Exchange.

- **Microsoft Exchange Site Replication**   You can disable this service unless you require compatibility with previous versions of Exchange.

- **NNTP**   You can disable this service unless you require newsgroup functionality. The service is required for installation but does not need to be enabled.

Protocol Logging

Protocol logs track the commands that an Internet protocol virtual server receives from clients over a network, and you can also use them to track outgoing commands. By setting the configuration properties of the virtual server associated with each messaging transport protocol, you can audit client operations and protocol traffic. You can then take steps to protect your mail system if suspicious traffic is detected.

The Internet protocols (SMTP, HTTP, and NNTP) enable you to use logging to track the commands the virtual server receives from clients. For example, for each message, you can view the client IP address, client domain name, date and time of the message, and number of bytes sent.

When protocol logging is used with Windows 2000 event logs, the protocol log enables you to audit the use of the virtual server and identify problems.

Logging Formats

You can specify the logging format that Exchange uses for recording information. You can either use an ASCII-based format or you can create an Open Database Connectivity (ODBC) database. The ASCII logs can be read in a text editor but are generally loaded into a report-generating software tool. ODBC logging format is a record of a fixed set of data fields that can be read by ODBC-compliant database software, such as Microsoft Access or SQL Server.

Protocol logs are, by default, saved in the C:\WINNT\System32\LogFiles directory tree. For example, log files for the Default SMTP virtual server are stored in C:\WINNT\System32\LogFiles\SmtpSvc1.

The ASCII format options are as follows:

- W3C Extended log file format
- Microsoft IIS log file format
- NCSA log file format

W3C Extended and NCSA formats will record data in a four-digit year format, while the Microsoft IIS format uses a two-digit year format and is provided for backward compatibility with earlier systems.

If you want to enable logging in an ODBC format, then you must specify the database you want to be logged to and set up the database to receive the logging data. You do not need to be a database programmer to administer Exchange, however. Fortunately, setting up an ODBC database is a relatively straightforward operation.

You create an ODBC-compliant database by using a database program such as Access or SQL Server. You need to create a table in the database that contains the fields listed in Table 11-5. In Access, varchar(255) is equivalent to a Text data type with a Field Size setting of 255.

Table 11-5   ODBC-Compliant Database Fields

Field name	Data type
ClientHost	varchar(255)
Username	varchar(255)
LogTime	datetime
Service	varchar(255)
Machine	varchar(255)
ServerIP	varchar(50)
ProcessingTime	integer
BytesRecvd	integer
BytesSent	integer
ServiceStatus	integer
Win32Status	integer
Operation	varchar(255)
Target	varchar(255)
Parameters	varchar(255)

Practice: Enabling and Configuring Protocol Logging

The method you use to enable and configure protocol logging varies depending upon the virtual server you are configuring. HTTP servers, including the Exchange virtual server (that is, the Default HTTP virtual server), are configured using IIS Manager. SMTP and NNTP virtual servers are configured using Exchange System Manager.

Exercise 1: Enable Logging for SMTP and NNTP Virtual Servers

This procedure is performed on the Default SMTP virtual server on Server01. The same procedure can be used for any SMTP or NNTP virtual server.

To enable and configure protocol logging on the selected server, perform the following steps:

1. Open Exchange System Manager.

2. Navigate to Administrative Groups\First Administrative Group\Servers\Server01\Protocols\SMTP, right-click Default SMTP Virtual Server, and then click Properties.

3. On the General tab, select the Enable Logging check box.

4. In the Active Log Format drop-down list, select the log file format, and then click Properties. The default log file format for SMTP is W3C Extended Log File Format (for NNTP, it is Microsoft IIS Log File Format).

5. On the General tab of the Logging Properties dialog box, shown in Figure 11-13, under New Log Schedule, select one of the following options:

   ❏ Hourly

   ❏ Daily (this is the default)

   ❏ Weekly

   ❏ Monthly

   ❏ Unlimited File Size (this appends data to the same log file)

   ❏ When File Size Reaches (this creates a new log file when the size reaches the amount you specify in MB)

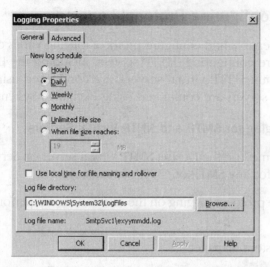

Figure 11-13   Scheduling logging and specifying the file location

6. Under Log File Directory, specify the log file location.

7. If you have selected the W3C Extended logging format, then you can select the Advanced tab and select the items you want to track. Although the names of these settings are based on WC3 conventions, they apply to specific SMTP values. For a full description of these extended properties, click Help in the Logging Properties dialog box.

8. Click OK.

9. Click OK again to close the Default SMTP virtual server Properties box.

Exercise 2: Enable and Configure Logging for the Exchange Virtual Server

The Exchange virtual server, or Default HTTP virtual server, implements the default Web site provided by IIS. You cannot manage this virtual server using Exchange System Manager. It must be administered from the IIS Manager console. In this console, the Exchange virtual server appears as Default Web Site. A similar procedure can be used to configure additional HTTP virtual servers.

To enable and configure protocol logging for the Exchange virtual server, perform the following steps:

1. Start IIS Manager on Server01.

2. Expand Server01\Web Sites, right-click Default Web Site, and then click Properties.

3. On the Web Site tab, select the Enable Logging check box.

4. In the Active Log Format drop-down list, select the log file format, and then click Properties. The default log format is W3C Extended Log File Format.

5. In the Logging Properties dialog box, on the General tab, select the time interval to write to the log file, the log file size, the directory where the log file exists, and other parameters, depending on the type of format you selected.

6. If you selected W3C Extended Log File Format in the Logging Properties dialog box, then you can access the Advanced tab and specify Extended Logging Options. For example, you can log the client's IP address (c-ip) and the protocol command or method sent by the client (cs-method).

7. Click OK. Click OK again to close the Default Web Site Properties box.

8. Verify that you can also right-click HTTP_server1 on the IIS console and configure logging for that virtual server using the same procedure. (You created the HTTP virtual server HTTP_Server1 in Chapter 9.)

Lesson Review

The following questions are intended to reinforce key information presented in this lesson. If you are unable to answer a question, review the lesson materials and then try the question again. You can find answers to the questions in the "Questions and Answers" section at the end of this chapter.

1. You are considering disabling Microsoft Exchange Management on a front-end Exchange server. Can you disable this service? What other considerations do you need to take into account?

   _____

   _____

2. Which of the following services are required to administer Exchange Server 2003? (Select all that apply.)

   a. Microsoft Exchange System Attendant

   b. Microsoft Exchange Management

   c. NNTP

   d. Windows Management Instrumentation

   e. Exchange MTA Stacks

   f. IPSEC Services

3. What is the default log file format for SMTP?

   a. W3C Extended log file format

   b. ODBC format

  c. Microsoft IIS log file format

  d. NCSA log file format

Lesson Summary

- Services should be disabled on an Exchange server if they are not required. Disabling a service closes the port that the service uses so that it is not available to an attacker. Note that unused ports should also be blocked at the firewall.

- The services that can be disabled mostly depend upon whether the server is a back-end or front-end server.

- Protocol logging provides an audit of all the operations performed by HTTP, NNTP, and SMTP virtual servers.

- Protocol logging can be in ASCII or ODBC format.

- You use Exchange System Manager to configure protocol logging for SMTP and NNTP virtual servers, and you use IIS Manager to configure protocol logging for HTTP virtual servers.

Case Scenario Exercise

You are the Exchange Full Administrator in a branch of Woodgrove Bank. Your Exchange organization comprises four front-end Exchange Server 2003 servers configured as a network load sharing cluster and two back-end Exchange Server 2003 servers configured as a Windows cluster to provide failover protection. Your domain controllers and member servers are all Windows Server 2003 servers.

Security is a major issue. Senior management needs to be assured that viruses, worms, and Trojan horses cannot attack the intranet. Spam and junk e-mail are particular areas of concern as they waste staff time and resources. Confidential e-mails containing financial information need to be encoded, and the senders of such e-mails need to be verified.

You have strong firewall protection for your domain controllers and back-end Exchange Server 2003 servers. However, your front-end Exchange Server 2003 servers are in a DMZ. Your organization uses POP3 clients but not IMAP4 clients. Financial information is sent to your Web server using SSL encryption. Employees are permitted to download their personal files onto laptops so that they can work on them at home. Currently, the Encrypting File System (EFS) is used to encrypt these files.

- **Requirement 1** You need to upgrade your antivirus software. You need to be assured that this software is compatible with Exchange Server 2003 servers. You also need to ensure that security patches and virus signatures are downloaded regularly and that immediate downloads occur if there is a known Internet threat.

- **Requirement 2**   Management accepts that unsolicited commercial mail cannot always be blocked. Nevertheless, you are required to minimize the level of such traffic. In particular, mail from known spamming organizations must be blocked.

- **Requirement 3**   You need to block all unused ports on your firewall. In addition, you need to disable any services that are not required. Your organization should offer the smallest possible target to an attacker.

Requirement 1

The first requirement involves upgrading your antivirus software.

1. You have been asked to find an antivirus software package that will protect your organization. This software must be fully compatible with Exchange Server 2003. Commercial antivirus software that was previously installed on the system has been found to be unsatisfactory. You need to identify a reputable company that can provide a professional product. How do you proceed?

    _____

    _____

2. Your chief information officer (CIO) wants to ensure that viruses never enter the intranet. She wants you to block them at the firewall. Therefore, she sees no need for antivirus software on the servers or clients. Do you agree with her? Why or why not?

    _____

    _____

3. A user reports that a self-extracting zip file that was e-mailed to him as an attachment did not unzip. When a zip file that was not self-extracting was sent to him, he was able to unzip it without any problems. How do you explain this to him, and what action (if any) do you take to remedy this situation?

    _____

    _____

Requirement 2

The second requirement involves minimizing unsolicited commercial e-mail and blocking e-mail from known spammers.

1. You have a block-list service provider configured, but you continue to receive unsolicited commercial e-mail from several senders. You have identified _nwtrad-_

ers.com and *treyresearch.com* as junk mail senders. They are not on your RBL. How can you block the messages coming from them?

_____

_____

2. You have shown your chief executive officer (CEO) how he can configure Outlook 2003 on his client machine to filter out junk mail from a known sender. He is now concerned about the amount of time that needs to be spent configuring Outlook on all the client machines and listing all possible junk e-mail sources. What do you tell him to put his mind at rest?

_____

_____

Requirement 3

The third requirement involves ensuring that your firewall is as secure as possible and stopping any unnecessary services.

1. Given the scenario described, what ports need to be open on your firewall?

_____

_____

2. What services should you disable on your front-end servers? List only the services that are definitely not required, rather than the ones which can optionally be disabled.

_____

_____

Troubleshooting Lab

In this lab, you identify a source of junk e-mail and block it at the Exchange Server 2003 server level. You then discover that the source has been spoofed but that this problem has now been solved. As a result, you no longer want to block e-mails from that source.

To complete this lab, you need to have your test network configured as described in the "Before You Begin" section of this chapter. In particular, you will be blocking and then permitting e-mail from a specific user in the *tailspintoys.com* domain. If your domain has a different name, substitute your domain name in the exercises.

Exercise 1: Sending a Junk E-Mail

This could be considered a trivial exercise, but if you refine the technique, you will never starve. To send junk e-mail, perform the following steps:

1. On Server02, log in as Don Hall. Open Internet Explorer and access OWA (*http:// server02/exchange*).

2. Send an e-mail message to *administrator@tailspintoys.com*. The text in this message is entirely your choice, but it could be on the lines of "I want to play guitar like Will Willis. Please send me lots of money for lessons."

3. On Server01, log on as administrator and open your Inbox. Read and delete the offending message.

Exercise 2: Block Junk E-Mail from Specified Domains

Outlook is set with a junk-mail filter that prevents e-mail from sources on your RBL being read by clients. However, when e-mail is coming from junk-mail domains, you want to block it before it enters your organization. You should therefore filter it out at the default SMTP virtual server on your front-end Exchange server.

To block Internet e-mail from specified domains and users, perform the following steps:

1. Open Exchange System Manager.

2. Browse to Administrative Groups\First Administrative Group\Servers\Server02\ Protocols\SMTP, right-click Default SMTP Server, and then click Properties.

3. On the Access tab, under Connection Control, click Connection.

4. In the Connection dialog box, ensure that All Except The List Below is selected, and then click Add.

5. In the Computer dialog box, select Domain.

6. Read the warning in the SMTP Configuration box, and then click OK.

7. Type **nwtraders.com** in the Name box, and click OK.

8. Click Add in the Connection dialog box, and then select Domain in the Computer dialog box.

9. Type **treyresearch.com** in the Name box, and click OK.

10. The Connection dialog box should look similar to Figure 11-14.

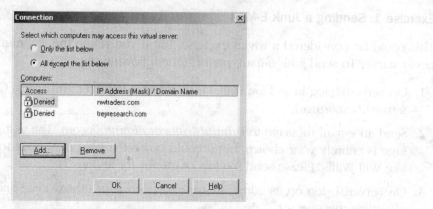

Figure 11-14   Blocking junk-mail domains

11. Click Add in the Connection dialog box, and then select User in the Computer dialog box.

12. Type **d.hall@tailspintoys.com** in the Name box, and click OK.

13. Click OK.

14. Click OK again to close the Default SMTP Virtual Server Properties box.

15. Send an e-mail from Don Hall to *administrator@tailspintoys.com*. Check that the e-mail is blocked.

Real World   Have You Blocked Junk E-Mail?

In the real world, it is difficult to test that you have blocked a junk e-mail sender, unless you have software that will spoof that sender. Whether you want to obtain such software, and encourage its supplier, is debatable. In practice, scan e-mail carefully and ensure that nothing more is received from the sender in question.

Exercise 3: Remove an Entry from the Block List

You now want to receive e-mail from Don Hall. To remove him from the block list, perform the following procedure:

1. Open Exchange System Manager.

2. Browse to Administrative Groups\First Administrative Group\Servers\Server02\Protocols\SMTP, right-click Default SMTP Server, and then click Properties.

3. On the Access tab, under Connection Control, click Connection.

4. In the Connection dialog box, ensure that All Except The List Below is selected, click *d.hall@tailspintoys.com*, and then click Remove.

5. Click OK.

6. Click OK again to close the Default SMTP Virtual Server Properties box.

7. Send an e-mail from Don Hall to *administrator@tailspintoys.com*. Check that the e-mail is received.

Chapter Summary

- You can place a front-end Exchange Server 2003 server behind the intranet firewall or in the DMZ. Back-end Exchange Server 2003 servers should be behind the firewall.

- MAPI clients such as Outlook can access an Exchange server through a firewall using RPC over HTTP.

- You can protect against viruses, worms, and Trojan horses at the client, at the server, and at the firewall. You need to keep your software, operating system, and signature files up to date.

- You need to have a virus-clean policy in place before you are attacked.

- You can filter junk e-mail in Exchange Server 2003 and in Outlook 2003.

- You can protect user messages from interception and alteration by using encryption and digital signatures.

- You can delegate administration by creating administrative groups and assigning administrative roles.

- You should disable unnecessary services and audit activity on your virtual servers by using protocol logging.

Exam Highlights

Before taking the exam, review the key points and terms that are presented in this chapter. Return to the lessons for additional practice.

Key Points

- A firewall protects your network by blocking traffic through unwanted TCP ports and by filtering traffic through permitted ports. Exchange back-end servers require strong firewall protection. Exchange front-end servers can be in the DMZ, or perimeter network.

- You need to keep your operating systems, applications, antivirus software, and virus signature files up to date to protect against viruses, worms, and Trojan horses. Virus-clean policies need to be in place before a virus attack occurs.

- You can filter junk e-mail based on the address of a single sender, on a domain name, or on the recipient address (or lack of one). An RBL provides a third-party solution to the junk e-mail problem.

- Encryption ensures that only the person for whom a message is intended can read it, and a digital signature proves the sender's identity and gives an assurance that the message has not been altered in transit.

- You can delegate various levels of administrative control over an administrative group to users and to security groups.

- Disabling a service closes the port that the service uses so that it is not available to an attacker.

- You use Exchange System Manager to configure protocol logging for SMTP and NNTP virtual servers, and you use IIS Manager to configure protocol logging for HTTP virtual servers.

Key Terms

firewall   A combination of hardware and software that provides a security system, usually to prevent unauthorized access to an intranet.

virus, worm, and Trojan horse   Executable code that can damage data, applications, operating systems, and (sometimes) hardware. The difference between the three is in the method they use to spread through a network.

junk mail   Unsolicited commercial e-mail, also known as *spam e-mail*.

administrative group   A collection of Active Directory objects that are grouped together for the purpose of permissions management. An administrative group can contain policies, routing groups, public folder hierarchies, servers, and chat networks.

public key infrastructure (PKI)   A system of digital certificates, certification authorities, and other registration authorities that verify and authenticate the validity of each party involved in an electronic transaction.

Questions and Answers

Page
11-11 **Lesson 1 Review**

1. What is the advantage of using RPC over HTTP to allow a MAPI client such as Outlook to connect to Exchange through a firewall?

   Configuring RPC over HTTP eliminates the need for a VPN connection when a user is accessing Exchange information. Users running Outlook can connect directly to an Exchange server over the Internet by using HTTP, even if both the Exchange server and Outlook are behind firewalls and located on different networks.

2. What TCP ports do you need to open on a firewall to allow HTTP, SMTP, and HTTP over SSL traffic? (Select all that apply.)

   a. Port 21

   b. Port 25

   c. Port 80

   d. Port 110

   e. Port 119

   f. Port 143

   g. Port 443

   h. Port 563

   The correct answers are b, c, and g.

Page
11-20 **Lesson 2 Review**

1. What is the difference between a virus and a worm?

   Unlike a virus, a worm does not require a host program and can replicate itself automatically whenever an application or the operating system transfers or copies files.

2. How does a Trojan horse spread?

   A Trojan horse cannot replicate itself. It relies on users to spread the program through e-mail.

3. Which Microsoft utility checks for missing patches, blank or weak passwords, and operating system vulnerabilities?

   a. SMS

   b. SUS

   c. MBSA

   d. Security Notification Service

   The correct answer is c.

Page
11-29

Lesson 3 Review

1. How does Exchange Server 2003 filtering work, and what do you need to configure in order to use it?

   Exchange Server 2003 filtering examines e-mail headers and checks them against established filter rules. To use the Exchange filtering features, you must first configure the properties of the global Message Delivery object to create global filters. Then you need to configure SMTP virtual servers to use these global filters.

2. An e-mail message has an SCL value of 3. Which of the following statements is true?

   a. The sender was found on the Deny list.

   b. The sender was found on the Accept list.

   c. The message probably is not junk e-mail.

   d. The message probably is junk e-mail.

   The correct answer is d.

Page
11-35

Lesson 4 Review

1. Which PKI component defines the content and purpose of a certificate?

   a. Certificate template

   b. CA

   c. CRL

   d. Certificate publication point

   The correct answer is a.

2. Don Hall sends an encrypted message to Kim Akers. How does Don encrypt it, and how does Kim read it?

   Don encrypts the message using Kim's public key. Kim decrypts it using her private key.

3. Kim Akers wants to send a message to Don Hall, but Don needs to be certain that the message really is from Kim. How can he verify this?

Kim signs the message using her private key. Don decrypts the signature using Kim's public key. This assures him that the message is from Kim and that it has not been intercepted and altered by a third party.

Page
11-44
Lesson 5 Review

1. You use Exchange System Manager to delegate control of an administration group to Don Hall. The administration group contains three Exchange Server 2003 servers called Server A, Server B, and Server C. You give Don the Exchange Administrator role. Don reports that he is unable to carry out any administration on the servers. What do you need to do?

   You need to make Don a local administrator on Server A, Server B, and Server C.

2. You want to grant advanced permissions on an administration group. You make the necessary registry changes, then try to add the ASDI edit snap-in to the Microsoft Management Console. ASDI Edit is not on the list of snap-ins. What have you forgotten to do?

   You have forgotten to install the Windows Server 2003 support tools.

3. You create a new routing group and find that the group inherits permissions from the administrative group in which it was created. You want different permissions applied to the new routing group object. What do you do?

   Access the routing group object's Properties box and use the Advanced option on the Security tab to block permission inheritance.

Page
11-55
Lesson 6 Review

1. You are considering disabling Microsoft Exchange Management on a front-end Exchange server. Can you disable this service? What other considerations do you need to take into account?

   You can disable this service without affecting the core functionality of Exchange. However, the service is also required for message tracking, which you may need to audit Exchange functionality.

2. Which of the following services are required to administer Exchange Server 2003? (Select all that apply.)

   a. Microsoft Exchange System Attendant

   b. Microsoft Exchange Management

   c. NNTP

   d. Windows Management Instrumentation

   e. Exchange MTA Stacks

   f. IPSEC Services

   The correct answers are a, b, and d.

3. What is the default log file format for SMTP?

    a. W3C Extended log file format

    b. ODBC format

    c. Microsoft IIS log file format

    d. NCSA log file format

The correct answer is a.

Page 11-57

Case Scenario Exercise: Requirement 1

1. You have been asked to find an antivirus software package that will protect your organization. This software must be fully compatible with Exchange Server 2003. Commercial antivirus software that was previously installed on the system has been found to be unsatisfactory. You need to identify a reputable company that can provide a professional product. How do you proceed?

You access *http://www.microsoft.com/exchange/partners/antivirus.asp*. Although Microsoft makes no warranties or representations with regard to these products or services, it is likely that an organization on the list will provide a professional product. If the supplier permits, download a trial version of the software. Test the software against criteria such as whether it is compatible with Exchange Server 2003, whether it updates its virus signatures automatically, how often it does so, and whether it blocks viruses, worms, and Trojan horses.

2. Your chief information officer (CIO) wants to ensure that viruses never enter the intranet. She wants you to block them at the firewall. Therefore, she sees no need for antivirus software on the servers or clients. Do you agree with her? Why or why not?

The CIO is mistaken. Antivirus software installed at the firewall can stop viruses entering or leaving your intranet. However, the front-end servers in the DMZ also need to be protected because employees are allowed to do corporate work on laptops at home. Although an employee is supposed to work on files downloaded while at work, there is nothing to stop him or her plugging an external modem into the laptop and connecting it to the Internet. If the machine is unprotected, it can pick up a worm, which can then affect your intranet when the laptop is connected to it. Therefore, antivirus software needs to be installed on the firewall, on servers, and on client machines.

3. A user reports that a self-extracting zip file that was e-mailed to him as an attachment did not unzip. When a zip file that was not self-extracting was sent to him, he was able to unzip it without any problems. How do you explain this to him, and what action (if any) do you take to remedy this situation?

Client e-mail software such as Outlook filters out certain types of files as potential risks. In particular, exploitable file types, such as .bat, .com, .scr, .vbs, and embedded HTML scripts are often either deleted or converted to text files. Self-extracting zip files are .exe files. While possibly less of a risk than the other file types mentioned, .exe files are executable code and can be used to transmit viruses. In the environment described in the scenario, where security is paramount, it is unwise to alter any settings that would allow .exe files to be sent to your users. You should instead inform users (and management) about known exploitable file types and explain why they cannot receive them as e-mail attachments.

Page
11-57

Case Scenario Exercise: Requirement 2

1. You have a block-list service provider configured, but you continue to receive unsolicited commercial e-mail from several senders. You have identified *nwtraders.com* and *treyresearch.com* as junk mail senders. They are not on your RBL. How can you block the messages coming from them?

RBLs cannot completely prevent unsolicited commercial e-mail because domains will always exist that are not included or that have been created subsequent to the block list. You need to be vigilant about monitoring your incoming e-mail and add any domains that are identified as junk mail senders to the junk mail list on the Connection tab of your SMTP virtual servers' Properties dialog boxes.

2. You have shown your chief executive officer (CEO) how he can configure Outlook 2003 on his client machine to filter out junk mail from a known sender. He is now concerned about the amount of time that needs to be spent configuring Outlook on all the client machines and listing all possible junk e-mail sources. What do you tell him to put his mind at rest?

Although users may want to configure Outlook to block particular junk mail sources on their client computers, particularly if they are also using these computers at home, the bulk of the junk e-mail sent to your organization can be blocked at the Exchange Server 2003 servers by configuring the SMTP virtual servers. Commercially available RBLs contain the domain names of most e-mail servers, and you need only add new sources as necessary rather than needing to generate a block list from scratch.

Page
11-58

Case Scenario Exercise: Requirement 3

1. Given the scenario described, what ports need to be open on your firewall?

You need to open TCP port 25 for SMTP. The scenario does not state whether your users access the Internet, but it would be unusual if TCP port 80 were not opened for HTTP. It is likely that your secure Web server is behind your firewall, so TCP port 443 needs to be opened for HTTP using SSL. The Exchange Server 2003 servers in your DMZ will use Active Directory, so TCP port 389 needs to be opened for LDAP. If RPC is blocked, nothing much else works, so TCP port 135 needs to be opened. Note that strict filtering conditions should be applied to all open ports.

There is no indication that Kerberos authentication will be needed across the firewall or that an X.400 connector is used. NNTP is not mentioned in the scenario. There are no IMAP4 clients, and it is not clear whether POP3 clients require access through the firewall. Nor is it certain that global catalog look-ups across the firewall are required. Therefore, TCP ports 88, 102, 110, 119, 143, 563, 636, 993, 995, 3268, and 3269 should be closed initially. They can be opened (and strictly filtered), if required.

2. What services should you disable on your front-end servers? List only the services that are definitely not required, rather than the ones which can optionally be disabled.

You can disable the following services in this scenario:

❑ *Microsoft Exchange IMAP4*—You have no IMAP4 clients.

❑ *Microsoft Exchange Information Store*—This service can be disabled because your front-end servers do not contain user data.

❑ *NNTP*—The scenario does not specify any newsgroup functionality.

❑ *Outlook Mobile Access*—The scenario does not specify that you require Outlook Mobile Access.

12 Backup and Restore

Exam Objectives in this Chapter:

■ Manage, monitor, and troubleshoot data storage

■ Perform and troubleshoot backup and recovery

Why This Chapter Matters

> Disaster recovery is a critical area in Microsoft Exchange Server 2003 design and implementation. In today's business environment, e-mail is possibly the most used method of communication, and private and public stores contain large volumes of valuable information. The survival of most organizations is dependent upon the safety and stability of this information. Therefore, information backup and restore and the management of information storage are crucial, and the exam reflects the importance of these topics.

Lessons in this Chapter:

■ Lesson 1: Managing Data Storage. 12-3

■ Lesson 2: Backing Up Exchange Server 2003 12-16

■ Lesson 3: Restoring Exchange Server 2003 12-28

Before You Begin

To perform the exercises in this chapter, you need the following hardware and software:

■ Two Microsoft Windows Server 2003, Enterprise Edition, servers installed in the *tailspintoys.com* Active Directory directory service domain. Server01 should be a domain controller, and Server02 should be a member server. Server01 should be multihomed. Server02 is reconfigured as a recovery server in the troubleshooting lab in this chapter.

> **Note** If your Active Directory domain is not called *tailspintoys.com*, there is no need to rename it. Instead, use your domain name rather than *tailspintoys.com* whenever the latter is mentioned in the chapter exercises.

- Exchange Server 2003, Enterprise Edition, should be installed on both servers.

- In the exercises in this chapter, the folder D:\Mybackup on Server01 is used as the backup location. If your servers have tape drives, then these can be used instead to bring the exercises closer to what happens in the real world.

- You need to create folders for backup and for transaction log files. As the exercises are written, these are D:\Mybackup and D:\My Transaction Logs on Server01.

- A Domain Name System (DNS) server needs to be available. Typically, DNS is installed on the domain controller.

Lesson 1: Managing Data Storage

The principles of data backup and restoration are well known, but a good backup strategy is not in itself sufficient to ensure the survival of your organization in today's information-intensive business environment. Unless accompanied by a sound and well-understood storage strategy, a restore operation can only restore data that was up to date the last time it was backed up, possibly the day before. Few businesses can afford to lose a day's data. Also, backup and restore does not provide failover protection. A store needs to be taken offline, or *dismounted*, in order to restore lost data, and users are then unable to access their mailboxes until the restore is complete and the mailbox stores are mounted again. In this lesson, you learn how redundant disk systems can protect against data loss and provide failover support, and how correct management of your storage will enable you to restore lost data up to the point of failure.

After this lesson, you will be able to

- Explain the various disk systems that are used to provide disaster protection and failover support
- Explain the functions of the various types of files in which Exchange Server 2003 data is stored
- Determine which type of disk configuration is best suited to storing which type of file
- Explain how transaction log files can assist in restoring data up to the point of failure
- Explain the relationship between backup types and transaction log files
- Explain circular logging and enable it, if appropriate
- Explain how storage area networks (SANs) are used to store Exchange data

Estimated lesson time: 60 minutes

How Exchange Server 2003 Manages Data

Exchange Server 2003 handles various data types, which have differing requirements and compete for storage resource. The most significant competition is between transaction log and database files. This lesson explains why these types of files do not coexist happily on the same disk and should whenever possible be stored on separate drives.

Exchange stores data using the Extensible Storage Engine (ESE) database structure. The Exchange store can be separated into transactions and messages. Messages are stored in .edb and .stm database files, and transactions are stored in transaction log files. In addition to messages, database files contain attachments, folders, rules, indexes, and everything else the store needs.

The log files and database files behave differently from each other. When a user creates a new message, the change is not immediately written to the database file because that would seriously limit performance. Instead, changes are written to log files that write the transactions sequentially to a numbered file. Data in a log file is written to the database later. Exchange creates a new transaction log file when the one it is currently using reaches 5 megabytes (MB) in size.

Log files are always written to in sequential order, while database files are read and written to in a random manner. Therefore, an Exchange Server 2003 server needs to be able to read and write randomly to a large database file, sending the disk drive heads back and forth among the platters, while simultaneously writing to transaction logs in a sequential manner. The patterns of disk usage are at variance with each other and this leads to a loss of performance, particularly if you have many users.

You need to place the transaction logs and database files on disk systems that do not compete and are optimized for the types of activity you expect. Placing the transaction log files and database files on different disk drives (or *spindles*) is an obvious step, but organizations of any significant size use disk arrays rather than single disks. You need to decide the disk configuration that gives the best balance of performance, data protection, and cost.

EDB and STM Files

The raw format of an e-mail message is usually the Multipurpose Internet Mail Extensions (MIME) standard. Some e-mail systems (such as Microsoft Exchange Server 5.5) convert incoming messages from MIME into Rich Text Format (RTF). Exchange Server 2003 (and Exchange 2000 Server) uses the simpler MIME format to reduce processor loads and stores those unconverted messages in .stm files.

As Simple Mail Transfer Protocol (SMTP) messages arrive on your Exchange Server 2003 server, they are "streamed" into the .stm files without conversion. If the message is destined for a user's mailbox, then the message-header information is stored in the Messaging Application Programming Interface (MAPI) tables in the .edb file. If a user opens the item using a MAPI client such as Microsoft Outlook 2003, then the header information is copied into the .edb database. If the user modifies the item, it moves into the .edb database.

Disk Arrays

The use of redundant array of independent drives (RAID) systems is well known and is reviewed only briefly here. There are software and hardware implementations, and these can vary between manufacturers. One supplier's RAID-0+1 can be another's RAID-1+0. We shall consider only the common implementations most used in Exchange Server 2003.

> **Note**   Depending upon the book you read, RAID can also stand for redundant array of independent disks and redundant array of inexpensive disks. Microsoft expands the acronym as redundant array of independent drives, and therefore that term is used here.

RAID-0 Disk Striping

RAID-0 requires a minimum of two drives and implements a striped disk array. The data is broken down into blocks, and each block is written to a separate disk drive in turn. Input/output (I/O) performance is enhanced because you can read from and write to all the disks in the array at the same time. If you have many channels and drives, then you can expect a corresponding improvement in performance, particularly when data is striped across multiple controllers with only one drive per controller. This is a simple design and is easy to implement, and there is no overhead due to parity calculation and no loss of usable disk capacity.

However, RAID-0 is not fault-tolerant. Parity information is compressed data from one disk that is stored on another to provide failover protection. Not generating such information improves performance and lowers cost, but data is unprotected. In fact, a RAID-0 array is less reliable than a single disk. It takes only one disk to go down for all the data in the array to be lost. The use of RAID-0 should be avoided in mission-critical environments.

> **Exam Tip**   Examiners have been tripping up unwary candidates for years by proposing RAID-0 as a fault-tolerant solution. There is no reason to believe they are going to stop doing so now.

RAID-1 Mirroring or Duplexing

In RAID-1, all the data that is written to one disk is also written simultaneously to a mirror disk. Thus if one disk goes down, the data is still available on the other. Duplexing is where you use a separate disk controller for each disk. This increases reliability because if one controller goes down, the other is still available. It can also improve performance because data can be written to both disks simultaneously. RAID-1 gives good read performance as data can be read from both disks at the same time.

> **Note**   Some configurations and RAID controllers will support simultaneous writes with only one controller, but you will not get the same reliability improvements as you would with a dual-controller setup.

RAID-1 requires a minimum of two drives to implement. There is total data redundancy, so a rebuild is not necessary in the case of a disk failure. However, RAID-1 is expensive. You need to double the disk capacity to support the same volume of data. Also, it may not provide instantaneous failover protection, depending upon hardware and software configuration considerations and which one of a mirrored disk pair fails. Also, if one disk goes down, the data on the remaining disk is no longer protected, and software implementation of RAID-1 adds to the load on the processor, possibly degrading throughput at high activity levels. Microsoft recommends hardware implementation, preferably with *hot-swapping* facilities where a faulty disk can be replaced and brought online without powering down or dismounting the array.

RAID-0+1 Mirrored Stripes

RAID-0+1 consists of two striped arrays that are then mirrored. This gives the redundancy of mirrored disks combined with the performance benefits of striping. RAID-0+1 requires a minimum of four drives to implement. It has the same overhead as RAID-1; you need twice the disk capacity as a standalone disk to store the same amount of data. If a single disk goes down, a RAID-0+1 array becomes a RAID-0 array with no data protection. If a second disk goes down on the same side of the mirror, then your data is retained. However, if disks on both sides of the mirror fail, then your data is lost and needs to be restored from backup when the faulty disks are replaced.

Because only one disk in a striped array needs to go down to bring down the entire array, RAID-0+1 is inherently less reliable than RAID-1, with the same overhead. This, however, should be balanced against the enhanced I/O performance that it provides. Typically, a RAID-0+1 array is a hardware implementation that supports hot swapping.

RAID-5 Striping with Parity

A RAID-5 array writes data on disk stripes, but for every row of stripes, it allocates one stripe per disk to hold parity information, which is compressed information about the data in all the other stripes of the same rank on the other disks. The parity stripes are distributed on all the disks in such a way that if one disk fails, the data on that disk is held in compressed form in stripes on all the other disks.

RAID-5 requires a minimum of three drives to implement. It offers excellent read performance because all the disks can be read simultaneously. Write performance is good, but not usually as good as that of RAID-0, because parity information needs to be generated and written to the parity stripes (although in modern RAID-5 configurations, this is hardware-based and relatively fast). The configuration gives immediate failover protection. If a disk goes down, then the parity stripes on the other disks continue to supply the data needed to support users. However, that data needs to be decompressed on read and compressed on write, so there is a significant drop in performance. Also, a striped array with a failed disk offers no data protection. If a second disk goes down, then the data is lost and needs to be restored from backup. Therefore, a failed disk in a RAID-5 system needs to be replaced and the data regenerated from the parity stripes on the other disks as soon as possible.

RAID-5 is not as expensive as RAID-1, but there is some reduction in total capacity because disk space is needed to store parity information. In the worst case, with three disks, one third of the total capacity is used for this purpose. If four disks are used, then one quarter of the total disk space is needed for parity information, and if five disks are used, then one fifth of total capacity is lost, and so on.

Software implementations of RAID-5 significantly load the processor. Systems with software RAID-5 also are unable to boot to the RAID-5 set because Windows needs to load the drivers for RAID-5 before it can recognize the array. Microsoft recommends the use of hardware RAID-5 in an Exchange Server 2003 organization.

Storing Transaction Logs and Databases

On any Exchange Server 2003 organization of a significant size (say over 100 users), you should store the transaction log files on a different disk from the database files. Exchange Server 2003 writes transactions to the log in sequential order, appending new transactions to the end of the log. These writes generate I/O activity, and the disks on which you store the transaction log must support a heavy I/O write load. The disks that contain the databases experience read and write activity when users access items in their mailboxes or when the information in the transaction log is written to a database. This is a comparatively small amount of I/O activity, except on servers that host multiple directory-replication connectors.

Because transaction logs require high-performance disks, a RAID-0 configuration would be ideal, except that it provides no data protection. The loss of transaction log data may not seem as serious a matter as the loss of database data, because only the transactions that have yet not been written into the database files are completely lost. However, the loss of transaction log data curtails your ability to recover lost database information up to the point of failure. Transaction log data therefore needs protection. The use of RAID-0+1 for storing transaction log files is a reasonable compromise. If a sensible backup regime is implemented, the total size of all the transaction log files should not be excessive, and the cost of RAID-0+1 storage can therefore be accepted.

Mailbox and public folder data is essential to your organization and must be protected. There is no requirement for exceptional I/O performance like there is for transaction log files. RAID-1 gives very safe and reliable data storage. However, mailbox and public folder stores can be very large indeed, and the cost of RAID-1 may be unacceptable. In this case, RAID-5 will provide data protection and good read performance at a reasonable cost.

Real World   Don't Rely Totally on RAID

There is an unfortunate belief held by some organizations that, because they protect data by using RAID systems, they do not require backup and restore policies. This is not the case. There are ways of losing, deleting, and overwriting essential data other than physical disk failure. Data needs to be backed up regularly and archived either in a fireproof safe or off-site, or preferably both.

How Transaction Logs Protect Your Data

If you store your transaction log files on a separate hard disk from your database files, then you improve your overall disk performance, and you also have protection against loss of recent data. When a transaction is completed, it is written into the transaction log. Each storage group has its own set of transaction log files. Periodically, the information in the transaction log is *committed*—that is, it is written into the storage group's database file. However, that information is *not* deleted from the transaction log. Transaction logs are deleted only when you do a full online backup of all the databases in the storage group. You should not delete transaction log files manually. A checkpoint file is used to indicate which transaction log entries have been written to a database file.

Soft Recovery

If you lose the hard disk containing the storage group databases, you can replace the damaged disk and then restore the most recent database backups. If you then delete the checkpoint file, then an automatic log file replay of all transactions that occurred after the backup transfers the recorded transactions from the log files to the databases. This is known as a roll-forward or a soft recovery.

Hard Recovery

It is possible that transaction log files were backed up subsequent to the database file backup. Transaction files are typically much smaller than database files and are backed up more regularly. An incremental backup backs up all the information that has been written to the transaction log since the last full or incremental backup. A differential backup backs up all the transaction log files whether they have previously been backed up or not. Neither incremental nor differential backups delete the transaction log files, nor do they back up the database files.

If you have backed up transaction log files since the last full backup, you can perform a hard recovery. Hard recovery is the process of replaying transaction log files from backup medium after you restore a database from an online backup. After the hard recovery, if Exchange determines that additional log files are available on the server for replay, then a soft recovery process restores these additional log files into the restored database.

ACID Properties

Transactions are not written to the transaction log files until they are completed. Such transactions are said to have *ACID properties*, where the acronym stands for Atomicity, Consistency, Isolation, and Durability. Put simply, this means that a transaction is either completed or it is not. Uncompleted transactions are rolled back, so that no transaction is ever partially completed. Suppose, for example, that somebody is sending an e-mail message with a large attachment to one of your users, and connectivity is lost due to a hardware fault in your server. In this case, the transaction does not complete and is rolled back, so the message is queued on the sending server. If you fix the hardware fault before the message times out, then the message is delivered. If not, a non-delivery report (NDR) is sent to the sender. Both are preferable options to the message disappearing in transit or being delivered without its attachment.

Loss of Transaction Log Files

If you lose the hard disk containing the transaction log files, but not the disk containing the databases, then you do not have to restore any storage group data from backup. However, you cannot replay transactions that are recorded to log files but not recorded to the physical database files on disk. This means that you can lose data that is not preserved either in the log files or in the last backup. If your backup strategy includes differential or incremental backups, then you can restore the transaction log files from this backup, but you will still lose recent transactions. However, if you have a well-designed backup strategy, the total size of all the transaction log files should not be excessive, and neither should the cost of RAID-based failover protection.

Tip You can minimize the time it takes to recover from a hard disk failure if you keep each of your Exchange storage groups on a separate hard disk or hard disk array. Then if only one disk fails, you need to restore only the storage group that is kept on the failed disk.

Circular Logging

Microsoft designed Exchange Server 2003 for the enterprise, but the software also works well in organizations that have few users. *Circular logging* is Microsoft's solution for companies that do not want transaction logs to use too much disk space. It can also be used where it is not essential to protect the information being transferred to a storage group, for example, in a Newsgroup server. Circular logging saves disk space by reusing transaction log files. Instead of accumulating a set of logs that contain all the transactions that have occurred since the last full online backup, circular logging marks a log file for reuse after an Exchange Server 2003 server commits transactions to the database. Typically, circular logging uses four (sometimes five) files, or 20 MB of disk space.

Suppose you are storing your transactions in log files E0000010.log, E0000011.log, E0000012.log, and E0000013.log. When all four log files are full, ESE will rename the log file E0000010.log to E0000014.log and start overwriting its data. The exception to this rule occurs when the checkpoint file is still pointing to E0000010.log, indicating that not all of the transactions in E0000010.log have been written to the database (and none of the transactions in the other logs). In this case, ESE creates a fifth log file (E0000014.log) and does not overwrite E0000010.log.

Circular logging is used where there is a shortage of disk space to store transaction logs. However, Exchange Server 2003 keeps transaction logs so you can recover transactions when you need to restore a database during a backup. If Exchange Server 2003 reuses the logs, then you cannot recover the old transactions. Do not use circular logging in an environment where data recovery is important.

> **Real World   Circular Logging**
>
> Circular logging is often used incorrectly in the real world. If an organization has no backup policy, or a badly designed one that does not implement full online backups, then transaction logs will eventually grow to fill the available disk space. Circular logging is not the answer to this situation; a good backup policy is. A transaction log takes up only 5 MB, which is not a huge amount given the current sizes of available hard drives. Unless your organization is very large and very busy (in which case you can afford the disk capacity), there really is very little excuse for having more than a few hundred MB filled with transaction log files.

Storage Technologies

There are several types of storage technologies that can be deployed with Exchange Server 2003. Your choice will depend on the size of your Exchange Server 2003 organization and how the vendor has implemented the solution.

> **Exam Tip**   Microsoft defines a typical exam candidate as having at least one year of experience implementing Exchange Server messaging systems in environments supporting from 250 to 5,000 or more users. It is likely (but not inevitable) that questions will be asked about storage systems capable of supporting that number of users.

It is probable that an Exchange Server 2003 organization will use one of the following storage technologies:

- External storage array (ESA)
- Network attached storage (NAS)
- Storage area network (SAN)

External Storage Array

The ESA storage solution uses an external Small Computer System Interface (SCSI) drive cabinet to house multiple SCSI disk drives, usually configured as one or more RAID sets. SCSI cables connect the disk drives directly to an Exchange Server 2003 server. This type of storage provides good performance but has limited scalability. It needs to be managed on a per-server basis. Microsoft recommends that ESAs, otherwise known as *direct attached storage (DAT)*, be used by smaller Exchange organizations.

> **Off the Record**   Microsoft does not define "smaller." This is wise. An organization with 300 users, all of whom use e-mail as their main method of communication, might have more complex requirements than an organization with 1,000 users, most of whom seldom use e-mail at all. As a very general rule of thumb: if you have 500 or more users, then start thinking about a solution more scalable than ESA.

Network Attached Storage

An NAS solution has its own network Internet protocol (IP) address rather than being attached to an Exchange Server 2003 server. SCSI or fiber channel connections attach the storage device to the Ethernet network. The Exchange Server 2003 server maps file requests to the NAS server.

Exchange Server 2003 has local data access and bandwidth requirements that are incompatible with NAS products, and Microsoft does not recommend NAS technology. However, some NAS devices can be directly attached to a Windows 2003 server and appear on the hardware compatibility list.

Direct Access Storage

Microsoft recommends that you use a storage area network (SAN) for the storage of your Exchange Server 2003 files in a medium to large Exchange organization. This configuration optimizes server performance and reliability. A SAN provides storage and storage management capabilities for enterprise data and uses *fiber channel* switching technology to provide fast and reliable connectivity between storage and applications.

A SAN has three major component areas:

- Fiber channel switching technology
- Storage arrays on which data is stored and protected
- Storage and SAN management software

Hardware vendors, such as Intel, IBM, and Conexion, sell complete SAN packages that include the necessary hardware, software, and support. SAN software manages network and data flow redundancy by providing multiple paths to stored data, and facilitates connectivity between multivendor systems with different operating systems, and storage products from multiple vendors. Although deployment cost can be a barrier, a SAN solution may be preferable because the long-term total cost of ownership (TCO) can be lower than the cost of maintaining many direct-attached storage arrays.

The following are advantages to implementing a SAN solution in your Exchange Server 2003 organization:

- Exchange Server 2003 requires high I/O bandwidth that is supported only by a SAN-attached storage array.
- Exchange Server 2003 requires that mailbox and public folders stores exist on a drive that is local to the Exchange Server 2003 server. This requirement is met by SAN solutions that connect to Exchange servers through a local fiber channel connection.
- SANs are highly scalable. As mail data grows and mailbox limits are continually challenged, you need to increase storage capacity and I/O rates. As your organization expands, a SAN helps you to easily add disks.
- A SAN lets you expand your Exchange organization by adding servers. You can connect multiple Exchange servers to multiple storage arrays and then divide the storage among them.

Practice: Managing Storage

In this practice, you create a storage group, dismount a data store, move the transaction log files, enable circular logging, and mount the store.

Exercise 1: Create a Storage Group

In this exercise, you create a storage group. The data in the user mailboxes in this group does not require to be restored to the point of failure in the event of a crash, and you can therefore enable circular logging. To create this storage group, perform the following steps:

1. Start Exchange System Manager.

2. Navigate to Administrative Groups\First Administrative Group\Servers.

3. Right-click Server01, click New, and then click Storage Group.

4. On the General tab of the Properties page, type **My Storage Group** in the Name box.

5. Click OK.

6. In Exchange System Manager, expand Server01, right-click My Storage Group, click New, and then click Mailbox Store.

7. On the General tab of the Properties page, type **My Mailbox Store** in the Name box.

8. Click OK. Click Yes to mount the store.

Note   You would typically enable circular logging (if required) and specify a new location for the transaction log files when you create the storage group. However, this practice simulates the management of a working storage group, which should be dismounted before changes are made.

Exercise 2: Manage a Storage Group

In this exercise, you dismount a storage group, specify a location for the transaction log files, enable circular logging, and mount the database. In a real-world situation, if you were enabling circular logging, there would be little point in moving the transaction log files, which cannot be used for data recovery once circular logging is enabled. The purpose of this exercise is to become familiar with the procedures.

To manage a storage group, perform the following steps:

1. Start Exchange System Manager.

2. Navigate to Administrative Groups\First Administrative Group\Servers\Server01 \Storage Groups\My Storage Group.

3. Expand My Mailbox Store and click Logons to check that no users are connected.

Tip   In this exercise, no users will be connected. In the real world, however, you should warn users that the store is being dismounted and ask them to disconnect.

4. Right-click My Mailbox Store, and then click Dismount Store.

5. A warning appears telling you that all users will be disconnected. Click Yes.

6. Right-click My Storage Group, and then click Properties.

7. On the General tab, select the Enable Circular Logging check box, and then click Apply.

8. Read the warning, and then click Yes.

9. Specify a new location for the transaction log files. This should be a different volume, preferably on a different disk drive or array. Figure 12-1 shows this procedure.

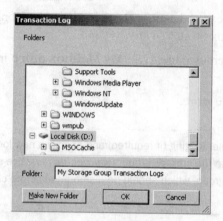

Figure 12-1   Specifying a new location for the transaction log files

10. Click OK.

11. Read the warning, and then click Yes.

> **Tip**   The warning indicates that all stores in the storage group will be dismounted to move the transaction log files. From this, you might deduce that you do not need to dismount any stores before starting the procedure. However, it is good practice to check for connected users and then dismount the stores before you start. This prevents users connecting to a store while you are specifying its properties.

12. The transaction log files are moved and My Mailbox Store is mounted automatically. Click OK to close the information box.

13. Click OK again to close the My Storage Group Properties dialog box.

Lesson Review

The following questions are intended to reinforce key information presented in this lesson. If you are unable to answer a question, review the lesson materials and then try the question again. You can find answers to the questions in the "Questions and Answers" section at the end of this chapter.

1. The Sales storage group database files are stored on a four-disk RAID-0 disk array. The transaction log files are stored on the same array. Circular logging is not

enabled. You do a full backup on Monday night and an incremental backup on Tuesday night. On Wednesday at 3:00 P.M., one of the disks in the array fails. Which of the following statements is true?

    a. You cannot retrieve any data that was written to the array on Tuesday or Wednesday.

    b. You can restore the data up to the Tuesday night backup.

    c. You can restore the data backed up on Tuesday night and then do a roll-forward to restore data up to 3:00 P.M. on Wednesday.

    d. You do not need to restore data. It is on a fault-tolerant array.

2. Which storage technology typically has its own IP address?

    a. RAID

    b. SAN

    c. ESA

    d. NAS

3. Your transaction log files are held on a four-spindle RAID-0+1 disk array. Disks A and B form a striped volume, as do disks C and D. The two striped volumes are mirrored. Disk A experiences a hardware failure. While replacing Disk A, your assistant accidentally damages Disk B. How do you recover from this situation?

_____

_____

Lesson Summary

- If you store database and transaction log files on the same disk drive and that disk goes down, then you can only restore up to the last backup. If the transaction log files are on a different disk and circular logging is disabled, then you can restore database files up to the point of failure by using the last backup and the transaction log files.

- RAID systems can protect data and provide failover protection. The exception is RAID-0, which gives enhanced I/O performance but does not protect data.

- Microsoft recommends ESA disk storage technology for small Exchange Server 2003 organizations and SAN disk storage technology for medium and large organizations.

Lesson 2: Backing Up Exchange Server 2003

The first line of defense in the event of a disaster is to make sure that critical information is backed up. This lesson introduces you to the various concepts and procedures for backing up Exchange Server 2003. Several third-party suppliers offer backup software suitable for Exchange Server 2003 servers, but this lesson concentrates on the backup utility included with Microsoft Windows 2003.

After this lesson, you will be able to

- Identify the types of data to back up
- Explain backup strategies
- Perform a full online backup
- Explain offline backup
- Start the volume shadow service
- Identify guidelines for backing up Exchange clusters
- Re-create full-text indexes
- Identify guidelines for verifying that backups are complete

Estimated lesson time: 90 minutes

Types of Data to Back Up

In the event of a disaster, it is important that you have backed up all the critical data for your company. This data includes the contents of your users' mailboxes and the configuration data that is needed to operate servers running Exchange Server 2003. Make sure that you have backups of all your management scripts and of all your Exchange stores.

You need to back up two types of data: static data and dynamic data.

Static Data

This type of data either does not change or does not change very often. Examples are as follows:

- Windows Server 2003 operating system software, along with any service packs or software updates
- Packaged application software (for example, Exchange Server 2003, Enterprise Edition)
- Supporting software, such as third-party backup or system management software

- User application software, such as Active Server Pages (ASP) applications, mailbox agents, and workflow software
- Management scripts

Dynamic Data

Dynamic data changes frequently. Examples are as follows:

- Exchange Server 2003 databases and log files
- Active Directory data
- Microsoft certificate services data
- Site Replication Service (SRS) databases
- System state data, including the Microsoft Internet Information Services (IIS) metabase
- Cluster quorum data (if your Exchange organization uses clusters)

Backup Strategies

You can use Windows 2003 Backup to implement different backup strategies. If you choose instead to use a third-party backup utility that is supported for Exchange Server 2003, the backup strategies remain the same. The backup strategy that you choose will have a direct impact on the restore process. You can choose from the following strategies:

- Full (sometimes known as normal)
- Full plus incremental
- Full plus differential
- Copy
- Copy plus incremental

Full Backup

Full backups copy both the database files and the transaction log files. At the completion of a full backup, transaction log files that have been committed to the database are deleted from the server. If your strategy is to use full backups only, then you should perform one every day.

Full Plus Incremental

Exchange databases can be very large, and it is often impractical to back them up every day. You can therefore choose to perform a full backup periodically, say once per week, and to supplement this by performing an incremental backup each day between full backups. The incremental backup captures only the transaction log data that has changed since the last full or incremental backup. This backup strategy copies only the transaction log files and not the database files. It is not available if you have enabled circular logging. Transaction log files are not deleted from the server at the completion of an incremental backup.

Full Plus Differential

You can also choose to perform a full backup periodically and to supplement this full backup with a daily differential backup. A differential backup backs up all the transaction files whether they were backed up previously or not. It is not available if you have enabled circular logging. Transaction log files are not deleted from the server at the completion of a differential backup.

Copy Backup

A copy backup is the same as a full backup, except that no file marking is performed. This means, for example, that performing an incremental backup after performing a copy backup is equivalent to performing the same incremental backup before that copy backup. You can use a copy backup to create a full backup of Active Directory or of the Exchange store without disturbing the state of any scheduled incremental or differential backups. Transaction log files are not deleted from the server at the completion of a copy backup. Typically, copy backups are used to create archived data that can be stored off-site.

Copy Plus Incremental

You can perform a copy backup in conjunction with incremental backups. This preserves all the transaction log files. With the other strategies (other than a straight copy), you delete committed log files during a full backup, thus limiting your ability to roll forward from any backup other than your very last full backup. With copy plus incremental, you can roll forward from any copy backup you have, just by adding all the incremental backups since the time the copy backup was taken.

To implement this strategy, you must begin the backup cycle with a full backup. Then you perform an incremental backup and continue alternating copy and incremental backups, typically doing an incremental each day immediately after the copy backup finishes. While this is a very safe strategy, it does not delete committed transaction log files, which could eventually fill your hard disk. You need to do a full backup every so often to prevent this.

Backup Size Implications

If you do a full backup every day, then this uses a lot of resource and a lot of backup media. You can perform online backups, so you do not need to dismount an information store to back it up. Nevertheless, there will be some degradation in performance. Full plus incremental backup has the least impact on performance. A full backup can be done during a quiet period (for example, the weekend), and incremental backups are relatively small. However, if you need to restore a database from backup, then you need to restore from the last full backup and then replay all the incremental backups performed since that full backup. If you use full plus differential backup, then in the same situation you need to restore from the last full backup and then replay only the last differential backup.

Performing Backups

Typically, you perform backups online, but offline backup is also available. You can also use the Volume Shadow Copy Service (VSS) to manage snapshot backups. The processes for backing up Exchange Server 2003 clusters are similar to those for backing up mailbox and public folder stores on Exchange clusters. Finally, you should be aware that backing up a database does not back up the indexes used for full text indexing, and you should know how to re-index data on your Exchange Server 2003 database.

Online Backups

When Exchange Server 2003 performs an online backup, all services, including the Exchange store, continue to run normally throughout the backup process. This allows users to continue to use their mailboxes during a backup process, whether the backup is incremental, differential, or full.

During a full online backup, the .edb, .stm, and .log files that comprise the Exchange store are backed up and checked for corruption at the file system level. Unreliable hardware, firmware, or disks can all cause file system corruption. The check verifies the checksums on each 4-kilobyte (KB) block or page in the database. If there is a checksum failure, backup aborts.

Therefore, after an online backup is complete, you should check the Event Viewer to find out whether your Exchange store is corrupted. If you see a failed backup with a page read error event in Event Viewer, there may be a problem in the database.

Offline Backups

Offline backup is not a recommended solution. To perform an offline backup of Exchange Server 2003 databases, you need to dismount the mailbox and public folder stores and then back up the database and transaction log files manually. However, you may need to perform an offline backup if your online backup failed, for example, due to an error such as a checksum-1018 JET_errRead Verify Failure.

You also need to perform an offline backup if you are using third-party backup software that does not support Exchange online backup application programming interfaces (APIs).

The disadvantages of offline backup include the following:

- You need to stop database services, and users will not be able to access their mailboxes during the backup.
- Transaction log files that contain transactions already written to the database files are not purged.
- The database is not checked for corruption during an offline backup.
- The chance of data loss is increased.

Volume Shadow Copy Service

One of the practical limits to the number of users supported on a single server is the time it takes to back up the mail storage. You can significantly reduce this limit by using VSS in Windows Server 2003 to help you create almost instantaneous backups of Exchange data at a specific point in time.

While an Exchange database is mounted, e-mail transactions can occur at any time. If you try to make a quick backup of the data at a particular point in time (a shadow copy), e-mail transactions may occur while the backup is progressing. As a result, when the backup finishes, it may contain an inconsistent copy of the data. If, in particular, you follow Microsoft's recommendation and store databases and transaction log files on separate volumes, this can lead to inconsistencies during a shadow backup.

If your backup software does not support VSS, the way to work around this problem is to conduct backups while the database is offline. This approach poses scheduling problems and negates any benefit of shadow copy backups. It also makes it difficult to complete backups because of the increasing demand for systems to be available 24 hours per day, seven days per week.

The VSS backup method solves this problem by creating a consistent point-in-time shadow copy of data while the system is online. After receiving a backup request, VSS notifies Exchange services that a backup is about to occur. Exchange then prepares for the backup by cleaning up on-disk structures and flushing caches.

Software that supports VSS (such as Windows 2003 Backup) can create a shadow copy of the disk at the beginning of the backup process. The software then creates the backup by using the shadow copy rather than the working disk. This method offers the following advantages:

- It produces a backup of a volume that reflects the state of that volume at the instant the backup started, even if the data changes while the backup is in progress.

- All the backup data is internally consistent and reflects the state of the volume at a single point in time.

- It notifies applications and services that a backup is about to occur. The services and applications can then prepare for the backup.

VSS support is at the storage group level and provides two disaster recovery packages that can be leveraged by software vendors. These are as follows:

- Point in time (no transaction log files are replayed)
- Full recovery (transaction log files are replayed)

Important   Exchange Server 2003 supports VSS for full and copy backups but not for incremental or differential backups.

Backing Up Exchange Clusters

The disk resources shared in an Exchange Server 2003 cluster include the quorum disk resource and the resource that contains the Exchange Server 2003 stores. Any of the nodes in a cluster can access the shared disks, and all nodes rely upon the data on these disks. Your disaster recovery strategy therefore requires that you back up these resources.

Exchange Server 2003 database files and transaction log files are stored on one or more of the shared disk resources of the cluster. Each Exchange virtual server located on a node in a cluster has its own set of databases and log files. To recover from a failure of one of the shared disk resources that contains your Exchange database and transaction log files, you must perform a separate backup of those files.

The quorum disk resource maintains the consistency of your cluster. It ensures, for example, that the cluster databases that reside in the Windows registries of each node in the cluster are consistent. These cluster databases contain information about all physical and logical elements in a cluster, including object properties and configuration data. To enable recovery from a failure in the quorum disk resource, you need to perform either a full computer backup or a Windows backup on the node that owns the quorum disk resource.

You can use the Microsoft cluster tool (Clustool.exe) to back up the configuration of an entire cluster. Clustool.exe can perform cluster configuration backups after your initial cluster configuration is complete, and after you make any configuration changes to the cluster.

Repairing Indexes

Full-text indexing (also known as content indexing) is an optional Exchange Server 2003 feature that allows users to perform full-text searches across both messages and attachments within messages. Full-text indexes are not stored with Exchange databases. By default, they are located in the Program Files\Exchsrvr\ExchangeServer_*Server Name* \Projects directory and are managed by the Microsoft Search service.

Full-text indexes are not backed up as part of your Exchange Server 2003 database backups. If a disaster occurs and you need to rebuild your server, then you also need to re-create your full-text indexes. To repair full-text indexes that are corrupt or are not synchronized with your Exchange databases, you must re-index the data on your Exchange databases. If Microsoft Search is damaged, you must restore the service as part of your full-text indexing repair.

Verifying Backups

To verify the success of your backup procedures, you need to check that the backup occurred and that it ran without error. You should examine the Windows Server 2003 backup log for the backup event that you are verifying, and then review the events in the Windows Server 2003 event log to ensure that your backup was completed as scheduled and without errors. If you identify any errors or inconsistencies in these log files, you need to resolve them as soon as possible.

You can also verify that data has been backed up successfully by restoring that data to another computer during a trial restore. This procedure is described in Lesson 3 of this chapter.

Practice: Performing Backups

In this practice, you back up a storage group, enable VSS, and delete and re-create full-text indexes. You need to perform a backup in order to practice restoring the storage group databases in Lesson 3.

Exercise 1: Back Up a Storage Group

In this exercise, you perform a full online backup of a storage group. The exercise gives a backup location on another volume of the same computer. If you want, you can change this either to a folder on the same volume or to a folder on your second computer on which you have granted the appropriate write permissions. If you choose to specify a different backup path, you need to specify the same path when you perform a restore in the next lesson.

To back up a storage group online, perform the following steps:

1. On Server01, from the Start menu, point to All Programs, point to Accessories, point to System Tools, and then click Backup.

2. In the Backup Or Restore Wizard, on the Welcome To The Backup Or Restore Wizard page, click Next.

3. On the Backup Or Restore page, ensure that Back Up All Files And Settings is selected, and then click Next.

4. On the What To Back Up page, select Let Me Choose What To Back Up, and then click Next.

5. On the Items To Backup Up page, in the Items To Back Up box, expand Microsoft Exchange Server, expand Server01, expand Microsoft Information Store, select the My Storage Group check box as shown in Figure 12-2, and then click Next.

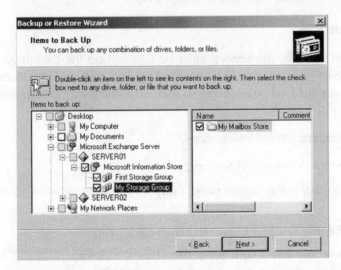

Figure 12-2   Specifying what to back up

6. On the Backup Type, Destination, And Name page, click Browse.

7. In the Save As dialog box, browse to D:\Mybackup. In the File Name box, type **Mybackup.bkf**, and then click Save.

8. On the Backup Type, Destination, And Name page, click Next.

9. On the Completing The Backup Or Restore Wizard page, click Finish.

10. When the backup is finished, click Report in the Backup Progress dialog box.

11. Verify that no errors are listed in the backup log, as shown in Figure 12-3. If no errors are listed, the backup was successful. Close the backup log window.

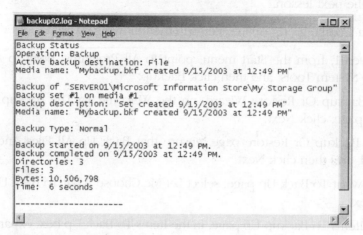

Figure 12-3   The backup log

12. In the Backup Progress dialog box, click Close.

Exercise 2: Enable VSS

To enable support for VSS, the service must be enabled on the Exchange server, and the backup software must support the new backup and restore APIs. In this exercise, you enable VSS on your Exchange server so that a backup program can perform a volume shadow copy.

To enable VSS, perform the following steps:

1. Open the Services console on Server01.

2. In Services (Local), in the details pane, right-click Volume Shadow Copy, and then click Start.

3. Right-click Volume Shadow Copy, and then click Properties.

4. In the Volume Shadow Copy Properties (Local Computer) dialog box, in the Startup Type box, select Automatic, and then click OK.

5. Close Services.

Exercise 3: Create a Public Folder Index

In order to practice deleting, re-creating, and repairing indexes, you must first index your public folder store. To enable full-text indexing on a public folder store, perform the following steps:

1. Open Exchange System Manager.

2. Navigate to Administrative Groups\First Administrative Group\Servers\Server01 \First Storage Group, and then click First Storage Group.

3. Right-click Public Folder Store (SERVER01), and then click Create Full-Text Index.

4. Click OK to accept the default catalog location.

5. Right-click Public Folder Store (SERVER01), and then click Start Full Population.

> **Tip**   This procedure assumes that you are building the index for the first time. Otherwise, unless there is a problem with your index, you would use incremental population.

6. Click Yes to close the warning box and start the update process. Click Yes again to close the subsequent warning box.

7. The update process can take a few minutes. Expand Public Folder Store (SERVER01) and click Full-Text Indexing. In the details pane, check that the Last Build Time is today's date. You may need to press F5 to refresh the window.

Exercise 4: Delete and Re-Create Indexes

Re-indexing the data on your Exchange databases requires that you remove full-text indexing information and re-create full-text indexes. To delete the damaged indexes and re-create them, perform the following steps:

1. Open Exchange System Manager.

2. Navigate to Administrative Groups\First Administrative Group\Servers\Server01 \First Storage Group, and then click First Storage Group.

3. In the details pane, right-click Public Folder Store, click Delete Full-Text Index, and then click Yes to continue.

4. From the Start menu, click Run, type **regedit**, and then click OK.

5. In Registry Editor, navigate to HKEY_LOCAL_MACHINE\SOFTWARE\Microsoft \Search\1.0\Databases, and then expand Databases.

6. Under Databases, click ExchangeServer_SERVER01.

7. In the details pane, next to Log Path under Data, locate the folder where the property store and log files are kept. Record the path to this folder because you need it for the next step. By default, the folder is C:\Program Files\Exchsrvr \ExchangeServer_SERVER01.

8. In Microsoft Windows Explorer, open the folder that you recorded in the previous step.

9. In the open folder, verify that the Projects and GatherLogs subfolders are empty. Do not delete the Projects and GatherLogs folders, but if there are any files in them, then delete the files. Figure 12-4 shows the GatherLogs folder.

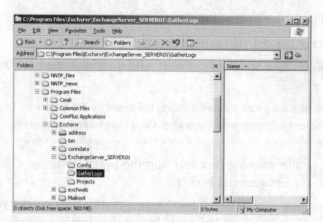

Figure 12-4 Checking that the GatherLogs folder is empty

10. Close Windows Explorer and close Registry Editor.

11. In Exchange System Manager, right-click Public Folder Store, and then click Create Full-Text Index.

12. In the Public Folder Store (SERVER01) dialog box, click OK to accept the default location for the catalog.

13. In Exchange System Manager, right-click Public Folder Store (SERVER01), click Start Full Population, click Yes to continue, and then click Yes again to close the subsequent warning box.

14. Right-click Public Folder Store (SERVER01), and then click Properties.

15. In the Public Folder Store (SERVER01) Properties dialog box, select the Full-Text Indexing tab.

16. On the Full-Text Indexing tab, select the This Index Is Currently Available For Searching By Clients check box, click OK, and then click OK again to acknowledge the warning.

17. Click OK to close the Public Folder Store (SERVER01) Properties dialog box.

Lesson Review

The following questions are intended to reinforce key information presented in this lesson. If you are unable to answer a question, review the lesson materials and then try the question again. You can find answers to the questions in the "Questions and Answers" section at the end of this chapter.

1. You store your databases and transaction log files on different hard disks. Circular logging is not enabled. You perform a differential backup every weekday night. Over the weekend, you perform a copy backup and archive the tape. It is taking longer each night to perform your differential backup and you are receiving warnings that the hard disk containing your transaction log files is nearing capacity. How do you deal with the situation?

   _____

   _____

2. You decide to use third-party backup software that uses the shadow copy method. You do not want to perform offline backups, and you want to ensure that your backed up databases are consistent. What do you need to check, and what step do you need to take?

   _____

   _____

3. What do you need to do to ensure that your Exchange Server 2003 organization can recover from the failure of a quorum disk resource?

   _____

   _____

Lesson Summary

- Copy and full backups back up both database and transaction log files. Incremental and differential backup types back up only the transaction logs. Full backup truncates the transaction logs—that is, it deletes the logs that contain transactions that have been written to the database.

- VSS gives backup software the facility to create a snapshot of file contents and to perform a backup from that snapshot.

- All files in a storage group can be backed up while the storage group is online.

- Full-text indexes are not backed up as part of your Exchange Server 2003 database backups. If a disaster occurs and you need to rebuild your server, then you also need to re-create your full-text indexes.

Lesson 3: Restoring Exchange Server 2003

If a disaster occurs, you may need to restore one or more databases from backup. You need to know how to do this, but you also need to know how to ensure that you do not make the situation worse. Sometimes a damaged database can contain retrievable information, and you should protect that information from being overwritten by a restored database that turns out to be unreadable. This lesson covers the principles behind restoring data and how you can verify your backups before you use them in a restore operation.

After this lesson, you will be able to

- Identify guidelines for restoring stores from online backups
- Explain the methods for restoring an offline backup
- Recover mailboxes and messages
- Explain how to recover public folders
- Restore clusters
- Restore Active Directory by using the Windows Server 2003 Backup utility
- Restore an Exchange Server 2003 server
- Configure a recovery server
- Explain how to perform a test restore on a recovery server

Estimated lesson time: 120 minutes

Recovering Databases

If a server running Exchange Server 2003 is still functional after a disaster, you can use the Windows Server 2003 Backup utility to restore the stores that you want to recover. To recover one or more stores, first make sure that the Exchange store is running. In addition, make sure that the Exchange store or stores that you want to restore are dismounted. You need only dismount the specific Exchange store or stores that you want to restore. This allows users to continue to access all of the other Exchange stores in the storage group.

Exchange contains a built-in mechanism that uses signature values to prevent you from accidentally replaying log files from a different storage group against the Exchange store you are restoring. Each storage group has a log file signature value, and each log file in the sequence has the signature stamped on it. The corresponding .edb file stores this signature value in its header information.

Using the Windows Server 2003 Backup Utility to Restore Stores

Before performing a restore from an online backup, you should make a copy of all existing database files, even if these files are damaged. Until your backup set is fully restored and verified, you cannot assume that your store has been successfully restored. If the attempted recovery fails, it might still be possible to repair the existing store from its copy, although you will probably lose at least some data during the repair process. When you have created copies of the database files that you want to restore, you should then attempt a recovery from your online backup.

> **Tip**   When you are restoring from a backup set, your current database files are overwritten as soon as the process begins. Rename the database files that you are restoring before you begin the restore process. Also, ensure that your database drive is at least half empty. Otherwise, you will not be able to restore from backup because you will not have enough space for the restore.

The Microsoft Exchange Information Store (IS) service manages the restore operation. After you dismount the store or stores, the restore process will perform the following operations:

- Replace the existing database files with the restored database files.
- Copy the log files that are on the backup media into a temporary log directory.
- Create the Restore.env file for each restore operation in progress in the same directory as the log files that are restored from backup media.
- Check the log file signature of all temporary log files to verify that the restored log files correspond with the storage group that manages the database being restored. Replay and apply the restored log files to the database.
- Replay and apply the active storage groups' log files to the database.
- Delete the log files from the temporary log directory.

Restoring Multiple Stores

You can restore multiple stores to multiple storage groups at the same time by running multiple instances of the Windows Server 2003 Backup utility. However, because each storage group is a backup set and log files are shared, it is best to perform one restore per storage group at a time. You can restore multiple stores in a storage group simultaneously; but you should not replay the log files simultaneously.

For example, if you have a single backup set that contains six databases, you can restore all six in a single operation, and a single shared Restore.env file will control hard recovery. If, on the other hand, you have six backup sets that you are restoring in parallel from six separate instances of your backup application, then you need to define separate temporary folders for each restore, and you should manually run hard recovery against each restore one at a time, so they don't all try to do hard recovery simultaneously.

To restore multiple backup sets in parallel from the same storage group, you need to do the following:

- Restore each backup set from backup media to its own temporary log directory.
- Ensure that the Last Backup Set check box is not selected.
- Use the Last Backup Set option to trigger hard recovery.
- Run the eseutil utility with the /cc switch in each temporary directory that contains restored transaction log files.

Restoring an Offline Backup

You have two methods of restoring an offline backup of Exchange databases: a point-in-time restoration or a roll-forward restoration. To perform either of these restorations, you need to ensure that the databases in the storage group that will be restored are dismounted and consistent.

A point-in-time restoration is when the database is restored but no log files are replayed into the database. All the data that was created after the backup is lost. You use point-in-time restoration to restore from an offline backup when circular logging is enabled on your Exchange server. Because circular logging reuses log files, not all of the log files required to update your database are available, and you would only be able to restore up to when the backup was made.

A roll-forward restoration is when the database is restored and the log files that were created after the backup are played into the database. If all the log files are available, all the data that was created after the backup can be restored. For roll-forward restorations, all the log files that were created after the time that the backup was taken must exist (including the current transaction log file). You delete the checkpoint file and shut down all the other databases in the storage group. Roll-forward automatically replays your log files into the restore database to make it current.

Recovering Mailboxes

As part of your disaster recovery process, you may need to recover a deleted mailbox or a message that a user has deleted in a mailbox. You should plan for this risk by enabling the deletion setting on the mailbox store to retain mailboxes and deleted items for a specified number of days.

When the mailbox retention option is enabled, the default retention period is set to 30 days. If a mailbox is deleted, and if restoration is requested within the 30-day retention period, then you can recover and reconnect that mailbox without restoring the entire database.

If the retention period has expired and you need to recover a mailbox, you need to use a recovery server. In this case, you need to perform the following tasks:

- Install the recovery server in a different Active Directory forest from the forest in which the original server is located.

- Install Exchange Server 2003 on the recovery server by using the same organization name that was used in the original organization.

- Recover the database to an administrative group in which the legacyExchangeDN values match the legacyExchangeDN values in the administrative group from which the database was originally located.

- Name the restore storage group and the restore logical database so that their names match the original storage group and logical database names.

- Create a .pst file and move all data that you need to recover into the .pst file.

- Open the .pst file on the production server and move the data back to the appropriate location.

Recovering Messages

Exchange Server 2003 performs both backup and restore tasks at the physical page level rather than at the mailbox level. Because of this, you cannot easily restore individual messages in a mailbox from a backup. If you want to allow users to retrieve messages from the Deleted Items folder in Outlook or Outlook Web Access (OWA), then you can do so by enabling the Keep Deleted Items For (Days) option for individual users in Active Directory, as shown in Figure 12-5. Alternatively, you can create a new mailbox policy using Exchange System Manager and set a retention policy, as shown in Figure 12-6. To restore an individual message, a user selects the Deleted Items folder and uses the Recover Deleted Items option from the Tools menu in Outlook, or from the Options menu in OWA.

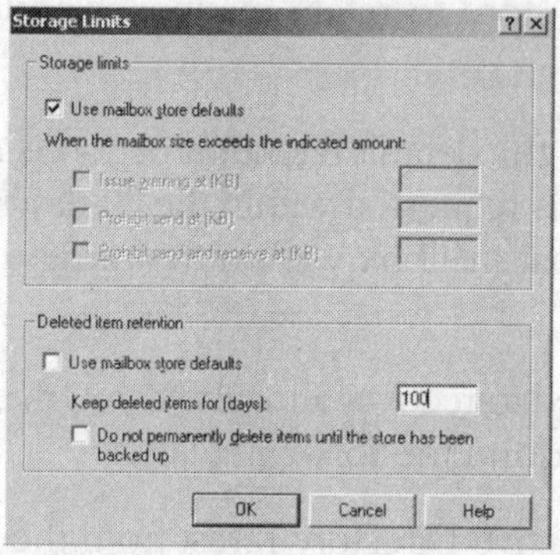

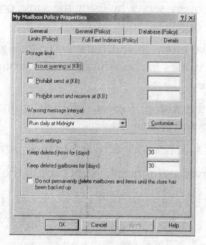

Figure 12-5 Setting a mailbox retention period for an individual user

Figure 12-6 Setting a mailbox retention policy

If you choose not to configure Exchange to allow users to retrieve messages from the Deleted Items folder, then you need to restore the entire mailbox to a recovery server, extract the message from the mailbox into a .pst file, and have the user import the message from the .pst file into his or her mailbox.

Restoring Public Folders

The difficulty with restoring public folders is that if you restore the public folder store, then not only will you restore the public folder that you are trying to recover, but you will also replace all the other existing public folders with the information contained in the backup set. This difficulty is reduced if you create a replica of the folder on another server, which allows you to replicate a copy of the public folder to the server where it was lost. If, however, you have only one server or have a dedicated public folder server, you need to use a recovery server to restore the public folder from your backup media.

The procedure for recovering a public folder is very similar to recovering an individual mailbox. To recover a public folder from backup media, you need to perform the following operations:

- Configure a recovery server to restore the public folder store.
- Use Windows Server 2003 Backup to restore the public folder store.
- Log on to the recovery Exchange server, open Outlook, and then copy the public folder to a .pst file.
- Log on to the production server, load the .pst file into your profile, and copy the folder back to the public folder tree of the production server.

Caution   Do not copy the restored public folder store into the production system. On the recovery server, new system folders are typically created in the public folder store. If you copy the public folder store on to the production server, then these folders will conflict with existing system folders.

Using Exmerge.exe To Restore Mailboxes

After you restore a database to the Recovery Storage Group, you can use the Exmerge.exe utility to move the recovered mailbox data to the regular storage group. You can use this method to recover an entire database or just a single mailbox. Mailboxes in the Recovery Storage Group are disconnected and are not accessible to users with mail clients.

To use a Recovery Storage Group, you must meet the following requirements:

- You must be logged in with an account (such as Backup Operators) that has Receive As and Send As permissions on all the Exchange mailboxes.

Tip   To grant these permissions, you can create a security group (called, for example, mailboxrecovery), add your logon account to this group, and then grant the group full permissions on the database object in Exchange System Manager.

- You must create a Recovery Storage Group on your Exchange server.
- You must verify that the original database and mailbox still exist in Active Directory.

To use a Recovery Storage Group to restore mailbox data, you must complete the following steps:

- Set up the Recovery Storage Group:

  ❑ Use the context menu of the server object to set up the Recovery Storage Group.

  ❑ Specify the transaction log and system path locations.

  ❑ Add the database to be recovered to the Recovery Storage Group by using the context menu of the Recovery Storage Group.

- Restore the mailbox database to the Recovery Storage Group:

  ❑ Use your backup and restore application and select the database and log files that you want to restore.

  ❑ Define your temporary file directory and indicate if this is the last backup to be restored in the set.

  ❑ Mount the store after the restore is complete.

- Merge the mailbox data from the restored database to the original database:

  ❑ Start the Microsoft Exchange Mailbox Merge Wizard (Exmerge.exe) from the command prompt.

  ❑ Follow the instructions in the wizard to specify the export method and the source and destination server (when the Recovery Storage Group is on the same server as the database you are working with, this is a single server).

  ❑ Select only the databases that are in the Recovery Storage Group to be restored.

  ❑ Select individual or multiple mailboxes that you want to restore.

  ❑ If necessary, specify the appropriate locale.

  ❑ Specify a temporary folder.

  ❑ Follow the remaining instructions to finish the wizard and move the mailbox data.

The wizard will copy data from mailboxes in the recovery database and merge it with data in the corresponding mailboxes in the original database.

Restoring Clusters

The disaster recovery processes for restoring Exchange Server 2003 clusters are similar to the processes for restoring data on standalone Exchange Server 2003 servers. You will encounter one of the following scenarios when you restore an Exchange cluster:

- Recovering a single server node in a cluster

- Recovering a lost cluster quorum

- Recovering the shared disk resource where Exchange databases reside

Recovering a Single Server Node   When a single node in a cluster fails, the Exchange resources running on the node are moved to another available node in the cluster. Exchange databases remain intact on shared storage and can be accessed by the Exchange virtual server from another node in the cluster. This security feature provides reliability when disaster occurs on a single cluster node. When resources are moved to an available node in the cluster, perform the following procedure to remove the non-functioning node and replace it with a new node:

1. Use Cluster Administrator to evict the lost server node from the cluster.

2. Build a new server node for the cluster by installing Windows 2003 on the new computer and provide a new computer name.

3. Rejoin the server node to the cluster.

4. Install Exchange on the server node and move resources back to the node.

Recovering a Lost Cluster Quorum   You can recover from a cluster quorum failure if you have backed up the cluster quorum resource. If, for instance, the cluster quorum resource is lost on a shared disk along with the Exchange databases, then you need to restore the cluster quorum resource from backup.

To restore the quorum from backup, perform the following procedure:

1. If the signature of the quorum disk has changed since you made the backup, then use the Windows Server 2003 Resource Kit dumpconfig utility to restore the signature.

2. Stop the Cluster Service on all cluster nodes.

3. Use Windows Server 2003 Backup to restore the system state data, which contains the contents of the cluster quorum disk.

4. Do not restart the computer when prompted; instead run the Clusrest.exe Resource Kit tool to restore the content of the Systemroot\Cluster\Cluster_backup directory to the cluster quorum disk.

5. Restart the computer.

Recovering the Database Shared Disk Resource   If the shared drive that Exchange uses for its databases is lost, you need to restore your Exchange databases from backup. To restore Exchange Server 2003 databases from backup, perform the following procedure:

1. Select the Do Not Mount At Startup check box for databases owned by the Exchange virtual servers on the cluster.

2. Perform the steps described in the exercise "Restore a Mailbox Store From Backup" in this lesson.

> **Tip** On a cluster server, you must verify that the shares where Exchange databases reside are available to, and can be accessed by, the cluster node that owns the disk resource.

3. Use Exchange System Manager to verify that databases are mounted.

4. Use Event Viewer to check the Event log.

5. Clear the Do Not Mount At Startup check box for each database that is successfully restored.

Backing Up and Restoring System State Data

Because Exchange Server 2003 relies on Active Directory, you may need to restore Active Directory information during some disaster scenarios. You can use Windows Server 2003 Backup to back up and restore Active Directory on domain controllers. You can perform a backup operation while the domain controller is online. You can perform a restore operation only when the domain controller is booted into Directory Services Restore mode by pressing the F8 key when the server is booting. Backing up Active Directory requires that you back up your Windows Server 2003 system state data.

The procedures for backing up and restoring system state data are described in exercises in this lesson.

Restoring Entire Servers

A full server recovery involves restoring both Exchange Server 2003 and Windows 2003. When you perform a full server recovery, you must reinstall Exchange Server 2003 in Disaster Recovery mode before recovering any Exchange Server 2003 data. You must reinstall Exchange Server 2003 while the Exchange server object for that server still exists in Active Directory. Running Setup in Disaster Recovery mode does not modify or re-create any Active Directory objects for the server being recovered. If you run Setup in any mode other than Disaster Recovery mode, the setup will fail because a duplicate server name will be detected.

> **Important** When you recover an Exchange server, always use the /DisasterRecovery switch. If you run Setup without using this switch, then Setup runs in Reinstall mode and automatically mounts the mailbox stores and public stores after the setup process completes. Mounting mailbox stores and public folder stores before restoring your Exchange databases can cause problems, including the potential loss of e-mail messages.

You can prepare to recover a server running Exchange Server 2003 by meeting the following requirements:

- Replace any failed hardware.
- Have the Windows 2003 and Exchange Server 2003 installation CDs available, including any applicable service packs or software updates.
- Have full backups of the system drive available.
- Have backups of all Exchange Server 2003 databases available. Verify that all member server objects exist in Active Directory.
- If the server running Exchange Server 2003 that you are restoring is a member server in the local domain, make sure that Active Directory still contains a server object for that server.
- Have a backup of your domain controller available if it is the only domain controller in your domain.
- Have a recent Windows 2003 system state backup set available.

Performing a Trial Restore

You can verify that data has been backed up successfully by restoring that data to another computer during a trial restore. It might not be feasible to verify backups on every server, particularly in a large installation. However, you can test the integrity of the system and identify any potential problems by performing a restore and verification process on selected servers or backup devices.

> **Real World   Delegate Trial Restores**
>
> You can train new administrators by asking them to perform trial restores. This is a safe way to ensure that they know how to perform a restore, and it can be done outside the stressful situation of having to recover from a real disaster. It also saves you from having to perform what can become a repetitive and tedious task.

Practice: Recovering from a Disaster Using Restore

In this practice, you recover a mailbox store, recover a deleted message, and back up and restore system state data. The practice also includes an exercise in restoring a complete server. This last exercise is too lengthy to describe mouse-click by mouse-click. Nevertheless, if you have completed all the other exercises in this chapter, you should be able to attempt it.

Exercise 1: Restore a Mailbox Store from Backup

In this exercise, you restore a mailbox store from its backup. In order to complete the exercise, you must have already performed a full online backup of My Storage Group.

1. Open Exchange System Manager.

2. Navigate to Administrative Groups\First Administrative Group\Servers\Server01 \My Storage Group, and then click on My Storage Group.

3. In the details pane, right-click Default Mailbox Store, click Dismount Store, and then click Yes to continue.

4. From the Start menu, click Run, type **C:\Program Files\Exchsrvr\My Storage Group**, and then click OK.

5. In C:\Program Files\Exchsrvr\Default Storage Group, select all the files, right-click them, and then click Copy.

6. Open Windows Explorer. Create a new folder C:\Temporary Logs, open Temporary Logs and create a new folder named Backup, open Backup, and then paste the copied files into C:\Temporary Logs\Backup.

7. Close C:\Temporary Logs\Backup.

8. From the Start menu, click All Programs, point to Accessories, point to System Tools, and then click Backup.

9. In the Backup Or Restore Wizard, on the Welcome To The Backup Or Restore Wizard page, click Next.

10. On the Backup Or Restore page, select Restore Files And Settings, and then click Next.

11. On the What To Restore page, in the Items To Restore box, expand File, expand Mybackup.bkf, select the Server01\Microsoft Information Store\My Storage Group check box, and then click Next.

12. In the Restore Database Server dialog box, in the Temporary Location For Log And Patch Files box, type **C:\Temporary Logs**, select the Last Restore Set (Log File Replay Will Start After This Restore Completes) check box, and select the Mount Database After Restore check box. The wizard page should look similar to Figure 12-7. Click Next.

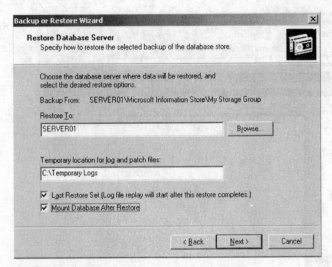

Figure 12-7   Setting the restore parameters

13. On the Completing The Backup Or Restore Wizard page, click Finish.

14. If the Check Backup File Location box appears, check that it contains the correct location of your backup file, and then click OK.

15. When the restore is complete, click Report in the Restore Progress dialog box.

16. Verify that no errors are listed in the backup log, and then close the log.

17. In the Restore Progress dialog box, click Close.

Exercise 2: Use OWA To Recover Deleted Messages

In this exercise, you delete messages from your mailbox and then use OWA to recover them. You need to have at least one item in your Deleted Items folder. To recover deleted messages, perform the following steps:

1. Open Internet Explorer and connect to *http://Server01/exchange*.

2. In the Folders list, click Deleted Items.

3. In Deleted Items, on the toolbar, click Empty Deleted Items, and then click OK to close the warning box. The Deleted Items folder should now be empty.

4. In Deleted Items, on the toolbar, click Recover Deleted Items, as shown in Figure 12-8.

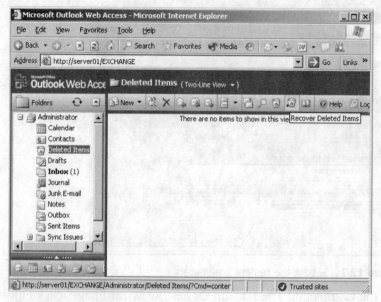

Figure 12-8   Recovering deleted messages

5. In the Recover Deleted Items window, select the message or messages that you want to recover, and then click Recover.

6. In the Recover Deleted Items window, click Close.

7. In the Deleted Items folder, verify that any messages that you recovered are listed. Move the items to your Inbox.

8. Close OWA.

Exercise 3: Back Up System State Data

In some disaster recovery scenarios, you need to restore system state data from a backup. To back up system state data, perform the following steps:

1. On Server01, close all applications.

2. From the Start menu, click All Programs, System Tools, and then click Backup.

3. In the Backup Or Restore Wizard, on the Welcome To The Backup Or Restore Wizard page, click Next.

4. On the Backup Or Restore page, select Back Up Files And Settings, and then click Next.

5. On the What To Back Up page, select Let Me Choose What To Back Up, and then click Next.

6. In the Items To Back Up box, expand My Computer, select the System State check box, and then click Next.

7. Type **D:\Mybackup** in the Choose A Place To Save Your Backup box, type **SystemState** in the Type A Name For This Backup box, and then click Next.

8. The backup can take a considerable time. Click Report to ensure that no errors occurred. Close the backup log and the Backup Progress dialog box.

Exercise 4: Restore System State Data

If you have backed up system state data, then you can restore Active Directory information on a domain controller. To restore the system state on a domain controller, perform the following steps:

1. Restart Server01 and press F8 when prompted to boot into Directory Services Restore mode.

2. Log on with the same administrator account and password that you used as credentials when promoting the server to a domain controller.

3. You are warned that your computer is starting in Safe mode. Click OK to close the warning box.

4. From the Start menu, click All Programs, point to Accessories, point to System Tools, and then click Backup.

5. In the Backup Or Restore Wizard, on the Welcome To The Backup Or Restore Wizard page, click Next.

6. On the Backup Or Restore page, select Restore Files And Settings, and then click Next.

7. On the What To Restore page, in the contents pane, double-click SystemState.bkf.

8. In the Items To Restore pane, select the check box next to System State. Double-click System State and ensure that SYSVOL appears in the contents pane, as shown in Figure 12-9. Click Next.

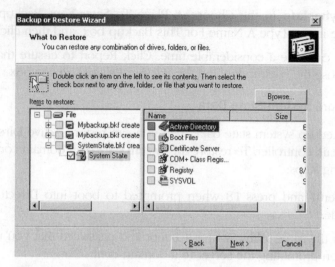

Figure 12-9   Specifying a System State restore

9. On the Completing The Backup And Restore Wizard page, click Advanced.

10. On the Where To Restore page, ensure that Original Location is specified, and then click Next.

11. Click OK to close the warning box.

12. On the How To Restore page, ensure that Leave Existing Files (Recommended) is selected, and then click Next.

13. On the Advanced Restore Options page, ensure that Restore Junction Points, But Not The Folders And File Data They Reference is selected, as shown in Figure 12-10. This ensures that sysvol junction points are re-created. Click Next.

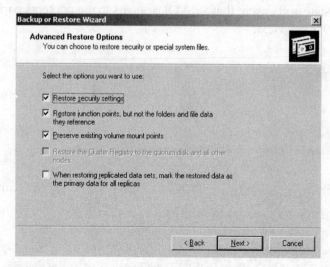

Figure 12-10   Specifying the advanced restore options

14. Click Finish.

15. When the restore has finished, click Report in the Restore Progress dialog box.

16. Ensure that no errors are reported, and close the backup log.

17. Click Close to close the Restore Progress box.

18. Click Yes to restart Server01.

Exercise 5: Restore an Exchange Server 2003 Member Server

In this exercise, you restore an entire Exchange Server 2003 member server. As stated previously, this exercise is too complex to describe mouse-click by mouse-click. Nevertheless, if you have performed all the exercises in this and previous chapters, you should be able to attempt this one. To restore an Exchange Server 2003 member server, perform the following steps:

1. If you can still access the hard disks of the damaged server, copy the Exchange Server 2003 database files from that server to a folder on a network share or to a removable storage device.

2. Replace any damaged hardware. If possible, ensure that all replacement hardware in the server you are rebuilding is identical to the hardware that existed in the server that experienced the disaster.

3. Install Windows 2003 on the server that you are rebuilding.

4. Restore the Windows backup set that was performed on the damaged server to the server you are rebuilding. Restoring the Windows backup set restores the Windows 2003 system files, including the registry database and Internet Information Services (IIS) metabase files. This process also provides the server that you are rebuilding with its original NetBIOS name and returns it to the correct domain. If you do not perform this step, you cannot properly run Setup in Disaster Recovery mode.

5. Install any Windows 2003 service packs and software updates that were running on the damaged server to the server you are rebuilding.

6. Install any applications (other than Exchange Server 2003) that run on the server.

> **Tip**   Install the applications to the same locations and with the same configurations as the applications that were installed on the damaged server.

7. Restore any additional data backups that were performed on the damaged server.

8. Run Exchange Server 2003 Setup in Disaster Recovery mode. This process installs Exchange applications and any necessary Exchange files to the server you are rebuilding. This process also uses the configuration information that is stored on the Exchange Server object in Active Directory to reclaim the configuration of the original server. The configuration information that is reclaimed includes the Exchange storage group names, mailbox store names, public folder store names, and virtual server configuration settings. When you run Exchange in Disaster Recovery mode, ensure that all the components that existed on the damaged server are selected.

9. If not already selected, select Disaster Recovery for each component that was installed on the damaged server.

10. Install Exchange Server 2003 to the same drive and directory that it was installed to on the damaged server. At a minimum, you should ensure that all the drive letters on which databases and log files were kept are available.

11. Install any Exchange Server 2003 hotfixes that were running on the damaged server.

12. Install in Disaster Recovery mode any Exchange Server 2003 service packs that were running previously on the damaged server to the server. Installing Exchange Server 2003 service packs in Disaster Recovery mode prevents the Exchange databases from being mounted at the end of the service pack installation process, which enables you to proceed directly to restoring the Exchange databases from backup.

13. If the drives that contain the Exchange database files and log files were also lost in the disaster, restore the Exchange Server 2003 databases that existed on the damaged server.

14. If you were able to archive the log files from the damaged server as recommended in step 1 of this procedure, copy these files to the correct location on the recovery server. If you do not copy the most recent log files to the proper locations on the server that you are rebuilding, you will lose changes that were made to Exchange databases up to the time the disaster occurred.

15. If the server that experienced the disaster included any Exchange full-text indexes, repair full-text indexing by re-creating full-text indexes on the server you are rebuilding.

Lesson Review

The following questions are intended to reinforce key information presented in this lesson. If you are unable to answer a question, review the lesson materials and then try the question again. You can find answers to the questions in the "Questions and Answers" section at the end of this chapter.

1. You want to restore three storage groups, each of which contains five databases. How many restore operations do you need to perform?

_____

_____

2. Your Exchange Server 2003 organization has a dedicated public folder server. You want to restore a single public folder store from backup. What difficulty do you face, and how do you accomplish your goal?

_____

_____

3. You have backed up system state data on a domain controller. What must you do to restore this data?

_____

_____

4. What happens to the Exchange Server 2003 resources running on a single node in a cluster if that node fails?

_____

_____

Lesson Summary

- To recover a damaged Exchange Server 2003 storage group, dismount the storage group and restore it from backup. If transaction log files are available, the databases can be rolled forward to the point of failure.

- If you need to restore a deleted mailbox within its retention period, then you can recover and reconnect the mailbox without restoring the entire database. If the retention period has expired, then you need to use a recovery server to recover the mailbox.

- You can allow users to retrieve messages from the Deleted Items folder in Outlook or OWA.

- If you need to restore Active Directory data in a domain controller, for example, when it is the only domain controller in the domain, then you should back up system state data. You can restore this data by booting the server up in Directory Services Restore mode.

Case Scenario Exercise

You are the Exchange and domain administrator for Tailspin Toys. Your Exchange Server 2003 organization has a dedicated public server. Your backup strategy is to do a full backup of all Exchange stores every weekend and incremental backups on weekdays. Tailspin Toys has recently purchased an additional server that you intend to configure as a recovery server and domain controller in a separate forest to the *tailspintoys.com* Active

Directory forest. Some senior managers are dubious about the value of configuring an expensive computer so that it is not part of the Tailspin Toys Exchange organization.

- **Requirement 1**   Management has mandated that an internal e-mail facility must be available 24 hours per day, seven days per week.

- **Requirement 2**   An employee left the company six months ago, and her mailbox was deleted. There is important information in the mailbox, and you are asked to recover it.

- **Requirement 3**   Tailspin Toys's chief information officer (CIO) requires evidence that both private and public store data can be restored in the event of a disaster. Also, he wants assurance that an individual public folder can be restored without restoring every folder in the group.

Requirement 1

The first requirement involves implementing an internal e-mail facility that will be available 24 hours a day, seven days a week.

1. Your chief executive officer (CEO) knows that you can do online backups but that mailbox stores need to be dismounted in order to restore data. She is also convinced about the value of trial restores. Previously, you have used recovery storage groups to restore test your restore process, but this is not seen as a totally satisfactory solution as data cannot be restored to exactly the same mailbox store unless you dismount that mailbox store. What do you tell the CEO?

_____

_____

2. Your CIO wants to know how you intend to configure an Exchange server in a different Active Directory forest when Tailspin Toys has only one forest. He also wants to know whether this server will be physically connected to the Tailspin Toys network. What do you tell him?

_____

_____

Requirement 2

The second requirement involves recovering important information from a deleted mailbox.

1. You need to recover a mailbox that was deleted six months ago. What information do you need to obtain about that mailbox?

_____

_____

2. What tool can you use to edit the properties of the configuration container on your recovery server in Active Directory?

_____

_____

Requirement 3

The third requirement involves proving that both private and public store data can be restored in the event of a disaster.

1. Your CIO requires proof that you can restore both public and private stores from backup. What proof can you give him?

_____

_____

2. Your CIO wants reassurance that you can restore a specified public folder in a public store without replacing the information in all the other public folders. What do you tell him?

_____

_____

_____

Troubleshooting Lab

In this lab, you configure Server02 so that it can act as a recovery server for your Tailspin Toys Exchange Server 2003 organization. Server02 will be promoted to the first domain controller in the _contoso.com_ forest. You must match all the following names used by your recovery server to those used by your original Exchange server (Server01):

- Organization name
- Administrative group name
- Storage group name
- Logical database name

Before proceeding with this lab, you must meet the system requirements outlined in the "Before You Begin" section at the beginning of this chapter.

Exercise 1: Reconfigure Server02 as a Recovery Server

To reconfigure Server02 as a recovery server, perform the following steps:

1. On Server02, access the Control Panel and open Add Or Remove Programs.

2. Select Microsoft Exchange, and then click Change/Remove.

3. On the Microsoft Exchange Installation Welcome page, click Next.

4. On the Component Selection page, click the left column of the Component box beside Microsoft Exchange, select Remove, and then click Next.

5. On the Installation Summary page, click Next.

6. Exchange Server 2003 uninstalls.

> **Caution**   Do not remove Server02 from the TailspinToys domain before you have uninstalled Exchange. If you do this, the computer can take an excessively long time to boot and to complete a logon.

7. Click Finish on the Completing The Microsoft Exchange Wizard page.

8. Close Add Or Remove Programs.

9. From the Start menu, click My Computer, and then click Properties.

10. On the Computer Name tab, click Change.

11. Select Workgroup and type **WORKGROUP** in the Workgroup Name box.

12. Click OK.

13. Specify the administrator account and password that you used when you configured this server, and then click OK.

14. Click OK when welcomed to the workgroup. Click OK again and restart the computer.

15. Log on using the same administrator account and password that you specified in step 13, and promote the server to a domain controller in the *contoso.com* domain.

> **Tip**   Detailed instructions for promoting a server to a domain controller in a new forest are not given. If you have any problems with this procedure, then refer to the Windows Server 2003 help files.

16. Log on to Server01 using the same credentials and install Exchange Server 2003, Enterprise Edition. Remember that this is a new forest and you need to run Forest-Prep and DomainPrep. The organization name should be the same as the Exchange Server 2003 organization on Server01 (TailSpinToys).

17. Use the Active Directory Domains And Trusts console to create a non-transitive two-way trust between the *contoso.com* and *tailspintoys.com* domains. This is to let you access the D:\Mybackup folder on Server01 from Server02.

18. On Server01, share D:\Mybackup. Ensure that *contoso.com* domain administrators have read permission on the folder.

19. On Server02, configure Exchange System Manager to display Administrative Groups and Routing Groups. Create a storage group and call it My Storage Group.

20. Delete Server02 from the TailSpinToys Active Directory. Delete the MX record for Server02 in the *tailspintoys.com* DNS zone. Create an MX record for Server02 in the *contoso.com* DNS zone.

21. Enable zone transfers in the *tailspintoys.com* and *contoso.com* DNS zones.

22. On Server02, create a secondary DNS zone for the *tailspintoys.com* Active Directory Integrated zone on Server01.

23. On Server01, create a secondary DNS zone for the *tailspintoys.com* Active Directory Integrated zone on Server02.

24. Close all open consoles. Reboot Server02.

Chapter Summary

- If you store database and transaction log files on the same disk drive and that disk goes down, then you can only restore up to the last backup. If the transaction log files are on a different disk and circular logging is disabled, then you can restore database files up to the point of failure by using the last backup and the transaction log files.

- RAID systems can protect data and provide failover protection. Microsoft recommends ESA disk storage technology for small Exchange Server 2003 organizations and SAN disk storage technology for medium and large organizations.

- Copy and full backups back up both database and transaction log files. Incremental and differential backup types back up only the transaction logs. Full backup truncates the transaction logs.

- To recover a damaged Exchange Server 2003 storage group, dismount the storage group and restore it from backup. If transaction log files are available, the databases can be rolled forward to the point of failure.

- If you need to restore Active Directory data in a domain controller, for example, when it is the only domain controller in the domain, then you should back up system state data. You can restore this data by booting the server up in Directory Services Restore mode.

Exam Highlights

Before taking the exam, review the key points and terms that are presented in this chapter. Return to the lessons for additional practice.

Key Points

- You can restore databases to the point of failure only if circular logging is not enabled and the transaction log files are stored on a different disk from the database files.

- RAID-1, RAID-0+1, and RAID-5 systems can protect data and provide failover protection. RAID-0 improves I/O performance but provides no fault tolerance.

- Full online backup truncates the transaction logs. No other type of backup deletes committed transaction logs, and you should not delete them manually.

- To recover deleted mailboxes after the retention period has expired, you need a recovery server. You also use a recovery server to restore a public store on a dedicated public folder server. A recovery server needs to be in a separate Active Directory forest.

Key Terms

transaction log   A combination of hardware and software that provides a security system, usually to prevent unauthorized access to an intranet.

Windows 2003 Backup   The backup and restore utility that is provided with Windows Server 2003. The utility may be used to back up and restore Exchange Server 2003 storage groups.

circular logging   An option that re-uses transaction log files and prevents them from filling the hard disk. If you enable circular logging then you cannot use transaction log files to restore an Exchange store up to the point of failure.

Volume Shadow Copy Service   A Windows Server 2003 service that enables backup software (such as Windows 2003 Backup) to create a snapshot of Exchange Server 2003 data at a specific point in time and back up from that snapshot.

recovery server   An Exchange Server 2003 server in a different forest from your Exchange Server 2003 organization. A recovery server enables you to recover a deleted mailbox after its retention time has expired, to restore public stores, and to perform test restores without dismounting any of your production storage groups.

Questions and Answers

Page
12-14
Lesson 1 Review

1. The Sales storage group database files are stored on a four-disk RAID-0 disk array. The transaction log files are stored on the same array. Circular logging is not enabled. You do a full backup on Monday night and an incremental backup on Tuesday night. On Wednesday at 3:00 P.M., one of the disks in the array fails. Which of the following statements is true?

   a. You cannot retrieve any data that was written to the array on Tuesday or Wednesday.

   b. You can restore the data up to the Tuesday night backup.

   c. You can restore the data backed up on Tuesday night and then do a roll-forward to restore data up to 3:00 P.M. on Wednesday.

   d. You do not need to restore data. It is on a fault-tolerant array.

   The correct answer is b.

2. Which storage technology typically has its own IP address?

   a. RAID

   b. SAN

   c. ESA

   d. NAS

   The correct answer is d.

3. Your transaction log files are held on a four-spindle RAID-0+1 disk array. Disks A and B form a striped volume, as do disks C and D. The two striped volumes are mirrored. Disk A experiences a hardware failure. While replacing Disk A, your assistant accidentally damages Disk B. How do you recover from this situation?

   Because Disks A and B are both on the same side of the mirror, a copy of all the transaction log files is held on the undamaged Disks C and D. You need to replace Disks A and B and ensure that all data from the volume implemented by C and D is copied to the volume implemented by A and B when you re-create the mirror. It would be wise to first back up the transaction log files, if you have not already done so.

Page
12-26

Lesson 2 Review

1. You store your databases and transaction log files on different hard disks. Circular logging is not enabled. You perform a differential backup every weekday night. Over the weekend, you perform a copy backup and archive the tape. It is taking longer each night to perform your differential backup and you are receiving warnings that the hard disk containing your transaction log files is nearing capacity. How do you deal with the situation?

Perform a full backup. This will truncate your transaction log files. Because neither a copy nor a differential backup deletes committed transaction log files, undeleted files are filling your disk. You also need to revise your backup strategy and implement periodic full backups.

2. You decide to use third-party backup software that uses the shadow copy method. You do not want to perform offline backups, and you want to ensure that your backed up databases are consistent. What do you need to check, and what step do you need to take?

You need to check that the third-party backup software supports Microsoft VSS. You need to enable this service on your Exchange Server 2003 servers and set the startup type to automatic.

3. What do you need to do to ensure that your Exchange Server 2003 organization can recover from the failure of a quorum disk resource?

To enable recovery from a failure in the quorum disk resource, you need to perform either a full computer backup or a Windows backup on the node that owns the quorum disk resource.

Page
12-44

Lesson 3 Review

1. You want to restore three storage groups, each of which contains five databases. How many restore operations do you need to perform?

Three. Because each storage group is a backup set and log files are shared, it is best to perform one restore per storage group at a time. You can restore multiple stores in a storage group simultaneously.

2. Your Exchange Server 2003 organization has a dedicated public folder server. You want to restore a single public folder store from backup. What difficulty do you face, and how do you accomplish your goal?

If you restore a single public folder store from backup, then not only will you restore the public folder that you are trying to recover, but you will also replace all the other existing public folders with the information contained in the backup set. If you have a dedicated public folder server, then you need to use a recovery server to restore the public folder from backup media.

3. You have backed up system state data on a domain controller. What must you do to restore this data?

You restart the domain controller and press the F8 key when the server is booting. You select to boot into Directory Services Restore mode and perform a restore operation in that mode.

4. What happens to the Exchange Server 2003 resources running on a single node in a cluster if that node fails?

When a single node in a cluster fails, the Exchange Server 2003 resources running on that node are moved to another available node in the cluster. Exchange databases remain intact on shared storage and can be accessed by the Exchange virtual server from another node in the cluster.

Page
12-46

Case Scenario Exercise: Requirement 1

1. Your chief executive officer (CEO) knows that you can do online backups but that mailbox stores need to be dismounted in order to restore data. She is also convinced about the value of trial restores. Previously, you have used recovery storage groups to restore test your restore process, but this is not seen as a totally satisfactory solution as data cannot be restored to exactly the same mailbox store unless you dismount that mailbox store. What do you tell the CEO?

You intend to create a recovery server. The recovery server will contain mailbox stores with exactly the same configuration as the stores in your current organization. You can perform trial restores on the recovery server without disrupting service to the Tailspin Toys Exchange organization.

Tip   Recovery storage groups are described in Chapter 14, "Troubleshooting Microsoft Exchange Server 2003."

2. Your CIO wants to know how you intend to configure an Exchange server in a different Active Directory forest when Tailspin Toys has only one forest. He also wants to know whether this server will be physically connected to the Tailspin Toys network. What do you tell him?

To create a recovery server, you need to configure an Exchange Server 2003 server in a different forest from your Exchange organization. Because you do not have another forest, you need to promote the server to a domain controller. The computer can be connected physically to your network.

Page
12-46

Case Scenario Exercise: Requirement 2

1. You need to recover a mailbox that was deleted six months ago. What information do you need to obtain about that mailbox?

You need to know the LegacyExchangeDN attribute of the administrative group that contains the mailbox you want to recover. The LegacyExchangeDN values for /O=<*Organization name*> and /OU=<*Site name*> in the configuration container in Active Directory on the recovery server must match the LegacyExchangeDN attributes of your production server.

2. What tool can you use to edit the properties of the configuration container on your recovery server in Active Directory?

You can use the Active Directory System Interface (ADSI) Edit tool to edit these properties.

Page 12-47 ## Case Scenario Exercise: Requirement 3

1. Your CIO requires proof that you can restore both public and private stores from backup. What proof can you give him?

When you have configured the recovery server, you can restore public and private stores to that server. You can do this without disrupting Tailspin Toys's e-mail or public store services.

2. Your CIO wants reassurance that you can restore a specified public folder in a public store without replacing the information in all the other public folders. What do you tell him?

If you attempt to restore a public folder on the same public store server then you also replace all the other existing public folders with the information contained in the backup set. This difficulty is reduced if you create a replica of the folder on another server, which allows you to replicate a copy of the public folder to the server where it was lost. Where you have a dedicated public folder server and cannot replicate a copy of the public folder on another server in your Exchange Server 2003 organization, then you need to use a recovery server to restore the public folder. You can then export the public folder data to a .pst file that you can load into your profile on the production server.

13 Monitoring Microsoft Exchange Server 2003

Exam Objectives in this Chapter:

- Manage, monitor, and troubleshoot server health
- Manage, monitor, and troubleshoot data storage
- Monitor, manage, and troubleshoot infrastructure performance

Why This Chapter Matters

You should monitor Microsoft Exchange Server 2003 services and resources to identify problems before they have an impact on your users. Monitoring also allows you to identify trends that indicate future problems and to plan for future growth. Critical services need to be monitored on a daily basis to ensure they are running properly. Scheduled monitoring allows you to accumulate the data you require for trend analysis and capacity planning. If daily or scheduled monitoring identifies a potential problem, or if a user reports a problem, then on-demand monitoring techniques are used to isolate and to help solve that problem. Both Exchange Server 2003 and Microsoft Windows Server 2003 provide tools to monitor system performance and to repair the problems that the monitoring process identifies. Monitoring is an important part of your work as an administrator and will be tested in the exam.

Lessons in this Chapter:

- Lesson 1: Performing Daily Exchange Server 2003 Monitoring and Maintenance. 13-3
- Lesson 2: Performing Scheduled Exchange Server 2003 Monitoring and Maintenance 13-20
- Lesson 3: Performing On-Demand Exchange Server 2003 Monitoring and Maintenance 13-35

Before You Begin

To perform the exercises in this chapter, you need the following hardware and software:

- Two Windows Server 2003, Enterprise Edition, servers. Server01 should be a domain controller installed in the *tailspintoys.com* Active Directory directory service domain, and Server02 should be a domain controller installed in the *contoso.com* Active Directory domain. Server01 should be multihomed. Local Area Connection on Server01 should be on the same network as Local Area Connection on Server02. Local Area Connection 2 on Server01 simulates an external network. It does not need to be connected to anything, but if you want, you can use it for Internet access.

> **Note**   If your Active Directory domains are not called *tailspintoys.com* and *contoso.com*, there is no need to rename them. Instead, use your domain names rather than *tailspintoys.com* and *contoso.com* whenever these names are mentioned in the chapter exercises.

- Exchange Server 2003, Enterprise Edition, should be installed on both servers. Server02 should be configured as a recovery server for Server01. Server02 was configured as a recovery server in Chapter 12, "Backup and Restore."

Lesson 1: Performing Daily Exchange Server 2003 Monitoring and Maintenance

After this lesson, you will be able to

- List the monitoring tasks that need to be performed daily
- Explain the guidelines for checking logs
- Explain the guidelines for monitoring services and cluster resources
- Examine and interpret Exchange store statistics
- Monitor Event Viewer entries for potential problems
- Check Monitoring And Status in Exchange System Manager
- Monitor queues by using Queue Viewer

Estimated lesson time: 90 minutes

Daily Monitoring Tasks

You need to monitor critical Exchange Server 2003 server services on a daily basis to ensure they are running properly. Daily monitoring should identify problems before they have an impact on your users. Monitoring also helps you to identify trends that indicate future problems and allow you to plan for future growth. Both Windows Server 2003 and Exchange Server 2003 provide utilities, such as Event Viewer, System Monitor, and Exchange System Manager, that monitor and analyze server components and Exchange Server 2003 server performance.

Maintenance tasks that you should perform on a daily basis include the following:

- Monitor Event Viewer for error and warning events.
- Check connector status and Exchange Server 2003 server status.
- Use Queue Viewer to view the message load on your Exchange Server 2003 servers.
- Review the logs generated by Event Viewer, the Performance console, virtual servers, and your antivirus product.
- Check the available disk space on volumes that store Exchange Server 2003 logs and databases.
- Monitor the required services for Exchange Server 2003 and Windows Server 2003.
- Use the Windows Performance console to monitor Windows Server 2003 server and Exchange Server 2003 server performance.
- Use Cluster Administrator to monitor failovers.

- Use Active Directory Sites And Services to verify replication.

- Use Exchange System Manager to examine Exchange Server 2003 store statistics.

Checking Logs

Much of the monitoring you perform on a daily basis is based on logs generated by the various logging tools, such as Event Viewer. Before looking at the specific tools, review some of the general guidelines for checking logs.

If you know what log content is typical in your environment, you can identify potential errors or anomalies to which you must respond immediately. In addition to checking event logs, performance logs, antivirus logs, and protocol logs daily, you should also archive logs so you can review them to obtain historical data and to identify trends that will require future action.

Event Viewer logs provide you with information about service failures, Active Directory replication errors, and warnings when system resources such as virtual memory or available disk space are running low. You should review Windows event logs daily because both Exchange Server 2003 and Windows Server 2003 report warning and error conditions to event logs. For example, if a volume has 10 percent or less disk space available, Windows Server 2003 reports this as "Event ID 2013: The disk is at or near capacity. You may be required to delete some files."

You can use system management utilities, such as the Performance console, to monitor the performance and capacity of your Exchange Server 2003 servers. You should configure these utilities to issue alerts when performance and capacity measurements fall outside normal operating parameters. You can, for instance, enable an alert if there is excessive memory paging or processor use. You also need to capture performance data to establish a performance baseline, and use the baseline for comparison against daily monitoring results in order to identify trends.

> **Caution**   You can also configure the Performance Logs And Alerts tool to alert you when the usage of a physical disk or logical disk volume reaches a predefined percentage of total capacity. However, Microsoft recommends that you do not enable disk counters unless you have a very good reason for doing so. Disk counters use a significant amount of resource and can degrade performance. They are disabled by default and must be enabled using the Diskperf.exe utility. This having been said, some experienced administrators do enable these counters, believing that the performance loss is more than counterbalanced by the ability to continuously and automatically monitor disk usage.

Antivirus logs tell you when the last virus scan was performed, what was scanned, and what the results were. Review this information to ensure that the antivirus product is working correctly. If your log file indicates that a virus exists that cannot be removed, search the Web site of your antivirus vendor for a possible solution. In this case, you should also review the frequency with which you download virus signature files and security updates.

Simple Mail Transport Protocol (SMTP), Network News Transfer Protocol (NNTP), and Hypertext Transfer Protocol (HTTP) virtual servers generate logging information that tracks the commands the virtual server receives from client computers. You can, for example, view the client computer's IP address and domain name, the date and time of the message, and the number of bytes, for each message sent. You should use these log files to identify unusual activities, such as messages with suspicious attachments. If you identify unusual activity, you should review your security settings to prevent undesirable mail from being delivered to your server.

Monitoring Services and Resources

Exchange Server 2003 server performance degradation can result from service failures, insufficient system resources, network performance problems, and server performance problems. If you are using clustering, then cluster problems can also degrade performance. You need to monitor your servers, your network services, and your network daily to ensure that Exchange Server 2003 is performing as expected. If you are using clusters, then you also need to use the Cluster Administrator tool on a regular basis. Because clusters provide failover support, it is sometimes not immediately obvious when a cluster node fails.

Network Performance   If the network is slow, then your Exchange organization is slow. You can verify the performance by using Network Monitor to capture, display, and analyze network traffic. You can also use Network Monitor to locate client-to-server connection problems, to find a computer that makes a disproportionate number of work requests, and to identify unauthorized users on your network.

> **Note**   The version of Network Monitor supplied with Windows Server 2003 captures only network traffic into and out of the machine on which it is installed. If you want to capture frames that are sent between remote computers, then you must use the Network Monitor component that ships with Microsoft Systems Management Server (SMS).

Server Performance   If Windows 2003 is not performing properly, then an Exchange Server 2003 server experiences performance problems. You can obtain information about programs and processes running on your computer by using Task Manager. You can use Task Manager, for example, to identify a process that consumes too much CPU or memory resource and to view pagefile and memory usage. This information helps you determine whether applications running on your Exchange Server 2003 server should be moved to another server or upgraded, or whether you must tune system resources or perform system upgrades.

The Performance console contains two utilities: System Manager and Performance Logs And Alerts. Both utilities monitor performance counters. You can monitor hardware counters and Exchange counters to determine whether performance bottlenecks exist, to identify trends, and to plan for upgrades.

Windows Services   Incorrect configuration of Windows services also degrades Exchange Server 2003 server performance. The first indication you get about this problem is typically through Event Viewer. If you receive such an indication, you may need to verify or modify the configuration of the relevant service.

You should monitor Active Directory performance daily because Active Directory configuration has an immediate impact upon the performance of an Exchange organization. Monitoring Active Directory indicators lets you identify trends before actual problems occur. For example, a slow response during the authentication of client computers or the slow appearance of newly configured objects in Exchange Server 2003 indicates problems with the Active Directory directory service. You can use the Active Directory Sites And Services console to review your Active Directory configuration.

You also need to monitor Domain Name System (DNS) indicators regularly. Exchange Server 2003 depends on DNS for name resolution. If you see DNS errors in Event Viewer, or if you experience communication problems between your Exchange Server 2003 servers, then you should review your DNS settings. You can use the DNS Management console to ensure that address records exist for your domain controllers and global catalog servers, and that Host (A) and Mail Exchanger (MX) records exist for your Exchange Server 2003 servers.

The Internet Information Services (IIS) service provides access to Exchange Server 2003 servers through HTTP. You should monitor the IIS performance indicators daily. If performance problems are detected, you should review your default Web site configuration.

Cluster Resources   You should use Cluster Administrator daily to monitor Exchange Server 2003 server clusters for failovers. Such monitoring is particularly important in an active/active cluster during a failover to ensure that enough resources are available to provide your users with the same level of performance that they experienced before the failover.

When you deploy Exchange Server 2003 server clusters, you should monitor virtual memory counters daily to determine when an Exchange virtual server must be restarted due to memory fragmentation. When the Microsoft Exchange Information Store (IS) service logs Event ID 9582, this can indicate that memory has become excessively fragmented.

Exchange Store Statistics

Exchange Server 2003 servers need free disk space to store and manipulate user databases and transaction logs and to run maintenance utilities. If you monitor Exchange store statistics daily, you can determine when free disk space is running low and take the appropriate action. You may need to add extra resources, but sometimes running a full backup and truncating the transaction log files will solve the problem. Event ID 1113 in the application event log indicates that an Exchange Server 2003 server is short of disk space.

You should use Windows Explorer daily to check the available free space. You can compare the available disk space on each of the Exchange Server 2003 server disk volumes with the expected rate of growth that you predict for your databases and transaction log files to determine when you will need additional disk resources. If you decide to enable the disk counters, you can also use System Monitor to check disk usage.

You also need to ensure that sufficient free disk space exists to run maintenance utilities by viewing the statistics for each of the Exchange databases and comparing these statistics with the available free space. As a general rule, available free disk space on a single drive must be equal to or greater than 110 percent of the size of the largest database.

Using Exchange System Manager, you can obtain additional information about the Exchange stores. Expanding a mailbox or public folder store lets you view the logged-on users. This functionality is useful if you need to perform maintenance and have to request connected users to close their mailboxes.

You can also use Exchange System Manager to view the size of individual mailboxes and identify the users who are consuming the most resources. You can obtain indexing statistics by viewing the index state, number of documents indexed, index size, last build time, index name, and index location. Finally, you can determine the size of individual public folders, the last time a folder was accessed, and the last time a replica was received. Figure 13-1 shows access and logon statistics for a public folder store.

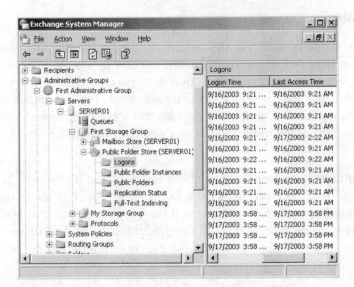

Figure 13-1 Public folder access and logon statistics

> **Real World** **Removing a Public Folder**
> If you suggest removing a public folder to free disk resources, there will inevitably be someone who objects. Knowing the last time the folder was accessed can provide powerful support to your argument.

Event Viewer

Event Viewer is a Windows utility that you can use to monitor hardware and software activities. Exchange Server 2003 uses the application log in Event Viewer to record errors, warnings, and information events. You can review the data in the application log to identify problems that have occurred and to anticipate problems before they occur. For example, a corrupt database will log errors in Event Viewer during online maintenance and online backups. By monitoring Event Viewer, you can identify a corrupt database and repair it before the symptoms of the fault impinge on your users.

You need to distinguish between Event Viewer entries that indicate normal behavior for the Exchange Server 2003 server and events that indicate a problem. By reviewing the event logs daily, you can establish a baseline of typical events that will save you time in identifying the events that need your attention.

Normal Events

Table 13-1 lists some of the events you might see during normal operation. Such events are logged as information events. Figure 13-2 shows an Event Viewer event report.

Table 13-1 Normal Exchange Server 2003 Events

Event number	Indication
700 and 701	Online defragmentation is beginning or has completed a full pass.
1206 and 1207	Starting cleanup of items past retention date for item recovery, or cleanup is complete.
1221	The database "...." has x megabytes of free space after online defragmentation has terminated.
9531 and 9535	Starting cleanup of deleted mailboxes that are past the retention date, or cleanup is complete.

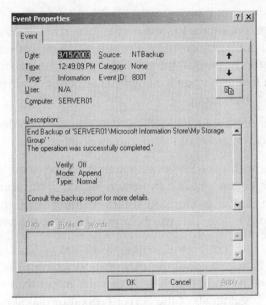

Figure 13-2 An Event Viewer event report

Abnormal Events

Table 13-2 lists some of the events you might see if Exchange Server 2003 is experiencing problems. Such events are logged as warning or error events.

Table 13-2 Exchange Server 2003 Error or Warning Events

Event number	Indication
2064 and 2069	Directory service access problems caused by incorrect DNS configuration.
9582	Virtual memory is low or fragmented.
1018, 1018, and 1022	Joint Engine Technology (JET) error events that indicate possible file-level damage to an Exchange database.

You can select an event source in Event Viewer to monitor events related to specific functions. You should monitor the following on a regular basis:

- **MSExchangeTransport**   Select this event source to view events recorded when SMTP is used to route messages. Event ID 4000 indicates that a connection has failed for a reason other than a specific protocol error. DNS problems, the server not being online, and connections that are dropped when the server is overloaded or hits internal errors can also cause connection failures.

- **MSExchangeAL**   Select this event source to view events related to the service that addresses e-mail through address lists. Event ID 8026 indicates problems with network connectivity or Lightweight Directory Access Protocol (LDAP) configuration.

- **MSExchangeIS**   Select this event source to view events related to the service that allows access to mailbox and public folder stores. Event ID 9518 indicates a failure while starting an Exchange storage group—for example, if all databases in a storage group are offline or if an Extensible Service Engine (ESE) error occurred while starting a database within a storage group.

- **MSExchangeSA**   Select this event source to view events that are recorded when Exchange uses Active Directory to store and share directory information.

If you identify potential problems with your Exchange Server 2003 server during your daily monitoring, you can control the amount of information logged in the application log by increasing the logging level. The higher you set the logging level, the more events you can view in the application log. This can help you diagnose the problem.

You can open the application log in Event Viewer, access Event Source, and select an Exchange-related event source. You can configure diagnostic logging to set Event Viewer's logging level. This is done in Exchange System Manager rather than in Event Viewer itself. On the Diagnostics Logging tab of the Server Properties dialog box, you can configure the logging level for each service and category for which you want to configure diagnostic logging. Be aware that if you increase the logging levels for Exchange services, you may experience some performance degradation.

> **Tip**   If you increase the logging levels on your Exchange server, also increase the size of the application log to contain all the data produced. Otherwise, you will receive frequent reminders that the application log is full.

The Monitoring And Status Utility

The Monitoring And Status utility provided as part of Exchange System Manager monitors key Exchange Server 2003 services by default. In addition, you can configure the utility to constantly monitor the performance level of other network and application services. You should use the Monitoring And Status utility daily to monitor the status of your servers and connectors and to determine if they are functioning properly.

You can use the Status column in Monitoring And Status to determine whether any service failures exist, whether system resources are running low, or whether messages are not flowing. Table 13-3 describes what each server status level indicates.

Table 13-3   Server Status Levels

Server status	What it indicates
Unreachable	One of the main services on the server is down or, if a server is in a different routing group, a connector between routing groups may be down or may not exist.
Unknown	System Attendant cannot communicate with the local server.
Critical or Warning	A monitored resource has reached the critical or warning state defined for that resource.
Unavailable	A communication service, such as the routing service, is not functioning on this connector.

Queue Viewer

You can use the Queue Viewer utility in Exchange System Manager to maintain and administer messaging queues in your Exchange organization. In Queue Viewer, the following queues can be displayed from either a local or a remote computer:

- An SMTP virtual server queue
- A Microsoft message transfer agent (MTA) object queue
- A connector queue
- DNS messages pending submission
- A failed message retry queue
- Messages queued for deferred delivery

As shown in Figure 13-3, the Queue Viewer utility provides the Disable Outbound Mail, Settings, and Find Messages options. There is also a pane (blank in the figure) for displaying additional queue information. You can monitor queues on a daily basis, and the utility is also used to identify problems that require on-demand maintenance.

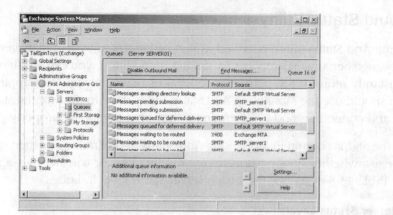

Figure 13-3   The Queue Viewer utility

Disable Outbound Mail

You can use the Disable Outbound Mail option to disable outbound mail on all SMTP queues. You may need to do this if, for example, a virus is active in your organization. The option does not disable the MTA or System queues.

If you want to prevent outbound mail from transmitting from a particular remote queue, then you can freeze the messages in that queue instead of disabling all SMTP queues. To do this, right-click the queue and then click Freeze. Right-click the queue and then click Unfreeze to unfreeze the messages.

Settings

You can use the Settings option to determine the frequency with which the queues are refreshed. The default refresh rate is once every two minutes. You can set the refresh rate to once every minute, every five minutes, every 10 minutes, or to Never Refresh. If you are trying to resolve a delivery problem, you may want to set the refresh interval to a small value, such as one minute, so that you can see changes to the queues sooner.

Find Messages

You can use the Find Messages option to display messages in the queue or to search for messages by specifying search criteria, such as the sender or recipient and the message state. You could, for example, search for all frozen messages. You can also specify the number of messages that you want your search to return. You can use this option if you are searching for a particular message or if you want to list the messages in the queues to see when the oldest message was submitted.

Additional Queue Information

You can use the Additional Queue Information option to view troubleshooting information about a particular queue. It also displays information about errors returned from Exchange-specific extensions to the SMTP service and indicates when a queue is unavailable—for example, when a service is not started.

Using Queue Viewer to Find Potential Problems

Exchange Server 2003 uses queues to hold messages while they are being processed for routing and delivery. If messages remain in a queue for an extended period, a problem may exist, such as an Exchange server not being able to connect to the network. It is therefore your responsibility as an Exchange Full Administrator to monitor Exchange queues daily.

You should first list messages in a queue by selecting the queue and by using the Find Messages feature. You can use Queue Viewer to determine if a problem exists with that queue. You can then review the State column in your search results to see which state the queue is in. Table 13-4 lists the message states.

Table 13-4   Message States in Queue Viewer

Message State	Description
Active	Indicates that a link queue has an active connection. No action is required.
Ready	Indicates that a link queue is ready to have a connection allocated to it. No action is required.
Retry	Indicates that a connection attempt has failed and that the server is waiting for a retry. You should review the State column again after a short period of time to ensure that this state has changed. If the message is still in the Retry state, then you need to identify the problem that is preventing the queue from delivering messages.
Scheduled	Indicates that the queue is waiting for a scheduled connection attempt. No action is required.
Remote	Indicates that the queue is waiting for a remote dequeue command. No action is required.
Frozen	Indicates that no messages can leave the link queue. Messages can be inserted in the queue if the Exchange routing categorizer is still running. If you have frozen the queue for a particular reason, such as during a virus attack, you need to unfreeze the queue when the virus problem is resolved.

You then need to review the Number Of Messages and Total Message Size (KB) columns to see if a large number of messages are backed up in the queue or if the message size of any message is too large for your Exchange organization. If a large number of messages are backed up in the queue, you can force a connection by right-clicking the queue and clicking Force Connection. If you have an extremely large message that is preventing other messages from being delivered, you should consider deleting the message.

You can also use the Find Messages feature to locate a specific message in the message queues. Typically, you look for a message in a queue if a user reports that he or she sent an important message that was not received. In this case, you can use the Search Results pane to view information about the messages located in the queue, such as whether the message is in the Retry state, what the size of the message is, what time the message was submitted, and at what time the message will expire. This information will help you to identify potential or current problems.

Practice: Configuring Diagnostic Levels and the Monitoring And Status Utility

You can control the events that are recorded in the application log of Event Viewer by changing the diagnostic logging level and by specifying events using the Monitoring And Status utility.

Exercise 1: Configure Diagnostic Logging

In this exercise, you check Event Viewer to determine whether any Exchange errors exist. You then change the diagnostic logging level and inspect the more detailed information that results from this configuration change. To view the application log and configure diagnostic logging, perform the following steps:

1. On Server01, from the Start menu, point to Administrative Tools, and then click Event Viewer.

2. In Event Viewer, in the console tree, click Application.

3. In the details pane, browse through the events, paying particular attention to any red stop events and yellow warning events.

4. Minimize the Event Viewer window.

5. Start Exchange System Manager.

6. Navigate to Administrative Groups\First Administrative Group\Servers. Right-click Server01, and then click Properties.

7. Select the Diagnostics Logging tab.

8. On the Diagnostics Logging tab, under Services, expand MSExchangeIS, and then click Mailbox.

9. Under Category, click General.

10. In the Logging Level box, select Maximum, as shown in Figure 13-4, and then click OK.

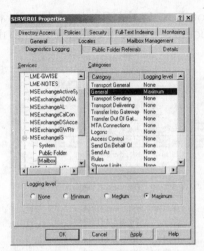

Figure 13-4   Setting a diagnostic logging level

11. Expand the Event Viewer window (or open Event Viewer if you closed it earlier).

12. On the View menu in Event Viewer, click Filter. This lets you filter the log and list entries for a specific type of Exchange-related event.

13. In the Application Properties dialog box, in the Event Source drop-down list, click MSExchangeIs Mailbox Store, as shown in Figure 13-5.

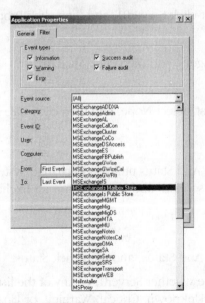

Figure 13-5   Selecting an event source

14. In the Application Properties dialog box, in the Category drop-down list, click General, and then click OK. You should see a list of events similar to those shown in Figure 13-6.

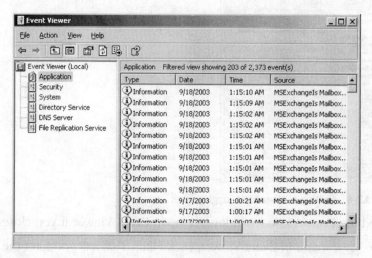

Figure 13-6   MSExchangeIS mailbox store events at maximum diagnostic logging level

15. On the View menu, click All Records to view all events, and then close Event Viewer.

16. In Exchange System Manager, right-click Server01, and then click Properties.

17. Select the Diagnostics Logging tab.

18. Under Services, expand MSExchangeIS, and then click Mailbox.

19. Under Categories, click General.

20. In the Logging Level drop-down list, select None, and then click OK.

Exercise 2: Specify Events to Monitor

In this exercise, you use the Monitoring And Status utility in Exchange System Manager to configure monitoring levels for key services and resources on an Exchange Server 2003 server.

1. Start Exchange System Manager.

2. Expand Tools, expand Monitoring And Status, and then click Status.

3. Check the details pane to determine whether Server01 or any of the listed connectors have a status of Unreachable, Unknown, Critical, Warning, or Unavailable.

4. Double-click Server01.

5. Click Add on the Monitoring tab.

Note   You can access the same control by navigating to Administrative Groups/First Administrative Group/Server/Server01, right-clicking Server01, clicking Properties, and then selecting the Monitoring tab.

6. In the Add Resource box, click Available Virtual Memory, and then click OK.

7. Specify virtual memory thresholds, as shown in Figure 13-7, and then click OK.

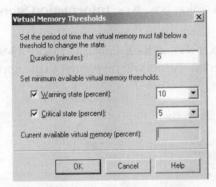

Figure 13-7   Specifying the virtual memory threshold levels

8. Click Add on the Monitoring tab.

9. In the Add Resource box, click CPU Utilization, and then click OK.

10. Specify CPU utilization thresholds, as shown in Figure 13-8, and then click OK.

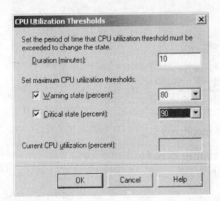

Figure 13-8   Specifying CPU utilization threshold levels

11. Repeat the same procedure to specify free disk space thresholds. If you have more than one disk volume, you can repeat the procedure for each of them.

12. Specify SMTP queues growth and X.400 growth thresholds.

13. Click Add, then click Windows 2000 Service, and then click OK.

Off the Record Currently, this says "Windows 2000 Service" rather than "Windows 2003 Service."

14. In the Services dialog box, in the pull-down menu next to When Service Is Not Running Change State To, select Critical, and then click Add.

15. Select Microsoft Exchange Information Store, and then click OK.

16. In the Name box, in the Services dialog box, type **Information Store**, and then click OK.

17. Your Server01 Properties dialog box should look similar to Figure 13-9. When the limits that you specified are exceeded, events will be written to the application log in Event Viewer.

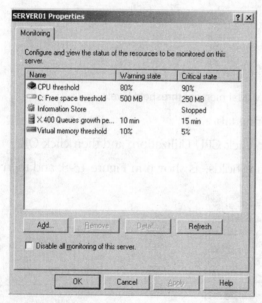

Figure 13-9 Configuring events to be monitored

18. Click OK to close the Properties dialog box.

Lesson Review

The following questions are intended to reinforce key information presented in this lesson. If you are unable to answer a question, review the lesson materials and then try the question again. You can find answers to the questions in the "Questions and Answers" section at the end of this chapter.

1. A user reports that she sent important information to a colleague some time ago, but the message has not been received. A non-delivery report (NDR) has not been returned to the sender. What tool do you use to investigate, and what message parameters should you look at?

   _____

   _____

2. You want to monitor free disk space on an Exchange Server 2003 server and obtain a notification if this drops below a threshold value. You use the Monitoring And Status utility in Exchange System Manager to configure the free disk space monitoring level. Where would you look for notification that free disk space has dropped below the threshold level?

   a. In your Inbox

   b. In the system log in Event Viewer

   c. On the Monitoring tab of the Server Properties dialog box in Exchange System Manager

   d. In the applications log in Event Viewer

3. You want to view events recorded when SMTP is used to route messages. Which event source should you monitor in Event Viewer?

   a. MSExchangeTransport

   b. MSExchangeAL

   c. MSExchangeIS

   d. MSExchangeSA

Lesson Summary

- You should review the following on a daily basis: the message load on your Exchange Server 2003 servers, the logs generated by Event Viewer, the Performance console, virtual servers, and your antivirus product. You should also check the available disk space on volumes that store Exchange logs and databases.

- Events related to Exchange Server 2003 server operation are recorded in the applications log in Event Viewer. You can use the diagnostic logging function in Exchange System Manager to configure the detail of events that are logged.

- You can use the Monitoring And Status utility in Exchange System Manager to monitor Exchange Server 2003 services, and Queue Viewer to monitor queues and get details of messages in these queues.

- If you use Windows clustering, you should use Cluster Administrator daily to monitor Exchange Server 2003 server clusters for failovers. You use the Active Directory Sites And Services tool to monitor Active Directory replication.

Lesson 2: Performing Scheduled Exchange Server 2003 Monitoring and Maintenance

Scheduled monitoring enables you to accumulate data that provides the information you require for trend analysis and capacity planning. By measuring system performance over time, you can identify the need for new resources before that need becomes critical, and use the collected data to troubleshoot your servers before faults occur that affect your users.

After this lesson, you will be able to

- List the maintenance tasks that you need to schedule
- Generate reports and identify trends
- Review protocol logs
- Explain the purpose of HTTP Monitor
- Manage mailbox limits
- Manage the Badmail folder
- Manage the postmaster mailbox

Estimated lesson time: 90 minutes

Scheduled Maintenance Tasks

To keep your Exchange organization running smoothly and to provide the level of service that users demand, you need to perform regular, scheduled maintenance tasks. You must define these tasks and the frequency with which you perform them. Typically, you need to perform the following tasks:

- Generate reports and identify trends by using System Monitor, Microsoft Operations Manager, or third-party utilities to capture performance data. This data allows you to identify potential bottlenecks and, for example, to estimate when a server must be upgraded.

- Use protocol logs to track commands that are sent and received by SMTP, NNTP, and HTTP virtual servers. Reviewing these logs can help you troubleshoot messaging problems and identify potential problems.

- Use HTTPMon to monitor your Outlook Web Access (OWA) servers and ensure that client computers are not experiencing connection or performance problems.

- Determine which users consume the most resources on your servers because this information helps you configure and maintain your Exchange storage.

- Monitor the Badmail folder to identify trends and prevent messages from building up. Messages that cannot be delivered and cannot be returned to the sender are sent to the Badmail folder. Over time, these messages can accumulate and use up disk resources.

- Manage the postmaster mailbox, which is used for NDRs. You should define which e-mail account is associated with the postmaster account and monitor and respond to NDR messages when necessary.

Generating Reports and Identifying Trends

Your first task when generating reports and identifying trends is to gather sufficient information to establish a baseline for the performance of each Exchange Server 2003 server. This information allows you to manage your servers proactively and perform trend analysis and capacity planning. You should create a baseline when you first deploy your server, and then re-baseline whenever changes in hardware or usage occur.

To create a baseline and then use deviations from that baseline to track trends and identify potential problems, you must create procedures to monitor your Exchange Server 2003 server. These procedures gather information about server resources such as memory usage, processor utilization, hard disk space utilization, disk performance, and network performance. In addition, performance indicators specific to Exchange Server 2003 server, such as Exchange store performance, message delivery rates, and message queue problems, are included. Your system monitoring procedures should specify the frequency of monitoring tasks, the baseline data to be captured, and the appropriate procedures for managing any problems that may arise.

System measurement is implicit within system monitoring. System measurement parameters include standards for the types of information measured, measurement sampling rates, methods used to analyze data, data storage formats, and reporting formats.

Capacity Planning

Capacity planning enables you to allocate system resources to ensure that optimal system performance is maintained as the system load increases. It is, however, not sufficient to carry out capacity planning using current data, to allocate the appropriate resources, and then to take no further action. Capacity planning is a continuous process that requires that you establish baselines for each service and then monitor all levels of system operations.

The Performance Console

The Performance console is used to gather and display information about performance objects and related counters. The console contains two tools, or snap-ins: Performance Logs And Alerts and System Monitor.

The Performance Logs And Alerts snap-in records and logs system activity over a period of time. The tool enables you to collect data at regular intervals for the counters you select. You can retain logs over extended periods of time by storing data in a database created by Microsoft Access or Microsoft SQL. If you store the data in a database, you can use the reporting features of the database program to create reports that can be used to assess overall performance and to perform trend analysis and capacity planning. Performance Logs And Alerts can also be configured to generate an alert if a counter value either exceeds or drops below a predefined value. The alert, by default, will record an event in Event Viewer, but you can configure it to send an administrative message or to initiate a program.

The System Monitor snap-in lets you chart activity in real time. You also use it to display information captured in log files by the Performance Logs And Alerts snap-in as reports, graphs, or histograms. You can use System Monitor to view server activity whenever server performance degrades. You can, for example, analyze processor activity and queues and use this information to isolate problems with specific components.

Configuring a Performance Console

You should configure the Performance console so that you can determine what is normal system behavior and what modifications you can make to improve performance. You need to know the average number of messages received per user per day and the total number of messages downloaded in a predefined period of time. You also need to know the frequency with which users open folders.

If you have these statistics, you can calculate the number of additional users that each of your servers can support. However, this is anything but a straightforward calculation. E-mail traffic is not smooth, but rather is notoriously peaky. You also need to know the peak delivery rate, the peak period during the day, the peak day of the week, and whether monthly or quarterly peaks exist.

To obtain this information, you need to create a Performance console that allows you to see the entire system environment and that registers changes in the performance of your servers. The guidelines for creating a Performance console are as follows:

- Create a Performance console that has two different sample times, for example:
    - ❑ 900 seconds for a 24-hour view
    - ❑ 10 seconds to catch short-lived spikes
- Include a minimal set of counters in each console, for example:
    - ❑ Memory\Pages/sec
    - ❑ Processor(_Total)\% Processor Time
    - ❑ Process(store)\% Processor Time
    - ❑ MSExchangeIS\RPC Requests
    - ❑ MSExchangeIS\RPC Operations/sec
    - ❑ PhysicalDisk(_Total)\Disk Transfers/sec
    - ❑ SMTP Server\Local Queue Length
    - ❑ SMTP Server\Messages Delivered/sec
    - ❑ MSExchangeIS Mailbox\Local Delivery Rate
    - ❑ MSExchangeIS Mailbox\Folder Opens/sec
    - ❑ MSExchangeIS Mailbox\Message Opens/sec
- Examine your busiest server to understand why it is busy and what performance problems can be resolved.
- Save your reference log files so that you can develop historical baseline data that allows you to see what changes have occurred and to accommodate for additional growth over time.

Analyzing Trends

By analyzing the reports you create using your data, you can uncover patterns and predict future trends. This trend analysis assists you to determine what steps you can take to prevent problems on your Exchange Server 2003 servers in the future. For example, you can predict when normal growth, such as mailbox growth, will require you to upgrade your storage.

Protocol Logs

Protocol logs were introduced, and protocol logging configured, in Chapter 11, "Microsoft Exchange Server 2003 Security." You can use protocol logging to track commands that an HTTP, SMTP, or NNTP virtual server receives from client computers and to track outgoing commands. You should establish a schedule for reviewing protocol logs, and you should also review the log files if your users are experiencing problems.

You can select from four types of file formats, depending on how you want to store the information. Table 13-5 describes these formats.

Table 13-5   Protocol Log File Formats

Format	Description
IIS Log	The information is written to a comma-delimited ASCII text file. The data is fixed, which means that you cannot customize the log.
NCSA Common Log	The information is written to an ASCII text file that uses the National Center for Supercomputing Applications (NCSA) format. The data is fixed, which means that you cannot customize the log.
ODBC Logging	The information that is logged is written to a database. You must set up an open database connectivity (ODBC)–compliant database before using this format.
W3C Extended Log	The information is written to an ASCII text file. The World Wide Web Consortium (W3C) Extended Log file format is the most flexible format because the data is variable, which means that you can choose what you want to track.

You enable protocol logging and select the log file format for an SMTP or NNTP virtual server by using Exchange System Manager to configure the virtual server properties. You can also specify the schedule for creating new log files and the location of these files (except for ODBC format). If your log file format is W3C Extended Log File Format, you can select the items that you want to track.

You manage HTTP protocol logging by using the IIS Manager console to configure the Web site properties. By default, protocol logging is enabled, and the log file format is set to W3C Extended Log File Format.

Using a Protocol Log File

You can use a protocol log file for general troubleshooting. Suppose, for example, users report that they are receiving messages when their addresses do not appear on the To or Cc lines. In this case, you can use SMTP log file data to compare the recipients specified in a rcpt to command with addresses posted in a message header or in the To and Cc lines of the message. Another example is when you search the SMTP log file for the message identity (ID) of a remote system so that you can collaborate with another system administrator to trace a message.

You can look for response codes that a receiving server returns after your server issues an ehlo command to determine the maximum-size message that a server will accept (for example: 250-size 60000000). You can also use the log data to generate reports. If another server attempts to use your server as a relay (assuming your server is properly configured to prevent unauthorized SMTP relaying), the log file posts a numeric response code of 550, which corresponds to Relaying Prohibited, in the protocol status (sc-status) field. You could write a script to search this field and tally the number of reported 550 codes.

HTTP Monitor

You can use the HTTP Monitor (HTTPMon) Resource Kit utility to monitor Web sites or applications. HTTPMon can check Web sites and report the results to either a log file in comma-separated values (CSV) format or in the Windows Server 2003 server event log. You can then either use Windows Management Instrumentation (WMI) to monitor the event log or import the CSV output into a Microsoft Excel or SQL database for further analysis.

The utility enables you to test that the Exchange Web site is responding to requests from client computers in a timely fashion. It lets you test several sites simultaneously to ensure that they are up and that they are responding within reasonable times. You can use HTTPMon to monitor OWA servers and identify and troubleshoot problems. You should establish a schedule for monitoring OWA on a regular basis.

HTTPMon comprises the following three components:

- **Realtime Sampling Service**   The real-time monitoring service.
- **SQL Reporting Server**   Pulls data from monitor servers and loads it into Microsoft SQL Server.
- **Client Monitor**   A set of Web pages that displays the results from the SQL Reporting Server database.

Installing HTTPMon

Currently, the HTTP Monitoring Tool is available only in the Windows 2000 Resource Kit and is not installed by the Resource Kit Setup program. To install it, insert the Windows 2000 Resource Kit companion CD into your CD-ROM drive. When the Setup screen appears, click Explore The CD. In the *<cdroot>*\apps\httpmon directory, double-click Setup.exe and follow the directions that appear on your screen.

When you install the HTTP Monitoring Tool, the information file (Readme.txt) and the user's guide (HTTPMon_whitepaper.doc) are also installed. Access these files for information on configuring and using the tool. They are both located in the directory where you install the tool (C:\Program Files\Httpmon in the default installation).

Tip   You can also download the HTTP Monitoring Tool installation file from *ftp:// ftp.microsoft.com/bussys/utilities/httpmon*.

Mailbox Limits

You need to manage mailbox limits on a regular basis. By default, Exchange Server 2003 permits large mailbox sizes, and this allows users to store a great deal of information in their mailboxes. However, this can lead to some users having excessively large mailboxes. You can use Exchange System Manager to manage mailbox limits and Event Viewer to check whether mailbox sizes have reached the various limit stages that you configured.

If you access the mailbox node in Exchange System Manager, then you can modify the mailbox view to include the Storage Limits column. This column provides feedback on whether certain limits have been enforced for a specific mailbox and, if so, what condition the mailbox is in. You can then use Event Viewer to view the events recorded when a mailbox reaches a limit threshold. Microsoft recommends that you monitor mailbox sizes at least once per week. Table 13-6 describes the limit settings that you can specify in the Storage Limits column.

Table 13-6   Mailbox Limit Settings

Limit	Description
No Checking	Mailbox limits are not enabled for the mailbox.
Below Limit	The mailbox has limits set, but the mailbox usage is below these limits.
Issue Warning	The mailbox size has reached the Issue Warning limit and a warning message is delivered to the mailbox.
Prohibit Send	The mailbox size has reached the Prohibit Send limit and the mailbox-enabled user is no longer able to send messages.
Mailbox Disabled	The mailbox size has reached the Prohibit Send and Receive limit and the mailbox is set to Disabled. The mailbox-enabled user cannot send messages from this mailbox, and the mailbox is unable to receive messages.

You can configure diagnostic logging on an Exchange Server 2003 server to enable you to view events in the application log in Event Viewer that indicate when mailboxes reach the various stages of storage limit warnings. You can also use the mailbox management process, otherwise known as Mailbox Manager, to manage oversized mailboxes.

Mailbox Manager is defined as a recipient policy and can be used to create reports or take actions to clean old mail from users' mailboxes. You can schedule the mailbox management process to run at a specific time for regularly scheduled cleanups, or you can run it manually. You should run the process manually if you are in immediate need of mailbox statistics or if you need to clear mailboxes of old mail immediately.

You start the process by starting Exchange System Manager, navigating to the relevant server, right-clicking the server, and then selecting Start Mailbox Management Process. Mailbox management starts after a short delay, which depends on the level of resource use on the server.

The Badmail Folder

If a message has reached the retry limit and an NDR cannot be delivered to the sender, a copy of the message is placed in the Badmail folder. Messages placed in this folder cannot be delivered or returned.

Over time, messages can accumulate in the Badmail folder. If you do not monitor the Badmail folder regularly, your Exchange Server 2003 server can run out of disk space. This causes the Microsoft Exchange Information Store service to shut down. You need to establish policies for monitoring the folder and removing messages after a certain age. Microsoft recommends reviewing the content of the Badmail folder on a weekly basis.

Another reason for monitoring the Badmail folder is that it could contain messages from an external user who is attempting to relay spam e-mail through your Exchange organization.

By default, the Badmail folder is located in the virtual server's home directory. You can relocate the folder by using Exchange System Manager to access the Messages tab in the relevant virtual server's Properties dialog box. You can use Windows Explorer to check the contents of the Badmail folder. A large number of undelivered messages could indicate delivery problems such as a DNS or network failure, or potential security problems due to spam e-mail. You should delete messages from the Badmail folder based on your organization's policies. For example, you could delete messages once per week.

The Postmaster Mailbox

The postmaster account is configured to receive NDRs and is used to send the delivery status of a message to the sender. By default, Exchange Server 2003 creates the postmaster proxy address and assigns this address to the administrator who created the Exchange organization. It is good practice to change this default setting so that the name of this administrator account is not exposed to outside users.

 Note   Request for Comments (RFC) 822 defines a reserved address for the postmaster. To access RFCs, browse to *http://www.rfc-editor.org/rfc.html*.

To designate a specific user's mailbox as the postmaster mailbox for a local SMTP domain, you add the proxy *postmaster@localdomainname* to the user's list of SMTP proxy addresses. You can associate an existing e-mail account with the postmaster or create a dedicated postmaster account from which the NDRs will be sent.

If you decide to create a dedicated postmaster account, you can log on using that account by using an Outlook profile and respond to the account messages. Alternatively, you can delegate Send As permissions on the account to the person to whom you have delegated the task of managing the mailbox, and add the mailbox to that person's Outlook profile.

You should establish a regular schedule for reviewing and responding to the delivery reports contained in the postmaster mailbox. This schedule should be based on your organization's requirements. Some organizations make this a daily task in an effort to reduce the number of e-mail messages that are delivered to users who are no longer with the organization, while others companies make this a weekly or monthly maintenance task.

Practice: Using Performance and Protocol Logs and Managing Mailbox Limits

In this practice, you configure the Performance Logs And Alerts tool to create a performance log for trend analysis and to generate a report when an Exchange counter exceeds a predefined value. You also check the SMTP protocol log for problems and check for oversized mailboxes.

Exercise 1: Configure a Performance Log

In this exercise, you configure a performance log by adding the counters that you want to monitor and by specifying a sample time. For the purposes of this exercise, a five second sample period is specified. If you wanted to log activity over a long period of time, you would specify a larger sample period, because otherwise the performance log file could grow to an excessive size.

To configure a performance log, perform the following steps:

1. On Server01, from the Start menu, click Administrative Tools, and then select Performance.

2. In the console tree, expand Performance Logs And Alerts.

3. Right-click Counter Logs, and then click New Log Settings.

4. In the New Log Settings Name box, type **MyLog** and then click OK.

5. On the General tab of the MyLog dialog box, check that the current log file name is the default, C:\PerfLogs\MyLog_000001.blg.

6. Click Add Counters. In the Add Counters dialog box, select Use Local Computer Counters.

7. In the Performance Object drop-down menu, select Processor.

8. Choose the Select Counters From List option. In the scroll box below this option, select %Processor Time.

9. Choose the Select Instances From List option and select _Total.

10. Click Explain to obtain a description of this counter, and then click Add.

11. Use the same technique to add the Process(store)\% Processor Time counter. Figure 13-10 shows this counter being added.

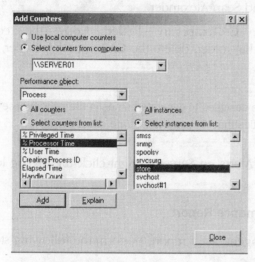

Figure 13-10   Adding the Process(store)\% Processor Time counter

12. Add the MSExchangeIS\RPC Requests and the MSExchangeIS\RPC Operations/sec counters.

13. Add the MSExchangeIS Mailbox\Local delivery rate, the MSExchangeIS Mailbox\Folder opens/sec, and the MSExchangeIS Mailbox\Message opens/sec counters.

14. Add the PhysicalDisk(_Total)\Disk Transfers/sec counter.

15. Add the Memory\Pages/sec counter.

16. Add the SMTP Server\(_Total)Local Queue Length and the SMTP Server\(_Total)Messages Delivered/sec counters.

Note   You can choose instances of SMTP Server because you created an additional SMTP virtual server in Chapter 9, "Virtual Servers." If you did not do so, or if you have since deleted that virtual server, then add the SMTP Server\Local Queue Length and the SMTP Server\Messages Delivered/sec counters.

17. Click Close.

18. On the General tab of the MyLog dialog box, set the Sample Interval to **5** seconds.

19. Click OK. If you are prompted to create the C:\Perflogs folder, click Yes.

20. On the Performance console, click Counter Logs and check that the MyLog counter log is running. It should be green in color, and if you right-click it, Start should be dimmed.

21. On Server02, use OWA to send an e-mail to *administrator@tailspintoys.com*, with copies to *d.hall@tailspintoys.com* and *s.alexander@tailspintoys.com*.

22. On Server01, use Outlook 2003 to send an e-mail to *administrator@contoso.com*, with copies to Don Hall and Sean Alexander.

23. On Server01, create a C:\Temporary folder. Copy the contents of C:\Windows\Drivers into that folder, delete the C:\Temporary folder, and empty the Recycle bin.

> **Note** Steps 21, 22, and 23 are designed to generate entries in the performance counters being monitored. Any other activities that you want to test are equally valid.

24. In Performance Logs And Alerts on Server01, right-click the MyLog log file, and then click Stop.

Exercise 2: Generate a Performance Report

To read the MyLog log file and generate a report, perform the following steps:

1. On Server01, from the Start menu, click Administrative Tools, and then select Performance.

2. In the console tree, click System Monitor.

3. In the details pane, on the toolbar, click View Log Data.

4. In the System Monitor Properties dialog box, access the Source tab, click Log Files, and then click Add.

5. In the Select Log File dialog box, browse to C:\Perflogs in the Look In box (unless already selected).

6. Click the MyLog_000001.blg log file, and then click Open.

7. In the System Monitor Properties dialog box, select the Data tab, and then click Add.

8. In the Add Counters dialog box, add all the counters for all the available performance objects, and then click Close.

9. Click OK to close the System Monitor Properties dialog box.

10. Use the toolbar to view the data in graph, histogram, and report format. Figure 13-11 shows report format.

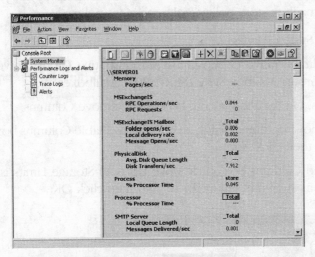

Figure 13-11   Captured data displayed in report format

11. Examine the data that you collected to determine whether any performance problems exist that you should act on.

Exercise 3: Read the Default SMTP Protocol Log File

In Chapter 11, you investigated the configuration of protocol logs in general terms. In this exercise, you look at a specific log file. This exercise assumes that you have enabled logging in your SMTP virtual server and that, therefore, the SMTPSVC1 folder exists. If that is not the case, use Exchange System Manager to navigate to the Default SMTP virtual server Properties dialog box, enable protocol logging, and then send an e-mail message to *administrator@contoso.com*.

1. On Server01, from the Start menu, click Run, type **C:\Windows\System32\Log-Files\SMTPSVC1**, and then click OK.

2. In the C:\Windows\System32\Logfiles\SMTPSVCl window, open any log file.

3. Read the log file.

4. If the W3SVC1 folder exists, read any log files in that folder. Some log files can hold a lot of information.

5. Close the log files.

Exercise 4: Create a Mailbox Store Policy and a Recipient Policy, and Check for Oversized Mailboxes

In this exercise, you check for oversized mailboxes. In order to do so, you must first create and apply a mailbox store policy and a recipient policy.

1. Start Exchange System Manager.

2. Navigate to Administrative Groups\First Administrative Group\Servers\Server01 \First Storage Group\Mailbox Store (SERVER01)\Mailboxes.

3. Click Mailboxes. On the View menu, click Add/Remove Columns.

4. In the Add/Remove Columns dialog box, in the Available Columns box, click Storage Limits, and then click Add.

5. In the Displayed Columns box, click Move Up until Storage Limits is the second item in the list, as shown in Figure 13-12, and then click OK.

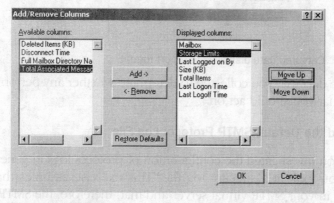

Figure 13-12   Configuring Mailbox View to view storage limits

6. In the Mailboxes details pane in Exchange System Manager, view the Storage Limits column to determine whether any mailboxes are over their limit.

> **Tip**   Click the Storage Limits column header to sort the data by storage limit status. This lets you locate large mailboxes more easily.

7. To delete items from an over-large mailbox, in Exchange System Manager, navigate to Administrative Groups\First Administrative Group\Servers\Server01, right-click Server01, and then click Start Mailbox Management Process. Mailbox Manager deletes items based on the recipient policy configured for your user mailboxes.

- Protocol logs can record all the t· **and Exchange Server 2003**
  a log file can be stored in one of
  ging format lets you select what ·

- The Badmail folder stores mail wh·ow, they can become fragmented. This creates
  sent to the sender. The postmaste·. Inconsistencies in Exchange databases can be
  to non-existent users in your dom·003 tools and utilities. You can also monitor
  You can monitor mailbox size a· of your Exchange Server 2003 servers to help
  Viewer when specified limits are· ypically, the on-demand maintenance tasks that
  Monitor to view mailbox properti· at have been reported by monitoring utilities or
  · maintenance activities are described in this les-
  · ues are discussed in detail in Chapter 14, "Trou-
  · 2003."

·ks
· the database
·r stores
·o verify mailbox and public folder store integrity
·ng queues

·quired to resolve issues that are identified by
· a result of problems reported by users. Typical
·llows:

·ic folder stores As they grow over time,
·res can become noncontiguous or fragmented,
·ns. You can defragment Exchange databases by
·iguous storage space and can also reduce the

·r store integrity You can use Isinteg.exe to
·e Server 2003 databases. The utility can both
·and repair errors in the database.

·sson 1, you can use Queue Viewer to monitor
·y normal and abnormal activity and to analyze
·s backed up in the queue can indicate a secu-
·ork performance issue.

Offline Defragmentation

Offline defragmentation creates a new, defragmented database and reduces database size. A badly fragmented database may not accept messages fast enough to keep up with the incoming volume. Offline compaction and defragmentation creates a new version of the database that is both smaller and faster than the original.

If you want to defragment a database offline, you need to dismount it. You also need to ensure that the free disk space is at least 110 percent of the size of the database being processed. If free space is not available on the volume where the database is held, you must either free up space or move the database to a volume that has enough free space to enable the eseutil utility to run.

Eseutil is a command-line utility that is used to defragment the mailbox and public folder stores in Exchange Server 2003. The utility examines the structure of the database tables and records. This activity can include reading, scanning, repairing, and defragmenting the database.

Table 13-7 lists the eseutil operation modes.

Table 13-7   The eseutil Operation Modes

Operation mode	Function
eseutil /d	Performs an offline compaction of a database.
eseutil /r	Performs a recovery and brings all databases to a consistent state.
eseutil /g	Verifies the integrity of a database.
eseutil /m	Generates a formatted output of various database file types.
eseutil /p	Repairs a corrupted or damaged database.
eseutil /c	Restores information.
eseutil /k	Verifies database checksums.
eseutil /y	Copies a database streaming file or log file.

Defragmenting Exchange Stores

When you defragment a database in a storage group, the process makes the used storage contiguous, eliminates unused storage, and compacts the database by copying the database records to a new database. When the defragmentation is complete, the original database is deleted or saved to a user-specified location, and the new version is renamed as the original. Only one database in any storage group can be defragmented at any given time. However, databases from different storage groups can be defragmented at the same time provided there are resources available for the process.

To defragment a database, you first use Exchange System Manager to dismount the Exchange store that you want to defragment and then run the eseutil /d utility at the command prompt.

Verifying Exchange Store Integrity

Sometimes headings, pointers, or other indicators in an Exchange store become corrupted. This results in the integrity of the store being compromised. Any of the following situations indicate that an integrity check is required:

- **An item count on a mailbox is inconsistent**   If, for example, a mailbox that you know contains 100 messages reports its size as anything other than 100, then some of the counters and pointers in your mailbox store may be corrupt.

- **You cannot move a mailbox**   If the Move Mailbox command or the exmerge utility fails on a particular mailbox, then the mailbox structure or the structure of a message inside the mailbox may be corrupt.

- **The Exchange store or mail client computer crashes frequently**   If, for example, Outlook crashes repeatedly when a user tries to access a particular mailbox or a specific message within a mailbox, then the mailbox structure or the structure of a message inside the mailbox may be corrupt.

If you suspect a loss of integrity, then you can use the isinteg command-line utility to identify and possibly correct the error. Isinteg searches through an offline Exchange store for integrity weaknesses. It first checks to see whether the MSExchangeIS service is stopped. If that service is stopped, isinteg displays the message "Error: unable to get databases status from server. The reason could be either wrong server name or networking problems," and then isinteg stops.

If the service is not stopped, isinteg displays a list of databases. When you select a database, isinteg checks the cross-reference tables in that database for errors. To do this, it first builds an Exchange database, called *refer.mdb*, of reference counts for the cross-reference tables. It then browses the tables and compares the counts found to the counts in refer.mdb. If you run isinteg with the -fix switch, these counts are updated to the true values, as determined by isinteg. Finally, isinteg performs the "named to ID" or "named properties cleanup" check to remove unused named properties.

Table 13-8 lists the switches that can be used with the isinteg utility.

Table 13-8   isinteg Switches

Switch	Function
-fix	Fixes any inconsistencies in the selected database.
-verbose	Displays a detailed report of the inconsistencies that isinteg discovers.
-test *TestName*	Defines the tests that isinteg will perform when it runs (for example, to perform all tests available, use -test alltests).

Exam Tip You can use eseutil with the /g and /p switches to check and repair database integrity. However, there are limitations to the type of database and the type of fault that can be repaired. Isinteg is the tool of choice for database integrity problems. If you are asked what tools *can* be used, the answer is isinteg and eseutil. If you are asked what the *best* tool is to use, the answer is isinteg. A good way of remembering this is that isinteg is an abbreviation of information store integrity.

Checking Queues

You can use the Queue Viewer tool to maintain and administer your Exchange organization's messaging queues and to identify mail-flow problems. You must first develop a queue baseline so that you can identify the difference between normal and abnormal behavior. Typically, on-demand use of the Queue Viewer results from a user support call indicating that e-mail delivery is slow or a message has not been delivered. You can use Queue Viewer to check for the following items:

- **Extended periods of queues** Typically, an Exchange Server 2003 server will not queue messages for an extended duration. Extended periods of queuing indicate an abnormal system event that you need to investigate. You should review performance metrics to see if some other problems (such as excessive load) are causing mail to be queued. If not, look for connectors or servers that are down or not functioning.

- **Spikes in queued messages** Spikes in queued messages can occur when someone sends a message to a large distribution list, an extremely large message to many people, or a message whose destination is across a slow network link.

Real World **Do Not Panic (Yet)**

Extended periods in queues and spikes happen. They are not typically a cause for alarm. However, you do need to take immediate action if you find a large number of messages queued to the same account. This can be the symptom of a spam or Denial of Service (DoS) attack. If you find a large number of messages queued to a specific server or domain, then maybe the server is down, a service is stopped, a domain is unreachable, or a network connection cannot be made.

Exchange Server 2003 Management Tools

Microsoft Operations Manager is included with Exchange Server 2003. It collects performance data that is generated by your Exchange Server 2003 servers to a central location. It filters, analyzes, reports, and responds to these events. You can use Microsoft Operations Manager to automate the monitoring of large numbers of servers to provide the best level of service for client computers.

The Microsoft Exchange Application Management Pack includes key performance metrics that monitor the overall performance of an Exchange organization and alert you to critical performance issues. By using Microsoft Operations Manager reporting, you can analyze and display this performance data to understand usage trends, to perform accurate load balancing, and to manage system capacity.

Practice: Defragmenting Exchange Stores and Checking Their Integrity

In this practice, you use the eseutil and isinteg command-line utilities to defragment a mailbox store and to check mailbox store integrity.

> **Note**   You need to dismount the mailbox store before performing either operation.

Exercise 1: Defragment a Mailbox Store

To use eseutil to defragment a mailbox store, perform the following steps:

1. Start Exchange System Manager.

2. Navigate to Administrative Groups\First Administrative Group\Servers \Server01\First Storage Group and expand First Storage Group.

3. In the console tree, right-click Mailbox Store (SERVER01), and then click Dismount Store.

4. In the warning box, click Yes to dismount the mailbox store.

5. Open the Command console on Server01.

6. At the command prompt, type **cd \program files\exchsrvr\bin** and then press ENTER.

7. At the command prompt, type **eseutil /d "c:\program files\exchsrvr\mdb-data\priv1.edb"** and then press ENTER.

8. View the output of eseutil in the command prompt window to verify that the defragmentation process completed successfully, as shown in Figure 13-13.

Figure 13-13   eseutil output

9. In Exchange System Manager, right-click Mailbox Store (SERVER01), click Mount Store, and then click OK to acknowledge that the mailbox store was successfully mounted.

Exercise 2: Verify a Mailbox Store

To use isinteg to verify the integrity of a mailbox store, perform the following steps:

1. Start Exchange System Manager.

2. Navigate to Administrative Groups\First Administrative Group\Servers \Server01\First Storage Group.

3. Expand First Storage Group, right-click Mailbox Store (SERVER01), and then click Dismount Store.

4. In the warning box, click Yes to dismount the mailbox store.

5. Open the Command console on Server01.

6. At the command prompt, type **cd \program files\exchsrvr\bin** and then press ENTER.

7. At the command prompt, type **isinteg -s server01 -test allfoldertests** and then press ENTER.

8. When prompted to specify a number to select a database, type the number that corresponds to Mailbox Store (SERVER01) and then press ENTER. The number that is associated with the Mailbox Store will vary depending on how many Exchange stores you have created on your server.

9. When asked whether to continue with your selection of First Storage Group/ Mailbox Store (Server01), type **Y** and then press ENTER.

10. View the results in the Command console, as shown in Figure 13-14, to verify that no errors occurred, and then close the Command console.

Figure 13-14   isinteg output

11. In Exchange System Manager, right-click Mailbox Store (SERVER01), and then click Mount Store. Click OK to acknowledge that the mailbox store was successfully mounted.

Lesson Review

The following questions are intended to reinforce key information presented in this lesson. If you are unable to answer a question, review the lesson materials and then try the question again. You can find answers to the questions in the "Questions and Answers" section at the end of this chapter.

1. You attempt to move a mailbox to a different storage group but are unable to do so. Which utility is most likely to fix the problem?

    a. eseutil

    b. isinteg

    c. exmerge

    d. Queue Viewer

2. You use Queue Viewer and determine that messages sent to a particular mailbox store are being held in the queue for an excessive amount of time before being delivered. There has been no increase in the volume of traffic. What is the problem and how would you fix it?

Lesson Summary

- On-demand maintenance is required when your regular monitoring activities detect a potential issue or when a user reports a problem.

- On-demand maintenance tasks can include defragmenting Exchange databases and repairing their integrity. For these purposes, you use the eseutil and isinteg tools, respectively. You need to dismount the database before carrying out either operation.

- If checking Queue Viewer indicates excessive queue length or if messages remain in queues for an extended duration, then there could be issues with mailbox stores. If there is excessive queue length or duration associated with a specific mailbox or server, then the situation should be investigated immediately.

- Additional Microsoft management tools include Microsoft Operations Manager and the Microsoft Exchange Application Management Pack.

Case Scenario Exercise

You are the Exchange Full Administrator for Fabrikam, Inc. Fabrikam employees use e-mail extensively for both internal and external communication, and management regards an efficient e-mail organization as an essential part of the company's operation. You need to respond promptly to reports that e-mail messages are not being delivered in a timely fashion. Also, you need to design and implement a comprehensive monitoring strategy that identifies potential problems before they impinge on users and that ensures that performance does not degrade over time.

The users at Fabrikam are technically sophisticated and frequently check their mailbox statistics. Any discrepancies in these statistics are reported as errors. Fabrikam is growing, and you cannot keep up with your daily maintenance tasks. Management has permitted you to appoint an assistant, and you need to delegate some of your duties.

Management has asked you to address any problems that users have identified, to prepare a monitoring and maintenance schedule, and to submit a report indicating what tasks you intend to delegate.

- **Requirement 1**   You need to identify the tasks that you should perform on a daily basis, on a weekly basis, and on demand. You also need to decide what tasks you can delegate.

- **Requirement 2**   You need to respond to user reports that e-mail is not being delivered at all, or is not being delivered in a timely fashion.

- **Requirement 3**   Your users' mailbox stores should return correct statistics and there should be no degradation in the performance of your Exchange databases over time. You need to check and repair database activity and to defragment databases as required.

Requirement 1

You need to decide what tasks should be delegated to your assistant, and you need to identify the tasks that need to be performed on a daily basis, on a weekly basis, and on demand.

1. Which of the following Exchange Server 2003 maintenance tasks should you (or your assistant) perform on a daily basis, which on a weekly basis, and which on demand?

   a. Review antivirus logs.

   b. Check the integrity of information stores and repair them as necessary.

   c. Check the application log in Event Viewer for error and warning events.

   d. Review performance logs to identify trends.

   e. Review protocol logs.

   f. Check the available disk space on volumes that store Exchange 2003 databases.

   g. Check the Badmail folder. Monitor the application log in Event Viewer for warnings and errors.

   h. Defragment Exchange databases.

   i. Check mailbox limits.

2. You want to delegate responsibility for dealing with service failures and for gathering Exchange 2003 store statistics. Which specific daily monitoring tasks should you delegate to your assistant?

   _____

   _____

Requirement 2

You need to respond to e-mail delivery problems that users report to you.

1. Sean Alexander, an executive at Blue Yonder Airlines, has sent an e-mail to your chief executive officer (CEO). The message is not in your CEO's mailbox, nor is it in the Badmail folder. Sean has not received an NDR. Where should you look to find the message, and what action can you take to expedite delivery?

   _____

   _____

2. You receive a report from Don Hall that he is receiving NDRs when he sends e-mail to Kim Akers. You know that Kim still works for Fabrikam and that her mailbox is not disabled. You ascertain that the e-mails sent did not have excessively large attachments. Other users report that they have no problems sending e-mail to Kim. You suspect that Don is consistently misspelling Kim's username. How can you quickly check this?

_____

_____

Requirement 3

You need to repair any problems that occur due to Exchange store fragmentation or loss of integrity.

1. You are receiving reports from several users on one of your Exchange stores that the counter for unread messages does not accurately reflect the actual number of unread messages in their inboxes. You verify that the users do not have filters on their inboxes. What should you do next?

_____

_____

2. You suspect that an Exchange mailbox store has become fragmented and that there may also be integrity errors. You attempt to use the isinteg and eseutil command-line utilities, but they will not run for that store. What have you forgotten to do?

_____

_____

Troubleshooting Lab

Network Monitor is one of the main tools used in Windows Server 2003 and Exchange Server 2003. It lets you see exactly what is happening on your network, right down to the bit level. You can identify the types of frames that are being transmitted or received by any computer, determine if a computer is excessively loaded, and analyze the traffic that is loading it. You can determine the proportions of broadcast, unicast, and multicast traffic on a network.

In this lab, you install the version of Network Monitor that comes with Windows Server 2003. This enables you to look at packets received or sent by the server (Server01) on which it is installed. You then use the tool to capture and examine packets between Server01 and Server02 and set up display filters to display the information you require. You can use a similar technique to set up a capture filter so that you capture only the information you want to look at.

You can view a subset of the data that you captured using Network Monitor by using a control known as a decision tree, which lets you specify what you want to see using Boolean logic. This process is not as complex as it sounds. For example, you can specify that you only want to view frames that use Transmission Control Protocol (TCP), or you can specify that you want to see all the captured frames *except* those that use TCP. You can specify that you want to view only the frames sent to a specified host or received from that host. You can combine conditions so that, for example, you view only TCP frames that are sent to the specified host.

Decision trees and Boolean logic are best explained by using them. This lab introduces you to both.

Before you begin this lab, ensure that your test network is set up as described in the "Before You Begin" section of this chapter. You also need to have a Windows Server 2003, Enterprise Edition installation CD in hand.

Exercise 1: Install and Use Network Monitor

To install and use Network Monitor, perform the following steps:

1. On Server01, insert the Windows Server 2003, Enterprise Edition, installation CD.

2. Open the Command console, type **ipconfig /all** and then press ENTER. Note the Physical or Media Access Control (MAC) address of Local Area Connection.

3. Open Add/Remove Programs in Control Panel.

4. Select Add/Remove Windows Components.

5. In the Windows Components Wizard, select Management And Monitoring Tools, and then click Details.

6. Select the Network Monitor Tools check box, and then click OK. When Network Monitor is installed, close Add/Remove Programs.

 Note   Installing Network Monitor tools automatically installs the Network Monitor driver.

7. Access Start\Programs\Administration Tools, and then select Network Monitor.

8. Because this is the first time Network Monitor has been accessed, you are prompted to select a network. Expand Local Computer, click Local Area Connection, check that the MAC address is as recorded, and then click OK.

9. The Network Monitor capture window appears. On the Capture menu, click Start.

10. Open Outlook on Server01.

11. Send an e-mail to *administrator@contoso.com* (where *contoso.com* is the domain in which you have installed Server02). In the body of the message, type **Now is the time for all good men to come to the aid of the party**.

12. Ping Server02 by fully qualified domain name (FQDN) and by IP address.

13. On the Network Monitor Capture menu, click Stop And View. The Network Monitor capture summary window appears.

14. On the Display menu, click Colors. Select ICMP, choose a foreground color (for example, red) and then click OK. All ICMP frames are then displayed in that color.

15. Double-click the first frame on the list. Your screen should look similar to Figure 13-15. This shows (from the top) the Summary, Detail, and Hex panes.

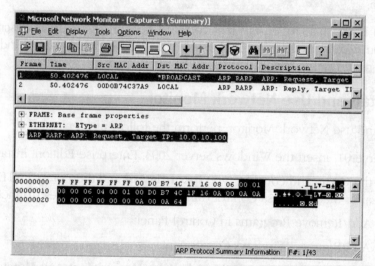

Figure 13-15   The Summary, Detail, and Hex panes in Network Monitor

16. Scroll down through the entries in the Summary pane. You will find the e-mail message you sent on the Hex pane in a TCP frame, as shown in Figure 13-16.

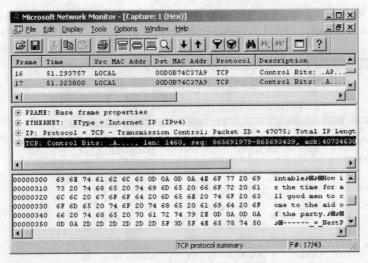

Figure 13-16   Frame containing e-mail message text

17. In the Detail pane, expand IP and scroll through the details. You can, for example, identify the source and destination addresses in the frame.

18. Save your capture by clicking Save As in the File menu and specifying a file name. By default, the capture is saved as a .cap file. If you start a new capture or attempt to exit Network Monitor without saving your capture, you will be prompted to save it.

> **Note** Only a small number of frames are captured in this procedure. If you had captured a large number, possibly over an extended period, then color highlighting might not be an adequate method of viewing the frames associated with a particular protocol. In this case, you can specify a display filter so that only frames that meet specific criteria are displayed. You can use the capture you saved to demonstrate this technique.

19. To configure a display filter, open the capture file you have just created from the Network Monitor File menu. Note that you could have continued the exercise without saving and reloading the file, but it is good practice to save the files you are working with.

20. On the Display menu, click Filter.

21. In the Display Filter dialog box, click Expression and select the Protocol tab.

22. Click Disable All.

23. In the Disabled Protocols box, select TCP.

24. Click Enable.

25. Click OK. Click OK again to close the Display Filter dialog box. Network Monitor will now display only TCP frames, as shown in Figure 13-17.

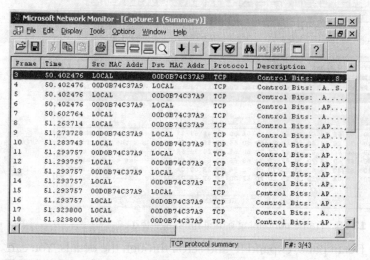

Figure 13-17   Filtering out all frames except TCP frames

> **Note**   Disabling a protocol does not always result in that protocol's frames not appearing in Network Monitor capture screens. A protocol that contains subprotocols, for example, the Service Message Block (SMB) protocol, will still be displayed if its subprotocols remain enabled.

26. If you want to display all the frames except TCP frames at this point, access the Display Filter dialog box, select the TCP protocol in the decision tree, and click NOT, and then click OK. To return to the previous filter, access the Display Filter dialog box and double-click the NOT box beside the protocol until it displays AND.

27. To refine the protocol filter still further by filtering by specific properties, such as source IP address or source MAC address, select Filter from the Display menu on the Network Monitor capture summary screen.

28. In the Display Filter dialog box, click Expression.

29. Select the Address tab, and set the condition that Station 1 is specified by the IP address of Local Area Connection on Server01. Also highlight the single arrow in the Direction pane, as shown in Figure 13-18.

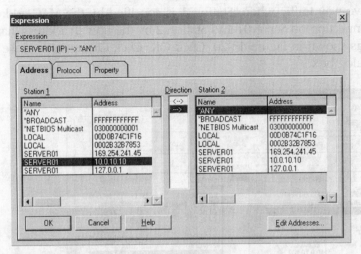

Figure 13-18   Filtering by IP address and direction

30. Click OK. Click OK again to exit the Display Filter dialog box. Network Monitor will now display only the TCP frames that Server01 transmits on to the internal network. It will not, for example, display frames sent from Server02 to Server01.

31. On the Display menu, select Filter and highlight the filter condition that you created. In the Delete section, click Line, and then click OK. The capture summary screen will now display all captured frames.

32. To display all the traffic between your server and one particular host on the network, whatever protocols are used, and to filter out traffic to and from other hosts, click Filter on the Display menu.

33. In the Display Filter dialog box, click Expression.

34. In the Expression dialog box, select the Address tab, and then click Edit Addresses.

35. Click Add, and add the IP address of Server02, as shown in Figure 13-19. Click OK, and then click Close.

Figure 13-19   Specifying an address for filtering

36. Select two-way traffic where Station 1 is specified by the MAC address of Local Area Connection on Server01 and Station 2 by the host IP address that you've just added, as shown in Figure 13-20. Click OK. Click OK again to close the Display Filter dialog box.

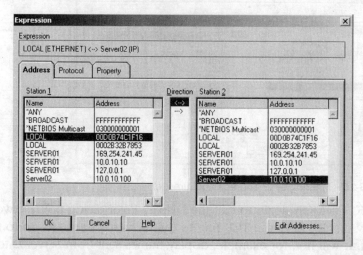

Figure 13-20 Specifying two way traffic between Server01 and Server02

37. Check that the frames displayed contain traffic between Server01 and Server02.

38. On the Display menu, click Filter. Highlight and delete the line you've just added to the decision tree.

39. Repeat the filter setup to display the broadcast traffic that your server puts on your subnet. Select the MAC address of Local Area Connection on Server01 for Station 1, the single arrow, and the broadcast address for Station 2. Check that only broadcast frames are displayed.

40. Close Network Monitor.

Tip The display filter decision tree is a very powerful and flexible tool. If you are familiar with Boolean logic, you can set up some very sophisticated filter criteria using this tool. The only way to learn this technique is by practice.

Chapter Summary

- You need to check certain logs, such as the application log in Event Viewer, on a daily basis. You can use the diagnostic logging function in Exchange System Manager to configure the detail of events that are logged. You need to check the message load on your Exchange Server 2003 servers and the logs generated by your virtual servers, and your antivirus product. You should also check the available disk space on volumes that store Exchange logs and databases.

■ You should monitor and review other logs and monitor information on a regular basis. You need to review performance logs and protocol logs, manage mailbox limits, manage the Badmail folder, and manage the postmaster mailbox. You can use HTTP Monitor to monitor Web sites and OWA servers.

■ On-demand maintenance is typically required when regular logging indicates a potential problem. Typically, you may need to defragment databases, check and restore database integrity, and deal with queuing issues.

Exam Highlights

Before taking the exam, review the key points and terms that are presented in this chapter. Return to the lessons for additional practice.

Key Points

■ The application log in Event Viewer records Exchange Server 2003 events. Tools such as diagnostic logging and the Monitoring And Status utility determine the events and event levels that are recorded in Event Viewer.

■ You use Exchange System Manager to configure protocol logging on NNTP and SMTP virtual servers. However, you need to use IIS Manager to configure protocol logging on HTTP virtual servers. Only the W3C Extended Logging format lets you choose what events to track.

■ The Performance console contains two snap-ins. The Performance Logs And Alerts tool is used to configure performance logs and set up alert conditions. System Monitor displays counters in real time and is also used to display logs.

■ The eseutil utility is used to defragment databases; the isinteg tool checks database integrity and repairs it as necessary. A fragmented database is larger and slower than it should be; a database that has lost its integrity may not be able to be moved and displays incorrect statistics.

Key Terms

Monitoring And Status utility   A tool provided with Exchange System Manager that monitors the status of Exchange Server 2003 servers and connections and logs events to the application log of Event Viewer when the level of these resources reaches a warning or a critical state.

Performance console   The Performance console measures the performance of objects in Windows Server 2003 and Exchange Server 2003 by means of performance counters. The console has two snap-ins: System Monitor and Performance Logs And Alerts.

isinteg utility   A command-line utility that tests and repairs the integrity of an Exchange information store.

eseutil utility   A command-line utility that defragments Exchange databases.

Network Monitor   A powerful tool that can capture all the frames set to or transmitted by a host and analyze the contents of these frames at the bit level.

Questions and Answers

Lesson 1 Review

1. A user reports that she sent important information to a colleague some time ago, but the message has not been received. A non-delivery report (NDR) has not been returned to the sender. What tool do you use to investigate, and what message parameters should you look at?

   You would use the Find Messages option in Queue Viewer to locate the message in the message queues. You can view the information in the Search Results pane to determine whether the message is in the Retry state, what the size of the message is, what time the message was submitted, and at what time the message will expire.

2. You want to monitor free disk space on an Exchange Server 2003 server and obtain a notification if this drops below a threshold value. You use the Monitoring And Status utility in Exchange System Manager to configure the free disk space monitoring level. Where would you look for notification that free disk space has dropped below the threshold level?

   a. In your Inbox

   b. In the system log in Event Viewer

   c. On the Monitoring tab of the Server Properties dialog box in Exchange System Manager

   d. In the applications log in Event Viewer

   The correct answer is d.

3. You want to view events recorded when SMTP is used to route messages. Which event source should you monitor in Event Viewer?

   a. MSExchangeTransport

   b. MSExchangeAL

   c. MSExchangeIS

   d. MSExchangeSA

   The correct answer is a.

Page
13-33

Lesson 2 Review

1. You configure protocol logging on your Default NNTP virtual server and your Default SMTP virtual server. You use Exchange System Manager to access the Properties dialog box of your Exchange virtual server, but the controls to configure protocol logging do not exist. How can you configure protocol logging on your Exchange virtual server?

   You need to open IIS Manager and access the Properties dialog box for the default Web site. You can configure protocol logging on the Web Site tab.

2. You enable and configure protocol logging on the Default SMTP virtual server on one of your Exchange Server 2003 servers. You do not want to log all available items, but instead want to select the items to track. Which log file format should you specify?

   a. IIS Log

   b. NCSA Common Log

   c. W3C Extended Log

   d. ODBC Logging

   The correct answer is c.

3. A user reports that when she sends an attachment to a particular recipient, she receives an NDR. You suspect that the Exchange Server 2003 server used by the recipient has a size limit for inbound messages. How can you determine what this size limit is?

   Review the SMTP protocol log-file data for the response codes that the receiving server returns after your server issues an ehlo command. Look for the response code 250-size xxxxxx, where xxxxxx is the maximum message size that the server can accept.

Page
13-41

Lesson 3 Review

1. You attempt to move a mailbox to a different storage group but are unable to do so. Which utility is most likely to fix the problem?

   a. eseutil

   b. isinteg

   c. exmerge

   d. Queue Viewer

   The correct answer is b.

2. You use Queue Viewer and determine that messages sent to a particular mailbox store are being held in the queue for an excessive amount of time before being delivered. There has been no increase in the volume of traffic. What is the problem and how would you fix it?

The mailbox store has become fragmented. You need to dismount the store and run the eseutil /d utility to create a smaller, faster database.

Page 13-43

Case Scenario Exercise: Requirement 1

1. Which of the following Exchange Server 2003 maintenance tasks should you (or your assistant) perform on a daily basis, which on a weekly basis, and which on demand?

   a. Review antivirus logs.

   b. Check the integrity of information stores and repair them as necessary.

   c. Check the application log in Event Viewer for error and warning events.

   d. Review performance logs to identify trends.

   e. Review protocol logs.

   f. Check the available disk space on volumes that store Exchange 2003 databases.

   g. Check the Badmail folder. Monitor the application log in Event Viewer for warnings and errors.

   h. Defragment Exchange databases.

   i. Check mailbox limits.

   You should perform tasks a, c, and f on a daily basis. You should perform tasks d, e, g, and i on a weekly basis. You should perform tasks b and h on demand.

2. You want to delegate responsibility for dealing with service failures and for gathering Exchange 2003 store statistics. Which specific daily monitoring tasks should you delegate to your assistant?

   You should delegate the following tasks:

   ■ Daily monitoring of Event Viewer to identify event information about service failures, Active Directory replication errors, and low-disk-space warnings.

   ■ Checking Monitoring And Status daily to view connector status and Exchange server status.

   ■ Daily monitoring of Exchange and network services to detect problems with services startup, Active Directory replication, and network health.

   ■ Daily review of Exchange store statistics to determine whether the Exchange store is mounted, what users are logged on, the state of public folder replication, and the state of full-text indexing.

Page
13-43

Case Scenario Exercise: Requirement 2

1. Sean Alexander, an executive at Blue Yonder Airlines, has sent an e-mail to your chief executive officer (CEO). The message is not in your CEO's mailbox, nor is it in the Badmail folder. Sean has not received an NDR. Where should you look to find the message, and what action can you take to expedite delivery?

   The message is probably queued for delivery. You can use the Find Message utility in Queue Viewer to find the message. If there is no particular property (such as excessive size) that is preventing delivery of the message, then you can force a connection by right-clicking the queue and clicking Force Connection.

2. You receive a report from Don Hall that he is receiving NDRs when he sends e-mail to Kim Akers. You know that Kim still works for Fabrikam and that her mailbox is not disabled. You ascertain that the e-mails sent did not have excessively large attachments. Other users report that they have no problems sending e-mail to Kim. You suspect that Don is consistently misspelling Kim's username. How can you quickly check this?

   Look in the postmaster mailbox. If, for example, mail has been sent to k.*ackers@fabrikam.com* instead of to k.*akers@fabrikam.com*, then NDRs should be stored in that mailbox. The Badmail folder will not store this e-mail traffic because NDRs can be returned to the sender.

Page
13-44

Case Scenario Exercise: Requirement 3

1. You are receiving reports from several users on one of your Exchange stores that the counter for unread messages does not accurately reflect the actual number of unread messages in their inboxes. You verify that the users do not have filters on their inboxes. What should you do next?

   You should use the isinteg utility to test the integrity of that Exchange store. Based on the information that isinteg provides, you may need to repair the Exchange store.

2. You suspect that an Exchange mailbox store has become fragmented and that there may also be integrity errors. You attempt to use the isinteg and eseutil command-line utilities, but they will not run for that store. What have you forgotten to do?

   You have forgotten to dismount the store.

14 Troubleshooting Microsoft Exchange Server 2003

Exam Objectives in this Chapter:

- Install, configure, and troubleshoot Microsoft Exchange Server 2003
- Install, configure, and troubleshoot Exchange Server 2003 in a clustered environment
- Configure and troubleshoot Exchange Server 2003 for coexistence with other exchange organizations
- Configure and troubleshoot Exchange Server 2003 for coexistence with other messaging systems
- Configure and troubleshoot for coexistence with other Simple Mail Transport Protocol (SMTP) messaging systems
- Manage, monitor, and troubleshoot server health
- Manage, monitor, and troubleshoot data storage
- Perform and troubleshoot backups and recovery
- Manage and troubleshoot public folders
- Manage and troubleshoot Internet protocol virtual servers
- Manage and troubleshoot front-end and back-end servers
- Manage and troubleshoot connectivity
- Manage and troubleshoot connectivity across firewalls
- Manage and troubleshoot permissions
- Manage and troubleshoot encryption and digital signatures
- Diagnose problems arising from host resolution protocols
- Diagnose problems arising from Active Directory directory service issues
- Diagnose network connectivity problems

Why This Chapter Matters

A review of the syllabus for Exam 70-284, or of the exam objectives listed above, indicates the importance of troubleshooting, both in the exam and in the real world. It is your job to install an Exchange Server 2003 organization, to ensure that it works securely and smoothly, and to monitor it to discover trends. However, where you are seen to earn your pay—where your skill, knowledge, and experience are most on public view—is when something goes wrong and you need to fix it. The importance of this chapter cannot be emphasized enough, and troubleshooting will be tested thoroughly in the exam.

Lessons in this Chapter:

- Lesson 1: Troubleshooting Exchange Server 2003 server migration and interoperability 14-4
- Lesson 2: Troubleshooting Exchange Server 2003 servers 14-16
- Lesson 3: Troubleshooting the Exchange Server 2003 organization 14-26
- Lesson 4: Troubleshooting Security 14-36
- Lesson 5: Troubleshooting Technologies that Support Exchange Server 2003 14-45

Before You Begin

To perform the exercises in this chapter, you need the following hardware and software:

- Two Microsoft Windows Server 2003, Enterprise Edition, servers. Server01 should be a domain controller installed in the *tailspintoys.com* Active Directory domain, and Server02 should be a domain controller installed in the *contoso.com* Active Directory domain. Server01 should be multihomed. Local Area Connection on Server01 should be on the same network as Local Area Connection on Server02. Local Area Connection 2 on Server01 simulates an external network. It does not need to be connected to anything, but if you want, you can use it for Internet access.

> **Note**   If your Active Directory domains are not called *tailspintoys.com* and *contoso.com*, there is no need to rename them. Instead use your domain names rather than *tailspintoys.com* and *contoso.com* whenever these names are mentioned in the chapter exercises.

- Exchange Server 2003, Enterprise Edition, should be installed on both servers. Server02 should be configured as a recovery server for Server01. Server02 was configured as a recovery server in Chapter 12, "Backup and Restore."

- Network Monitor should be installed on Server01. This was done in Chapter 13, "Monitoring Microsoft Exchange Server 2003."

- Windows Server Support tools should be installed on Server01. The installation file is located in the Support\Tools folder on the Microsoft Exchange Server 2003 installation CD.

Lesson 1: Troubleshooting Exchange Server 2003 Server Migration and Interoperability

Clean installations of Exchange Server 2003 and migration from earlier Exchange systems are straightforward, well-defined processes. Nevertheless, they can fail if all the requirements are not in place. Removal of an Exchange Server 2003 server from an organization is more complex, particularly if private stores exist on the server. Coexistence and interoperability with foreign messaging systems requires careful configuration so that encoding problems can be avoided.

After this lesson, you will be able to

- Troubleshoot installation and enumerate the reasons that a clean install of Exchange Server 2003 could fail
- Remove an Exchange Server 2003 server from an Exchange Server 2003 organization, list the reasons that such an operation could fail, and explain the workaround in that situation
- Check connectivity and Domain Name System (DNS) and Active Directory availability using the appropriate command-line tools
- Troubleshoot migration and interoperability issues

Estimated lesson time: 60 minutes

Troubleshooting Installation

An Exchange Server 2003 organization may be created by migration from Exchange 2000 Server or Exchange Server 5.5. However, you may also need to install an Exchange Server 2003 server, or even an entire Exchange Server 2003 organization, from scratch. Installation was covered in Chapter 2, "Planning a Microsoft Exchange Server 2003 Infrastructure." Normally, Exchange Server 2003 installation is a straightforward process, but things can go wrong. A clean installation of Exchange Server 2003 can fail for a number of reasons:

- The target server does not meet hardware requirements.
- The target server does not meet software requirements.
- You do not have the appropriate permissions.
- The appropriate services are not running, or services are running that should not be.
- Active Directory is not available.
- ' ForestPrep and DomainPrep have not been run.
- The DNS service is not available.

When you try to install Exchange Server 2003 and not all the conditions are met, the installation program typically responds with a list of all the required conditions. It is then up to you to determine what conditions you have failed to meet. It is therefore wise to go through a checklist before starting to install the software. The first page of the installation setup guidance that appears after you select New Exchange 2003 installation gives you this checklist. It also gives links to ForestPrep and DomainPrep.

Hardware and software requirements are listed in Chapter 2, "Planning a Microsoft Exchange 2003 Infrastructure." The information is repeated here deliberately so that it can be seen from a troubleshooting viewpoint and to save you from having to check back to obtain it.

Hardware Requirements

The minimum processor requirement is a Pentium 133. However, a Pentium III 500 processor is recommended for Exchange Server 2003, Standard Edition, and a Pentium III 733 for Exchange Server 2003, Enterprise Edition. It is unlikely that the processors on all but your most out-of-date servers fall below the minimum installation requirements, but severe performance problems will result in all but the smallest Exchange Server 2003 organizations if the recommendations are not followed.

The minimum memory requirement is 256 megabytes (MB). It is possible that this could be a source of failure if you are installing on a Windows 2000 Server machine. Windows 2000 Server will install on 128 MB. However, such an inadequate machine would be a strange choice for an Exchange Server 2003 server. What is more likely is that you will experience performance problems if your server memory is below the recommended 512 MB.

Installation will fail if you do not have 200 MB free space on your system drive and 500 MB free space on the partition where Exchange Server 2003 is installed. In practice, you will experience severe problems if your free disk space drops to anywhere near these limitations. An Exchange Server 2003 server will typically use disk arrays for performance and failover protection, and will store at least transaction logs, and possibly also Exchange binaries, on separate disks from the Exchange databases. Disk storage systems were discussed in Chapter 12.

It is unlikely that the machine chosen for Exchange Server 2003 installation will not have a CD-ROM drive or VGA graphics. It is, however, necessary to ensure that all disk partitions involving Exchange Server 2003 are NTFS. Typically, all partitions in Windows Server 2003 servers and Windows 2000 Server servers are NTFS unless the machines are dual boot.

Software and Service Requirements

Exchange Server 2003 will not install unless the target machine is running either Windows Server 2003 or Windows 2000 Server with Service Pack 3 (SP3) or later installed. If you want to use Windows clustering services for failover protection, then either Windows 2000 Advanced Server or Windows Server 2003, Enterprise Edition, is required. Network Load Balancing can be implemented on Windows 2000 Server or Windows Server 2003, Standard Edition. The SMTP, Network News Transport Protocol (NNTP) and World Wide Web (WWW) services must be installed and enabled on the server before you start Exchange Server 2003 installation, and the Post Office Protocol version 3 (POP3) service should not be installed. NNTP is required for installation, but you should subsequently disable it unless newsgroup functionality is required.

If your server is running Windows Server 2003, then Active Service Pages (ASP.NET) must be installed. It must also be enabled using the Internet Information Services (IIS) Manager console. Windows Server 2003 has Microsoft .NET Framework built into the operating system and you do not need to install it.

> ### Real World   An Installation Oddity
>
> Some people who have successfully installed Exchange Server 2003 on Windows 2000 Server member servers have found that the installation failed on Windows Server 2003 member servers. Because ASP.NET and .NET Framework did not exist when Windows 2000 Server was introduced, Exchange Server 2003 installs them automatically during the Setup process on a Windows 2000 Server member server. However, it does not install ASP.NET on installation of an Exchange Server 2003 server on a Windows Server 2003 member server. Instead, you need to first install ASP.NET manually using Add/Remove Programs in Control Panel and enable it using IIS Manager. It seems to confuse people mightily that they need to perform additional steps when installing on the newer system.

Active Directory access is required. Notice that this does not mean that you need to install Exchange Server 2003 on a domain controller; indeed it would be most unwise to do this on a production network. However, the server you choose needs to be a member server in either a Windows 2000 or Windows 2003 Active Directory domain. Exchange Server 2003 requires DNS, but so does Active Directory. Therefore, the availability of Active Directory implies that the DNS service is also available.

Permission Requirements

You need to run ForestPrep when you install the first Exchange Server 2003 server in a forest and hence create an Exchange Server 2003 organization. ForestPrep can take some time—often an hour or more—to complete.

You need to run DomainPrep on the forest root domain, on all domains that will contain Exchange Server 2003 member servers, and on all domains that will contain Exchange Server 2003 mailbox-enabled objects. Most administrators remember that they need to run DomainPrep on child domains in their forests, but it is easy to forget that you also need to run it on the forest root domain directly after running ForestPrep.

To run ForestPrep for the first time in a forest, you need to be a member of the Schema Admins and Enterprise Admins groups. The Administrator account on the first domain on the first tree of a forest is by default a member of both groups, but it is good practice to use that account as seldom as possible. If you need to run ForestPrep again, then you can do so if you have Exchange Full Administrator permissions at the Exchange organizational level. The same level of permissions is also required to install the first Exchange Server 2003 server in a domain or to install an Exchange Server 2003 server with the Site Replication Service (SRS) enabled. To install additional services in a domain, you need to have Exchange Full Administrator permissions at the administrative group level. To run DomainPrep, you need to be a member of the Domain Admins group in the target domain. If you do not have sufficient permissions, then the installation will fail.

> **Important**   It is tempting to do all your installation using the highest level of permissions that you have—typically the Administrator account for the forest root domain. Please resist this temptation. This practice is insecure. Also, if you are not familiar with the lower permission levels required for some of the tasks, then you will find it more difficult to delegate these tasks.

Removing an Exchange Server 2003 Server

The Exchange Server 2003 server installation wizard is also used to remove an Exchange Server 2003 server from an Exchange Server 2003 organization. You need the same level of permissions to remove a server that you do to add one. However, you can have problems that you need to troubleshoot when removing servers. For example, the wizard will not remove a server unless you have deleted or moved all the mailboxes on that server. In this case, the wizard stops with an error message, and you have two choices:

- You can move or delete all the mailboxes.
- You can forcibly remove the Exchange Server 2003 server from the organization.

The second process will result in the loss of any data held in public stores or mailboxes on the server. It is carried out using Exchange System Manager, and you need to power the server down or else an error will occur. This implies that the server you are removing cannot be the only machine on which Exchange System Manager is installed. (It would be very bad practice if it were.)

Forcible removal of an Exchange Server 2003 server is described in detail in Chapter 2, "Planning a Microsoft Exchange Server 2003 Infrastructure."

Troubleshooting Connectivity

Another possible reason for installation failure is that your target server is not connected to the services that you think it is. You can perform simple tests such as pinging a domain controller and a DNS server, or using the nslookup utility. However, more powerful tools are included in the Support/Tools folder on the Windows Server 2003 installation CD. The netdiag utility is used to test network connectivity, and the dcdiag utility can test both network connectivity and DNS resolution.

The netdiag command-line diagnostic utility is used to isolate networking and connectivity problems by performing a series of tests to determine the state of your server. This tool has a number of switches that let you specify specific tests, and to fix simple faults. However, a major advantage of the tool is that it can run without specifying any parameters or switches. You can therefore focus your efforts on analyzing the output rather than on training users how to use the tool.

The dcdiag command-line diagnostic utility analyzes the state of domain controllers in a forest and reports any problems. It is a powerful tool, with a large number of (optional) switches, which provides you with detailed information that lets you identify abnormal behavior in the system. The tool consists of a framework for executing tests, plus a series of tests that verify different functional areas of the system.

Troubleshooting Migration

Migration is discussed in detail in Chapter 5, "Migrating from Microsoft Exchange Server and Other Mail Systems." Migration is designed to be straightforward and can be rolled back if problems occur. Problems, and hence troubleshooting requirements, are mainly associated with transferring user mailboxes. In Exchange 2000 Server, as in Exchange Server 2003, there is a one-to-one relationship between user accounts and mailboxes. However, Exchange Server 5.5 maintains its own directory independent of Windows, and a single Windows user account could be associated with multiple Exchange Server 5.5 mailboxes. This can cause problems when migrating Exchange Server 5.5 to Exchange Server 2003.

Exam Tip   Remember that the migration wizard and other migration tools move mailboxes from one organization to another. You should use the Active Directory Users And Computers console to move mailboxes within an organization.

If you use the Active Directory Connector to move mailboxes, it creates a new disabled user account when it cannot match a mailbox to an existing user account. The problem with this method is that the newly created user accounts have different security identifiers (SIDs) than the accounts currently in use in the source organization. As a result, they have no permissions configured, and they are not the mailbox owners for the corresponding mailboxes. To work around this problem, you need to enable each account manually and then grant that account permissions to the associated mailbox.

The preferred migration technique is to use the Active Directory Migration Tool, which is found in the \I386\ADMT folder of the Windows Server 2003 installation CD. This tool migrates the SID history of the user account, which enables accounts to retain their permissions after the migration. However, a problem can occur when using the Active Directory Migration Tool. If you find that the user passwords have not been migrated, and that as a result you need to set the passwords manually, then you may have used an old version of the tool. Version 2 on the Windows Server 2003 installation CD can migrate passwords. Previous versions cannot.

> **See Also**   The README.DOC document in the same folder of the CD merits careful study. Pay particular attention to the "Known Issues" section, which contains a substantial amount of troubleshooting information.

Another problem that can occur during migration involves the use of connectors. If the Exchange Server 5.5 server was configured with an Internet Mail connector, then you need to configure an SMTP virtual server on the Exchange Server 2003 server and change the Mail Exchanger (MX) record in DNS to point to the new server. There will be a disruption in Internet mail delivery while this information propagates over the Internet. This is unavoidable, and the changeover should be done at off-peak server usage times. If the changeover is not done, the Exchange Server 2003 organization will continue to use the Internet Mail connector. In this case, when you take the Exchange Server 5.5 server out of service, internal mail is unaffected but all Internet mail stops. The temporary workaround is to put the Exchange Server 5.5 server back on the network, but you should switch to the SMTP virtual server as soon as possible.

Troubleshooting Interoperability

When your Exchange Server 2003 organization is interoperating with other e-mail systems, problems can occur due to formatting incompatibility or to the use of Exchange-specific functions such as calendaring. For example, Exchange Server 2003 sends messages across an X.400 connection in native Exchange format. This works when the system at the other end of the connection is also running Exchange, but if the destination system is, for example, UNIX, then the message will be garbled. The solution to this problem is to clear the Allow Exchange Contents option on the X.400 connector and allow standard X.400 formatting to be used.

Sometimes an X.400 connector is the solution rather than the problem. By default, Exchange Server 2003 routing groups are connected by routing connectors. If, however, the connection is unreliable or non-persistent (a demand-dial connection, for example), then transfer reliability can be improved by using an X.400 connection, which uses message-based data transfer rather than remote procedure call (RPC).

You also need to take care how you specify encoding formats for your POP3 and Internet Message Protocol version 4 (IMAP4) clients on the relevant virtual servers. This was discussed in Chapter 9, "Virtual Servers." If your clients use UNIX to UNIX encoding (uuencode), then your virtual servers need to be set up appropriately. For Macintosh clients, you need to specify uuencode and then select BinHex for Macintosh.

Microsoft Outlook users tend to take calendaring for granted because it is a built-in Outlook function. However, the Calendar Connector's properties are set not to synchronize calendar data by default. Thus when Outlook users attempt to view the schedules of users on foreign systems, for example Lotus Notes, the information could be out of date.

Exam Tip   If you get a question about interaction with a foreign system, read it carefully to determine if you are getting no communication with the foreign system, in which case a connector is down or a virtual server has failed. If, on the other hand, you are getting a connection but the messages are garbled, then the encoding format may be specified incorrectly.

Practice: Using the Netdiag and Dcdiag Command-Line Utilities

The netdiag utility tests network connectivity. The tool lets you specify a number of optional parameters, such as /test: to run a specific test and /d: to specify a domain. However, it is typically run either with no parameters or with the /fix switch to repair minor errors and the /debug switch to give detailed output. The output from the tool can be redirected to a text file for analysis.

The dcdiag utility is mainly used to test domain controller operation, but it also tests DNS availability. If there is a problem with your Active Directory domain or your DNS server, then Exchange Server 2003 will not install and dcdiag can help troubleshoot the failure. The utility has a number of parameters, all of which are optional. You can use the /s: switch to specify a domain controller, the /u: switch to specify a user (by username and domain name), and the /p: switch to specify a password. If you do not supply any of these parameters, then the utility will test the host on which it is run in the context of the logged in user. The /fix switch fixes the Service Principal Names (SPNs) on the specified domain controller, and the /test: switch allows you to specify particular tests. All tests except DcPromo and RegisterInDNS must be run on a domain controller.

> **See Also**   Details of the netdiag and dcdiag tests and parameters may be obtained from the Windows Server 2003 help files. Search under "Support Tools."

In this practice, you create files to hold the output of the tests, run the netdiag tests on a normal system and on a faulty system, compare the outputs, and then do the same with the dcdiag tests.

Exercise 1: Create Files to Hold the Test Output

To create files to hold the test output, perform the following steps:

1. On Server01, create a new folder named C:\Tests.

2. In the C:\Tests folder, create the following empty text files:

   ❑ Netdiag1.txt

   ❑ Netdiag2.txt

   ❑ Dcdiag1.txt

   ❑ Dcdiag2.txt

> **Note**   Some administrators do not create the required folder and files before using command-line utilities such as netdiag and dcdiag, because the utilities create them automatically. However, not all command-line utilities do this. Arguably, it is good practice to create files before you run any utility that uses them.

Exercise 2: Use Netdiag to Check Network Connectivity

To use netdiag to test network connectivity on Server01, perform the following steps:

1. On Server01, open the Command console.

2. Enter **netdiag /debug /fix > c:\tests\netdiag1.txt**.

3. Open the Netdiag1.txt file using Microsoft Notepad.

4. Read the test output. Use the search function to find "Errors," "Warning," or "Failed." A section of the test output is shown in Figure 14-1.

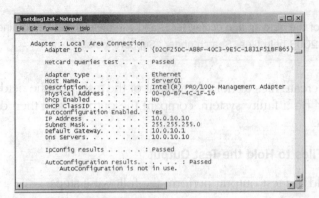

Figure 14-1   Netdiag output

Exercise 3: Use Netdiag to Find a Connection Fault

To create a connection fault on Server01 and use netdiag to diagnose the fault, perform the following steps:

1. On Server01, unplug the connector from Local Area Connection.

2. Open the Command console.

3. Enter **netdiag /debug /fix > c:\tests\netdiag2.txt**.

4. Open the Netdiag2.txt file using Notepad.

5. Read the test output. Use the search function to find "Fatal." The relevant section of the test output is shown in Figure 14-2.

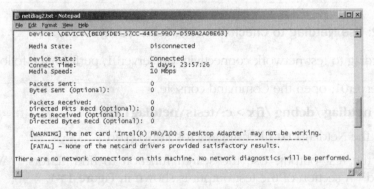

Figure 14-2   Netdiag output showing a fatal error

6. Replace the network connector for Local Area Connection. Test the connection by pinging Server02.

Exercise 4: Use Dcdiag to Test Server02

In this exercise, you run dcdiag from Server01 to test Server02. If Server02 is not a domain controller on your test network, then test Server01 instead. To test Server02 using dcdiag, perform the following steps:

1. On Server01, open the Command console.

2. Enter **dcdiag /s:server02 /n:contoso.com /u:contoso.com\administrator /p:* /v /f:c:\tests\dcdiag1.txt /fix**.

3. Enter the password for the *contoso.com* administrator when prompted. The test completes as shown in Figure 14-3.

Figure 14-3   Running dcdiag on Server02

4. Open the Dcdiag1.txt file using Notepad and read the results. A section of the test output is shown in Figure 14-4.

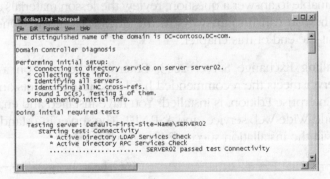

Figure 14-4   Output of dcdiag test on Server02

Exercise 5: Use Dcdiag to Detect a Fault on Server02

In this exercise, you stop the DNS service on Server02 and then run dcdiag from Server01 to test Server02. To use dcdiag to detect a fault on Server02, perform the following steps:

1. On Server02, open the DNS console, right-click SERVER02, and then click Stop.

2. On Server01, open the Command console.

3. Enter **dcdiag /s:server02 /n:contoso.com /u:contoso.com\administrator /p:* /v /f:c:\tests\dcdiag2.txt /fix**.

4. Enter the password for the *contoso.com* administrator when prompted.

5. Open the Dcdiag2.txt file using Notepad and read the results. The relevant section of the test output is shown in Figure 14-5.

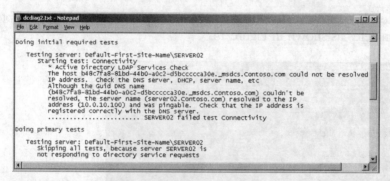

Figure 14-5   Dcdiag failure notification on Server02

6. Start the DNS service on Server02.

Lesson Review

The following questions are intended to reinforce key information presented in this lesson. If you are unable to answer a question, review the lesson materials and then try the question again. You can find answers to the questions in the "Questions and Answers" section at the end of this chapter.

1. You are installing Exchange Server 2003, Enterprise Edition, on a standalone server. The server meets the recommended hardware requirements and Windows Server 2003, Enterprise Edition, is installed. You have installed and enabled SMTP, NNTP, the World Wide Web service, and ASP.NET. The server is a standard primary DNS server. Will the installation succeed? If not, why not?

   _____

   _____

2. You migrate an Exchange Server 5.5 organization to Exchange Server 2003. You use the Active Directory Migration Tool to migrate the mailboxes. You find that the mailboxes have migrated with all the user permissions intact, but user passwords have not migrated. What is the probable reason?

   _____

   _____

3. Your Exchange Server 2003 organization connects to a UNIX e-mail system over an X.400 connector. You establish connectivity with the system, but e-mail messages are garbled. How do you solve the problem?

_____

_____

Lesson Summary

- Exchange Server 2003 will fail to install if your hardware resources are inadequate, if your member server does not have the appropriate operating system, or if Active Directory or DNS are not accessible.

- Other reasons for installation failure are that SMTP, NNTP, and the World Wide Web service are not installed and running and that POP3 is installed. When installing on a Windows Server 2003 member server, you also need to install and enable ASP.NET.

- Migration from Exchange systems requires that mailboxes be migrated. When migrating to Exchange Server 2003 you should use version 2 of the Active Directory Migration Tool, which will migrate mailboxes that are associated with user accounts and will also migrate passwords. You need to configure an SMTP virtual server to replace the Internet Mail connector used by Exchange Server 5.5 and configure DNS accordingly.

- When you need to coexist with foreign e-mail systems, it is important to check your encoding. Exchange Server 2003 defaults are not always suitable for this coexistence.

- You can use support tools such as netdiag and dcdiag to check network connectivity and DNS and Active Directory operation.

Lesson 2: Troubleshooting Exchange Server 2003 Servers

The performance of an Exchange Server 2003 server depends upon the efficiency of general server processes, such as memory and processor operation, in addition to the processes specific to Exchange. Troubleshooting server health involves interpreting the values of the appropriate counters recorded in a performance log and taking action as required. If you suspect that a fault is occurring that could result in an unusually high or low counter reading, you can set thresholds to trigger an alert. The alert could in turn initiate logging of other counters.

Loss of data is a very serious matter in an Exchange organization, and you need to be proactive in troubleshooting data storage to prevent a disaster. If a disaster does occur, you need to have confidence that your data recovery process is operating correctly. If your servers are clustered to provide failover or load sharing, then you need to have procedures in place to ensure that those clusters are operating correctly and to repair any failures before they affect your users.

After this lesson, you will be able to

- Interpret a Windows Server 2003 server performance log and take action, as appropriate
- Troubleshoot data storage and ensure that disk performance and failover protection are maintained
- Troubleshoot Exchange Server 2003 server clusters
- Troubleshoot backup and recovery operations

Estimated lesson time: 90 minutes

Troubleshooting Server Health

Chapter 13 described how you can configure a performance log and diagnostic logging in order to monitor counters and resources on an Exchange Server 2003 server. In this lesson, you learn the significance of the results obtained and the action that you can take when these results indicate a problem.

You can also set up alerts to indicate when resource usage or a performance counter exceeds a critical limit. There are many counters and instances of counters in an Exchange Server 2003 server. The following are among the most commonly used to diagnose problems with server health:

- **Memory\Pages/sec** This counter indicates the rate at which pages are read from or written to disk to resolve hard page faults. It is the sum of Memory\Pages Input/sec and Memory\Pages Output/sec, and indicates the type of faults that cause system-wide delays. It includes pages retrieved to satisfy faults in the file system cache (usually requested by applications) and non-cached mapped memory files. If the counter value increases over time, it could indicate that memory is becoming a bottleneck. It can also indicate "leaky" applications that use memory when running but do not release it when they stop. Typically, the counter value should not exceed five. A value of 20 or more indicates a problem.

- **Processor\% Processor Time**   This is the percentage of elapsed time that the processor spends to execute a non-idle thread. The counter is the primary indicator of processor activity and displays the average percentage of busy time observed during the sample interval. It is quite normal for this counter to reach 100 percent. However, a value in excess of 80 percent averaged over a period of time indicates that the processor may be overloaded. If you have a symmetrical microprocessor (SMP) computer, then each processor is monitored as an instance of this counter. If you discover high readings for one processor and low readings for another, then you should use Task Manager to discover what processes have a hard affinity to the first processor.

- **Process\% Processor Time**   This indicates the percentage of elapsed time for which all of the threads of a process used the processor to execute instructions. An instruction is the basic unit of execution in a computer, a thread is the object that executes instructions, and a process is the object created when a program is run. Because there are many processes created in an Exchange Server 2003 server (or any server), there are many instances of this counter (for example, store). Use the counter instances to keep track of key processes. There is no "correct" value for this counter. You need to establish a baseline for normal operation and compare your current readings against this. If the processor time used by a particular process increases over time, you need to judge whether there is a problem with the process or whether this is normal behavior that indicates that you may eventually need to upgrade the processor.

- **MSExchangeIS\RPC Requests**   The MSExchangeIS object represents the service that allows access to mailbox and public folder stores. Remote Procedure Call (RPC) Requests is the number of client requests that are currently being processed by the information store. The RPC protocol is used to transfer messages between computers and across connectors. You need to look at the value of this counter, together with the readings for MSExchangeIS\RPC Packets/sec (the rate that RPC packets are processed) and MSExchangeIS\RPC Operations/sec (the rate that RPC operations occur) to determine whether there is a bottleneck in the system.

- **PhysicalDisk\Disk Transfers/sec**   The value in this counter indicates the rate of read and write operations on a physical disk. A physical disk can contain several logical disks or volumes. Conversely, if disk arrays are used, a logical disk can contain several physical disks. You can add this counter to a performance log, but you will get a value of zero unless the disk counters are enabled using the diskperf command-line utility. Do not enable disk counters unless you have a problem that you need to solve, and do not enable them for any longer than you must. Enabling disk counters can seriously degrade server performance.

- **SMTP Server\Local Queue Length**   This indicates the number of messages in the local queue on an SMTP server. You can get the same information from Queue Viewer, but a performance log lets you view a report over time and track trends. You should look at this counter in conjunction with the SMTP Server\Messages Delivered/sec counter, which indicates the rate at which messages are delivered to local mailboxes. It is possible that there are a lot of messages in a queue, but the queue is being processed at a rate sufficient to ensure that the messages are delivered promptly. You can also set alerts on counters such as SMTP Server\Bad-mailed Messages (No Recipient) so that you are warned if an excessive amount of anonymous mail is delivered, possibly indicating spamming or a Denial of Service (DoS) attack.

- **MSExchangeIS Mailbox\Local Delivery Rate**   This is the rate at which messages are delivered locally. The MSExchangeIS Mailbox object counters specifically measure mailbox, as opposed to both mailbox and public folder, traffic. Other counters that you might need to monitor are MSExchangeIS Mailbox\Folder Opens/sec, which is the rate that requests to open folders are submitted to the Information Store, and MSExchangeIS Mailbox\Message, which is the rate that requests to open messages are submitted to the information store. You need to compare these counter values against performance baselines to determine whether a bottleneck exists and to track trends over time.

Troubleshooting Data Storage

Chapter 12 discussed the various redundant array of independent drives (RAID) configurations that can be used to store Exchange Server 2003 server databases and transaction logs. We saw in that chapter that recovery to the point of failure is possible only if circular logging is disabled (the default) and transaction logs are stored on separate disks or disk arrays from databases. We also saw that a well-designed backup strategy could prevent disks from being filled with an excessive number of transaction logs.

With the exception of RAID-0, the failure of a disk in an array is not always immediately obvious. It is possible to generate an alert if a counter such as Physical\Disk Transfers/sec drops to zero, but this would necessitate having the disk counters enabled (and may be a good reason for enabling these counters). You can also configure Monitoring And Status in Exchange System Manager to write an event to the application log in Event Viewer if free disk space in the array falls below a predefined limit, and you can configure Notifications in the Monitoring And Status tool to notify you by e-mail or by some other method specified in a script file when the event occurs. This will alert you if there are capacity problems, but will not indicate a disk failure in an array because the loss of a spindle in an array does not affect free disk space.

However, it is important that you deal with a disk failure immediately because your array is no longer fault-tolerant. If you are using RAID-5, then the loss of a spindle will result in noticeable performance degradation; basically everything slows down. In RAID-1 and RAID-0+1 arrays, however, the degradation in read performance may not be immediately noticeable, especially during quiet periods. Commercial hardware RAID systems can generate visual and audible warnings of disk failure, and you should take this functionality into account when choosing a system.

Mailbox and Public Store Policies

You can create mailbox and public store policies for any administrative group by expanding the administrative group in Exchange System Manager, right-clicking System Policies, and then specifying either a new mailbox or a new public store policy. Chapter 7, "Managing Recipient Objects and Address Lists," and Chapter 8, "Public Folders," discuss policies in detail. From a troubleshooting viewpoint, limiting the size of public and mailbox stores, specifying a retention policy for deleted items, and not permanently deleting mailboxes until the store has been backed up are the most useful components of these policies. In Chapter 13, you learned how to monitor mailbox sizes and start the mailbox management process.

These procedures help to troubleshoot storage, because problems can occur when databases grow too large. Enforcing mailbox limits can prevent such problems. Proactive troubleshooting—that is, preventing problems from occurring—is the hallmark of the efficient administrator.

> ### Real World   But There's Hardly Anything in My Mailbox!
> Not all users will see mailbox limits as good proactive troubleshooting. They will assure you that they regularly read and delete items and download extensions to their local disk. You need to explain that unless an e-mail message with a large extension is deleted, it will remain in the mailbox, and that deleted items are kept in mailboxes until they are backed up. Carefully note details of any issues that a user has with your policies. The information can be very useful when the same user asks you to retrieve a message that he or she deleted six months ago.

Troubleshooting Clusters

When a cluster node goes down and failover occurs, it is not always immediately obvious that you have a problem. You need to use Cluster Administrator on a daily basis to check the health of your clusters.

One of the main problems when using clusters is virtual memory fragmentation. You need to monitor the following virtual memory counters for each node in the cluster to determine when an Exchange virtual server must be restarted due to this fragmentation:

- **MSExchangeIS\V Largest Block Size**   When this counter drops below 32 MB, Exchange Server 2003 logs a warning in the Event Viewer application log (Event ID=9582). It logs an error if the counter drops below 16 MB.

- **MSExchangeIS\VM Total 16MB Free Blocks**   You should monitor the trend on this counter to predict when the number of 16-MB blocks is likely to drop below three. When this number drops below three, you should restart all the services on the node.

- **MSExchangeIS\VM Total Free Blocks**   This counter enables you to calculate the degree of fragmentation of available virtual memory. The smaller the average block size, the greater the fragmentation. You also need the value returned by the store instance of the Process\Virtual bytes counter. The average block size is the Process (store)\Virtual Bytes value divided by the MSExchangeIS\VM Total Free Blocks value.

- **MSExchangeIS\VM Total Large Free Block Bytes**   If the value in this counter drops below 32 MB on any node in the cluster, failover the Exchange virtual servers, restart all the Exchange services on the node (or restart the server), and then failback the Exchange virtual servers.

Troubleshooting Backup and Restore

As you learned in Chapter 12, an online backup uses a checksum to check files for corruption and writes events to the application log of Event Viewer if any inconsistencies are found. In addition, a backup log is generated. Thus if an online backup runs with no errors recorded, you can have a good degree of confidence that the data has been backed up correctly.

Sometimes an offline backup is necessary, either when an online backup fails or when third-party software is used that does not support online backups. In this case, you can use the eseutil command-line utility with the /k switch to verify the backup copy.

No matter how confident you may be about your online backup, it is wise to perform a practice restore. You can perform a practice restore on a recovery server, which is also used to recover deleted mailboxes after their retention periods have expired. A recovery server needs to be in a separate forest. You can also restore on the same server, or on a server in the same organizational group, by using a recovery storage group.

Recovery Storage Groups

A recovery storage group is a specialized storage group that can exist alongside the regular storage groups in an Exchange Server 2003 server (even if the server already has four normal storage groups). You can restore mailbox stores from any normal Exchange Server 2003 storage group to the recovery group. You can then, if appropriate, use the exmerge command-line utility to move the recovered mailbox data from the recovery storage group to the regular storage group.

Recovery storage groups allow you to restore without overwriting the data in the stores you backed up. This is important when you suspect there may be a problem with backups and you do not want to risk overwriting your current data with corrupted backup data. In addition, you can recover an entire mailbox store (all of the database information, including the log data) or just a single mailbox.

If you have confidence in your backup and restore processes, then backup becomes a troubleshooting tool rather than a troubleshooting problem. You can restore the last full backup and, when appropriate, the last differential backup or series of incremental backups. You can then replay any transaction logs that are stored on a separate disk to restore the data on up to the point of failure.

Practice: Configuring an Alert

In this practice, you configure an alert that triggers if 20 or more messages are waiting to be sent out from the Server01 mailbox. In your test network, this number is an arbitrary choice. On a production network, you would use a performance log and monitor Queue Viewer to create baselines for normal and busy periods. The number of queued messages that you choose to trigger the alert should be higher than the highest anticipated number during busy periods, and therefore indicate a fault in the messaging environment.

Exercise 1: Configure a Queue Alert

To configure a queue alert, perform the following steps:

1. On Server01, open the Performance console.
2. Expand Performance Logs And Alerts, right-click Alerts, and then click New Alert Settings.
3. In New Alert Settings, in the Name box, type **Send Queue Alert** and then click OK.
4. On the General tab of the Send Queue Alert dialog box, type **Alert if 20 messages**, and then click Add.
5. In the Add Counters dialog box, in the Performance Counters drop-down menu, select MSExchangeIS Mailbox. In the Select Counters From List box, select Send Queue Size (normally selected by default), and in the Select Instances From List box, select First Storage Group–Mailbox Store (SERVER01), as shown in Figure 14-6.

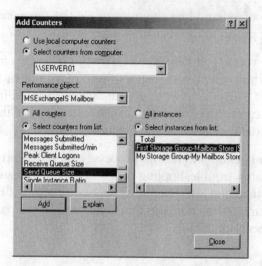

Figure 14-6   Selecting a performance object, counter, and instance

Note   You have a choice of instance because you created the My Storage Group–My Mailbox Store in Chapter 12. If you did not do this and there is no choice of instance, then the First Storage Group–Mailbox Store (SERVER01) will be monitored by default.

 6. Click Add to add the counter, and then click Close.

 7. In the Alert When Value Is box, select Over.

 8. In the Limit box, type **20**.

Exam Tip   The Alert When Value Is box can be set only to Over or Under. Therefore, Over means "greater than or equal to," and Under means "less than or equal to." So if you want the alert to trigger at 20 messages, you set "Over 20." If you did not know this, you might assume that "Over 19" would trigger on 20. Examiners sometimes test areas where the intuitive answer is not the correct one.

 9. Ensure that the sample interval is at the default value of 5 seconds. Figure 14-7 shows the alert settings.

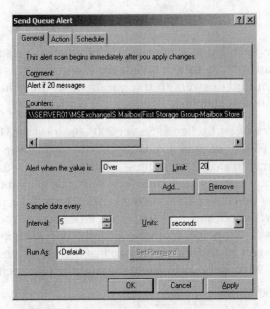

Figure 14-7   Settings for the send queue alert

10. On the Action tab, select Send A Network Message To and type **Administrator** in the associated box.

> **Note**   This sends a network message to any PC (assuming it has a Windows NT, Windows 2000, Windows Server 2003, or Windows XP operating system and the messenger service is enabled) where you are logged on using the Administrator account. You might want to consider sending messages to the ordinary user account that you created for yourself according to the Principle of Least Privilege. In a production network, you should log on using the Administrator account as seldom as possible. Also note that by default an event is logged in the applications log in Event Viewer, that you can start a performance log if an alert is triggered, and that you can run an executable file. This file could send you an e-mail message or, if you have the appropriate technology installed, could trigger a personal bleeper.

11. Click OK.

12. In the Performance console, click Alerts. In the details pane, right-click the alert and confirm that it has started (Start is unavailable).

> **Warning**   You can also determine that an alert is running because it is green, but this method is not infallible. A newly created alert may be started but appear as red until the first time you click it. Also, those who are prone to color blindness easily confuse red and green.

Lesson Review

The following questions are intended to reinforce key information presented in this lesson. If you are unable to answer a question, review the lesson materials and then try the question again. You can find answers to the questions in the "Questions and Answers" section at the end of this chapter.

1. You are the administrator of an Exchange Server 2003 organization. During busy times the performance of one of your Exchange Server 2003 servers slows. The server uses a RAID-1 array to store system files, a RAID-5 array to store database files, and a RAID-0+1 array to store transaction logs. Currently all of the disk arrays are used at less than 60 percent of total capacity. You check your performance counters during a busy period and find that your Processor\%Processor Time counter is consistently at 70 percent or above and your Memory\Pages/sec counter is typically between 30 and 40. You notice that there is an unusually high amount of disk activity. What is the most likely cause of the poor performance?

    a. A disk in one of your arrays is faulty.

    b. One of your disk controllers is faulty.

    c. The server needs additional memory.

    d. You need to upgrade your processor.

2. You set alerts on all the nodes on a cluster group to warn you if the value that the MSExchangeIS\VM Total 16m Free Blocks counter returns is three or less. What action should you take on any node on which the alert is triggered?

    _____

    _____

3. You want to test your backup and restore procedures by restoring a mailbox store. You do not want to dismount the store while you are performing the restore, and you do not want to overwrite the data in the store with backed up data that might be faulty. You do not have a recovery server. How can you test the restore?

    _____

    _____

Lesson Summary

- Performance logs can be used for troubleshooting server health. An alert can be set to indicate a problem associated with a particular resource.

- Faults in data storage are sometimes not immediately obvious but can affect the failover protection that RAID systems provide. Disk storage systems need to be monitored frequently. Limiting the size of mailboxes and public stores can lessen storage problems.

- Problems can occur in clusters where a node failure may not be immediately obvious. Memory fragmentation is a problem in clusters, and several counters are available to help monitor the problem.

- Recovery storage groups can be used to test backup and restore.

Lesson 3: Troubleshooting the Exchange Server 2003 Organization

While some faults are restricted to specific Exchange Server 2003 servers, others affect the entire Exchange Server 2003 organization. Problems with public folders can affect everyone in your organization, as can problems with virtual servers. If you use a back-end/front-end configuration, it is easy to misconfigure certain parameters, and you also need to ensure that your front-end and back-end servers can communicate through your firewall. Connectivity problems can prevent your Exchange Server 2003 servers from accessing Active Directory and DNS, which will in turn affect your whole organization.

After this lesson, you will be able to

- Describe the problems that can occur with public folders, and restrict the ability to create top-level public folders to selected users or groups
- Explain how diagnostic and protocol logging can help troubleshoot problems on virtual servers
- Describe the problems associated with a front-end/back-end server configuration
- List the tools that you can use to troubleshoot connectivity problems within your Exchange Server 2003 organization

Estimated lesson time: 45 minutes

Troubleshooting Public Folders

Public folders can contain internal company information and can also be used for collaboration projects with partner organizations and to give information about your company to external users. Problems in public folders therefore impinge upon the image that your organization presents to its own employees, to its partner organizations, and to the world at large. Any problems that affect public folders need to be resolved urgently.

Some of the problems that can occur with public folders concern the limits imposed by any public store policies that you decide to create. There are sound reasons for limiting the size of public folders and the size of individual items within any folder. However, you need to be proactive in deleting any items that are no longer required. Users who can post items to a public folder will report warnings and write prohibitions as errors. Also, it reflects badly on your organization if some of the content of a public folder is irrelevant or out of date. You can delegate the task of ensuring that obsolete items are deleted. Indeed, you should do so. As an administrator, you are not in a position to judge whether items posted by, for example, the human resources department can be deleted. However, you do need to keep a close eye on folder size.

If you have a dedicated public folder server, the task of restoring public folders can lead to failure reports because you need to dismount a public folder to restore it. Sometimes this is inevitable, for example, if the data in a public folder is corrupt. Trial restores of public folders, however, should be done on a recovery server in this instance.

Another possible source of error is when you have a public folder that should be accessible through e-mail. Public folders are not mail-enabled by default, and you need to enable this function. The procedure to do this is described in the troubleshooting lab in Chapter 8.

However, the main source of errors in public folders is incorrectly configured permissions. If, for example, you allow too many users to create top-level folders, then your folder tree will become large, unorganized, and difficult to browse or manage. You can control permissions to create top-level folders by right-clicking your Exchange organization in Exchange System Manager and granting the permission only to selected individuals or groups. Figure 14-8 shows the Create Top Level Public Folder permission being granted to Don Hall.

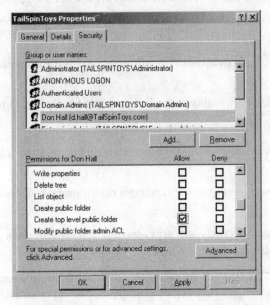

Figure 14-8   Granting the Create Top Level Public Folder permission

Another common permission problem occurs when users who should only be permitted to read items in a public folder are also granted write or delete permission. In general, users should have only read permission to public folder items, with write and delete permissions being granted very sparingly. Remember also that permissions granted on a high-level public folder will, by default, propagate to lower-level folders. If permissions are changed at the wrong level, errors can result.

Troubleshooting Virtual Servers

Chapter 9 and Chapter 13 discussed many of the techniques that are used for managing virtual servers and monitoring their performance. Protocol logs provide a powerful method of recording every detail of every event that occurs in each individual virtual server. If, for example, a message is rejected because it is oversized, this can be deduced from the SIZE *xxxxxxx* entry in the SMTP virtual server's protocol log. Diagnostic logging is configured using Exchange System Manager, except for Hypertext Transport Protocol (HTTP) virtual servers, for which you use IIS Manager and configure diagnostic logging for the Web site associated with the virtual server.

Diagnostic Logging

Diagnostic logging can assist in troubleshooting both virtual servers and the general health of an Exchange Server 2003 server and of the Exchange Server 2003 organization. You can configure the level of diagnostic logging on the following services:

- **IMAP4SVC** This service allows users to access mailboxes and public folders through IMAP4. Detailed logging can help locate faults on IMAP4 virtual servers.

- **MSADC** This service runs connection agreements if the Active Directory Connector is installed.

- **MSExchangeAL** This service allows users to address e-mail through address lists.

- **MSExchangeDSAccess** This service allows Exchange access to Active Directory.

- **MSExchangeIS** This service allows access to the Information Store.

- **MSExchangeMTA** This service allows X.400 connectors to access the message transfer agent (MTA).

- **MSExchangeMU** This service replicates Exchange configuration information changes to the IIS metabase.

- **MSExchangeSA** This counter records an entry when Exchange uses Active Directory to store and share directory information.

- **MSExchangeSRS** This counter records an entry whenever Site Replication Services are used to replicate computers running Exchange 2000 Server or later with computers running Exchange Server 5.5.

- **MSExchangeTransport** This counter records an entry whenever SMTP is used to route messages. Configuring the diagnostic logging level can assist in troubleshooting SMTP virtual servers.

- **POP3SVC** This counter records an entry whenever POP3 is used to access e-mail. Configuring the diagnostic logging level can assist in troubleshooting POP3 virtual servers.

Encoding and Relaying

Errors can occur in IMAP4 and POP3 virtual servers if incorrect encoding methods are specified. Often you can solve the problem by creating an additional virtual server and allowing access to a group of clients with particular encoding requirements. If only a few clients have requirements that differ from those of the majority, then you can configure client settings on a per-client basis. This is discussed in Chapter 9.

Open relaying can cause problems with SMTP virtual servers. Relaying is disabled by default, but IMAP4 and POP3 clients need to use the facility so that they can use SMTP to send e-mail. Relaying can be enabled for specific clients, but it is usually better practice to create an additional SMTP virtual server that permits relaying and allows access only to POP3 and IMAP4 clients. This is also discussed in Chapter 9.

Troubleshooting Front-End and Back-End Servers

There are several advantages to a front-end and back-end configuration. Front-end servers do not host mailboxes and can be located outside the main firewall. Back-end servers can use the Microsoft Cluster Service for failover protection while front-end servers can use Network Load Balancing to enhance performance. The use of front-end servers means that mailboxes on your domain can be accessed using a single Uniform Resource Locator (URL), no matter what back-end server you put them on. You can move mailboxes from one back-end server to another, and such a move is invisible to the end user.

However, the advantages that the configuration offers bring their own troubleshooting issues. Front-end servers need to be able to communicate with back-end servers through your firewall without compromising either security or usability. Load balancing clusters are not applicable to back-end servers, nor are Windows clusters to front-end servers, and incorrectly configured clustering can lead to problems. A failure of a mailbox store or a virtual server on a back-end server can look like a fault on a front-end server, and it is important to track messages and find out where the fault occurred.

You need to create a virtual HTTP server on each back-end server to handle front-end requests. A failure on any one of these servers can result in Outlook Web Access (OWA) clients being unable to send mail to or receive mail from your domain.

For all of these reasons, the techniques for troubleshooting communication across a firewall, the use of Cluster Administrator, and the use of virtual server troubleshooting techniques such as protocol logging become even more important when you have a back-end/front-end configuration. The following problems are also common in this configuration:

- **Authentication is misconfigured** The implementation of authentication settings varies between server roles. On front-end servers, IMAP4 and POP3 virtual servers use basic authentication, and this cannot be changed. On POP3 and IMAP4 virtual servers on back-end servers, you can select basic authentication or Integrated Windows Authentication. Integrated Windows Authentication cannot be specified on front-end HTTP virtual servers. Because authentication methods vary with the server type (for good reasons), it is sometimes difficult to work out the settings that meet your required objectives and easy to misconfigure authentication.

- **Users are disconnected when downloading messages**   On back-end servers, the connection timeout setting limits the length of time for which a client is permitted to remain connected to the server without performing any activity. On front-end servers, the connection timeout setting limits the total length of the client's session, regardless of client activity. A common configuration error is to set back-end connection timeout values on front-end servers. You need to configure this setting on your front-end servers so that your users can download the maximum message size permitted over the slowest supported connection speed without being disconnected.

- **Calendaring settings on front-end POP3 and IMAP4 virtual servers are ignored**   Exchange Server 2003 does not recognize any URL settings configured on the Calendaring tab of IMAP4 and POP3 virtual servers on your front-end servers unless you configure the corresponding virtual servers on your back-end servers to use front-end settings.

Troubleshooting Connectivity

Because connectivity problems can prevent Exchange Server 2003 from installing, the netdiag utility was discussed in Lesson 1 of this chapter. In addition to netdiag, you can use ping to test connectivity with domain controllers, DNS servers, Exchange Server 2003 servers, IIS servers, and other significant hosts on your network. If you can ping by Internet Protocol (IP) address but not by hostname, then this indicates name resolution problems and possibly a problem with DNS.

You can use telnet to check whether a TCP port (for example port 25 for SMTP) can be opened to a receiving host and whether the receiving host is responding. Telnet is useful for testing connectivity over a firewall that blocks the Internet Control and Messaging Protocol (ICMP) on which ping depends.

You can use the nslookup command to query DNS to confirm that DNS is working properly and that MX and A (host) records exist for a particular Exchange Server 2003 server or for all such servers in a domain. You can, for example, use the **nslookup –querytype=mx tailspintoys.com** command to return all the MX records for the *tailspintoys.com* domain.

Practice: Limiting Write and Delete Permissions to Public Folders

In your organization, only the senior managers group, which contains users Sean Alexander, Don Hall, and Kim Akers, is permitted to place information in public folders. Only Don Hall is permitted to delete files in public folders. Domain administrators have full control over public folders for administrative purposes. All other users have only read permission. This practice sets up these permissions.

Exercise 1: Create the Senior Managers Security Group

This exercise assumes that mail-enabled accounts exist for Kim Akers, Don Hall, and Sean Alexander. These accounts were created in Chapter 9. If the accounts do not exist, use the Active Directory Users And Computers console to create them before you start this exercise.

To create the Senior Managers security group, perform the following actions:

1. On Server01, open the Active Directory Users And Computers console.
2. Expand TailSpinToys.com, right-click Users, click New, and then click Group.
3. On the New Object–Group page, in the Group Name box, type **Senior Managers**.
4. Ensure that the Group Scope is Global and the Group Type is Security, as shown in Figure 14-9. Click Next.

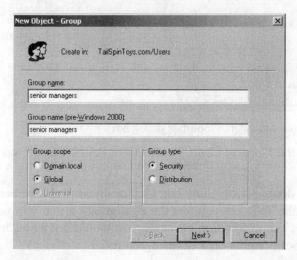

Figure 14-9   Specifying the Senior Managers global security group

5. You have the option at this stage of mail-enabling the group. However, the use of mail-enabled global security groups is not recommended and is not appropriate in this exercise. Click Next.
6. Click Finish.

7. In the details pane of Active Directory Users And Computers, right-click Senior Managers, and click Properties.

8. On the Members tab, click Add.

9. In the Enter The Object Names To Select box, type **Don Hall**.

10. Click Check Names, and then click OK.

11. Repeat the procedure described in steps 8, 9, and 10 to add Kim Akers and Sean Alexander to the security group.

12. The Senior Managers Properties dialog box should contain the entries shown in Figure 14-10. Click OK to close the dialog box.

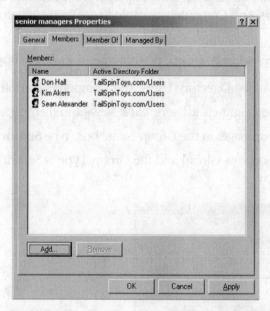

Figure 14-10   The Senior Managers Properties dialog box

13. On Server01, open the Domain Controller Security Policy console and click User Rights Assignment.

14. In the details pane, double-click Allow Log On Locally and add the Senior Managers group to that right. This lets you test the configuration that you will carry out in the next exercise. In a production network, you would not typically grant ordinary users log on locally rights on a domain controller.

Exercise 2: Configure Permissions on a Public Folder Store

In this exercise, you configure permissions such that the Senior Managers group can add files to the public folder store and amend files, but only Don Hall can delete files that were created by other users.

To configure permissions on a public folder store, perform the following actions:

1. Start Exchange System Manager.

2. Navigate to Administrative Groups\First Administrative Group\Servers\Server01 \First Storage Group\Public Folder Store (Server01).

3. Right-click Public Folder Store (Server01), and then click Properties.

4. On the Security tab, click Add.

5. In the Enter The Object Names To Select box, type **users** and then click OK.

6. In the Group Or User Names box, click Users. In the Permissions For Users box, clear all the Allow check boxes except Read, Execute, Read Permissions, List Contents, and Read Properties.

7. Click Add. In the Enter The Object Names To Select box, type **Senior Managers** and then click OK.

8. In the Group Or User Names box, click Senior Managers. In the Permissions For Users box, clear all the Allow check boxes except Read, Write, Execute, Read Permissions, List Contents, and Read Properties. Figure 14-11 shows permissions being specified for the Senior Managers group.

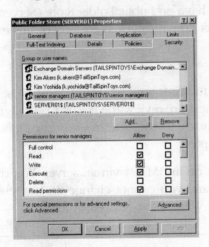

Figure 14-11   Specifying permissions for the Senior Managers group

9. Click Add. In the Enter The Object Names To Select box, type **Don Hall** and then click OK.

10. In the Group Or User Names box, click Don Hall. In the Permissions For Users box, clear all the Allow check boxes except Read, Write, Execute, Delete, Read Permissions, List Contents, and Read Properties.

> **Note** Write permission enables users to create files, change the content of files, and delete files that they created. Delete permission allows users to delete files that were created by other users.

11. Click OK to close the dialog box.

12. Open Outlook and create a new public folder called My Public Folder. Post a message to that public folder.

13. Log off, and then log on as Kim Akers. If you set up the accounts as specified in Chapter 9, then the username is k.akers and the password is password&2.

14. Open Outlook and investigate what you can and cannot do in My Public Folder. You should, for example, be able to post items to the folder.

15. Log off, and then log on as Don Hall. If you set up the accounts as specified in Chapter 9, then the username is d.hall and the password is password&2.

16. Open Outlook and investigate what you can and cannot do in My Public Folder. Discover whether Don Hall has any more rights than Kim Akers.

17. Experiment with changing the permissions that the Senior Managers group and Don Hall's individual user account have on Public Folder Store (Server01). Ensure, however, that you are logged on as Administrator at the end of this exercise.

Lesson Review

The following questions are intended to reinforce key information presented in this lesson. If you are unable to answer a question, review the lesson materials and then try the question again. You can find answers to the questions in the "Questions and Answers" section at the end of this chapter.

1. You are configuring authentication on an IMAP4 virtual server. You discover that the check boxes appear dimmed, and you cannot change the authentication setting, which is basic authentication. What is the reason for this?

_____

_____

2. Files in a public folder are being added and deleted without official sanction. How can you prevent this happening?

_____

_____

3. You want to increase the amount of information that is written to the application log in Event Viewer. What should you configure?

    a. Protocol logging

    b. Diagnostic logging

    c. Performance logging

    d. Event filtering

Lesson Summary

- You need to restrict write and delete permissions on public folders and the ability to create top-level public folders to carefully selected users or groups. Many of the problems related to public folders are caused by incorrect permission settings.

- Protocol logging provides a detailed record of every event on a protocol virtual server. You can also increase the range of events that are written to event viewer by configuring diagnostic logging.

- Authentication settings available on protocol virtual servers on a front-end server can be different from those on the same type of protocol servers on a back-end server. You also need to take care when configuring time-out and calendaring settings.

- The netdiag and dcdiag utilities run a series of tests that check connectivity, Active Directory access, DNS access, and the general health and interoperability of your Exchange Server 2003 organization.

Lesson 4: Troubleshooting Security

Security troubleshooting can be a complex and difficult process. Traffic can be filtered at a firewall, at a router, or at a virtual server. If a particular type of traffic or traffic from a particular source is getting through when it should not or is not getting through when it should, then it can be difficult to locate the problem. Troubleshooting permissions can also be problematic. Permission inheritance is a very useful function, but sometimes it is not easy to discover the level at which a permission is defined. The use of security certificates is typically invisible to the ordinary user, but you need to know what to do if a certificate is compromised or corrupted.

After this lesson, you will be able to

■ List the protocols and services that you may want to pass through your firewall and their associated ports

■ Describe the functions of firewall and virus logs

■ Troubleshoot permissions and permission inheritance

■ Describe the uses of public and private keys and troubleshoot encryption and digital signatures

Estimated lesson time: 60 minutes

Troubleshooting Connectivity Across Firewalls

You can secure network applications and services by restricting connections to their associated ports. TCP port filtering on a firewall enables you to control the type of network traffic that reaches your Exchange Server 2003 servers and network devices. Correctly configured firewalls are stable and sturdy devices, invisible to the legitimate user, but a barrier to the attacker. However, like everything else, firewalls may not do what you intended them to, and troubleshooting is required.

Real World   Good and Bad Firewall Problems

Your users will probably not agree with this, but there are good and bad firewall problems. Good problems are when the good guys cannot get past the firewall to do what they need to do. They may be unhappy, but you can solve their problems. Bad firewall problems are when the bad guys get past your firewall and do unpleasant things to your intranet. Accept the criticism you get for limiting the good guys. Concentrate on foiling the bad guys.

Back-end servers contain private stores and sensitive public stores and need strong protection. Front-end servers typically require weaker protection and more functionality.

Therefore, many organizations implement light (or no) firewall protection between front-end servers and the outside world and strong firewall protection to protect back-end servers and other sensitive parts of the intranet. The front-end servers are then said to be in a demilitarized zone (DMZ), also known as a perimeter network.

Troubleshooting firewall connections requires that you allow only essential connections. If you allow a TCP port to connect, ensure that only the hosts that need to make a connection are allowed through the firewall. If you have to err at all, err on the side of blocking access rather than enabling it. Table 14-1 is taken from Chapter 11, "Microsoft Exchange Server 2003 Security," and is important enough to reproduce in this chapter. These are the ports that Exchange Server 2003 server might need. Open as few of them as possible.

Table 14-1   Exchange Server 2003 Ports and Services

Port	Service
25	SMTP
80	HTTP
88	Kerberos
102	Message Transfer Agent (MTA)-X.400 connector over TCP/IP
110	POP3
119	NNTP
135	Client/server communication RPC Exchange administration
143	IMAP4
389	Lightweight Directory Application Protocol (LDAP)
443	HTTP using Secure Sockets Layer (SSL)
563	NNTP using SSL
636	LDAP using SSL
993	IMAP4 using SSL
995	POP3 using SSL
3268 and 3269	Global catalog lookups

In addition to opening and closing ports, firewalls also filter traffic by blocking or allowing specific addresses, ranges of addresses, and domains. Selected protocols can also be blocked. It is, for example, common practice to block ICMP packets. Incoming traffic often has different filtering conditions to outgoing traffic. Also, filtering can be set up on connectors and virtual servers, and on routers. Blocking and filtering can therefore be complex, and it can be difficult to determine where it has been incorrectly configured. The key to troubleshooting in this area (as in most others) is good documentation that records all the configuration changes that you make.

Network Address Translation

Network Address Translation (NAT) is often implemented by the firewall, although Routing and Remote Access servers can also provide this service. The computers in your DMZ, including front-end Exchange Server 2003 servers, need public Internet IP addresses to communicate externally. They also need private IP addresses to communicate with your intranet. Because the public IP addresses of these computers should not change, your NAT service needs to permanently associate a public address with each private address allocated to them. This allocation is known as a *special port*. If external users report disruption in accessing your Exchange Server 2003 organization, then check that NAT has been set up correctly. The IIS server that hosts your organization's public Web page also requires a special port. If external users also report problems accessing this Web site, then incorrect NAT configuration is probably the problem.

Virus Protection

Virus protection can be implemented on your firewall, on your servers, and on your clients. You should check virus logs on a daily basis. Microsoft does not offer any antivirus products, so the format and content of your virus logs will depend upon the third-party antivirus product that you choose. Virus protection is discussed in depth in Chapter 11.

Firewall Logs

Firewall devices, and software firewall programs, produce logs. These are invaluable in troubleshooting inappropriate firewall operation and also for detecting attempts to attack your system. The logs give you details of attempts to communicate through blocked ports and various Transmission Control Protocol/User Datagram Protocol (TCP/UDP) probes that the firewall has intercepted. Attempts on the same set of ports from a number of sources on the Internet probably indicate that your organization is being subjected to a decoy scan. One of these attempts is an attack; the others are not. Firewall logs can also detect Trojan horse probes, such as GirlFriend (port 21544) or GateCrasher (port 6969). SubSeven (ports 1243, 6711, and 27374) is a particularly powerful probe widely used by hackers.

If details of such probes appear in your firewall log, then your firewall is doing its job and is blocking them. However, such entries indicate that your organization is under attack, and you need to find out more about the attackers. There is not sufficient space in this book to cover this topic fully, but an Internet search for "firewall logs" is highly recommended.

Real World   Honeypots

A *honeypot* is when you set up what appears to be a vulnerable Web presence and then analyze the methods used to attack it. This can give you information about the attackers and also diverts them away from your real organization. There is not sufficient space here for a full discussion of this topic, but an Internet search is recommended.

Troubleshooting Permissions

You can use the Exchange Administration Delegation Wizard in Exchange System Manager to control access to the Exchange objects contained within your Exchange organization or administrative group. These objects include public folder trees, address lists, message databases (MDBs), protocols, and connectors. Exchange Server 2003 uses Active Directory permissions such as read, write, and list contents, and Exchange extended permissions such as Create Public Folder and View Information Store Status. If you look at an object's permissions, Active Directory permissions are listed first, followed by Exchange extended permissions.

Permissions may be inherited from a parent object, or applied directly to an Exchange object. Because permissions give considerable flexibility, they can also introduce complexity. You need to troubleshoot permissions when you first set up your Exchange Server 2003 organization, and again if the organization changes significantly and new objects are added. You can make your permissions structure more robust by allowing permissions to groups rather than individual users and by using deny permissions as sparingly as possible.

An example of a permission problem is when two organizations are unable to send authenticated messages to each other over SMTP connectors. The problem is that the required Send As permission has not been granted on the SMTP virtual servers in both organizations for the account used for authentication. Without this additional permission, messages sent between the servers will be denied, because the server performs a check to see if the authentication account has permissions to send as the user who sent the mail.

You can view the permissions that a user or group has on any Exchange object by navigating to that object in Exchange System Manager and then accessing the Security tab in the object's Properties dialog box. If the Allow and Deny check boxes for a permission are shaded, the object has inherited permissions from its parent object. You can change inherited permissions, or you can click Advanced and block inheritance. If you choose to do the latter, then you have the option of either removing all the inherited permissions or copying them so that the object retains its permission settings, but they are no longer inherited. Figure 14-12 illustrates this option.

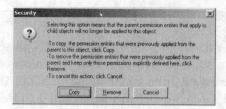

Figure 14-12   Copying or deleting inherited permissions

One of the most common errors when setting permissions is that the administrator decides that the inherited permissions are not appropriate, blocks inheritance, removes all the inherited permissions, sets a required permission, but neglects to restore those inherited permissions that are essential for correct operation. If you are changing permissions, and especially if you are delegating that task, then all changes must be carefully documented.

Troubleshooting Encryption and Digital Signatures

Exchange Server 2003 uses Transport Layer Security (TLS) to encrypt and digitally sign SMTP communications. Other Internet protocols use SSL. Both TLS and SSL require certificates that you obtain from a certification authority (CA). A certificate consists of a public key, which can be made available to anyone, and a private key known only to its owner.

If you use basic authentication, then a user's username and password will be transmitted in plain text unless the entire communication is encrypted. Encryption protects the contents of a message from being intercepted and read, and from being altered in transit. The sender encrypts the message using the recipient's public key and the recipient decrypts it using his or her private key. Only the recipient can decrypt the message.

A sender digitally signs a message using his or her private key. The recipient uses the sender's public key to validate the signature. Only the sender could have sent the message because only the sender has the private key.

Encryption and digital signatures can fail for the following reasons:

- **The certificate has been revoked**   Typically, certificates are revoked if an administrator believes they may have become compromised. If, for example, a third party has obtained a private key, the certificate is no longer secure.

- **A key has been corrupted**   A user's private key is stored in that user's profile and can become corrupt. In this case, an administrator needs to revoke the certificate and issue a new one.

- **The certificate is not accepted**   If you have Certificate Services installed in a server in your Active Directory domain, then you can issue certificates. Such certificates can be used within your organization but are unlikely to be trusted externally. To encrypt and digitally sign Internet mail, you need a third-party certificate from a trusted supplier such as VeriSign.

Practice: Checking That E-Mail is Encrypted

In this practice, you send an e-mail from Server01 to Server02 and capture the contents using Network Monitor. You then obtain a certificate and use this to encrypt outgoing mail. You then send another e-mail and check that the contents are encrypted. The practice assumes that Network Monitor has been installed and that this is not the first time it has been used. The instructions for installing Network Monitor are given in Chapter 13. If this is the first use of Network Monitor, you need to instruct it to monitor Local Area Network when prompted.

The practice also assumes that you have not already obtained a certificate and encrypted e-mails. If so, use the certificate wizard to remove the certificate before you start. Finally, the practice assumes that Certificate Services is installed on Server01.

Exercise 1: Capture an Unencrypted E-Mail Message

This exercise is similar to a section of the troubleshooting lab in Chapter 13. Nevertheless, it is only a short exercise and is required for the remainder of the practice.

To capture an unencrypted e-mail, perform the following steps:

1. On Server01, open Network Monitor.

2. On the Capture menu, click Start.

3. Open Outlook and send a message to *administrator@contoso.com*. In the message body, type **Now is the time for all good men to come to the aid of the party**.

4. On the Capture menu, click Stop And View.

5. In the details pane (the top pane), scroll through the captured frames until you locate the message, as shown in Figure 14-13.

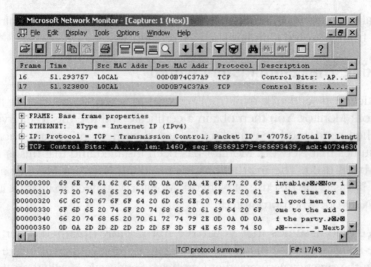

Figure 14-13   An intercepted, unencrypted e-mail message

6. Close Network Monitor. Do not save the capture.

Exercise 2: Obtain a Certificate and Configure Encryption

In this exercise, you obtain a certificate and configure encryption. You then test that e-mail traffic is encrypted.

To secure your e-mail traffic by using encryption, perform the following steps:

1. On Server01, start Exchange System Manager.

2. Navigate to Administrative Groups\First Administrative Group\Servers\Server01 \Protocols\SMTP\Default SMTP Virtual Server.

3. Right-click Default SMTP Virtual Server and click Properties.

4. On the Access tab, click Certificate.

5. The Web Server Certificate Wizard opens. Click Next.

6. Select Create A New Certificate, and then click Next.

7. Select Send The Request Immediately To An Online Certification Authority, and then click Next.

8. Click Next again to accept the defaults on the Security Name And Settings page.

9. Ensure that the Organization is Tailspintoys and the Organizational Unit is Administration. Click Next.

10. Ensure the Common Name is Server01. Click Next.

11. Ensure that the Geographical Information is correct. Click Next.

12. Select a certificate authority to process your request, as shown in Figure 14-14.

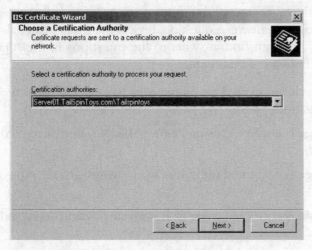

Figure 14-14   Selecting a certificate authority

13. Click Next. Click Next again to submit the request.

14. Click Finish to close the wizard.

15. The Communication button on the Access tab of the Default SMTP Virtual Server Properties dialog box no longer appears dimmed. Click that button.

16. Configure the security settings to use a secure channel, as shown in Figure 14-15.

Figure 14-15   Specifying security settings

17. Click OK. Click OK again to close the Properties dialog box.

18. Repeat the procedure in Exercise 1 to send an identical e-mail message to *administrator@contoso.com* and capture that message. This time, however, you should be unable to read the message body contents in Network Monitor.

Lesson Review

The following questions are intended to reinforce key information presented in this lesson. If you are unable to answer a question, review the lesson materials and then try the question again. You can find answers to the questions in the "Questions and Answers" section at the end of this chapter.

1. Kim Akers sends an encrypted e-mail message to Don Hall. Which of the following statements is true?

   a. The message is encrypted using Don's public key and decrypted using Don's private key.

   b. The message is encrypted using Kim's private key and decrypted using Kim's public key.

   c. The message is encrypted using Don's private key and decrypted using Don's public key.

   d. The message is encrypted using Kim's public key and decrypted using Kim's private key.

2. You suspect that someone is attacking your organization with Trojan horse probes. Where would you look to confirm this suspicion and to find out what ports are under attack?

   _____

   _____

Lesson Summary

■ A firewall can block all incoming or outgoing traffic (or both) through a port. It can also filter traffic depending upon the source.

■ Firewall and virus logs contain information about attacks that have been made on your organization. You should check them regularly.

■ Permissions and permissions inheritance can cause problems. You need to know what permissions are assigned at what level and what permissions are inherited from a higher level. Take care to document all permission changes.

■ Problems with encryption and digital signatures are often due to certificates being revoked or reaching their expiration dates. Internally issued certificates may not be accepted by other organizations.

Lesson 5: Troubleshooting Technologies That Support Exchange Server 2003

In this lesson, you learn about Windows Server 2003 technologies that operate in the background, supporting the Exchange Server 2003 organization. Although these technologies are not directly concerned with e-mail, public stores, or newsgroups, Exchange Server 2003 needs them in order to work. If Exchange Server 2003 servers cannot resolve the hostnames of clients and other servers to IP addresses, and in turn resolve these IP addresses to Media Access Control (MAC) addresses, then Exchange will not operate. If access to Active Directory fails, then Exchange will fail.

In Lesson 1, you learned how the netdiag and dcdiag utilities can be used to diagnose connectivity problems within an Exchange organization. You also need to know how to check connectivity to other networks, including the Internet. A number of command-line utilities exist for testing connectivity, and you need to become familiar with their use.

After this lesson, you will be able to

- Explain how the Address Resolution Protocol (ARP) works and use the arp command-line utility to manage the ARP cache
- Use the nslookup and ipconfig command-line utilities to diagnose and debug common DNS problems
- Troubleshoot Active Directory problems
- Use command-line utilities such as ping, tracert, ipconfig, and pathping to diagnose network connectivity problems

Estimated lesson time: 90 minutes

Troubleshooting Host Resolution

Hosts on a network identify each other using a MAC address, which is a unique 48-bit number programmed into to every network interface card (NIC). When a host needs to locate another host by hostname, the hostname is first resolved into an IP address (typically by DNS) and then ARP resolves the IP address into a MAC address.

How ARP Works

Typically, ARP operation is invisible to the user. If anything does go wrong, however, you need to examine the ARP cache or use Network Monitor to look at the content of ARP frames. To make sense of the information that these tools provide, you need to know how ARP works.

ARP resolves IP addresses used by TCP/IP-based software to MAC addresses used by network hardware, such as Ethernet. As each outgoing IP datagram is encapsulated in a frame, source and destination MAC addresses must be added. ARP determines the destination MAC address for each frame.

When ARP receives a request to resolve an IP address, it first checks to ascertain whether it has recently resolved that address or whether it has a permanent record of the MAC address that corresponds to the IP address requested. This information is held in the ARP cache. If it cannot resolve the IP address from cache, ARP broadcasts a request that contains the source IP and MAC addresses and the target IP address. When the ARP request is answered, the responding PC and the original ARP requester record each other's IP address and MAC address in their ARP caches.

Resolving a Local Address   ARP operation is best illustrated by considering examples of local and remote address resolution. In the first example, Host A, Host B, and Host C are on the same subnet. A ping command is issued on Host A, specifying the IP address of Host C. ICMP instructs ARP to resolve this IP address.

ARP checks the cache on Host A. If the IP address cannot be resolved from cached information, then an ARP request is broadcast to all the hosts on the subnet. The ARP broadcast supplies the source IP and MAC addresses and requests a MAC address that corresponds with the IP address specified. Because the ARP frame is a broadcast, all hosts on the subnet will process it. However, hosts that do not have the corresponding IP address (such as Host B) reject the broadcast frame. Host C recognizes the IP address as its own and stores the IP address/MAC address pair for Host A in its cache. This process is illustrated in Figure 14-16. The target address shown in this figure is the Ethernet address for a broadcast frame (FFFFFFFFFFFF). The MAC address of the target host is not known and is assigned the value 000000000000.

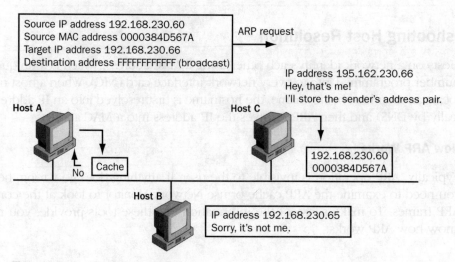

Figure 14-16   The ARP request

Host C sends an ARP reply message that contains its MAC address directly back to Host A. When Host A receives this message, it updates its ARP cache with Host C's address pair. Host A can now send the ICMP ping datagram (or any IP datagram) directly to Host C. This process is illustrated in Figure 14-17.

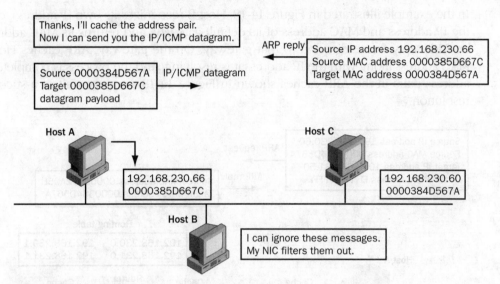

Figure 14-17   The ARP reply

Resolving a Remote Address   When the target address of an IP datagram is on a remote subnet, ARP will resolve the IP address to the MAC address of the NIC in the router gateway that is on the source host's local interface. In this example, Host A and Host B are on different subnets. A ping command issued on Host A specifies the IP address of Host B.

As in the previous example, ARP first checks its cache on the source host (Host A). If the destination IP address cannot be resolved from cache, an ARP request is broadcast. ARP does not know that the target host is remote because routing is an IP function, not an ARP function. The ARP request to resolve a remote IP address is therefore exactly the same as the ARP request to resolve a local address.

All the ordinary hosts on the local subnet reject the request because none of them has a matching IP address. The router, however, checks its routing table and determines that it can access the subnet for the remote host. It then caches the IP address/MAC address pair for Host A and sends back an ARP reply that specifies the MAC address of its gateway NIC. On Host A, ARP caches that MAC address with the IP address it is resolving. As far as ARP on Host A is concerned, it has done its job. Thus, Host A resolves a remote IP address to the MAC address of its default gateway.

At this stage, ARP on the router takes over the task of IP address resolution. First, it checks its cache for the target host's interface. If it cannot resolve the target host's IP from cache, it broadcasts an ARP request to the target host's subnet, supplying the IP address and MAC address of the gateway NIC that accesses the target host's interface.

In the example illustrated in Figure 14-18, Host B recognizes its own IP address, caches the IP address and MAC address of its default gateway, and returns its MAC address in an ARP reply frame directed to that gateway. On the gateway, ARP caches Host B's MAC address along with the IP address it is resolving, and the process is complete. The address pairs in the ARP caches shown in Figure 14-18 are the result of a successful resolution.

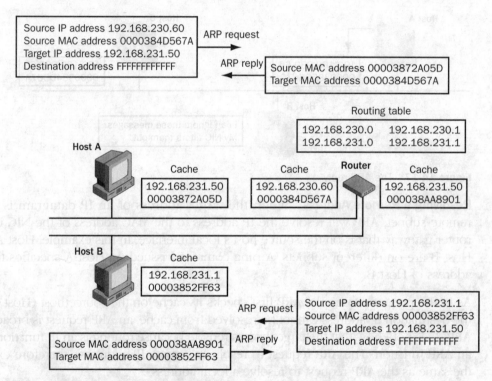

Figure 14-18   Resolving a remote IP address

Troubleshooting DNS

Several methods are available for resolving a hostname to an IP address. If the same hostname was resolved recently, the information will normally be available in the host's DNS cache. Cache resolution is quick and efficient and is always the first resolution method that is attempted. Static host files can resolve hostnames, but these require a lot of administrative effort because you need to put them on every computer. NetBIOS methods such as the Windows Internet Name System (WINS) are useful in mixed-mode domains. However, in Windows Server 2003 (and Windows 2000 Server), dynamic DNS (DDNS) is available and is the resolution method of choice. In the remainder of this section, when we consider hosts registering their DNS records dynamically, functionality assumes that DDNS is used.

DNS is discussed in several chapters of this book. In particular, Chapter 10, "SMTP Protocol Configuration and Management," describes the creation of MX records. DNS needs to be available for Active Directory and hence for Exchange Server 2003 server installation. Therefore you can assume that DNS was available and correctly configured on installation, and you need to identify what could cause DNS to fail during Exchange Server 2003 server operation.

Failure of a DNS Server

It is unusual for DNS to fail completely in an Active Directory domain. Typically, Active Directory–integrated DNS is available on more than one domain controller to provide failover support. If Active Directory DNS is not used, then a secondary DNS server is used to back up the primary DNS server. A primary DNS server that is not Active Directory–integrated is a single source of failure. If it goes down, you cannot add new entries to the DNS zone file. However, the secondary will continue to provide a name resolution service, usually for a length of time sufficient to bring the primary DNS server back on line.

However, the failure of a DNS server can cause problems if a host is not configured with the IP address of at least one alternative DNS server. If a host is configured with only one DNS server's IP address and that server goes down, then the host is unable to resolve hostnames, even though the DNS service is available on the other server. Typically, client machines are configured through the Dynamic Host Configuration Protocol (DHCP) and receive a list of all the available DNS servers. However, servers such as Exchange Server 2003 servers are usually configured manually. It is easy to forget to add alternative DNS servers, and everything will work perfectly unless the DNS server fails.

The dcdiag utility described in Lesson 1 of this chapter is mainly used to troubleshoot Active Directory problems, but it can also check DNS operation. The netdiag utility, described in the same lesson, also runs a DNS test. The nslookup utility described in Chapter 10 obtains DNS statistics and lists available DNS servers. You can test connectivity to a DNS server by pinging its IP address. However, possibly the simplest and most useful test is provided by the ipconfig /all utility, which lists the primary and alternative DNS servers available to any host. It is wise to use ipconfig /all to test all your Exchange Server 2003 servers and ensure that they are configured with a list of the IP addresses of all available DNS servers.

A Server Does Not Register in DDNS

When a new server comes online, it takes some time (sometimes as long as 15 minutes) for it to register dynamically in DDNS. If the services provided by that server are required immediately, then you can force registration by opening the Command console and entering the following commands in succession:

- ipconfig /registerdns
- net stop netlogon
- net start netlogon

You need to check Event Viewer for errors if registration fails to occur. However, unless there are other errors, you should see the server's A (host) record appear in DNS almost immediately.

Negative Caching

If DNS resolves a hostname to an IP address, the hostname/IP address pair is held in cache on the host that originated the request (the resolver). However, if resolution is unsuccessful, that information is also cached. This is to stop the waste of resources when a user types in a hostname incorrectly. Suppose, however, that the hostname is correct but because of some fault, the resolution does not take place. This negative information is cached. Suppose that the fault is then fixed. Now every client can resolve the hostname except for the client that tried to do so earlier. It attempts to resolve the hostname from cache, obtains the negative information, and returns an error. You can solve the problem by opening the Command console on that client and entering **ipconfig /flushdns**.

> **Real World   The No-Effort Solution**
>
> There is an alternative method of solving a negative caching problem that is useful if the client machine is too far away for you to get to easily, and if the user is not sufficiently skilled to access the command prompt and type in the necessary command. Tell the user to take a lunch or coffee break, and the problem will be solved when he or she gets back. Cache entries (including negative entries) time out, typically in an hour or less.

DHCP Problems

Sometimes a client machine cannot access any servers on a network or resolve any hostnames, when all the other clients are having no problems. In this case, check the configuration of the client using the ipconfig utility. There is a good chance that the client's IP address will be in the 169.254.x.x range. What has happened is that the DHCP service has stopped for some reason, or has run out of leases, and the host has been configured through automatic private IP addressing (APIPA). If you fix the DHCP problem, then the client will obtain a DHCP lease in approximately five minutes and the problem is solved. If you need an immediate solution, then open the Command console on the client and enter the following commands:

- ipconfig /release
- ipconfig /renew

 Note   It is sufficient to enter only **ipconfig /renew** when converting an APIPA address to a DHCP lease. However, it is good practice always to release an IP configuration before you renew it.

Troubleshooting Active Directory Issues

As with DNS, Active Directory must be available in order to install Exchange Server 2003 and create an Exchange Server 2003 organization. Active Directory is robust because the Active Directory database is replicated between domain controllers. Unless you have only one domain controller (not recommended), there is no single point of failure for the entire Active Directory.

However, Active Directory uses operations masters, and the failure of an operations master affects the functionality of the Active Directory directory service. Typically, the following problems are associated with operations masters:

- **You cannot create security principals**   Assuming that you have sufficient permissions to create a security principal, then typically this problem occurs when the Relative Identity (RID) master is not available or has failed to replicate. This may be caused by a network connectivity problem or may be due to the failure of the computer holding the RID master role. This fault can also occur when the Access This Computer From The Network user right is not assigned to the appropriate groups on the RID master.

- **You cannot change group membership**   Assuming that you have the necessary administrative credentials to manage group membership, this problem typically occurs when the infrastructure master is not available. This may be caused by a network connectivity problem. It may also be due to a failure of the computer holding the infrastructure master role.

- **Users cannot authenticate**   This can be a problem in mixed mode domains in which some clients are not Active Directory–aware. Typically, it happens when the user's password has expired and the primary domain controller (PDC) emulator master is not available. This may be caused by a network connectivity problem. It may also be due to a failure of the computer holding the PDC emulator master role.

In all of these cases, you can identify the computer holding the RID master role, the infrastructure master role, or the PDC emulator role by issuing the **netdom query fsmo** command from the Command console of any host in the domain, as shown in Figure 14-19. You can then repair or replace the computer holding the appropriate operations master role. You may need to seize the operations master role. Alternatively, you may need to resolve the network connectivity problem.

Figure 14-19   Identifying operations masters

The dcdiag utility, described in Lesson 1 of this chapter, is a powerful tool for checking the general health of Active Directory. As previously stated, Active Directory is robust. Provided that it was configured correctly when Exchange Server 2003 was installed, very few Active Directory problems are likely to occur.

Important   If you have any Windows 2000 domain controllers in your domain, ensure that SP3 or later is installed on them. Otherwise, Exchange Server 2003 cannot access them.

Troubleshooting Network Connectivity

Lesson 1 of this chapter discussed the netdiag utility and Chapter 10 discussed the telnet and nslookup utilities. In this lesson, we saw how the ipconfig utility is used to display a host's IP configuration, to register a host in DDNS, to clear the DNS cache, and to obtain a DHCP lease. In this section, we discuss various other command-line utilities that can be used to troubleshoot network connectivity.

Ping

The ping utility uses ICMP echo commands to test IP connectivity. Some firewalls and routers filter out ICMP packages, and you cannot ping across them. In spite of this limitation, ping remains one of the most useful and widely used troubleshooting tools. You can test that TCP/IP is correctly installed on a host by pinging the loopback address 127.0.0.1. You can ping all the interfaces on your local computer. You can ping another host on your subnet by both IP address and hostname to test connectivity and name resolution. You can ping all the servers that you need to connect to. Finally, you can ping a host on a distant subnet to test internetwork connectivity.

Ping lets you set a number of parameters to specify, for example, the size of the ping packets, how many packets to send, whether to record the route used, what time-to-live (TTL) value to use, and whether to set the "do not fragment" flag. If you open the Command console and enter **ping /?** you can obtain details about these options.

For example, **ping -n 6 -l 2000 -w 10000 10.0.10.100** pings the host with IP address 10.0.10.100 six times using a ping packet 2,000 bytes in size. By default, ping waits for up to 4,000 milliseconds for each response to be returned before it displays the "Request Timed Out" message. If you are pinging a remote system across a slow link, then you can use the –w (wait) option to specify a longer timeout. In the example given, the timeout is 10 seconds.

Arp

You can use the arp command-line utility to manage the ARP cache, which is a table that stores IP address/MAC address pairs. Whenever a source computer resolves a target IP address using an ARP request broadcast, the address pair for the target computer is stored in the source computer's cache. Similarly, when a target computer responds to an ARP request with an ARP reply, the address pair of the source computer is stored in the target computer's cache. Cache entries generated automatically by ARP resolution are called dynamic entries. They remain in the cache for a specified TTL (2 minutes by default) and, if not accessed during that time, are then discarded. If an entry is referenced again before it is removed, its TTL is increased by another two minutes. Thus, a frequently referenced entry can increase its TTL up to a maximum of 10 minutes.

Address pairs for frequently accessed targets, such as default gateways or member servers, can be entered manually. Manually entered address pairs are called static entries; they persist in cache until the host is rebooted or until they are manually deleted.

Tip   Static arp cache entries are deleted on reboot. If you want them to be persistent, create a startup script that re-enters them.

Nbtstat

Network basic input/output system (NetBIOS) over TCP/IP (NetBT) resolves NetBIOS names to IP addresses. TCP/IP provides many options for NetBIOS name resolution, including local cache lookup, WINS server query, broadcast, DNS server query, and lmhosts and hosts file lookup. In theory, DDNS is the main name resolution method in native mode Windows 2003 and Windows 2000 Active Directory domains, and NetBT can be disabled. In practice, many services and BackOffice products (for example, Systems Management Server) use NetBT. You need to investigate very carefully if you want to remove it.

You can use the nbtstat command-line utility to troubleshoot NetBIOS name resolution problems. The available options are as follows:

- **nbtstat -n**   Displays the names that were registered locally on the system by programs such as the server and redirector.

- **nbtstat -c**   Shows the NetBIOS name cache, which contains name-to-address mappings for other computers.

- **nbtstat -R**   Purges the name cache and reloads it from the lmhosts file.

- **nbtstat -RR**   Releases NetBIOS names registered with a WINS server and then renews their registration.

- **nbtstat -a name**   Performs a NetBIOS adapter status command against the computer specified by *name*. The adapter status command returns the local NetBIOS name table for that computer plus the MAC address of the adapter.

- **nbtstat -S**   Lists the current NetBIOS sessions and the status of each, including statistics.

> **Note**   The nbtstat utility was developed for UNIX and is case-sensitive.

Netstat

You can use the netstat command-line utility to display protocol statistics and current TCP/IP connections. The available options are as follows:

- **netstat -a**   Displays all connections.

- **netstat -r**   Displays the route table plus active connections.

- **netstat -o**   Displays process identities so that you can view the port owner for each connection.

- **netstat -e**   Displays Ethernet statistics.

- **netstat -s**   Displays per-protocol statistics.
- **netstat -n**   If you use this option, addresses and port numbers are not converted to names.

Tracert

You can use the tracert command-line utility to determine the path that an IP datagram takes to reach a destination. The utility uses the IP TTL field and ICMP error messages to determine the route from one host to another through a network. Because it uses ICMP, tracert will not work across firewalls and routers that block ICMP frames. You can try **tracert www.microsoft.com**. This may or may not work depending on the route the IP datagram takes to its destination. You can also use tracert to trace the path of a datagram through your intranet. The utility is useful for troubleshooting large networks where several paths can be taken to arrive at the same point. The tracert command has the following syntax:

tracert [–d] [–h *maximum_hops*] **[–j** *host-list*] **[–w** *timeout*] *target_name*

The options are described in Table 14-2.

Table 14-2   Tracert Command-Line Options

Option	Description
–d	Specifies that IP addresses are not resolved to host names.
–h *maximum_hops*	Specifies the number of hops to allow in tracing a route to the host named in *target_name*.
–j *host-list*	Specifies the list of router interfaces in the path taken by the tracert utility packets.
–w *timeout*	Waits the number of milliseconds specified by *timeout* for each reply.
target_name	Name or IP address of the target host.

Pathping

The pathping utility is a route tracing tool that combines the features of ping and tracert and gives additional information that neither of those tools provides. The utility sends packets to each router on the way to a final destination over a period of time and then computes results based on the packets returned from each hop. Because the command shows the degree of packet loss at any given router or link, you can determine which routers or links might be causing network problems. A number of options are available, as shown in Table 14-3.

Table 14-3 Pathping Options

Option	Name	Function
–n	Hostnames	Does not resolve addresses to host names.
–h	Maximum hops	Maximum number of hops to search for target.
–g	Host-list	Loose source route along the host list.
–p	Period	Number of milliseconds to wait between pings.
–q	Num_queries	Number of queries per hop.
–w	Time-out	Pathping waits this many milliseconds for each reply.
–i	address	Instructs pathping to use the specified source address.
–4	IPv4	Forces pathping to use IP version 4.
–6	IPv6	Forces pathping to use IP version 6.

The default number of hops is 30, and the default wait time before a timeout is three seconds. The default period is 250 milliseconds, and the default number of queries to each router along the path is 100.

When you run pathping, you first see the results for the route as it is tested for problems. This is the same path that the tracert command shows. The pathping command then displays a busy message typically for the next 125 seconds (this time varies depending upon the hop count). During this time, pathping gathers information from all the routers previously listed and from the links between them. At the end of this period, it displays the test results.

Practice: Managing the ARP Cache and Analyzing an ARP Packet

In this practice, you manage the ARP cache and use Network Monitor to capture and analyze an ARP packet. As did the previous practice, this practice assumes that Network Monitor has been installed and that this is not the first time it has been used. The instructions for installing Network Monitor are given in Chapter 13. If this is the first use of Network Monitor, you need to instruct it to monitor Local Area Network when prompted.

Exercise 1: Manage the ARP Cache

To manage the ARP cache on Server01, perform the following steps:

1. On Server01, open the Command console.

2. Enter **arp**. When entered with no arguments, the utility lists the command syntax (as does **arp /?**).

3. Enter **arp -a**. This displays the current ARP cache, as shown in Figure 14-20.

Figure 14-20   The ARP cache

4. Because Server01 is multihomed, you can use the interface addresses to display the ARP cache for each interface. Enter **arp -a -N** *ip_address*, where *ip_address* is the IP address of Local Area Connection on Server01, as shown in Figure 14-21.

Figure 14-21   Displaying the ARP cache for a specified interface

5. Enter **arp -d** without arguments to delete all cache entries.

> **Note**   The command **arp -d** *ip_address* will delete an individual cache entry.

6. Enter **ping server02**.

7. Enter **arp-a** to display the IP address/MAC address pair that the ping operation places in the arp cache, as shown in Figure 14-22.

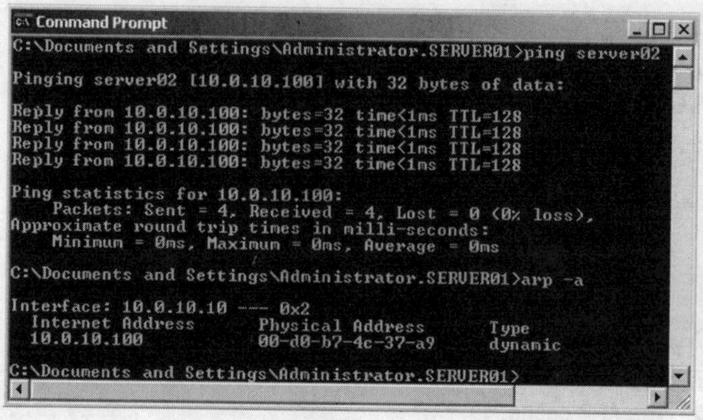

Figure 14-22   The ping command adds an entry to the ARP cache

8. Frequently accessed machines on your subnet, such as the default gateway, should be placed in the ARP cache as static entries. Enter **arp -s 10.0.10.1 00-d0-b7-4c-56-a8** to add a static entry. Both the IP address and the MAC address in this step are examples and their values are not significant.

9. Enter **arp-a** to view the ARP cache. Both the static and dynamic entries should be present.

10. Wait for approximately 10 minutes, and then enter **arp -a** to list the ARP cache entries. The dynamic entry is removed because its TTL has expired. The static entry will remain until Server01 is rebooted.

11. Static entries can, however, be removed using the **arp -d** command. Enter this command to clear the ARP cache.

Exercise 2: Use Network Monitor to Display the Contents of an ARP Broadcast Frame

Before you start this exercise, ensure that the ARP cache is clear. If it holds entries for Server02, then the broadcast frames that you want to analyze will not be sent.

To use Network Monitor to display the contents of an ARP broadcast frame, perform the following steps:

1. On Server01, open Network Monitor. On the Capture menu, click Start.

2. Do not close Network Monitor. On Server01, open the Command prompt and enter **ping server02**.

3. In Network Monitor, on the Capture menu, click Stop And View.

4. There should be two ARP-RARP frames at or near the top of the list in the Summary pane. (Note that Network Monitor calls ARP frames ARP-RARP, where *RARP* stands for Reverse ARP.) Click on the Request frame (the first one), expand the list in the detail pane, and read the source IP and MAC addresses, as shown in Figure 14-23.

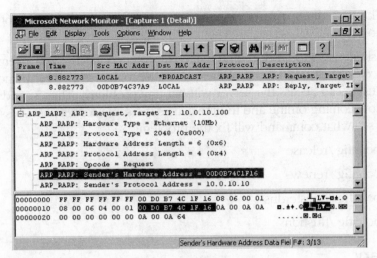

Figure 14-23   Analyzing the ARP-RARP Request frame

5. Analyze the Reply ARP-RARP frame in the same way.

Lesson Review

The following questions are intended to reinforce key information presented in this lesson. If you are unable to answer a question, review the lesson materials and then try the question again. You can find answers to the questions in the "Questions and Answers" section at the end of this chapter.

1. You suspect that a router somewhere in your intranet is causing transmission delays and may be dropping frames. Which tool would give you the most information about the problem?

    a. pathping

    b. ping

    c. tracert

    d. netstat

2. You successfully ping a host on a remote network. You examine the ARP cache on your computer and find that it contains one IP address/MAC address pair. What are these addresses?

    a. The IP address and MAC address of your default gateway

    b. The IP address and MAC address of the remote host

    c. The IP address of the remote host and the MAC address of your default gateway

    d. The IP address of your default gateway and the MAC address of the remote host

  3. You ask all users to work offline while you fix a connectivity problem. When the users come back online, one of them is unable to access a server by hostname. All other users can access the server without any problems. The user admits that he was slow coming offline and tried to access the same server unsuccessfully before doing so. What command will fix the problem?

    a. ipconfig /release

    b. ipconfig /renew

    c. ipconfig /registerdns

    d. ipconfig /flushdns

Lesson Summary

- ARP resolves IP addresses to MAC addresses. You can use the arp utility to display and manage the ARP cache.

- You can use the nslookup and ipconfig command-line utilities to diagnose and debug common DNS problems. Also, you can use ipconfig to diagnose incorrect TCP/IP configuration.

- The dcdiag utility can be used to diagnose Active Directory problems. Sometimes you may need to transfer or seize an operations master role.

- You can use command-line utilities such as ping, tracert, ipconfig, and pathping to diagnose network connectivity problems. Nbtstat and netstat return NetBIOS and TCP/IP statistics, respectively.

Case Scenario Exercise

You administer the Exchange Server 2003 organization at Coho Vineyard, and your duties include maintaining and troubleshooting four Exchange Server 2003 servers. Two of these are front-end servers configured to use Network Load Balancing, and two are back-end servers. A hardware firewall is installed and the front-end servers are in the DMZ. Three Windows Server 2003 servers are configured as domain controllers. One of these servers is scheduled for replacement. All the servers at Coho use Windows Server 2003, Enterprise Edition, but client operating systems include Microsoft Windows NT 4 Workstation, Windows 2000 Professional, and Windows XP Professional.

- **Requirement 1** The size of Coho's network does not, in the opinion of management, justify a recovery server. Nevertheless, management wants the reassurance that mailbox storage group restores are reliable and wants to minimize the time that mailbox stores are dismounted. Management accepts that public stores need to be dismounted to be restored. To minimize this downtime, strict limits are required for the size of public stores, and on the number of people who can add and delete public store items.

- **Requirement 2** The number of users is greater than the number of client machines. Any user should be able to log on and be authenticated at any client computer.

- **Requirement 3** One of the domain controllers has only 256 MB of memory. This is the computer that is scheduled for replacement, and its memory will not be upgraded. How soon the replacement occurs will depend upon how often that computer experiences problems and the severity of the problems. The chief information officer wants documentary proof of problems in that computer and wants to be informed when problems become severe.

Requirement 1

The first requirement involves minimizing the time that mailbox stores are dismounted by imposing strict limits for the size of public stores and on the number of people who can add and delete public store items.

1. You need to be able to restore mailbox stores and individual mailboxes. You do not want to restore on top of existing data in case restore errors cause the data to be lost. You do not have a recovery server. How do you solve the problem?

_____

_____

2. You recover a mailbox that has been corrupted. Your chief executive officer (CEO) asks if you can also recover a lost file that was in the public store. She does not want the store dismounted, and she wants to recover only the one item, not the entire store. What do you tell her?

_____

_____

3. You have restricted write and delete rights to the public store to a very small group and have limited the size of the store. However, users report that they are having problems finding items in public stores and that the public store hierarchy is becoming complex. What other limitation should you impose?

_____

_____

Requirement 2

The second requirement involves ensuring that any user is able to log on and be authenticated at any client computer.

1. A user reports that he was unable to log on and be authenticated on one of the client machines. When he tried another computer, he was required to change his password, but otherwise had no problems. What is the likely cause, and how do you confirm it?

   _____

   _____

2. NetBT is still widely used on Coho's network. What tool can you use to troubleshoot NetBIOS name resolution and obtain NetBIOS statistics?

   a. netstat

   b. nslookup

   c. ipconfig

   d. nbtstat

Requirement 3

The third requirement involves determining when the domain controller that has only 256 MB of memory should be replaced.

1. You want to be informed when the suspect domain controller is experiencing memory problems. You want a message sent to yourself and to your chief information officer, an entry written to Event Viewer, and a performance log started. What counter do you use and how should you set it up?

   _____

   _____

2. You have been asked to produce statistics that can be used to analyze the performance of the suspect domain controller over a period of time. What tool will give you the information you want in a suitable format?

   a. System Monitor

   b. The report view of a performance log

   c. The applications log in Event Viewer

   d. Diagnostic logging

Troubleshooting Lab

If you do not need to perform test restores of public storage groups, and if your budget or organizational policies do not permit a recovery server, then you can restore individual mailboxes or mailbox stores to a recovery storage group. In this lab, you troubleshoot backup and restore by restoring a previously performed full backup to a recovery storage group. When you are satisfied that the restore completed without errors, you can then merge the recovered mailbox data with regular mailbox groups.

In order to perform this lab, you need to have the hardware and software configuration described in the "Before You Begin" section of this chapter.

Exercise 1: Set Up the Recovery Storage Group

To set up the recovery storage group, perform the following steps:

1. Start Exchange System Manager.
2. Navigate to Administrative Groups\First Administrative Group\Servers\Server01.
3. Right-click Server01, click New, and then click Recovery Storage Group.
4. Click OK to accept the default file locations specified in the Transaction Log Location and the System Path Location boxes. The new recovery storage group will appear in the server's list of storage groups.
5. Right-click Recovery Storage Group and click Add Database To Recover.
6. In Select Database To Recover, click Mailbox Store (Server01), and then click OK.
7. In Mailbox Store Properties, review the mailbox store's properties, and then click OK to accept the default settings.

> **Important**   If you are restoring multiple stores at the same time, the stores must all be from a single storage group.

Exercise 2: Back Up the First Storage Group

In this exercise, you create a backup of the First Storage Group that you will subsequently restore to the recovery storage group that you created in Exercise 1. You created a backup of My Storage Group in Chapter 12, but that backup may not be suitable for Exercise 4 of this lab because there is no guarantee that it contained any mailboxes. Before starting this exercise, ensure that you have a suitable folder for holding the backup—for example, D:\Mybackup.

To create a backup of the First Storage Group, perform the following steps:

1. On Server01, from the Start menu, click Run, type **ntbackup**, and then click OK.

2. The Backup Or Restore Wizard starts. Click Next.

3. Click Back Up Files And Settings, and then click Next.

4. Click Let Me Choose What To Back Up, and then click Next.

5. Expand Microsoft Exchange Server\Server01\Microsoft Information Store, select First Storage Group, and then click Next.

6. In the Choose A Place To Save Your Backup box, browse to a suitable folder (for example, D:\Mybackup). Type **Firstbackup** in the Type A Name For This Backup box, and then click Next.

7. Click Finish. When backup completes, click Close to close the Backup Progress box.

Exercise 3: Restore a Mailbox Store to the Recovery Storage Group

In this exercise, you restore from the backup of First Storage Group to the recovery group.

To restore a mailbox store to a recovery storage group, perform the following steps:

1. On Server01, from the Start menu, click Run, type **ntbackup**, and then click OK.

2. The Backup Or Restore Wizard starts. Click Next.

3. Click Restore Files And Settings, and then click Next.

4. In Items To Restore, select Server01\Microsoft Information Store\First Storage Group, and then specify that you want to restore Log Files and Mailbox Store (Server01).

5. Click Next.

6. On the Restore Database Server page, ensure that Server01 is specified in the Restore To box, type **D:\Mybackup** (or the path to your chosen backup folder) in the Temporary Location For Log And Patch Files box, and then select Last Restore Set.

7. Click Next. Click Finish to close the wizard and start the restore process.

8. If prompted, click OK in the Backup File Location box.

9. When the restore is complete, click Close to close the Restore Progress box.

10. In Exchange System Manager, check that Mailbox Store (Server01) is in the Recovery Storage Group container.

11. Open Event Viewer and check that the restore procedure did not generate any errors in the applications log.

12. In Exchange System Manager, right-click Mailbox Store (Server01) in the recovery storage group, and then click Mount Store. In the warning dialog box, click Yes. Click OK when you are informed that the store was successfully mounted.

Exercise 4: Merge the Recovered Mailbox Data with My Mailbox Store

If the restore completes without errors, you may decide to merge the stored data with the current contents of the appropriate mailbox store. To perform this procedure, you need the Microsoft Exchange Mailbox Merge Wizard (Exmerge.exe). Exmerge.exe is usually installed into the C:\Program Files\Exchsrvr\bin folder. If it is not available on your server, you can download Exmerge.exe from *www.microsoft.com/exchange/2003/ updates*. This exercise assumes that you have downloaded Exmerge.exe and installed it into the C:\Program Files\Exchsrvr\bin folder.

To merge recovered mailbox data with regular user mailboxes, perform the following steps:

1. On Server01, from the Start menu, click Run, type **C:\program files \exchsrvr\bin\exmerge\exmerge.exe**, and then click OK.

Tip   If you have problems running Exmerge.exe, then try copying the file Exchmem.dll from the C:\Program Files\Exchsrvr\bin folder to the C:\Program Files\Exchsrvr\bin\Exmerge folder.

2. The Mailbox Merge Wizard opens. Click Next.

3. Select Extract Or Import (One Step Procedure) and click Next. (If the recovery storage group were on a different server from the original mailbox store, you would use the two step procedure.)

4. Type the names of the source server and the domain controller in the appropriate boxes. (In this exercise, the source server and domain controller are both Server01.) Type **389** in the Port Number For LDAP Queries box. Click Next.

5. Type the names of the destination server and the domain controller in the appropriate boxes. (In this exercise, the destination server and domain controller are both Server01.) Type **389** in the Port Number For LDAP Queries box. Click Next.

6. On the Database Selection page, select Recovery Storage Group/Mailbox Store (Server01), and then click Next.

7. On the Mailbox Selection page, select the mailboxes to restore. You can select individual mailboxes or multiple mailboxes. Click Next.

8. Click Next to specify the default locale.

9. On the Target Directory page, click Change Folder. Browse to D:\Mybackup, and then click OK. Click Next.

10. On the Save Settings page, click Next.

11. Click Finish. If errors were encountered, check the Exmerge.log file in the C:\Program Files\Exchsrvr\bin\Exmerge folder.

Chapter Summary

- Exchange Server 2003 will fail to install if hardware resources are inadequate, if the operating system is not as specified, if necessary services are not started, or if Active Directory or DNS are not accessible. When installing on a Windows Server 2003 member server, you also need to install and enable ASP.NET.

- You can use support tools such as netdiag and dcdiag to check network connectivity, and DNS and Active Directory operation. Performance logs can be used for troubleshooting server health. An alert can be set to indicate a problem associated with a particular resource.

- Disk storage systems need to be monitored frequently. Limiting the size of mailboxes and public stores can lessen storage problems. Memory fragmentation is a problem in clusters, and several counters are available to help monitor the problem. Recovery storage groups can be used to test backup and restore. Many of the problems related to public folders are caused by incorrect permission settings and by not restricting the right to create top-level public folders.

- Protocol logging provides a detailed record of every event on a protocol virtual server. You can also increase the range of events that are written to event viewer by configuring diagnostic logging. Firewall and virus logs contain information about attacks that have been made on your organization. You should check them regularly.

- ARP resolves IP addresses to MAC addresses. You can use the arp utility to display and manage the ARP cache. You can use command-line utilities such as ping, tracert, ipconfig, and pathping to diagnose network connectivity problems. Nbtstat and netstat return NetBIOS and TCP/IP statistics, respectively.

Exam Highlights

Before taking the exam, review the key points and terms that are presented in this chapter. Return to the lessons for additional practice.

Key Points

- You need to install and enable ASP.NET when installing Exchange Server 2003 on a Windows Server 2003 member server but not on a Windows 2000 Server member server. A Windows 2000 Server member server needs to have SP3 or later installed.

- You can use the netdiag, ping, tracert, pathping, and telnet utilities to troubleshoot connectivity problems. You can use ipconfig to troubleshoot TCP/IP configuration problems. You can also use ipconfig and nslookup to troubleshoot DNS problems, and dcdiag can troubleshoot Active Directory problems. Nbtstat and netstat return NetBIOS and TCP/IP statistics, respectively. The arp utility displays the ARP cache.

- You can use recovery storage groups to recover mailbox stores and individual mailboxes. The exmerge tool lets you merge data restored to a recovery storage group with the data in an existing mailbox store.

- If you block permission inheritance from a parent object, you can choose to remove all inherited permissions or to copy them.

Key Terms

alert   You configure an alert to warn you if the value in a performance counter exceeds or drops below a defined level. An alert writes an event to the application log in Event Viewer, and can also send a message to a specified user, start a performance log, and run an executable file.

recovery storage group   You can restore mailbox stores and individual mailboxes to a recovery storage group and then merge them with the contents of the original stores or mailboxes. You cannot restore public folders to a recovery storage group.

netdiag   Netdiag is a Windows Server 2003 support tool that performs a series of tests that check services and connectivity within an organization.

dcdiag   Dcdiag is a Windows Server 2003 support tool that tests the operation of Active Directory. You can also use it to test DNS operation.

Questions and Answers

Page
14-14

Lesson 1 Review

1. You are installing Exchange Server 2003, Enterprise Edition, on a standalone server. The server meets the recommended hardware requirements and Windows Server 2003, Enterprise Edition, is installed. You have installed and enabled SMTP, NNTP, the World Wide Web service, and ASP.NET. The server is a standard primary DNS server. Will the installation succeed? If not, why not?

   The installation will fail because the server is standalone and Windows Server 2003 requires access to Active Directory.

2. You migrate an Exchange Server 5.5 organization to Exchange Server 2003. You use the Active Directory Migration Tool to migrate the mailboxes. You find that the mailboxes have migrated with all the user permissions intact, but user passwords have not migrated. What is the probable reason?

   You have probably used version 1 of the Active Directory Migration Tool. You need version 2 to migrate passwords.

3. Your Exchange Server 2003 organization connects to a UNIX e-mail system over an X.400 connector. You establish connectivity with the system, but e-mail messages are garbled. How do you solve the problem?

   You clear the Allow Exchange Contents option on the X.400 connector and allow standard X.400 formatting to be used.

Page
14-24

Lesson 2 Review

1. You are the administrator of an Exchange Server 2003 organization. During busy times the performance of one of your Exchange Server 2003 servers slows. The server uses a RAID-1 array to store system files, a RAID-5 array to store database files, and a RAID-0+1 array to store transaction logs. Currently all of the disk arrays are used at less than 60 percent of total capacity. You check your performance counters during a busy period and find that your Processor\%Processor Time counter is consistently at 70 percent or above and your Memory\Pages/sec counter is typically between 30 and 40. You notice that there is an unusually high amount of disk activity. What is the most likely cause of the poor performance?

   a. A disk in one of your arrays is faulty.

   b. One of your disk controllers is faulty.

   c. The server needs additional memory.

   d. You need to upgrade your processor.

   The correct answer is c.

2. You set alerts on all the nodes on a cluster group to warn you if the value that the MSExchangeIS\VM Total 16m Free Blocks counter returns is three or less. What action should you take on any node on which the alert is triggered?

If the value in this counter drops below 3, it is an indication that memory has become fragmented in the node. You should restart all the services on the affected node.

3. You want to test your backup and restore procedures by restoring a mailbox store. You do not want to dismount the store while you are performing the restore, and you do not want to overwrite the data in the store with backed up data that might be faulty. You do not have a recovery server. How can you test the restore?

You need to create a recovery group. You can then restore to that recovery group and examine the contents.

Page
14-34
Lesson 3 Review

1. You are configuring authentication on an IMAP4 virtual server. You discover that the check boxes appear dimmed, and you cannot change the authentication setting, which is basic authentication. What is the reason for this?

The IMAP4 virtual server is on a front-end server and can only use basic authentication. You can, however, specify encryption, assuming you have obtained the necessary certificate.

2. Files in a public folder are being added and deleted without official sanction. How can you prevent this happening?

You need to review the permission settings on the public folder. It is probable that a group such as Users or Everyone has write and delete permissions. Such groups should have (at most) read, execute, read permissions, and list contents permissions. You should severely restrict write and delete permissions to public folders.

3. You want to increase the amount of information that is written to the application log in Event Viewer. What should you configure?

   a. Protocol logging

   b. Diagnostic logging

   c. Performance logging

   d. Event filtering

The correct answer is b.

Page
14-44

Lesson 4 Review

1. Kim Akers sends an encrypted e-mail message to Don Hall. Which of the following statements is true?

   a. The message is encrypted using Don's public key and decrypted using Don's private key.

   b. The message is encrypted using Kim's private key and decrypted using Kim's public key.

   c. The message is encrypted using Don's private key and decrypted using Don's public key.

   d. The message is encrypted using Kim's public key and decrypted using Kim's private key.

   The correct answer is a.

2. You suspect that someone is attacking your organization with Trojan horse probes. Where would you look to confirm this suspicion and to find out what ports are under attack?

   You would look in virus logs, which list identified viruses, worms, and Trojan horses (described in Chapter 11). You would also look in firewall logs, which identify (among other things) the ports that are under attack.

Page
14-59

Lesson 5 Review

1. You suspect that a router somewhere in your intranet is causing transmission delays and may be dropping frames. Which tool would give you the most information about the problem?

   a. pathping

   b. ping

   c. tracert

   d. netstat

   The correct answer is a.

2. You successfully ping a host on a remote network. You examine the ARP cache on your computer and find that it contains one IP address/MAC address pair. What are these addresses?

   a. The IP address and MAC address of your default gateway

   b. The IP address and MAC address of the remote host

   c. The IP address of the remote host and the MAC address of your default gateway

   d. The IP address of your default gateway and the MAC address of the remote host

   The correct answer is c.

3. You ask all users to work offline while you fix a connectivity problem. When the users come back online, one of them is unable to access a server by hostname. All other users can access the server without any problems. The user admits that he was slow coming offline and tried to access the same server unsuccessfully before doing so. What command will fix the problem?

   a. ipconfig /release

   b. ipconfig /renew

   c. ipconfig /registerdns

   d. ipconfig /flushdns

   The correct answer is d.

Page
14-61
Case Scenario Exercise: Requirement 1

1. You need to be able to restore mailbox stores and individual mailboxes. You do not want to restore on top of existing data in case restore errors cause the data to be lost. You do not have a recovery server. How do you solve the problem?

   You create a recovery storage group. If you had more than one administrative group, you would create a recovery storage group for each administrative group, but this is unlikely in this size of organization. You can restore an entire mailbox store or a single mailbox to the recovery group and merge the data with that in the appropriate mailbox store after you ascertain that the restore ran without errors.

2. You recover a mailbox that has been corrupted. Your chief executive officer (CEO) asks if you can also recover a lost file that was in the public store. She does not want the store dismounted, and she wants to recover only the one item, not the entire store. What do you tell her?

   Recovery storage groups cannot be used to restore public stores. Without a recovery server, the only way to restore a public store item is to restore to the same public store that was backed up. You have to restore the entire store and cannot restore just a single item. You need to dismount the public store while you are restoring it.

3. You have restricted write and delete rights to the public store to a very small group and have limited the size of the store. However, users report that they are having problems finding items in public stores and that the public store hierarchy is becoming complex. What other limitation should you impose?

You should limit the right to create a top-level public store to an even more select group (possibly only yourself).

Page
14-62

Case Scenario Exercise: Requirement 2

1. A user reports that he was unable to log on and be authenticated on one of the client machines. When he tried another computer, he was required to change his password, but otherwise had no problems. What is the likely cause, and how do you confirm it?

The user probably tried to log on at a Windows NT 4 Workstation after his password had expired. If the PDC emulator operations master were offline, then none of the other domain controllers would be able to implement the password change. When the user subsequently logged on at a client that was Active Directory-aware, another domain controller could process the password change. It may be the case that the domain controller that is experiencing reliability problems is the PDC emulator. If you enter the command **netdom query fsmo** from the Command console, you can confirm the identity of the PDC emulator. You can then find out whether it is operational and connected to the network and transfer, or, if necessary, seize the operations master role.

2. NetBT is still widely used on Coho's network. What tool can you use to troubleshoot NetBIOS name resolution and obtain NetBIOS statistics?

    a. netstat

    b. nslookup

    c. ipconfig

    d. nbtstat

The correct answer is d.

Page
14-62

Case Scenario Exercise: Requirement 3

1. You want to be informed when the suspect domain controller is experiencing memory problems. You want a message sent to yourself and to your chief information officer, an entry written to Event Viewer, and a performance log started. What counter do you use and how should you set it up?

You use the Performance Logs And Alerts tool to generate an alert when the Memory\Pages/sec counter reaches a critical level (such as over 20). You can configure this alert to send messages to you and your chief executive officer and to start a performance log. It will write an entry to the application log in Event Viewer by default.

2. You have been asked to produce statistics that can be used to analyze the performance of the suspect domain controller over a period of time. What tool will give you the information you want in a suitable format?

   a. System Monitor

   b. The report view of a performance log

   c. The applications log in Event Viewer

   d. Diagnostic logging

The correct answer is b.

Glossary

A

access control entry (ACE)   An entry within an access control list (ACL) that grants or denies permissions to users or groups for a given resource.

access control list (ACL)   A list that contains a set of access control entries that define an object's permission settings. ACLs enable administrators to explicitly control access to resources.

ACE   *See* access control entry (ACE).

ACL   *See* access control list (ACL).

Active Directory   The Microsoft Windows Server directory service that forms the basis for centralized network management on Windows 2000 Server and later networks, providing a hierarchical view of network resources.

Active Directory Account Cleanup Wizard   A utility that allows you to merge two Active Directory users, or a user and a contact. This is useful if after a migration you have duplicate accounts and each account contains information that needs to be saved.

Active Directory Connector (ADC)   The Microsoft Exchange Server 2003 service that allows for the replication of information between Active Directory and a Microsoft Exchange Server 5.5 directory.

Active Directory Migration Wizard   A utility that allows you to migrate Active Directory user accounts and mailboxes from one domain to another, across Microsoft Exchange Server organizations.

Active Directory Service Interfaces (ADSI)   A directory service model implemented as a set of COM interfaces. ADSI allows Microsoft Windows applications to access Active Directory, often through Microsoft ActiveX interfaces such as VBScript.

Active Directory Users And Computers console   The primary systems administrator utility for managing users, groups, and computers in a Microsoft Windows 2000 Server and later domain, implemented as a Microsoft Management Console (MMC) snap-in.

ADC   *See* Active Directory Connector (ADC).

ADC Tools   A Microsoft Exchange Server 2003 set of tools that provides a wizard interface for going step-by-step through the deployment of the Active Directory Connector.

address list   A list used to organize the Global Address List (GAL) into smaller, more manageable groupings. Address lists in Microsoft Exchange Server 2003 are formed through administrator-defined Lightweight Directory Access Protocol (LDAP) queries.

address (A) record   The most basic type of resource record on a Domain Name System (DNS) server. Every client that registers with DNS has an associated A record that maps its name to its Internet Protocol (IP) address.

address space   The part of an address that specifies the system that will receive a message. It is a subset of a complete address—for example, in the e-mail address *willis@contoso.com*, *@contoso.com* is the address space.

administrative group   A Microsoft Exchange Server 2003 organizational concept that defines the administrative topology for an organization. Administrative groups can be used to limit the scope of administration to a specific grouping of Exchange Server 2003 servers, rather than the entire organization.

administrative rights (public folder)   These rights control the users and groups that can use Exchange System Manager, a custom Microsoft Management Console (MMC) console, or any other administrative utility to change the replication, storage limits, and other settings for a public folder.

administrative role   Microsoft Exchange Server 2003 supports three administrative roles that can be delegated using Exchange System Manager: Exchange Full Administrator, which can manage anything in the organization, including permissions; Exchange Administrator, which can manage everything in the organization except permissions; and Exchange View Only Administrator, which has read-only administrative access to the Exchange organization.

ADSI   *See* Active Directory Service Interfaces (ADSI).

alert   You configure an alert to warn you if the value in a Performance counter exceeds or drops below a defined level. An alert writes an event to the application log in Event Viewer and can also send a message to a specified user, start a performance log, and run an executable file.

American Standard Code for Information Interchange (ASCII)   A standard set of codes used worldwide, where each letter of the English language is represented by a code. The ASCII standard allows disparate e-mail systems to exchange messages with each other in a format that can be read anywhere. ASCII is commonly referred to as "plain text."

ASCII   *See* American Standard Code for Information Interchange (ASCII).

attribute   The basic unit of an object, an attribute is a single property that through its values defines an object. For example, an attribute of a standard user account is the account name.

auditing   A security process that tracks the use of selected network resources, typically storing the results in a log file.

authentication   The process by which a user's logon credentials are validated by a server so that access to a network resource can be granted or denied.

B

bridgehead server   The contact point for the exchange of directory information between Active Directory sites. When bridgehead servers are used, traffic is funneled from all Microsoft Exchange servers in a site through a single bridgehead server, which transfers the data out of the network.

C

CA   *See* certificate authority (CA).

certificate   Binds together the public and private keys that are used for the secure communication and exchange of data, typically over the Internet. Certificates are digitally signed to ensure their validity.

certificate revocation list (CRL)   A document that is maintained by the certificate authority (CA), which lists all certificates that have been revoked. It is used to keep revoked certificates from being misrepresented as valid.

certificate trust list (CTL)   A list published by the certificate authority (CA) that contains a list of certificates that are trusted for a designated purpose such as digitally signing e-mail.

certificate authority (CA)   An issuer of digital certificates that authorizes and vouches for the validity of the certificates it issues and other CAs that it is associated with.

checkpoint file   A file that indicates the location of the last information successfully written from the transaction logs to the database. In a data recovery scenario, the checkpoint file indicates where the recovery or replaying of data should begin.

circular logging   When a log file fills up, it is overwritten with new data rather than having a new log file created. This conserves disk space but can result in data loss in a disaster recovery scenario, as you would be required to restore back to the last full backup.

cluster group   A collection of cluster resources that is used to define the settings that make up a virtual server on a cluster. When a failover occurs on a node of the cluster, it is the cluster group that fails over to another node.

cluster resource   A cluster resource is an individual component of a cluster virtual server, such as an Internet Protocol (IP) address, a network name, or a physical disk. Cluster resources are collected into groups. When a resource fails, it restarts according to a configurable policy. If a resource exceeds its restart threshold, it can force a failover of the entire group it belongs to.

clustering   The process of combining the resources of multiple physical servers to appear to network clients as a single server. Clusters are used to increase fault tolerance and performance.

Configuration Naming Partition   Stores information about the physical structure of the Microsoft Exchange organization, such as routing groups and connectors.

connection agreement   Used by Active Directory Connector to control replication between Active Directory and the Exchange Server 5.5 directory. Connection agreements can be used to replicate from Exchange Server 5.5 to Active Directory, or vice versa, or in both directions.

contact   A mail-enabled object on a Microsoft Exchange server that links to an external e-mail address. Contacts do not have mailboxes on the Exchange server and serve to provide a convenient means of accessing frequently used external e-mail addresses.

container   An object in Active Directory that is capable of holding other objects. An example of a container is the Users folder in Active Directory Users And Computers.

convergence   The method used by network load balanced clusters to mark a server node as non-responsive and to remove it from the cluster. Convergence begins when a server does not respond to five consecutive heartbeat packets.

CRL   See certificate revocation list (CRL).

CTL   See certificate trust list (CTL).

D

dcdiag   A Microsoft Windows Server 2003 support tool that tests the operation of Active Directory. You can also use it to test Domain Name System (DNS) operation.

delegation of authority   The process of offloading the responsibility for a given task or set or tasks to another user or group. Delegation in Microsoft Exchange Server 2003 involves granting permission to someone else to fill a specific administrative role, such as Exchange Full Administrator, Exchange Administrator, and Exchange View Only Administrator.

Deleted Item Retention   A configurable period of time that items deleted from a user's mailbox will be retained for before being permanently deleted and recoverable only from backup.

Deleted Mailbox Retention   A configurable period of time that a mailbox will be retained for before being permanently deleted and recoverable only from backup.

diagnostics logging   A feature of Exchange System Manager that lets you define the level at which the events written to the application log in Event Viewer are logged.

digest authentication   An industry standard authentication scheme that allows clients to authenticate using a sequence of challenges and responses carried over Hypertext Transfer Protocol (HTTP).

directory rights (public folder)   These rights control which users and groups have permission to change e-mail-related attributes of a mail-enabled public folder.

dismount   A term associated with information stores. Dismounting a store refers to taking a store offline (such as for maintenance).

distinguished name   The name that uniquely identifies an object, using the relative distinguished name, domain name, and the container holding the object. An example would be CN=Willis,CN=Contoso,CN=COM. This refers to the Willis user account in the *contoso.com* domain.

distribution group   A type of Microsoft Windows Server 2003 Active Directory group that is used to define e-mail distribution lists. Distribution groups have no security context and cannot be used to grant permissions to resources, but they are useful for grouping users that share a common purpose, such as all employees at a branch location.

DNS   *See* Domain Name System (DNS).

domain   A collection of Microsoft Windows Server 2003 computers, users, and groups that share a common directory database. Domains are defined by an administrator.

domain controller   A server that is capable of performing authentication. In Microsoft Windows Server 2003, a domain controller holds a copy of the Active Directory database.

Domain Name System (DNS)   A hierarchical name resolution system that resolves host names into Internet Protocol (IP) addresses and vice versa.

DomainPrep   A Microsoft Exchange Server 2003 Setup switch that prepares an Active Directory domain for an Exchange Server 2003 installation. DomainPrep is also used when installing the Exchange Server 2003 Active Directory Connector as a precursor to installing Exchange Server 2003 into an existing Microsoft Exchange Server 5.5 organization.

DSAccess   Implements a directory access cache that stores recently looked-up information for a configurable period of time.

DSProxy   A Microsoft Exchange Server 2003 proxy service that functions as an intermediary between the client and the global catalog.

E

ESE   *See* Extensible Storage Engine (ESE).

eseutil utility   A command-line utility that defragments Microsoft Exchange databases.

Exchange Deployment Tools   A collection of pre-installation tools that can be run individually or through a wizard-like interface. The Exchange Deployment Tools are used to collect information about the current environment and to prepare the environment for a successful deployment of Microsoft Exchange Server 2003.

Exchange System Manager   The primary administrative tool for configuring a Microsoft Exchange Server 2003 organization.

Exchange Task Wizard   A wizard used to enable or disable Microsoft Exchange Server–related services on Active Directory objects. The Exchange Task Wizard can be used to create or delete a mailbox, create or delete an e-mail address, move a mailbox, and so on.

Exchange virtual server   The Exchange virtual server is the Default HTTP virtual server. It manages the default Web page. By default, it manages Outlook Web Access (OWA) and Web Distributed Authoring and Versioning (WebDAV) access.

expansion server   A server that is used to resolve or expand the membership of a mail-enabled group whenever a message is sent to that group.

Extended Simple Mail Transfer Protocol (ESMTP)   An extension of the basic Simple Mail Transfer Protocol (SMTP) that provides additional commands for server communication.

Extensible Storage Engine (ESE)   The Active Directory database engine, ESE is an improved version of the older Jet database technology.

F

failback   A term that defines how failed over application services are moved back to the original server node once the node is back online. *See also* failover.

failover   A term associated with cluster servers, this refers to the ability of a backup server to immediate begin servicing requests if a primary server fails, without an interruption in servicing user requests. *See also* failback.

filter rules   Rules created using recipient policies. Filter rules are generated using Lightweight Directory Access Protocol (LDAP) syntax and allow you to specify what kind of e-mail address is generated for each recipient object.

firewall   A hardware and software security system that functions to limit access to network resources across subnets. Typically, a firewall is used between a private network and the Internet to prevent outsiders from accessing the private network and limiting what Internet services users of the private network can access.

forest   A grouping of Active Directory trees that have a trust relationship between them. Forests can consist of noncontiguous namespace and, unlike domains and trees, do not have to be given a specific name. An Active Directory forest can only support a single Microsoft Exchange Server 2003 organization.

ForestPrep   A Microsoft Exchange Server 2003 Setup switch that prepares Active Directory for the Exchange Server 2003 installation by extending the schema to support the Exchange Server 2003–specific attributes and classes.

forest root domain   The first domain created in an Active Directory forest.

FQDN   *See* fully qualified domain name (FQDN).

front-end/back-end   A Microsoft Exchange Server 2003 configuration where servers are used either strictly for authentication and fault tolerance (front-end) or to physically store data (back-end).

fully qualified domain name (FQDN)   A Domain Name System (DNS) domain name that unambiguously describes the location of the host within a domain tree. An example of an FQDN is *www.contoso.com.*

G

GAL   *See* Global Address List (GAL).

Global Address List (GAL)   The address list that contains all mailbox-enabled and mail-enabled objects in the Microsoft Exchange Server organization.

global catalog   This contains a partial replica of every Microsoft Windows Server 2003 domain within Active Directory, enabling users to find any object in the directory. The partial replica contains the most commonly used attributes of an object, as well as information on how to locate a complete replica elsewhere in the directory, if needed.

global catalog server   The Microsoft Windows Server 2003 server that holds the global catalog for the forest.

globally unique identifier (GUID)   A hexadecimal number supplied by the manufacturer of a product, which uniquely identifies the hardware or software. A GUID is in the form of eight characters followed by four, by four, by four, by 12. For example, {15DEF489-AE24-10BF-C11A-00BB844CE637} is a valid format for a GUID (braces included).

GUID   *See* globally unique identifier (GUID).

H

heartbeat   A special type of network packet that is sent out to each server node participating in a cluster to determine the responsiveness of a node. Server nodes that do not respond to heartbeat packets for a configurable period of time are marked as inactive.

hierarchical namespace   A namespace, such as with Domain Name System (DNS), that can be partitioned out in the form of a tree. This allows great flexibility in using a domain name, since any number of subdomains can be created under a parent domain.

hop   Used to describe how many routers a packet must travel through in order to reach its destination. For example, a message that passes through four routers is said to have taken four hops.

I

IFS   *See* Installable File System (IFS).

IMAP4   See Internet Message Access Protocol version 4 (IMAP4).

Information Store   The Microsoft Exchange Server 2003 service that is responsible for managing the storage groups, and mailbox and public store databases. If the Information Store service is not running, databases cannot be mounted for use.

Installable File System (IFS)   A Microsoft Windows Server 2003/Exchange Server 2003 storage technology that makes mailboxes and public folders accessible through the file system.

Integrated Windows Authentication   Internet Information Services (IIS) authentication in which the password is encrypted for security. This form of authentication does not work through firewalls and proxies.

Internet Message Access Protocol version 4 (IMAP4)   An Internet messaging protocol that enables a client to access mail on a server rather than downloading it to the computer. IMAP4 is designed for environments where users log on to the server from a number of different workstations, or log in remotely from outside of a firewall without a virtual private network (VPN) connection.

Internet protocol virtual server   Microsoft Exchange Server 2003 uses virtual servers to handle e-mail messages that use the various Internet protocols. Exchange Server 2003 uses Hypertext Transfer Protocol (HTTP), Simple Mail Transfer Protocol (SMTP), Network News Transfer Protocol (NNTP), Internet Message Access Protocol 4 (IMAP4), and Post Office Protocol version 3 (POP3) virtual servers.

isinteg utility   A command-line utility that tests and repairs the integrity of a Microsoft Exchange information store.

J

junk e-mail   Unsolicited commercial e-mail, also known as spam e-mail.

K

Kerberos   An Internet standard security protocol that has largely replaced the older LAN Manager user authentication mechanism from earlier Microsoft Windows NT versions.

L

LDAP   *See* Lightweight Directory Access Protocol (LDAP).

Lightweight Directory Access Protocol (LDAP)   The Microsoft Windows Server 2003 protocol that allows access to Active Directory. LDAP is an Internet standard for accessing directory services. Microsoft Exchange Server 2003 leverages LDAP for querying such things as address list membership and distribution list membership.

M

mail-enabled   An Active Directory object that has been configured with an e-mail address but does not have a mailbox in the Microsoft Exchange Server 2003 organization. User accounts, groups, contacts, and public folders can be mail-enabled in Exchange Server 2003.

mailbox-enabled   An Active Directory user account that has been configured with a Microsoft Exchange Server 2003 mailbox and can receive mail in the Exchange Server 2003 organization.

Mailbox Merge Wizard   A Microsoft Exchange Server 2003 utility designed to move mailboxes in bulk between Exchange Server 2003 organizations.

Mail Exchanger (MX) record   A Domain Name System (DNS) record that defines an e-mail server.

MAPI   *See* Message Application Programming Interface (MAPI).

masquerade domain   A configuration option that allows you to specify a different domain name in the From and Mail From fields for outgoing Simple Mail Transfer Protocol (SMTP) e-mail messages.

Message Application Programming Interface (MAPI)   The API used by Microsoft Outlook to access collaboration data. MAPI is also used as the transport protocol between Outlook clients and Microsoft Exchange Server servers.

message transfer agent (MTA)   A Microsoft Exchange component that uses the X.400 protocol to route messages to other Exchange MTAs, information stores, connectors, and third-party gateways.

metabase   A store that contains metadata, such as that used by Internet Information Services (IIS).

metadata   Data that describes other data, such as that within Active Directory or the structure of an information store.

Microsoft Cluster Service   A Microsoft Windows Server 2003 service that allows for the creation of active/active and active/passive clusters. Microsoft Cluster Service clusters are application-aware and can fail over services from one node to another. These types of clusters do not provide fault tolerance benefits.

Migration Wizard   A Microsoft Exchange Server 2003 utility used to migrate mailboxes from one organization to another. The Migration Wizard is often used in conjunction with the Active Directory Migration Tool to migrate user account information in the process.

MIME   *See* Multipurpose Internet Mail Extensions (MIME).

mixed mode   The default operation of Microsoft Exchange Server 2003, mixed mode provides backwards compatibility with Microsoft Exchange Server 5.5 servers in an organization at the expense of being able to use certain Exchange Server 2003–only features.

Monitoring And Status utility   A tool provided with Exchange System Manager that monitors the status of Microsoft Exchange Server 2003 servers and connections and logs events to the application log of Event Viewer when the level of these resources reaches a warning or a critical state.

mount   A term associated with information stores, it refers to the process of making a store available for use.

MTA   *See* message transfer agent (MTA).

Multipurpose Internet Mail Extensions (MIME)   A standard that allows multiple files of various content types to be encapsulated into one message. Request for Comments (RFCs) 2045 through 2049 currently define MIME and are considered to be one single standard.

MX record   *See* Mail Exchanger (MX) record.

N

Name Service Provider Interface (NSPI)   Part of the DSProxy process that can accept Microsoft Outlook client directory requests and pass them to an address book provider.

namespace   A collection of resources that have been defined using some common name. Domain Name System (DNS) namespace is hierarchical and can be partitioned, whereas Microsoft Windows NT 4 and earlier used a flat namespace.

naming context   Active Directory is partitioned into three naming contexts: Domain Naming context, Configuration Naming context, and Schema Naming context. These naming contexts are used to store information about the Microsoft Exchange Server 2003 organization in Active Directory.

native content file   One of the two files that make up a Microsoft Exchange Server 2003 database, the native content file or streaming file (ending in .stm) holds all non–Message Application Programming Interface (MAPI) information.

native mode   A Microsoft Exchange Server 2003 organization that has been converted from mixed mode after it no longer contains any Microsoft Exchange Server 5.5 servers. Native mode organizations can support both Microsoft Exchange 2000 Server and Exchange Server 2003 servers and provide access to all the features of Exchange Server 2003 at the expense of breaking backwards compatibility with Exchange Server 5.5.

NDR   *See* non-delivery report (NDR).

netdiag   A Microsoft Windows Server 2003 support tool that performs a series of tests that check services and connectivity within an organization.

Network Load Balancing   A clustering technology of Microsoft Windows Server 2003 that load balances network client requests between multiple services.

Network Monitor   A powerful tool that can capture all the frames set to or transmitted by a host and analyze the contents of these frames at the bit level.

Network News Transport Protocol (NNTP)   A Microsoft Windows Server 2003 service managed by Internet Information Services (IIS) that allows for discussion forum–type of messages to be stored, created, and read by client software. NNTP was one of the first collaboration protocols on the Internet, used with USENET. Microsoft Exchange Server 2003 provides NNTP virtual server capabilities for hosting newsgroups in public folders.

node   A server that is a member of a cluster.

NNTP   *See* Network News Transport Protocol (NNTP).

non-delivery report (NDR)   An automatically generated e-mail message that notifies a user (and possibly the Microsoft Exchange administrator) if the Exchange Server system was unable to deliver a message to the intended recipient.

NSPI   *See* Name Service Provider Interface (NSPI).

O

object   A distinct entity represented by a series of attributes within Active Directory. An object can be a user, computer, folder, file, printer, and so on.

operations masters   Most Active Directory domain controller functions are multi-master, meaning any domain controller in the domain can handle the function at any given time. However, five roles are reserved as single-master: the PDC Emulator, Schema Master, RID Master, Infrastructure Master, and Domain Naming Master.

organization   Defines the common security context of a collection of Microsoft Exchange Server systems and their resources. An Active Directory forest can support a single Exchange Server 2003 organization, and an organization can be thought of conceptually as being like an Exchange Server–specific forest.

organizational unit (OU)   An Active Directory container object that allows an administrator to logically group users, groups, computers, and other OUs into administrative units. An OU is the smallest administrative unit in Active Directory that permissions can be assigned to.

OU   *See* organizational unit (OU).

Outlook Web Access (OWA)   A Microsoft Exchange Server feature that integrates with Internet Information Services (IIS) and allows mailbox-enabled users to log in and manage their mailboxes through a Web browser. OWA is not as full-featured as Microsoft Outlook but provides access to calendaring and groupware functionality not available through Post Office Protocol version 3 (POP3) and Internet Message Access Protocol 4 (IMAP4).

P

Performance console   The Performance console measures the performance of objects in Microsoft Windows Server 2003 and Microsoft Exchange Server 2003 by means of performance counters. The console has two snap-ins: System Monitor and Performance Logs And Alerts.

PKI   *See* public key infrastructure (PKI).

policy   Policies enable an administrator to configure settings in one location in a flexible manner and have them apply to a large number of users based on their membership in mailbox or public stores, or address lists. When policies are applied, the settings cannot be overridden on an individual basis.

POP3   *See* Post Office Protocol version 3 (POP3).

port filtering   A firewall-type technology that limits the traffic that can pass from an external network to hosts on an internal network based on port numbers. Port filtering is commonly used to increase protection for Microsoft Exchange Server 2003 servers by limiting communications to only port 25 (SMTP) and possibly 110 and 143 (POP3 and IMAP4, respectively).

Post Office Protocol version 3 (POP3)   An Internet protocol that allows messages to be downloaded from a server to the local computer. This is effective for systems that cannot maintain a continuous connection with the server.

public folder   A collaboration feature of Microsoft Exchange Server that creates a repository of information that is accessible to any user who has been granted permissions to the folder. A public folder can contain mail items, calendar items, task items, or custom forms.

public folder referral   The process by which when a user connects to a public folder store and the store does not contain a copy of the content the user is requesting, Microsoft Exchange Server 2003 automatically redirects the user to a server that does contain the content.

public folder tree   A hierarchy of public folders contained in a public store. There are Default public trees and General Purpose public trees. You can have only one

Default public tree in a Microsoft Exchange Server 2003 organization, but you can have multiple General Purpose trees. Messaging Application Programming Interface (MAPI) clients such as Microsoft Outlook and Outlook Web Access (OWA) can only access the Default public tree, but other applications can access General Purpose trees.

public key infrastructure (PKI)   Industry standard technology that allows for the establishment of secure communication between hosts based on a public key/private key or certificate-based system. It is a system of digital certificates, certificate authorities (CAs), and other registration authorities that verify and authenticate the validity of each party involved in an electronic transaction.

Q

query-based distribution group   Enables you to use a Lightweight Directory Access Protocol (LDAP) query to specify membership in the distribution group dynamically. The result is that membership is automatically determined by attributes of a user account, such as department, reducing the amount of administration required to manage distribution lists.

quorum disk   A disk resource that contains the configuration information about the cluster and must be accessible by each server node in the cluster.

R

recipient policy   Used as a quick and easy way to define different e-mail addresses for different users in an organization. Rather than having to edit the properties of individual users in the organization, you can create a policy to apply to a large number of users at once.

Recipient Update Service (RUS)   Updates recipient e-mail addresses and distribution list membership and replicates this information on a schedule to other Microsoft Exchange Server 2003 servers in the domain.

recovery server   A Microsoft Exchange Server 2003 server in a different forest from your Exchange Server 2003 organization. A recovery server enables you to recover a deleted mailbox after its retention time has expired, to restore public stores, and to carry out test restores without dismounting any of your production storage groups.

recovery storage group   You can restore mailbox stores and individual mailboxes to a recovery storage group and then merge them with the contents of the original stores or mailboxes. You cannot restore public folders to a recovery storage group.

referral   When a user attempts to access a public folder on a public folder server and the server does not contain the content the user is looking for, a referral is made to another public folder server. Referral servers are configured by default to use routing group membership, but an administrator can also configure a custom referral list to be used.

registry   A data repository stored on each computer that contains information about that computer's configuration. The registry is organized into a hierarchical tree and is made up of hives, keys, and values.

replica   A copy of a public folder that is placed in a public store on another server and kept synchronized through replication.

replication   The process of synchronizing information between multiple servers, replication can take place within a local area network (LAN) or across wide area network (WAN) links.

Request for Comments (RFC)   An official document that specifies protocols or networking standards

resource records   Standard database record types used in Domain Name System (DNS) zone database files. Common types of resource records include Address (A), Mail Exchanger (MX), Start of Authority (SOA), and Name Server (NS), among others.

RFC   *See* Request for Comments (RFC).

Rich Text File   One of the two files that make up a Microsoft Exchange Server 2003 database, the rich text file (ending in .edb) holds mail messages and Message Application Programming Interface (MAPI) content.

routing group   A collection of Microsoft Exchange Server 2003 servers that are all well connected and reachable in one hop. Routing groups form the physical routing topology for replication traffic.

routing group connector   Connects routing groups. Configuration is one-way and requires specification of a bridgehead server and optionally a schedule and other details.

RUS   *See* Recipient Update Service (RUS).

S

schema   In Active Directory, a description of object classes and attributes that the object class must possess and can possess.

schema naming partition   This contains information about all the object classes and their attributes that can be stored in Active Directory.

security group   A Microsoft Windows Server 2003 Active Directory group type that can be used for assigning permissions to resources and can be mail-enabled and used as a distribution list.

security identifier (SID)   A unique identifier associated with every Active Directory user account and security group. SIDs are never reused, so if an account is deleted and then recreated with the exact same name and information, it is seen as an entirely new object to Active Directory.

service account   A special account created for use by an application's services. Service accounts are used when specific security contexts are needed that you don't want to grant to an existing user account (such as the Administrator account), and you want to be able to specify account settings that will not be subject to domain policies.

service dependency   Services often rely on other services running in order to be able to run. If a service that has a number of dependencies is stopped, intentionally or not, all dependent services will also stop.

SID   *See* security identifier (SID).

Simple Message Transfer Protocol (SMTP)   The native transport protocol of Microsoft Exchange Server 2003, SMTP is a standards-based protocol that allows for the transfer of messages between different messaging servers. SMTP is defined under Request for Comment (RFC) 821 and uses simple command verbs to facilitate message transport over TCP/IP port 25.

Single Instance Storage (SIS)   A feature of Microsoft Exchange Server 2003 that reduces the overall size of an information store by creating only one instance of a message and using pointers to refer multiple users back to it. If a message sent to a distribution list is deleted by one user, only the pointer is deleted for that user. The message itself is not deleted until the last user's pointer is removed.

SIS   *See* Single Instance Storage (SIS).

site   A well-connected Transmission Control Protocol/Internet Protocol (TCP/IP) subnet. The term site refers either to a grouping of Active Directory servers or to a grouping of Microsoft Exchange Server 5.5 servers. With Microsoft Exchange Server 2003, sites are divided into administrative groups and routing groups.

Site Replication Service (SRS)   Works in conjunction with Active Directory Connector to provide replication services from Active Directory to the Exchange 5.0 Directory Service and Exchange 5.5 Directory Service.

source domain and target domain   When you use either the Active Directory Migration Tool or the Migration Wizard, you define a source domain that contains the accounts and mailboxes you are migrating and a target domain that is the destination for the migration.

SRS   *See* Site Replication Service (SRS).

storage group   A collection of mailbox stores and public folder stores that share a set of transaction log files. Microsoft Exchange Server 2003, Enterprise Edition, supports up to four storage groups per server, and each storage group can contain up to five stores.

store   Implemented using the Extensible Storage Engine (ESE), a store is a database that can be for storing either mailbox information (mailbox stores) or public folders (public stores). Stores are contained within storage groups, and a single storage group can hold up to five stores.

subnet   A collection of hosts on a network that are not separated by routers. A basic corporate local area network (LAN) with one location would be referred to as a subnet when it is connected by a router to another network, such as that of an Internet service provider.

System Attendant   One of the core Microsoft Exchange Server 2003 services, the System Attendant performs various functions such as generating address lists, offline address books, and directory lookup facilities. The System Attendant must be running before other key services, such as the Information Store and the Directory Service, can start.

system policies   Sets of rules configured to apply to servers, mailbox stores, and public folder stores.

T

TCP port   Used to define a common communications channel for Transmission Control Protocol/Internet Protocol (TCP/IP) applications. For example, the Simple Mail Transfer Protocol (SMTP) protocol uses port 25 to communicate, which allows mail servers that otherwise would not know of each other to successfully exchange data.

Time to Live (TTL)   The amount of time a packet destined for a host will exist before it is deleted from the network. TTLs are used to prevent networks from becoming congested with packages that cannot reach their destinations.

top-level folder   In a Microsoft Exchange Server 2003 public folder hierarchy, a top-level folder is the highest-level folder in the tree. By default, users can create top-level folders, but a common security practice is to remove this permission so that only administrators can create top-level folders and users can create subfolders.

transaction logs The primary storage area for new transactions made to Extensible Storage Engine (ESE) databases. Data is written to the logs sequentially as new transactions occur. Changes in the logs are later committed to the actual databases. Transaction logs in Microsoft Exchange Server 2003 are always 5 megabytes (MB) in size, and when a log reaches 5 MB, a new log is created.

Trojan horse A computer program that appears to be useful but that actually does damage. *See also* virus, worm.

TTL *See* Time to Live (TTL).

V

virtual server A collection of services that appears to clients as a physical server. Microsoft Exchange Server 2003 uses Internet protocol virtual servers for Simple Mail Transfer Protocol (SMTP), Hypertext Transfer Protocol (HTTP), Post Office Protocol version 3 (POP3), Network News Transfer Protocol (NNTP), and Internet Message Access Protocol 4 (IMAP4). Virtual servers are also used when configuring instances of Exchange Server 2003 on cluster servers running the Microsoft Cluster Service.

virus Code written with the express intention of replicating itself. A virus attempts to spread from computer to computer by attaching itself to a host program. It may damage hardware, software, or data. *See also* Trojan horse, worm.

Volume Shadow Copy Service (VSS) A Microsoft Windows Server 2003 service that enables backup software (such as Windows 2003 Backup) to create a snapshot of Microsoft Exchange Server 2003 data at a specific point in time and back up from that snapshot.

VSS *See* Volume Shadow Copy Service (VSS).

W

WAN *See* wide area network (WAN).

Web Distributed Authoring and Versioning (WebDAV) Defined in Request for Comment (RFC) 2518, an extension to the Hypertext Transfer Protocol (HTTP) version 1.1 standard that is defined in Request for Comment (RFC) 2518. Microsoft Exchange Server 2003 services that use HTTP, such as Outlook Web Access (OWA), rely on this technology.

Web storage system A storage platform that provides a single repository for managing multiple types of unstructured information within one infrastructure. Web storage systems combine the features and functionality of the file system, the Web, and a collaboration server (such as Microsoft Exchange Server) through a single,

URL-addressable location for storing, accessing, and managing information, as well as building and running applications.

WebDAV   *See* Web Distributed Authoring and Versioning (WebDAV).

well-connected network   A network that contains only fast connections between domains and hosts. The definition of "fast" is somewhat subjective and may vary from organization to organization.

wide area network (WAN)   Multiple networks connected by slow connections between routers, WAN connections are typically 1.5 megabytes (MB) or less.

Windows 2003 Backup   The backup and restore utility that is provided with Microsoft Windows Server 2003. The utility may be used to back up and restore Microsoft Exchange Server 2003 storage groups.

worm   A subclass of virus. A worm generally spreads without user action and distributes complete copies (possibly modified) of itself across networks. A worm can consume memory or network bandwidth, thus causing a computer to stop responding. *See also* Trojan horse, virus.

X

X.400   A messaging standard that can be used by many messaging systems.

X.400 Connector   A Microsoft Exchange Server component that is integrated with the message transfer agent (MTA) and can be configured to connect routing groups within Exchange or to route messages to foreign X.400 systems.

X.500   A set of standards developed by the International Standards Organization (ISO) that define distributed directory services.

X.509   A standard certificate format developed by the International Telecommunication Union - Telecommunication (ITU-T). X.509 version 3 is the industry-standard format used by Microsoft Windows Server 2003 certificate-based security processes.

Index

A

Active Directory, 1-1 to 1-21
  case scenario exercise, 1-15 to 1-16, 1-20 to 1-21
  changing configuration partition, 10-8
  connecting with Exchange Server 5.5, 4-3 to 4-22
  defined, 1-7
  domains, 1-2 to 1-3
  forests, 1-2, 2-29, 2-34, 2-46
  function of, 1-2
  global catalog, 1-4 to 1-5
  installing ADC, 4-3 to 4-5, 4-9 to 4-10
  integrating Exchange Server with, 1-8 to 1-11
  integration with Windows domain infrastructure, 1-1
  key terms, 1-17
  merging duplicate accounts, 4-34 to 4-42
  operations masters, 1-5 to 1-7
  OUs, 1-3 to 1-4
  overview, 4-3
  practice exercises, 4-8 to 4-20
  questions and answers, 1-6 to 1-7, 1-10 to 1-11, 1-18 to
      1-21, 4-21 to 4-22, 4-47 to 4-48
  schema, 1-3
  searching for mailbox stores, 7-22
  setting up connection agreement manually, 4-6 to 4-8,
      4-17 to 4-20
  sites, 1-3
  summary points, 1-7, 1-11, 1-16 to 1-17, 4-22
  synchronizing with ADC tools, 4-5 to 4-6, 4-11 to 4-16
  troubleshooting, 14-51 to 14-52
Active Directory Account Cleanup Wizard, 4-34 to 4-35,
    4-38 to 4-41
Active Directory Migration Tool, 5-8, 5-13 to 5-22
Active Directory Users And Computers console, 4-33, 5-44,
    14-8
active/active clusters, 6-9, 6-26, 6-37
active/passive clusters, 6-26, 6-37
ADC (Active Directory Connector), 4-3 to 4-5
  diagnostic logging, 4-37 to 4-38
  handling mailboxes tied to user accounts, 5-7
  installing, 4-3 to 4-5, 4-9 to 4-10
  planning for deploying, 4-4
  summary points, 4-22
  synchronizing with ADC tools, 4-5 to 4-6, 4-11 to 4-16
  troubleshooting checklist for connections, 4-35 to 4-36
ADC Setup Wizard, 4-5
ADCConfigCheck tool, 4-25
ADCObjectCheck tool, 4-25
ADCUserCheck tool, 4-25
ADCUserScan tool, 4-25
address lists
  about, 7-58 to 7-59
  administering, 7-62 to 7-64
  creating, 7-59 to 7-61, 7-69 to 7-70
  key terms, 7-77
  modifying, 7-61 to 7-62
  offline, 7-66 to 7-67, 7-70
  practice exercises, 7-69 to 7-70
  questions and answers, 7-70 to 7-71, 7-78 to 7-85
  setting permissions, 7-62 to 7-63
  summary points, 7-72, 7-76 to 7-77
  updating lists manually, 7-64
Address Resolution Protocol. See ARP (Address Resolution
    Protocol)
addresses. See e-mail addresses; IP addresses
administering public folders, 8-13 to 8-25. See also public
    folders
  mail-enabling folders, 8-13, 8-23 to 8-24, 8-37
  managing e-mail properties, 8-13 to 8-17
  moving folders, 8-19
  practice exercises, 8-23 to 8-24
  public folder referrals, 8-22 to 8-23
  questions and answers, 8-24 to 8-25, 8-40 to 8-41
  replication, 8-19 to 8-22, 8-24
  setting storage limits, 8-18 to 8-19
  summary points, 8-25
  tasks in, 8-13
administrative groups
  about, 3-13 to 3-14, 11-36
  adding, 11-36 to 11-37
  administrative models for, 3-14 to 3-15
  advantages of native mode for, 3-24
  creating, 3-17, 11-39 to 11-40
  defined, 11-62
  delegating control, 11-40 to 11-42
  enabling, 3-14
  public folders and, 8-17
  questions and answers, 3-18 to 3-19
  routing groups vs., 3-15
  summary points, 3-19 to 3-20, 11-45
  unable to move mailboxes between, 7-31
administrative permissions, 11-36 to 11-45. See also
    administrative groups
  administrative groups, 3-13 to 3-15, 3-17 to 3-20, 3-24,
      11-36, 11-39 to 11-42
  Adsiedit.exe utility, 11-39
  configuring, 11-37 to 11-38
  public folder, 8-27, 8-31 to 8-32, 8-34
  questions and answers, 11-44, 11-65
  setting advanced security permissions, 11-38 to 11-39,
      11-42 to 11-44
  summary points, 11-45
administrative role, 3-36
Adsiedit.exe tool
  about, 11-39
  changing Active Directory configuration partition, 10-8
  changing organization names with, 2-24
  summary points, 11-45
  viewing read-only permissions, 11-37

age limits on public folder storage, 8-19
alerts, 11-18, 14-21 to 14-23, 14-67
aliases for e-mail addresses, 7-15 to 7-16, 8-14 to 8-15
/All switch, 2-21
anonymous authentication, 9-41, 10-23
anonymous relays, 10-32
antivirus software
    choosing, 11-16
    client-side, 11-14
    downloading, 11-20
    firewall, 11-15
    operating system updates needed as well, 11-14
    server-side, 11-15
    updating, 11-15
architecture for storage groups, 7-46 to 7-47
ARP (Address Resolution Protocol)
    displaying contents of ARP broadcast frame, 14-58 to
        14-59
    how it works, 14-45 to 14-46
    managing ARP cache, 14-56 to 14-58
    requests and replies in, 14-46 to 14-47
    resolving addresses, 14-46 to 14-48
    summary points, 14-60
ARP cache, 14-56 to 14-58
arp command-line utility, 14-53
ASP (Active Server Pages), 2-8 to 2-10
ASP.NET, 2-8 to 2-9, 14-6
assigned permissions, 8-26 to 8-27
authenticating virtual servers, 9-41 to 9-51
    authentication methods, 9-41 to 9-42
    on back-end server, 9-45 to 9-47
    certificate for IMAP 4 server on front-end server, 9-44 to
        9-45
    configuring incoming SMTP messages, 10-27 to 10-28
    default HTTP virtual server on front-end server, 9-47 to
        9-49
    encryption, 9-42
    forms-based authentication, 9-29 to 9-30
    methods used for, 9-43, 10-23
    POP3 settings on front-end server, 9-49 to 9-50
    practice exercises, 9-44 to 9-50
    questions and answers, 9-50 to 9-51, 9-61
    SASL, 9-42
    setting up client access to protocols, 9-43 to 9-44
    summary points, 9-51, 14-35
    troubleshooting authentication problems, 14-29 to 14-30,
        14-35

B

back-end servers, 3-28 to 3-32. *See also* front-end servers
    authentication on, 9-45 to 9-47
    benefits of, 3-28 to 3-29
    clustering, 6-30 to 6-31
    configuring for virtual servers, 9-23 to 9-24
    key terms, 6-37
    optional services, 11-51
    questions and answers, 3-31, 3-41 to 3-42, 6-33, 6-40 to
        6-41

required services, 11-50
    standard topology, 3-29 to 3-30
    troubleshooting authentication problems, 14-29 to 14-30
    unexpected timeouts during large downloads, 9-24
backup log, 12-24
Backup Or Restore Wizard, 12-23, 12-39, 12-42
backups, 12-16 to 12-27
    case scenario exercise, 12-45 to 12-47
    copy, 12-18, 12-21
    copy plus incremental, 12-18
    data size and types of, 12-19
    dynamic data, 12-16 to 12-17
    exchange cluster, 12-21 to 12-22
    full, 12-17, 12-21
    full plus differential, 12-18
    full plus incremental, 12-17 to 12-18
    historical baselines for system restores, 11-17
    key terms, 12-50
    offline, 12-19 to 12-20
    online, 12-19
    overview, 12-1, 12-16
    practice exercises, 12-22 to 12-26
    questions and answers, 12-26 to 12-27, 12-52
    recovery storage group, 14-64
    repairing indexes, 12-22
    static data, 12-16 to 12-17
    summary points, 12-27, 12-49 to 12-50
    system state data, 12-36, 12-40 to 12-41
    troubleshooting, 14-20 to 14-21
    verifying, 12-22
    Volume Shadow Copy Service (VSS), 12-20 to 12-21
Badmail folder, 10-8, 13-27
basic authentication, 9-41, 10-23
BinHex format, 9-40
bridgehead server, 3-16
browsing public folder trees, 8-10 to 8-11

C

caching, 14-48, 14-50, 14-56 to 14-58
centralized administrative model, 3-14 to 3-15
certificates
    deploying digital signature and encryption, 11-32 to
        11-35
    obtaining and installing for IMAP4 server, 9-44 to 9-45
    troubleshooting, 14-40 to 14-41
child folders, 8-26 to 8-27
/ChooseDC *dcname* switch, 2-19
circular logging
    defined, 7-48, 7-77, 12-50
    incorrect uses of, 12-10
    saving disk space with, 12-9 to 12-10
client workstation requirements, 3-7 to 3-8, 3-12
clients. *See also* IMAP4 clients; POP3 clients
    client-side antivirus software, 11-14
    configuring access to virtual server protocols, 9-43 to
        9-44
    experimenting with additional client hosts, 10-2
    HTTP, 10-39 to 10-41

disk space requirements for restoring data, 12-29
dismounting
    storage groups, 12-13 to 12-14
    stores, 12-3
display filter decision tree, 13-50
distribution groups, 7-5
DMZ (demilitarized zone), 11-3, 11-5, 14-37
DNS (Domain Name System)
    configuring support for SMTP message transfer, 10-9 to
        10-10
    confirming functioning of, 14-30
    MX records for organization managing own, 10-9 to
        10-10
    troubleshooting, 14-48 to 14-51
DNS Mail Exchanger (MX) records. *See* MX records
domain controllers
    configuring all for RPC proxy server, 11-7
    interoperability with Exchange Server 2003, 14-52
    operations master roles assigned to, 1-8
    setting for Recipient Update Service, 7-65
    specifying during Setup, 2-19
Domain Name System. *See* DNS (Domain Name System)
domain names, 9-13
domain naming context, 1-8, 1-11, 1-17
Domain Naming Master, 1-5, 1-17
DomainPrep, 2-15 to 2-16, 2-18, 2-20, 2-46
domains
    about, 1-2 to 1-3
    blocking, 11-27 to 11-28
    integrating Active Directory with, 1-1
    limiting number for message relay, 10-14 to 10-15
    masquerade, 9-23
    message defaults for SMTP messaging systems, 10-44 to
        10-46
    preparing forests and, 2-15 to 2-16
    questions and answers, 2-17, 2-48 to 2-49
    selecting in User Account Migration Wizard, 5-16
    trust between migrating, 5-14 to 5-15
    upgrading to Active Directory, 5-4
DoS (Denial of Service) attacks, 13-38
downloading
    antivirus software, 11-20
    blocking, 11-14
    virus signatures, 11-19
DSAccess service, 1-9
DSConfigSum tool, 4-24
DSObjectSum tool, 4-24
DSProxy service, 1-9
dynamic data, 12-16 to 12-17
Dynamic Domain Name System. *See* DDNS (Dynamic
    Domain Name System)

E

E00.chk file, 7-46
E00.log file, 7-46
E00tmp.log file, 7-47
.edb files, 7-46, 12-4
e-mail. *See also* e-mail addresses; junk e-mail; mailboxes
    customer feedback, 8-3
    identifying delivery failures, 10-27, 14-30

IMAP4 and POP3 unable to deliver, 10-36, 10-41
    intercepting unencrypted, 14-41 to 14-42
    managing public folder e-mail properties, 8-13 to 8-17
    overriding global delivery restrictions, 10-38
    pulling queued mail from another server, 10-34
    recovering messages, 12-31 to 12-32
    relaying POP3 and IMAP4 client mail, 10-43
    removing viruses, 11-17
    restricting Internet, 10-24 to 10-25
    security guidelines for, 11-24 to 11-25
    virus transmission, 11-13
e-mail addresses
    aliases for, 7-15 to 7-16, 8-14 to 8-15
    blocking, 11-27 to 11-28
    customer feedback, 8-3
    forwarding mailboxes to other, 7-28 to 7-29, 7-42
    hiding from GAL, 7-14
    offline address lists, 7-66 to 7-67, 7-70
    recipient policies for, 7-67 to 7-69
enabling
    administrative groups, 3-14
    ASP in IIS, 2-9 to 2-10
    connection filtering, 11-26 to 11-17
    NNTP service, 10-44
    OWA, 10-40 to 10-41
    virtual servers, 9-15 to 9-17
    VSS, 12-24
encoding, 14-29
/EncryptedMode switch, 2-20
encryption
    encrypting SMTP messages for POP3 and IMAP4 clients,
        10-26
    function of, 9-42
    implementing, 11-33 to 11-35
    intercepting unencrypted mail, 14-41 to 14-42
    Outlook certificates for, 11-34
    required for basic authentication, 10-23
    securing e-mail traffic with, 14-42 to 14-43
    SMTP, 10-23 to 10-24
    summary points, 11-61, 14-44
    TLS, 9-15
    troubleshooting, 14-40 to 14-43
encryption certificates, 9-44 to 9-45, 11-32 to 11-35, 14-40
    to 14-41
Enterprise edition of Exchange Server 2003, 3-14, 9-59
ESAs (external storage arrays), 12-11, 12-15
eseutil utility
    defined, 13-52
    defragmenting mailbox stores, 13-39 to 13-40
    operation modes, 13-36, 13-38
    output of, 13-40
    summary points, 13-51
ESMTP (Extended Simple Mail Transport Protocol)
    common commands, 10-6 to 10-7
    defined, 10-57
    implementing connection, 10-5 to 10-8
    overview, 10-1
    testing connections, 10-7 to 10-8
    vrfy command, 10-6, 10-7
etrn command, 10-6, 10-34

EULA (End User License Agreement), 2-22, 2-25
Event Viewer, 13-8 to 13-10, 13-51
Exchange Administration Delegation Wizard, 11-37 to
        11-38, 14-39
Exchange Administrator, 11-38
Exchange cluster backups, 12-21 to 12-22
Exchange Deployment Tools, 4-23 to 4-26
Exchange Domain Servers global group, 2-15
Exchange Enterprise Servers local group, 2-15
Exchange Full Administrator, 11-37
Exchange organizations. See organizations
Exchange Server 5.5. See Microsoft Exchange Server 5.5
Exchange Server 2003. See Microsoft Exchange Server 2003
Exchange Server Deployment Tools windows, 4-29 to 4-32
Exchange Server Migration Wizard
    assigning source Exchange server, 5-22 to 5-23
    designating information for migration, 5-23
    limitations of, 5-10 to 5-11
    migrating from other messaging systems, 5-39 to 5-40
    options in, 5-39 to 5-40
    selecting accounts for migration, 5-24
    setting migration destination, 5-22
    summary points, 5-45
    tasks performed by, 5-9 to 5-10
    troubleshooting migrations with, 5-44
Exchange System Attendant resource, 6-26 to 6-28
Exchange System Manager
    configuring client permissions, 8-28 to 8-29, 8-34
    confirming database move in, 7-53
    creating public folders in, 8-5 to 8-7
    mail-enabling public folders in, 8-13
    monitoring Exchange stores with, 13-7 to 13-8
    moving storage groups and databases, 7-52 to 7-54
    starting Exchange Task Wizard in, 7-30
Exchange Task Wizard
    Available Tasks page, 7-8
    deleting mailboxes, 7-10 to 7-11
    Establish E-mail Address page, 7-8
    Move Mailbox page, 7-29 to 7-30
    starting in Exchange System Manager, 7-30
Exchange View Only Administrator role, 3-36, 11-38
Exchange virtual server, 9-59. See also HTTP virtual servers
exdeploy.exe command-line utility, 4-26
Exmerge.exe tool, 11-17, 12-33 to 12-34
expansion servers, 7-38
extended periods in queues, 13-38

F

failback, 6-6, 6-20 to 6-23
failover, 6-6, 6-20 to 6-23
failover ring, 6-7
failures
    identifying message delivery, 10-27
    installing Exchange Server 2003, 14-4 to 14-7
    minimizing recovery time from hard disk, 12-9
    notification of in dcdiag, 14-14
fault tolerance. See RAID (redundant array of independent
        drives)

files
    associating MIME types with file extensions, 10-44
    blocking downloading, 11-14
    creating for practice exercise test output, 14-11
    .edb and .stm, 12-4
    file formats for protocol logs, 13-24
    log and database, 12-4
    renaming before restoring database, 12-29
filtering
    address lists, 7-61 to 7-62
    message, 11-22 to 11-25
    Network Monitor, 13-47 to 13-50
    recipient, 11-25
    sender, 11-25
    TCP port, 11-4 to 11-5
firewall antivirus software, 11-15, 14-38
firewall logs, 14-38
firewalls, 11-3 to 11-11
    benefits of front-end and back-end servers for, 3-29
    blocking unused ports at, 11-46
    defined, 11-62
    DMZs and front-end servers, 11-3
    front-end server behind, 3-30
    IFC, 11-10 to 11-11
    MAPI client connections through, 11-5
    proxy servers, 11-3
    purpose of, 11-3
    questions and answers, 11-11, 11-63
    RPC over HTTP, 11-5 to 11-6, 11-8 to 11-10
    RPC proxy server configuration for specific ports, 11-7 to
        11-8
    RPC virtual directory configuration, 11-6
    summary points, 11-11, 11-61, 14-44
    TCP port filtering, 11-4 to 11-5
    troubleshooting connectivity, 14-30, 14-36 to 14-39
folders. See also public folders
    Badmail, 10-8, 13-27
    granting permissions to Outlook, 7-27
    moderated, 8-30 to 8-32
    Queue, 10-8
Folders container, 8-6
ForestPrep
    defined, 2-46
    function of, 2-20
    running, 2-12 to 2-16, 2-18, 14-6 to 14-7
    time required for completing, 2-12
forests
    about, 1-2 to 1-3, 1-17
    migrating user accounts within, 5-7
    preparing domains and, 2-15 to 2-16
    questions and answers, 2-17, 2-48 to 2-49
    support for single Exchange organization, 2-29, 2-34,
        2-46
forms-based authentication, 9-29 to 9-30
forwarding
    mailboxes, 7-28 to 7-29, 7-42
    unresolved messages to smart hosts, 10-13 to 10-14

front-end servers, 3-28 to 3-32. *See also* back-end servers
   accessing calendaring information for, 9-24
   behind firewall, 3-30
   benefits of, 3-28 to 3-29
   clustering, 6-30 to 6-31
   DMZs and, 11-3
   examining POP3 settings on, 9-49 to 9-50
   installing Exchange as, 6-29 to 6-30, 6-32
   installing IMAP4 certificate on, 9-44 to 9-45
   key terms, 6-37
   load balancing on, 3-30
   optional services, 11-49 to 11-50
   questions and answers, 3-31, 3-41 to 3-42, 6-33, 6-40 to
      6-41
   required services, 11-48
   standard topology, 3-29 to 3-30
   troubleshooting, 14-29 to 14-30
   unexpected timeouts during large downloads, 9-24
   virtual servers configured on, 9-23 to 9-24, 9-47 to 9-49
full backups, 12-17, 12-21
full plus differential backups, 12-18
full plus incremental backups, 12-17 to 12-18
functional levels. *See* mixed mode; native mode

G

GAL (Global Address List), 7-4, 7-14
General Purpose public folder trees, 8-7 to 8-8, 8-29
General tab (Microsoft Calendar Connector), 5-30 to 5-31
Global Address List (GAL), 7-4, 7-14
global catalog, 1-4 to 1-5, 1-9
global catalog servers, 1-5, 1-7
global delivery restrictions, 10-38
global security groups, 14-31 to 14-32
global settings feature, 10-37 to 10-38
group recipients, 7-5 to 7-6
groups
   administrative, 3-13 to 3-15, 3-17 to 3-20, 3-24, 11-36,
      11-39 to 11-42
   integration with Active Directory, 1-10
   mail-enabled, 7-37 to 7-40, 7-43
   removing rather than denying permissions, 10-54
   routing, 3-15 to 3-20, 3-23 to 3-24, 3-38 to 3-39
   security, 2-15 to 2-16, 2-18, 2-46
   storage, 6-11, 7-77
   troubleshooting, 14-51

H

hardware
   hardware-related installation failures, 14-5
   optimal hard disk configuration for Exchange Server
      2003, 7-50 to 7-51
Hex pane (Network Monitor), 13-46
hiding
   mailboxes, 7-14 to 7-15
   mail-enabled groups, 7-40
historical baselines, 11-17
honeypots, 14-39
host programs, 11-12

host resolution, 14-45
hot-swapping drives, 12-6
HTTP (Hypertext Transport Protocol)
   Exchange Server support of, 10-36
   public folder tree access through, 8-7, 8-10 to 8-11
HTTP clients, 10-39 to 10-41
HTTP Monitoring Tool, 13-25
HTTP virtual directories, 8-9 to 8-10, 9-12, 10-40
HTTP virtual servers
   additional, 9-20, 9-46, 10-39
   authentication methods, 9-43, 9-46
   browsing General Purpose public folder trees, 8-7
   configuring, 9-18, 9-21, 9-27 to 9-29, 9-47 to 9-49
   controlling access to, 9-13
   creating, 9-12, 9-26 to 9-27
   default, 9-59
   logging for, 11-54 to 11-55
   overview, 9-11 to 9-12, 9-19
   public folder and mailbox access in virtual directories,
      10-40
   setting up back-end server as, 6-31
   support for OWA, 9-13, 10-36

I

ICFs (Internet Connection Firewalls), 11-10 to 11-11
IIS 6
   enabling ASP in, 2-9 to 2-10
   Exchange Server integration with, 10-36
   integration with Exchange Server, 1-12 to 1-15
   questions and answers, 1-14, 1-20
   summary points, 1-14 to 1-15
IIS Certificate Wizard, 14-43
IIS Manager console, 2-10
IMAP4 (Internet Message Access Protocol version 4)
   defined, 10-57
   fast message retrieval support, 9-40
   unable to deliver e-mail, 10-36, 10-41
IMAP4 clients
   accessing Exchange mailbox with, 10-36
   configuring, 10-47 to 10-49
   encrypting SMTP message delivery for, 10-26
   per-user options, 10-48 to 10-49
   relaying mail for, 10-43, 10-55
   supporting, 10-41 to 10-42
IMAP4 virtual servers
   additional, 9-20
   Application event log entry for, 9-58
   assigning IP addresses, 9-17 to 9-18
   authentication for, 9-43, 9-46
   certificate on front-end server, 9-44 to 9-45
   configuring, 9-21 to 9-22, 9-33
   enabling and starting, 9-16 to 9-17
   overview, 9-7 to 9-8, 9-19
   summary points, 9-51
   viewing and managing connected users on, 9-53
indexes, 12-22, 12-24 to 12-26
information stores, 7-46 to 7-57
   adding storage groups and databases, 7-48 to 7-52, 7-54

information stores, *continued*
  moving storage groups and databases, 7-52 to 7-55
  multiple databases and storage groups, 7-47 to 7-48
  overview, 7-46
  practice exercises, 7-54 to 7-55
  questions and answers, 7-55 to 7-56, 7-79 to 7-81
  about storage group architecture, 7-46 to 7-47
  summary points, 7-57
Infrastructure Master, 1-6, 1-17
inherited permissions, 8-26 to 8-27, 14-36
installing
  Active Directory Connector, 4-3 to 4-5, 4-9 to 4-10
  ASP.NET on Windows Server 2003 servers, 14-6
  Network Monitor, 13-45 to 13-50
installing Exchange Server 2003, 2-3 to 2-11. *See also*
    Microsoft Exchange Installation Wizard
  in clustered environments, 6-3 to 6-18
  combinations of Exchange and Windows Server
    supported, 2-3 to 2-5
  creating service account, 2-6 to 2-7
  into existing 5.5 organization, 4-23 to 4-33
  failures, 14-4 to 14-7
  front-end server for, 6-29 to 6-30, 6-32
  hardware requirements for, 2-5 to 2-6, 2-45
  monitoring installation, 2-20
  into new organization, 2-21 to 2-26
  practice exercises, 2-8 to 2-10, 4-29 to 4-32
  questions and answers, 2-33 to 2-34, 2-50 to 2-51, 4-32
    to 4-33, 4-48, 6-16 to 6-17, 6-38 to 6-39
  services added while, 3-2 to 3-3
  summary points, 2-11, 2-34, 4-33, 6-18, 14-15
  unattended setup, 2-28 to 2-34
  Windows services required before, 2-7 to 2-10
integrated Windows authentication, 9-41 to 9-42, 10-23
integrity checks
  repairing database integrity, 13-52
  situations indicating mailbox needs, 13-37
  verifying integrity of mailboxes, 13-35, 13-37
Internet. *See also* ISPs (Internet service providers)
  configuring SMTP connections for message transfer,
    10-11 to 10-12
  preventing users from sending mail on, 10-30 to 10-31
  restricting e-mail from, 10-24 to 10-25
  SMTP message formats and delivery parameters for,
    10-12
Internet Connection Firewalls (ICFs), 11-10 to 11-11
Internet Information Services. *See* IIS 6
Internet mail connectors. *See* SMTP connectors
Internet Mail Wizard, 10-12
Internet protocol virtual servers, 9-59. *See also* virtual
    servers
IP address resource, 6-23 to 6-24
IP addresses
  ARP host resolution of, 14-46
  assigning for IMAP4 virtual servers, 9-17 to 9-18
  filtering in Network Monitor, 13-48 to 13-49
  resolving local, 14-46 to 14-47
  resolving remote, 14-47 to 14-48

ipconfig command-line utility, 14-49 to 14-51, 14-60
ISA Server, 11-6
isinteg utility
  checking database integrity with, 13-38
  defined, 13-52
  output for, 13-41
  summary points, 13-51
  switches for, 13-37
  verifying mailbox stores with, 13-40 to 13-41
ISPs (Internet service providers)
  MX records in namespace,10-10
  retrieving mail from dial-up connection, 10-26 to 10-27

J

junk e-mail
  blocking from specified domains, 11-58 to 11-60
  defined, 11-62
  message filtering, 11-22 to 11-23
  removing entry from block list, 11-60
  sending, 11-58
  spam vs., 11-22
  summary points, 11-61
  testing blocks for, 11-60
Junk E-Mail feature, 11-22, 11-25 to 11-26

L

LDAP port
  changing, 4-44 to 4-45
  defined, 4-46
  for Exchange Server 5.5, 4-11
LDAP queries
  creating address lists via, 7-58, 7-60 to 7-61
  query-based distribution groups and, 7-38 to 7-40
licensing agreements, 2-22, 2-25
Lightweight Directory Access Protocol (LDAP). *See* LDAP
    port; LDAP queries
load balancing on front-end server, 3-30
logging. *See also* transaction logs
  checking logs, 13-4 to 13-5
  circular, 7-48, 7-77, 12-9 to 12-10, 12-50
  diagnostic, 4-37 to 4-38, 9-53, 9-56 to 9-59, 13-14 to
    13-16
  firewall, 14-38
  about log files, 12-4
  protocol, 11-46 to 11-56, 11-61, 11-65 to 11-66
lost cluster quorum, 12-35
Lotus Notes, 5-26 to 5-32
  configuring Connector for Lotus Notes, 5-26 to 5-30
  installing Connector for Lotus Notes, 5-26
  synchronizing with Exchange Server, 5-30 to 5-32, 5-45

M

MAC (Media Access Control) addresses, 14-45
mailbox queue alert, 14-21 to 14-23
mailbox stores
  adding, 7-54
  assigning offline lists to, 7-70
  defragmenting, 13-39 to 13-40

information stores and, 7-46
mounting before restoring, 12-36
moving mailboxes to other, 7-29
recovering, 12-28
restoring, 12-29 to 12-30, 12-38 to 12-39, 14-64 to 14-65
storage limits, 7-19 to 7-23
verifying, 13-40 to 13-41
Windows Server 2003 Backup utility for restoring, 12-29
mailbox-enabled users, 7-4, 9-25, 10-46 to 10-47
mailboxes, 7-10 to 7-37. *See also* junk e-mail; mailbox
     stores; Resource Mailbox Wizard
accessing Exchange inboxes, 10-36
alias for addresses, 7-15 to 7-16, 8-14 to 8-15
blocking e-mail address and domain, 11-27 to 11-28
configuring mailbox queue alert, 14-21 to 14-23
creating for recipients, 7-7 to 7-9
defaults for SMTP messaging systems, 10-38 to 10-39
defragmenting, 13-35
deleted mailbox retention period, 7-11 to 7-12, 7-77
deleted message recovery, 12-31 to 12-32, 12-39 to 12-40
deleting, 7-10 to 7-11, 7-15, 7-41
delivery restrictions, 7-27 to 7-28
enabling connection filtering, 11-26 to 11-17
forwarding to other e-mail addresses, 7-28 to 7-29, 7-42
guidelines for security, 11-24 to 11-25
handling with ADC, 5-7
hiding from GAL, 7-14 to 7-15
Junk E-Mail feature, 11-25 to 11-26
management tasks for, 7-10
managing mixed-mode servers, 4-27 to 4-28
merging recovered mailbox data, 14-65 to 14-66
message filtering, 11-22 to 11-24
migrating, 5-11, 5-22 to 5-24, 5-44, 14-8
moving, 7-29 to 7-37, 7-42
permissions, 7-24 to 7-27
primary and resource, 4-12
questions and answers, 11-29, 11-64
reconnecting, 7-12 to 7-13, 7-41, 7-77
recovering, 7-12, 12-30 to 12-31
relationship between user accounts and, 5-7
restoring with Exmerge.exe, 12-33 to 12-34
security, 11-22 to 11-29
storage limits, 7-17 to 7-24, 14-19
summary points, 11-29
verifying integrity of, 13-35, 13-37
mail-enabled groups, 7-37 to 7-40, 7-43
mail-enabled users, 7-4
mail-enabling
existing accounts, 7-7 to 7-8
public folders, 8-13, 8-23 to 8-24, 8-37
security groups, 7-5
maintaining virtual servers
diagnostic logging, 9-53, 9-56 to 9-59
questions and answers, 9-53 to 9-54, 9-61
starting, stopping, pausing, and restarting servers, 9-52
summary points, 9-54
viewing and managing users and connections, 9-52 to
    9-53

Majority Node Set server clusters, 6-6
managing clusters, 6-19 to 6-28
adding disk resource to virtual server, 6-25 to 6-26
creating IP address resource, 6-23 to 6-24
creating network name resource, 6-24 to 6-25
creating virtual server, 6-19 to 6-20, 6-23
Exchange System Attendant resource, 6-26 to 6-28
practice exercises, 6-23 to 6-27
questions and answers, 6-27 to 6-28, 6-39 to 6-40
summary points, 6-28
manual connections to Active Directory, 4-6 to 4-8, 4-17 to
    4-20
manual replication of public folder tree, 8-21 to 8-22, 8-24
MAPI (Mail API), 8-7, 8-37 to 8-38, 11-5
masquerade domains, 9-23
MBSA (Microsoft Baseline Security Analyzer), 11-19
Media Access Control (MAC) addresses, 14-45
merging duplicate accounts, 4-34 to 4-35, 4-38 to 4-41
message filtering, 11-22 to 11-25
Message Transfer Agent (MTA), 6-9
message transfer in SMTP, 10-3 to 10-20. *See also* SMTP
    (Simple Mail Transport Protocol); SMTP connectors
asymmetric request-response protocol, 10-3 to 10-4
authenticating incoming SMTP messages, 10-27 to 10-28
common commands, 10-4
common reply codes, 10-5
configuring Internet connectivity, 10-11 to 10-12
creating MX records, 10-15 to 10-16
message formats and delivery parameters, 10-12
overview, 10-1
SMTP connector, 10-3 to 10-5, 10-11 to 10-12
SMTP relaying, 10-12 to 10-15
messaging systems, 5-26 to 5-38, 10-36 to 10-52. *See also*
    Lotus Notes; X.400-compliant messaging systems
associating MIME types with extensions, 10-44
configuring domain message defaults, 10-44 to 10-46
creating mailbox-enabled users, 10-46 to 10-47
experimenting with other, 10-2
global settings features, 10-37 to 10-38
HTTP client support, 10-39 to 10-41
IMAP4 client support, 10-41 to 10-42, 10-47 to 10-49
Lotus Notes, 5-26 to 5-32
mailbox defaults for, 10-38 to 10-39
message defaults for, 10-38
migrating from other, 5-1, 5-39 to 5-42
mission critical nature of, 6-1
NNTP client support, 10-43 to 10-44
overview, 10-36 to 10-37
POP3 client support, 10-42 to 10-43, 10-49 to 10-51
practice exercises, 5-33 to 5-36
questions and answers, 5-37, 5-41, 5-48 to 5-49, 10-51,
    10-60 to 10-61
summary points, 5-38, 5-41 to 5-42, 10-51 to 10-52
troubleshooting interoperability with other, 14-9 to 14-10
X.400-compliant messaging systems, 5-32 to 5-36
Microsoft Active Directory Connector Setup component,
    4-9 to 4-10
Microsoft Baseline Security Analyzer (MBSA), 11-19

Microsoft Calendar Connector, 5-30 to 5-32

Microsoft Cluster Service, 6-3, 6-5 to 6-8
  Enterprise Edition needed for, 9-59
  Network Load Balancing vs., 6-8 to 6-9, 6-37
  summary points, 6-18
  types of configurations for, 6-6

Microsoft Exchange 2000 Server, 5-5

Microsoft Exchange Application Management Pack, 13-39

Microsoft Exchange Installation Wizard, 2-19 to 2-21
  Component Progress page, 2-26
  Component Selection page, 2-14, 2-22 to 2-23
  displaying user interface in unattended mode, 2-20
  Installation Summary page, 2-24 to 2-25
  Installation Type page, 2-23
  installing Exchange Server with, 2-21 to 2-26
  Licensing Agreement page, 2-25
  Organization Name page, 2-23 to 2-24
  removing Exchange Server with, 2-35 to 2-37
  types of installation, 2-19 to 2-21

Microsoft Exchange Mailbox Merge Wizard, 7-31 to 7-37
  Destination Server page, 7-35 to 7-36
  Folders page, 7-34
  Mailbox Selection page, 7-36
  Procedure Selection page, 7-31
  Source Server page, 7-32
  Target Directory page, 7-37

Microsoft Exchange Server 5.5, 4-1 to 4-50
  case scenario exercise for migrating from, 4-42 to 4-44, 4-50
  changing LDAP port, 4-44 to 4-45
  checklist for basic troubleshooting, 4-35 to 4-36
  configuring connection agreement, 4-44
  connecting to Active Directory, 4-3 to 4-22
  diagnostic logging for, 4-37 to 4-38
  incompatibility with native mode, 3-24
  installing Exchange Server 2003 into Exchange Server 5.5 organization, 4-23 to 4-33
  interoperability in mixed mode, 3-22 to 3-23
  key terms, 4-46
  merging duplicate accounts, 4-34 to 4-35, 4-38 to 4-41
  overview, 4-1 to 4-2
  practice exercises, 4-8 to 4-20, 4-29 to 4-32
  questions and answers, 4-21 to 4-22, 4-32 to 4-33, 4-41 to 4-42, 4-47 to 4-50
  replication from Active Directory to Exchange Server 5.5, 4-36 to 4-37
  replication from Exchange Server 5.5 to Active Directory, 4-36
  Site Replication Service troubleshooting, 4-38
  summary points, 4-22, 4-33, 4-42, 4-45
  synchronizing with Active Directory, 4-5 to 4-6, 4-11 to 4-16
  troubleshooting connections to Active Directory, 4-34 to 4-42

Microsoft Exchange Server 2003. *See also* planning Exchange Server infrastructure
  adding and removing components, 3-8, 3-10
  administrative groups in Enterprise edition of, 3-14
  certificates for digital signatures and encryption, 11-34
  coexisting with Exchange 2000 Server in native mode, 3-22
  configuring to use RPC over HTTP, 11-5 to 11-6
  data storage in, 12-3 to 12-4
  /DisasterRecovery switch, 2-20
  global settings feature, 10-37 to 10-38
  installing, 2-3 to 2-11
  integrating with Active Directory, 1-8 to 1-11
  integrating with IIS 6, 1-12 to 1-15
  mixed mode administration, 3-23
  optimal hard disk configuration for, 7-50 to 7-51
  ports, 11-4, 11-6
  removing, 14-7 to 14-8
  restoring entire servers, 12-36 to 12-37
  services used, 3-3, 11-4, 11-46 to 11-51
  supported Exchange and Windows Server installations, 2-3 to 2-5
  types of installations for, 2-19 to 2-21
  unattended installations, 2-28 to 2-34
  Windows 2000 Server or Windows Server 2003 installations, 4-23

Microsoft Exchange System Management tools, 3-7 to 3-8, 3-12

Microsoft Internet Security and Acceleration Server (ISA), 11-6

Microsoft Mail, 10-36

Microsoft Operations Manager, 13-38 to 13-39

Microsoft Outlook 2003
  certificates for digital signatures and encryption, 11-34
  configuring client permissions in, 8-28 to 8-29, 8-32, 8-34
  creating profile for RPC over HTTP, 11-8 to 11-10
  creating public folders in, 8-3 to 8-4
  evaluating unauthenticated mail in, 11-24
  granting permissions to folders in, 7-27
  Junk E-Mail feature, 11-25 to 11-26
  MAPI client connections through firewalls, 11-5

Microsoft Security Notification Service, 11-18

Microsoft Security Web site, 11-18

Microsoft Software Update Services (SUS), 11-19

Microsoft Systems Management Server (SMS), 11-19

Microsoft Windows 2000 Advanced Server, 6-4

Microsoft Windows 2003 Backup, 12-50

Microsoft Windows NT 4 Advanced Server, 6-4

Microsoft Windows NT 4 Datacenter Server, 6-4

Microsoft Windows Server 2003
  Active Directory troubleshooting issues, 14-51 to 14-52
  analyzing ARP packet, 14-58 to 14-59
  ASP.NET installation, 14-6
  Backup utility, 12-29
  DNS troubleshooting, 14-48 to 14-51
  Exchange Server 2003 installation failures on servers with, 14-8
  installing required Windows services, 2-7 to 2-10
  managing ARP cache, 14-56 to 14-58
  network connectivity and, 14-52 to 14-56
  questions and answers, 14-59 to 14-60
  summary points, 14-60

support tools, 11-42
supported combinations of Exchange and, 2-3 to 2-5
troubleshooting, 14-45 to 14-60
Microsoft Windows Update, 11-18
migrating to Exchange Server, 5-1 to 5-50
   case scenario exercise, 5-42 to 5-43, 5-49 to 5-50
   coexisting with other messaging systems, 5-26 to 5-38
   creating X.400 transport stack, 5-33 to 5-36
   key terms, 5-45 to 5-46
   Lotus Notes, 5-26 to 5-32
   Migration Wizard for, 5-39 to 5-42
   from other messaging systems, 5-39 to 5-42, 5-48 to 5-49
   overview, 5-1 to 5-2
   practice exercises, 5-14 to 5-24, 5-33 to 5-36
   preparing users, 5-40
   questions and answers, 5-24 to 5-25, 5-37, 5-41, 5-47 to
      5-50
   summary points, 5-25, 5-38, 5-41 to 5-42, 5-44 to 5-45
   troubleshooting, 14-8 to 14-9
   troubleshooting lab, 5-43 to 5-44
   upgrading from Exchange 2000 organization, 5-11 to
      5-14
   upgrading from Exchange Server 5.5 organization, 5-3 to
      5-11
   X.400-compliant messaging systems, 5-32 to 5-33
Migration Wizard. See Exchange Server Migration Wizard
MIME (Multi-Purpose Internet Mail Extensions) format,
      9-40, 10-44
mirrored system disks, 7-50
mirrored transaction log disk, 7-50
mixed administrative model, 3-14 to 3-15
mixed mode, 3-21 to 3-27
   benefits and limitations of, 3-22 to 3-24
   concepts behind, 3-21 to 3-22
   converting to native mode, 3-24 to 3-25
   managing mixed-mode servers, 4-27 to 4-28
   prerequisites for coexisting with Exchange 2000 and 5.5,
      4-30
   questions and answers, 3-26 to 3-27, 3-38 to 3-41
   summary points, 3-27
moderated folders, 8-30 to 8-32
Monitoring And Status utility, 13-11, 13-16 to 13-18, 13-51
monitoring Exchange Server, 13-1 to 13-56. See also daily
      monitoring and maintenance; on-demand
      monitoring and maintenance; scheduled tasks
   Badmail folder, 13-27
   capacity planning, 13-21
   case scenario exercise, 13-42 to 13-44, 13-55 to 13-56
   checking queues with Queue Viewer, 13-38
   configuring protocol logs, 13-23 to 13-25, 13-28 to 13-30
   defragmenting mailbox stores, 13-39 to 13-40
   diagnostic logging, 13-14 to 13-16
   during installation, 2-20
   eseutil operation modes, 13-36
   Event Viewer for, 13-8 to 13-10
   generating reports and identifying trends, 13-21, 13-30 to
      13-31
   hardware and software for exercises, 13-2
   HTTP Monitoring Tool for, 13-25

isinteg switches, 13-37
key terms, 13-51 to 13-52
list of, 13-3 to 13-4
mailbox policies and oversized mailboxes, 13-32
management tools for, 13-38 to 13-39
managing mailbox limits, 13-26 to 13-27
Monitoring And Status utility for, 13-11
offline database defragmentation, 13-36
overview, 13-1 to 13-2
Performance console for, 13-22 to 13-23
postmaster mailbox, 13-27 to 13-28
questions and answers, 13-18 to 13-19, 13-33, 13-41,
      13-53 to 13-56
Queue Viewer utility for, 13-11 to 13-14
reading default SMTP protocol log file, 13-31
reviewing logs, 13-4 to 13-5
server performance, 14-16 to 14-18
services and resources monitoring, 13-5 to 13-6
specifying events to monitor, 13-16 to 13-18
stores, 13-7 to 13-8
summary points, 13-19, 13-33 to 13-34, 13-42, 13-50 to
      13-51
tasks for, 13-35
troubleshooting lab with Network Monitor, 13-44 to
      13-50
types of, 13-20 to 13-21
verifying store integrity, 13-37, 13-40 to 13-41
moving
   mailboxes, 7-29 to 7-37, 7-42
   public folders, 8-19, 8-25
MTA (Message Transfer Agent), 6-9
multimaster replication model, 8-21
MX records
   function of, 10-9
   for ISPs, 10-10
   for organization managing own DNS, 10-9 to 10-10
   practice exercise creating, 10-15 to 10-16
   verifying, 10-15 to 10-16

N
N+I hot-standby server, 6-6 to 6-7
naming contexts, 1-8 to 1-9, 1-11, 1-17
NAS (network attached storage), 12-11
NAT (Network Address Translation), 14-38
native mode, 3-21 to 3-27
   advantages of, 3-24 to 3-25
   coexistence of Exchange versions in, 3-22
   concepts behind, 3-21 to 3-22
   converting to, 3-24 to 3-25
   questions and answers, 3-26 to 3-27, 3-38 to 3-41
   summary points, 3-27
nbstat command-line utility, 14-54
NDRs (non-delivery reports), 12-9
NetBIOS spam, 11-18
netdiag command-line utility
   checking network connectivity, 14-11 to 14-12
   defined, 14-67
   finding connection fault, 14-12
   function of, 14-8, 14-10

netdiag command-line utility, *continued*
  output illustrated, 14-12
  practice exercises, 14-10 to 14-14
  summary points, 14-15
netstat command-line utility, 14-54 to 14-55
network connectivity, 14-52 to 14-56
Network Load Balancing, 6-3 to 6-5
  load balancing on front-end server, 3-30
  Microsoft Cluster Service vs., 6-8 to 6-9
  servers supporting, 6-4
  summary points, 6-18
  unable to monitor application services in, 6-37
  virtual servers and, 9-4
Network Monitor, 13-44 to 13-50
  defined, 13-52
  displaying contents of ARP broadcast frame, 14-58 to
    14-59
  filtering frames by criteria, 13-47 to 13-48
  installing and using, 13-45 to 13-50
  IP address filtering, 13-48 to 13-49
  overview of, 13-44 to 13-45
  Summary, Detail, and Hex panes in, 13-46
  versions of, 13-5
network name resource, 6-24 to 6-25
Network News Transfer Protocol. *See* NNTP (Network
    News Transfer Protocol) service
New Server Cluster Wizard, 6-13 to 6-15
N-node failover pairs, 6-6
NNTP (Network News Transfer Protocol) service
  accessing General Purpose public folder trees in, 8-7
  IIS built-in, 1-13
  installing, 2-7 to 2-8
NNTP clients, 10-43 to 10-44
NNTP virtual servers
  additional, 9-20
  authentication methods supported, 9-43
  configuring, 9-22
  creating, 9-33 to 9-34
  disabled by default, 10-44
  enabling and starting, 9-16 to 9-17
  overview, 9-8 to 9-10, 9-19
  protocol logging for, 11-53 to 11-54
  specifying paths for internal and newsgroup files, 9-34
nodes, 6-4 to 6-5, 6-37
/NoErrorLogging switch, 2-21
/NoEventLog switch, 2-20
Novell GroupWise, 5-45
nslookup, 10-27, 14-30, 14-60

O

ODBC-compliant database fields, 11-52
offline address lists, 7-63, 7-66 to 7-67, 7-70
offline backups, 12-19 to 12-20, 12-30
on-demand monitoring and maintenance, 13-35 to 13-42
  checking queues, 13-38
  defragmenting mailbox stores, 13-39 to 13-40
  eseutil operation modes, 13-36
  isinteg switches, 13-37
  management tools for, 13-38 to 13-39
  offline database defragmentation, 13-36
  questions and answers, 13-41, 13-54 to 13-55
  summary points, 13-42
  tasks for, 13-35
  verifying store integrity, 13-37, 13-40 to 13-41
online backups, 12-19
operating system updates, 11-14
operation modes for eseutil utility, 13-36, 13-38
operations masters, 1-5 to 1-7, 1-17
organizational units (OUs), 1-3 to 1-4, 5-18
organizations
  changing names, 2-24
  connectivity problems, 14-30
  defined, 2-46
  diagnostic logging for virtual servers, 14-28
  forest support for single, 2-29, 2-34, 2-46
  front-end and back-end server configurations for, 14-29
    to 14-30
  incorrect encoding and relaying for, 14-29
  installing Exchange Server 2003 into 5.5, 4-23 to 4-33
  installing Exchange Server into new, 2-21 to 2-26
  limiting permissions to public folders, 14-31 to 14-34
  migrating to new Exchange 2003, 5-8 to 5-9
  migrating to other, 5-7 to 5-8
  problems with public folders, 14-26 to 14-27
  questions and answers, 14-34 to 14-35
  removing Exchange Server from, 2-35 to 2-40
  summary points, 14-35
  troubleshooting, 14-26 to 14-35
  upgrading from Exchange Server 5.5 in same, 5-4 to 5-7
OrgCheck tool, 4-24
OrgNameCheck tool, 4-24
OUs (organizational units), 1-3 to 1-4, 5-18
Outlook. *See* Microsoft Outlook 2003
Outlook Web Access. *See* OWA (Outlook Web Access)
OWA (Outlook Web Access)
  browsing public folder trees, 8-10 to 8-11
  creating public folders in, 8-4 to 8-5
  defined, 1-13 to 1-15
  enabling or disabling, 10-40 to 10-41
  forms-based authentication, 9-29 to 9-30
  HTTP virtual server support for, 9-13, 10-36
  recovering deleted messages with, 12-39 to 12-40

P

packet filters, 11-3
parent folders, 8-26 to 8-27
password migration, 5-18 to 5-20
/Password *password* switch, 2-20
payload, 11-12
PDC Emulator, 1-6, 1-17
performance
  accelerating front-end servers, 3-29
  monitoring network, 13-5
Performance console
  configuring, 13-22 to 13-23
  defined, 13-51

summary points, 13-51
System Manager and Performance Logs And Alerts, 13-6
performance counters, 14-16 to 14-18
adding, 14-21 to 14-22
diagnosing server health with, 14-16 to 14-18
virtual memory fragmentation, 14-19 to 14-20, 14-25
Performance Optimizer, 7-52
perimeter network. *See* demilitarized zone (DMZ)
permissions
administrative, 11-36 to 11-45
allowing Relay Permissions for POP3 and IMAP4 users, 10-55
clustering and, 6-11
configuring on public folder store, 14-32 to 14-34
incorrectly configured, 14-27
installation failures and sufficient, 14-6 to 14-7
mailbox, 7-24 to 7-25, 7-28 to 7-29, 7-42
public folder, 8-28 to 8-32, 14-31 to 14-34
questions and answers, 11-44, 11-65
removing groups rather than denying, 10-54
required for Exchange installation, 2-7
setting on virtual directory, 9-28
summary points, 11-45
troubleshooting, 14-39 to 14-40, 14-44
write and delete, 14-34 to 14-35
per-user options
IMAP4 client, 10-48 to 10-49
overriding global defaults with, 10-56
POP3 clients, 10-50 to 10-51
Pickup folder, 10-8
ping utility, 14-53, 14-57 to 14-58
PKI (public key infrastructure), 11-31, 11-62
planning Exchange Server infrastructure, 2-1 to 2-54
case scenario exercise, 2-40 to 2-43, 2-52 to 2-54, 3-42 to 3-44
creating service account, 2-6 to 2-7
forest and domain preparation, 2-12 to 2-18, 2-46
.ini file for unattended setup, 2-28 to 2-32
installation hardware requirements, 2-5 to 2-6, 2-45
installing Exchange Server, 2-19 to 2-27
key terms, 2-46
overview, 2-1 to 2-2
practice exercises, 2-8 to 2-10, 2-15 to 2-16
preparing for installation, 2-3 to 2-11
questions and answers, 2-10 to 2-11, 2-17, 2-26 to 2-27, 2-33 to 2-34, 2-39 to 2-40, 2-47 to 2-54
removing Exchange Server from organization, 2-35 to 2-40, 2-44 to 2-45
required Windows services, 2-7 to 2-10
summary points, 2-11, 2-18, 2-27, 2-34, 2-40, 2-45 to 2-26
supported combinations of Exchange and Windows Server, 2-3 to 2-5
unattended setup, 2-28 to 2-34
PolCheck tool, 4-24

POP3 (Post Office Protocol version 3)
about, 1-13
accessing Exchange inboxes with, 10-36
allowing Relay Permissions for users, 10-55
defined, 10-57
encrypting SMTP message delivery for clients, 10-26
unable to deliver e-mail, 10-36, 10-41 to 10-42
POP3 clients
calendaring with, 10-43
configuring, 10-42 to 10-43, 10-49 to 10-51
per-user options, 10-50 to 10-51
relaying mail with SMTP virtual server for, 10-43
SMTP support for sending e-mail for, 10-42
POP3 virtual servers
additional, 9-20
authentication options on back-end server, 9-46
configuring, 9-21 to 9-22
creating, 9-30
enabling and starting, 9-16 to 9-17
examining settings on front-end server, 9-49 to 9-50
overview, 9-5 to 9-7, 9-19
SASL authentication for clients, 9-42
SSL for, 9-6
summary points, 9-51
supported authentication methods, 9-43
ports
blocking unused, 11-46
configuring RPC proxy server to use specific, 11-7 to 11-8
Exchange Server, 11-6, 14-37
special, 14-38
TCP port filtering, 11-4 to 11-5
postmaster account, 10-38 to 10-39
postmaster mailbox, 13-27 to 13-28
practice exercises
address lists and recipient policies, 7-69 to 7-70
authenticating virtual servers, 9-44 to 9-50
backups, 12-22 to 12-26
configuration steps after installation, 3-8 to 3-10
connecting with Exchange Server 5.5 with Active Directory, 4-8 to 4-20
information stores, 7-54 to 7-55
installing Exchange Server, 2-21 to 2-26, 4-29 to 4-32, 6-12 to 6-16, 6-29 to 6-30, 6-32
limiting permissions to public folders, 14-31 to 14-34
managing Exchange Server cluster, 6-23 to 6-27
merging duplicate accounts, 4-38 to 4-41
migrating Active Directory user accounts, 5-15 to 5-22
MX records, 10-15 to 10-16
netdiag and dcdiag command-line utility, 14-10 to 14-14
on-demand monitoring and maintenance, 13-39 to 13-41
preparing forests and domains, 2-15 to 2-16
public folder trees, 8-8 to 8-9
public folders, 8-23 to 8-24, 8-32

practice exercises, *continued*
  restoring data, 12-37 to 12-44
  security, 11-5 to 11-6, 11-20, 11-32 to 11-35
  service account, 2-8 to 2-9
  SMTP, 10-27 to 10-34, 10-41 to 10-49
  SMTP connectors, 10-17 to 10-18, 10-30
  unattended Exchange Server installation, 2-31 to 2-32
  virtual servers, 9-15 to 9-18, 9-25 to 9-39, 9-45 to 9-50,
    9-53
preparing forests and domains, 2-12 to 2-18
  DomainPrep, 2-15 to 2-16, 2-18, 2-46
  ForestPrep, 2-12 to 2-16, 2-18, 2-46
  overview, 2-12
  practice exercises, 2-15 to 2-16
  questions and answers, 2-17, 2-48 to 2-49
primary and resource mailboxes, 4-12
Principle of Least Privilege, 9-16, 10-27, 14-23
private keys, 11-31
PrivFoldCheck tool, 4-25 to 4-26
protocol logging, 11-46 to 11-55
  configuring, 11-53 to 11-55, 13-23 to 13-25, 13-28 to
    13-30
  defined, 11-51
  formats for, 11-51 to 11-52
  overview, 11-46
  questions and answers, 11-55 to 11-56, 11-65 to 11-66
  summary points, 11-56, 11-61, 14-35
protocol virtual servers. *See* virtual servers
proxy servers, 11-3
PubFoldCheck tool, 4-24 to 4-25
public folder indexes, 12-24 to 12-25
public folder recipients, 7-6
public folder referrals, 8-22 to 8-23
public folder stores
  configuring permissions on, 14-32 to 14-34
  creating, 8-8 to 8-9
  defragmenting, 13-35
  policies for, 14-19
  storage limits, 8-18 to 8-19
  verifying integrity of, 13-35
public folder trees, 8-7 to 8-8
  accessing, 8-10 to 8-11
  creating, 8-8 to 8-9
  Default, 8-7, 8-12
  defined, 8-39
  General Purpose, 8-7 to 8-8
  manual replication of, 8-21 to 8-22
  practice exercises for, 8-8 to 8-9
  questions and answers, 8-11 to 8-12, 8-40
public folders, 8-1 to 8-44. *See also* public folder trees
  administrative rights for, 8-27, 8-31 to 8-32, 8-34
  age limits on storage, 8-19
  case scenario exercise, 8-34 to 8-36, 8-43 to 8-44
  configuring folder e-mail addresses, 8-13 to 8-14
  creating, 8-3 to 8-7, 8-9
  Default public folder trees, 8-7, 8-12
  directory rights for, 8-27, 8-31, 8-34
  function of, 8-1 to 8-2
  General Purpose public folder trees, 8-7 to 8-8

inherited and assigned permissions, 8-26 to 8-27
key terms, 8-38 to 8-39
limiting permissions, 14-31 to 14-34
mail delivery restrictions, 8-14 to 8-16
mail-enabling folders, 8-13, 8-23 to 8-24, 8-37
managing e-mail properties, 8-13 to 8-17
monitoring, 13-7 to 13-8
moving, 8-19, 8-25
permissions, 8-26 to 8-32, 14-31 to 14-34
practice exercises, 8-8 to 8-9, 8-23 to 8-24, 8-32
public folder trees, 8-7 to 8-8
questions and answers, 8-11 to 8-12, 8-24 to 8-25, 8-33
    to 8-34, 8-40 to 8-44
referrals, 8-22 to 8-23
removing, 13-8
replication, 8-19 to 8-22, 8-24
restoring, 12-32 to 12-33, 14-27
security, 8-26 to 8-34
setting storage limits, 8-18 to 8-19
summary points, 8-12, 8-25, 8-34, 8-37 to 8-38
tasks in, 8-13
top-level folders, 8-39
troubleshooting, 14-26 to 14-27
troubleshooting lab, 8-36 to 8-37
using, 8-2 to 8-3
Public Folders container, 8-6
public key encryption, 11-30 to 11-31
public key infrastructure (PKI), 11-31, 11-62
public stores. *See* public folder stores
pull relationship, 10-26

Q

query-based distribution groups, 7-38 to 7-40
Queue folder, 10-8
Queue Viewer, 13-11 to 13-14
  Additional Queue Information option, 13-13
  checking queues, 13-35, 13-38
  disabling outbound mail, 13-12
  displaying messages in queue, 13-12
  finding potential problems, 13-13 to 13-14
  illustrated, 13-12
  message states in, 13-13
  queues displayed in, 13-11
  setting queue refresh frequency, 13-12
  summary points, 13-42
queues
  checking, 13-35
  configuring mailbox queue alert, 14-21 to 14-23
  displaying messages in, 13-12
quorum disks, 6-10 to 6-11, 6-37

R

RAID (redundant array of independent drives)
  backing up and restoring, 12-8
  configurations for storing transaction logs, 12-7 to 12-8
  RAID-0+1 mirrored stripes, 12-6
  RAID-0 striping, 12-5
  RAID-1 mirroring or duplexing, 12-5 to 12-6

RAID-5 striping with parity, 12-6 to 12-7
server configurations for Exchange Server 2003, 7-50 to
    7-51
summary points, 12-15
random failover, 6-7
RARP (Reverse ARP), 14-58 to 14-59
RBL (Relay Blocking List), 11-23
Recipient Connection Agreement, 5-7
recipient filtering, 11-25
recipient objects, 7-3 to 7-45. *See also* address lists;
    information stores; mailboxes
  adding mailbox stores, 7-54
  case scenario exercise, 7-72 to 7-75, 7-83 to 7-85
  contact recipients, 7-5
  creating, 7-6 to 7-9, 7-41
  group recipients, 7-5 to 7-6
  hiding from GAL, 7-14
  information stores, 7-46 to 7-57
  key terms, 7-77
  mailbox management, 7-10 to 7-37
  mail-enabled users, 7-4
  managing mail-enabled groups, 7-37 to 7-40
  overview, 7-1 to 7-2
  practice exercises, 7-41 to 7-43, 7-54 to 7-55, 7-69 to 7-70
  public folder recipients, 7-6
  questions and answers, 7-43 to 7-44, 7-55 to 7-56, 7-70
      to 7-71, 7-78 to 7-85
  recipient policies, 7-67 to 7-69, 7-75 to 7-76
  recipient update service, 7-64 to 7-65
  summary points, 7-45, 7-57, 7-72, 7-76 to 7-77
  troubleshooting lab, 7-75 to 7-76
  types of recipients, 7-3 to 7-9
  user recipients, 7-3 to 7-4
recipient policies
  creating and applying, 7-67 to 7-69, 7-75 to 7-76
  managing recipient update service, 7-64 to 7-65
Recipient Update Service, 7-64 to 7-65, 7-77
RecipientDSInteg tool, 4-26
reconnecting mailboxes, 7-12 to 7-13, 7-41
recovering data. *See also* restoring data
  database shared disk resources, 12-35 to 12-36
  /DisasterRecovery switch, 2-20
  lost cluster quorum, 12-35
  minimizing recovery time from hard disk failure, 12-9
  recovering deleted mailboxes, 7-12
  single server node, 12-35
  soft recovery with transaction logs, 12-8
recovery server
  defined, 12-50
  reconfiguring, 12-48 to 12-49
  summary points, 12-50
recovery storage groups, 14-20 to 14-21
  backing up first, 14-64
  defined, 14-67
  merging recovered mailbox data, 14-65 to 14-66
  restoring mailbox store to, 14-64 to 14-65
  setting up, 14-63 to 14-64
recurring viruses, 11-19

redundant array of independent drives. *See* RAID
    (redundant array of independent drives)
referrals, 8-22 to 8-23, 8-38
Relative ID (RID) Master, 1-6, 1-17, 14-51
Relay Blocking List (RBL), 11-23
relaying. *See also* SMTP relays
  defined, 10-20
  incorrect, 14-29
Remove Server task (Exchange System Manager console),
    2-36
removing Exchange Server, 2-35 to 2-40
  forcibly, 2-36 to 2-39
  with Microsoft Exchange Installation Wizard, 2-35 to
      2-37
  questions and answers, 2-39 to 2-40
  summary points, 2-40, 2-45
  troubleshooting lab for, 2-44 to 2-45
removing Exchange Server 2003 server, 2-36 to 2-39, 14-7
    to 14-8
repairing
  database integrity, 13-52
  indexes, 12-22
replicas, 8-19 to 8-20, 8-38
replication
  Active Directory to Exchange, 4-19, 4-36 to 4-37
  defined, 4-46
  Exchange to Active Directory, 4-18, 4-36
  General Purpose public folder trees, 8-7
  initiating manual, 4-8
  manual replication of public folder tree, 8-21 to 8-22,
      8-24
  public folders, 8-19 to 8-22, 8-24
  Site Replication Service, 4-38
reply codes for SMTP, 10-5
Res1.log file, 7-47
Res2.log file, 7-47
resolving naming conflicts, 5-21 to 5-22
Resource Mailbox Wizard
  configuring default destination, 4-13 to 4-14
  configuring site connection agreements, 4-14 to 4-15
  installation summary, 4-15 to 4-16
  overview of, 4-6
  selecting primary and resource mailboxes, 4-12
  setting site credentials, 4-13
resources
  adding disk resource to virtual server, 6-25 to 6-26
  cluster, 6-37
  monitoring services and, 13-5 to 13-6
  recovering database shared disk, 12-35 to 12-36
  requirements and dependencies for virtual servers, 9-4
      to 9-5
restoring data, 12-28 to 12-45
  case scenario exercise, 12-45 to 12-47
  clusters, 12-34 to 12-36
  disk space requirements for, 12-29
  entire servers, 12-36 to 12-37
  Exchange Server 2003 member server, 12-43 to 12-44
  key terms, 12-50

restoring data, *continued*
  mailbox stores, 12-29 to 12-30, 12-38 to 12-39, 14-64 to
    14-65
  mailboxes, 12-30 to 12-31, 12-33 to 12-34
  offline backups, 12-30
  overview, 12-1, 12-28
  performing trial restore, 12-37
  practice exercises, 12-37 to 12-44
  public folders, 12-32 to 12-33, 14-27
  questions and answers, 12-44 to 12-45, 12-52 to 12-53
  reconfiguring recovery server, 12-47 to 12-49
  recovering messages, 12-31 to 12-32, 12-39 to 12-40
  renaming files before, 12-29
  stores, 12-28 to 12-29
  summary points, 12-45, 12-49 to 12-50
  system state data, 12-41 to 12-43
  troubleshooting, 14-20 to 14-21
restricting access to mail-enabled groups, 7-40, 7-43
Reverse ARP (RARP), 14-58 to 14-59
reverse DNS lookup, 10-24
roles
  administrative, 3-36
  Exchange View Only Administrator, 3-36, 11-38
  operations master roles assigned to domain controllers,
    1-8
  required for Exchange installation, 2-7
root directory permissions, 9-29
Routing and Remote Access, 10-33
routing groups
  about, 3-15 to 3-16
  administrative groups vs., 3-15
  advantages of native mode for, 3-24
  creating, 3-17 to 3-18
  organizations in mixed mode and, 3-23
  questions and answers, 3-18 to 3-19, 3-38 to 3-39
  summary points, 3-19 to 3-20
RPC over HTTP
  defined, 1-14, 1-17
  Outlook profile for, 11-8 to 11-10
  using, 11-5 to 11-6
RPC proxy server
  configuring for specific ports, 11-7 to 11-8
  configuring on front-end server, 11-5
Rpc/HTTP NSPI port setting, 11-7 to 11-8
runas utility, 10-27

S

SAN (storage area networks), 12-11 to 12-12, 12-15
SASL (Simple Authentication and Security Layer), 9-42
scheduled tasks, 13-20 to 13-34
  capacity planning, 13-21
  configuring protocol logs, 13-23 to 13-25, 13-28 to 13-30
  creating mailbox policies and checking for oversized
    mailboxes, 13-32
  generating reports and identifying trends, 13-21, 13-30 to
    13-31
  HTTP Monitoring Tool for, 13-25
  managing mailbox limits, 13-26 to 13-27
  monitoring postmaster mailbox, 13-27 to 13-28

  Performance console for, 13-22 to 13-23
  questions and answers, 13-33, 13-54
  reading default SMTP protocol log file, 13-31
  reviewing Badmail folder, 13-27
  summary points, 13-33 to 13-34
  types of, 13-20 to 13-21
Schema Master, 1-8, 1-17
schema naming context, 1-9, 1-11, 1-17
schemas, 1-3, 1-7
SCL (Spam Confidence Level), 11-24
Secure Multi-Purpose Internet Mail Extensions (S/MIME),
    11-31
Secure Sockets Layer (SSL). *See* SSL (Secure Sockets Layer)
security
  administering from client workstations, 3-7 to 3-8
  administrative permissions, 11-36 to 11-45
  antivirus software, 11-14 to 11-16
  blocking junk e-mail, 11-58 to 11-60
  case scenario exercise, 11-56 to 11-58, 11-66 to 11-68
  checking e-mail encryption, 14-41 to 14-44
  connectivity across firewalls, 14-36 to 14-39
  delegating administrative authority, 3-6
  digital signatures and encryption, 11-30 to 11-35
  disabling services, 11-46 to 11-51, 11-55 to 11-56
  downloading antivirus software, 11-20
  encryption and digital signatures, 14-40 to 14-41
  firewalls, 11-3 to 11-11, 11-61, 11-63, 14-44
  flaws in basic authentication, 9-41
  key terms, 11-62
  mailbox, 11-22 to 11-29, 11-64
  overview, 11-1
  permissions problems, 14-39 to 14-40, 14-44
  protocol logging, 11-46 to 11-56, 11-61, 11-65 to 11-66,
    14-35
  public folders, 8-26 to 8-34, 8-41 to 8-42
  questions and answers, 11-11, 11-20 to 11-21, 11-29,
    11-35, 11-44, 11-55 to 11-56, 11-63 to 11-68, 14-44
  security updates, 11-18 to 11-19
  SMTP, 10-21 to 10-35
  spam masquerading as administrator alert, 11-18
  strategies for, 11-13 to 11-15, 14-38
  summary points, 11-21, 11-29, 11-56, 11-60 to 11-61,
    14-44
  troubleshooting, 14-36 to 14-44
  types of, 11-12 to 11-13
  virus protection, 11-12 to 11-21
security groups
  created by DomainPrep, 2-15 to 2-16, 2-18, 2-46
  creating global, 14-31 to 14-32
  mail-enabling, 7-5, 8-17
security identifiers. *See* SIDs (security identifiers)
security principals, 14-51
security updates, 11-18 to 11-19
Send On Behalf permissions, 7-24 to 7-25
sender filtering, 11-25
Senior Managers security group, 14-31 to 14-32
servers. *See also* back-end servers; front-end servers; virtual
    servers
  accelerating front-end, 3-29

clustering, 6-3
customizing list of referral, 8-22 to 8-23
expansion, 7-38
front-end and back-end, 3-28 to 3-30, 3-36
installing Exchange Server 2003 on existing, 2-6
mixed mode, 3-22 to 3-24, 4-27 to 4-28
restoring, 12-36 to 12-37, 12-43 to 12-44
starting and stopping virtual, 9-52
supporting Network Load Balancing, 6-4
upgrading from Exchange Server 5.5 on different, 5-5 to 5-7
troubleshooting, 14-16 to 14-25
server-side antivirus software, 11-15
service accounts
about, 2-6 to 2-7, 2-11
creating, 2-8 to 2-9
defined, 2-46
service dependencies, 3-4 to 3-5, 3-36
service logon accounts, 3-5
services
added in typical installation, 3-2 to 3-3
Exchange Server ports and, 14-37
modifying, 3-9
monitoring, 13-6
monitoring resources and, 13-5 to 13-6
optional for front-end and back-end servers, 11-49 to 11-51
required for front-end and back-end servers, 11-48, 11-50
service dependencies, 3-4 to 3-5, 3-36
stopping prior to rebooting, 3-5
/ShowUI switch, 2-20
Shutdown.exe file, 3-5
SIDs (security identifiers)
conflicting IDs for migrated user accounts, 5-7
defined, 5-45
migrating history of user account, 5-8
Simple Mail Transport Protocol. *See* SMTP (Simple Mail Transport Protocol)
Single Node server clusters, 6-6
Single Quorum Device server clusters, 6-6
site connection agreements. *See* connection agreements
site credentials, 4-13
Site Replication Service, 4-28 to 4-29, 4-33, 4-38
sites, 1-3, 1-7, 3-36
smart hosts
configuring SMTP virtual servers to use, 10-13
forwarding unresolved messages to, 10-13 to 10-14
on SMTP connectors, 10-14
S/MIME (Secure Multi-Purpose Internet Mail Extensions), 11-31
SMS (Microsoft Systems Management Server), 11-19
SMTP (Simple Mail Transport Protocol). *See also* ESMTP (Extended Simple Mail Transport Protocol); SMTP relays; SMTP virtual servers
associating MIME types with extensions, 10-44
asymmetric request-response protocol, 10-3 to 10-4
authentication, 10-23, 10-27 to 10-28

case scenario exercise, 10-52 to 10-54, 10-61 to 10-62
common commands, 10-4
common reply codes, 10-5
configuring Exchange for other SMTP messaging systems, 10-36 to 10-52
connecting to Internet with Routing and Remote Access, 10-33
creating mailbox-enabled users, 10-46 to 10-47
defined, 10-57
DNS support, 10-9 to 10-10
domain message defaults, 10-44 to 10-46
encryption, 10-23 to 10-24
global settings features, 10-37 to 10-38
HTTP clients, 10-39 to 10-41
identifying message delivery failures, 10-27
IMAP4 clients, 10-41 to 10-42, 10-47 to 10-49
implementing SMTP connection, 10-3 to 10-5
incoming connection options, 10-21 to 10-22
installing, 2-7 to 2-8
Internet connectivity with, 10-11 to 10-12
junk e-mail prevention, 10-25 to 10-26
key terms, 10-57
mailbox defaults, 10-38 to 10-39
managing message transfer support, 10-3 to 10-20
message defaults, 10-38
MX records, 10-15 to 10-16
NNTP clients, 10-43 to 10-44
outgoing connection options, 10-22
overview, 10-1 to 10-2, 10-21, 10-36 to 10-37
POP3 clients, 10-42 to 10-43, 10-49 to 10-51
practice exercises, 10-27 to 10-34
provided by Windows Server 2003, 1-13
pulling queued e-mail from another server, 10-34
questions and answers, 10-19 to 10-20, 10-34 to 10-35, 10-51, 10-58 to 10-62
relaying, 10-12 to 10-15, 10-31 to 10-32
restricting Internet e-mail, 10-24 to 10-25, 10-30 to 10-31
retrieving mail from ISP dial-up connection, 10-26 to 10-27
reverse DNS lookup, 10-24
security and advanced options, 10-21 to 10-35
SMTP connectors, 10-11 to 10-12, 10-32 to 10-33
summary points, 10-20, 10-35, 10-51 to 10-52, 10-56
TLS encryption, 10-29 to 10-30
troubleshooting lab, 10-54 to 10-55
SMTP connectors
configuring credentials of, 10-12
configuring for only receiving or sending e-mail, 10-12
creating with Internet Mail Wizard, 10-12
implementing, 10-3 to 10-5
limiting scope of, 10-11
overriding relay settings on virtual server, 10-32 to 10-33
practice exercises, 10-17 to 10-18, 10-30
setting to only receive or send mail, 10-12
smart hosts with, 10-14
SMTP relays, 10-12 to 10-15
configuring relay host, 10-14, 10-18
defined, 10-20

SMTP relays, *continued*
   forwarding unresolved messages to smart host, 10-13 to
     10-14
   limiting domains for, 10-14 to 10-15
   overview, 10-12 to 10-13
   preventing open relaying, 10-31 to 10-32
   relaying mail for IMAP4 clients, 10-43
   restricting servers relaying e-mail messages, 10-14
   troubleshooting junk mail, 10-54 to 10-55
SMTP virtual servers
   additional, 10-11
   configuring, 9-14 to 9-15, 9-22 to 9-23, 9-37 to 9-38
   creating, 9-21, 9-36 to 9-37
   enabling protocol logging for, 11-53 to 11-54
   incoming connection options for, 10-21 to 10-22
   limiting domains for relay messages, 10-14 to 10-15
   masquerade domains, 9-23
   outgoing connection options, 10-22
   overview, 9-14, 9-19
   relaying mail for POP3 and IMAP4 clients, 9-40, 10-43
   restricting servers relaying e-mail messages, 10-14
   setting up as relay host, 10-14
   summary points, 9-51
   supported authentication methods, 9-43
   using smart hosts, 10-13 to 10-14
software-related installation failures, 14-6
source domains, 5-46
spam. *See also* junk e-mail
   extended periods in queues as symptom of, 13-38
   junk e-mail vs., 11-22
   masquerading as administrator alert, 11-18
Spam Confidence Level (SCL), 11-24
special ports, 14-38
spikes in queued messages, 13-38
SSL (Secure Sockets Layer)
   benefits of front-end and back-end servers for, 3-29
   combining TLS with, 10-29
   enabling on POP3 virtual server, 9-6
Standard edition of Exchange Server 2003, 3-14
starting and stopping virtual servers, 9-52
static data, 12-16 to 12-17
static IP addresses, 6-10, 6-37
.stm files, 7-46, 12-4
storage area networks (SANs), 12-11 to 12-12, 12-15
storage groups. *See also* recovery storage groups
   adding, 7-48 to 7-52, 7-54
   architecture of, 7-46 to 7-47
   backing up, 12-22 to 12-24
   circular logging, 7-48, 7-77
   creating, 12-12 to 12-13
   data storage for minimizing recovery time, 12-9
   defined, 7-77
   dismounting, 12-13 to 12-14
   managing, 12-13 to 12-14
   moving, 7-52 to 7-55
   multiple databases and, 7-47 to 7-48
   recovery, 14-20 to 14-21, 14-63 to 14-67
   support for, 6-11

storage limits
   mailbox, 7-17 to 7-24, 14-19
   public folder, 8-18 to 8-19
stores. *See also* information stores; mailbox stores; public
     folder stores; public stores
   defragmenting, 13-36
   monitoring Exchange store statistics, 13-7 to 13-8
   restoring, 12-29
   verifying integrity of, 13-35, 13-37, 13-40 to 13-41
strong passwords, 2-9
subnets, 9-31 to 9-32
Summary pane (Network Monitor), 13-46
SUS (Microsoft Software Update Services), 11-19
switches for Microsoft Exchange Installation Wizard, 2-19
     to 2-21
synchronizing Lotus Notes with Exchange Server, 5-45
system state data
   backups of, 12-36, 12-40 to 12-41
   restoring, 12-36, 12-41 to 12-43

T
target domains, 5-46
Task Manager, function of, 13-5
tasks after Exchange Server installation
   delegating administrative authority, 3-5 to 3-6, 3-9 to
     3-10, 3-36
   modifying services, 3-9
   practice exercises, 3-8 to 3-10
   questions and answers, 3-10 to 3-11, 3-37 to 3-38
   service dependencies, 3-4 to 3-5, 3-36
   service logon accounts, 3-5
   services added in typical installation, 3-2 to 3-3
   stopping services prior to rebooting, 3-5
   summary points, 3-12
TCP port filtering, 11-4 to 11-5
TCP/IP X.400 Service Transport Stack, 5-33 to 5-34
teaming, 6-7
telnet, 10-27, 14-30
test output files, 14-11
testing server with dcdiag utility, 14-13
TLS (Transport Layer Security) encryption
   about, 9-15, 10-24
   configuring, 10-29 to 10-30
   requiring clients to use, 10-29
   troubleshooting, 14-40 to 14-41
Tmp.edb file, 7-47
top-level folders, 8-39
tracert command-line utility, 14-55
transaction logs, 7-49 to 7-50, 7-77, 12-50. *See also* circular
     logging
   ACID properties of files, 12-9
   circular logging, 12-9 to 12-10, 12-50
   defined, 12-50
   hard recovery, 12-8 to 12-9
   loss of files, 12-9
   RAID configurations for storing, 12-7 to 12-8
   summary points, 12-49

Transport Layer Security (TLS) encryption. *See* TLS
    (Transport Layer Security) encryption
trial restores, 12-37
Trojan horse, 11-13, 11-62
troubleshooting, 14-1 to 14-73
    Active Directory, 4-34 to 4-42, 14-51 to 14-52
    analyzing ARP packet, 14-58 to 14-59
    backing up and restoring servers, 14-20 to 14-21
    case scenario exercise, 14-60 to 14-63, 14-71 to 14-73
    checking e-mail encryption, 14-41 to 14-44
    configuring mailbox queue alert, 14-21 to 14-23
    connectivity problems, 14-8, 14-30, 14-36 to 14-39
    data storage, 14-18 to 14-19
    diagnostic logging for virtual servers, 14-28
    DNS, 14-48 to 14-51
    encryption and digital signatures, 14-40 to 14-41
    extended periods in queues, 13-38
    forcing component installation in Setup, 2-21
    front-end and back-end server configurations, 14-29 to
        14-30
    Groups, 14-51
    handling corrupted e-mail messages, 7-30
    hardware and software requirements, 14-2 to 14-3
    host resolution, 14-45 to 14-48
    identifying message delivery failures, 10-27
    incorrect encoding and relaying, 14-29
    Information Store service transaction logs, 7-49
    installation failures, 14-4 to 14-7
    interoperability, 14-9 to 14-10
    key terms, 14-67
    managing ARP cache, 14-56 to 14-58
    migration and interoperability, 14-8 to 14-9
    monitoring server performance, 14-16 to 14-18
    netdiag and dcdiag for, 14-10 to 14-14
    network connectivity, 14-52 to 14-56
    organizations, 14-26 to 14-35
    overview, 14-1 to 14-2
    permissions problems, 14-39 to 14-40, 14-44
    public folders, 14-26 to 14-27, 14-31 to 14-34
    questions and answers, 4-41 to 4-42, 4-49, 14-14 to
        14-15, 14-24, 14-34 to 14-35, 14-44, 14-59 to 14-60,
        14-68 to 14-73
    removing Exchange Server 2003 server, 14-7 to 14-8
    security, 14-36 to 14-44
    servers, 14-16 to 14-25
    setting mailbox and public store policies, 14-19
    situations indicating mailbox needs integrity check,
        13-37
    summary points, 4-42, 14-15, 14-25, 14-35, 14-44, 14-60
    TLS encryption, 14-40 to 14-41
    troubleshooting lab, 14-63 to 14-66
    unexpected timeouts during large downloads, 9-24
    virtual memory fragmentation in clusters, 14-19 to 14-20,
        14-25
    Windows Server 2003 technologies, 14-45 to 14-60
troubleshooting labs
    blocking junk e-mail, 11-58 to 11-60
    Microsoft Exchange Server 5.5, 4-44 to 4-45

migrating to Exchange Server, 5-43 to 5-44
with Network Monitor, 13-44 to 13-50
public folders, 8-36 to 8-37
recipient objects and address lists, 7-75 to 7-76
reconfiguring recovery server, 12-48 to 12-49
for removing Exchange Server, 2-44 to 2-45
setting diagnostic level and reading log, 9-56 to 9-58
setting mail relaying restrictions, 10-54 to 10-55
troubleshooting, 14-63 to 14-66
using Network Monitor, 13-44 to 13-50
virtual servers, 9-56 to 9-58
trust between migrating domains, 5-14 to 5-15

U

unattended setup, 2-28 to 2-34
    creating .ini file for, 2-28 to 2-32
    overview, 2-28
    performing, 2-31 to 2-32
    questions and answers, 2-33 to 2-34, 2-50 to 2-51
/UnattendFile filename.ini switch, 2-20
unified namespace, 3-28 to 3-29
uninstalling Exchange Server, 2-36 to 2-39
updating
    address lists manually, 7-64
    antivirus software, 11-15
    operating system, 11-14
    security bulletin services, 11-18
upgrading
    about, 2-4
    configuring trust between migrating domains, 5-14 to
        5-15
    from Exchange 2000 organization, 5-11 to 5-14
    from Exchange Server 5.5 organization, 5-3 to 5-11
    installation checklist for, 4-31
    practice exercises, 5-14 to 5-24
    questions and answers, 5-24 to 5-25, 5-47
    sequence for front-end and back-end servers, 3-36
User Account Migration Wizard
    account transition options, 5-19 to 5-20
    configuring user options, 5-20
    domain selection, 5-16
    organizational unit selection, 5-18
    password options, 5-18
    resolving naming conflicts, 5-21 to 5-22
    specifying object property exclusions, 5-20 to 5-21
    user selection, 5-17
user accounts
    configuring options in User Account Migration Wizard,
        5-20
    migrating, 5-7 to 5-8, 5-15 to 5-22
    selecting for migration in Exchange Server Migration
        Wizard, 5-24
    selecting in User Account Migration Wizard, 5-17
user recipients, 7-3 to 7-4
UserCount tool, 4-24
users
    creating mailboxes for, 7-7 to 7-9
    disconnected when downloading messages, 14-30

users, *continued*
  explaining mailbox and public store policies to, 14-19
  introducing mailbox storage limits to, 7-24
  mail-enabled and mailbox-enabled, 7-4
  preparing for migrations, 5-40
  restricting mail sent over Internet, 10-30 to 10-31
  unable to authenticate in Active Directory, 14-51 to 14-52
  viewing and managing on IMAP4 server, 9-53
  viewing and terminating connections, 9-52 to 9-53
uuencode format, 9-40

V

VerCheck tool, 4-24
verifying
  backups, 12-22
  Exchange store, 13-37
  mailbox stores, 13-40 to 13-41
  mailboxes, 13-35, 13-37
  MX records, 10-15 to 10-16
  public folder stores, 13-35
virtual directories
  creating, 8-9 to 8-10
  HTTP, 8-9 to 8-10, 9-12, 10-40
  public folder and mailbox access in, 10-40
  RPC, 11-6
  setting permissions, 9-28
virtual memory fragmentation, 14-19 to 14-20, 14-25
virtual organizations, 10-3, 10-9
virtual server protocols, 9-43 to 9-44
virtual servers, 9-1 to 9-62. *See also specific virtual servers*
  adding disk resources to, 6-25 to 6-26
  additional, 9-20 to 9-21
  assigning IP addresses to, 9-17 to 9-18
  authentication methods, 9-41 to 9-51
  calendaring settings ignored on front-end POP3 and IMAP4, 14-30
  case scenario exercise, 9-54 to 9-56, 9-62
  clustering and, 6-9
  configuring, 9-21 to 9-23
  creating, 6-19 to 6-20, 6-23
  defined, 6-31, 6-37
  diagnostic logging, 9-53, 9-56 to 9-59, 14-28
  enabling and starting, 9-15 to 9-16
  front-end and back-end configuration, 9-23 to 9-24
  HTTP, 9-11 to 9-13, 9-19, 9-21, 9-26 to 9-29
  icons indicating stop or pause in service, 9-17
  IMAP4, 9-7 to 9-8, 9-16 to 9-17, 9-19, 9-21 to 9-22, 9-33
  Internet protocol, 9-59
  key terms, 9-59
  maintaining, 9-52 to 9-54
  in network load balancing environment, 9-4
  NNTP, 9-8 to 9-10, 9-16 to 9-17, 9-19, 9-22, 9-33 to 9-36
  overriding relay settings with SMTP connectors, 10-32 to 10-33
  overview, 9-1
  POP3, 9-5 to 9-7, 9-16 to 9-17, 9-19, 9-21 to 9-22, 9-30 to 9-32

  practice exercises, 9-15 to 9-18, 9-25 to 9-39, 9-44 to 9-50
  questions and answers, 9-19, 9-39 to 9-40, 9-50 to 9-51, 9-53 to 9-54, 9-60 to 9-62
  resource requirements and dependencies for, 9-4 to 9-5
  SMTP, 9-14 to 9-15, 9-19, 9-22 to 9-23, 9-36 to 9-38, 10-11, 10-21 to 10-22
  starting and stopping servers, 9-52
  summary points, 9-19, 9-40, 9-51, 9-54, 9-58 to 9-59
  troubleshooting lab, 9-56 to 9-58
  in Windows clustering environment, 9-3
virus protection, 11-12 to 11-21
  antivirus software, 11-14 to 11-16
  downloading antivirus software, 11-20
  questions and answers, 11-20 to 11-21, 11-63 to 11-64
  security updates, 11-18 to 11-19
  sensible precautions against, 11-12
  spam sent as administrator alert, 11-18
  strategies for, 11-13 to 11-15, 14-38
  summary points, 11-21
  types of, 11-12 to 11-13
  virus transmission, 11-13
  virus-clean policies and procedures, 11-16 to 11-17
virus signatures, 11-19
viruses, 11-12 to 11-13, 11-62
VMWare, 10-2
vrfy command, 10-6 to 10-7
VSS (Volume Shadow Copy Service), 12-20 to 12-21, 12-24, 12-50

W

Web Server Certificate Wizard, 9-45, 10-29 to 10-30
WebDAV (Web Distributed Authoring and Versioning), 10-36
Windows 2000 Advanced Server, 6-4
Windows 2003 Backup, 12-50
Windows NT 4 Advanced Server, 6-4
Windows NT 4 Datacenter Server, 6-4
Windows Server 2003. *See* Microsoft Windows Server 2003
Windows Server 2003 Backup utility, 12-29
worms, 11-13, 11-62
write permissions, 14-34 to 14-35
WWW (World Wide Web) service, 1-13 to 1-14

X

X.25 X.400 Service Transport Stack, 5-33
X.400-compliant messaging systems
  configuring Exchange to coexist with, 5-32 to 5-33
  creating X.400 transport stack, 5-33 to 5-36
  defined, 5-46
  types of transports for, 5-33

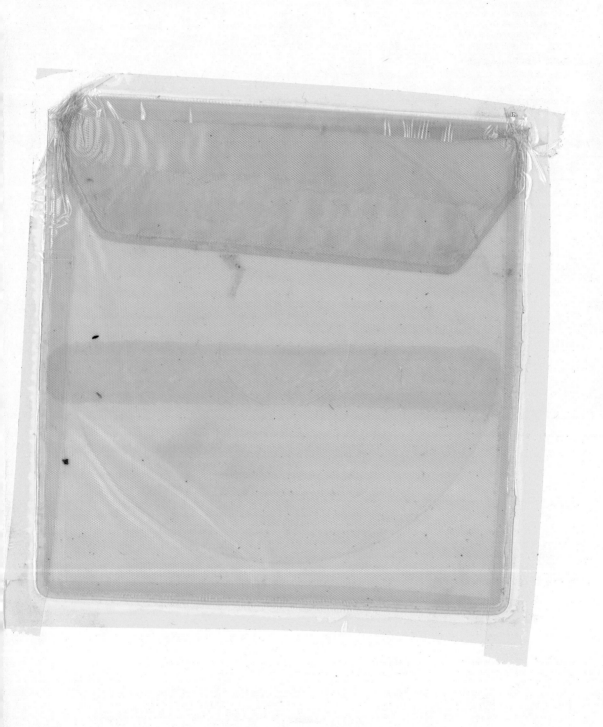

MCSA and MCSE for Microsoft Windows Server 2003

The Microsoft Certified Systems Engineer (MCSE) credential is the premier certification for professionals who analyze the business requirements and design and implement the infrastructure for business solutions based on the Microsoft® Windows Server™ 2003 platform and Microsoft Windows Server System. Implementation responsibilities include installing, configuring, and troubleshooting network systems.

The Microsoft Certified Systems Administrator (MCSA) credential proves that you have the skills to successfully implement, manage, and troubleshoot the ongoing needs of Windows Server 2003–based operating environments.

For information on study materials, training, and certification for Microsoft Windows Server 2003, please visit: **www.microsoft.com/traincert**.

MCSA/MCSE Core Requirements

MCSA

Three core exams, including:

■ Two Networking System exams

■ One Client Operating System exam

MCSE

Six core exams, including:

■ Four Networking System exams

■ One Client Operating System exam

■ One Design exam

Networking System Exams

MCSA (Two Exams Required)	MCSE (Four Exams Required)	Core Exams: Networking System	Microsoft Press® Study Materials	ISBN
✔	✔	Exam 70-290: Managing and Maintaining a Microsoft Windows Server 2003 Environment	MCSA/MCSE Self-Paced Training Kit (Exam 70-290): Managing and Maintaining a Microsoft Windows Server 2003 Environment	0-7356-1437-7
			MCSE Self-Paced Training Kit: Microsoft Windows Server 2003 Core Requirements, Exams 70-290, 70-291, 70-293, 70-294	0-7356-1953-0
✔	✔	Exam 70-291: Implementing, Managing, and Maintaining a Microsoft Windows Server 2003 Network Infrastructure	MCSA/MCSE Self-Paced Training Kit (Exam 70-291): Implementing, Managing and Maintaining a Microsoft Windows Server 2003 Network Infrastructure	0-7356-1439-3
			MCSE Self-Paced Training Kit: Microsoft Windows Server 2003 Core Requirements, Exams 70-290, 70-291, 70-293, 70-294	0-7356-1953-0
N/A	✔	Exam 70-293: Planning and Maintaining a Microsoft Windows Server 2003 Network Infrastructure	MCSE Self-Paced Training Kit (Exam 70-293): Planning and Maintaining a Microsoft Windows Server 2003 Network Infrastructure	0-7356-1893-3
			MCSE Self-Paced Training Kit: Microsoft Windows Server 2003 Core Requirements, Exams 70-290, 70-291, 70-293, 70-294	0-7356-1953-0
N/A	✔	Exam 70-294: Planning, Implementing, and Maintaining a Microsoft Windows Server 2003 Active Directory® Infrastructure	MCSE Self-Paced Training Kit (Exam 70-294): Planning, Implementing, and Maintaining a Microsoft Windows Server 2003 Active Directory Infrastructure	0-7356-1438-5
			MCSE Self-Paced Training Kit: Microsoft Windows Server 2003 Core Requirements, Exams 70-290, 70-291, 70-293, 70-294	0-7356-1953-0

Client Operating System Exams

MCSA (Choose One)	MCSE (Choose One)	Core Exams: Client Operating System	Microsoft Press Study Materials	ISBN
✔	✔	Exam 70-270: Installing, Configuring, and Administering Microsoft Windows® XP Professional	MCSE Training Kit (Exam 70-270): Windows XP Professional	0-7356-1429-6
✔	✔	Exam 70-210[1]: Installing, Configuring, and Administering Microsoft Windows 2000 Professional	MCSA/MCSE Self-Paced Training Kit (Exam 70-210): Microsoft Windows 2000 Professional, Second Edition	0-7356-1766-X

Design Exams

MCSA (Not Applicable)	MCSE (Choose One)	Core Exams: Design	Microsoft Press Study Materials	ISBN
N/A	✔	Exam 70-297[2]: Designing a Microsoft Windows Server 2003 Active Directory and Network Infrastructure	MCSE Self-Paced Training Kit (Exam 70-297): Designing a Microsoft Windows Server 2003 Active Directory and Network Infrastructure	0-7356-1970-0
N/A	✔	Exam 70-298[2]: Designing Security for a Microsoft Windows Server 2003 Network	MCSE Self-Paced Training Kit (Exam 70-298): Designing Security for a Microsoft Windows Server 2003 Network	0-7356-1969-7

1 Candidates who passed Windows NT 4.0 Exams 70-067, 70-068, and 70-073 had the option to take the comprehensive Exam 70-240: Microsoft Windows 2000 Accelerated Exam for MCPs Certified on Microsoft Windows NT 4.0. By passing this exam, candidates met the MCSE exam requirement for 70-210. Exam 70-240 is no longer available.

2 Exams 70-297 and 70-298 may each count once as either one core design exam or one elective exam.

 = qualifying exam